The Possibility/Imp‹

Critical Language in Education

MW00862130

EDUCATIONAL FUTURES
RETHINKING THEORY AND PRACTICE
Volume 44

Series Editors
Michael A. Peters
University of Illinois at Urbana-Champaign, USA

Editorial Board

Michael Apple, *University of Wisconsin-Madison, USA*
Miriam David, *Institute of Education, London University, UK*
Cushla Kapitzke, *Queensland University of Technology, Australia*
Simon Marginson, *University of Melbourne, Australia*
Mark Olssen, *University of Surrey, UK*
Fazal Rizvi, *University of Illinois at Urbana-Champaign, USA*
Linda Tuahwai Smith, *University of Waikato, New Zealand*
Susan Robertson, *University of Bristol, UK*

Scope
This series maps the emergent field of educational futures. It will commission books on the futures of education in relation to the question of globalisation and knowledge economy. It seeks authors who can demonstrate their understanding of discourses of the knowledge and learning economies. It aspires to build a consistent approach to educational futures in terms of traditional methods, including scenario planning and foresight, as well as imaginative narratives, and it will examine examples of futures research in education, pedagogical experiments, new Utopian thinking, and educational policy futures with a strong accent on actual policies and examples.

The Possibility/Impossibility of a New Critical Language in Education

Ilan Gur-Ze'ev (author/editor)
University of Haifa, Israel

SENSE PUBLISHERS
ROTTERDAM/BOSTON/TAIPEI

A C.I.P. record for this book is available from the Library of Congress.

ISBN: 978-94-6091-270-2 (paperback)
ISBN: 978-94-6091-271-9 (hardback)
ISBN: 978-94-6091-272-6 (e-book)

Published by: Sense Publishers,
P.O. Box 21858,
3001 AW Rotterdam,
The Netherlands
http://www.sensepublishers.com

Printed on acid-free paper

All Rights Reserved © 2010 Sense Publishers

No part of this work may be reproduced, stored in a retrieval system, or transmitted in any form or by any means, electronic, mechanical, photocopying, microfilming, recording or otherwise, without written permission from the Publisher, with the exception of any material supplied specifically for the purpose of being entered and executed on a computer system, for exclusive use by the purchaser of the work.

DEDICATION

To my beloved children—Hadas, Nimrod and Keyla

TABLE OF CONTENTS

ILAN GUR-ZE'EV

1. TOWARD A NEW CRITICAL LANGUAGE IN EDUCATION[1] (INTRODUCTION)

To take love seriously and to bear and to learn it like a task, this is what people need... For one human being to love another, that is perhaps the most difficult of all our tasks, the ultimate, the last test and proof, the work for which all other work is but a preparation. (Rainer Maria Rilke, 1904)

Yes, Critical Pedagogy and the possibility of counter-education are tremendously meaningful for me; even today, at its worst stage, when its fashioned politically-correct rhetoric has the upper hand and is so irritating to me, and certainly at its best, when realizing its respond-ability (Gur-Ze'ev, 2005, p. 26) in an attempt to edify a new human gaze and fresh eavesdropping in face of what seems from the outside as an ongoing silence.

This is where my response to the shortcomings of present-day Critical Pedagogy comes from. It relates to what Critical Pedagogy should become—a ladder to the possibilities for a worthy overcoming of the factuality signified and re-produced by Critical Pedagogy. Maybe we should talk here about the "various Critical Pedagogies" and not so much about "Critical Pedagogy" as such, since, there is no such thing as one, unified, agreed "Critical Pedagogy". Nevertheless from time to time I will speak here of "Critical Pedagogy" and I must beg my listeners' forgiveness already at this stage.

At today's meeting of friends of Critical Pedagogy with some of its most serious critics I would suggest the following: we cannot be content with transcending Critical Pedagogy. We should take it solely as *a starting point*, part of our self-education in order to prepare ourselves to go down deeper and climb higher. We should conquer the impulse to defend the theory that is devoted to justice and to the protection of fundamental human interests. Why do I think that we should not hold on to Critical Pedagogy and protect its conventions at all cost? Why should we refuse loyalty to it? Because we should be responsive to the quest that in spite of everything is still incubating in its original telos. We should *dislearn* and prevail over conventional rhetorical, ideological and philosophical conventions if we genuinely care about justice for actual people, for the fundamentals of the concept of justice, for the invitation of Love of Life. When we seriously respond to its present-day invitation to rethink ourselves, the self-evidence and the celebrated disorientations and their fashionable syncretisms and mishmashes, we should try, and in a worthy manner overcome, not the present manifestations of Critical Pedagogy alone but even some of the central elements of the Critical Theory that enabled Critical Pedagogy in its very beginning to move toward new forms of homelessness and Diasporic existence (Gur-Ze'ev, 2005a, pp. 343–365).

I. Gur-Ze'ev, The Possibility/Impossibility of a New Critical Language in Education, 1–13.
© 2010 Sense Publishers. All Rights Reserved.

What is so important in our meeting today? I hope we have not come to New College, and met here as part of the rituals in academic production, or even as part of a serious attempt to hunt for a neo-Marxist, post-structuralist, or other saviour that will redeem Critical Pedagogy after all. When I say "Critical Pedagogy" in this respect I mean the entire baggage: the educational framework, the ideological construction that justifies and elaborates it, the philosophical vocabulary that cultivates its fruits, and our entire social context and material realities. Saving not the "world" of the "I" but the poiesis of dwelling or being in a worthy exile from it, or in it, is what is at stake here. This is what brought many of us here, much more than academic rituals and productivity. For my part, dear friends, I do not search, nor do I invite you to explore, for a more creative "synthesis". No. This meeting is not an invitation to a new attempt to sail for the still undiscovered shores of integration of the current most fashionable academic cultural commodities with the traditional ethos of critical education. Already at this stage of our meeting I will say loud and clear: I oppose these attempts, as presented at their best by some of our friends participating in today's Oxford critical dialogue here at New College.

Before unfolding my reflections on Critical Pedagogy today, I would like to add another personal note: this is a talk that comes from Love and ultimately concerns Love. Critique that abandons love will not help us to transcend any Platonic "cave", nor any Weberian "iron cage", nor will it enable us to offer our hand to a friend in his suffering or respond in a worthy manner to the possibility of revealing, creating, or receiving meaning concerning that which is going on around and within us. Unfortunately, rarely is critical education attracted by questions of *loss* and the possibilities to open new, poetic and moral gates to unknown possibilities for us in face of the triumph of meaninglessness, productive violence and dogmatic counter-productive resistance. Quite often it runs too hastily to questions of efficient "critique" or "resistance" or to the most recent critical rhetoric, abandoning the original invitation to love, creation, physical edification and poetic existence and their relation to the loss that is inflicted by "theory", "politics" and normalizing education in a post-metaphysical moment.

In other words, the critique of Critical Pedagogy—in its current various trends and paths teaches me not only the shortcomings of various versions of Critical Pedagogy. No less important, it offers an invitation to a reflection on the limitations, costs, and open horizons of "critique" itself. It is an *invitation to transcend "critique"* as such. But what alternative do we have, and from where or with what ears might we listen to the music of the new call? What is it that awaits us outside the critical tradition that in an unproblematic manner we could use, internalize, or surrender ourselves to? Nothing of that kind awaits us. Nevertheless its possibility or the quest for redemption of the Messianic call, or even the possibility of meaning and worthy life of an eternally-becoming individual is so important for our rethinking Critical Pedagogy today. It illuminates the quest for a possibility of meaningful paths: roads toward transcendence from the continuum of meaninglessness, from the omnipotence of thingness that swallows every possibility of a vivid otherness and genuine transcendence of a Diasporic improviser in the immanence of the current dull historical moment.

Such questions reintroduce us to *Utopia*. They reintroduce us to the Utopia of the possibility of happiness of the kind that is neither made possible nor advocated by self-abandonment and enslavement/destruction of the otherness of the Other and the "I". This, as I have argued on so many other occasions, causes me not to abandon the telos of Critical Theory.

My refusal to abandon Critical Theory's telos springs from here; at its best, as in the case of mature Adorno, it offers no "solutions", "victories of the oppressed", and "emancipation", neither does it promise "peace" and unproblematic "consensus". On the contrary: all the eternal open, Diasporic individual can hope for is worthy Diasporic Love of Life, creativity, mature forms of togetherness, and eternal nomadism as a manifestation of co-poiesis.

Today, as we are gathered here to discuss the possibility/impossibility of a new critical language in education, let's begin with some of the main difficulties I find in present day Critical Pedagogies. This is my way to welcome the lovers of Critical Pedagogy who have come to this Oxford Critical Pedagogy symposium from so many countries and different continents to pay their respects and to contribute to the prospects of critical education today.

The various Critical Pedagogies known to me suffer from weaknesses which call us to attend, again, to the fundamentals, the origins, the telos, the impasse and the possibilities of life at present. Only after that, or, on a second level, are we invited to rethink the language and the relations between ourselves, practice, and theory. Let us be more specific here, even if the full elaboration of this issue is beyond the scope of this talk: we are confronted, more than invited, by a call to rethink the theoretical, to de-experience and re-establish the existential, bodily, aesthetic, ethical, political and material-physical preconditions and realities of the Critical Theory upon which Critical Pedagogies are constructed. This is a challenge critical thinkers rarely dare to respond to, maybe because not many are ready to respond properly to the call or even able to dance with the invitation and to associate with the offsprings of such a dance. Instead, a good number of them try to "improve" or "strengthen" Critical Pedagogy by importing into it every morning anew the most up-to-date fashions of the academic culture industry and the latest approved conceptions of its politically-correct moral police.

To my mind, this afternoon and on other occasions we, friends of Critical Pedagogy, should confront its apparent demolished relevance and courageously recount its sources, address its reasons, and face its fruits. We should not do what Giroux and many other critical educators do, following the projectionists of the Copernican cosmology in the 17th century when trying to defend the good old Aristotelian-Ptolemaic astronomy: to add ever more suppositions and artificial "corrections" and epicycles to curves of the stars according to the obsolete astronomical theory, its cosmology, and the ideologies it supports and justifies. There is a difference, however. The traditional astronomers, clergy, and educators defended in the 17th century a scientific theory and a cosmology that ultimately manifested or glorified *the sacred*; they tried to sacrifice whatever possible to defend what they believed was the true, the just, and the most beautiful; they struggled to defend worthy life and the possibility of salvation and resurrection, nothing less then that. And even within this struggle many Jesuit scientists were open listening to and embracing the new astronomical theories, even the pope, as long as people like Galileo did not insist on the theological implications of the new scientific findings and theories. In this sense their ecstatic reactionary mission was worthy of defense in face of a then still problematic scientific alternative.

Today's critical pedagogues who are so productive in introducing into their Critical Pedagogy almost every latest fashionable cultural commodity do it neither as a sacred deed nor as a genuine religious commitment. Often I have the impression that they do it just to be intact with the celebration, only for the joy of being celebrities, being cited, interviewed, or looked upon in admiration in a post-metaphysical historical moment; at its best they accept the new "progressivism" as a quasi-religious alternative, in a range which includes sensitivity for the silenced voice and suffering and resistance to universal-absolutist assertions to celebrating Western decolonization and the counter-violence of its victims. At best they do it because they know no better, in the absence of a new Jesus, Moses, Mohammad or Marx, namely in face of the endless, changing, non-hierarchially replacements for the voice of God and the exile of the humanist killer of God. Their *self-forgetfulness* must ensure the forgetfulness of their self-forgetfulness and the exile of Spirit. All that is left to these Critical Pedagogues is *speeding* intelligent recycling and transgressions within the immanence in face of the exile of erotic transcendence. There is neither room in present-day Critical Pedagogy for religious, erotic acts of dislearning, nor for new, great creations, unless they are swallowed by the new anti-Semitism and come up with an ecstatic "critique", postcolonial "resistance" and quasi-religious false counter-education.

We should educate ourselves to be open to searching in new ways for a new search; to revolutionize—in the Copernican sense of the word—thinking and existence that is currently being so sophistically enhanced and fruitfully misrepresented by the diminishing possibilities to offer courageous replies to aporia, the impasse and endless ways opened by the present moment. More than once this aporia reveals itself as new technological-cultural-political possibilities; as promising hybrid spaces that celebrate the exile of censorship, hierarchies, hegemony, false claims to universally valid truths and values, and so much more. We should learn how to unveil this Maya curtain while overcoming the deceiving power of optimistic promises for easy, or, at least unproblematic "solutions", carried out by the armies of the new puritans such as radical "Greens", postcolonialist NGOs, "genuine" democrats, "peace activists", and so many more.

In saying this I do not mean that there is no merit in much of the invested critique, the good will, and the practice of such organizations and ideologies. Of course there is. Particularly in face of the racist, chauvinist, nihilistic and neo-liberal alternative agendas. I would like to stress, however, that what we need today, desperately, as the Sahara Desert needs sweet water, is *to overcome the rhetoric of "solutions"* and "crisis solving" agendas on the illusionary path to postcolonialist world-peace, "justice", "radical democracy" (Kellner, 1996) or "cyberfeminism" (Gur-Ze'ev, 1999, pp. 437–455). We need to reposition ourselves anew toward Life as a wonderful-serious-voyage from autopoiesis toward co-poiesis especially when entering the era of mega-speed and the exile of solitude and togetherness in face of the deconstruction of holiness. We should not satisfy ourselves with new vocabularies, language games and ideological ecstasies, let alone with new imports to be incorporated into the old habits, dogmas and fears. The new progressive thinking is not totally wrong when it calls us to reposition ourselves in the sense of de-territorializing ourselves, not merely re-territorializing and surrendering ourselves in new ways to the continuum of the Same and be swallowed by the thingness that as it were awaits our "homecoming" each moment anew. Deterritorialize ourselves, after the loss of that intimacy which allowed poiesis and aletheia (at least as an ecstatic transgrssion). This form of new progressive *self-forgetfulness*, however, has its roots in "old" progressivism that by the same token also enhanced progress in techno-scientific and political terms. The new progressivism, in opposition to the "old" humanistic-oriented progressivism led us to exile Eros, deconstructing creative-co-poiesis and simple manifestations of compassion, replacing them with the extravagant promises of the Pleasure Machine or quasi-idealist promises about the "true" revolution/critique/deconstruction/parody. In the last generation even these possibilities became ridiculed, deconstructed, and contextualized. A mockery to be defended as a dogma of a closed "critical" cult with problematic connections to organizations and ideologies such as the North Korean dictatorship, the Palestinian death cult[2] and Iranian revolutionary fundamentalism, on the one hand, and Deleuzian and Foucaultian Torah of the "death of the subject", on the other. What is the habitus for beauty or co-mpassion in face of the new progressive celebration of the "death of the subject", mega-speed "hyper-realities" or, alternatively, when approaching with Zizek the genuine Leninist revolution?

The present critical prospects are embarrassingly diverse and conflictual and include the World of Jihad and the McWorld, revolutionary utopian modernism and poststructuralist celebration of difference and heterogeneity. Anti-religious, ultra religious and quasi-religious quests for redemption in a post-metaphysical moment collaborate with the disciples of deconstruction of any transcendental claim and so much more. And yet, their diverse version of "critique" is an ontological sign that unites us in face of a totalizing challenge of the nearing probability of an End to all Life on earth. In this unique moment these diverse versions of "critique" are also united in an anti-democratic coalition. Pre-modern (Ahmadinejad), modern (Zizek, Badiou, Ceresole, Chavez) and postmodern (Deleuze, Butler, Pappe, Briadotti) alike are united in the form of an anti-progressive progressivism, or, in other words, as the heroes of the new anti-Semitism. This coalition offers "resistance" to democracy, humanism and free spirit as an ecstatic, redeeming way of life. In front of such wretched new progressivism what we desperately need is a tiger leap; nomadic dwelling beyond the agenda of "critique", "resistance" and new progressive religiosity that celebrates the exile of holiness, the deconstruction of com-passion, and the metamorphosis of the courage for self-overcoming and Diasporic improvisation.

The new language has not yet honored us with its blessed presence; we are still deprived of its responsibilities, possibilities, and imperatives, and yet, we already must respond to the most urgent realities in a responsible manner and to the possibility of struggling to overcome the new realm of self-evidence. But might some new possibilities already await us, with growing impatience, beyond the locked door of our habits, fears and hubris? Have we genuinely tried to overcome the language of "emancipatory education", and open ourselves to the *essence* of the saying of the aporia of our era? Have we tried to overcome the satisfaction of effective "critique", playful deconstruction, and self-indulgent pessimism and its adjunct possibilities, dead-ends, and mounting dangers to the very survival of the planet? Have we genuinely tried to get beyond the critique of dangerous ideologies and policies risky for human nature and for the nature of love, creation and transcendence in face of mega speed realities and the near end of all life on earth? *What, dear friends, is our present reply to this challenge* to the very possibility of friendship, love, thinking, and Life?

Very seldom, if at all, have we, critical educators, dared to look into the eyes of *the call* back, "home", to the promised harmony of nothingness and meaninglessness, even in the form of postcolonial emancipatory ecstatic "critique" and cathartic, quasi-spiritual "counter-violence". As critical educators, within the framework of Critical Pedagogy we have not tried enough to *dislearn* and to overcome the fear of dancing with-in ambivalence, heteronomy and danger, especially when offered the "radical" language of "critique" within which everything is known and controlled by Gurus and political-correct police while praising "diversity" and new-pantheism as against Judeo-Christian violent "Monotheism" and its offsprings. We have not created and have not put together strong enough efforts to re-educate ourselves in *listening* to the saying whose meaning goes so far beyond that which was said by "critique". Freire did not introduce us to a legacy, to an ethos, surely not to pathos of taking seriously *the saying of the immanence*; addressing the invitation of the music of the production of meanings and drives that generates in the womb of our generation's conflicting unbeatable language games and the market's ever-changing fashions as the manifestation of an ecstatic **Same**.

Immanence, today, is not disturbed by the abandonment of *intimacy with the cosmos* of the kind we experienced before the constitution of the first religions and the furthering of the division of production relations. Meaninglessness is not troubled at all by the exile of the quest for a non-dogmatic "homecoming", by the loss of a call to search for the key to the locked door that might unveil the way to *becoming-toward-the-world* as a form of being-together as open Diasporic learners, and as being-toward-the-Godless-world (Gur-Ze'ev, 2005, p. 18). The celebrated return of the lost intimacy with immanence, and today it puts forward for us quite a few ways for self-forgetfulness: 1. Quest to be swallowed by the postmodern suggestive powers of the omnipotent Pleasure Machine. 2. Rebelion against the McWorld under the banner of the Jihad. 3. Postcolonialist "resistance" and "critique". 4. Continuing one of the numerous utopist, modernization projects which offer "homecoming" or transforming reality into a worthy "home" within the framework of a vivid nation-building project, socialism, feminism or even liberalism. 5. Ensuring self-forgetfulness within the framework of individualistic and ethnocentrist fragment-alism which is committed to cannibalistic deconstruction of any consensus, ethos, sensitivity to self-constitution, or other potentials for transcendence. Critical Peda-gogies, today, dwell in different degrees of comfort and productivity in three of the five alternative ways open for self-forgetfulness. Yhey rarely reach their destined path: the way toward religious Diasporic response-ability and improvising co-poiesis. It never enters the path of the *Orcha*.

Effective meaninglessness has a much stronger suggestive power and relevance for critical education in "our" post-metaphysical moment; its very existence drives out an alternative desire—the quest to eavesdrop to the music of the cosmos, the music of Love of Life or even the most microscopic manifestations of com-passion. Its very presence exiles the quest to become closer to the call of the truth of Being (Heidegger, 1996, p. 223). It is philosophical in the Deleuzian sense of producing strong, vivid, creative concepts (Deleuze, 1994, p. 9) and young reactions. It manifests the omnipotence of the new immanence and the strength as well as the creativity of the *illusion* of ecstatic self-forgetfulness as a substitute for transcendence within this immanence; where there is no difference which makes a difference. The false promise of quasi-emancipation by the new technologies and the newly created fields of human intersubjectivity manifest this illusion and its sophisticated castrating power; it reveals its vigor to chain Eros to the service of Thanatos as a form of giving-birth, as a vivid manifestation of genuine *Spirit*, as a path to true deification of humans; the final triumph over the loss of original intimacy with the cosmos, on the one hand and the alternative Utopia of "homereturning" in the form of turning the earth into a genuine Garden of Eden, on the other.

The new technologies, however, do not contain the dialectic and the promise Marx could unveil in the capitalist mode of production of his day. The transition from Fordism into post-Fordist (Ash-Amin, 2003, pp. 1–40) relations of production, representation, distribution, and consumption manifest in a much clearer way the productive, progressive, reifications of human existence, its fragmentation and its *surrendering to the postmodern Pleasure Machine* and its contingencies.

These contingencies host countless, diverse, particular interests, worldviews, political practices and alternative educational agendas, among which Critical Pedagogy has its legitimate rituals, mantras, masters, enemies and disciples. This position, however, is very different from the role of Ideology Critique and the proletariats' educational and political vanguard's praxis as conceived and realized in the Marxist tradition. In arenas of mega-speed and hyper reality it is impossible to see Critical Pedagogy retaking the role of the vanguard, dear friends, even if some of us would like it so much.

The McDonaldized realities of today not only recycle themselves under the banner of diversity, locality, freedom of choice (of the customer), and democracy—they facilitate and re-produce critique and "resistance" to the system as part of its own ornamentalization and fertilization; "critique" is accepted and even encouraged as underground music and exotic folklorist tendencies that are allowed while encouraged to be a little "wild"—only to become ever more creatively integrated and efficiently swallowed by the self-recycling of the capitalist globalization process and its eroding any potentially antagonistic remnant (Gur-Ze'ev, 2000, pp. 209–231). Within the same process of exiling the killer-of-God-each-moment-anew it becomes part and parcel of the new anti-Semitism as the new world religion of the progressive circles. It is impossible to disconnect the preconditions of the ideology of "the special rights of the client" and preconditions of the ideology of "the special rights of the victims of Western oppression". The cathartic ecstasies of the two arenas of symbolic exchange enables self-forgetfulness of the kind that will tell us that there is a substitute to God and there is a "worthy" alterative to the holiness of the humanist Utopia of killing-God-each-moment-anew within *the new nomadism* as a sacred existence offered by the postmodern Pleasure Machine on the one hand and the new anti-Semitism (and Critical Pedagogy included) on the other.

Given the current symbolic order of things and the current technological, economic, and political developments, critical hopes for cyberdemocracy, cyber communities and not-hegemonic de-territorializations necessarily become part and parcel not only of the global entertainment economy but of the further *spiritualization* of life within the McWorld. It is but a fraction of the postmodern omnipotent Pleasure-Machine which produces meanings as the fruits of meaninglessness and "horizontal" ecstasies which serve as gates, paths and "walks" toward *the End*. The critique and the pantheistic "daily spirituality" of the oppositional voices (where there is no essential difference that makes a difference between Bin Laden, Dalai Lama, Zizek, Baudrillard or Bill Gates) are instrumental; enhancing further the productivity and the effectiveness of the globalization process: it becomes a vital contribution to the global, standardized, forming of the quest for ecstasies in the form of "resistance", "consuming" and "horizontal" everyday spirituality in a world where the quest for transcendence was deconstructed, exiled or ridiculed to non-tragic-death.

The United Nations and NGOs charters and practices integrate to the same symbolic, contingent, multicultural order, and represent the integration of the contextual/local to the unavoidable/global parallel to the fabrication of the glocali-zation processes as part of life in the McWorld. There is no special, universal, yet un-fundamentalist solution to the philosophical impasse of our historical moment. As Alan Badiou rightly claims there is no *hope* in texts such as the Human Rights Charter. It does not represent "progress" nor is it part of a development that will enhance bettering of human conditions in Sudan, China or France.

Optimism concerning the work of the NGOs, the UN declarations, and the new technologies, however, are of much help for the setting up of standardization and self-regulation of a new totality, which allows endless "free", "diverse", "multicultural", "unique" contexts and fields that are all committed to and depend upon, or actually become part and parcel of, *the omnipotent immanence*; the Platonic cave that is ruled by the logic of capitalism. All are determined by, obey, and unconditionally support global, coordinated practices (as an alternative to the strength of the locality and the concreteness of shared poiesis, love, ideals, and worthy suffering as experienced by the free citizen in the Roman Republic). They support and strengthen the system even when using their cell-phones and credit cards in order to construct resistance to globalization or against new threats to the environment.

While searching for the possibilities opened by the dialectical dimensions within this historical advance we should acknowledge that these developments pursue and enable the customers "democratic" approval of capitalistic dehumanization practices of/by the new technologies; with the further reification of life, productivity, pleasure, resistance, and "critique" as part and parcel of the new daily spirituality. And it goes along with the establishment of the McWorld and the post-Fordist reality. What is their philosophical and political axis? Their limit is *the very existence of life on the planet*. Are we still faced with a dialectical development and is it in spite of everything still possible and desirable to teach Ideology Critique as an educational tool? Should Critical Pedagogy continue to search for realizing a positive Utopia in face of mega speed realities, deconstruction of pre-conditions for transcendence and the rapidly growing probability of bringing an end to all life on earth as a manifestation of progress that went mad in a post-metaphysical moment?

Any present-day attempts to rearticulate Critical Theory should take into consideration the following: in face of the threat to the very existence of the planet we are challenged by *the exile of the pre-conditions and the very quest for transcendence and the irrelevance of love, intimacy, creativity, meaning, and exclusively valued aim*; at the same time we stand before the rise of the world of *Jihad*: a totalistic-oriented spiritual alternative of the victims of the holiness of killing-God-each-moment-anew in the form of armed, dogmatic, fanatic, fundamentalism that is ready and willing for a total destruction of the present order of things, with the technological potential almost at hand to destroy the entire human civilization or, at least, Western civilization as we know it (Althourity, 2006). One of the master signifiers of this alternative is the slogan "Death to Freedom!" This is the meeting point of the disciples of Nasrallah, Chavez and Bill Gates. What is the stance of "critique" in face of anti-democratic victims that are committed to reaching world hegemony and establishing a totalitarian world order, or commit nothing less than total destruction of any otherness, or, alternatively, destruction for the sake of ecstasies as spectacle that inherits holiness which was possible in the world of transcendence, love and mysterium? What are the prospects of a new critical language in education in face of "the general skepticism about theory in anything stronger than its ironic or deconstructive forms, and the general feeling of helplessness in face of impersonal forces and the fragmentation of life" (McCarthy, 2001, p. 428)? What are the prospects for a new critical language in education in light of current Critical Pedagogy's' celebration of Badiou and Zizek who promise us a rebirth of Leninist violence and "a genuine" revolution even more radical than the Pol Pot experiment with the lives of the Cambodian people while supporting the projects of Chavez, Nasrallah, Ahmadinejad and Kin Jon-il against "Western colonialism" or Jewish Monotheism? How should we understand current Critical Pedagogy as part of the new progressivism that supports anti-humanist ideologies and struggles against liberal, democratic and humanistic-oriented "old" progressivism as the manifestation of Lucifer or "Empire"?

Critical Pedagogies today have abandoned altogether their responsibility for a Critical Theory that will be the framework and foundation of current critical education. Many critical pedagogues accept poststructuralist deconstruction cynically or in a naïve manner and celebrate anti-democratic agendas and the most violent ethnocentrism "of the victims" such as those of Hamas and Hezbollah while offering "critique" and "resistance" to democracy, humanism or "whiteness"; they "resist" any humanist-oriented general Critical Theory that dares to present itself as universally valid or, at least, as the one committed to reaching closer to the truth or even to fairness and care; these critical pedagogues reject any educational project that conceives itself as more than contingent, contextualized, fruit of violent-meaningless-aimless-power-relations which for them are legitimate pragmatically, contingently or as an empowerment of the self-evidence and the counter-violence of the victims of the "Empire" or the victims of the Judeo-Christian civilization. At best it tries to offer a universally valid ethical framework for counter-education that unites pluralism and rejection of any claim for monopoly, total resistance to any exclusivity—on knowledge, meanings, ethical and moral judgment—(Offir, 1996) which is so problematic for the exclusive mission of this Critical Pedagogy itself.

Today, dear friends, we are not faced with the challenge of "correcting" or "saving" Critical Pedagogy. We stand before the challenge of finding/constructing *a new critical language* that will go beyond the limitations of the present dogmatized-eclectically-rearticulated Critical Pedagogies. While we continue this elaboration the reality that demanded Critical Pedagogy in the first place is becoming ever more acute; new threats to the future of the very survival of humanity and the earth are gathering momentum every day, as part of the techno-scientific progress, the new technologies, and the empowerment of some of the most miserable victims of capitalistic colonization. At the same time outside the borders of the world of Jihad, within the framework of the McWorld, other victims of this historical development become ever more enthusiastic supporters of their victimization apparatuses and their ideological frameworks. What we are facing presently is the *simultaneous* processes of deconstruction of the pre-conditions for transcendence (and therefore also for edifying "critique") and the surrendering of the victims to their victimization processes and some of their counter-violence ideals and practices, in educational, political, military, and existential terms.

Examples of this one can meet in the way our kids surrender themselves to the logic of capitalism and to the quest of pleasurable self-forgetfulness in cyberspace, or in the coalition between revolutionary Venezuela and fundamentalist Iran or in the cult of death and anti-reflectivity in the Palestinian nation-building project.

These, and so many others, are normally unmet by serious responses by today's various Critical Pedagogies. New, rearticulated, evaluations and fresh responses are urgently needed. But in what language should we reevaluate the very concepts of "compassion", "autonomy", "independence", "victimization", "emancipation", "truth", "solidarity", "dialogue", "critique", "education" and "peace"? Not only is it not enough to present a new rhetorical fashion and new forms and norms of politically-correct anti-intellectual tools and agreements. What we genuinely need is far beyond that. What we need is a shift, a rebirth, a new beginning in face of *the End*.

Time is here critical: 1. In the sense of the loss of historical perspective as part of the exile of transcendental holiness and the deconstruction of "Monotheism". 2. In the form of universally-valid quests, hierarchies, linear history, values and ideals (in cyberspace and in the youth culture, to name two examples). 3. In the potential of self-edification in the totality of the autopoiesized moment. 4. In face of the growing probability of bringing an end to all life on earth as a side effect of present technological progress.

And until then? In the absence of a new Moses, Buddha, or Jesus, what we are permitted to seek for and counter-educate to is *a new respond-ability*. Responsibility of the kind that response-ability precedes (Gur-Ze'ev, 2005, pp. 26–30). It is not primarily "theoretical" nor is it first and foremost political as a tool or even an aim: it is related to the ethical sphere and to the existential more than to the moral-historical-political arenas of human existence and human work.

Situated in *Diaspora* as a Utopian existence, Diasporic responsibility unites response-ability and respond-ability. An unsolvable tension, an abyss, exists between the two; even if both are authentic manifestations of the richness of Life, part of the *derech eretz* of the *Orcha*. Respond-ability is enabled, enhanced and challenged in the historical-political level of existence. It relates to the questions of freedom and emancipation from oppressive manipulations in the conscious, intellectual, and psychological level of moral life, the life of the human as a political agent. On this level the original intimacy with the world is replaced by the philosophical-political alternative which is "natural" and committed to effective manipulation of nature and humans. It extends and sometimes transforms the Godly project of "homecoming", and calls for the psyche while abandoning or negating the pneuma. Response-ability, by contrast, relates first and foremost to the pneuma: to the Spiritual, unarticulated brink of existence. Here the psyche, the moral-historical, and even the natural order of things are conceived much as in the Gnostic tradition, as a triumphant violence that exiled the original order of things. In this sense, response-ability overcomes dogmatized, psychologically justified conventions and the various fruits of normalized education and the order it makes possible. Diasporic existence manifests response-ability; it represents genuine creativity and togetherness with the cosmos as a Diasporic wholeness whose victory over the primordial is never complete, or must be "punished" as Anaximander teaches us already before the quest for transcendence in the Platonic tradition. The present historical situation and the stance of Critical Theory and Critical Pedagogy *open new possibilities* for a counter-education that will manifest genuine response-ability. In this sense we are on the edge of a new beginning, even if not in the sense of a new, positive, Utopia, but much more of the kind symbolized in the tradition of Negative Theology. Within the framework of the new anti-Semitism we are so close to overcome monotheism itself as it is invested in the historical development of Western philosophy and techno-scientific progress realized and manifested in the spirit and practice of capitalism.

If true to itself, today's counter-education must go beyond the ability to propose fresh articulations and more effective "emancipatory" didactics. It must reach beyond the overcoming of current trends in Critical Pedagogy. Today's Diasporic counter-education has the titanic mission of evisiting the lost language that was spoken by the builders of the Tower of Babel. The true reappearance of the silenced/deconstructed language might come true only in a negative manner, as a *Utopia*; as the presence of the absence, in face of the new realities and the impasse of Western culture and the self-cannibalism enacted by its spiritual techno-scientific advance, its economic progress, and by the counter-offensive of the demons it summons to counter-attack the ugliness and demanding penance for its killing of

God/absolute. This is the gate for new anti-Semitism as the grad spiritual alternative to Judeo-Christian false promise of personal redemption and universal emancipation. The new anti-Semitism, however, with all its relevance and creativity is essentially anti-Diasporic. However, with all its importance as a new meta-narrative for the progressive circles (in different degrees and various prisms) I still insist on a Diasporic, on a genuine Diasporic addressing the challenges of a post-metaphysical historical moment.

As part of this responsibility I would say that today's counter-education should not run away from the current absence of intimate relations and mutual fertilization between the existential dimension, the philosophical dimension, the physical dimension, the ethical dimension, the aesthetic dimension and the political dimension in Life. Reestablishing intimacy is not easy, and is far from being a mere fruit of a strong will. As an *act of will*, as a conscious effort it can only be realized negatively and individually. It must also address the question *who is the sovereign of "my" "free will"?* Negativity and individuality, however, when struggled for or when realized it has so many faces, some of which are "positive", durable, communicative, and even part of a new togetherness. And even so, only for the individual or for a twinkling of an eye. What we are talking about here is nothing less than a *turn*, a new beginning. Its spaces are historical, political, and physical, yet they turn to transcend the given facts and the present order as long as they are a-historical and refuse political "success".

Response-ability and responding are very different from the mechanical responses, from the reactions that fears and habits enhance or other manners of self-forgetfulness enrich. Human creation as part of overcoming the call for self-forgetfulness is unavoidably realized in ways relevant to saving the otherness of the human as an individual, as a unique, autonomous, potentially self-edifying human. This is so, while the "risk society" (Beck, 2004) not only inflicts polluted rivers, shrinking forests and dehumanized or uprooted communities: it endangers the very existence of the earth and offers total McDonaldization of reality. The fragmented, isolated *cracks* as well as the new technologically enhanced possibilities are united in the saying of the world of Jihad as against the optimism of the McWorld: risk, danger, suffering and tragedy manifest today, in their peculiar ways, the presence of hope, love, and rebirth.

Poetry and dance, gymnastics and spiritual edification as part of the realization of response-ability might after all offer new possibilities for renewed being-toward-a Godless-world, a renewed relation to the meaning of holiness and the holiness of meaning might become possible precisely within the dullness of "our" historical moment. The holiness of meaning and the meaning of holiness are not abstract. It is the guide of Diasporic existence toward responsible-improvised-co-poiesis; in the form of com-passion it is a way of life. It is the impetus of the *Orcha* and the present-day actual Diasporic relation between knowledge and intimacy. And here I would like to conclude with the words of Rilke that opened this meeting which concern the possibility of a new critical language in education:

If true to itself it is Diasporic. And if it is genuinely Diasporic it is all about Love.

NOTES

[1] Reworked paper presented at the Critical Theory and Critical Pedagogy International Workshop, Oxford, New College, 2 April 2006.
[2] Hamas encouraging children to become living bombs See: http://www.al-fateh.net/

REFERENCES

Althouiry, I. (2006, March 4). Second in rank to Bin Laden. http://www.memri.org.il/memri/LoadArticle Page.asp?enttype=4&entid=1937&language=Hebrew

Amin, A. (2003). Post-Fordism: Models, fantasies and phantoms of transition. In A. Amin (Ed.), *Post-Fordism—A reader* (pp. 1–40). Oxford: Blackwell.

Beck, U. (2004). *Risk society—toward a new modernity* (M. Ritter, Trans.). London: Sage Publications.

Deleuze, G., & Guattari, F. (1994). *What is philosophy?* (H. Tomlinson & G. Burchell, Trans.). New York: Columbia University Press.

Gur-Ze'ev, I. (1999). Cyberfeminism and education in the era of the exile of spirit. *Educational Theory, 49*(4), 437–455.

Gur-Ze'ev, I. (2000). Critical education in the cyberspace? *Educational Philosophy and Theory, 32*(2), 209–231.

Gur-Ze'ev, I. (2005). Critical theory, critical pedagogy and diaspora today. In I. Gur-Ze'ev (Ed.), *Critical theory and critical pedagogy today—toward a new critical language in education*. Haifa: Faculty of Education, University of Haifa.

Gur-Ze'ev, I. (2005a). Adorno and Horkheimer: Negative theology, diasporic philosophy and counter-education. *Educational Theory, 55*(3), 343–365.

Heidegger, M. (1996). Letter on humanism. *Basic writings*. London: Routledge.

Kellner, D. (1996, February). Techno-Politics, new technologies, and the new public spheres. http://www.uta.edu/huma/illuminations/kell32.htm

McCarthy, T. (2001). Critical theory today: An interview with Tomas McCarthy. In S. O'Neill, & N. Smith, W. Rehg, & J. Bohman (Eds.), *Pluralism and the pragmatic turn—the transformation of critical theory*. Cambridge, MA: The MIT Press.

Offir, A. (1996). Postmodernism—a philosophical standpoint. In I. Gur-Ze'ev (Ed.), *Education in the era of the postmodern discourse*. Jerusalem: The Magnes Press. (Hebrew)

Rilke, R. M. (1975). *Rilke on love and other difficulties* (J. L. Mood, Trans.). New York: W. W. Norton.

ILAN GUR-ZE'EV

2. CRITICAL THEORY, CRITICAL PEDAGOGY AND DIASPORA TODAY

Critical Pedagogy faces today a very strange situation. While being positioned in a seemingly comfortable position and warmly received by so many liberals, post-colonialists, multi-culturalists, postmodernists, and feminists (to name only few of the long list of its adorers), it is being domesticated, appeased, or even castrated by the present order of things. It became too successful, under different titles, while under the flag of Critical Pedagogy it became domesticated, disoriented, or dogmatized. Today it has become difficult to speak of "Critical Pedagogy"; it is quite ambitious even to articulate the essential elements common to the various and conflicting pedagogies that propagate themselves under the banner of "Critical Pedagogy".

Critical Pedagogy was constituted on the central concepts of Critical Theory and on the material, social, and cultural conditions that enabled the critical Utopia. It was part of a rich Western tradition, not just a sign of a dramatic crisis in modern thought and reality. If in classical times the whole was conceived as prior to the parts, and harmony preceded differences and otherness, the imperial Roman era already acknowledged the turn away from the wholeness of the cosmos. Stoa and Gnosis represented it in rich, different, ways. For Gnosis *Being is temporary*; not eternal. *Being is essentially split* and antagonistic to itself. The temporality of Being and its infinite not-identical-with-itself is acknowledged also by St. Augustine in the tenth book of his *Confessions* as well as in the first Letter to Thessalonians in the New Testament. Without abandoning truth, it faced the retreat of classical togetherness of humans and the wholeness of the cosmos, as well as the priority and supremacy of the whole over its individual parts. Cosmic intimacy and unproblematic self-evidence were replaced by alienation; alienation between the parts and the whole, and alienation within the individual himself. Medieval Christianity offered an alternative—via the "homereturning" project. With the assistance of dogma and well kept walls between classes in society, and between Christian and Jewish sacred truth and existence, it maintained a fairly stable illusion of coherent, steady, relations between the intellect, moral faculty and the aesthetical dimensions of life, and the body. This relative stability was perceived as part of a redeemed, yet fragile and threatened whole: between the Christian, the world, the Other, and knowledge about worthy knowledge. This stable hierarchy, which divided Spirit and body, supra-human and worldly-life, was never genuinely harmonious, stable, coherent, or wholly penetrating. In actuality it did not safely protect the hegemonic social order and its realms of self-evidence: it was actually questioned time and again by rebellious poor farmers, well-educated heretics, witches, madmen, children, women, Jews,

I. Gur-Ze'ev, The Possibility/Impossibility of a New Critical Language in Education, 15–38.
© *2010 Sense Publishers. All Rights Reserved.*

and other Others. And yet, it enjoyed relative success in hiding its *immanent violence*, which offered, aside from inequality (after death), suffering, ignorance, and effective silencing of the free spirit. At this price, however, it offered *meaning* to the given reality and *hope* for transcendence. The demolition of the medieval Western Christian world was brought about by the strengthening and by the universalization of two versions of its arch-rival: the alliance of classical Greek thought and Judaism. Herman Cohen emphasized the *universal realization of Judaism as the expression of the critical spirit and humanism* (Choen, 1972)—Karl Marx (Marx, 1919) emphasized the *universal realization of Judaism as manifested by the logic and practice of capitalism* (Gur-Ze'ev, 2005, pp. 256–299). The medieval Christian world could not very long resist such united, erotic, transcending powers.

The medieval order could not sustain durable resistance to the new philosophical and scientific revolutionary developments (Horkheimer, 1985, VIII., p. 286), or to the economic, social, technological, and national challenges imposed by the spirit of capitalism. In modernity the critical project was aimed at a positive mission: reestablishing the world as a "home"; *offering a "home returning" project for humans, back to a (pre)meaningful wholeness* enhanced by rational, solidarian, dialogical, individuals. Within the framework of Enlightenment individuals committed themselves to re-constitute the Garden of Eden on earth via critical thinking and collective rational-political praxis. The Critical Theory thinkers of the Frankfurt School were faced with the problematic of the unattainable metaphysical assumptions for this mission. They also acknowledged the new, irrelevant, social conditions for the realization of the Enlightenment's educational project—and along with Heidegger and existentialism, they not only refused any metaphysic, they further developed a *Diasporic philosophy*—one that addressed humans' ontological *Diasporic existence*. They responded to the human condition as "being-thrown-into-the-world", meaninglessness, and omnipotent-cannibalistic-violence that enhances "culture" and "progress" only as new forms of nihilistic negation of love of Life in its wholeness.

For late Adorno and Horkheimer, this was the beginning of a new, vivid, thinking, not the end of their Utopian undertaking. Even if they were not aware of it, we can still identify in their later work that the dissolution of the promise of modernity became, actually, a gate for a new beginning. Earthly, Diasporic, life disconnected from the Exile-Redemption narrative, became an entry for a renewed, negative, ecstatic, intimacy with the world. Out of awareness of the existential situatedness as *being-thrown-into-the-world* they articulated a concept of *living-toward-the-not-yet-in-a-Godless-world*, in the totality of each moment. Living, here, is not so much in the sense of self protection and reproduction as in the sense of "becoming", of commitment for self-constitution and edification. Diasporic life enabled creative improvisations and births, which made meaninglessness an impetus to new possibilities for happiness, meaning, aim, and togetherness.

Within the framework of mature Critical Theory the concept of *Diaspora* was developed even beyond the Gnostic division between the exiled, hidden, God and the evil God of creation/reality; a division between evil nature and meaningless laws and fabrications—and the wholeness and supremacy of nothingness/chaos.

The contribution of Critical Theory to the history of Diasporic Philosophy was made possible by the change of stance of the concepts, ideals, symbols, strivings, and other signifiers which were dissolved, ridiculed, or forgotten in the era of advanced capitalism and its fully administered world in which progress paralleled the broadening of the possibilities for emancipation on the one hand, and the empowerment of the oppression of the individual to the level of the instincts, on the other (Horkheimer, 1974, p. 141). Not only the promise of Enlightenment became irrelevant: the traditional Gnostic rejection of the world of facts and its entire negative alternative became anecdotal at best, in face of the life conditions dictated by the omnipotence of Instrumental Rationality and advanced capitalism and its Culture Industry.

Some Critical Pedagogy thinkers such as McLaren, Gruschka, Mason, Tubbs, De-Olivera, Zeichner, Roth and Weiler insist on the modernistic-oriented humanist project. Others, such as Michael Peters, Patti Lather, and Gert Biesta, emphasize the new possibilities within the framework of the postmodern discourses and the postmodern conditions. Still others, such as Colin Lankshear, Wendy Kohly, Nicholas Burbules, Raquel Moraes, Mark Olssen, Elisabeth Heilman, Eduardo Duarte and Henry Giroux, search for a creative synthesis between modern and postmodern sensitivities, conceptions, practices, technologies and paths for communication, existence and education. But this is far from being the only dichotomy. Other dichotomies crisscross Critical Pedagogy today on the level of gender, multiculturalism, postcolonialism, and queer conflicting theories. Sometime the line of division crisscrosses not solely critical thinkers and agendas—they oppose each other even in their own educational philosophy. Other critical philosophers, such as Jan Masschelein, refuse to identify themselves further with Critical Pedagogy, and search for a worthier alternative by long meditative walking in silence and in other paths. Regardless to the degree of identification with Critical Pedagogy, it seems to me that many critical pedagogues are today ready for, or actually searching for *a new critical language in education* that will go beyond the achievements and limitations of Critical Pedagogy.

In itself this is nothing to regret or to be sorry for. What is regrettable, however, is that so much of Critical Pedagogy has become dogmatic, and sometimes anti-intellectual, while on the other hand losing its relevance for the people it conceived as victims to be emancipated. Why is this regrettable? Because the erotic telos of Critical Pedagogy insists on poetic, religiously anti-dogmatic, worthy Life as a manifestation of Love, not of fear or of heated "critique". Because it symbolizes the quest for freedom and refusal of meaningless suffering in face of the *loss of naïve intimacy with the world* and with the truth of Being, and because, sometimes, it actually enhances equality and resists oppression; even if actually it normally promotes new forms of oppression and enhances new ways for *self-forgetfulness*. In detaching itself from the rich works of Adorno, Benjamin, Horkheimer, and the other thinkers of Critical Theory, Critical Pedagogy in its different versions has abandoned its attunement to *Life* itself in so many respects.

Currently next to no attempts are being made to confront Critical Pedagogy with reality in actual, enduring, pedagogical engagements. No wonder then that next to

17

no attempts are being made to articulate an educational framework for critical teachers' training either, and certainly no ongoing practice of teachers' training at schools. Important exceptions here are the theoretical and practical contributions of Kenneth Zeichner (Zeichner, 1990, pp. 105–131; Zeichner, 1993, pp. 1–13), Daniel Liston (Liston, 2000, pp. 81–102), and Andreas Gruschka (Gruschka, 1986). All this, in face of deceptive calls from the various symbols, strivings, and technologies of globalizing capitalism, and alongside the actuality of anti-reflective and ethnocentric-oriented construction of collective identities of many of the oppressed groups that are so enthusiastically idolized by many disciples of Critical Pedagogy. These are but fragmentary examples of the detachment of current Critical Pedagogies from the wholeness, depths, abysses, dangers, and richness of Life.

Critical Pedagogy contributed more than its fair share in an ongoing attempt to be relevant to political challenges, especially for marginalized and oppressed groups. This is an attempt of vital importance, especially when it is conducted in the wider context of the current crisis in the stance of humanistic-oriented knowledge and its dynamics (as in the work of Burbules, Peters, Heilman, Biesta, Tubbs, Rimon-Or, Marshall, Mason, Gruschka, and Masschelein), or within the context of historical cultural, and economic changes (as in the case of McLaren, Apple, Kellner, and Duarte). The present historical moment, however, needs so much more than that. And overcoming any historical moment and its imperatives, walls, and possibilities calls for even more than that. We cannot, however, offer, arbitrarily, new master signifiers, strivings, or openness, nor a new critical language, at the present historical moment.

A new critical vocabulary, and not-yet-born master-signifiers, along with other genuine manifestations of **the totally other** (Heidegger, 1993, p. 258; Horkheimer, 1985, VII., pp. 385–404), cannot appear out of the blue, on demand. Master-signifiers, new horizons, and historical shifts are parts of the rich affluence of Being and are manifested differently in all parts and dimensions of the cosmos, preceding any abstraction, law, or control. They might be approached by humans as *manifestations of Love vs. Metaphysical Violence*, or as the infinite/restrained presence of *affluence as Metaphysical Violence*. In any case, these do not behave like domesticated pets, and are never at humans' mercy. They are true manifestations of the infinity and freedom of Being. The new master-signifiers are essentially unforeseeable, uncontrollable, and never totally deciphered, or truly to be mobilized for further productivization, preservation, or enrichment of the instrumental ways for being-in-the-world. They burst into reality—or do not appear at all, beyond determinism, contingency, and unpredictability. Their possible appearance enables freedom and necessity, yet it is not conditioned by laws of freedom, determinism, or representation.

When **the totally other** bursts into a specific historical moment the realm of self-evidence is cracked by this manifestation of "messianic time" (Benjamin, 1980, p. 695), and "now-time" (ibid., p. 701) is irreparably shattered by "redemption"; the epoch of the essentially newly born possibilities becomes not only possible but actually inevitable. It is the moment for untouched horizons, fresh master-signifiers, and fruitful, dynamic, new creations, reactions, and life-and-death wars.

The truth of Being and the hidden violence of the historical moment might become unveiled by poetry, philosophy, art, dance, and singing. At such a rare moment dialogue with the world (that conditions any genuine human communication and "dialogue") and self-reflection face newly born possibilities. The very possibility of such a moment is a precondition for transcendence and for counter-education, which will uncover fresh forms of intimacy and creation with and amid distorted Being.

The possibility of a new critical language in education and of spanking new possibilities for approaching the nearness of truth and the richness of Life are always a matter for human concern. But even at the best of times it is in our hands only partially and always merely conditionally, fragmentarily, and frigidly. And this too, only for a fleeting moment. This is an important positive dimension of Negative Utopia: it means that there is so much that we can do, under the present conditions— actually, under any conditions! And yet, essentially, there is always a limit not only to our possibilities within the historical moment: the very existence of meaningful horizons and their specific material, symbolic, and existential characteristics are essentially *not ours* but a challenge to overcome, a potential to transcend.

Present-day Critical Pedagogy faces, as the authors of this collection manifest, challenges of different kinds, and it responds to these challenges in various, different, and at times conflicting, ways. Among these challenges the contributors to this collection note globalizing capitalism, the introduction of new technologies in communication, the change in the stance and function of knowledge, the dramatic shift in the structure of society, and the transformation of relations between work, finance, and the state in the era of the McWorld (Barber, 1995).

Obsolete conceptions of class-struggle and traditional emancipatory sensitivities, vocabularies, and practices are deconstructed, consumed, reified and neutralized in the present historical moment, while marginalization, suffering, injustice, and structural blocking from cultural and political capital become ever more sophisticated and harsh for ever more people around the globe. Under these circumstances normalizing education becomes a vital element of the oppression, not solely as part of the direct and indirect violence inflicted on the poor, the homeless, mino-rity races, ethnicities, cultures, and other Others. It becomes at the same time an almost *omnipotent de-humanizing power* by the minorities, the oppressed, and the marginalized—against their own Others, against their oppressive powers and against free spirit, thinking, and Life.

Critical Pedagogy, in its different versions, has usually failed to meet this challenge of emancipatory pedagogy, becoming part and parcel of normalizing education (Gur-Ze'ev, 1998, pp. 463–486). Its identification with the marginalized and the oppressed, and its commitment to a positive Utopia, allowed it to sharpen its critique and become instrumental in many academic radical circles. Committed to its various positive Utopias in the fields of feminist, multi-cultural, race, class, post-colonial, and queer struggles, the different versions of Critical Pedagogy have more than once become dogmatic, ethnocentrist, and violent. Concurrently, they have become increasingly popular in ever widening academic circles, and decreasingly relevant to the victims it is committed to emancipate. What is to be done, for that which the different versions of Critical Pedagogy treat to be seriously re-approached? For a genuine rejection of injustice and the nearness *to truth as Love and as violence, as affluence and as scarcity/fright, as the presence of Eros and the presence of Thanatos,* not to be abandoned in favor of fashionable, domesticating "radical" rhetoric? I limit myself to six aspects of this manifold and rich challenge, from the perspectives of Diasporic Philosophy and counter-education.

I believe I do not run the risk of exaggeration by asserting that in fact *all current versions of Critical Pedagogy have lost their intimate connections to the Critical Theory of the Frankfurt School*; not much is left of its original relation with the Frankfurt School that was an enrichment so fruitful for the very possibility of Critical Pedagogy; for Paulo Freire and early Henry Giroux, Peter McLaren, Michael Apple, Ira Shor, and other founders of the unexpected present popularity (and irrelevance) of the different versions of Critical Pedagogy. This historical and philosophical gap is not a regretful condition per se; if only a fruitful transformation and a rich, elevating, alternative had lifted Critical Pedagogy beyond Critical Theory! How regrettable that this promise is still not- actualized. It has not happened, even if the influences of postmodernism, post- structuralism, postcolonialism, new versions of feminism, multiculturalism, and queer theories have indeed enriched many aspects of current Critical Pedagogy. What is it that is lost, and should be courageously addressed?

Most versions of Critical Pedagogy opened themselves up to the influences of postmodern and post-colonialist academic rhetoric, which has become so popular in American and European universities. In their rush to become politically active and relevant in the field of education the Critical Pedagogy thinkers overlooked the essential instincts, ideals, and telos of Critical Theory that Critical Pedagogy, at its best moments, committed itself to "realize".

Critical Pedagogy thinkers forgot that mature Critical Theory was a *Negative Utopia*—not a Positive Utopia (Gur-Ze'ev, 1998a, pp. 119–155). Later Horkheimer and Adorno dismissed any "revolutionary", "radical", or "emancipatory" project that promised reconciliation, "just peace", an "end to suffering", "salvation" for the victims, or even advancement on this road. Demolition of terror would inevitably result in cultural and social deconstruction, according to Adorno and Horkheimer (Adorno & Horkheimer, 1988, p. 225), and Benjamin asserted that there is no cultural document that was not a manifestation of barbarism Benjamin, 1999, p. 256). Even the idea of approaching "truth" via ideology-critique was problematic for them, since, according to Adorno, cultural critique itself had become reified, and critical spirit, when content with itself, cannot challenge the total reification of the present historical moment (Adorno, 1993, p. 157).

The mature work of Adorno and Horkheimer is not optimistic, yet it insists on the Utopian axis of *Life* in all its manifestations—as a Negative Utopia. Philosophical pessimism makes the Messianic impulse possible, and redemption is what is being addressed here (Horkheimer, 1985, VII., p. 231), while insisting on what in Negative Theology was conceived as *the presence of the absence of God.* Horkheimer notes explicitly in his diary entry for 5 July 1923 that this is his personal impetus for philosophizing (Horkheimer, 1987, XI., p. 235). There is such a rich, infinite, space for creative courage, Love of Life and transcending power in awareness of the presence of meaninglessness in face not of the absence of truth—but on the contrary, in face of the presence of the successful (contingent) production of truths, values, and yardsticks for evaluation of rival values, truths, and passions! All this in the service of a life-and-death struggle between rival arenas of truths-and-values-production, in support of nihilistic *self-forgetfulness* of humans' being-toward-life.

In light of the tradition of Diasporic Philosophy the mature Critical Theory of Adorno and Horkheimer conceived the unbridgeable tension between equality and freedom; the abyss between human culture and the harmonic, beautiful-meaningless self-contentment of nature as a starting point for their (negative) Utopia; without being swallowed by false promises to overcome the dialectics of Life, the abysses and dangers facing true love and genuine creativity, and certainly *without promising social "emancipation" or "revolution"* (Horkheimer, 1985, VII., p. 341; Horkheimer, 1985, VIII., p. 346) or a true, unproblematic, educational alternative of the kind Critical Pedagogy educators normally are so quick to promise us in so many voices and agendas (Gur-Ze'ev, 1998, p. 469).

When Horkheimer declares his abandonment of Marx in favor of Schopenhauer (Horkheimer, 1985, VIII., p. 339) he actually comes very close to some of the central Gnostic conceptions within the framework of a Diasporic Philosophy. The foundations and the telos of the Enlightenment's modern emancipatory tradition and its Marxian versions are fundamentally challenged in the later works of Adorno and Horkheimer. Even the young Horkheimer already noted in his diary that he was most uncomfortable with the tranquilizing dimension of the Marxian Utopia (Horkheimer, 1987, XI., p. 269). This part of their work is too often ignored by today's radical and emancipatory educators. Here it might be worth bearing in mind that for the Gnosis authentic freedom is never to be related to the human mind or psyche—which are constructed and policed by historical power-relations and violent manipulations (much in the same manner as the body is enacted by the physical law). Solely the Spirit, the *pneuma*, the foreign, never-to-be-defined-nor-controlled element in Life manifests genuine freedom. Human psyche and mind are part of the evil creation of the *Demiurgus* that rules over all the world of individual existence and thingness.

Late Adorno and Horkheimer did not satisfy themselves in recycling a Gnostic concept of salvation within the framework of the reformulated late Critical Theory; they further developed (a beginning) of a *Diasporic Philosophy*, which refuses to offer any "solution", "method", or "salvation" (Gur-Ze'ev, 2003, pp. 17–35). Their later work acknowledges the *Diaspora* as the gate to rich alternative thinking and becoming-toward-the-world.

This gate I understand as an important starting point for a present-day Diasporic counter-education. Of special importance here is their refusal of any version of Positive Utopia and of all calls for "salvation", "emancipation", "effectiveness", or "success". This is also a refusal of any kind of nihilism and abandonment of hope and Love of Life. For Diasporic humans, here the return to the (absent) wholeness and richness of nature is part of (re)establishing (negative) cosmic intimacy. Adorno and Horkheimer are much closer here to Hans Jonas and Immanuel Levinas than to Heidegger, who, as Jonas rightly noted, had no respect for nature (Jonas, 1992, p. 339).

Parallel to their intensive efforts to become "relevant", "involved", "effective", and "emancipating", the current different versions of Critical Pedagogy lost not only Negative Utopia. Today's Critical Pedagogy lost another essential element of Critical Theory—the attempt to transcend itself and to enable a worthier nearness to dialectical intimacy to the richness of Life in its wholeness. Critical Pedagogy abandoned the Negative Utopian kind of commitment to transcendence in favor of another: commitment to successful political activity and effective practical involvement that will ensure us being successfully swallowed by the continuum of the immanence; a successful return into thingness. This is a switch from a Diasporic project, which is committed to a never-concluding-effort of *transcendence*, to a different one, which while paying lip service to "resistance" and "emancipation" is totally committed to a nihilistic devotion to the closure of *immanence*. It runs away from eternal worthy suffering that is part and parcel of Diasporic nomadism and its struggle for a never-concluding-effort at transcendence—not for a reconciling "homereturning" project (which frequently praises exile too—only to end in nirvana, "redemption", "tragic heroism", "consistent nihilism" or other forms of Thanatos). This turn was paralleled in the last thirty years by overemphasis on either the intellectual aspects of education (ideology-critique, conscious awareness enhancement, and so forth), or on the subjective "experience" of the oppressed pupil and the self-evidence of diverse conflicting, marginalized collectives that strive for hegemony and "emancipation" that will ultimately effectively enslave their Others, without leaving traces or exacting too high a price.

Contrary to this trend, the Frankfurt School critical thinkers, while opposing the tradition of "life-philosophy", took all kinds of existential self-evidence and philosophical self-contentment as a challenge that might effectively destroy or exile the transcending potential of human existence (Horkheimer, 1990, pp. 276–299). They did not try to establish intimacy with the self-evidence of hegemonic or marginalized collectives. They conceived *self-evidence* as collective closure and as a great danger for the free human spirit. Intimacy, patriotism, and dogmatism for them were threats of being swallowed by thingness, nature, and myth.

As Diasporic thinkers, they centered their thought on the relation between the human subject and the world. Subject and object were not mere abstract theoretical categories for Adorno and Horkheimer. The human and nature, and especially the estrangement between the two, enforced by Western Instrumental Rationality, were a starting point for Enlightenment, and therefore also for Critical Theory, which acknowledges that all along history humans had to decide between two possibilities: enslaving nature or being enslaved by it (Adorno & Horkheimer, p. 71). For them the acknowledgement of humans' homelessness in a Godless world was the gate to the elaboration of possibilities for a worthy response and for the possibility of cultivating what I call *Diasporic response-ability*.

Diasporic response-ability addresses the affluence of meaninglessness and violence since the destruction of the chaos/nothingness and the history of Godly creation/ human "progress". Response-ability in this sense is not merely passive and not solely active; it is not a mere manifestation of affluence in Life, nor is it exclusively a manifestation of human scarcity. If, true to its Diasporic essence, it does not offer counter-violence against nature and against humans, nor does it offer what Nietzsche called slave morality as a gate for transcendence: it refuses all calls for escape in self-protection and pleasure/truth as the ultimate goal of Life. Here response-ability acknowledges meaninglessness and suffering, and does not try to escape them or the danger of self-destruction: it transcends them within the creativity of Love, Diasporic, non-sentimental Love of Life and its abysses (Horkheimer, 1987, XI., p. 366). It transcends them in the sense that it challenges the traditional lines of division between "transcendence" and "immanence", "home" and "homelessness". The various conflicting collective Positive Utopias, and individual escapist, nihilist, and relativist "homereturning" projects, were for them a manifestation of the forgetfulness of human forgetfulness; not a worthy response to this challenge, which in advanced capitalism became stronger and more sophisticated than ever. In their mature work, after the publication of the *Dialectic of Enlightenment*, they searched for a third, Diasporic, path between the Scylla of collectivism-dogmatism and the Charybdis of selfish, relativist-oriented Instrumental Rationality that sees nature and the Other as a mere standing reserve, an object of manipulation or a source of terrible danger. The Diasporic counter-education that we can reconstruct from the tradition of Diasporic Philosophy (and here Adorno and Horkheimer are of special relevance to us) challenges modern nihilism, in all its forms. It maintains both dualism and dialectics, yet insists on Love and intimacy in a Godless world, where human rationality cannot establish any alternative Garden of Eden, meaning, aim, or an authentic "I".

Current Critical Pedagogy either continues the anti-Diasporic conception of the human as a mere "rational animal", or is swallowed by the sweet soporific power of the reformulated Sirens who call us with their irresistible beauty, as with Odysseus in his day, to come back *"home" to harmonious nature*: to the homogeneous-totalistic-infinity of the thingness; a safe "homereturning" to the infinity and the beauties of nature and harmonious thingness; back to nothing-ness, after finally defeating and abandoning the wonder, danger, and openness of otherness in Being and in the human being. In these two versions of Critical Pedagogy, its thinkers reveal a lack of attention and the importance of their avoidance; the significance of neglect of a theoretical, practical, physical, and existential synthesis.

This neglect offers a synthesis between human and world; a synthesis, yet never a symbiosis, between the moment and eternity, signifier and signified, becoming and nothingness, Diaspora as an ontological, epistemological, existential attunement to the call to self-creation, as against self-forgetfulness; as an alternative to being swallowed by all "homereturning" appeals and all salvation/emancipation agendas and educational projects that offer to constitute the "I" via the "we" and the self-evident, true, or relevant values, truths, ideals, and strivings.

Critical Pedagogy's abandonment of Critical Theory's Diasporic Philosophy is constructive indeed. This desertion enables its easygoing disregard for the educational connections between and among dance, poetry, play, singing, responsibility, intellectual edification, and non-oppressive political involvement. Critical Theory's Diasporic Philosophy's addressing the richness, meaninglessness, and potentialities of being-toward-the-Godless-world, with no absolute, with no undeceiving "home-returning" telos, is the only gate for hope (Gur-Ze'ev, forthcoming). Here we should remind ourselves that hope was so central to Critical Theory (Horkheimer, 1985, VII., p. 386), not part of a normalizing education that calls us to be swallowed by ethnocentrism and dogma as an alternative to an irrational intimacy with the cosmos, but on the contrary, as the only open gate to a mature, Diasporic, intimacy with loving, creatively improvising, Life in a Godless world. It is a Godless world not in the sense that there is no meaning to God but in the sense of the meaningful absence of God, and the *presence of creative metaphysical violence*, suffering, and meaninglessness in a human life.

Critical Pedagogy, in all its versions, did not even try to develop a serious response to the theological and philosophical challenges presented by "environmental" education at its best (Bowers, 2001; (de Haan, 2001; Palmer, 1998). This absence also signifies the lack of courage to search for a connection between (*a*) passions, intellect, the ethical-I, imagination, responsibility, and creative-improvisation; (*b*) human and nature, or Being and human beings; (*c*) the totality of eternity and (the totality of) "the moment"; (*d*) signifier and signified (which are dissociated only as an abstraction). This neglect is not a mistake, a short-coming, or an abandonment, to be "fixed" by the new masters of Critical Pedagogy. It is essential to the very philosophical foundations of current Critical Pedagogy.

The various versions of current Critical Pedagogy do not continue the attempt of Critical Theory to offer a holistic (negative) Utopia, within which new, yet, essential, *connections are established between the aesthetic, the ethical, the intellectual, the existential, and the political*. Surely it does not follow Horkheimer's critique of Marx, according to which his work misses too much when it disregards Love. Current Critical Pedagogy, so it seems, rejects any effort to become an actual attempt at a counter-educational Eros, that refrains from becoming "a project", a "system/dogma", or a new form of collectivism.

And last but not least, current Critical Pedagogy has lost the connection to *Love of Life*. I have to say these hard words even when they refer to some of my best friends: their "critique" does not manifest love and distances itself from Life, packs itself into the mechanical, abstract, and violent level of the political and the historical; it is not only far from becoming creative—it is ultimately even irrelevant, dogmatic, and normalizing, and of the kind it is committed to emancipate us from.

Critical Theory in its mature form manifested *religiosity* as a relation to the cosmos. It was aware and proud of it. The present versions of Critical Pedagogy, while normally being committed anti-traditionalist and anti-religious, tend to assume an anti-religious position to the kind of religiosity that Adorno and Horkheimer praised in Judaism (Horkheimer, 1985, VIII., pp. 182–183). At the same time Critical Pedagogy itself has become more of a religion in the traditional, institutional, dogmatic, and oppressive sense.

Much more than a religious-creative-cathartic experience and an erotic dialogical edification, the "implementations" of the ideas of Adorno and Horkheimer by Critical Pedagogy masters tend to become rival, close ideologies, reproduced by closed sects of naïve, fanatic devotees. Their coldness, mechanism, and commitment to "effectiveness" distance them not only from the Critical Theory, but from *Life* and from possibilities of genuine creativity and worthy struggles to transcend educational violence.

Present-day versions of Critical Pedagogy tend to reproduce and defend collectivism and self-evidence (even if only that of the oppressed and not that of their victimizers). In their commitment to defend the victims and support their efforts to regain security, honor, wellbeing, and possibilities for rich development, Critical Pedagogy masters tend so often to justify and enhance the self-evidence and ethnocentrism of the marginalized and the oppressed. Here too in distancing themselves from the mature Critical Theory they have aligned themselves with greatest threats to the autonomy, happiness, responsibility, creativity, and solidarity of humans, as understood by Benjamin, Adorno, and Horkheimer. And they have surely missed the self-irony that was so much part of the religiosity of Adorno, Horkheimer, and Benjamin. That is why these versions of Critical Pedagogy, for all their importance— and they are so important in so many ways, are to be considered much more as part of normalizing education and less as part of current worthy counter-education.

What is there to be said about counter-education in relation to the current versions of Critical Pedagogy? Much is to be said about the relation between the possibilities of present-day counter-education in relation to Critical Pedagogy. This is because Critical Pedagogy, even when it collapses into dogmatic, non-creative, and ethnocentrist practices of "emancipation" and "critique", still symbolizes the quest for **the totally other**; a refusal to be swallowed by the temptations, imperatives, and fashions of the world of facts, the productivity of its power-relations and the limits set by its historical horizons; transcending what Gnosis considered the manifestations of the (evil) presence of the God of creation. Even in face of an anti-Utopian "reality" it still symbolizes the essence of the Utopian commitment—even if against its own will. Its critical impulse[1] still symbolizes in its essence the possibilities for genuine, transcending, anti-collectivistic, and anti-instrumental-oriented reflection; its essence still insists on calling for *the birth of the nomadic eternal-improviser*. Critical Pedagogy, when true to itself, might still summon humans to overcome the reality it serves and represents; its call, however, if true to itself, is always negative, and it could only become a not-yet-deciphered *invitation*. As such, and only as such, it should send an invitation to transcend the numerous assorted temptations and practices that each moment join forces anew to push humans back into thingness; into the meaningless continuum of the immanence. This is where genuine counter-education might embark on its awakening; here is the potential starting point of Diasporic philosophy and its relevance to the field of education. This is where today's Critical Pedagogy, at best, is silent. This is where, at its best, it could learn so much from Critical Theory.

Critical Theory of the second stage in the development of the Frankfurt School might be considered part of a philosophical tradition with roots much deeper than those of critical philosophy and modern revolutionary praxis; one might consider its roots in Gnosis, or even in the philosophy of Heraclites; maybe even in that of Anaximander and the problematization of Being and nothingness, thinking, and cosmos in light of the principle of individuation and Life and its inevitable suffering, punishments, and redemption (Anaximander, 1986, p. 29). Here I shall be content with only few words on Diasporic Philosophy and its implications for counter-education in light of the shortcomings and relevance of current Critical Pedagogy. To this topic I have devoted some effort on other occasions (Gur-Ze'ev, 2007, pp. 386–381).

I begin with the assertion that Diasporic Philosophy is more than a philosophical "stance" or "orientation"; it has a rich, deep, and wide-ranging past—if we dare to reconstruct and re-interpret in this light works of thinkers such as Heraclites, Marcion, Pascal, de Montaigne, Kierkegaard, Nietzsche, Schopenhauer, Kafka, Heidegger, Blanchot, Bataille, Adorno, Camus, Derrida, Levinas, Rushdie, Deleuze, Zizek and Badiou, to name only a few. Some non-Western cultures have given rise to other important Diasporic thinkers. Not all cultures have done so, however, certainly not in the same forms and with equal richness. Nevertheless, their philosophical importance is vital for any further enhancement of a future genuine cosmopolitic Diasporic Philosophy that will offer a serious counter-education. What we are facing here is the possibility of counter-education in a multicultural world governed by Instrumental Rationality, global capitalism, and the reactions of the world of Jihad to the McWorld in face of the speedy, daily, McDonaldization of reality (Lash & Urry, 1991).

Diasporic Philosophy—of which I consider Critical Theory in its second stage of development a part—has no starting point; nor does it have a telos or a territory; and it undoubtedly distances itself from all forms of "homereturning" projects (Gur-Ze'ev, 2004, p. 71). Still, above all Diasporic Philosophy manifests *the erotic essence of Being itself as Diasporic, never at home.* Love of Life—not "critique" or a claim for justice to the oppressed, or revenge, is essential to it. Eagerness and dynamism, creation and renewal of creation in face of production toward nothingness; creation as a birth of Love, as a loving impetus—all these are essential. Its very existence, however, inevitably faces violence, meaninglessness, anti-creative horizons, and de-humanizing preconditions for any authentic creativity, for any quest for nearness to the truth of Being, for any responsibility that is more than an echo of the original, innovative, violence that enforced it, and for thinking itself.

Not being at "home" at all cost; refusing becoming swallowed by the self-evidence, self-content, and the negation of the Other at "home" and "there" is essential to Diasporic Philosophy. Refusing any identity thinking (Adorno, 1999) or any positive Utopia is essential here ontologically, epistemologically, ethically, existentially, and politically. This runs counter to the historic tension between the concepts of Diaspora and Redemption, which was traditionally conceived within a framework of a promised synthesis, "salvation", or "solution"; even if in the form offered by Pyrrho the skeptic, who insisted on a concluding, total, silence; or Philipp Mainlander, who asserted that the act of suicide of entire humanity and the destruction of all the world will invite a renewed pre-creationist harmonious nothingness (Mainlaender, 1876).

Diasporic Philosophy refuses all forms of positive Utopia in theory and practice. It overcomes any theoretical or political "home", self-evidence, truth, self-content, nirvana, and all other manifestations of Thanatos. In this sense it insists on consistent negativity as a form of Life.

Diasporic Philosophy emphasizes, but does not idolize, difference, *improvised continuation* as an alternative to *deterministic-mechanistic continuum*; it seriously faces *immediacy* in its intimate relation to *eternity, meaninglessness, violence, and historical productivity.* At the same time, it refuses relativism, nihilism, and pragmatism, and insists on religious existence, poetic creativity and courageous nomadism. It calls for a responsible self-constitution and reflection as one of the manifestations of human uniqueness in an infinite cosmos that is present in eternity as well as in the totality of each and every moment. It is focused on the presence of *the not-yet*, the potential, **the totally other**, and its wholly-presence in a Life which, ultimately, is not to be totally represented, controlled, or predicted.

The human being, as part of the infinite openness of Being, is essentially *free* because it is lost; it is lost in the cosmos, and as such it is in the state of becoming-toward-the-world and becoming-in-the-world alike. The human is potentially open to overcoming the successes of normalizing education, which is committed to turn him or her from *some-one* into *some-thing*.

Critical Pedagogy keeps aloof from the birth-giving tension between humans and cosmos. This challenge was essential to Critical Theory throughout its evolution. Critical Pedagogy abandoned even the standard topics that are regularly dealt with in the framework of "environmental education": issues such as global responsibility for conservation of natural beautiful sites and important recourses; sustainability of the planet and resistance of humanity to dangerous practices of control and consumption of nature; education to critical reconstruction of economic and political interests that legitimate and drive the destruction of inner and outer nature and resistance to their treatment of ecology; and finally, education to responsibility for the future coexistence of humanity and nature.

Until today, Critical Pedagogy almost completely disregarded not just *the cosmopolitic aspects of ecological ethics* in terms of threats to present and future life conditions of all humanity. It disregarded the fundamental philosophical and existential challenges of subject-object relations, in which "nature" is not conceived as a standing reserve either for mere human consumption or as a potential source of dangers, threats, and risks. In many respects the ecological dimensions of Ulrich Becks' concept of "the risk society" (Beck, 2004) are much more advanced and promising than the ecological dimensions in the work of Henry Giroux.

Critical Pedagogy disregarded the *intimate* relations between humans and the cosmos, an intimacy that Diasporic Philosophy conceives as an abyss and mystery, and at the same time as an impetus for Life, Hope, Love, and creativity. Here "nature", "environment", and "ecology" are conceived in a much deeper and wider

sense, and are identified in the Other, in one's self, and in the world of representations and their fruits. Counter-education that takes the tradition of Diasporic
Philosophy seriously begins here, in the fundamentals of existence, as Heidegger
articulated it, in the relations between Being and human beings, or the challenge
that humans face according to the myth of Odysseus and the Sirens as interpreted
by Adorno and Horkheimer. According to them, this dichotomy is the precondition
for the dialectic of Enlightenment and the possibility of the enslavement of humanity
to Instrumental Rationality that was supposed to enslave and consume nature in the
service of humanity. Effective conquest of the cosmos as a form of "homereturning"
after *the Fall* is revealed historically as an anti-diasporic stance that ultimately
internalized violence and is in the end is directed not solely against brute "nature"
as potential human "resources" but against other humans and against the individual
himself or herself. Diasporic philosophy might offer here hope, imagination, alternative logics and alternative creative responses to the human situatedness between
cosmic exile and scarcity (from human's point of view) and *inhuman cosmic
affluence*.

Counter-education that takes the tradition of Diasporic Philosophy seriously
makes an attempt to establish a Diasporic relation with the "successful", instrumental,
enslavement of "nature". The governing borders, disciplines, dichotomies and life
possibilities that are founded on instrumental subject-object relations are transcended. Homelessness in the various manifestations of the subject-object dichotomies
enable a kind of diasporic life that reopens (negative) intimacy in the cosmos. This
intimacy in and with the cosmos is enriched by alienation, sensitivity for suffering
and enslavement of other people, creatures, and representations, and opens the gate
to Diasporic hope. This hope makes possible Diasporic morality and Diasporic
creativity, which manifest love of Life, and not dissatisfaction, greed, fear, and
colonialism as a starting point for an alternative relation to the world.

Love, as the opposite of violence, stands along with hope, imagination, and
authentic, improvising creativity in contrast to fear, self-forgetfulness, greed, and
conquest. Diasporic Philosophy represents a kind of homelessness that is opposed to
the *self-forgetfulness* manifested in love of God, dedication to control-oppression-
mere survival and to any other forms of enslavement to Thanatos.

Contradiction, negation, and tension are not in opposition to Love. On the
contrary, according to Diasporic Philosophy *Love* is manifested in Life; and there
is no Life but amid, within, and against contradictions, abysses, dangers, and self-
constitution amid suffering, meaninglessness, and dialectical dynamics. Love of
Life is love of creativity from, against, and towards difference, plurality, impasse
and contradiction; yet it represents being-towards, becoming, and transcendence. This
is why counter-education, as a manifestation of love, transcends meaninglessness
and insists on revealing as creating meaning, aim, and alternative togetherness with
the world and Others. Precisely because homelessness is its home it enables
(negative) intimacy with the world and its realities and with the Others without a
false promise of final reconciliation that actualizes nirvana, or "homereturning".
This is the gate to counter-education that enhances genuine creativity that is fertilized
by sensitivity to suffering, imagination, hope, and commitment to self-constitution

and transcendence; a kind of creativity that is so much more than "art education" or "critical cinema studies" of the kind that are sometimes advanced within the framework of current Critical Pedagogy. Here creativity is an *ecstatic* experience that is essentially religious and manifests love of Life that might become poetically meaningful, good, and beautiful because there is no final point for the "home-returning" project nor any "solution" to meaninglessness, suffering, and loneliness. Love of Life, here, accepts Life as the rich presence of the absence, the absence of the absolute, the endlessly new manifestations of the *not-yet*, the potential. This is why the Diasporic human, as a loving, creative, human, is actually an eternal improviser.

Diasporic Counter-Education might offer new possibilities for human creativity that goes beyond the limits of "art education" which even in its limited form was foreign to most versions of Critical Pedagogy. Diasporic Philosophy faces the instrumentalization of Eros and poiesis as a precondition for culture and successful social structures. Creativity is recruited in the service of teleological collective and dogmatic "projects", represented and served by all versions of normalizing education. The autonomy of the human subject and genuine creativity, in all spheres of life, not solely in the arena of what is determined as "art", are a threat to normalizing education, to "law and order", and to "peace". Critical Pedagogy is no exception here.

For Critical Pedagogy too, authentic creativity and its affluence in all spheres of life are a huge threat. Original creativeness is a great peril to the ideology of "emancipation" and to the truths, values, and collectives it is committed to. Genuine counter-education, however, will offer a Diasporic relation to the present achievements of cultures and ideologies, their truths, interests, symbols, agendas, and enemies. In face of meaninglessness, from the edge of the abyss of homelessness in the world of representations, abstractions, and violence it might enable the attendance or at least the quest for the eternal-improviser. The eternal-improviser does not simply abandon "critique". Neither are responsibilities as a citizen and a fellow human neglected: they are transcended.

The eternal-improviser tries to develop an alternative *gaze* and an alternative *eavesdrop*. Such a Diasporic existence makes possible much more than an alternative "art education"; it opens the gate to *Life as a form of art*, while offering a kind of homelessness than enables a new, nomadic, intimacy with the cosmos and all its forms of creativity/destruction. For the Diasporic human, as an eternal-improviser, this new embrace of Being is not in the sphere of abstraction. It is not an ideal to live by, or a mere "inner absolute imperative"; it is beyond "external" and "internal" power; it transcends the dividing line between two versions of metaphysical violence: scarcity as manifested by alienation and fear of the totality of the moment on the one hand, and being swallowed by/open to the *affluence* of intimacy with/against the infinity of eternity on the other. Creativity as a manifestation of Love of Life, for the eternal-improviser here is a manifestation of challenging metaphysical violence in the name of hope by the power of Love and creativity, without being overwhelmed by an optimistic, sentimentalist, or abstract conception of life, art, and education.

Counter-education here goes beyond the best achievements of Critical Pedagogy, yet it does not abandon them. Here ideology critique and empowering the skills and tools of deciphering the politics of cultural reproduction become an important part of art education; and art education becomes integrated with physical education, environmental education, critical cyberspace education, cooking, car repairing education, history lessons, literacy, economics, and so much of the canon. And yet, counter-education transcends all these not solely on the pedagogical level: it transcends all these in a religious sense by re-introducing poiesis in a postmodern world.

Re-approaching the original act of the human hands and reintroducing the body, poetry, play, and erotic togetherness are not abstract and mere fantasy. They are actual life possibilities for mature, religious humans, especially when they are young. As such, they are innovative and inviting. They invite creativity of the kind that opposes and overcomes the reification of art in face of globalizing capitalism and its culture industry. Counter-education here is Diasporic, refuses the calls for consensual reception and embrace by the fashion and hegemonic ideologies and institutions. Here too creativity, if true to itself, must be homeless and not strive for domesticating acknowledgement, consensus, admiration, and domesticating rewards. At the same time, however, it is part of a *nomadic life*, whose happiness and creativity amid suffering, meaninglessness, aimlessness, and misrecognition on the way to an alternative togetherness are enabled by the affluence of Love and the imaginative potential of hope. This path does not lead to nihilism, relativism, solipsism or cannibalistic joy, nor to irresponsibility. On the contrary, for the creative, nomadic, eternal-improviser, response-ability is a precondition for genuine creativity, for re-entering togetherness in a mature manner, and for caring and edifying all loving and transcending manifestations of courageous Life.

Diasporic Philosophy is in a sense immoral. Still, it negates all forms of nihilism. It is beyond the hegemonic moral politics because it relates seriously to the possibility of an "ethical I" (Levinas, 1987, p. 56). It relates in the most intimate way to the infinite richness of the world and its beauty, meaninglessness, and suffering in the totality of the moment on one level, and to the Other and the political arena on another, historical, level, as one, unifying (yet not systematic), Diasporic existence. On the one level it relates primarily to *response-ability*. On the other level it relates primarily to *respond-ability*. *Response-ability precedes respond-ability.* It is related more to the ethical sphere and to the existential more than to the moral-historical-political arenas of human existence and human work. The two are not opposed to genuine responsibility, while they are opposed to the hegemonic social conditions, philosophical foundations, political practices, and fruits of normalized morality. An unsolvable tension, if not an abyss, exists between the two, even if both are authentic manifestation of the richness of Life.

Situated in Diaspora as a Utopian existence, Diasporic responsibility unites response-ability and respond-ability. It addresses the *infinity of the moment* in its endless creative possibilities, dangers, and abysses. It calls for a fundamental communication with the otherness of the Other, which precedes cultural borders, political interests, race, national, gender, and other differences. It precedes yet enables truly rational moral elaborations and critiques. As such it relates to the most intimate manifestations of *becoming-toward-the-world*, the Other, and one's self as a challenge and as an object of shared responsibility, love, creation, and happiness (which might include suffering).

At the same time, however, Diasporic responsibility must also be ready to address the historical moment. And when the moment comes, also to position itself against injustice and even join a wider political practice. It must be relevant to the cognitive, historical, and political dynamics. Yet *it cannot ensure a non-violent consensual historical action* concerning the ongoing silenced genocide in Southern Sudan, and so much more.

For Diasporic Philosophy, all calls to respond are manifestations of Life as a *call*, as a challenge, as a potential to be addressed and creatively surmount. In face of *the abyss between the ethical and the political* it insists on nomadism and love, creativity and negativity. And as such, it cannot share the positive Utopia of Levinas, who to a question in an interview replied: "Yes, an agreement between the ethics and the State is possible. The just State will be the work of just people and the saints, rather than of propaganda and preaching". It insists on what Adorno told us so many years ago, namely "a philosophy forswearing all of that must in the end be irreconcilably at odds with the dominant consciousness. Nothing else raises it above the suspicion of apologetics. Philosophy that satisfies its own intention, and does not childishly skip behind its own history and the real one, has its lifeblood in the resistance against the common practices of today and what they serve, against the justification of what happens to be the case" (Adorno, 1998, p. 6).

Diasporic Philosophy tries, negatively, yet as a form of Love of Life, to address the question of *The Good*. Benjamin, Adorno, and Horkheimer are of vital importance for us today, in responding in a worthy way to the calls of Life and their challenges. Responding here is active. While acknowledging the importance of contemplation, reflection, gaze, openness, and silence, it is directed to *giving birth*. It concerns actual activity not philosophical challenges as a closed arena; it directs philosophy as an art of life to calls and challenges that are material, physical, emotional, and spiritual, "inner" and "exterior" ethical, aesthetic, existential, and political. It relates also to the conditions of "the call" as well as to the possibilities of a worthy response and their all-embracing practices.

Responding in a worthy manner is never given, easy, or without a price. Nor is it a skill to be developed by normalizing education. By itself it is a *possibility* as well as an *imperative* for worthy Life that resists becoming swallowed by any "home-returning" project; nor does it abandon responsibility to creation and Love. As such, it is "practice oriented". Its ultimate test is in actuality, in creation, deeds, actions, endeavors that are fundamentally authentic or inauthentic, relate to worthy eavesdropping or to its negation—to its replacement by instrumentalist-oriented focusing. Its actuality is in the attempt to approach new ways to gaze, overcoming the calls to satisfy itself in mere "rationalist" and instrumentalist-oriented use of the eyes. It even directs itself to abandon the collective and positive attempts to unveil the inner truth and the potentials of "the object" of manipulation. Active, responsible, involvement in the world presumes response-ability. In its absence humans' poiesis deteriorates into instrumental-oriented consumption and oppression that begins in self-oppression and concludes in the neglect or oppression of fellow citizens of the cosmos.

Response-ability is born each moment anew among the plants, among the animals, and in the birth of each new human baby. The human, however, treats this potential in a unique manner. So normally, this potential is robed, reworked, and productivized by the system at the instant of the new baby's birth. For humans within sophisticated cultural systems it is a neglected potential, not a given skill. In the framework of the political arena it is to be historically re-created, edified, cultivated, and protected only at the cost of its transformation into its opposite.

Response-ability is not only a potential: for the ethical I it is a gate to being true to oneself, a way for self-constitution as some-one and not as some-thing. Response- ability is a potential transcendence that does not disregard the whole and the call to retreat into the infinity of immanence. It aims at transcending thingness. At the same time, it is committed to *overcoming the division between immanence and transcendence.* It acknowledges this challenge as an ethical moment that is also an ontological sign. It does so even if in postmodern conditions humans are urged to self-forgetfulness and loss of genuine response-ability in the most efficient ways, in the name of promised pleasure, economic, emotional, and political rewards, and other agents of self-forgetfulness that work in the service of normalizing education. Diasporic Philosophy offers ontological signs and ethical calls that enable re-facing response-ability, at least as a (negative) Utopia. It enables a kind of counter-education that will call for, never ensure, overcoming self-forgetfulness and normalized morality, nihilism, ethnocentricity, and other "homes" that guard the hegemonic legitimacy of the discourse concerning moral and responsibility.

Diasporic nomadism invites the human; it cannot do more than that. It cannot guarantee or offer anything, not even a clear dividing line between its alternative and other, more attractive or "rewording" alternatives. If true to itself it can only invite the human to follow indirect paths to re-work his or her gaze while widening it and enriching it in new ways and towards more manifestations of Life, in the infinity of each moment. It invites the cultivation of a gaze that is beyond the industrialized focus, as it is developed within the framework of the system that is committed to the fabrication of the "rational human". It invites a different kind of focus; a focus that opens itself to attunement, to a happy attunement to each every degree out of the 360; an attunement that relates also to that which is absent but not from a standpoint of anger, revenge, or greed. It is a focus that enhances new kind of listening. Eavesdropping to each and every voice of the cosmic music, like the one we had as babies and lost with the success of normalizing education. Like the one poetry, music, and dance offer us again and again at rare moments of transcendence. Diasporic life here questions, deconstructs, subverts, yet preserves, accepts, and transcends. It does not offer an abstract negation, abandonment, or forgetfulness of politics, culture, habits, friendships, or experiences—it relates to them differently and overcomes their limiting, domesticating, enclosing effects. In this light it also relates to the category of responsibility.

By *overcoming responsibility in terms set by patriotism, devotion to the class, commitment to a race (or against a certain race), dedication to individual "achievements" or narcissistic-oriented enjoyment*, this counter-education does not put forward an ethical desert: it presents an alternative kind of ethics, a new, Diasporic, response-ability. Diasporic response-ability goes beyond the normalized responses to the post-modern reality on "authentic" paths that enable penetration into "the real" or new age "spiritual" moral transcendence. The gate to genuine response-ability is opened at the moment of accepting responsibility for overcoming the fruits of the violence of normalizing education in the form of aggression, fear, greed, narcissism, and "responsibility" in light of the self-evidence and the other manifestations of "home".

Homelessness without the promise of an emancipatory "homereturning" project in face of the presence of the absence of "God" opens the gate to *true responsibility*. This kind of responsibility is not only opposed to the one constructed by the various human "homes" and "homereturning" projects. It is opposed to the fundamental philosophy of "home", which also offers a kind of psychology that pretends to justify "home" and clarifies its inevitability from a psychological point of view. Diasporic Philosophy opposes the philosophical foundations of this psychology while offering a dialectical critique of the concept of "home" and the kind of responsibility it offers.

Responsibility, within the framework of Diasporic Philosophy, is part of and enables The Good, yet it is a Diasporic Good, not a domesticated good. The Good here accepts and responds to *Life* in an *eternal Diaspora* as a starting point for any reflection on historical and political arenas of human life and the possibility of an alternative philosophy of education. Responsibility here is grounded in Diasporic response-ability as a worthy response to Diaspora in history and Diaspora in politics, and only as such is it true responsibility that enables *The Good*. A true response to the infinite, uneducable otherness of the Other and a worthy response to the richness and meaninglessness of Life unite here in a new, Diasporic, kind of responsibility.

True responsibility is aware of the absence of God, it faces the withdrawal of the Absolute, the arbitrariness of master-signifiers, and the contingency of omnipotent effectiveness of meaninglessness. Today, it must challenge, beyond the dichotomies between modernism and postmodernism, immanence and transcendence, the very possibility of meaning and human activity as becoming-toward-the-world. It must search for new, Diasporic, ways to question that which produces (contextual) truths, (contextual) valid values, (contextual) yardsticks, and (contextual) safe havens and realms of self-evidence. This is the starting-point for a Diasporic *responsible response* to humans' being-in-the-world as becoming-toward-the-world. There is an abyss between *being-in-the-world* and *becoming-toward-the-world*. This tension, however, is a possible gate to caring for the self, for the edification of one's own difference in its relations to the world and to the otherness of the Other (Levinas, 1996, p. 9).

But how relevant is it to the ongoing silenced genocide in the Southern Sudan, to the systematic starvation of entire populations by the interest rate of loans sent by "the free play" of world exchange centers? Or for the future of women's, or children's rights in the Arab world? It is exactly in light of *the abyss between the ethical and the political* that a Diasporic responsibility might enable responsibility also in the historical moment; as an active citizen and as a politically engaged man or woman who is not a prisoner of the Platonic cave, who is not a mere echo/construct/product/agent of contingent power relations and violent educational manipulations. Such a citizen is a Utopia. It is, however, a concrete Utopia. It is so far from what (even at their best) the hegemonic program of democratic education, peace education, and Critical Pedagogy offer us today.

The political aspect of Diasporic responsibility is not relevant solely to the politics of the construction of the human and the effective reproduction of her impotence for reflection, self-constitution, and worthy response-ability to its Diasporic situatedness in Life. It is at the same time of vital importance for the relation between this kind of becoming-toward-the world and worthy *response-ability* as against being-in-the-world and the possible *respond-ability* as a human situatedness in a specific historical moment, as a counter-educator.

Diasporic response-ability in the physical, psychic, spiritual, existential, ethical, and poetical aspects is a precondition for a worthy respond-ability in the social arena. In many respects it challenges the political dimensions of life and enables the nomadic eternal-improviser to free herself from the limits, imperatives, and manipulations of "the political". Diasporic counter-education must be very clear on this point: it is political in the sense that it challenges the political. It does not disregard the historical moment and the specific material, social, political, and cultural context. It relates to the historical sphere and the social arena in the most specific and concrete manner—in order to avoid being swallowed by their manipulations.

Does this mean that Diasporic counter-education is escapist and apolitical, and actually offers a tempting retreat into the "inner" world of the elect?

Late Horkheimer explicitly asserts that not "the revolution" is the aim of mature Critical Theory but the struggle of and for the autonomy of the "spiritual" individual. (Horkheimer, 1985, VII., p. 341) My reply would be that such a counter-education would become politically involved and would not abandon politics. But it will become politically involved in the most responsible manner, namely engaging the contextual social realities in order to enable the individual to realize his or her respond-ability; respond-ability whose actualization will offer creative possibilities for doing *The Good* while *overcoming the logic of the politics altogether*. Here many of the fruits of Critical Theory would be very relevant and productive. Again, all this only to direct a critique and to respond to injustice not within the framework of an alternative collective or worthier dogma. Counter-education here offers an invitation to a kind of political involvement that manifests the situatedness of the ethical within the framework of the political only to overcome the political and to transcend the historical moment—not to enslave one's life to the imperatives, limits, and possibilities of the political. Again, it is not the bridge between the ethical and the political; it is the situatedness of the Diasporic eternal-improviser in the specific historical moment that enables his or her involvement in the social arena. And such an involvement is not only unavoidable, it is a worthy manifestation of the attempt to approach the truth of counter-education and the Diasporic existence.

In another sense, the "realization" of Diasporic counter-education in the social arena in each historical moment is never solely critical of and negative toward politics. It must become dialectically engaged in manners that will give birth to new possibilities for human togetherness. Of special importance it is for such a countereducation to open the way to *new kinds of togetherness* amid suffering, injustice and manipulations, for victims and victimizers alike, freeing them from their "homes" and normalized responsibilities. There should be a way for forgiveness and charity to all humans—yet not for all human deeds.

Central to a Diasporic counter-education are the sensitivity and self-directedness to human life as *becoming-toward-the world*. It manifests self-accepted transcendence as Love of life, and not as a mere echo, or a reaction of fear. As counter-education it does not educate to fear *loneliness in the Godless world*. As a Diasporic alternative it tries to offer concrete practices for edifying skills, sensitivities, knowledge, and practices that will enable the existence of the nomadic human that maybe we could call *the eternal-improviser*. The nomadism of the eternal-improviser enhances skills and knowledge of various kinds. Of vital importance among these is the response-ability to a changing and ever-veiling dynamics. Authentic responses are potentials of Life as a serious play, as a form of art; (Marcuse, 1967, pp. 863–870) they edify creativity as an ethical, physical, and intellectual becoming-toward-the-world. It is a nomadic becoming on all levels, and as such it challenges the fruits of normalizing education and the subjectification processes that precondition "home", "responsibility", stable "I", social order, and cultural progress. Like freedom, however, the connection between response-ability and respond-ability cannot be guaranteed, delivered or "correctly realized" in advanced—it must be freely decided, struggled for, each moment anew under odd conditions.

And yet, responding in a worthy manner to the call of **the totally other** and the new possibilities, it might (or might not) introduce/impose a potential that might be learned and cultivated. But it assumes a different kind of learning and a new kind of thinking. It relates very much to what Adorno conceived as educated maturity.

Here the responsibility of the counter-educator will be actualized in self-education and in inviting other individuals to self-education in manners, by skills, with and against methods, and practices that are already elaborated and partially realized in the history of counter-education. Here too, Critical Pedagogy, when it is true to Critical Theory, might become of much relevance. But ultimately response-ability and respond-ability as manifestations of Diasporic responsibility are not to be ensured or authentically delivered. Openness, danger, and Eros, here too, must have the last word. It is always put to the test in relation to the connection of human life to the moment, to history, and to eternity. Critical Pedagogy restricted itself to the historical sphere and the social arena. Diasporic counter-education that takes seriously the work of the Frankfurt School thinkers, however, might contribute so much if it related to the tensions, gaps, and connections of the moment, history, and eternity, for humans, animals, plants, and other manifestations of Life as a source of hope and transcendence, not solely as different manifestations of the Platonic cave. Politics or the world of contingent power-relations and violent symbolic and direct dynamics, here becomes a very relevant factor, yet never has the upper hand. The Diasporic eternal-improviser, when true to himself or herself, is never a totally controlled citizen of *The Earthly City*; he or she resists becoming-swallowed-by-the-system, the historical facts, or the social horizons. He or she crosses from the infinity of each moment to eternity or from eternity retreats to the historical sphere and to the infinity of a fleeting moment. Parallel to the asymmetry and the absence of hierarchy and determined order between the *moment, history,* and *eternity* is the absence of hierarchy and determinism between *reality and its hermeneutical depths*. It parallels also to the *"cosmic music"* of that which is symbolized by "reality", its representations, its courageous-edifying critique and its creative-transformative interpretations. These two levels are parallel, but do not constantly relate to each other in the same order. So "the moment" relates to "the deeper meaning of reality"; "history" relates to "reality" and its power-relations; and "eternity" relates to "that to which the meaning and telos of history/reality refers too. This third element is not a mere abstract metaphysical category. Not only does it enable the moment and history—it also bursts into the continuum in all its richness, from time to time, in the form of Hope, **the totally other**, or the not-yet. For the Diasporic eternal-improviser, as a genuine nomad, this third, uneducable, uncontrollable, element of Life is of outmost importance. It enables the Diasporic existence to become-toward-the-world in infinite ways beyond being swallowed by the immanence and beyond being fragmented and disappearing in one of the "homereturning" projects that promise transcendence and an end to homelessness. Only within this framework is politics challenged from a Diasporic perspective in a way that enables *The Good* in its concrete material, historical and social context.

Counter-education from the sources of Diasporic Philosophy counters collectivism, combats dogmatism, and opposes all other "homes". It refuses any plea or call for recycling, defending or enhancing the present order of things and its realms of self-evidence. Normalizing processes cannot but end up in collectives that surrender themselves to the destruction of the otherness of the Other as a concrete form of "salvation" (Gur-Ze'ev, 2003a, pp. 1–24). Diasporic existence is anti-collectivist-oriented and anti-dogmatic. It refuses the self-abandonment of the individual that is so vital for the historical production of a stable collectives and progressive cultures. This is true not solely in pre-modern and modern spaces, which are so quick to summon their armies, habits, and temptations against the otherness of the Other. It is valid also in postmodern spaces such as the cyberspace. Maybe the Hacker, or that which the Hacker symbolizes, is one of the very few exceptions (Gur-Ze'ev, 2004, pp. 77–92).

Here, in light of a never-ending struggle for overcoming any "home" and collectivism, new possibilities are opened. New prospects are given birth not solely for the self-constitution of the eternal-improviser as a genuine nomad: new leeway is opened for genuine solidarity and for new kinds of togetherness.

The new kinds of togetherness are not committed to the imperative of normalizing education to destroy the otherness of the "ethical I" and the otherness of the Other. *Becoming-toward-the-otherness-of-Being* and the infinite expressions of Love of Life might enable a kind of togetherness with the cosmos and all other Life manifestations on new paths that Diasporic self-constitution will pave. This new

Diasporic togetherness with the otherness within the "I", the Other, and the world might crisscross "the moment", "history", and "eternity". Such a self-positioning amid and against Being might enable a better eavesdropping to *the call*, when and if it comes. It might enable a worthy response in the right moment toward and with other Diasporic humans in ways that will give birth to *a new, Diasporic, togetherness.*

A community, not a collective, is here enabled, for a moment, solely for a fragile moment, among Diasporic individuals. If true to themselves they will cherish moments of togetherness as creative, improvising, responsible, Diasporic, individuals, yet will refuse any institutionalization or dogmatization of their—yes, their—togetherness. The moment such counter-education is self-content and domesticated it will immediately transform itself into nothing but an old-new collective and an old-new form of normalizing education.

NOTES

[1] Even when articulated in a manner that serves nothing more than an alternative, rival, violent realm of self-evidence that will enhance the violent productivity of the "we" against the "they" and their otherness.

REFERENCES

Adorno, T., & Horkheimer, M. (1988). *Dialektik der Aufklaerung*. Frankfurt a. Main: Suhrkamp.

Adorno, T. (1993). Culture critique and society. In T. Adorno & M. Horkheimer (Eds.), *The Frankfurt school*. Tel Aviv: Sifriat Poalim. (Hebrew)

Adorno, T. (1999). *Negative dialectics* (E. B. Ashton, Trans.). New York: Continuum.

Alexander, H. (2001). *Reclaiming goodness—education and the spiritual quest*. Notre-Dame, IN: University of Notre Dame Press.

Anaximander. (1986). *The presocratic philosophers* (J. Barnes, Ed.). London and New York: Routledge.

Barber, B. (1995). *Jihad vs. McWorld—How globalism and tribalism are shaping the world*. New York: New York Times Books.

Beck, U. (2004). *Risk society—toward a new modernity* (M. Ritter, Trans.). London: Sage Publications.

Benjamin, W. (1980). ueber den Begriff der Geschichte. In *Gesammelte Schriften*, I.2. Frankfurt a. Main: Suhrkamp.

Benjamin, W. (1969). *Illuminations* (H. Zohn, Trans.). New York: Schocken.

Bowers, C. A. (2001). *Education for eco-justice and community*. Athens, GA: University of Georgia Press.

Cohen, H. (1972). *Religion of reason out of the sources of judaism* (S. Kaplan, Trans.). New York: F. Unger Publications.

Derrida, D. (1978). *Writing and difference* (A. Bass, Trans.). Chicago: University of Chicago Press, 1978.

de Haan, G., Mann, J., & Others (Eds.), *Educating for sustainability*. Frankfurt a. Main: Per Lang.

Gruschka, A. (1986). *Negative Paedagogik—Einfuerung in die Paedagogik mit Kritische Theorie*. Muenster: Pandora.

Gur-Ze'ev, I. (1986). *The Frankfurt school and the history of pessimism*. Jerusalem: Magnes Press. (Hebrew).

Gur-Ze'ev, I. (1998, Fall). Toward a nonrepressive critical pedagogy. *Educational Theory*, *48*(4), 463–486.

Gur-Ze'ev, I. (1998a). Walter Benjamin and Max Horkheimer: From Utopia to redemption. *Journal of Jewish Thought and Philosophy, 8*, 119–155.

Gur-Ze'ev, I. (2003). Critical theory, critical pedagogy and the possibility of counter-education. In M. Peters, C. Lankshear, & M. Olssen (Eds.), *Critical theory and the human condition—founders and praxis* (pp. 17–35). New York: Peter Lang.

Gur-Ze'ev, I. (2003a). *Destroying the other's collective memory.* New York: Peter Lang.

Gur-Ze'ev, I. (2004). *Toward diasporic education—multiculturalism, postcolonialism and counter-education in the post-modern era.* Tel Aviv: Resling. (Hebrew).

Gur-Ze'ev, I. (2005). The university, the eternal-improviser, and the possibility of meaning in a post-modern era. In I. Gur-Ze'ev (Ed.), *The end of Israeli academia?* (pp. 256–299). Haifa: The Faculty of education, University of Haifa. (Hebrew)

Gur-Ze'ev, I. (2007, November). Diasporic philosophy, counter-education and improvisation. *Studies in Philosophy and Education, 28,* 386–381.

Gur-Ze'ev, I. (forthcoming). Max Horkheimer's political theology as a new Jewish diasporic philosophy. In C. Schmidt (Ed.), *Political theology today.*

Mainlaender, P. (1876). *Philosophie der Erloesung.* Berlin (A new reprint: Hildesheim 1996). Marx, K. (1919). *Zur Judenfrage.* Berlin: Rowohlt.

Hall, S. Brave new world: The debate about post-fordism. *Socialist Review, 2*(1), 57–64.

Heidegger, M. (1996). The end of philosophy and the task of thinking. In D. F. Krell (Ed.), *Martin Heidegger—basic writings.* London: Routledge.

Heidegger, M. (1993). *Letter on humanism. Basic Writings.* London: Routledge.

Horkheimer, M. (1974). *Eclipse of reason.* New York: Oxford university Press.

Horkheimer, M. (1985). *Gesammelte Schriften* VIII. Frankfurt a. Main: Fischer.

Horkheimer, M. (1985). *Gesammelte Schriften* VIII. Frankfurt a. Main: Fischer.

Horkheimer, M. (1990). *Gesammelte Schriften* X. Frankfurt a. Main: Fischer.

Horkheimer, M. (1985). *Gesammelte Schriften* XII. Frankfurt a. Main: Fischer.

Jonas, H. (1992). *The Gnostic religion.* Boston: Beacon Press.

Lash, S., & urry, J. (1991). *The end of organized capitalism.* Madison, WI: The University of Wisconsin Press.

Levinas, E. (1987). *Collected philosophical papers of Emmanuel Levinas* (A. Lingis, Trans.). Dordrecht: M. Nijhoff.

Levinas, E. (1996). *Emmanuel levinas—basic philosophical writings* (A. T. Perezk, S. Critchley, & R. Bernasconi, Eds.). Bloomington & Indianapolis, IN: Indiana University Press.

Liston, D. (2000). Love and despair in teaching. *Educational Theory, 50,* 81–102.

Marcuse, H. (1967, November–December). Die Zukunft der Kunst. *Neues Forum,* 863–870.

Zeichner, K. (1993). Traditions of practice in U.S. preservice teacher education programs. *Teaching and Teacher Education, 9*(1), 1, 1–13.

Zeichner, K. (1990). Changing directions in the practicum: Looking ahead to the 1990's. *Journal of Education for Teaching, 16*(2), 105–131.

Zizek, S. (2002). *Welcome to the desert of the real—five essays on September 11 and related dates.* Tel Aviv: Resling. (Hebrew).

ILAN GUR-ZE'EV

3. CONFLICTING TRENDS IN CRITICAL THEORY AND DIASPORIC COUNTER-EDUCATION TODAY

A courageous revisiting of the progressivism of the Frankfurt School Critical Theory today is an extraordinary act. It is a daring act in face of the triumph of the new progressivism; both new neo-Marxists such as Badiou and Zizek, on the one hand, and celebrated poststructuralists such as Deleuze, Baudrillard and Judith Butler, on the other hand offer today a new kind of progressivism: a new kind of progressive thinking that presents "old" humanist-oriented progressivism as nothing but a manifestation of Judeo-Christian immanent violent colonial-drive and as the fruit of its unrestrained racist-oppressive impulse. In the field of critical education for current poststructuralists and new neo-Marxist alike Adorno, Horkheimer or Thomas Mann became less relevant than the proto-Nazi thinkers and their post-structuralist disciples. For the new progressivists Nietzsche, Heidegger and Carl Schmitt or Blanchot, Bataille, Baudrillard and the anti-Enlightenment tradition became much more fruitful than the traditional humanist critical thinkers. Most of the heroes of current critical pedagogues represent strong anti-democratic, anti-humanist and anti-Semitic commitments, rhetoric and policies. It is no wonder that so many of today's Critical Pedagogy theorists and activists present ecstatic support for the redeeming postcolonialist agenda of Hugo Chavez, Kim Jong-il, Ahmadenijad or Nasrallah who only last week declared how happy he is for the concentration of six million Jews in Israel since it will enable the Hezbollah to exterminate all Jews on one strike without troubling to chase them all over the globe. Experiencing the strengths of the current transformation of progressive thinking the work of the Frankfurt School thinkers should be considered of vital importance for addressing the possibility of a new critical language in education in "our", dull, post-metaphysical moment.

The Critical Theory of the Frankfurt School is of special importance today in face of the exile of holiness; addressing the attempt to offer "critique" and "resistance" while resisting the quest for transcendence and the calls of Eros in arenas governed by mega-speeds (most critical pedagogues today will alternatively insist on the challenge of "the Empire", "whiteness" or "Zionism"). The Frankfurt School thinkers addressed the acceleration of movements and speeding social changes, but their Critical Theory could not confront the reality of mega-speed, the exile of Eros and the deconstruction of (humanist-oriented) holiness that presently we face on a global scale. This is why they still could offer a religious commitment to secular holiness and transcendence; response-ability toward the negative Utopia of Godless meaning, co-poiesis and Diasporic religiosity, rather than "truth" and "emancipation".

I. Gur-Ze'ev, The Possibility/Impossibility of a New Critical Language in Education, 39–67.
© *2010 Sense Publishers. All Rights Reserved.*

Up to the Holocaust Theodor Adorno and Max Horkheimer interlaced the goals of Critical Theory with the Marxian revolutionary project. The development of their thought led them to criticize orthodox Marxism and ended with a complete break with that tradition, (Gur-Ze'ev, 1996, p. 115) as they developed a quest for a religiosity of a unique kind, emanating from Judaism. This unique religiosity offers a reformulated *negative theology* within the framework of what I call *"Diasporic philosophy"* (Gur-Ze'ev, 2003; Gur-Ze'ev, 2007, p. 3; Gur-Ze'ev, 2010). This shift enabled them to offer us, even if only implicitly, a blueprint, and more then that, the sensitivity, for the quest for what I call "counter-education" (Gur-Ze'ev, 2003a, p. 62; Gur-Ze'ev, 2003, pp. 1–24), challenging normalizing education, that is so vividly manifested in the various, conflicting, versions of collectivist-oriented revolutionary and emancipatory traditions.

Diasporic philosophy worthy the name is very different from what Zizek celebrates on his way toward a worthy new Leninist dictatorship and it represents a *nomadic*, hence "Diasporic" relation to the world, to thinking and to existence (Gur-Ze'ev, 2004, p. 9). Its starting point is the presence of the *absence* of truth, God, and worthy hedonism. Diasporic philosophy is positioned against any secular and theist philosophical, existential, and political projects that represent positive Utopias and reflect *"homereturning"* quests. While thus rejecting all dogmas and other forms of closure and *sameness,* it also refuses all versions of nihilism and relativism, and opens the gate to counter-education. Critical Pedagogy, even in its most advanced versions, manifests the birthmarks of the first stage in the development of Critical Theory, namely, normalizing education that Critical Theory in its second stage was committed to overcome. In my view, later Critical Theory was in its essence such a *Diasporic philosophy*; an existential self-positioning and counter-educational erotic endeavor that opens for us the possibility of non-repressive creation, happiness, responsibility, and worthy suffering that is most relevant to us today. This especially so in face of contemporary new progressive rhetoric and fundamentalist calls for worthy homelessness or unrestrained ethno-centrism of the victims of the Jewish Monotheism on the way to a postcolonialist Garden of Eden.

It is important to go into this neglected issue for many reasons, one of which is that the direct and indirect influences of the Critical Theory on generations of philosophers of education and the current transformation of Critical Pedagogy in light of the triumph of the new anti-Semitism and the new progressive mind and psyche. The manifestations of these transformations go far beyond the horizons of Critical Pedagogy as the concrete realization of Critical Theory in the schooling process. Even within the limited concept of education as schooling, feminist pedagogies, multi-cultural and post-colonial theories of education, cultural studies, as well as critical literacy or aesthetic education are all seen to be influenced by the ideas of Theodor Adorno, Max Horkheimer, Herbert Marcuse, Walter Benjamin, Erich Fromm, and the other members of the Frankfurt School. Some of the influences of Critical Theory are more obvious and explicitly acknowledged by Paulo Freire, Peter McLaren, Douglas Kellner, Henry Giroux, and Kathleen Weiler, and some are less explicit and are subterranean or are realized indirectly.

It is not uncommon that some of these influences are dressed in postmodern garb and are offered—how ironic—as an alternative to the modernity of Critical Theory and the Enlightenment's arrogance and its self-defeating educational project.

The main argument below is that the foremost philosophers of education who were explicitly and even enthusiastically influenced by Critical Theory were influenced by the work of Herbert Marcuse and by the first stage in the development of Adorno and Horkheimer's thought. According to this argument, the second stage in the development of Adorno and Horkheimer's thought was disregarded by most philosophers of education and did not illumine the paths chosen by the various versions of Critical Pedagogy.

When the main version of Critical Pedagogy became defensive and apologetic in face of the critique of the academic left it turned to the postmodern alternatives for help.[1] It was part of a more general transformation of reality and the symbolic sphere in face of post-Fordist production, new media technologies and the deconstruction of holiness that inflicted the triumph of the new progressive thinking and its various Critical Theories. This unfortunate situation was instrumental in allowing the development of original, influential, and progressive educational theories such as those of Giroux, Lather, McLaren, Weiler, Aronowitz, and Ellsworth. It was most unhelpful, however, for the task of establishing a reflective counter-education. For all its importance, it also contributed to the establishment of oppressive and uncritical trends within Critical Pedagogy itself. The thoughts of Adorno and Horkheimer in the second stage of the development of their Critical Theory, I argue, could have been and still are potentially open to the creation of a genuine counter-educational struggle—of the kind that will path ways beyond the prospects of hegemonic Critical Pedagogy.

The part in Critical Theory that was not ignored and was even praised by most educational theoreticians was fundamentally optimistic, revolutionary, and positive, at least on first sight. Its Marxist birthmarks were still very present at this stage. In the tradition of Critical Pedagogy this part of the work of Horkheimer and Adorno was conceived in a manner that deprived Critical Theory of its self-reflection and its dialectical dimensions. The thinkers of Critical Pedagogy normally underestimate Adorno and Horkheimer's anti-Utopianism and self reflection. They over-emphasize Adorno's optimism about the possibility of the constitution of a theoretical and educational framework that will enhance a praxis which will overcome the logic of capitalism and other forms of oppression.

The third issue of the sixth volume of *Zeitschrift fuer Sozialen Forschung*, the official journal of the Frankfurt School, which was published in 1937, can serve as a vivid manifestation of the complexity of the smilingly explicit anti-Utopian commitment of Horkheimer of that time. In "a contribution" to Marcuse's main article in that issue he goes out of his way to criticize "those who call themselves critical theoreticians"—namely, Marcuse—who's Utopianism "contradicts genuine Critical Theory" (Horkheimer, 1985, V., p. 224). He criticizes Marcuse's "philosophical Utopianism", likening it to other dangerous versions of Utopianism. He especially targets the liberal version—for manifesting "saintly egoism", which ultimately opens the way to nihilism and National Socialism, and the orthodox

Marxist version, which is "mechanistic and non-dialectical" (ibid., p. 223). Already in 1931 when the theologian Paul Tillich described capitalism as "the devil" both Adorno and Horkheimer were quick to criticize him for the kind of Utopianism that constituted this unworthy critique (Horkheimer, 1985, p. 410). The two colleagues attacked those intellectuals who attempted to find a philosophical ground for the "genuine revolution". They criticized those who saw capitalism as "the ultimate kingdom of evil, the bad form of human togetherness" and who "expect the ultimate truth on earth" (ibid., p. 264) to be realized in actual history. Their evaluation and critique of the ideological dimensions of hegemonic knowledge, in that period, was still guided by the Marxist claim of anti-idealism and anti-transcendentalism, founded on materialist reality, class interests, and economic developments. Adorno and Horkheimer of that period, however, favored the possibilities of a proletarian revolution and more than once even found themselves siding with the kind of Utopianism they so strongly opposed. It was Horkheimer himself who wrote then, "Maybe they are right. Maybe socialism does bring with it the kingdom of the millennium and the prophecies of the old testaments prophets will be realized after all" (ibid., p. 226).

The standard position of the Critical Theory thinkers of this period is, however, that theory is never neutral—and this is valid in respect of Critical Theory itself. The very foundation of Critical Theory is not justified merely on theoretical grounds: "a vision of a worthier human reality guides it" (Horkheimer 1985 III., p. 105). And yet, with all its explicit anti-Utopian commitment, already in his 1935 "Notes for philosophical anthropology" one encounters other trends, whereby Critical Theory commits itself to the mission of "a happier humanity" (ibid., p. 226). In 1936 Horkheimer explicitly speaks of the possibility of

> future circumstances [in which] efficiency and consciousness will constitute a common interest for human beings; 'the destruction drive' will no longer disturb them... (ibid., p. 86)

This trend is visible even in "Traditional Theory and Critical Theory", probably the most important publication of Critical Theory in its first stage of development (1937). Critical Theory is here explicitly presented as "a moment" of revolutionary praxis towards "new social forms". While still founding his perspectives for future society on materialist grounds and not on philosophical speculations Horkheimer explicitly speaks here of the importance of the idea of a future free human community ("as much as it is allowed by the technical conditions"). At the same time, however, he develops a vision of *the realization of Reason* and overcoming of alienation between thinking and reality, rationality and sensuality; in an almost Marcusian spirit he speaks even of "future freedom and spontaneity". This positive Utopian trend is manifested also in "Montaigne and the function of skepticism" (1938). Here Critical Theory is presented as directed to nothing less than "*the establishment of a brand new world*" (Horkheimer, 1985, IV, p. 289). At this period both Horkheimer and Adorno offer a promising, progressive, revolutionary theory of knowledge promising the overcoming of oppressive social realities and ideological manipulations. While doing very little in the field of explicit educational theory, their Critical Theory is of much relevance for criticizing established leftist and rightist pedagogical theories and they draw the framework for a possible revolutionary pedagogy. In this respect Paulo Freire, Peter McLaren, Michael Apple, Henry Giroux, Patti Lather, Ira Shor, Kathleen Weiler and other teachers of Critical Pedagogy are not totally mistaken in their implementation of Critical Theory as Critical Pedagogy. Still, as I will show this project is far from being unproblematic.

Freire's Critical Pedagogy has more then one source of inspiration, and among its most important ones I will name Christian theology, orthodox Marxism, and the works of the Frankfurt School thinkers. Here, however, it is of vital importance to note that it was their work in its *first* stage of development, the optimistic-oriented, oppressive one that became so relevant for him. He was totally unaware of the second stance, the Diasporic one, in their work, and this disregard of Freire influenced the paths chosen by Critical Pedagogy and its limitations until this very day. Freire's Critical Pedagogy should be considered, even in its best, as part and parcel of normalizing education in the sense that it was foundationalist and positivist, in contrast to his explicit negation of this orientation. It is a synthesis between dogmatic idealism and vulgar collectivism meant to sound the authentic voice of the collective, within which the dialogue is supposed to become aware of itself and of the world. The educational links of this synthesis contain a tension between its mystic-terroristic and its reflective-emancipatory dimensions. In Freire's attitude towards Fidel Castro and Che Guevara, the terroristic potential contained in the mystic conception of *the emancipated "group"*, "people", or "class" knowledge is revealed within the concept of a dialogue. Freire introduces Che Guevara as an ideal model for anti-violent dialogue between partners in the desirable praxis. Che Guevara, however, used a structurally similar rhetoric to that of Ernst Juenger and National Socialist ideologues on the creative power of war, the erotic, edifying sense of blood in combat, and sweat in the constitution of a new man, the worrier, as the real "proletarian" in South America. Freire gives this as an example of the liberation of the oppressed within the framework of new "love" relations which allow to speak the silenced "voice" (Freire, 1968, pp. 163–164).

His uncritical understanding of power/knowledge relations draws him to observe the de-colonization process in Africa and elsewhere (undoubtedly a progressive development in itself) as suitable contexts for national realization of Critical Pedagogy (Freire & Macedo, 1987, pp. 154–157). This is not mere naivety but a readjustment of the terroristic element of his Critical Pedagogy revealed earlier in his understanding of "Che" as an educator in his alliance with the national systematic oppression of "liberated" Third World. It is important to note that there is a connection between Freire's concept of love-emancipatory-violence-transcendence and his failure in the crucial theoretical and political concepts such as knowledge-power, consciousness and violence, as presented by Hegel, Marx, Adorno, and Foucault. That is why his emancipatory Eros sides implicitly with the anti-critical tradition of dogmatic revolutionary Christianity and voluntaristic revolutionary models of the anarchists, National Socialism, and South America's guerrillas. These are contrasted with the explicit devotion of his Critical Pedagogy to dialogue, non-functionalist Critical Thinking, as well as spiritual maturity.

Following the Frankfurt School's Critical Theory *in its first phase*, Freire's project is indebted to the "old" humanist progressive negation of present reality within the framework of an anti-Diasporic project; from within the quest for "home-coming", for appeasement, nirvana, rest, and other manifestations of Thanatos: it attempts to expropriate knowledge of oppressed groups as possessing special validity; from the totality governed by power to save a certain "authentic will" and consciousness which are devoted to an erotic praxis that will finally lead them "somehow" away from suffering, danger, and the presence of the absence of God; toward "authentic voice" to call them upon; toward truth, and uninterrupted pleasure as rearticulated Life in earthly Garden of Eden.

Even before this total redemption they are supposed to be *liberated* by their very entrance trough the gate of Critical Pedagogy and its erotic love as their genuine "home" as *Same* (Gur-Ze'ev, 2003b, p. 107). Within Critical Pedagogy they are supposed to be freed from the dynamics and internal logic of reality implicitly, in the name of the superiority of the essence of Being. In contrast to the Critical Theory's concept of love (Horkheimer, 1978, p. 127), this kind of love is immanently violent, even in the sense of political terror and the fabricating and controlling of collective as well as individual consciousness in the earthly Garden of Eden. Until this transformation it will have the last word in justifying "the counter-violence" of the oppressed and their self-evidence as an erotic spring for quasi-transcendence and "love" of the kind presently manifested by suicide bombers, mass killing of children and silencing reflection in the name of the "imperative of the revolution" in face of colonial oppression.

The central shortcoming of Freire's project, that gave birth to most of his failures—and to some of his most important contributions—is that *it is anti-Diasporic in its essence*. It is committed to establish a "homecoming" project for the oppressed as a collective and attempts to lead them into a non-nomadic human existence, and non-individualistic dwelling free from untruth, injustice, suffering, and meaningless-ness. A Gnostic perspective of homelessness and meaninglessness, worthy suffering in a Godless world are not even considered as an existential and philosophical option, surely not as a goal and locus of a genuine counter-education. This is why Freire is committed to a non-reflective, almost automatic preference for the self-evident knowledge of the oppressed to that of the oppressors is dangerous. The self-evidence of "the people" or a social or cultural group, especially when developed to reflectivity by a grand leader-educator, is not without a terroristic potential. On the one hand, the idea is that the educational leader is responsible for the success of the project, while by the same token he (not she) has to be *a total lover* and be totally loved. This is within praxis whose starting point is the self-evidence of the group and the imperatives of effective earthly politics (Gur-Ze'ev, 1998, p. 486) of the victims of Western colonialism and its arrogant emancipatory ambitions. This opens the gate to various forms of totalitarianism, nihilistic solipsism; swallowed by the system of truths, values, and strives on their path toward the post-colonialist earthly heaven. "Critique", "eroticism", and "resistance" can find in this arena of meaninglessness its home with no much difficulty. It is not only that the very language of "solutions" to such Titanic challenges is problematic in Freire's important work; more disturbing is the current lack of awareness that this attempt to avoid/address the challenge of the paradox of emancipatory education is actualized in a post-metaphysical moment and in light of the abandonment of the ideals of progress, transcendence and hierarchy by the new progressive thinking.

The optimistic-oriented self-indulgent attitude that in Freire's work is balanced by his self-reflection and courageous meeting with actual human experience has no much presence in the work of Henry Giroux.

In Giroux's project, even before his postmodern turn Critical Pedagogy's failure to transcend itself from normalizing education is grounded in its misunderstanding of the fundamentals of Critical Theory and in his disregard of the Diasporic philosophy of Benjamin and in the later works of Adorno and Horkheimer. While the pedagogical project of the early Giroux serves as a model for an educational project that almost disregards Adorno and Horkheimer's later work. At the same time it makes productive use of the other, less optimistic and less foundationalist dimensions, even in *the first stage* of the development of Critical Theory. Giroux expressly notes that his educational project is founded on the Critical Theory. The revolutionary potential of Critical Theory is explicitly of special importance in the early stage of the development of his thought (Giroux, 1983, p. 19). In another text he says that a precondition for a worthy pedagogical work is a worthy reading of the work of the Critical Theory thinkers (Giroux, 1981, p. 81). Here Giroux draws on the positive Utopianism of early Critical Theory, and following Freire he develops his project in accordance with the requirements of an optimistic revolutionary pedagogy.

According to Giroux, in the Critical Theory of the Frankfurt School every thought and theory is bound to a specific interest in the development of an unjust society. Of special importance for Giroux, as for other thinkers in Critical Pedagogy, is to present Ideology Critique—which challenges hegemonic knowledge and its claims—as a fundamentally unproblematic tool for *emancipatory education*. As a prima facie Critical-Theory-in-action, Critical Pedagogy, in this sense, becomes a transformative process, founded on the solid promise of a more humane future (Giroux & Aronowitz, 1981, p. 22). Giroux speaks here explicitly of Critical Theory as a transcending power within which critical thinking becomes a precondition for human freedom.

The central trend in Critical Pedagogy as here represented by Giroux not only contradicts the central massage of late Critical Theory as manifested by later Adorno and Horkheimer, but even the central commitments of *its first stage*, as laid down in the works of Benjamin, early Adorno, and early Horkheimer. Actually Giroux follows Herbert Marcuse and ignores the reservations of Adorno and Horkheimer concerning Marcuse's easy-going revolutionary project.

In the following I will show that *in the second stage* of the development of Critical Theory Adorno and Horkheimer not only abandoned their positive Utopianism, they forcefully cast aside its philosophical foundations and historical justifications. They rejected the entire tradition, which supported and manifested optimism about the possibility of a nonrepressive revolution and about an unproblematic emancipatory critique and the constitution of a new, genuine, "home" for the oppressed as a collective, always as a collective.

This is the theoretical arena out of which they developed their later negative Utopia and of "Diasporic philosophy" (Gur-Ze'ev, 2003c, pp. 17–35). It was based on the tradition of philosophical pessimism, which they elaborated into a transcendental dimension within their negative Utopianism. Since they refused to give up the Utopian axis they founded it in a most original way on Diasporic philosophy that offers a new negative theology, which they understood as essentially Jewish. This later work, as will be argued, is of vital importance in any attempt to develop current possibilities for counter-education in a postmodern era; hegemonic Critical Pedagogy was deprived of such possibilities since it ignored the mature part of Critical Theory. Nevertheless, when developing their Critical Pedagogy on Critical Theory's foundations, following Marcuse and avoiding the work of later Adorno and Horkheimer, Freire, Giroux, and their followers offered an important contribution to the development of a progressive Critical Pedagogy that emphasized "possibilities" without neglecting "critique". This progressive project, however, with all its importance, does not transcend from the framework of normalizing education. By holding on to this assertion one should acknowledge the progressive dimensions of this version of Critical Pedagogy and of its ways of negating *Life*. Not less important is to reconstruct the way Giroux's project consumes the work of the Frankfurt School thinkers only to offer a one-dimensional, non-dialectical, version of it in the field of education.

According to Giroux's Critical Pedagogy, when evaluating the schooling process it is wrong to disconnect the school curriculum and its other texts from its cultural and social contexts. In this sense school is a prima facie political arena, which plays an indispensable part in the production of discourses, meanings, identities, and subjects, and allows efficient control of their manipulated representation, distribution, and consumption. Following Critical Theory, Critical Pedagogy reveals the powers, interests, and ideologies beyond the *Maya* curtain of the school's declared commitment to the distribution of true/relevant knowledge/information. It critically reconstructs the abundant ways by which schools reflect and serve central social interests. This structural role of the school determines its function as a space dedicated to the organization of canonic knowledge, control of time, body, consciousness and conscious, and even constituting "valid" evaluation apparatuses, validating "the relevant" interpretive strategies. In this sense school functions as one of the cultural, social, and economic reproduction apparatuses in service of the dominant group and/ or the hegemonic master signifiers and their realm of self-evidence.

In contrast to the hegemonic pedagogical rhetoric, which is committed to depoliticizing the predicates and the sources of the representations of schooling, Giroux—following Adorno, Horkheimer, and Marcuse—acknowledges that at the present stage of capitalistic development there is no level or terra in society that is free of the presence of the hegemonic ideology.

Giroux explicitly identifies his Critical Pedagogy with the work of Marcuse, and commits himself to realizing this work in the field of education in order to develop a radical new pedagogical theory (Giroux, 1983, p. 2). Within this project, the Marcusian work is interpreted as a call for *intellectual activism* for teachers and students in the school arena. Teachers are called upon to become "transformative intellectuals" in schools and in society in general. As deeply committed intellectuals, they are obliged to develop every aspect of the formal educational process into an active and "popular" clash with the hegemonic order (Giroux, 1988, p. 37). In face of the obvious difficulties and limitations of Critical Pedagogy, that made it so irrelevant or even threatening for the oppressed it was committed to liberate and in light of the new intellectual bone tone in the academic left Giroux made a dramatic shift in the middle of the 1980's in his concept of Critical Pedagogy. He did not revisit the work of his heroes nor did he enter an articulation of an original philosophy of education. He went into the most updated politically correct ideologies and into their most fashioned postmodern and post-colonialist rhetoric implementations only to introduce them into traditional, modern, Marxist oriented Critical Pedagogy.

This shift has not only conceptual manifestations; it becomes clear even in other respects. It is not surprising, therefore, that in his 1981 *Ideology, Culture and the Educational Process* Marcuse is explicitly referred to in 22 pages, Adorno is mentioned in ten and Horkheimer in four. In his *Border Crossings* (1992), however, Adorno is mentioned only four times, and so is Horkheimer. Marcuse, from then on is not mentioned at all. Michel Foucault, who was mentioned only once in the text of 1981, has now become the hero of the reformulated Critical Pedagogy and is cited more than any other philosopher. It is not only that Giroux, like McLaren, Weiler, Lather, Shor, and other prominent American thinkers in the tradition of Critical Pedagogy, and to a certain degree also Paulo Freire, disregarded the mature work of Adorno and Horkheimer. Even within the part of Critical Theory that they did relate to they selected the more optimistic and foundationalist parts, especially in the work of Marcuse. They disregarded the complementary, Diasporic-anti-foundationalist aspects of Critical Theory, which is of vital importance even for the understanding of the immanent dialectic of Critical Theory in its first stage of development. The inner dialectics between these two dimensions is the gateway to understanding Critical Theory and its educational implications.

This dialectic is present not only in the work of Adorno, Horkheimer and Benjamin. It is there even in Benjamin's Utopianism, which was challenged along with that of Marcuse, even if for contrasting reasons.

The limits of Critical Pedagogy were challenged both within the tradition of Critical Pedagogy and "outside", by critics such as Elizabeth Ellsworth (Ellsworth, 1989, pp. 297–324). Until now, however, these difficulties were hardly met by an attempt to rearticulate Critical Pedagogy in light of a new reading of Critical Theory as a first step in countering new critical theories and trends within postmodern, post-colonialist, feminist, multiculturalist and queer theories and discourses. The effort to rearticulate Critical Pedagogy was made in an explicit attempt to be in line with the last fashions in current critical rhetoric (Giroux, 1996, p. 51). Among the very few prominent Critical Pedagogy thinkers who were not swallowed up by this trend one should mention McLaren. But he too did not respond to the limits of Critical Pedagogy by rethinking his conceptions of Critical Theory. He preferred to rearticulate orthodox Marxism in light of the current capitalistic globalization processes and in face of the dehumanization and the suffering it brings along with the "prosperity" it offers its elected ones (McLaren, 2000, pp. 25–33). Yet even

McLaren avoided the most important challenges that Benjamin and Late Adorno and Horkheimer presents us, when attempting to rearticulate Critical Pedagogy today in face of globalizing capitalism.

Before going into the issue of current possibilities and limitations of Critical Pedagogy or going beyond its horizons it is of vital importance to address in a much more detailed manner the change in Critical Theory of the Frankfurt School and to elaborate more on its Diasporic philosophy and its relevance for today's possible counter-education.

In the first stage of Critical Theory both Adorno and Horkheimer interlaced the goal of Critical Theory with the Marxian revolutionary project. In the second stage the turn away from Marx's main theses is evident. Marx's project was regarded as an element in the positive Utopian position, which by then they both rejected. Horkheimer expressly declares that it is a trend from the Marxian thought to that of Schopenhauer and the tradition of philosophical pessimism (Horkheimer, 1985 VII., pp. 339–340).

In the second stage of the development of Horkheimer's thought he is explicitly anti-revolutionary. *It is the nature of the revolutionary, every revolutionary, according to later Horkheimer, to become an oppressor* (ibid., p. 418). Every revolution, especially a "successful" one, is a manifestation of power. And justice, when it becomes powerful, is realized only at the cost of its transformation into oppression (ibid., p. 341). In contrast to the Marxian tradition, it is now conceived that as long as even some remnants of freedom survive violence will flourish (Horkheimer, 1989, p. 247).

> In the end, whatever hopes Marx did hold on behalf of true society, apparently they seem to be the wrong ones, if—and this issue is important to Critical Theory—freedom and justice are interrelated in mutual opposition. The more justice there is freedom will diminish accordingly. (ibid., p. 340)

The historical reconstruction of the Culture Industry with its limitations, about which Giroux was aware of and articulated of important implications in his Critical Pedagogy, is conceived here within the framework of a new, religious, Diasporic philosophy. For Adorno, "space is nothing but absolute alienation (Adorno, 1970, p. 205). For him this is the framework for viewing the whole historical reality of advanced technological society, in which everything has become "consumption", and life, with all its layers and dimensions, is nothing but "a fetish of consumption" (Adorno, 1970 III., p. 243).

In their *Dialectic of Enlightenment* Adorno and Horkheimer do not limit to the capitalistic logic and its realization in itself, or the other representations of totalitarianism such as the National-Socialist or the Stalinist. Ultimately they target culture itself:

> Culture has developed with the protection of the executioner…All work and pleasure are protected by the hangman. To contradict this fact is to deny all science and logic. It is impossible to abolish… terror and retain civilization. Even the lessening of terror implies a beginning of the process of dissolution. (Adorno & Horkheimer, 1988, p. 255)

The conception of revolution and Critical Theory within the framework of historically progressing human emancipation is conceived within a double-layered philosophy of history, one linear, the other circular.

From the viewpoint of circular conception of time there is no room for progress in the Kantian, Hegelian, or Marxian sense, which made possible the optimism of Critical Pedagogy.

According to Benjamin, there is no document of culture which is not at the same time a document of a barbarity (Benjamin, 1972, p. 696). For Adorno and Horkheimer all substantive levels of "progress" manifest an oppressive regression. In this sense, "adaptation to the power of progress involves the regression of power. Each time anew 'progress' brings about those degenerations. They manifest not the unsuccessful but successful progress to be its contrary" (Adorno & Horkheimer, 1988, p. 42).

On the other level of "progress", the explicitly historical one, unless an unpredictable interference occurs the good intentions and progressive talents of educators devoted to revolutionary education are of little use in halting the enhancement and sophistication of barbarism. The instrumentalization of rationality is reconstructed as representing and serving the growing needs of technological progress and economic development. Instrumental Rationality becomes "a magic essence". Instrumental Rationality is conceived here as a metaphoric revolt of instrumentalized nature, as a return of *mythos*, whose overthrow was the essential mission of Enlightenment. Mythical thought gave birth to Enlightenment in the form of *Bildung* and human emancipation. This is the reason that today, for its part, in its most "progressive" form Enlightenment returns to a more dangerous type of mythical thought (Horkheimer, 1989 XIII., p. 328) within what Horkheimer calls "the full-administered world".

In such a reality there is no room for non-repressive "progressive", positive, Utopianism, or for an objective, justifiable, education and praxis for resistance and overcoming the present reality (Horkheimer, 1974, p. 26). Does this mean that Adorno and Horkheimer abandoned Utopia altogether, that they gave up the essential commitment of Critical Theory, or ended their transformative-educational imperative? Not at all. On the contrary, they became devoted more than ever to the Utopian call.

Adorno and Horkheimer gave up the Marxist conception of progress, and in this sense their optimism as to a social revolutionary change, and even the goal, and to a certain degree also the means of critique. But they did not abandon the Utopian project and the essential imperatives of Critical Theory as an emancipatory dimension and political praxis. However, their definition of emancipation and the stance of realization of intellectual autonomy as praxis changed dramatically to become more in line with the Gnostic tradition and with Jewish negative theology, traditions that refused all versions of "redemption", "emancipation" and "homecoming" that were committed to solve human essential Diasporic existence in face, within, and as part of Being. Here Adorno and Horkheimer are much closer to Heidegger then to Marcuse. This understanding is of vital importance for any current attempt to face the limitations of Critical Pedagogy and go into the struggle for the constitution of counter-education in face of the exile of spirit and the omnipotence of globalizing capitalism and the advance in today's high-tech cultural and existential realizations.

While the first stage (the revolutionary-optimistic) of Critical Theory became the foundation of todays Critical Pedagogy, the second stage is a brilliant manifestation of *counter-education*, committed not only to criticize, but also to overcome all versions of normalizing education. Adorno's and Horkheimer's later work offers a framework for counter-educational praxis whose religiosity is fertilized by the alarming recognition of the impossible realization of the imperative of human "homecoming" to God, or domesticating absolute Spirit or Reason; the establishment of a genuine "home" or "homecoming" to the advancing true knowledge of genuine human interests and realization of their potentials is here a constitutive element of philosophy and politics. The current work of Slavoj Zizek, who writes that "the paradox of self-consciousness is that it is possible only against the background of its own impossibility" (Zizek, 1993, p. 15), is very close to this later work of Horkheimer and Adorno. In this sense the later Critical Theory writings, which I consider essentially *Diasporic* in the sense that they try to overcome the quest for "homereturning" in all its manifestations, became prima facie counter-educational, even if the word "education" is rarely mentioned and schooling is hardly tackled at all. This philosophy is a challenge to present relations between the hegemonic Critical Pedagogy and its roman with the new anti-Semitism.

The big challenge for the critical mind and for humanistic education is not so much *the fruit of alienation* but the disappearance of (the consciousness of) alienation within the totality, which is today governed by the various fruits of the post-metaphysical moment within the ether of holiness of the killing-God-each-moment-anew. This quest of the critical mind for transcendence in face of holiness in light of alienation and the challenges of the exile of critical Spirit and Love of Life mark the difference between critique of orthodox Marxist ideology and Horkheimer's and Adorno's conceptions. Governing Instrumental Rationality leaves no room for non-efficient and non-pragmatic considerations, and drives out the concepts, ideals, and traditions that allowed speculation and critique of the self-evident, and offered transcendence from the oppressive practices of all master signifiers. Instrumental Rationality is responsible for the current reality, in which the more progressive the processes of de-humanization become, the more efficient becomes the concealment of the oppression by present Culture Industry (Adorno, 2000, p. 233). The exile of Spirit and Love of life, and the bridging of the abyss between substance and subject, existence and meaning, creation/work and aim, Diasporic self-positioning and quests for "homecoming" are trivialized, and *Spirit* is again presented; but only as a commodity form that has lost its connection to its use value and functions primarily as a violent symbolic interchange, as part of what I call "the Pleasure Machine" that normalizing education is so quick to celebrate as "reality" (Gur-Ze'ev, 2003, p. 2). Reified consciousness (Adorno, 1994, p. 200) which is fabricated with less and less antagonistic dimensions by the present culture industry reaffirms "spirituality" and "spiritual education" as a power of anti-love-of-life, and occultists are celebrating their victory all over Western culture, especially when it presents itself as the redemptive Diasporic power at the present historical moment (ibid., p. 244).

According to Adorno and Horkheimer there is no *anchor*, stable ground or a perfect future to secure optimism; not even the very premises of Critical Theory, and a philosopher worthy of the name must become what I call "a Diasporic human being". The seeming political freedom, free opinion, and tolerance within present Western society conceal and actually serve the process of totalistic de-humanization.

> Not only does the mind mould itself for the sake of its marketability, and thus reproduce the socially prevalent categories. Rather, it grows to resemble ever more closely the status quo as its "home" even where it subjectively refrains from making a commodity of itself. The network of the whole is drawn ever tighter […] It leaves the individual consciousness less and less room for evasion, performs it more and more thoroughly, cuts it off as it were from the possibility of differentiating itself as all difference degenerates to a nuance in the monotony of supply. (Adorno, 2000, p. 198)

The critique of traditional Marxist ideology cannot have much use since culture itself "has become ideological" (ibid., p. 206). "Today", Adorno says, "ideology means society as appearance […]" (ibid., p. 207). However, since ideology is no longer conceived as a socially necessary appearance which veils the "facts", critique of ideology can no longer offer an emancipatory deciphering of "reality" and cannot claim to empower humanistic-oriented resistance to social oppression and to manipulative representations of histories, identities, and realities. Adorno offers a view that does not allow this kind of optimism, since

> Ideology today is society itself in so far as its integral power and inevitability, its overwhelming existence-in-itself, surrogates the meaning which that existence has exterminated. (ibid.)

Horkheimer is on the verge of acknowledging that there is no longer justification for a Critical Theory. In a personal letter to Adorno he says that nowadays "reflection [has become] senseless. Actually the world to which we saw ourselves as belonging is destroyed" (Horkheimer, 26 May 1960, Archive, VI., 13, 511). Elsewhere he writes that serious talk itself has become senseless and that those who refuse to listen—to the attempts to save meaning—are not totally wrong (Horkheimer, 1978, p. 129). Truth in this context is not absent; it is rather revealed in, swallowed and re-presented by, the present reality which as such ridicules any "critical" attempt to be put within brackets. Today it is the "critique" itself which can survive only within brackets, unless it accepts the ecstatic, purifying fire of the new anti-Semitism, on the one hand, or new age "everyday spiritualism", on the other. The issue at stake here is not solely truth or justice but the very *quest* for responsible Diasporic human as an eternal improviser, or, in other words, the possibility of transcendence (Adorno, 2000, pp., 65, 85) from meaninglessness and from "sameness" (Adorno, 2000, p. 236)—or what Levinas calls *the Same* (Levinas, 1987, p. 55)—*overcoming the hospitality* of being swallowed by the mere thingness of Being. Addressing the absence of the foundation for the quest for transcendence and facing its infinity as negative Utopia is an ontological sign of Diaspora that Critical Theory offers as an impetus for a possible present day counter-education.

In the work of later Adorno and Horkheimer, two very different conceptions of truth emerge. One is the hegemony that is established on the existing world of facts, which ultimately represents "power" (Adorno & Horkheimer, op. cit., p. 236). Here human existence in its essence is revealed at its full price: practical involvement, within which ideals transform into oppression (ibid.). The implicit negation of any optimistic positive emancipatory educational project of the kind that standard Critical Pedagogy is presently actualizing is mercilessly manifested here.

Within the framework of Critical Theory Adorno positions his philosophy against the fundamental assumption of all positive Utopias and all "homecoming" projects: the assumption that the power of thought is sufficient to grasp the totality of the real (Adorno, 2000, p. 24). In regard to an alternative concept of *truth*, homelessness and Diasporic existence are here connected to Adorno's central conceptions, among which a special role is reserved for dialectics, non-identity, negation, and reflection. For him

> The name of dialectics says no more, to begin with, than that objects do not go into their concepts without leaving a reminder that they come to contradict the traditional norm of adequacy [...] it indicates the untruth of identity, the fact that the concept does not exhaust the thing conceived. (ibid., p. 57)

In light of the centrality to Adorno's later thought of the concept of nonidentity, it is of vital importance to state that for him what I call "Diaspora" is not a merely epistemological dimension. It is even much more than a way of life, and surely it is not a temporary punishment of humans by God only to be overcome by redemptive "homecoming" to a cosmic harmony and non-alienated human existence. As in the Gnostic tradition, Adorno's rearticulated "exiled good God" is present as an absence in the reality of *the evil God* of historical existence and creative reality. This is why for him; while dialectics is the consistent sense of nonidentity it also assures the impossibility of any stable ground for "standpoint"—not only the "wrong stand-point" (ibid.). The aim of Adorno's Diasporic philosophy is Diasporic self-reflection, and self-overcoming. Diasporic self-overcoming will make possible transcendence, responsibility, improvisation and co-poiesis with no ground, ultimate end, or appeasing nihilistic pleasure, rational conclusion, totalizing synthesis, or any other kind of "home" or redemption.

In an imaginary conversation between the philosopher—an implicit reference to the masters of Critical Theory themselves—and the practical man, the philosopher is the one on the defensive, not his practical interlocutor. The genuine philosopher is introduced by Adorno and Horkheimer not as a promising educator but as *a neurotic*, who manifests his refusal to be cured when insisting on continuing his impossible project of curing normal, realistic-oriented, sane, people (Adorno & Horkheimer, op. cit., p. 255). Facing these conclusions one should ask, *what, if any, is the justification for Critical Theory and for Critical Pedagogy as emancipatory education in action, under conditions in which "serious philosophy has come to its end"?* (Horkheimer, 1985, VII., p. 404) One may ask if there is a secure or insecure yet worthy non-religious "home" even for counter-education, if Adorno is right in saying:

> Whatever wants nothing to do with the trajectory of history belongs all the more truly to it. History promises no salvation and offers the possibility of hope only to the concept whose movements follows history's path to the very extreme. (Adorno, 1998, p. 17)

The later Horkheimer presents mature Critical Theory as a Jewish Negative Theology. This change carries major educational implications. Following Benjamin, it was for him of vital importance that Judaism did not present God as a positive absolute. The negativity of this Utopianism is constituted of two elements: the first is rejection in principle of the possibility of a positive realization of any Utopia. Horkheimer refuses to imagine a positive picture of future society prior to its realization (Horkheimer, 1985, VII., p. 382). The second is his commitment to confront Critical Theory with its own negativity and its own impossibility. This is a challenge worthy of a Diasporic philosophy that cannot satisfy itself in a concluding synthesis, not even in its essential homelessness or negativity. It is this challenge that opens the gate to counter-education, and in many respects it is the gate itself. In Adorno's words

> The plain contradiction of this challenge is that of philosophy itself, which is thereby qualified as dialectics before getting entangled in its individual contradictions. The work of philosophical self-reflection consists in unrevealing that paradox. Everything else is signification, secondhand [...]. (Adorno, 2000, p. 60)

As genuine Diasporic philosophers both Adorno and Horkheimer refuse any philosophy that leads to consensus, synthesis, and the end of dialectics and worthy suffering. Yet at the same time they refuse to abandon the quest for the Messiah or human emancipation. The *quest*, as a Messianic tension, is central here, not its "successful" fulfillment. The messianic quest so often is interwoven in a positive Diasporic philosophy that it makes possible the institutionalization of religion and normalizing, repressive, religious, education which challenges genuine religiosity and authentic Diasporic existence. Adorno and Horkheimer are careful to position in the center of their counter-education a Diasporic attitude: different from to homocentric-oriented, reflection, and from humanistic transcendence. In his *Minima Moralia* Adorno concludes that

> The only philosophy which can be responsibly practiced in face of despair is the attempt to contemplate all things as they would present themselves from the standpoint of redemption. Knowledge has no light but that shed on the world by redemption: all else is reconstruction, mere technique. Perspectives must be fashioned that displace and estrange the world, reveal it to be, with its rifts and crevices, as indigent and distorted as it will appear one day in the messianic light. (Adorno, 1999, p. 247)

In contrast to present thinkers of the new ant-Semitism and to its education Judaism was so important for Horkheimer and his counter-education. He saw in it "a non-positive religion", "a hope for the coming of the Messiah" (Horkheimer, 1985, XIV., p. 331). Judaism, within this framework, is not a reality but a symbol for—non-violent—solidarity of the powerless (ibid., p. 140). As a Jewish Negative Theology, Critical Theory expresses, in his view, "a refusal to recognize power as an argument for truth" (ibid., p. 139). Horkheimer's contribution to the Diasporic perspective is here crystal clear when he identifies "Judaism", as a "non-positive religion," with Critical Theory. Adorno too understood the refusal of power, effectiveness, and domestication in the *Same* of the world of facts as a precondition for genuine counter-education that will challenge the present reality (Adorno, 1971, p. 147).

The conception of *dwelling in an ontological Diaspora* was vital for presenting late Critical Theory as a Jewish Negative Theology. The uniqueness of Judaism lies in its permanent demand for justice, emerging out of a hope with no real historical anchor: "Jewry was not a powerful state, but the hope for justice at the end of the world" (Horkheimer, 1978, p. 206). The idea that *the demand for justice essentially cannot obtain power*, and that *justice can be realized only at the cost of its transformation into its opposite—injustice*, is central to the educational implications of this version of Critical Theory.

It implies that counter-education must not attempt to transcend negativism; it is committed to anti-dogmatism and it must resist any manifestation of the self-evident, even that of the oppressed and the persecuted. It must resist popularization and political victories. At the same time its Messianic impulse is directed to resisting actual injustices in the present reality as the only manifestation of the quest for truth and justice. This version of Negative Theology as a mature Critical Theory in Horkheimer's thought complies with Adorno's concept of Negative Dialectics.

It was not in opposition to the view of the philosopher as a neurotic who refuses to be cured, but in compliance with this vision that Adorno articulated the "categorical imperative of philosophy" (Adorno, 2000, p. 53). There he concludes: "it does not hold the key to salvation, but allows some hope only to the moment of concept followed by the intellect wherever the path may lead" (ibid.). Yet Adorno's Diasporic philosophy is not consistent enough with itself.

Ultimately, Adorno presents Critical Theory as a path to salvation. This, however, is within a negative framework that leaves no room for any positive Utopia or actual salvation in the sense that traditional positive utopias or optimistic-oriented Critical Pedagogy can promise its disciples. In most of his educational texts Horkheimer too is short of consistent Diasporic philosophy and he offers optimism on the possibility of a worthier education—at the expense of counter-education, which if genuine must be truly Diasporic and refuse any optimistic version of normalizing education. The explicit philosophical texts of these thinkers in their second stage of development represent a much more consistent Diasporic philosophy.

Even in a post-metaphysical moment, according to Adorno, philosophy has not concluded its mission. However, it does not have any foundation, self-evidence, social strata, or pain on which to establish its critical education: "Philosophy offers no place from which theory as such might be concretely convicted of the anachronisms it is suspected of, now, as before" (Adorno, 2000, p. 55). Adorno, in accordance with Benjamin and Horkheimer, presents another kind of dialectics that stands in contrast to the orthodox Marxist concept of dialectics and its version of Ideology Critique (as an emancipatory overcoming of alienation and false consciousness, and as a precondition for a revolutionary praxis). As a genuine counter-educator he refuses any concept of dialectics, which promises victory, emancipation, or peace.

According to Adorno's ontology, human's homelessness is neither a temporary situation nor a punishment; ontologically it is rooted in the infinite rootlessness, in what Deleuze calls "becoming" (Deleuze & Guattari, 1995, p. 294) or "the rhizomatic" that opens the gate to nomadic existence. Adorno and Horkheimer are united here in refusing any manifestations of the absolute, the totality, the truth, or a positive justice on earth. Their philosophy refuses the post-structuralist celebration of the triumph of immanence over transcendence. Their responsibility is of vital importance in the present day of mega speeds and the near possibility of the end of all life on earth as a manifestation of human progress which challenges both the emancipatory concept of "progress" as conceived by the Hegelian tradition and the concept of existence as developed by the existentialist tradition. Does it enable or contradict counter-education?

Adorno is very much aware of the contradictions in the heart of his project. His Diasporic project rests here, on these contradictions precisely, as a way of overcoming meaninglessness and self-evidence of various kinds, including the revolutionary kind. "The work of philosophical self-reflection consists in unraveling that paradox. Everything else is signification, secondhand construction, pre-philosophical activity" (Adorno, 2000, p. 60). *What then remains for philosophy to do?* Is there still a mission it can devote itself to—without transforming itself into its negative and become a new, sophisticated, version of normalizing education?

Addressing the human condition in face of dangers and open possibilities such as non-manipulative presence/interpretation of the governing power-relations, sameness, the presence of **the totally other** as a pure manifestation of metaphysic violence becomes vital for any reflective attempt to genuinely listen, to present a meaningful question in a Godless world, to offer your hand to the Other without destroying his otherness. According to Adorno,

> To change this direction of conceptuality, to give it a turn toward nonidentity, is the hinge of Negative Dialectics. Insight into the constitutive character of the nonconceptual in the concept would end the compulsive identification, which the concept brings unless halted by such reflection. Reflection upon its own meaning is the way out of the concept's seeming being-in-itself as a unit of meaning. (Adorno, ibid., p. 63)

In this sense, and solely in this sense, for Adorno, "philosophy can make it after all" (ibid.). His Diasporic philosophy in this respect becomes the only way to resist the process of destruction of the autonomy of the human subject (Adorno, 1998, p. 5). It becomes the only manner of resistance to being overwhelmed by the one-dimensional functionality and thingness of the system (Adorno, 2000, p. 234) and its deceiving message of freedom in accordance with the laws of the market and the current world of facts (ibid., p. 198). As such, within its negativity, it incubates an alternative to the hegemonic educational message propagated by the Culture Industry: it offers nomadic, creative, religious existence and love via the possibility of refusal of the present process of subjectification; resistance to the reality of constructing the de-humanized agent. As such Diasporic philosophy offers a kind of thinking which allows hope of overcoming the current educational reality (ibid., p. 238) of which today's Critical Pedagogy is an important part.

Diasporic philosophy enabled Adorno and Horkheimer to not only effect a radical critical reconstruction of the present historical moment but to go further into offering an existential-philosophical counter-educational refusal to all manifestations of power in the present culture and society. The Diasporic philosophy constructed by them was actually a non-positivistic and anti-optimistic alternative; as in the Gnostic tradition, it was a call for the overcoming of the omnipotence of the presence of "the evil God". Such an alternative opened up when they insisted on transcend-ence, and (against the deceiving call for relativism, nihilism, or pragmatism) on love. They insisted in face of the dullness of the present historical moment on meaning, responsibility, and creativity that are not a mere echo of the hegemonic power-games of the totally administered world.

Critical Theory here becomes an introduction to a *renewal* of poiesis and ecstatic religiosity without becoming a new dogmatic religious, philosophical, or political "home". At the same time, however, dogmatic and institutionalized religion comes to have special relevance for the Frankfurt School thinkers: they struggled for the very possibility of Diasporic sensitivity to the pursuit for **the totally other**. Only within this Diasporic philosophy and its counter-educational alternatives are we to understand its refusal to abandon the imperative of responsibility to the yet unrealized human potentials. To this imperative, like to the presence of hope out of suffering, they offered only one possible way: that of *religious negation*. Holiness is Diasporically reclaimed in face of the absence of holiness, Love and the exile of meaning.

The message here has its origins in the Jewish messianic impulse, the commitment to transcendence from the secular order of things, from mere life as the aim of life, from the continuum and most importantly: from false sacredness or ecstatic meaninglessness which is a gate for self-forgetfulness: from any mani-festation of the self-evident and the *Same*; it is a call for a struggle to overcome meaninglessness in a Godless world. In this sense, here any possible educational "implication" should be negative, if it is to be true to itself. At the same time, as genuine counter-education it is a manifestation of **Love** and a concrete realization of joy and creativity, *tikun olam*. In this sense later Adorno and Horkheimer are so important in any attempt to keep alive the quest and the actual appearance of counter-education as a concrete Utopia of education for love in a postmodern condition.

For Adorno and Horkheimer, the transcendental dimension and the concept of the horizon as a limit that does not have the last word determine the frame of struggle which constitute the "genuine" human—a position that comes close to mystic tradition. According to Adorno, and here he is very close to Heidegger, from whom he and Horkheimer were so concerned to distance themselves.

> What is waiting in the objects themselves needs such intervention to come to speak, with the perspective that the forces mobilized outside [...]. (Adorno, 2000, p. 75)

This dimension is made especially clear in Horkheimer's unpublished works. In every single thing, he wrote in a private note, a higher aim dwells, which is channeled to external infinity, which transcends it. The negative Utopia of Diasporic philosophy is expressed here, on the one hand, by the deeds of the genuine philosopher, which manifest openness and readiness for being called upon, geared towards a total negation of the given reality as the actuality of "truth, beauty, and goodness" (Horkheimer, 1985, XIV., p. 162). Horkheimer's starting point, however, includes the acknowledgement that these dimensions reflect the absolute, which will forever remain concealed, unreachable, and misconceived. One must clarify the status of this *yearning*, a clarification that Horkheimer himself avoided and Adorno did only very little to address. Here we come up against the limits of their mature Critical Theory even when it becomes an implicit rich Diasporic philosophy.

With Horkheimer, as with Adorno and Benjamin, the struggle for the possibilities of transcendence from the boundaries of the horizons of the hegemonic reality transforms this praxis into *prayer,* a holy deed. Here too, holiness is not conditioned and determined by the level of its "success" but by openness and possibility. Also in Franz Rosenzweig's views on prayer.

> The question is not asked here whether the prayer will be answered and fulfilled. The context of the prayer is its fulfillment. The soul prays [...] for the capability of prayer [...] this ability to pray is the highest gift given to the soul in revelation. This gift is actually the capability of prayer. But by being superior it already passes the boundaries of the realm of capability. For, with the ability of prayer given, the necessity for prayer is also included. (Rosenzweig, 1970, p. 215)

In prayer, the yearning for a dialogue between the human as an infinite challenge to her finitude and "God" as a representation of infinity is realized. Intimacy with holiness is reestablished. The relation is a religious one. What establishes the religious dimension is not the establishment of an unproblematic meeting with "God" but the Diasporic facing of his absence and the meeting of the existential moment where Sisyphean *overcoming* of mere (pleasurable/painless/ "successful") human life is the aim of human life. A self-contained, domesticated, human subject cannot make possible a true human, since he is essentially Diasporic when true to himself; the human is conditioned by transcendence and improvisational challenging the immanence. The traditional concept of prayer (Dresner, 1957, p. 24) represented this idea in a manner still fruitful, especially in face of the absence of God. As happens so often with love, happiness, and creativity, prayer too, when instrumentalized and institutionalized, negates its own essence and becomes a devoted slave of the reality it is committed to transcend.

In order to realize the idea of the quasi-autonomous improvising subject, the human is normally educated to be overwhelmed by powerful inhumanity: a desire for power—a desire for "home" in the swallowing presence of the absolute immanence. Unless the Diasporic counter-education is offered, neither emancipation nor redemption awaits but nihilism and disintegration of human culture. Today it is so vividly manifested in the disintegration of Western culture that has lost its truth, its master signifiers, and its aim. Hence the central role played by the myth within the ideological system, which serves the hegemonic realm of self-evidence. A powerful desire such as this—one that allows the metaphysics and purpose of existence of every individual in such a society, may force its way in and erupt in various conceptual earthquakes, akin to Humanism, Nazism, early Judaism, Christianity, or total nihilism. This power may manifest itself as an ecstatic poiesis that springs from a rich cultural heritage which stands before these occurrences and calls them by names, catalogues them, and transforms them. The Diasporic community enriches itself by the presence of the absence of the absolute, which constitutes the longing for it. This negative presence, the presence of the absence, might reconnect us with the essence of religiosity that is so often misrepresented by the institutionalized religions that constitute the false quest for Diasporic existence as a prelude to "homecoming" to the lost Garden of Eden, nirvana, ultimate pleasure or other positive Utopian versions of human's self-forgetfulness. This made nomadism possible and enabled the posing of new philosophical questions, a lust which gave power to martyrs at the stake, to monks confronting ancient parchments as absent truths, or to women confronting the systematic oppression that was inflicted on them by the ever-growing sophistication of Western phallocentrism (Gur-Ze'ev, 1999, p. 452). The desire for **the totally other** as impetus of Love and authentic creativity made possible the reality in the system while challenging it. It also allowed transformation, transgression, and border-crossing from one system of self-evidence and "homecoming" project to a different one. It was not only co-opted for the reproduction of the order of things—it also was a power of change and altered systems on the existential level of every individual as well as on the level of the rises and falls of entire civilizations.

Gnosis was the struggle for the knowledge of "the good exiled God", the under-standing of which was unattainable. Hence its noble Diasporic position. Adorno and Horkheimer viewed the "understanding" of the given reality as stipulated in connection with the absolute; an affinity which is viewed as a certain type of knowledge, or conditioned in a specific type of knowledge, which is different from that which is reproduced in the hegemonic realm of self-evidence. In this manner even they, in their Diasporic philosophy, like Gnosis, sought after metaphysical knowledge, which can be defined as the "knowledge of the secrets of the universe". Only in this sense can a human hope to achieve salvation (ibid., p. 284). Within the framework of Critical Theory this is the quest for the secrets of the universe, as much as it is a human universe, open for co-poiesis, improvisation and Love that is actualized in resistance to injustice.

In opposition to the present new anti-Semitism as the meta-narrative of progressive thinking, the projects of Benjamin, Adorno, and Horkheimer are essentially Diasporic and as such are not founded on present reality; nor are they optimistic about their chances of finally having the upper hand. The philosophical anthropology of their Diasporic project presents intentionality as essential to the Diasporic human as "the genuine individual".

Horkheimer's Negative Utopianism as prayer and as Diasporic existence has three aspects. The first is the advent of an ideal Diasporic, anti-ethnocentristic-oriented community in which one can attempt to see levels of religion, or an established cult with a special jargon, rituals and gestures, common enemies, similar societal background, etc. within this Diasporic philosophy. Negative Utopianism is also *an invitation* to the Diasporic community as a sort of "praying congregation", present in writings of Rosenzweig, as well as the method of establishing this community. To a certain degree, this type of community already exists.

The second aspect is the establishment of the religious erotic dimension of this Diasporic philosophy in relation to the absence of the absolute. According to Heschel, the purpose of prayer in Jewish mysticism is to recall God to the world and to establish in it his kingdom (Heschel, 1954, p. 61). In this respect, *prayer* is the ladder towards the perfection over the horizon. With Horkheimer, the resting point of this ladder is the Diasporic existence and the awareness of the absence of the absolute. "The longing for heaven, where he will never enter" (Horkheimer, 1974, p. 212) relies on the existence of the absolute and supersedes it—and at the same time constitutes it. Horkheimer's endeavor as prayer is very close to that of the *Kabala* concerning the relationship between mystical prayer and divinity.

According to Moshe Idel, one of the *kabala* texts illustrating this belongs to Rabbi Elazar of Worms:

> Let there be the sound of prayer of Israel—for prayer travels upward towards the heavens above their heads and travels and rests on the head of the Almighty and becomes for him a crown [...] for prayer rests like a crown [...] Human prayers are transformed by their relation that they are transcended and become part of the divine escort: Divine Presence, a wreath on the head of God, and 'like the crown'. (Idel, 1988, p. 372)

Idell sees the composition of a "wreath" by means of prayer as a "crowning of a king". From this aspect he continues, "one can see the *Kabala* not only as caring for the garden but also caring for the gardener himself" (ibid., p. 197).

Adorno and Horkheimer's Diasporic projects are not very far from the essence of kabalistic yearning—the yearning of the homeless for **the totally other** than the totality of the immanence of the present reality as the manifestation of Being; the yearning for what Levinas calls **the infinite Other**, which is a condition for prayer, and at the same time its fruits.

With regards to the affinity to the absolute, the Diasporic project itself appears as a *prayer* of an eternal nomad, who refuses any positive God, refuses any of the positive Utopias and all alternative kinds of "homecoming" projects to the lost Garden of Eden or to its sub-mundane realizations. As such there is no place in it for prayer as a separate activity. This is based on the Gnostic view of true prayer: "prayer as a type of higher communication with supreme reality must be quietness" (Mortley, 1986, p. 37).

The third aspect of this Diasporic philosophy is the self-constitution of the "genuine individual" in the ideal Diasporic community. The ability of the true individual (the philosopher) to send *the invitation* to the critical conversation—where the possibility for the struggle for salvation of the soul lies—is also the moral duty which Horkheimer imposes on the Diasporic philosopher, and maybe on himself:

> Both prayer and romantic love have a common past. Today both are fading, and there is no better manifestation of it than the propaganda taking place in their name... the praise and the condemnation, the sanctions against the skeptic. If he remains purely negative, he contributes to the validity of regression. To be devoted one to another as man intended, in the past, to do with the assistance of prayer, even though the impotence of prayer and the insignificance of man became a well known thing; to transform into much love... to drive aside the skepticism whenever the social and psychological conditions were exposed and understood and from awareness to them: to drive aside the skepticism without forgetting what these skeptical matters brought about—this is the only resistance the individual can offer in face of the vain progress. It will not cease the decline; it will, however, bear witness on the right thing during the period of darkness. (Horkheimer, 1974, p. 206)

This responsibility of the Diasporic, religious, eternally-improvising human, who has no dogma, collective, pleasure, "truth", "revolution", Garden of Eden or God to enslave himself to, is born out of an the existential decision—similar to the Kierkegaardian "Either-Or"—which creates dislearning and manifests Love of Life. Adorno and Horkheimer's anthropology understands existence as dependent on that which is beyond it, hence the erotic commitment to transcendence above any given reality or above life as the ecstatic aim of life. Existence, here, is an endless religious, nomadic self-creation, a fulfillment as a departure into the realm of possibility, into a realm which has not yet been realized.

The Diasporic religiousness, which I credit to Adorno and Horkheimer, is similar to the existential religiousness that I find in Kierkegaard—something Adorno clearly states when speaking of Kierkegaard. Adorno and Horkheimer's religiousness is nothing but an interpretation of reality which becomes co-poiesis way of life that not only transcends the historical reality but even transforms the historical moment itself in the sense that it reveals its self-negation in face of the infinite Diasporic essence of Being itself.

As a way of life, as co-poiesis, Diasporic philosophy is not religiousness based on the fear of life but on the affirmation of life, while facing meaninglessness, suffering, and the rejection of all calls for "homecoming". This refusal makes nomadism possible as a religious way of life, as Love of Life. It gives life justification, not through purposefulness of the kind from which the concept of oppression is constituted. This justification is a manifestation of Love of Life and is a Sisyphean one, in the sense of the religion of the Greeks according to the Nietzschean interpretation. The Diasporic human, then, like the Nietzschean super-human, may be truly *happy* (which is in opposition to satisfaction by the furnishing of phony needs) from this tragedy. The Greek hero, Nietzsche's super-human, and Horkheimer's philosopher affirm life not only despite their suffering and meaninglessness but more than that out of meaninglessness, suffering, and the absolute absence of the Other as a friend.

The Diasporic identification of the possibilities for transcendence from the tyranny of the facts of the present reality is also present in Nietzsche's Dionysianism. While opposed to conventional religion, this, nevertheless is "the road towards life", which is essentially "religious", a tragic-"holy" struggle, an "aim" that overcomes "God" and redeems Life and "earth" (Nietzsche, 1999, p. 978). Horkheimer, for all his criticism, sees Nietzsche as a thinker who symbolizes a will and a way to salvation (Horkheimer, 1985, XIII., p. 258). The Diasporic religiousness to which we refer to is not stopped by the awareness of "death of God"; on the contrary, this is its starting point. Of this may be said what Victor Nouvo said of radical theology: "a new liberty is formed from the recognition of the death of man and the death of God. It is radical theology which opens the way to this new liberty" (Nuovo, 1966, p. 25).

In light of the present exile of holiness from the West, exile which is instrumental for the deconstruction of love and the flourishing of the new anti-Semitism we should remember that Adorno and Horkheimer's Diasporic philosophy does not lack holiness: it makes the overcoming of the belief in all forms of "God", the absolute or the positive, into a starting point of a re-articulated Gnostic counter-education for love. As such it sits well with the dealings of modern critical theologians who express true religious tension, which is dependent on "waiving the concept of God as the basis for work", in the words of Dietrich Bonhoffer (Bonhoffer, 1998, p. 191). This *disbelief* is close to the religiousness of Karl Barth, who states that today "[true] religiousness is disbelief" (Barth, 1957, p. 327). Even so, the denial of belief should not be seen as a forgoing of the absolute. It is *this* denial of dogmatic belief which makes possible a burst of vital, absolute belief which wills a life of wandering upon the skeptic. The holy deeds of the skeptic form the totality of his existence and the permanence of his Diasporic community. Historically, this is the difference between weak-spirited skepticism, which is pragmatic or carries the suffix "post", and skeptical religiousness, which enriches that same major religion—one which usually produces power and at the same time promises new eroticism. This Diasporic skepticism is the burning bush of the kind out of which God spoke to Moses (Exodus III, 4). This call out of the burning bush will never be easy to identify as other than the echo of the governing power-games and an effect of the immanence of the symbolic exchange. It will never be totally deciphered, classified, or evaluated; it will always remain beyond, other, an abyss, as understood by the deep religiousness of Moses, Pascal, Schopenhauer, Nietzsche, Benjamin, Adorno, Horkheimer, and Levinas. The idea of "the bush that is never consumed" is to be understood in its connection to Utopian tradition as well.

Adorno and Horkheimer's Diasporic religiousness is closer to the Gnostic tradition than to atheism. In light of the loss of the relevance of the traditional religions as

61

a manifestation of the overcoming of the bad God over Life, or over the primordial, exiled, God, they seeked to give "theism a new meaning [...] from within atheism itself" (Horkheimer, op. cit., p. 185). This is in order to save the "Judeo-Christian" Utopia of "unification of truth, love and justice, as expressed in the Messianic idea" (ibid., p. 186).

Central to Adorno and Horkheimer's Diasporic philosophy is Negative Utopianism. This is Negative Utopianism geared to the human field of struggle over the realization of its potential for being different, and in a sense more than being directed by the system. However, it is not the attainment of power that is here stressed but the Diasporic acknowledgement of the impotence of justice and of the human who challenges injustice.

Adorno and Horkheimer's Diasporic religiousness calls for "unification of religion and philosophy in the realm of true solidarity" (Horkheimer, 1985, III., p. 223). This type of solidarity is supposed to include science as a central element and to perceive it as a threatening enemy. This is not the concept of Utopian science which we find in Marcuse's "principle of the new reality", whose maximal Utopian version is supposed to be realized in the future society.

Within the framework of Adorno and Horkheimer's Diasporic philosophy the given reality is not in the realm of "the absolute", nor is it the place that one can decide in connection with this reality itself. Both thinkers came out against "dogmatic atheism" on the one hand and against dogmatic theism on the other (Horkheimer, ibid., p. 238).

Negative Utopianism is quintessential for Adorno and Horkheimer. They stress it with special clarity when relating to the implicit predecessors of Diasporic philosophy. This is why Horkheimer went so sharply against "Schopenhauer's dogmatic atheism", in which, in his opinion, the idea of "the nil" is no less subjective than the idea of "God", which he refuses to present in a positive manner, in line with the hermetic tradition, Master Eckhart, and Nicolas of Cusa's *De Docta Ignoratia* and its Negative Theology (Nicholas of Cusa, 1981, pp. 84–85). He made a crucial decision, and because of this refused to give up the Utopian desire. The only argument which can be found for this is a moralistic one: a refusal to acknowledge the hegemony of evil, which characterizes this world. In this context he explicitly speaks of "belief"—belief which is capable of unifying in a moralistic manner the community that holds that the terrible reality in the world will not have the last word. In other words, in some respects this is a yearning for "true" reality—that meant by the Utopian tradition and the tradition of religious salvation. Thus we conclude that ultimately, despite their important contribution to the history of Diasporic philosophy, Horkheimer and Adorno are not consistent in their Diasporic philosophy even in the second stage of their work, since they have not abandoned the idea of "the ultimate reality" or the "absolute" as an alternative that ultimately will be realized within the framework of historical reality.

As against this element in their thought it is important to stress that from a consistent Diasporic point of view the Diasporic essence of Being and human essential homelessness when true to itself is the possible arena for dancing with the immanence of the absolute. Only when overcoming the limits of their own work might Adorno and Horkheimer offer us such a transcending dance; a religious counter-education that will insist on transcendence from mere power-relations and meaninglessness. This, within the framework of Negative Dialectics and nomadism as a way of life. A mode of existence that develops special relations with the Jewish concept of an absent God and traditional Jewish anti-dogmatism and the rejection of any call to establish a national, intellectual or moral "home". This, only to ultimately overcome Jewish Messianism and all other forms of monotheism. This refusal of any attempts at domestication and normalization is the terra in which the negation of the present reality is anchored. Eternal and infinite Diaspora as the manifestation of the absolute makes possible "the grand refusal" of the open individual and empowers the overcoming of the call to reconcile with the reality and being swallowed by the historical moment. But what is the non-contingent framework or foundation of "the last truth" or for the negation of its production? Horkheimer's answer is: "the religion". Here the struggle for the salvation of religiousness appears to him synonymous with the struggle for realizing the essence or the aim of Western culture.

Even if only implicitly, Adorno and Horkheimer accept the *Diasporic essence of Being* and human life as a starting point for their mature, religious-oriented Critical Theory (Adorno, 1970, X., p. 137). This enables them to insist on their critique and on their reconstruction of the omnipotence of power and meaninglessness (namely the apparatuses that produce meanings, values, and strives) in current life, on the one hand, while insisting on transcendence from the present reality and insisting on creativity and moral responsibility, on the other.

> We must all be unified by the yearning, which takes place in this world, injustice and horror will not be the final word, what was the other... what is called religion [...] the idea of infinity, which was developed by religion—we must need it and not give up on it. Clearly, we must not turn it in to an example [...]. (Horkheimer, 1985, XIII., p. 343)

The second idea comes to light in the commandment of Jewish religion not to present a positive description of God (ibid.), an idea diametrically opposed to the Marcusian Utopia as a whole and realizes the Jewish commandment, "Thou shall not make a statue or mask" (Marcuse, 1964, p. 11). These are at the foundation of the Diasporic *great refusal*, which contains the same special knowledge that is included in the criticism in the laws of prayer; this is a privileged knowledge, an erotic response to the burst of **the totally other**.

Already the first phase of Adorno's and Horkheimer's contemplation includes a Diasporic recognition that one must not base values and goals and it is impossible to prove objective truths; central already here is the decision to believe; that only from the act of choosing to believe can the counter-educational project spring. The criticism, which positions this decision as an experiment to save the moral, still must explain in a rational manner how it is possible to see the preference of this move over remaining in relativism or subjectivism or replacing a specific belief system with one of its rivals. The absurd in the decision of Adorno and Horkheimer is that in the lack of the possibility for validity in a rational manner of their decision, the project takes place in the realm of struggle for the salvation of Enlightenment—which they criticize in an extreme manner as an expression of power and oppression. Their decision exists within the realm of their own religiousness, and only it can be used as a systematic base, just as it provides a Utopian purpose as well. But is it a decision, an act of free choice—or the reaction to the persuasive power of the arbitrariness of the voice of **the totally other**, that forced itself on them and made possible their free choice to believe? And in what sense is this arbitrariness and power essentially different from the deceiving power of present-day Sirens that counter-education directs us to overcome?

The explicit purpose of Adorno's and Horkheimer's Diasporic religiousness in the second phase of their thought is no longer a revolution, but rather a struggle for "the autonomy of the individual" (ibid., 341).

In the struggle for salvation, Horkheimer's *animal symbolicum* overpowers mere reality and continues on the paved way of the Cabbalists while he sees himself as continuing the position of Schopenhauer. According to this position reality is essentially not absolute and Life is not governed or reduced to "facts", but the product of the mind, symbols and allegories, objects for infinite creative interpretations.

> Each thing which turns into a symbol has the ability to bring us down into a gutter which cannot be described, to the aspect of nil. In all things and every phrase in the world a concealed brilliance of hidden life manifests itself for the Cabbalist, infinite life glows inward [...] It is possible to say that the whole world and all acts of genesis are nothing but style of speaking, as a symbolic expression of that layer of what the thought cannot afford, from it a post or a corner of each building which can be achieved by thought. (ibid., p. 227)

The place of Diasporic hope in Horkheimer's thought also matches its understanding by the theologians of salvation within genuine religiosity: salvation is, first and foremost, a *promise* that "its realization might remain no more than a hope" (ibid., p. 224). His "practical optimism" is not attuned to cosmic salvation. It is not even expressed in response to a Utopian invitation to an ideal dialogue; within the Diasporic project, on the basis of the hope which it generates, the purpose and the end result of counter-education. Then, and only then, is there room for "practical" optimism in relation to the text and the Other as partners to a responsible, creative, loving, nomadic, way of life. In other words, the "optimism" spoken of is found in the context and expresses a dimension of its action, and it is not a force or external condition which establishes this religiousness. In the long run, it is devoted to an existential decision, which molds a way of life which, in the eyes of the believers, is holy and meaningful. Adorno's and Horkheimer's Diasporic project expresses first and foremost yearning for holiness and belief which do not require approval and cannot be negated by the present reality and its logic.

The new Diasporic philosophy that Adorno and Horkheimer offer us is of the kind traditionally Judaism offered to the world—under the evil conditions set by postmodern global capitalism which develops along new destructions and distorted creative Eros also new possibilities for cosmopolitanism. This new cosmopolitanism transforms the Gnostic and Messianic traditions in face of postmodern and pre-modern fundamentalist-oriented postcolonialist alternatives. This Messianic moment, even as a potential, is normally distorted, misused, or forgotten. But in face of cultural, economic, political, and, ultimately, existential crisis it wakes. In face of *the End* as a probable possibility it reconnects us to holiness and enables (negative) intimacy with Love of Life. Life, improvised, endangered life, becomes an impetus for counter-education exactly against the exile of Spirit, the instrumentalization of reason, and the reification of the human relations. In opposition to the optimists who establish great hopes for "the chosen ones" in the form of "the victims" or even for all humanity as clients on the foundations of globalizing capitalism (Beck, 2004, pp. 234–235). I am offering a dialectical reconstruction of our post-meta-physical historical moment: it is the same globalizing capitalism which rationally sends entire populations into a "flexible job markets", rationalized starvation, structurally guaranteed poor health, and loss of self-respect in the margins of world affluent economy which also opens the door for the visibility of suffering, for universal needs and values, and for new possibilities for counter-education and Diasporic way of life which transcends ethnocentric solidarity, political borders, and contextual pragmatism and cynicism (Gur-Ze'ev, 2004, pp. 179–202).

The later work of Adorno and Horkheimer is an important manifestation of counter-education in the Gnostic sense. As such it manifests a Diasporic Philosophy that refuses all calls for "homecoming", to God, to the Garden of Eden, to the Patria, to truth, or to mere-pleasure and practical nihilism. Adorno's and Horkheimer's negative theology, while addressing the relevance of Jewish traditional anti-dogmatism and anti-collectivism, offers us today, more then ever, a goal, meaning, and love—without being swallowed by any Pleasure Machine, "truth" or "we". As Diasporic humans we are called upon by their counter-education to insist on transcendence co-poiesis and improvisation to actualize love in creativity and in a kind of togetherness that is dialogic and refuses any collectivism and all dogmas. As such, the later work of Adorno and Horkheimer makes a genuine contribution to counter-education, which is so much needed in face of the recent success of the educational violence of the new anti-Semitism and the fruits of its self-hatred. One of the first steps of current counter-education should be the synthesis of Adorno's and Horkheimer's critique of Western society and the logic of capitalism with present day analyses of capitalist globalization processes within the framework of risk society that at the same time opens new possibilities for Diasporic existence and new realizations of nomadism of the kind that a re-articulated Gnosis might make relevant. Such a counter-education should not abandon the critical tradition, yet it should insist on love of life, on responsible and improvisational co-poiesis in face of the nearing probability of *the End*. It should develop new connections between the aesthetic and the ethic, the intellectual and the physical, the political and the religious dimensions of life of an eternal improviser. How ironic it is that global capitalism and the new anti-Semitism, while exiling human spirit and enhancing the omnipotence of the creative "bad God", also opens new possibilities; possibilities for new forms of Gnosis and for new Diasporic individuals and communities within a dull historical moment of quasi-improvisation and ecstatic life where mega speeds replace the holiness of killing-God-each-moment-anew. This is the gate for a new kind of Diasporic life, free from the hospitality of the illusion of redemption and from the quest for escaping into nothingness.

NOTES

[1] In this article I do not prove this claim. I try to show its validity only by referring to Henry Giroux, who is undoubtedly one of the central figures in this field.

REFERENCES

Adorno, T. (1970). *Gesammelte schriften*, III. Frankfurt a.Main: Suhrkamp.

Adorno, T. (1970). *Gesammelte schriften*, X. Frankfurt a.Main: Suhrkamp.

Adorno, T., & Horkheimer, M. (1988). *Dialectik der Aufklaerung*. Frankfurt a.Main: Fischer.

Adorno, T. (1998). *Critical models*. New York: Columbia university Press.

Adorno, T. (1999). *Minima moralia—reflections from damaged life* (E. F. N. Jephhott, Trans.). New York: verso.

Adorno, T. (2000). Culture industry reconsidered. In B. O'Connor (Ed.), *The Adorno Reader*. Oxford: Blackwell.

Barth, K. (1957). *Kirchliche Dogmatik I*. Frankfurt a. Main: Fischer.

Beck, U. (2004). *Risk society—towards a new modernity* (M. Ritter, Trans.). London: Sage.

Benjamin, W. (1972). *Gesammelte schriften*, 1.2. Frankfurt a.Main: Suhrkamp.

Bonhoffer, D. (1998). *Widerstand und ergebung*. Muenchen: Christopher Kiser.

Deleuze, G., & Guattari, F. (1995). *A thousand plateaus—capitalism and schizophrenia* (B. Mussumi, Trans.). Minneapolis, MN: University of Minnesota press.

Dresner, S. H. (1957). *Prayer, humility and compassion*. Philadelphia: The Jewish Publication Society.

Ellsworth, E. (1989). Why doesn't it feel empowering? Working through the repressive myths of critical pedagogy. *Harvard Educational Review*, 297–324.

Freire, P. (1968). *Pedagogy of the oppressed* (R. Bergmann, Trans.). New York: Herder & Herder.

Freire, P., & Macedo, D. (1987). *Literacy: Reading the word reading the world*. London: Routledge and Kegan Paul.

Giroux, I. (1983). *Theory and resistance in education—a pedagogy for the oppressed*. South Hadley, MA: Bergin & Garvey.

Giroux, H., & Aronowitz, S. (1981). *Education under siege—the conservative, liberal, and radical debate over schooling*. South Hadley, MA: Bergin & Garvey.

Giroux, H. (1988). *Teachers as intellectuals*. New York: Bergin & Garvey.

Giroux, H. (1996). Is there a place for cultural studies in colleges of education? In H. Giroux, C. Lankshear, P. McLaren, & M. Peters (Eds.), *Counternarratives*. New York: Routledge.

Gur-Ze'ev, I. (1996). *The Frankfurt school and the history of pessimism*. Jerusalem: Magnes Press. (Hebrew)

Gur-Ze'ev, I. (1998, Fall). Toward a nonrepressive Critical Pedagogy. *Educational Theory*, 48(4), 463–486.

Gur-Ze'ev, I. (1999, Fall). Cyberfeminism and education in the era of the exile of spirit. *Educational Theory*, 49(4), 437–455.

Gur-Ze'ev, I. (2003). *Destroying the other's collective memory*. New York: Peter Lang.

Gur-Ze'ev, I. (2003a, Fall). Socrates, counter-education, and Diasporic love in a postmodern era. *Journal of Thought*, 38(3), 41–66.

Gur-Ze'ev, I. (2003b). Holocaust/Nakbah as an Israeli/Palestinian homeland. In R. Robin & B. Strath (Eds.), *Homelands—poetic power and the politics of space*. New York: Peter Lang.

Gur-Ze'ev, I. (2003c). Adorno, Horkheimer, critical theory and the possibility of counter-education. In M. Peters, C. Lankshear, M. Olssen (Eds.), *Critical theory and the human condition* (pp. 17–35). New York: Peter Lang.

Gur-Ze'ev, I. (2004). *Toward diasporic education*. Tel Aviv: Reseling. (Hebrew).

Gur-Ze'ev, I. (2007). *Beyond the modern-postmodern struggle in education—toward counter-education and enduring improvisation*. Rotterdam: Sense Publications.

Gur-Ze'ev, I. (2010). The death of God as progress, the death of the killer of God as the end of progress and education in the era of mega speed. *Tabur* (3). (Hebrew)

Heschel, A. J. (1954). *Man's quest for God*. New York: Schriber.

Horkheimer, M. (1974). *Eclipse of reason*, New York: Oxford university Press.

Horkheimer, M. (1978). *Dawn and decline: Notes 1926–1931 and 1950–1969* (M. Shaw, Trans.). New York: The Sabury Press.

Horkheimer, M. (1985). *Gesammelte Schriften*, III. Frankfurt a.Main: Fischer.

Horkheimer, M. (1985). *Gesammelte Schriften*, IV. Frankfurt a.Main: Fischer.

Horkheimer, M. (1985). *Gesammelte Schriften*, V. Frankfurt a.Main: Fischer.

Horkheimer, M. (1985). *Gesammelte Schriften*, VII. Frankfurt a.Main: Fischer.

Horkheimer, M. (1985). *Gesammelte Schriften*, XI. Frankfurt a.Main: Fischer.

Horkheimer, M. (1989). *Gesammelte Schriften*, XIII. Frankfurt a.Main: Fischer.

Horkheimer, M. (1985). *Gesammelte Schriften*, XIV. Frankfurt a. Main: Fischer.

Horkheimer, M. (1960, May 26). Max Horkheimer Archive VI. *13*, 511.

Idel, M. (1988). *Kabbalah—new perspectives*. New Haven, CT: Yale University Press.

Levinas, E. (1987). *Collected philosophical papers*. (A. Lingis, Trans.). Dordrecht: M. Nijhoff.

Marcuse, H. (1964, June 8). Marx, Freud und der Monotheismus. *Herbert Marcuse Archive*, 241.00, 11.

McLaren, P. (2000, April). Reconsidering Marx in Post-Marxist times. *Educational Researcher, 29*(3), 25–33.

Mortley, R. (1986). *From word to silence*, II. Bonn: Hanstein.

Nicholas of Cusa. (1981). *On learned ignorance*. (J. Hopkins, Trans.). Minneapolis, MN: The Arthur J. Banning Press.

Nietzsche, F. (1999). *Goetzen/Daemmerung*. Werke II. Muenchen: Carl Hanser verlag.

Nuovo, V. (1966). Some critical remarks on radical theology. *Union Seminary Quarterly Review, XXII*, 12–37.

Rosenzweig, F. (1970). *The star0 of redemption*. Jerusalem: Mossad Bialik. (Hebrew).

Zizek, S. (1993). *Tarring with the negative—Kant, Hegel and the critique of ideology*. Durham: Duke University Press.

ILAN GUR-ZE'EV

4. IMPROVISATION, VIOLENCE AND
PEACE EDUCATION

Peace education worthy the name is a religious work: an erotic relation to the loss of intimacy with Life, especially in the era of exile of holiness, meaning and Love. Peace education is currently working hard for achieving homogeneity and ethnocentristic-oriented togetherness in face of growing awareness to the philosophical challenges presented by post-structuralist philosophies. This awareness, however, did not yet culminate into systematic reflection on the central challenges, conceptions and aims of peace education neither on its cultural, political and philosophical pre-conditions, histories and fruits. Until this very moment, however, peace education is a field of research and a celebrated practice with no serious theoretical framework and grounding (Gur-Ze'ev, 2001). Peace education did not make the slightest effort to reconstruct its history let alone a critical history of peace education as a spiritual, educational and political effort that begins with the profits and the early church to various "heretic" movements and oppositions to the hegemonic theology, culture and social structures. Peace education is currently actualized and developed with no historical consciousness neither a systematic conceptual reflection on its central values, concepts and ideals. Systematic historic and conceptual analysis of the field and its main challenges are beyond the scope of this article. In this chapter I will restrict myself to a short reflection on the relations between three concepts: peace, violence and improvisation. I will try to show that the concept of *improvisation* might become of special relevance for any attempt to articulate and actualize counter-education which addresses the threats inflicted by present day peace education to free, anti-dogmatic, creative and erotic humans.

In my mind one of the shortcomings of the present hegemonic peace education as a practice, as an ideology and as a field of academic research is the missing elaboration of relations between peace and violence, peace and metaphysical violence, peace and structural violence, peace and counter-violence, peace and power, peace and revolt, peace and defiance, peace and insubordination, and peace and passive disobedience. There are other central concepts, such as "education" and "consensus" which should be systematically analyzed in this context and this is surely solely a partial list. Any attempt to conceptualize the practice of peace education and to critically reconstruct its practices and agendas should go into the analytics, evaluation and rethinking of these relations, concepts, and strives that are their impetus. If violence is seriously to be questioned it should be evaluated and addressed in face of well classified ends. It is time to ask: what is the aim of peace education? What should we learn from the tension between the explicit aims and the unconscious and sometime wordless telos of peace education? And even more so, *what is it that peace education veils-symbolizes, works for, and is a naïve agent of?*

I. Gur-Ze'ev, The Possibility/Impossibility of a New Critical Language in Education, 69–84.
© *2010 Sense Publishers. All Rights Reserved.*

The possibility of *justice* as a relevant ethical framework and as *a manifestation of overwhelming unjust power* is not to be disconnected from the challenge of a worthy facing the presence of effective violence. Violence which enables a specific order with specific borders, limits and conditions facilitates effective silent consumption and transformed reproduction of fruitful normalization processes. These normalization dynamics produce stable virtual "illusions" concerning the "reality" of harmony, tranquility and peace. In post-modern arenas peace is a precondition for reproducing *productive self-forgetfulness*, surrendering and enhancement of the "not-I" in the "I" as a loving, protected, edified human agent. Violence celebrates having the upper hand in the form of "peace" and "normality" that makes possible the invisibility of normalizing violence. This understanding calls on us to address the *essence* of violence and its truth. This is why it is so important to listen to Walter Benjamin when he tells us that

> the task of a critique of violence can be summarized as that of expounding its relation to law and justice. For a cause, however effective, becomes violent, in the precise sense of the word, only when it bears on moral issues. (Benjamin, 1978, p. 277)

The challenge of violence is properly addressed in relation to the truth of peace in its proper context. And the contexts vary historically and analytically. There are important differences between (1) the context of a religious perception of a pre-redeemed world controlled by anti-Christ and slow movements in changing worldviews, transportation and human nomadism and prayer, which is in search of transcendence as opposed to the animistic worldview and its immanence, (2) the context of a revolutionary tradition that relates to a *not-yet-emancipated order* of things within a framework of rapidly changing society, world views, human movement and spiritual transformations which strive for transcendence and "homereturning" projects in an ever speeding processes of modernization, and (3) the context of the McWorld as a post-Utopian arena which abandons the messianic/revolutionary strive for transcendence and homogeneity and enters the world of mega-speed, beyond the modern arenas of speeding and transcendence. The changing relations between space and movement culminate in rich influences on the human condition. Peace, in this sense is no exception. Peace-violence relations in the McWorld represent the human being as it is swallowed by *total immanence*. This is but a partial manifestation of immanence where capitalist globalization has the upper hand and plays the role of "the absolute", traditionally reserved to God, Universal Reason and the authentic "I". The McDonaldization of reality, in other words: postmodern normalizing education, *realizes* "peace" as an omnipotent, unchallenged, "neutral"/ absolute-moral(ess) totality that organizes, represents, consumes/destroys, recycles Being in its particularities.

Faced with an ever-disenchanting-hiding position, the truth of violence, with its tempting-fascinating ends and fruits, varies according to whether it is enacted/conceived in a pre-redeemed world, at a pre-liberated historical moment, or alternatively after its *realization* as peaceful diverse-dynamic-hybridic-ecstatic post-modern hyper-reality. It differs dramatically when it is in the service of redemption/emancipation or, as a realization of its opposite, in the form of a conservative, imperialist, dictatorial or "Luciferean" presence, to be met with morally justified (counter-) violence. "Peace education" in such a context could be realized, according to present postcolonialists such as Peter McLaren, Ilan Pappe and Howard Davidson, in *education for resistance and struggle* for a future peaceful, harmonious, post-revolutionary reality. Totalitarian good-natured postcolonialists presently extensively long for it in the academic ivory towers or in million-dollar roomy-tranquil apartments in prosperous suburbs.

This kind of *peace education in the form of education for resistance* might be realized in diverse forms: from direct and open war to defiance, insubordination and disobedience of various kinds: this is a difference that makes a difference.

This line of conceptualization studies violence in relation to sharp binary dichotomies such as justifiable-unjustifiable ends. It addresses the question of requirements for *defined* preconditions, limits and yardsticks for maintaining power in the form of law and order of the kind that makes peace possible. Here *power*, as Hannah Arendt claims, is not a synonym for *violence* but its opposite. Power makes possible the *res publica*, the public dimension, peace. Violence, on the other hand, bursts out in the absence of power, so according to Arendt

> the amount of violence at the disposal of a given country may no longer be a reliable indication of that country's strength or a reliable guarantee against destruction by a substantially smaller and weaker power. (Arendt, 1969, p. 2)

Still, in the first place it is violence, effective violence, that makes possible and constitutes the stability of power; the kind of power that forms law, order and official representations of justice and lawful executions; lawful destruction or re-education of "the violent ones" who threaten "peace", "law" and "order", within which is the kind of *vita activa* that Arendt presents as a civil virtue.

A serious philosophical elaboration of peace education cannot be content with socio-historical reconstructions which confirm the conceptual relations between peace and violence and represent "peace" as an extreme and highly effective manifestation of violence that hides its origin and telos in the form of lawfulness, security and peaceful normalization. If we could rest in face of such manifestations we would have "only" to evaluate and determine the preferable violence according to the higher and more valuable aims which justify this *violence on the path toward harmony, peace, or nothingness*. Peace education, however, cannot be satisfied even with such a titanic mission. Its challenge is even greater, more demanding and traumatic and far more dangerous if it is to be worthy of its name and true to its responsibility.

Recognition of the intimate relations between peace, as an absence and as a reality, and (different kinds and degrees of) violence is present in the cosmogony of many cultures have faced the challenge of Being and nothingness, existence and suffering/meaninglessness. In the most fundamental sense, the very creation of the world, its very existence as a *destruction of nothingness or the unlimited*, Being as an opposition to nothingness, is an offense against peace and justice, against the harmony within nothingness. According to Anaximander,

The unlimited (*apeiron*) is both principle (*arche*) and element (*stoicheion*) of things that exist, being the first to introduce this name of the principle. … it is neither water nor any other of the so-called elements, but some other unlimited nature, from which all the heavens and the worlds in them come about; and the things from which is the coming into being for the things that exist are also those into which their destruction comes about, in accordance with what must be. For they give justice (*dike*) and reparation to one another for their offence (*adikia*) in accordance with the ordinance of time (Anaximandrus, 1982, p. 29).

The Gnostic tradition addresses seriously the challenge of peace and violence. It offered an alternative from its early beginnings in the 1st and 2nd centuries in the Middle East to the 19th-century romantics and 20th-century philosophers, poets and political thinkers to the present new-age spiritual alternatives. Of special importance for us here is the Gnostic conception that *nature and history are the embodiment or the arena of the rule of an evil God*. It is the God of creation, of nature, of the body and psyche, of history; it is a wrathful God of peace-war, law, limits, productivity and history into which the human is thrown. The Other, the God of love, does exist, but is present only as an exile.

The human who is aware of his or her living on earth in Diaspora acknowledges that the triumph of the God of the Bible is, however, never complete. Diasporic life is still an open possibility — even in face of the ongoing triumph of the violence of the Evil God. This is because the exiled God is still traceable, and a leap into worthy existence is, despite all, possible in the life of the *pneuma*, the truly spiritual, undetermined, not-to-be-controlled human dimension. The psyche is mobilized by ethics and the body is controlled by physical law; these constitute false "peace" and adored-frightening violence that are responsible for the constitution of what Schopenhauer understood as "the Maya curtain" in human existence.

Normalized humans who are overwhelmed by effective education, physical needs and political manipulations forget their forgetfulness and cooperate with the exile of the true God. They disregard the possibility of Gnostic knowledge and the possibility of transcending existence that is ruled by the false dichotomy between peace and violence, good and bad, law and unlawfulness. However, Pneumaticos, the spiritual human, as already the excommunicated heretic Christian Gnostic Marcion thought in the 2nd century, might liberate himself and live *beyond good and evil* (Harnack, 1990). Here moral struggles are articulated in opposition to the hegemonic traditions, and in extreme cases of this tradition "peace" or "peace education" is conceived as a manifestation of *fundamental violence*.

Within this framework *peace is violence. But violence, even the worthiest, does not strive for "peace"* or for any other religious "homereturning" project. Any of these projects offers redemption and is necessarily reigned by the Evil God. It is present in nature, in history and in the "body", which the pneumatic human should do his or her best to transcend in light of ontological Diaspora. This position with various modifications and alterations does not apply only to the first centuries in the Middle East. It is a constant challenge to Western thinking and politics to this very day. It is of special relevance for Schopenhauer, Nietzsche, Heidegger and present-day post-structuralist philosophy, to which current peace education is in debt much more than it is aware of.

Another "pre-modern" challenge to the presumptions, conceptions and goals of present-day peace education comes from another version of Diasporic philosophy, which offers an alternative view of the relations between violence and peace. This challenge understands the relations between peace and violence by totally negating the Gnostic dualistic scheme. Here too, "peace" is a manifestation of evil. Yet the Gnostic Evil God is conceived here as the true God. His kingdom, as the universe after the exile of the God of love, is for the Gnostics "the Godly city". The true believer is conceived, however, as exiled in the "earthly city".

> I distinguish two branches of mankind: one made up of those who live according to man, the other those who live according to God. I speak of these branches also allegorically as two cities, that is, two societies of human beings, of which one is predestined to reign eternally with God and the other to undergo eternal punishment with the devil. For at the very start, when the two cities began their history through birth and death, the first to be born was the citizen of this world, and only after him came the alien in this world who is a member of the city of God, one predestined by grace and chosen by grace, one by grace an alien below and by grace a citizen above. (Augustine, 1957, p. 415)

For St. Augustine the preference for peace is to be decided not in a neutral way and not under any conditions. On the contrary, only under very specific conditions is "peace" desirable and a value whose realization is to be striven for as an ultimate, justifiable end: solely in the framework of *true belief* in the right way of the redemption of humans and the world. In this sense this conception of peace is opposite to the one praised by most secular peace-education activists. For in their mind earthly peace means homogeneity, harmony and human self-realization in this world as the perfect, or at least the best possible, "home". For Christian theology as represented by St. Augustine peace, genuine peace is only possible by transcending the "earthly city" and by dwelling in "the Godly city", its opposite.

Here St. Augustine follows the Socratic tradition and connects redemption to the possibility of transcendence as attaining the light of the true knowledge. This is one of the preconditions for the totalizing dimension of Western education and its being swallowed, reproduced, and re-presented in the service of hegemonic violence. Present peace education has lost its theological sources and its religious yearning. It has lost also its humanist orientation, as well as its total commitment to the imperatives of reason and to the revolutionization of the general human condition toward its full emancipation. But it has not lost its commitment to the fundamental "homereturning" project and the kind of fear of Apeiron, ambivalence and Life; of being situated between transcendence and immanence in eternal homelessness that cannot be calmed or appeased.

While speaking the language of the new anti-Semitism, much of present-day peace education fails to submit non-contingent justifications for its claims, practices, and hopes for a state of peace. It cannot offer foundations, claims and aims that transcend mere contextual violent/stable, political constructs. It fails to offer a relation of peace and violence that is self-evident, nor a peace philosophy that is sacred and transcends the endless productivity/futility of mere language games.

In the present-day postmodern condition there is no naïve-nostalgic-grotesque room for a serious challenge to the hegemonic claim to knowledge by **the totally other**. Present-day reality destroys any vivid Spirit. The McWorld has no room for a new Moses, Jesus, Buddha, or Marx, or for a new Hitler. In the modern and pre-modern conditions, the otherness of the Other is *terrorized while proclaimed as evil*, or as a dangerous epistemological gift. This is a hopeful situation where there is room for love, prayer and struggle. But what room is left for hope, love and struggle in the post-modern arenas amid mega-speed kaleidoscopic ecstasies? In cyberspace the otherness of the Other is ridiculed, presented as a grotesque or even internalized in the global Pleasure Machine as a mere "attractive" "link", "site", "item", or an "experience that can make it for you", as an ornament or a plaything to be consumed for a passing moment in a context where there is no transcendence or escape from immanence, from meaninglessness; not even a tragic exile that incubates a worthy-redeeming waiting. Peace, how terrible, has here the upper hand.

This conception is immanently committed to totalizing information and to purging the threatening gift or "saving" humanity from its danger by all necessary means. Inseparable here are the procedures of purging the Other of his or her epistemological otherness, structural violence, and the "direct" individual and collective violence. This is the Lebensraum of normalizing education. One of our aims should be to unveil the relation between the success of these violences and their invisibility as a manifestation of mental health and collective stability, order, law, and "peace". Within the framework of counter-education we are called to question beyond "critique" the present order of things and its "bettering". Such dichotomies prevent counter-education, which is beyond functionalism, critique and fear of Apeiron and Life that drive Western education toward "homereturning" projects. As manifested today by Levinas, within the Diasporic alternative peace is not an earthly stable power-relations with no effective opposition or "the return of the multiple to unity, in conformity with the Platonic or Neoplatonic idea of the one" (Levinas, 1996, p. 162).

However, within history, for St. Augustine it is impossible to conceive "the city of God" disconnected from "the earthly city": they are always to be envisaged in their mutual relation. Moreover, while real peace is only to be conceived in "the city of God", its rival city strives for peace too. The division is not only, as in current peace education, between a state of peace and a state of violence (or conflict), but in parallel also between two essentially different states of peace. One might also say between two different sets of violences, one secular, the other sacred violence, namely "peace".

"The earthly city" is in constant "pursuit of victories that either cut lives short or at any rate are short-lived" (Augustine, 1957, p. 425). Yet as the manifestation of triumphant violence, these victories contain also goods, albeit only "the lowest kind of goods". Among these "lowest kinds of goods" attained by warfare St. Augustine counts "earthly peace" (ibid.). The point that is important for St. Augustine, which is forgotten by today's peace education, is that (earthly) peace is only attainable by warfare:

> Thus to gain the lowest kind of good it covets an earthly peace, one that it seeks to attain by warfare; for if it is victorious and no one remains to resist it, there will be peace…(ibid.)

According to St. Augustine there are higher goods than earthly peace; these "belong to the city above, in which victory will be untroubled in everlasting and ultimate peace" (ibid.: 427). This other kind of peace is totally other than the peace that is tenable in the "earthly city", and it is even conditioned by transcending from the peace that the "earthly city" and its victories can offer. St. Augustine offers us two levels of analysis: on one level he represents a Western philosophical tradition which after being secularized by Kant, Hegel, and Marx could lead to a kind of universalism within which idealists, pragmatists, and even (very) "soft" postmodernists could share peace education. In peace education, as developed by pragmatists, feminists, multiculturalists, and certainly by positivistic-oriented functionalists who strive for social stability and free, prosperous national and international markets, all trends relate to human rights and resist direct and explicit violence in the name of universal rights such as freedom from persecution or exploitation. Here the division between peace and violence is clear-cut, and the very commitment and quest for peace is left unaddressed and unproblematized.

On the second level it is St. Augustine, more than present-day peace-education theorists and practitioners that follow his essentialism, who seriously addresses the issue of peace and problematizes the quest for peace in relation to the essence of the human and her ultimate goal. In Augustinian terms the ideal and the reality, which peace education strives for, is the "earthly city" in its most stringent form. For St. Augustine this is something unavoidable in this world, yet it is a challenge to overcome if redemption is to be realized.

We see St. Augustine's doctrine and the educational attitude he represents in Western thinking not solely, but part of, violent control of Western consciousness and a manifestation of epistemological violence enacted against its disciples. At the same time, however, it is worth acknowledging its dialectics and its transcendental element. It contains an antagonism to the whole order, of which "peace" as a desire, as an ideal, and as a reality, is but a part. As such, it is a constant challenge to this order, while being part of it, and it contains an important emancipatory potential. This dimension of challenging the hegemonic realm of self-evidence and the imperative to overcome philosophy and mere existence is unfortunately missing from the concept of peace which functions in the various trends in current peace education.

Following St. Augustine, we claim that what in the political arena is called "peace" is one of the extreme manifestations of successful terror. Levinas sees the seed of this condition already in "Greek wisdom" and pinpoints its violent nature in which human peace is awaited on the basis of the truth:

> Peace on the basis of the truth—on the basis of the truth of knowledge where, instead of opposing itself, the diverse agrees with itself and unites; where

the stranger is assimilated... Peace on the basis of the truth, which—marvel of marvels—commands humans without forcing them or combating them, which governs them or gathers them together without enslaving them, which through discourse, can convince rather than vanquish... (Levinas, 1996, p. 162)

This totalizing concept of peace in its relation to true knowledge allows *effective de-humanization* of humans and their formation into collectives. At its peak it makes possible and secures consciousness, which is committed to "true" solidarity. It creates and generously awards the willingness of the individual to sacrifice herself for the collective, its security, ideals, values, and horizons. As such it is part and parcel of the violence which produces borders, wars, and Others as objects of education, destruction, redemption and emancipation. Yet it is a concept of peace conditioned by abandonment of reflection and transcendence. It is a manifestation of one's being swallowed or constructed by the ruling realm of self-evidence. With the assistance of good parents, devoted teachers, supportive friends, beautiful texts, and endless other ways it produces brave warriors to protect its fears and destroy its internal and external enemies. As such, it actually manifests human forgetfulness of Diasporic love. It enhances domestication; empowers tranquilization that reflects the victory of normalizing education. It is peace as "repose among beings well-placed or reposing on the underlying solidity of their substance, self-sufficient in their identity or capable of being satisfied and seeking satisfaction" (ibid., p. 163).

This concept of philosophy, which was dominated by the Platonic quest for light and love of truth, is embarrassed and feels guilty in current Western thought. It finds it hard to

recognize itself in its millennia of fratricidal, political, and bloody struggles, of imperialism, of human hatred and exploitation, up to our century of world wars, genocides, the Holocaust, and terrorism; of unemployment, the continuing poverty of the Third World. (ibid.)

Modern peace education is very much influenced by the ideas of the Enlightenment and its visions of a future perfect world. In light of the exile of God and the overcoming of superstition, and with the power of rational critique, scientific reasoning and social progress in education, science and technology, it promises deification of humanity and eternal peace. Lessing, Kant, Condorcet, Rousseau and the false promises of the rosy future awaiting humanity after the beheading of Louis XVI are impossible to understand disconnected from the transformation of the idea of progress: from a religious teleological "homereturning" project to the secular Garden of Eden-like redemptive fulfillment. The secular "homereturning" project in the form of revolution or peace education becomes possible only by overcoming the promise of Godly redemption, but still in the framework of "homereturning" metaphysics. In its revolutionary and educational formats, it offers holiness: human progress as the manifestation of the edifying advance of earthly freedom, which inherits the religious metaphysical quest for transcendence and its victory over anti-Christ, Satan, or various manifestations of "the earthly city".

Franz Rosenzweig presents a very different version of an alternative to the hegemonic peace-education concept of "peace" as the antinomy of "violence". He challenges any attempt to present mundane politics as the genuine, appeasing, Garden of Eden, refusing to accept "emancipation" as the historic realization of the human potential totally to control nature, social reality, the mysterium and Fortuna. Rosenzweig goes farther than St. Augustine. He offers not just a different concept of historical progress toward peace and redemption but actually an alternative conceptual apparatus for the centrality of exile, nomadism and Diaspora. This apparatus offers a different kind of *religiosity* and *hospitality*: the hospitality of Diasporic life; an alternative co-poiesis amid nomadism, which replaces "peace" as standstill in the form of continuity with peace as the hospitality of love of an enduring improvisation of the one who actualizes eternal creative moral responsibility every moment anew (Peretz 2003: 17).

At the same time, however, Rosenzweig stands with St. Augustine against the Enlightenment's concept of progress and the promise of rational peace in the framework of secular history. His rejection, however, does not end up as a religious mirror-picture of humanist arrogance and violence. He presents a very different kind of Diaporic poiesis, poiesis which becomes co-poiesis; an alternative to the secular-revolutionary and Christian-positive-redemptive Utopias alike.

He offers the position of Judaism concerning the responsibility of the Jew. According to Rosenzweig, Judaism stands *detached from history*, refusing to become part of the normal power-game, its rules, strives and goals. The Christian, Rosenzweig tells us, anchors his belief to the past, to the beginning of the road, to the first Christian. "Although the center is only center between beginning and end, its main stress nevertheless moves towards the beginning" (Rosenzweig, 2005, p. 368). Rosenzweig nevertheless emphasizes that the Christian, when true to himself, is essentially Diasporic. This is because when "he thus turns alone toward the Cross, he may forget the judgment"—but he remains on the way, in eternal Diaspora, even if on the wrong homereturning path: "the Christian consciousness, absorbed entirely in faith, pushes toward the beginning of the way, to the first Christian, to the Crucified one (ibid.: 368.). It leads Christianity to "*expansion into everything*, simply into everything outside" (ibid., p. 369). While Jewish consciousness, "rooting into its own innermost" (ibid., p. 369), "gathered entirely in *hope*, toward the man of the last days, to David's royal shoot" strives toward the future (ibid., p. 368). Jewish history is a *separate* history (ibid.: 427), the history of a relic.

> If the Messiah comes 'today', the remnant is ready to receive him. Jewish history is, in defiance of all world history, history of this remnant" against "power as the fundamental concept of history" and against "All worldly history [that] is about expansion". (ibid., p. 427)

The Jew is therefore essentially and not temporarily or partly a Diasporic human, witnessing universal history while always within himself. The text/universe in its wholeness is his home, for all time in the *nowhere*, in the in-between: dwelling as an eternal nomad between the word and its meaning, between this world and the world-to-come; he forever "awaits salvation", eternally "on the shore" (ibid., p. 428) of transcendence as something "put into our blood at birth, toward the future coming of the Kingdom" (ibid.).

Diasporic counter-education does not annihilate itself in the form of a belief and praxis for paving the way to the Messiah/deliverer/genuine revolution within the framework of a positive Utopia, "peace". Here Messianism is true to itself by refusing any vision of a future peace, resisting any positive Utopia and any worldly, stable, appeasing "home". It insists on *eternal Diaspora* which negates its negation by realizing the ideal of transcendence from this world to the world-to-come: every day, every moment, is a flash-eternity of a possible change, an open gate for the appearance of **the totally Other**. It is the Messianic dimension. It is present in the form of the unique day of change eternally to be waited for. As such it is realized in facing *the presence of the absence of peace as a worthy gate* for the relation to the law of the Torah (ibid., pp. 428–429). Facing redemption as an eternal Messianic awaiting is actualized in the eternal anti-dogmatic reinterpretation of the text, rearticulating our relation to Life and the further study of the Torah which refuses any call to participate in the violence that promises "progress", redemption or "peace".

At the same time it commands responsibility and worthy addressing of any form and occasion of injustice. As in Stefan Heym's *Achashverosh, The Wandering Jew* (Heym, 1983), God is freedom (ibid., p. 227) and the Jew is in eternal Diaspora, wandering as an eternal critic, an eternal nonconformist, an eternal responsibility for *Tikun Olam*, an eternal Other to any king, priest and prophet. And as such he will never know, neither will he carry homogeneity, consensus or "peace".

Peace education that challenges the fruits of normalizing education should challenge both the quest of totalizing homogeneity and the dogmatic quest for difference as two alternatives which within the framework of peace education pave the path for the "homereturning" self-forgetfulness. Co-poiesis and enduring responsible improvisation might offer counter-education which will open the gate for an alternative for present peace education.

Counter-education that addresses seriously the challenge of loss, exile, and the deceiving "homereturning" projects accepts that no positive Utopia awaits us as "truth", "genuine life", "worthy struggle", "pleasure", "peace" or worthy/ unavoidable self-annihilation. Loss is not to be recovered or compensated; not for the individual nor for any kind of "we". And yet, Love of Life is the home of the Diasporic in the Socratic sense of Eros as an attracting absence of the beautiful. Counter-education should invite the Diasporic to the hospitality of responsible Love of Life. Such hospitality denotes the absence of non-consensual creativity and calls for overcoming conventional morality and the other imperatives of the ethnocentric "we", its self-evidence, its normality, its counter-resistance of the oppressed and its normalized patriotic citizenship.

Response-ability and respond-ability (Gur-Ze'ev, 2005, p. 26) toward noncollective, toward pre-subjective and existential kinds of homelessness, toward erotic Diasporic existence, might offer new beginnings and a kind of becoming-toward-the-world (ibid., p. 32) as against becoming-swallowed-by-the-matrix; an awakening.

Flourishing out of Love of Life, it might make possible an awakening, which will open the gate not to "emancipation" but to transcendence from the endless various and conflicting "homereturning" projects and their complementary forms of exile/ exiling, nomadism and slumber dwelling.

The determination for Diasporic life and the possibilities opened by Diasporic counter-education is always ironic. It is never at home, it is never in peace. It gives birth to something at all times immensely more important than the individuality of the Diasporic individual as in the relation of the artist to her great creation. It is creation. A symbol of Love of Life as creation that always transcends herself to the otherness of the Other as the Feminine to the Masculine and the born baby as an act of genesis, as Eros to the not-yet, as **the totally other** to the infinite not-yet fertilized potentials of each moment. The absence of "peace" is a pre-condition for the edification of these potentials. The absence of tranquility and of homogeneity is here of special importance and it gives honor to space, voice, sound, movement, visibility, smell and contact. The absence of "peace" and the overcoming of the illusion of peace is the birth moment of an *alternative togetherness* as offered by responsible improvisation which actualizes co-poiesis. The heart of improvisation is this movement within co-poiesis (Ettinger, 2005, pp. 703–713) as a togetherness offered by Love of Life. As shown by Ettinger who was instrumental in the development of this concept, it gives birth to the totally new and the wholly unex- pected. The Diasporic human faces its hospitality as *alterity* and togetherness, not as "peace"; a form of non-instrumental playfulness that manifests erotic responsibility to Life at its best. It is an invitation which offers hospitality, the *Not-Yet*, not "home" but the Spirit of Diaspora that is not threatened by silence, by the absence of ethnocentristic-oriented dogma, rituals or psychic structure that is pre-organized and demands surrender and playing by the rules. It is silence that hosts here, the self- educated gaze, the eye that meets again genuine religiousness and the responsibility that is realized with, in front of, and in preparation for the participation of the Otherness of the Other as a friend, as a companion, as a worthy rival, as an unanswered question, as an indispensable manifestation of the entire cosmos and its holiness. As such, *co-poiesis opens the gate to improvisation* that is part of the reply and part and parcel of the most concrete, daily manifestation of the "femininity", of the birth-giving spirit of the co-poiesis, which is so different from the "masculine", instrumental "homes" and political "peace".

Diasporic counter-education is part of an improvised-courageous facing the dangerous waters of the river of fear of ambivalence and rival "truths", strivings, and the fear of landing on the demanding never-satisfied banks of loss. This fear is a lieutenant of "the fall" and enhances the various and conflicting "homereturning" projects that are all united in one thing only: in the promise of an end to ambi- valence, alterity and Life; in the promise of an end to the Odyssey, in the promise of "peace". The togetherness that *responsible improvisation* offers as an alter- native to "peace" is not rational/irrational in the sense established by hegemonic philosophical and political discussions, nor is it ethically justifiable in normalized paths. It is pre-rational and pre-ethical, yet it has a form; it is aesthetically "justified", allowing ethics and rational deliberation. It is also beyond "negative" and "positive" Utopia. Still, improvisation does represent *hope* and manifests the possibility of **the totally other** within the actualization of co-poiesis which is more fundamental than "peace" and so much more than the promise to end alterity, alienation, and suffering by returning to the peace incubated within thingness and bestiality.

Peace education is part and parcel of the hegemonic normalizing education. Such awareness is a worthy introduction of an alternative kind of *togetherness*, Diasporic togetherness, where improvisation as a concept, as an ideal, as a way of life is central for the possibility of counter-education. In opposition to the various agendas in present-day peace education Diasporic togetherness as actualized in the dynamics of improvisation does not call us to return "home" to sentimentalist-ethnocentric alternatives or to anti-humanist mechanical "solutions" and compensations for the loss incubated by departing from nothingness, "homeland" or "the one".

Improvisation manifests the dialectics of response-ability and respond-ability (Gur-Ze'ev, 2005, pp. 26–27). It is not "constructive" nor is it merely "negative"; it is far from a manifestation of "resistance" to oppression or suffering and loss. Improvisation represents a creative-speculative attunement, a different kind of gaze and response-ability that makes possible responsibility that offers co-poiesis in the infinity of the moment, each moment anew. It involves a kind of intimacy with the richness of the cosmos and its inviting dynamics, impulses, drives and meaning-creation. Here hospitality enables creative compassion, where the alterity of the otherness of the Other is an unavoidable partner in creative realization of playful Love of Life that strives not back "home" but eternally toward the *Not-Yet*, the unknown and the never-in-peace happiness/suffering of the Other as alterity and companion.

Improvisation, when true to itself, transcends any limited context, border, dogma, regulations, drives, habits and fears—dwelling in the infinity of the moment and the ecstasies of the here and now. It is essentially dynamic, overcoming itself and the immanence that makes welcome the drive for transgression; it offers holiness each moment anew. It is a mimesis of Genesis; it dwells within the erotic unknown, attuned to the music of the not-yet gazing at the manifestations of Life, playfully responding to it in the right manner before any rational calculation and regardless of the will or direction of any colonizing power/temptation. Its acknowledged-blessed homelessness transcends suffering and fear into worthy suffering and responsibility as creative Love of Life, a kind of "peace" that does not serve the victory of violence that has successfully silenced its victims.

Improvisation is not rhetorical, rational and ethical in the traditional Western concept of knowledge and intersubjectivity. This is why normally it is conceived as irrelevant for peace education. It offers, however, a pre-rational and pre-ethical quest for the true, the beautiful and the right in a manner that transcends Western binary subject-object, body-spirit, natural-human, human-Godly dichotomies. These separations parallel Western detachment of the aesthetic, the ethical, the intellectual, the bodily and the political—detachments that are reflected also in the saying of the psyche and in somatic silence, dichotomies which are pre-conditions for "peace" and "war" (and other kinds of violence). Diasporic counter-education transcends hegemonic peace education and introduces improvisation as happy playfulness that weaves anew the symbolic, the existential, the musical and the intellectual creative attunement; a reply of responsible-playfulness to alterity, to suffering and to anti-erotic pleasures as a serious play, as co-poiesis; serious play as the wind of the wings of hope manifesting the concreteness of the presence of Love. *It is more fundamental then "peace"* as an a-historical moment—in a way an anti-historical and anti-peace moment. Within its never-set horizons *art becomes a form of life* in a specific, material historical moment that seeks or creates bodily conduct and genuine togetherness with the cosmos in its most specific, even microscopic, manifestations in the infinity of the instant.

Improvisation is of vital importance for a kind of peace education that will not be part and parcel of normalizing education: within co-poiesis improvisation offers a *togetherness* that is not pre-imposed or predicted-directed by someone or something: it is the manifestation of the spirit of freedom that meets the gate between silence and "voice", between respond-ability and response-ability; Love of Life communicates joyfully. The kind of peace it offers accepts the invitation of alterity and of the *Not-Yet*, creates each moment anew, without being imprisoned in any predetermined model, interest, habit, or violating threats or temptations. Only the imperative of refusing shekels and resisting any exterior limitation enlightens improvisation worthy of the name. Because it is not the fruit of subjectification processes, and since it is prior to "genuine intersubjectivity", such an overcoming of what is presently called "peace" makes possible happy, responsible nomadism. It opens the gate not to "peace" as totalizing homogeneity neither to endless meaninglessness fragmentation as a gate for postmodern salvation but to nomadism of an individual who is beyond subjectivism in the sense of "self-fulfillment". A nomad who is with herself as she is with the moment, dwelling in the cosmos in a de-territorialized and a-historical experience that is beyond her subjectivity, calculations and interests. In improvisation, she is partner to compassionate, never "peaceful", hospitality of a non-ethnocentric togetherness with the cosmos and with the Other—the Other as a homeless human who does not try to reeducate to a new "home", dogma or self-forgetfulness.

For a serious elaboration of present day peace education it is important to note that while improvisation is uncontrolled and resists functionalist and "effective" realization, evaluation, representation and constitution, it is, at least partially, to be edified, cultivated, enhanced, improved, or at least called for. Self-constitution and self-education (which also includes much dislearning) meets here the role of teachability and learning with, for and from the partners. Here there is even room for the master as an important, serious challenge to address and overcome as part of a co-poiesis that facilitates transcendence.

Precisely because it abandons the naivety of strive for "peace" or the strive for problematic consensus of the kind Habermas and all present day peace education experts promises us—improvisation facilitates transcendence from the quest to return "home", back to the infinity of nothingness and to the suggestive power of "peace", "consensus" and "harmony" which are the fruits of meaninglessness. Improvisation is not a medium, not a "function", not (as so popular in today's high-tech) an instrument that might offer big business and successful individuals "maximization of benefits", nor is it a fascinating entertainment or a reliable method for self-forgetfulness. It might become, however, a devoted agent of these and so many management experts offer today to their clients training in improvisation that will come-out in better management-employees relations, superior products and higher salaries. In opposition, Diasporic Life as offered by counter-education improvises a challenge to the traumatic-phallic-colonialist attitude to Life as actualized since the Socratic project and the beginning of the history of Monotheism which is nothing but the history of the search for the road to the lost "peace".

Diasporic co-poiesis improvises different relations with central dimensions of Life and with central concepts and realities such as "touch", "gaze", "attunement" and response-ability/responsibility which are central to any overcoming of present-day peace education. In the form of improvisation it furthers an attempt to re-unite or at least rearticulate the tensions, abysses and bridges between (pre-rational) thought and action, spirit/psyche and body, "I" and the otherness of the Other in a manner that transcends traditional Western relations of space and time. It also rearticulates the relations of the bodily and spiritual touch and infinity, read-dressing the relations of the moment and eternity. It facilitates that which has been so difficult for Western thought and human life since the departure from Orphic poetry and primitive nomadism: totally being in the infinity of the moment, totally dwelling in Love of Life. And it does—or does not—do so in the most concrete, embodied, deep-rooted manifestations of the de-territorialized space shared with others. That is why it is of vital relevance to exile and to nomadism of various kinds, including the collective, historical, forced exile as we know it only too well in the 20th and the 21st centuries.

Improvisation is of vital importance for any counter-education that is true to itself and is courageous to face the false promises of present-day peace education by offering not emancipating negativity and ultimately eternal and comprehensive "peace" but something very different: it offers *(re)birth*. It brings forth responsibility, a mature, speculative ear for, gaze at, and touch of the newly-born each moment anew. The de-territorialized "here" that is offered us within the endlessness of improvisation is a specific, the most specific and most concrete "here and now"; the here and now that offers not a false "home", "nirvana" or "pleasure". It offers nomadic hospitality, Diasporic hospitality of the co-poiesis kind. Such (re)birth is a concrete communicative creativity that has its roots in the nomadic ethics (Braidotti, 2006), within the techno-scientific realities of globalizing capitalism, in the pre-rational com-passion as offered by Ettinger (Ettinger, 2005, pp. 73–713) and the kind of togetherness that is to be educated to and trained by partners that show us and create with us new roads beyond the modern-postmodern struggle in education, and surely beyond contextuality and the horizons of the powers that form our "self"; beyond the tradition of "critique" into the era of co-poiesis, improvisation and new forms of togetherness challenge the given reality and the presence of injustice and meaninglessness. Imagination, passion and response-ability meet here in a kind of togetherness that Unger comes very close to articulating for us: "In the setting of our non-instrumental relations to one another, we come to terms with our unlimited mutual need and fear. This coming into terms is a search. It is a quest for freedom—for the basic freedom that includes an assurance of being at home in the world... The most radical freedom is the freedom to be, to be a unique person in the world as it is" (Unger, 1984, p. 109). Improvisation makes possible transcendence within the triumph of the context—not to manifest the omnipotence of the immanence and homogeneity but to open the gate to transcendence and heterogeneity. It calls for the transformation of respond-ability into co-response-ability, of passion into com-passion, of quasi-poiesis into co-poiesis; a kind of togetherness that does not free any of us from Diasporic existence, or from wars and the danger of self-forgetfulness, yet it opens the gate for something more fundamental than "peace": to serious playfulness with alterity in the Other and the "homereturning" quest within "our" self. It invites self-preparation and self-overcoming amidst the quest for total fragmentation and being swallowed by the immanence, on the one hand and the quest for objective, unifying "peace" on the other. It is not a "theory" neither is it a mere drive. And it is here, with us, around us, reminding us that togetherness must not culminate into oppressive collectivism and "emancipating" cruel "critiques "nor "legitimate counter-violence of the oppressed". Poiesis of the individual, of a genuine individual, opens here the gate for "co-poiesis" which is so much more fundamental and responsible than "peace". But the Diasporic counter-education is a path which still lacks the first step to prepare its leap. The first step toward this leap is overcoming the pre-assumptions, the passions and the telos of the hegemonic versions of present day peace-education.

REFERENCES

Anaximandrus. (1982). In J. Barnes (Ed.), *The presocratic philosophers* (pp. 19–37). London and New York: Routledge.

Arendt, H. (1969). Reflections on violence. Special Suppl. *New York Review of Books, 12*(4), 1–25.

Augustine, St. (1957). *The city of god against the pagans.* London and Cambridge: W. Heinemann.

Benjamin, W. (1978). *Reflections—essays, aphorism, autobiographical writings.* New York: Harcourt Brace Jovanovich.

Braidotti, R. (2006). *Transpositions: On nomadic ethics.* Cambridge: Polity Press.

Ettinger, B. (2005). Copoiesis. *Ephemera, 5*(X), 703–713.

Ettinger, B. (2005a). Compassion and com-passion. http://underfire.eyebeam.org/?q=node/512

Gur-Ze'ev, I. (2001). Philosophy of peace education in a post-modern era. educational *Theory, 51*(3), 315–336.

Gur-Ze'ev, I. (2005). Critical theory, critical pedagogy and diaspora today: Toward a new critical language in education (introduction) In I. Gur-Ze'ev (Ed.), *Critical theory and critical pedagogy today—toward a new critical language in education* (pp. 7–34). Haifa: Faculty of education the university of Haifa.

Gur-Ze'ev, I. (2009). Philosophy of peace education in a postmetaphysical era. In G. Salomon (Ed.), *Handbook for peace education.*

Gur-Ze'ev, I. (Forthcoming). Philosophy of peace education. *International encyclopedia of education* (3rd ed.).

Gur-Ze'ev, I. (2007). *Beyond the modern-postmodern struggle in education—toward counter-education and enduring improvisation.* Rotterdam: Sense Publishers.

Harnack, A. von (1990). *Marcion—The Gospel of the Alien God.* Durham: Labyrinth Press.

Heraclitus. (1987). *Fragments* (T. M. Robinson, Trans.). Toronto: University of Toronto Press.

Heym, S. (1983). *Achashveros—the wandering Jew*. Tel Aviv: Am Oved.

Levinas, E. (1996). Peace and proximity. In A. Peperzak, S. Critchley, R. Bernasconi (Eds.), *Emmanuel Levinas—basic philosophical writings*. Bloomington, IN: Indiana University Press.

Peretz, A. (2003). *The art of teaching and improvisation*. MA Thesis, The Israeli Branch of the University of Leeds. http://www.improvcenter.co.il/texts/thesis/synopsis-english.html

Rosenzweig, F. (2005). *The star of redemption* (B. Galli, Trans.). Madison, WI: The University of Wisconsin Press.

Unger, R. (1984). *Passion—an essay on personality*. New York: The Free Press.

ILAN GUR-ZE'EV

5. THE NEW ANTI-SEMITISM—TOWARD EDUCATIONAL CHALLENGES[1]

The "new anti-Semitism", some would claim, is nothing but a new rhetoric tool in the service of Zionist propaganda; an instrument that is to halt justified critique and enhance the efficiency of refusing moral responsibility to the fruits of the Israeli evil industry. Others claim that there is nothing new in anti-Semitism and, that, actually, the discourse that addresses "the new anti-Semitism" is misleading and turns the focus from genuine challenges to empty and misleading aims. Still others conceive "the new anti-Semitism" as a genuine, challenging new phenomenon. According to this view we should prepare ourselves for a worthy addressing of the new challenge since not only the new anti-Semitism offers an unknown de-legitimization of the very existence of the State of Israel—it might become a frame-work for a world politics which will threaten the prosperity and even before long endanger the very existence of the State of Israel.

The present conference will give room for these perspectives yet it will devote itself mainly to the more comprehensive and theoretical dimensions of new anti-Semitism. It will address the new anti-Semitism as an actual phenomenon which is not to be reduced to the rhetoric concerning "dangers" but should rather be addressed as a challenge; a challenge that we did not yet prepare ourselves to properly address. Why is it so that we are not properly prepared to address it and to respond to its possibilities and its fruits? Because we do not yet understand what we are faced with, in spite of the vitality, urgency and enormous embarrassment it faces us with. This conference will address with special focus the educational challenges of the new anti-Semitism.

As an introduction to the upcoming various and diverse discussions of the educational challenges of the new anti-Semitism herewith I offer one perspective, my own perspective concerning the new anti-Semitism. This introduction will hopefully give reason to the question why did I initiate this discussion and this meeting today?

*

Until recently "new anti-Semitism" as a phenomenon received its visibility, a proper name and fruits almost exclusively within the prism of reaction to the growing critique of Israeli policies and in face of a new, unconcealed de-legitimization of the very existence of the Jewish state.

Under the flag of "the new anti-Semitism" an attempt is actualized to unveil the roots of an alleged unfair critique of Israel and even hatred, which, according to this line of argument, contains so much unconscious and intellectual vitality within

I. Gur-Ze'ev, The Possibility/Impossibility of a New Critical Language in Education, 85–105.
© *2010 Sense Publishers. All Rights Reserved.*

the framework of the anti-Israeli rhetoric, which flourishes today in Western academic and intellectual centers, from where it is scattered to the public discussion, good-searching NGO's, progressive Websites, public opinion polls and to spontaneous reactions in the streets of Amsterdam, Dublin, Berkley, Sydney, Tokyo or Caracas to the Muslim quarter of Paris, Marcy or London.

Without underestimating the importance of this question it is my view that what we are actually facing here is a challenge of much higher magnitude; immensely richer, rooted profoundly deeper; a grave *threat to mankind as a whole* in the present historical moment and not a power that threatens solely the future of the Jewish people. Three seemingly disconnected dynamics are incubated in the present moment. The explosion of their togetherness offers hospitality to the weaker ones among us: the globalization of capitalist logic, the exile of the humanist killer of God, and the near-possibility of mankind bringing an *End* to all Life on earth by its own *Will to Power*; an *End* which the human race gathers all its resourcefulness for ensuring its realization as its most grandiose and everlasting spectacle.

The ongoing discourse which concerns the new anti-Semitism normally relates merely to the tip of this gigantic-ecstatic educational burning iceberg. In fact, as the strongest and richest *myth* of the present historical moment, new anti-Semitism offers to all an outstandingly fruitful critique, a unique powerful resistance and the last still possible quasi-religious-ecstatic creativity. New anti-Semitism is a total and ironically also universal substitute to the Enlightenment's telos; a transformation of progressivism from a humanist-oriented ethos committed to the Enlightenment into a new progressivism that is committed to destroy Enlightenment and finds much relevance in the tradition of 18 and 19th century counter-Enlightenment , in the proto-Nazi literature and in present new neo-Marxism and post-structuralist philosophies; an unrestrained ecstatic strive to *oppose and destroy the essence, the history and the aim of the West and its Judeo-Christian foundations.*

As an alternative to the possibility of the hospitality of an humanist-oriented emancipating telos new anti-Semitism offers humans of the present day rich theo-logical, philosophical, psychological and political constructs, strong symbols and ecstatic drives which enable an effective *self-forgetfulness* in a dull historical moment: these are of so much need in the era of the exile of the killer of God! In its explicit and "external" manifestations it is connected, actualized in and gives fruits to various and even conflicting arenas, fashions, interests and agendas. It has no specific one, unified, manifestation. It is realized in a thin, plentiful, quasi-religious, fragmentary range of high-speed changes and developments; it includes a range of varieties: from a reaction to the exile of God's holiness to the exile of the great humanist rebel against God and the desolation of *the holiness of killing-God-each-moment-anew*. The world that was freed of holiness and "vertical" spirituality acknowledges the richness and the excitement of the "thin", "horizontal" daily-spirituality and exchanges, the joy of experiencing "differences" which do not make a difference and the quasi-moral potential for ecstatic reaction of the nerve system as a joyous, quasi-spiritual resistance. "Resistance", no holy transcending history of progress toward redemption: resistance to any (immanently oppressive) quest for homogeneity, exclusivity, elitism, hierarchy and stability.

How ironic it is that the emancipatory tradition has become a homogenizing, elitist, exclusivist-oriented, hierarchal and racial commitment. As a pedagogical catharsis this new progressivism offers an alternative totality—against the whole-penetrating power of contingency, mega-speed, globalization and the near-possibility of realizing the human's potential for a celebrated destruction of all life on earth.

On the one, moderate, edge of the new anti-Semitism range we find post-colonialist sensitivity to suffering of the less lucky ones, empathy with the marginalized and care for the victims whose absence was so strongly experienced along the agonizing history of humanist education. On the other extreme of this range the new sensitivity is organized into "resistance" and terror, or, at least into "understanding" terror of the victims of the West. When on June 4 the "peace activists" on the *Marmara* heading to Gaza port were called by the Israeli navy to stop since they are approaching a zone of navel blockade the recorded reply of the radio of these new progressivists in the flotilla ship was: "shut up and go back to Auschwitz!" and also: "We are helping Arabs to fight the US. Don't forget September 11 guys" (http://www.youtube.com/watch?v=xkJVEYuF-lE).

This new kind of anti-Semitism is very different from what until now was understood as "anti-Semitism" as we can see in the open letters which were exchanged on this matter by Habermas, Brumlik and Honderich in light of the publication of *After the Terror* hailing Palestinian terror as morally justified. One should remember, however, that the "counter-violence" of the victims of the West is diverse and spread from Riyadh to Bagdad to New York; but its focus is Jerusalem, or, more precise: the Jewish Spirit and its alleged successful universalization in the form of Enlightenment, "western civilization" or "colonialism". Its roots are spiritual, theological and philosophical. Its manifestations and pre-conditions are global political, economic, technological, psychological and intellectual. Education worthy its name in such an historical moment cannot afford itself to disregard the challenge of this transformation. The educational fruits of this transformation constitute the horizons of the possibilities of our present gaze, eavesdrop, inclusiveness as well as our impending for a cultural rebirth.

The realization in actuality of this post-modern *Geist* within the post-colonialist political framework is unfeasible unless it has a durable, solid, representation apparatus and an effective educational implementation. And postcolonialism does educate. It does educate extremely lucratively! *Postcolonialism educates fundamentally for "resistance" to the victimization drive which is so essential to Judo-Christian monotheism/"the West"*; contra any claim for objective-universal truths and values; specially it is directed against (Western) pretentiousness to deliver the word of "redemption" or "liberation" in a genuine, just and universally valid manner: whether it is in the form of authority/hierarchy of the symbolic father, phallocentric logos and its fruits, an all-mighty God and the missionaries that represent "him" or in the form of the humanist universally valid Utopia, democracy, and the Enlightened pedagogues who are totally and genuinely devoted to its realization. The negation of this and other Western "liberating" projects is grounded on the understanding that in their service the foundations are set for the predatory practices of capitalism, oppression and destruction of the Others' identity, aims and ways of life in the margins of Western hegemonic culture and, especially, in the Third World. The impetus for this Western oppressive drive is the Jew. **The Jew** or the Jewish spirit is identified by its uniqueness. The Jew is different from all nations, from any "goy". The Jewish nation is holy and it has a holy mission since God is holy and he chose one nation from all nations, the Jewish nation. This self-understanding which was so problematic for Christianity with its universal truth claims and for traditional anti-Semitism is even more problematic for the postmodern philosophies and for the post-colonialist agenda. Judaism and the post-colonialist agenda are in life-and-death struggle: who is the true Other? Who is the deliverer of the alternative to the history of human violence and oppressive pedagogy? Who bears the genuine transcendence from the history of violence which Western colonialism, in its various forms, is the latest and most threatening manifestation? For the postcolonialist's and many of their post-structuralist masters the very claim for uniqueness of which no standard can match or judge; *holy exclusivity*, the very self-perception as "light for the nations" and the vanguard of morality in face of blindness or the non-Jews as darkness ("or lagoiim") culminates in the racist-oppressive existence of the State of Israel. This is quite a challenge for educators to address, especially in the era of globalization, fundamentalism and the post-modern zeitgeist which is anti-transcendent, anti-monotheistic, "pantheistic", yet needs badly quasi-holiness, quasi-transcendence in the form of the ecstasis of the kind suggested by the new anti-Semitism, on the one hand and globalizing capitalism, on the other.

The *resistance* to the actualization of the Judeo-Christian essential drive for elitism, exclusivism and colonization is realized under different flags and in countless arenas and contexts among which one could note the resistance to "Monotheism" (with the exception of Islam), resistance to "phallocentrism", resistance to "colonialism", resistance to "hegemonic sexual practices and ideals", resistance to "Israel and its oppressive racial policies" and so forth. These have their positive manifestations in the form of peace education, work for growing number of stimulating NGO's and especially in support for the Palestinians whom Pope Benedictus VIV just recently acknowledged in his visit to the holy land as "*God's chosen people*". What, if at all, could be in a post-metaphysical era the common denominator for phenomena as diverse as insisting to disregard China/Syria/Somalia/Russian/ Zimbabwe/ Venezuela's civil right's record, silence concerning Iranian official anti-Semitism, challenging "phallocentrism", resistance to "monotheism", "radical multicultural education" and "postcolonial activism"? The complex, rich nets and arenas of post-modern existence of which this list is only a reminder to, with all its important differences, share one, semi-religious holiness, which is actualized in education for "*resistance*" to *Western/monotheistic/Judeo-Christian oppressive essence*. In various and different degrees and actualizations it shares resistance to two conflicting trends: 1. A claim for moral uniqueness and exclusive mission in history. 2. *Any* claim for objective-universal truth, value or yardstick, humanism included.

The resistance to these Western but fundamentally Jewish educational agendas is grounded on the understanding that these agendas set the pre-conditions for oppressive capitalism, political enslavement, cultural a-symmetries and other forms of Western colonization—within the margins of the West and especially in the Third World. *Israel is here conceived as the most extreme, violent and fragile representative of the colonialist essence of the West* of which the impetus is its Judeo-Christian heritage. Jewish monotheism is the root of this heritage and postcolonial education must address these roots, this essence, if it is true to its commitment to overcome colonialism in all its forms and manifestations. Postmodern "resistance" is much more than political and educational praxis and it is ecstatic and quasi-religious alternative in an era from which not only God was exiled but even the exile of the holiness of killing-God-each-moment-anew was deconstructed, ridiculed and swallowed by the system. Derrida, Lyotard and surely Levinas did not explicitly implement it within the post-colonial prism but many of their pupils and epigones did. Within the post-colonial prism it easily becomes a new anti-Semitism. As Zizek himself admits, in a post-colonial moment the Jewish question reappears as our central challenge. Alan Badiou is not very far from this position when he establishes his "resistance" to democracy, humanism and Western immanent violence and run away from "the ethics of truths".

"Resistance" as quasi-religiosity is *actualized under different banners and in endless different arenas.* All these are united in facing *the truth of the post- metaphysical moment*; the exile of the holiness of transcendence or progress in the form of a humanist killing of God. It is a titanic educational challenge which demands our addressing. Most humanists, however, did not yet reach the conceptualization, sensitivity and courage to address this ecstatic-spiritual-psychological challenge and its political fruits. They are not alone: even the most enthusiastic partners to the creation of the *new anti-Semitism as an ecstatic spirituality* in a dull, post-metaphysical, historical moment are normally unaware of the powers manipulating them. In a totality within which changes become ever deeper and faster in all levels and dimensions of life there is only one arena or dynamic in which they are all united. They are all amalgamated in one *sacred work* in a world of which holiness, meaning and telos were exiled from: "resistance" to "Israel", "the Zionists", or, simpler after a drink or two: "the Jews".

The move from "resistance to homogeneity/hierarchy/universalism/exclusion" to "resistance to Western colonialism" to "resistance to Israel" to "resistance" to "the Jews" varies and is sometimes even sublime and sophisticated, but it becomes almost politically correct these days: so that Egypt's Minister of Culture Faruk Husni could be the surest candidate to be elected in October 2009 as the new head of UNRA even in light of countless explicit vulgar anti-Semitic expressions and calls to burn all Israeli books since, as he explained in another occasion "the Jews are known to steal the cultures of other people", and so forth. In face of his near election day he published today (28.5.2009) in the Le Monde an article which tries to explain that, actually, he is not a racist, only a genuine post-colonialist facing Israeli evil; an explanation which today is on the edge of politically correct and is received by his relevant readers in progressive intellectual and political circles with no much more than a slender amount of embarrassment.

In a hybridist, "plane" actuality within which contingency and mere power-relations are established as the sole rulers "resistance" to Israel becomes an *ecstatic quasi-holiness*, part of the new-age daily spirituality but also its exclusive alternative: "Israel" becomes an icon for all evil that is presently threatening but not unconditionally. The condition is in the space between the brackets and the fetishzed symbol. The target of transforming a representation of a political entity into a spiritual entity is a self-defeating project since Israel is by its very nature a symbol, a holy movement outside history that has received the alternative to its own "brackets" by the Zionist entering history and establishing the new dialectical dimension within the Jewish spirit by the establishment of the State of Israel as a normal state, as a nation among nations under un-normal conditions. The new anti-Semitic work that is done here is supposed to *edify* within contingency and immanence; as if transcendence, meaning and telos are still possible. The possibility is conditioned by exposing "Israel" as a unique entity which opens otherwise impossible possibilities in a post-metaphysical era. "Israel" saves the human in "our" post-metaphysical moment from meaninglessness, contingency and from the psychological fruits of the concept of "Difference", namely, the quest for "homereturning" into nothingness. Judaism, for the new anti-Semitism is arch-rival in its Love of Life, on the one hand and its universal mission, on the other, not in its claim for normality or the gravity of its policies. The State of Israel serves here both as an object for facing one-self by experiencing ecstasy via "resistance" to the claim for universalism, on the one hand and by the engagement with the horrific commitment to exclusivist sense of being "the(elected)-One", on the other. "Israel" is both the selected One and the elected One. The most Diasporic and its extreme negation.

It is worth nothing that not only on the psychological level post-colonial heroes such as Hugo Chavez, Ahmadinejad, Faruk Husni, Mikis Theodorakis or Nobel prize winner Saramago move smoothly from "resistance" to "Israel" to "resistance" to "Jews": within the post-colonialist philosophy it is almost a conceptual imperative, while explicitly keeping distance from traditional anti-Semitism. This is since the State of Israel is conceived as the incarnation of the Jewish Spirit that in light of post-structualist critique its monotheism is conceived *not any more as the Other of Western civilization but rather as the essence and impetus of Judeo-Christian civilization*, in sharp contrast to traditional Western anti-Semitism.

In all the diverse manifestations of the new anti-Semitism "Israel" is conceived and represented as the agent of "the West" and its immanent, multi-façade, oppressive colonialist drive. It serves as an extreme, "dense" manifestation of a general phenomenon that the spirit of Judaism initiates and realizes universally, in countless arenas and occasions. The explicit accusation of world "Jewish conspiracy" or "hegemony" is only the most primitive, obsolete articulation of this philosophy which in its more sophisticated versions post-colonial education offers us as the most progressive politically correct mantras of the day.

The aim of this conference is to focus attention of scientific research and of the public discourse to the ways in which postmodernism not only challenges modernism but, not less important, its "monotheistic" foundations: claim for objective and universal validity of a certain set of values and assertions; a linear conception of time; binary logic; telos who's aim is monolithic truth, ethnocentristic-oriented-universal-peaceful-order, and so forth. The "pantheistic" character of the postmodern discourse and its sensitivity and commitment to "difference", "multi-culturalism", "anti-phallocentrism", resistance to any hierarchy, stability, universalism and objectivism opposes existentially, philosophically, psychologically and politically the Jewishness of Enlightenment's emancipatory project and fruits. It opposes *the Jewish spirit* which is the constitutive element and the philosophical impetus of Western cruel oppressive colonialism. It all originates in the notion of one God, one chosen people, one Torah, one telos to be inflicted universally, at all cost, upon all others. This is the impetus of Western violence even if the concept of "chosen people" is transformed to anti-violent missionary agenda of the "chosen ones" who see their exclusiveness in readiness to suffer for the Other and self-sacrifice for the Other's re-education.

Present day new anti-Semitism is not entirely original. It has a (forgotten) history in modernity that it is important to critically reconstruct. What we presently face is a new version of new anti-Semitism. To the present, post-colonialist, version one should note Marx's new anti-Semitism and that of Nietzsche, which were new, comparing to traditional anti-Semitism. These continued traditional anti-Semitism in focusing on Jewish unique existence among other nations but their focal point was neither the religious nor the desolated stance of Jewish existence and its universal challenge to all others. For both Marx and Nietzsche the modern Jewish existence opened the gate for a dramatic transformation and for progress for all humanity, a mission which no other nation could undertake. The specific kind of progress and the victims of the universal realization of the spirit of Judaism was the focal point of the earlier stages of new anti-Semitism. This threatening side of the *universal realization of the essence of Judaism* is also in the centre of the present wave of the new anti-Semitism, which is a difficult phenomenon for a specific, comprehensive reduction that will offer an exact determination. This is since the new version of the new anti-Semitism is more of an uninstitutionalized religion in a godless world, a zeitgeist in a world from which Spirit was exiled so that some might think, not without reason, that "new anti-Semitism" is not the proper name for this phenomenon and others, also with good reasons, might claim that the new anti-Semitism is a phenomenon that by its nature cannot be described by any proper name and should not be reduced to any specific determination.

The present, post-colonial new anti-Semitism is different from that of Marx and Nietzsche. This is since the versions of Marx and Nietzsche, with all their differences, were united in presenting the reaction of the West to the killing of God by modernity and the constitution of an edifying mission to the killer of God—whether this deification relates to whole humanity or exclusively to the "superman". The present version of the new anti-Semitism recounts to the exile of the killer of God and the desolation of the historical deification of Man/humanity not to the killing of God, to the reaction to the deconstruction of the deification of humanity, not to the pre-modern sacredness which concerned the total presence of the goodness of God the almighty. The present version of the new anti-Semitism is a reaction. It is a reaction to holiness and edification being enthusiastically deconstructed and swallowed within the endless arenas and manifestations of the dullness of the present post-metaphysical historical moment; an historical moment which has neither space nor time for transcendence, to nothing more grand than temporary, individual "plain" pleasure, on the one hand and pragmatic struggle for the interests and self-evidence of the victims, on the other. This, unless it accepts the richness and holiness of the fundamentalist total alternative to the progressive humanist agenda, which has its coalitions with globalizing capitalism and post-colonialism and should be considered as part and parcel of the shallowness of the triumphant post-modern historical moment. If one would like to understand the ecstatic new progressivist support of the "go back to Auschwitz" Gaza flotilla one should address the intimate connection between the "critique" of "plane", Western democracy and its concept of freedom as articulated by Gill Deleuze, Alan Badiou and Slavoj Zizek to the "death to freedom" educational agenda of the Hamas regime in Gaza and more generally the Islamist principle rejection of democracy and freedom.

Counter-education in such days if worthy its name should alarm and awake. It should awake of its dogmatic slumber and encourage the humanists among us as well as the consistent Diasporic humans and present them the central challenges of this historical moment, its imperatives, invitations, threats and its new gates for hope. The present conference hopes to become part of such an awakening effort.

In face of such an invitation it is worthy the effort to emphasize the complexity of the category "new anti-Semitism" and its relation to post-structuralist philosophies and to the post-colonialist agenda. What we are presently facing is a transformation-in-process; a new "medieval" epoch on the edge of a total shift in space-speed relation, entering mega-speed actuality within which postcolonialism prospers. Postcolonialism, it should be added, is only one of many prisms that prosper in the present zeitgeist-without-Spirit. Among these prosperous prisms one can note multi-culturalism, radical feminism, queer theories and so many more which are all initiated by the spiritual suffocation inflicted by the desolation of the humanist project of deifying humanity within the realization of the holy responsibility to kill-God-each-moment-anew as part of transcendence toward Utopia.

The post-colonialist momentum is a genuine and fruitful *quasi-spiritual power* and it is neither merely a political might nor a mistake to be easily corrected. The "critique" and "resistance" to "Israel" within it is a much needed sacred-work, surely far from a kind of critical reasoning and argumentation that one can within it settle the disagreements between "the West and the rest" and between "Israel" and "the post-colonial alternative". Within it there is no room towards the prospects of dialogue of the kind Enlightenment offered for the last two centuries with so much enthusiastic optimism. Israel, here, is unredeemably destined to become "the Jew among nations", a demonic entity, not a concrete political reality; it becomes an entity that is *essentially* different from all other nations and political entities, even in light of the works of Hayden White, Benedict Anderson, Gill Deleuze, Alan Badiou or Michel Foucault to which they normally pay tribute as present day high priests of the new religion. To the "resistance" to "Israel" there is within the new anti-Semitism theological, philosophical, psychic and political meanings which transcend any specific disagreements such as the effectivity or legitimation of the blockade on the terroristic Islamo-fascist regime and its devastated population in Gaza, the number of unnecessary road blocks imposed in the West Bank by the IDF or the exact borders of the future Palestinian State: there is no rational discussion which can satisfy the post-colonial agenda on these disagreements and no room for a possible agreement—only total inhalation of the Jewish State, and this too, only as a first step toward "genuine decolonization". All possible agreements are conceived within this agenda as steps toward this aim of "genuine de-colonization".

There is a range of rhetorical differences between the "resistance" to "Israel" and the resistance to **The Jew**, and they have their psychological barriers, cultural barriers and politically-correct barriers. It is not (yet) politically correct to be explicitly anti-Jewish or a blunt anti-Semite in the traditional sense of the concept. The old blunt anti-Semitism is conceived in normative critical discussions as obsolete, primate, and unsuitable for the new progressivists. Even heroes such as Hugo Chavez or Faruk Husni deny their racism, rearticulate themselves or apologize when caught in too blunt anti-Semitic expressions. Others, less politically-correct, such as Jose Saramago do not make these differences within their post-colonialist critique, when offering their "critique" against "those experts in cruelty with doctorates in disdain, who look down on the world from the heights of the insolence which is the basis of their education. We can better understand their biblical god when we know his followers. Jehovah or Yaweh or whatever he is called, is a fierce and spiteful God, whom the Israelis always live up to". Sometimes, in respect to the mentioned barriers the "resistance" to the "Jews" is replaced with "resistance" to the "Zionists". Most new progressivists, among whom quite a few are Jews, do not see themselves as racists and as anti-Semites. Many of them are proud anti-racists and are explicitly and consciously against (old) anti-Semitism. It is quite a challenge for them to face their anti-racist credo as part and parcel of the new anti-Semitism. Either way the *resistance to the Jewish State of Israel becomes in the post-colonialist zeitgeist a universal moral question*, neither merely a political problem nor a rational challenge: it has vital existential, philosophical, political and educational dimensions which are central for the self-recognition of the West as colonialist who must redeem itself. According to this educational agenda, if the West is ever to purify itself of its impurities the West must go into genuine, courageous self-decolonization. The West, in its best, is presently struggling for the salvation of its soul by scarifying its Spirit. And the West is horrified. It is terrified from both its present identity, from its past memories as well as from the suggested medicine. So, it neither gives birth to children nor to great new ideas. This anxious effort for salvation in conditions of fright, however, has its toll: *hatred*. Ardent self-hatred. Its fire is focused on the essential of all in Western Spirit that is now acknowledged as a sin that it has to be cleansed of: its Jewish germ.

In a process of *projection* this threatening germ of Western civilization is enthusiastically *extroverted* as its Other. The Jew becomes, again, the Other of Western civilization and the object of torture, humiliation, and, finally annihilation attempts. That is how Christian civilization and Islam treated the Jews all along the history with short brakes of relative tolerance. The renewed emphasis on **the Jew** as *the Other* is currently even more fanatic and universal; enhanced by current capitalist globalization and the growing need for a substitute to the deconstructed **totally other** in a "flat", dull, multicultural reality. Presently, under the title "Zionism", "Israel" or as "unacceptable self-declared moral superiority" that is a gate for racism and victimization of the Other". In the West the internalized spirit of **the Jew** is to be sacrificed religiously as an educational process of *penance*. Hatred is here very much in the center. Self-hatred is presently being transformed into a new progressive "critique" and "resistance"; a penancing quasi-sacred work. A quasi-sacred work, however, is no easy thing in the dullness of the present post-metaphysical era; in face of the desolation of the pre-conditions for "moral", "meaning" and religious fanatisms of all kinds signified by the current McDonaldization of reality. The fanatism of the new anti-Semitism became only one dimension of the anti-fanatism of our era of McDonaldization: an imperative of dullness, the ecstatic dullness of the post-metaphysical moment. The current capitalist market as well as its cultural manifestations and the new progressivists share a common reaction to the exile of holiness and the deconstruction of transcendence. This reaction is an ontological sign, a strong sign for the era weakness that compensates itself by velocity and ever mounting ecstasies. For the post-Fordist markets as well as for the politics of the new progressivists any standard, any non-contingent drive or value, any practice or position, especially hierarchical, exclusivists, enduring and homogenic-oriented ideals have become "colonialist" power that springs from the spirit of Jewish monotheism. They should be totally annihilated unconditionally and with no mercy as the manifestations of a postmodern veiled Lucifer of the progressivists. How should we understand this transformation of progressive thinking?

What we are faced here with is an attempt for purification from a terrible sin within the framework of the myth which triumphs in the zeitgeist of the exile of Spirit. It is the *last possible quasi-religiosity* which differs from everyday new age spirituality and still contains a connection to religiosity; the last possible holiness in the era of the exile of the killer of God and the deconstruction of the ethos of universal Utopian emancipation.

Self-hatred and the hatred toward the *not-I* within the self, namely, commitment for purification of the otherness of the Jew within Western culture as the most infamous dimension of Judeo-Christian civilization join together not only psychologically but conceptually and spiritually. It is so important for us to remember that new anti-Semitism has rich psychological roots, strong and fruitful ideological frameworks as well as a redeeming (daily) mystical dimension. They give birth and re-present a new myth, a zeitgeist, quasi-spirituality and rhetorical fashions and even codes of politically-correct; these are not to be separated from global capitalism, massive immigration waves and the other manifestations of the present historical moment. In this sense *the new anti-Semitism is the disease of our time* as well as its constitutive myth and promise for cure. It is also the credo of the (new) progressive West for meeting itself purified, redeemed.

New anti-Semitism as the constitutive myth of the era of the exile of the killer of God is an *enabling power*. We should not underestimate this power. Presently there is no other, more fruitful quasi-religious suggestion other than the postmodern Pleasure Machine, on the one hand, and the Jihadist alternative, on the other. It enables psychological, intellectual and political changes and good-searching. These do challenge past and present dimensions of the West which do tend to oppression, totalitarianism, silencing and self-indulgence under the banner of redemption, emancipation, progress or universal truth. The election of Barack Hussein Obama to the presidency of the US could have been only a dream without this development. At the same time, however, it is important to note that this constitutive myth and the quasi-spirituality of the present zeitgeist is moving within a path that is far more dangerous than the present misdeeds and limits of Western culture.

Within the historical change from arenas of ever faster changes, higher speed and humanist holiness in killing-God-each-moment-anew to the exile of the killer of God, deconstruction of the humanist holiness and the entrance into mega-speed realities Western self-hatred replaced the spirit of reflection. It substituted the critical ethos and the spirit of homocentric "critique" which began its modern journey in Descartes' "cogito ergo sum" and came to its historical conclusion today in deconstructing "Spirit" itself. The power of anxiety, frustration and furiousness which are incubated in the new anti-Semitism are fertilized by the downfall of modern Utopia, and more specifically the dissolution of its last 1968 revolutionary experience. Post 1968 West is incompetent to face itself, its past and its telos in the era of mega-speed. No substitute has been created to the metaphysical anchor of Monotheism neither to the humanist revolt against it. No alternative was found nor created to progressive education as a secular sacred work. No substitute to the creative vitality of erotic humanism as a manifestation of progress, as transcendence toward worthy life. It is not the end of vitality but rather its transformation from an erotic one into a Thanatos-oriented vigour, from slow vertical poiesis to rapid horizontal ecstasis, from erotic dialectical existence back "home" to the harmony that celebrated itself until that unforgivable moment of "creation". The absence of erotic strength appears as *hospitality*; as hospitality of an invitation: invitation for "homereturning" into nothingness. Within this hospitality the West cannot avoid facing its past and present and the absence of new New Testament but by giving birth to quasi-spirituality, a return of the constitutive *myth* in the form of projection of its "Satanic" germ (in the words of Hugo Chavez, the undisputable hero of the post-colonialist ideology) and its purification in the fire of the altar of self-decolonization.

The theocentric era, in which humans devoted themselves to God and the next, homocentric, era in which human devoted themselves to the deification of humanity by killing-God-each-moment-anew is now replaced by a new era of the kind Marx, Nietzsche, Heidegger and Adorno could not even imagine. Two rival educational agendas flourish in this post-metaphysical era. They nourish each other and recycle a new myth, a new way of *self-forgetfulness* which enables human life even in the absence of holiness under the banners of the infinite right of the victim of the Judeo-Christian civilization on the one hand and under the banner of the infinite right of the client in the McWorld, on the other; life as an arena that initiates a kind of self-forgetfulness within ecstatic recycling of pleasures and symbols with no depth, telos or "meaning" beyond its "flat" recycling, on the one hand, and life as ecstatic "resistance" which actualizes itself in feminist, multi-cultural, post-colonialist and queer prisms, on the other. These seem as antagonistic trends yet they have so much in common. They represent two versions of anti-Diasporic existence: one path deconstructs Diasporic existence by enthusiastically being swallowed by the Pleasure Machine; celebrating ever growing speeds of recycling and exchange of fashions, commodities, symbols, passions and identities. The other path is the political ecstasy of quasi-spiritualist resistance to any genuine Diasporic existence and eternal improvisation-transcendence as offered by Judaism. The boundaries between these discourses are not always stable, clear and definite. They all drink from the post-structuralist well and from the postmodern culture which hails the local, partial, hybrid, contingent, heterogeneous and in the extreme also the call for *un-aimed-creative violence*, for the triumph of the aesthetic demon, for the return of the crazy gods. In the post-colonialist context, neither "justice" nor "truth" or universal human progress but rather the partial, the local, and the ethnocentric self-evidence of the victims and the creativity of counter-violence (of the victims, which, actually makes it at the same time to nothing but an echo of the victimizer's original sin) are to be the substitute to the Utopian telos of humanist education and its supposed immanent colonialist oppression. The quasi-religious nature of the ecstatic "resistance" to the originally Jewish homogenization drive of the West and to Western imposed hierarchies, to Western silencing, colonization and oppression becomes an *alternative to holiness* and to the essentially Jewish insistence on Love of Life; a post-modern alternative to Jewish-Western moral uniqueness in a Godless world from which even the killer of God has been exiled.

Universal, exclusivist Utopia and the promise for human emancipation were deconstructed and recycled as part of the new anti-Semitic myth; as the grand alternative to the Jewish monotheistic heritage and its alternative concepts of difference, uniqueness and nomadism. The burning excitement of this "resistance" constitutes a psychological-spiritual alternative: as the September 11 destruction of the symbol of Judeo-Christian synthesis shows—there is a powerful relevant reply to this dualistic phallic quest for transcendence and domination from the part of the coalition between postcolonialism and the world of Jihad. They are united in a strong commitment to level down the two rival manifestations of Judaism. The first is Jewish devotion to Love of Life and Diasporic devotion to its unique, Messianic-a-historical path. The second is the State of Israel and the Zionist quest to return to history and to mundane life. Before we turn to the Third World's reaction to the truth of the present historical moment we should ask: how does the West react to the untruth of the present historical moment? And in other words: what is "the meaning", or, what is the relevant substitute to "the meaning" and "mission" in face of the successful deconstruction of the revolt against God and the triumph of the Gnostic god? How could the West save itself from "homereturning" into haughty return into nothingness in face of the deconstruction of the pre-conditions for transcendence, in face of the triumph of relativism, contextualism and instrumental-oriented pragmatism that inherit metaphysic, holiness and the hospitality of *mysterium* on the one hand, and of rational deliberation, on the other?

What is the worthy deed in the era of the killing of God and the exile of the killer of God? Is a progressive act still possible in face of the transformation of progressive thinking into anti-democratic credo and new anti-Semitism as the quasi-religion of the 21st century? What is the worthy act in face of higher speeds within endless dull arenas which inherited the metaphysical, "dense" history where holiness hospitalized humanity under conditions of hope, happiness, truth, transcendence and worthy suffering? This transformation on the edge of entering the mega-speed arenas is a Gnostic road back, home, into *the end*. *The end* not as eschatological, religious or imaginary category. Not at all. *The End* in the era of global capitalism and mega-speed in "plane" and banal reality becomes a prosaic, reasonable, pragmatic adjunct to human progress which its realization becomes more probable by the day. The new anti-Semitism and the *end* are rivaling on the worthiest alternative in this dull historical moment. Presently we will not go into the rich philosophical, existential, spiritual and political meaning of *the end*. I will relate more to the new anti-Semitism, its affaire with the "homereturning" quest into nothingness and its post-modern manifestations.

The new anti-Semitism is a reaction to the post-metaphysical moment. This is since in a post-metaphysical moment the absence of ground for an anchor—psychological, spiritual and political ground—is a vivid absence that demands a reaction. It must impose a reaction. A highly creative reply to the silence of the killer of God. A response which its grandiose will match the greatness of the *loss* in face of the exile of the holiness of the pedagogy of the humanist killer of God. The philosophical and psychological loss unites in quest of a signifying compensation: a quasi-transcendence aim or at least an explicit, visible, detectable enemy; so that the post-modern nomad might struggle against and indulge in self-forgetfulness which offers an overwhelming illusion of *ecstatic catharsis* which will make bearable the loss of transcendence and the exile of holiness. The exclusivity and the meaning of such a struggle are irreplaceable. In the absence of negation, struggle and victory there is no life. The Gnostic redemption, revealing itself as a Paulinic-oriented renaissance, demands a struggle, needs a substitute to the exile of the killer of God and the missions and worthy suffering he could offer. It cannot abandon the promise invested in the need for arch-enemy and a redemptive struggle. This is the titanic mission the new anti-Semitism currently undertook in the West.

In the Third World, for marginalized groups, and the oppressed "resistance" to Israel has a different character. It derivates from the spiritual and political effort to establish a new, post-colonial, framework for meeting the West and re-establish new relations to it and more importantly—to itself. The attempt to enforce new, post-colonial, relations with the West is complimented by a gigantic educational effort; it became the framework for the change in the identity, for the representation of identity and the meeting of its Other. Within this pedagogical effort a place is reserved for the West for confession of its sins, for compensating its victims and for self-transformation (de-colonization) to its opposite on the background of the terrible moral a-symmetry that characterized their relations until presently. This post-colonialist pedagogical effort for transforming the economic, political, moral relations between the West and the rest actualized in the context of globalizing capitalism, which is also the era of change from higher speeds to mega-speed, which is also the post metaphysical moment which gave birth to the new anti-Semitism. In face of the exile of the killer of God new possibilities are opened in rich and different levels of existence. This is, however, also an actuality of greater inequalities, suffering for more people, economic disastrous "restructuring", cultural devastation and ecological ruin to huge populations matched by mass immigration and greater frustrations in the Third World. This is a fertile ground for the Third Worlds reception of the old anti-Semitism and not solely within Muslim communities. As such it might be considered part of the new anti-Semitism.

One should note that the post-modern dimensions of the new anti-Semitism is accompanied by a new bloom of good old anti-Semitism in the West and elsewhere, especially in Japan and South America after two generations of delegitimation of anti-Semitism following WWII. The structural economic changes inflicted by the change into a post-Fordist economy are paralleled, like in the turn of the 19th century and in 1929th crisis by an anti-Semitic bloom.

In Third World cultures the need of addressing the economic crisis and the drastic structural changes inflicted by capitalist globalization is accompanied by the destruction and restructuring of old traditions and the triumph of global culture industry which is in quest for spectacle, ecstasies and quasi-transcendence which will enable safe self-forgetfulness while enhance productivity in an ever more speedy and competitive market.

In face of these tendencies in the Third World and in the West the dullness of the post-metaphysical moment and the deconstruction of the Judeo-Christian mono-theism in the form of humanist education and its economic, cultural and existential pre-conditions give room for a search for an alternative for the quest for transcen-dence, holiness and telos, for an alternative for the possibility of *alethea*: a search for "horizontal" ecstatic experiences which will replace the quest for "vertical" transcendence, edification and redemption. Nerve-reactions to stimulus exiting self-forgetfulness inherit edifying holiness and religious sacred work. This intensification and quest for further outlandish intensification is a vital element of the new anti-Semitism in the era of high-speed and globalizing capitalism.

The economic reasons, the technological, ecological, cultural and political changes are of much relevance: they re-establish **The Jew** or "Israel" in the Muslim world but more generally in the Third World in a new-old centrality for the evaluation of ones stance in Life, wherever she is as against the traditional and the post-colonialist concept of the Other. The two rival concepts of otherness are in a fierce struggle each claiming to be the genuine Other, the ultimate victim and the true deliverer of the alternative pedagogy. It re-positions and de-territorializes the old centrality of **The Jew** as "the elected one" or the devil's deliverer. Old anti-Semitism targeted the Jews and their concept of one God, one Torah, one, holy, chosen nation. New anti-Semitism (re)elects "Israel", even if under the banner of "a Nazi-State", or the responsible to the economic crisis, to the violence of the Islamic world, to the oppressive nature of capitalism and so forth in a new context: in the context of *the absence of a true God*, in face of the need for self-forgetfulness, for an effective quasi-spirituality or for a substitute to the presence of Spirit and its edification, catharsis and salvation. It is an attempt to be completely swallowed, with no remnant, by self-forgetfulness and for being totally consumed and integrated in the quasi-spiritual experiences which post-colonial education offers. As such it justifies, glorifies and empowers the capitalist globalization to the very roots of the post-metaphysical soul of the individual. The infinity of the edifying rituals in the forms of endless *"rights of the victim"* of the Judeo-Christian civilization are integrated with infinity of *"the rights of the client"* which are, actually, the richness of the victimization process/ deconstruction/ differentialization, on the one hand and the response-ability of the cyborg in the present capitalist Pleasure Machine, on the other.

Old and the new anti-Semitisms, fanatic fundamentalists and new progressivists successfully join forces as partners to the "resistance" glorified by Chavez, Ahmadinejad, Nasrallah and Zizek. The new religion is widely internalized in various degrees and ways by the new progressivism that today even "light" leftists practice it with much devotion within the framework of the new anti-Semitism. This is the background for the famous remark of Helen Thomas who served many years as the white house columnist for the Hearst newspapers. Thomas declared recently that the Jews should "get the hell out of Palestine" and "go back home to live in Germany and Poland... Director Oliver Stone returning recently from a meeting in Teheran with president Ahmadinejad declared in this spirit that America's focus on the Holocaust was a product of the "Jewish domination of the media" and promised that his upcoming documentary series Secret History of America would put Hitler "in context"... The "go back to Auschwitz!" rhetorical flag of the Gaza flotilla is but a more dramatic manifestation of the same new progressive project. The case of Hugo Chavez, the Leader Maximus of Socialist Venezuela which made postcolonialism its ultimate emancipatory aim is paradigmatic in this case. It is wrong to address the "resistance" of Chavez's regime as a balanced or imbalanced criticism of Israel. In my mind it will be a mistake to relate to it as a particular case of old anti-Semitism. The agenda enhanced by Chavez—and he is but one explicit and especially effective manifestation of Third World's current postcolonialism—has its roots and connections, of course. It is, however, a new phenomenon. A new phenomenon which joins resistance to the traditional and new Jewish exclusivisms: 1. Reaction to the old Jewish claim for unique moral stance and exclusive universal spiritual mission as materialized by Jews and especially by the State of Israel. 2. Post-colonialist resistance to the oppressive homogeneity imposed by the West and its current most extreme emissary—the State of Israel as a representative of the wrong, misleading, otherness, in the name of *the genuine Other, the post-colonial victim* of Judeo-Christian civilization. Most of us are still unaware of its richness and potentials and surely we are not equipped properly to challenge and enhance its educational fruits.

Embarrassed are the humanists among us in face of the post-colonialist critique. They are speechless, disoriented and deprived of a grand emancipatory mission to struggle under its flag for a better future. It is not only that the post-colonialists took over much of the critical language that was so dear to the critical educators—it is the very fact of the near probability of *The End* of life as a manifestation of Western kind of progress, on the one hand, and the guilt, the terrible guilt of acknowledging

Judeo-Christian values and ideals as the grand oppressor in human history, on the other. At most, my humanist friends can hope for a fierce polemic or a strong apologia. Some, such as Bernard-Henri-Levi, Michael Walzer, Richard Wolin, Terry Eagleton, Charles Taylor or Allen Bloom still insist on refusing the suggested spiritual Hara-kiri of the kind offered to them by post-colonial education. But all this does not culminate into the ultimate philosophical deed: *commitment to worthy giving birth to children*, namely, to erotic response to the hospitality of Thanatos and its agents. In the meeting, at home, between those who experience the omnipotence and holiness of Allah as a living God and those experiencing the exile of the holiness of killing the Judeo-Christian God and its humanistic substitutes the birth ratio gap is currently 1.4 to the Europeans and 7.6 to the Muslim immigrants. Today about half of the newly born children in the Netherlands are Muslims. In the absence of a dramatic change it is not unlikely that in 46 years France will become an Islamic republic. Courageous counter-education should today both overcome Islamophobia and all kinds of racism and at the same time confront Western call for surrendering Life brought about by the new anti-Semitism.

These post-colonial spiritual, political and demographic dynamics in the West and in the Third World integrate within the capitalist globalizing developments. They have, of course, a strong presence in Israel and Palestine too. According to the demographical predictions, if no dramatic change suddenly appears secular Jews will be outnumbered by Islamists and Jewish Jihadists by 2020. How should the Judeo-Christian civilization respond once it abandoned all versions of its monotheistic holiness and quest for transcendence? It can choose between a rapid (post-colonialist) transformation, a gradual change and a renewed struggle for its Spirit. In the Israeli context one can meet the new anti-Semitism in three seemingly rival fronts: Muslim anti-Semitism which develops traditional anti-Semitism and enhances it with relevant aspects of the new anti-Semitism; post-colonialist new anti-Semitism, which brings together Jewish self-hatred/poststructuralist critique and Palestinian racism/postcolonial "resistance"; and New Age spiritualism as manifested in Cabalist anti-Semitism. Popular new anti-Semitism can be found in the works of Rabbi Philip Berg, the head of the "Center for Kabala" with famous disciples such as Madonna, Sarah Ferguson Duchess of York, Mick Jagger, Demi Moore and hundreds of thousands other supporters, visitors and disciples. According to Rabbi Berg, the Jews are responsible for anti-Semitism, actually for the universal run toward *Towu Va'avohu*, because of the Jewish refusal for universalization of the Kabala—a project he committed himself to, with much "success" in the form of neo-liberal-oriented centers of Kabala teaching its practical secrets and its magical power for the ones who are willing to pay all over the world.

In the Israeli context, the fruits of the Zionist insistence on Jewish return into secular history and its "homereturning" project, the traditional reaction of the Arab world and the new anti-Semitism have brought Israel to the situation within which *it has to pay in coins of worthy existence for ensuring its very existence*; the dialectics of Jewish life within/outside history, namely, the internal struggle of Jewish telos and the exile of Spirit brought Israel to become ever closer to some of the more disgusting anti-Semitic miss-representations of it. Paradoxically, at the same time the central part of Israeli society, under the influence of global capitalism and the new progressivist education, become rapidly more pragmatic, more neo-liberal and favors multiculturalism-light. It is longing for pragmatic compromises, good business and unthreatened plugging-in-into-the-post-modern-pleasure-machine: neither for heroic sacrifice nor for grand victories; because it lost its Spirit, telos and strives for transcendence along with the rest of the West.

These trends and the fashions they create are manifesting the third historical stage—the post-metaphysical stage, within which the exile of the killer of God is actualized. Holiness and mysterium are deconstructed. Its relics are swallowed in a quasi-religiosity of the neo-liberal creativity, on the one hand and the ecstatic postmodern "resistance", on the other, strengthened by the realities suggested by the world of Jihad.

Ambitious, indeed, is the task of the critical reconstruction of these developments. It is not easy a work to reconstruct and systematically show their roots, their dynamic-ever-changing synthesis and their unification within the framework of the new anti-Semitism as a burning quasi-spiritual ecstasy. Such a work is impossible task. However, we should not abandon our duty to address the suggestive power and fruits of the new anti-Semitism as the current strongest myth; to address the challenge of quasi-meaning as well as individual and collective telos in an era of successful deconstruction of the hubris of eternal truths, objective aims and worthy universal values. How ironic it is that *the triumph of the new anti-Semitism enables the rebirth of (counter) education.*

Counter-education worthy its name in such days must engage fierce rivals and titanic challenges in various levels: 1. Modern humanist education did not prepare us to address such challenges. It did neither imagine its pre-conditions and its commitment to establish a post-metaphysical reality nor did it acknowledge a dystopia or a rival Utopia exterior to the project of killing-God-each-moment-anew. The triumph of the Gnostic god was beyond the prospects of humanist educators from Lessing to Marx, Thomas Mann, Buber or Marcuse. 2. The new space-time relations appear in various, different and even conflicting arenas and prisms that as part of the fragmentation of reality in high-speed arenas or even in mega-speed realities are hard to detect. Even the justification of the expression "the present development" is problematic, an object for a post-structural deconstruction and post-colonial "resistance". It is especially important to note the complex relations between technological, political, cultural and psychic development in such an historical moment of mega-speed and fragmentation. 3. The evasiveness of the theoretical articulations and the unveiling of different arch-enemies to struggle against. The critique targets arch-enemies as diverse as "monotheism", "phallocentrism", "Judeo-Christian civilization", "The West", "America", "Empire" and so forth. All these culminate into one agreed immediate arch-enemy: "Israel". 4. The covenant between postmodern philosophies and capitalist globalization, between the special status of "the victim" of Judeo-Christian civilization and "the client" in a postmodern culture and in face of new age spirituality which is part and parcel of globalizing capitalism, yet incubates some particles of erotic light and remnants of Love of Life. Jewish monotheism, along classic Greek and Roman heritage, and its material and symbolic development as the focal point and impetus of Western spirit and its immanent colonialist drive are in *a moral dept that cannot be repaid*. The infinity and eternity of the West/ monotheism/Judaism and surely that of "Israel" are the two main pillars of the post-colonial political prism of actualizing post-structuralist thought. This is also the well from which steams the quasi-holiness of the counter-violence of the victims in a post-metaphysical era. In the era of the exile of transcendence holiness is deconst-ructed and re-introduced as immanent ecstatic celebration. In an era which surrenders to the dullness and "horizontal" "spiritual" experiences and mysticism of daily life, to the imperatives not of universal moral or almighty God but to those of the logic of the market and the fashion in which the victims are but one of the aspects of the symbolic exchange/recycling and the movement of products *new anti-Semitism becomes a must*. It enables quasi-freedom, quasi-moral excitement and quasi-meaning which are universal and transcending, enabling ecstatic self-positioning in the world.

The pre-conditions for the specific and concrete appearances of the new anti-Semitism are enabled effectively by globalizing capitalism. Globalizing capitalism is not a merely economic phenomenon and it has rich and vital sources, arenas and fruits: psychic, ecological, technological, political and cultural. It is wrong to separate between the privatization drive of current neo-liberalism which flourishes today all over the globe, the post-structuralist quasi-spirituality and the post-colonialist symbolic, emotional and political quasi-moral ecstasies in the midst of the post-metaphysical moment. It is wrong to disregard the connection between nihilism, narcissism and relativism which are so dominant in the rating culture governed by neo-liberalism and the highlighting of the hybrid, net-oriented self and her strong experiences as an "empowering" dimension of the quest for being swallowed by the post-modern Pleasure Machine, as much a mistake it will be to disconnect between post-Fordist economy and the threats to life on earth.

Globalization and its loyal adjunct, glocalization, are economically, culturally, and politically integrated. They co-exist and encourage *the return of the myth*, a zeitgeist in a world from which Spirit was exiled so that the gate was opened for the celebration of the local, the surrendering to the contingent, to the last fashion, to the marginal and to the ever-more-exotic or ever-more-ecstatic; to the various arenas of self-evidence and caprice of "the client" (actually it is "the market", or, to be more precise: the ecstatic-creative meaningless and its imperatives)—just the same as they unreflectively surrender to the self-evidence of the marginalized, the interests of the victims and the refusal to any hierarchy, any claim for a non-contingent yardstick or any claim for universality, objectivity or exclusivity of the kind introduced by the Jewish people and later by the West. The world of Jihad joins this critique and the anti-humanist agenda.

The McWorld, the world of Jihad and the post-colonialist agenda join forces and globalizing capitalism sets the conditions for materializing the common aims of this coalition. These are different manifestations of the post-metaphysical moment; funda-mentalism and "homereturning" into the fundamentals (the world of Jihad), McWorld (affirmation of the capitalist Pleasure Machine in the form of ecstatic daily spiritual experiences ranging from a new fast car to yoga or "kabala courses for daily life") and the quasi-moral excitement and sense of aim and meaning offered by post-colonialist "resistance" and the other prisms of the new myth. These are all manifestations of the (un)truth of the post-metaphysical moment, of the presence of the exile of the killer of God.

The fundamentalism of the world of Jihad, the capitalist Pleasure Machine and the post-colonialist resistance are united in celebrating the destruction of the *hope* of humanist education. Striving in different paths for desolating the processes of modernization as a road to emancipation they unite; they compose different manifestations of the truth of "our" historical moment. Globalizing capitalism, the ever-intensification of the speed of changes, movements and re-cycling in a "flat" world with no "vertical" axis for transcendence and the quasi-spiritual resistance to the Jewish spirit in the form of monotheism, phallocentrism, Enlightenment and Western colonialism are interwoven and united in the new anti-Semitism. It challenges both "Jerusalem" and "Athens" as the impetus and framework of Western God and the immanent colonizing teleological education of the humanist killer of God. New anti-Semitism as *the returning of myth* is dedicated to offer both a grand quasi-spiritual ecstasy and a political alternative within the post-metaphysical hyperreality so that self-forgetfulness will tell itself: "yes, even in our cynical world after all is said and done there is a difference that makes a difference! To enable it we should do more for the "back to Auschwitz" flotilla, reclaim goodness, salvage our soul and destroy the spirit of Jewish monotheism, Israeli ethnocentrism and Western racism by saving the blockaded children of Gaza from Israeli oppression".

These are the pre-conditions of the *new anti-Semitism as the great myth* of our time. **The Jew**, in the form of "the Jewish state", becomes, again, an acid test to the stance of the human: as a Westerner, as a victim of the West, or even as a Jew. The Jew and the Jewish State of Israel are leveled disregarding the theological and the existential tension between them. The new anti-Semite disregards the gap that creates the post-colonialist tension between the (Israeli) claim for nation state and the deconstruction, distrust and hostility toward the modern commitment to truth of the national narrative or the pre-modern imperative of the true religion in a post-metaphysical moment. He does not ask the question of rival moral claims when clashing through different time-space formats—one as a legitimate modern nation-building project and the other a post-colonialist deconstructive moral commitment. The new anti-Semite connects his post-colonial blindness to the truth of the gap between rival moral loyalties to the pre-modern, modern and post-modern Platonic caves to his devotion to the otherness of the victims of the otherness of the Jew as the ultimate Other. He must *destroy the Diasporic essence of the Jewish otherness;* since he is devoted to the truth of the post-colonialist dogma regarding true otherness, victimhood and nomadism. And this concept of *post-colonialist Other as the victim of the diabolic Other, namely, the Jew* is presently unique and irreplaceable. It is very important to elaborate on this question, the question of who is the genuine Other in the center of the new anti-Semitism and its post-colonial educational prisms. We should seriously relate to its devotion to resist both genuine Diasporic life as represented traditionally by Judaism and its *opposite* in the form of devotion for "homereturning" and national bloom as represented by the State of Israel. Sometime the post-colonialists do understand the opposition between Judaism and Zionism but even than they tend to de-legitimate "Israel" on the one hand and resist the truth of eternal Diasporic existence as represented by Judaism, on the other.

The progressive powers of the day, if they still dare to speak about "progress", echoing the logic of the neo-liberal market in a post-structuralist rhetoric relate to the importance of "re-mapping" or challenging "hierarchies" and do not claim to educate for universal values, surely not those of Western humanism or Judeo-Christian monotheism on the educational path toward Utopia. Quite the contrary: present-day post-colonial progressivism is devoted to overcome this emancipatory universalistic tradition which, according to its critiques, quests for *homogeneity* which unavoidably is exclusivist and oppressive as much as the Jewish God (or its universal secularization and materialization in the form of capitalism or Enlightenment) can be.

Post-colonial education offers a grand pedagogical alternative within a rapidly fragmentized world in reaction to and as part of affirming hybridity, contingency, locality, kaleidoscopic realities and quasi-eternal nomadism, on the one hand and ultra-ethnocentrist educational agendas under the flag of "diversity", "multiculturalism" or "post-colonialist education", on the other. The new progressivists are committed to give "voice" to the silenced ones on the road toward radical, multicultural democracy and other manifestations of eternal nomadism and a celebration of differences, clashes, dionystic temporarities, local and contingent alliances and agreements which, according to the post-colonialist promise, will give birth simultaneously to harmony, quasi-spiritual ecstasy and eternal-Diasporic life where everyone is flourishing in a "flat", post-violent reality. At best, it is a myth which brings with it a very naïve Utopia.

The new anti-Semitism is a genuine and most serious educational challenge. On the simplest level, it calls us to address the charge, justified so many times, to our shame, that the discourse concerning the new anti-Semitism actually serves Israel's avoiding moral responsibility to terrible acts. More challenging still is the facing up to the characteristics of the monotheistic tradition and its central concepts such as "chosen people", "universalism", "objective truth", "redemption" and so forth, in a post-metaphysical moment, namely, facing metaphysics and its deconstruction in light of the void left by the exile of the holiness in killing-God-each-moment-anew.

The educational challenge of the new anti-Semitism is here, now, and real. It invites us to courageously address the different responses to *the exile of holiness*, the presence of globalizing capitalism and the demolition of transcendence. It calls us to overcome the hospitality of the greatest, most sophisticated and most unarticulated of present day myths. As such, it enables counter-education to address the roots, the present and the open possibilities for genuine transcendence, or, genuine, responsible, improvised co-poiesis: Diasporic life in what I call *orcha*—the no-mans-land *between* immanence and transcendence. It offers us a serious addressing the spiritual struggle over the identity of the "I", meaning, aim and emancipation/redemption/meaninglessness of Jews, Westerners and all other humans in a post-metaphysical moment, where outside new age spirituality there is no room for "genuine transcendence", meaning and telos, only hatred, quasi-spiritual ecstatic political "resistance" or, alternatively, joining the capitalist Pleasure Machine.

In such a context the Jews, over again, become *the chosen people*; this time chosen by those claiming to be the genuine victims, the injured party of the Jew. In light of their commitment to the holiness of the one and only true God and everlasting anti-dogmatic interpretation: edification of moral imagination as a way of life, Jews became the holy people and its unique moral status and mission as an undefeated burning Love of Life was enabled. Hillel the elder, the most respected Jewish Rabbi tells us that all the Torah might be condensed into one sentence: "love your neighbor as yourself". It is wrong to divide here between love as an epistemological dimension, ethical dimension and ontological dimension. Love is the impetus of Diasporic existence and of Jewish refusal to power and normality. This exclusivist self-conception is represented as the impetus of Western colonialism and oppression and as its present most aggressive and explicit manifestation in the form of "Israel". The new anti-Semitism must unlash this satanic moral fire and destroy "Israel" if it is to save the world from a triumphant history of oppression. Nothing less than that will suffice.

To the complexity, richness and demanding qualities of the new anti-Semitism we are not yet fully equipped to respond. Not even courageous enough; not to mention the desolation of the Enlightened concepts, ideals and drives that are of no much use in face of the suggestive power of the new conquering myths in the dullness of the present historical moment. Maybe we should turn not for an alternative "homereturning" project or to a rival Utopia of perfect dwelling on the humanized earth but rather to a Diasporic hospitality, to an improvised co-poiesis which is essentially religious even in face of the exile of God as well as the exile of the killer of God. *Holiness* and transcendence are possible today from the presence of the infinite in our lives: the near probability of *The End, as the final, most glorious manifestation of human progress*; as a response-ability to the return from exile of the Gnostic god. A return with its awful truth: no "homereturning" exists. It unites us, all humans, conceptually and existentially; makes life as eternal erotic improvisation each-moment-anew relevant more than ever before. Yes, in contrary to the educational message of the new anti-Semitism it enables us to learn from Judaism and from other cultures that Diaspora is not solely a punishment, a disaster or the wrong nomadism leading to ethnocentrism and racism — it is a universal gate for eternal life as responsible, improvising nomads, as part of *derech-eretz* of *orcha*: to whom the new anti-Semitism is but another part of the eternal desert of Life, and as such also one of its oases to be respected, fertilized, yet never dwelt in.

NOTES

[1] Reworked "rational" of the conference, New anti-Semitism—Educational Challenges, University of Haifa June 22, 2009.

6. NEW ANTI-SEMITISM AS THE META-NARRATIVE OF THE NEW PROGRESSIVE THINKING AND CRITICAL PEDAGOGY TODAY

Ilan Gur-Ze'ev: Thank you, Professor Peter McLaren for enabling this conversation. I would suggest we begin our Odyssey by relating to the new challenges faced by the various versions of critical education. I think it is only fair to say that to this very day critical education has not offered a serious response to many of the fundamental changes in human existence, certainly not to the relations between these fundamental changes, their fruits and their implications. What do I mean by relating to the absence of "a serious response"? What I mean here is that assuming we can find common ground among the various trends in Critical Pedagogy, or even in respect of the version you consider the most important for you in light of the current fundamental changes in the human condition, we are called to make a distinction between (1) the general aims of Critical Pedagogy, (2) the standard argumentations and practices of current Critical Pedagogy, and (3) the impetus and the essence of the quest, of the spirit or pneuma that Critical Pedagogy is only an agent of. It is of vital importance for me, Peter, to insist that even if the transformation of the human condition does not allow justification of the standard rhetoric and many of the practices of hegemonic Critical Pedagogy, we should still make every effort to realize our responsibility for its ultimate aims and live in the light of the essence of Critical Theory and Critical Pedagogy. This is our impetus, this is the meeting point of its genesis; the ultimate mission which enables *hope* to become a constitutive and concrete dimension of our lives as creative-lovers, as erotic humans who are earnest concerning the edification of their response-abilities and their Diasporic, improvised co-poiesis. When we get to it in our conversation I will try to suggest that while the standard rhetoric of Critical Pedagogy was overwhelmed by the new anti-Semitism as the current meta-narrative of progressive thinking, it is still of utmost important to uphold our responsibility for the essence of our response-ability and the quest whose deliverer Critical Theory has cultivated itself to become. This essence of the emancipatory quest, however, is negated by current standard rhetoric of Critical Pedagogy. Its success loads additional responsibility onto the search for a new critical language in education and on the possibility of transcending "critique". Genuine counter-education, which will be true to the *essence* of Critical Theory and to the impetus of Critical Pedagogy as a negative Utopia, has become more urgent than ever before. Please, Peter, allow me to begin by relating to four major challenges which, to our shame, are not yet addressed by current new progressivism and critical education even though they have already made obsolete the revolutionary rhetoric of Critical Pedagogy and have unveiled the dangers of its post-colonialist practices. It is my intention

I. Gur-Ze'ev, The Possibility/Impossibility of a New Critical Language in Education, 107–164.
© *2010 Sense Publishers. All Rights Reserved.*

here to offer this reconstruction not in order to domesticate Critical Pedagogy but rather the opposite: to revitalize the Diasporic search and its poiesis to face the dangers, the abysses, the infinite possibilities it bears in their most concrete actualities so that true to its essence and its telos it will radically transcend its dogmatic "radicalism" and the bon ton offered in light of the current new anti-Semitism.

First, we are caught, or to put it in other words we are afflicted, by the brutal historical fact of *the exile of the (humanist) holiness of killing-God-each-moment-anew*. The second dimension of the crisis of "our" present situation contains the theological, philosophical and existential implications of global capitalism, its culture industry and its fruits. Of special importance here are *the intimate relations between the critical language of "the special rights of the victim" and "the special rights of the client"*. The third never-ever faced new reality in the human condition is the objective, yes, Peter, the objective fact that we, and here, finally, we can say unproblematically *"we", are the first humans ever who live in a world in which humanity is technologically capable of total destruction of all life on earth*. Today, *The End* is more real than ever and differs in its kind from previous conceptions of *End* and from previous reactions to the nearness of the end of human history. Its actualization becomes more likely and less troubling by the day, and it is my assertion that it transforms the stance of the human condition, of philosophy and of education. The fourth new aspect of the present change in the human condition is the fact of entering the era/ arena of *mega speed hyper realities*. Entering a radical change in space-time relations on the one hand, and the relations between eternity and the moment on the other; a world where transcendence is impossible nor is it even desired in face of the reaction to the invitation to return "home" into nothingness. All these, Peter, are framed today by the emerging progressive narrative of the new anti-Semitism which becomes, not without the support of Critical Pedagogy, a new universal quasi-spirituality. Presently I will try to show that new anti-Semitism is the new progressive alternative of vital importance for the possibility of the various hegemonic versions of critical education, even for the very quest of enhancing the possibilities of "critique" as transcendence, emancipation and growth.

Critical education today, if true to its telos, should address these four components, which are, of course, interwoven in rich dynamic relations, while nourishing some and abandoning, or losing in life-and-death battles, other peculiarities: interwoven in an ever more surprising manner that destroys, ridicules or re-organizes the optimism, the impetus and the emotional, intellectual, economic and technological preconditions for the project of Enlightenment via critical education. They challenge the idea of linear-accumulative rational-social progress and the very possibility of moral edification; and yet, they do not release us from our moral responsibility while opening new possibilities for meaningful action in the era of the exile of meaning. In this respect, Peter, how is it possible today to defend Critical Pedagogy as an emancipating power and the very Utopia of transcendence, meaning or universal progress? Why should we, and how is it still possible for us, under the new sky, to insist on revolutionary Critical Pedagogy which will be enhanced and guided by strong suggestive myths such as Spartacus on his horse with his big sword, Che Guevara on his motorcycle with his Kalashnikov, and Peter McLaren on the podium with his newest book? There is here a genuine quest for truth, Peter. A genuine striving for salvation. A genuine decision to abandon the Diasporic, sometimes lonely and dangerous path to transcendence. It is a surrender to the "homereturning" project of the ecstatic, consensual "we" and the quasi-religious cathartic breakthrough from current triumphant meaninglessness which should be appreciated. Why? Because they are sincere, Peter. Because fear of the pain of Diasporic existence, which is the essence of "critique" as transcending love, is "authentic": *as a genuine, burning, quasi-sacred self-forgetfulness*. But there are other manifestations of seriousness too, even in a post-metaphysical era. As I have tried to show on so many occasions, self-forgetfulness and the cult of "resistance" are not the only gate still open and Diasporic lovers should go on as an *Orcha* even when the endless desert does not offer "gates", "oases" or convenient enemies and domesticating mantras, Gurus and other pleasures of self-forgetfulness. And yet, while the human, as always and everywhere is attracted by the temptations and invitations of "homereturning" into nothingness, it is of vital importance to face the objective truth that the human condition has changed. We can no longer go on with what we have done until now even for very survival, certainly for *worthy life*. We ought to address the transformation of the preconditions and the possibilities still open for the relation between the human, the world and the holy. Peter, how do you rearticulate, or alternatively why do you resist rearticulating, the justification, the possibilities and the telos of your understanding of Critical Pedagogy in face of the *desolation of its preconditions* on the one hand, and in light of your genuine, religious quest for true quest turning into uncritical-dogmatic acceptance of the critical imagination by your disciples, on the other? How do you explain the truth of the roots of the established Guru-disciple relations in current Critical Pedagogy and the stance of Critical Pedagogy which encourages self-forgetfulness, making you "their" Guru and your deliberations "their" credo on the path to hatred, violence and dogmatism under the flags of "radical critique", "revolutionary multiculturalism" and "post-colonial struggle"? What is the connection between your transformation from a critical educator into a Guru and the transformation of Critical Pedagogy from a manifestation of a humanist attempt to actualize the values of the Enlightenment into a manifestation of the new progressive thinking that is committed to destroy Enlightenment, resist liberal democracy and enhance the ethnocentrism and violence of the most brutal anti-humanist regimes like in the case of Chavez, Ahmadinejad, Nasrallah and Kim Jong-il?

Peter McLaren: To speak of Critical Pedagogy, my good friend Ilan, is, as you must know, an ideological symptom in the same way it is symptomatic to speak of knowledge in the singular. Just as there are many knowledges and systems of intelligibility so are there many critical pedagogies. Even revolutionary critical pedagogies. But you have singled out the reference to a term that I have been using for the last decade of my work, a term that I have taken from the writings of Paula Allman, and understand that you have been following my specific use of the term. In this case, I would argue that your comment is ideologically symptomatic of my use of the term 'revolutionary' more than of my use of the term 'critical' so I will operate under that assumption. As I have written elsewhere, oftentimes when the word 'revolutionary' is used it is characterized—even by avowed leftists—in a way that is dripping with acrimony and derision. It is the stormy petrel of U.S. progressives and I dare say with progressives working, as you are, in other geopolitical contexts. To use the term 'revolutionary' is to cross the threshold of a sacrosanct boundary freighted with the danger of caricature. Here, Ilan, you appear to have ensepulchered the term in the rag-and-bone shop of what you have termed 'irrelevance, dogmatism and violence'. So your question betrays a symptom, one found among many on the left today, a symptom that regrettably reinforces the false perception that revolutionary Critical Pedagogy is a shopworn term that needs to be jettisoned, as if a great ontological divide has been given birth between the struggle for socialism and the struggle for democracy, so wide that one cannot bridge the chasm, forcing a false 'either/or 'choice—this is, after all, a double-sided fallacy, if not a crass caricature.

As an educational project aimed at creating the conditions of knowledge production for bringing about a socialism for the twenty-first century (not a monolithic socialism imposed from above but one contextually specific to its geopolitical conditions of possibility of creation from the ground up) revolutionary Critical Pedagogy cannot be denied on the grounds that socialist struggles in the past have often turned into their opposite. One of the questions Marxist humanists ask themselves is why so many revolutions have turned into their opposite. And that is a question that demands its own interview. And as for its irrelevance, the Venezuelan United Socialist Party has six million members, and clearly revolutionary Critical Pedagogy would not be as irrelevant there, as it is, perhaps, in the academy where both you and I work as academics. Venezuela has, after all, many more members than the 155 members of the Marxian Analysis of Schools, Society, and Education Special Interest Group of the American Education Research Association of which I am a member. I work a great deal in Latin America, and more recently in Europe, and from my own experience I would say that the struggle for socialism has never been more relevant than it is today. Revolutionary Critical Pedagogy is an attempt to bring knowledge into dialogue with other knowledges in a way that rearticulates the geopolitical order of knowledge production horizontally rather than vertically. Not only is it an attempt to re-cognize knowledge formation from a historical materialist standpoint, but to interrogate critically all knowledge production from a social, political and ethical standpoint as part of a larger project of creating a post-capitalist future. It includes questions of epistemology and epistemicide (the denaturing, despoiling and enfeebling of indigenous knowledges related to property, nature, and kinship and other contexts), but also participates actively at multiple levels of class struggle, recognizing that money buys only what we have lost, what alienation has vanquished among us, under capitalist social relations, relations which, of course, are constantly racialized, gendered, and sexualized according to the needs and purposes of the transnational capitalist class and reinitiated according to the strategies of the corporate elite. It is also an attempt to address the issue of xeno-racism (racism directed towards ex-colonial migrants in Western European countries). But this is not a call to mutilate racism, sexism, speciesism or white supremacy by imposing some monolithic version of universalism but a call to pluriversality. That is, to open up the veins of universalism to an infusion of voices from below, a collective expression that leads to a plurality of narratives and conceptions of what constitutes both consciousness and reason. There is no universalism that is not populated with the voices of others, that is innocent of the cries of the subaltern, of *les damnés* and these voices of people struggling from below need to be heard, not in some patronizing way, but by making the path as we walk, horizontally and not from a position of ascendancy, not from above. Here I would invoke the spirit and the praxis Zapatistas' "preguntando caminamos", or 'walking we ask questions'—the way of the guerrillero pedagogue. As an engineer friend of Eduardo Galleano told him: "único que se hace desde arriba son los pozos," (the only thing that you can make from up to down are holes"). So I see revolutionary Critical Pedagogy as a shared project of producing critical social thought, and fostering the creation of a theory and philosophy of praxis by which to interrogate the limitations of occidental thought and the circumscriptions afforded by Critical Theory, critical race theory, Marxist humanist discourse, and other languages of critique. Revolutionary Critical Pedagogy is an attempt to bring to the table other ways of thinking about and acting in relation to and against modernity/coloniality and the epistemologies of empire. These "other knowledges" attempt to disturb the hegemonic ontological categories that have saturated the imaginary of our age, imprisoning us in the normalcy of their ways of knowing. Because we know that there is knowledge that does not know itself, that there are disavowed beliefs and that there are suppositions in our work and in our daily life that we are not aware of adhering to ourselves, we must admit that Critical Pedagogy as the practice of freedom would only be fully possible in a society that no longer needed it. But even so, can we, as critical agents, act in such a way that our choices retroactively open up their own possibility so that our actions can alter the values of the propositions about the past that have excluded the possibility of alternatives to capitalism and its ensuing barbarism? Can we insert a new possibility into the past so that the present can be won for equality and social justice? Do we need to act as if the future one wants to bring about is already here, as a way of undoing the inevitable? Can we create an inedito viable, what Freire described as possible places for humanization? Or in asking such questions are we merely escaping into fantasies that are reliable only because they can never be attained? Are we simply, therefore, preempting experiences of the problem in our attempt to refine the future? Are we, in effect, dishonoring the disorder of experience? That being said, has Critical Pedagogy or revolutionary Critical Pedagogy been impervious to critique? It certainly has, at least in its historical formation, and of course it attempts to learn from its critics, and you have been one of its very honorable critics. Revolutionary Critical Pedagogy, as with any system of intelligibility, needs to be open to the strengths and limitations of different logics, rationalities, systems of classification and structures of power. After all, all of us would be better off if we would benefit from the epistemic force of the local histories of subaltern groups in enable to re-enunciate power in a democratic mode, to expand the potential for coordinated growth and development, making us an enemy of forgetfulness (rather than being committed, as you say we are, to self-forgetfulness) and to be committed to a protagonistic revolutionary praxis from the point of view of the most invisible among us—*los olvidados*—who have so treacherously been denied in the Anglosphere and elsewhere all bonds of human solidarity and compassion. As I have written at great length, many times, revolutionary Critical Pedagogy is about reading the word and the world dialectically, in the spirit of Freire, that is, it is about understanding and transforming the reciprocally revealed relationship between consciousness and the world, and that which lies beyond the world, by being attentive to the unity of diversities in the individual and in the world that unites both the large and the small, the powerful and the powerless, in the dinergic unity of social life. This is what I consider a philosophy of praxis, discovering the deep-rooted unity below the surface diversity of the world without imposing it. Revolutionary educators are committed to discovering it together, in our shared human wholeness, as enemies of deception and lies and as friends of the both human and non-human worlds. But here we must be cautious. Extremely so. We can't fall prey to grandiose illusions and must always be open to criticism. Your sage criticisms have helped us in this regard, Ilan. We might have grand ideals, but how are these to be put into effect in the world?

Critical Pedagogy should neither remain Olympian in its self-assurance nor condescending in its skepticism. Rather it must make its home in the provisional and promiscuous domain of praxis—in making the road by walking, without blueprints or prescriptions. As a language of the unacceptable, revolutionary Critical Pedagogy is a cultural artifact that needs to be protected from those who would condemn praxis as a distraction from high theory. Critical Pedagogy is not only about creating the pedagogical context for teaching ourselves the stories of others, but it is about a new way of hearing what we say that enables us to listen in new ways, and hopefully learn to speak in ways that are open to others, while recognizing that the choices we have made for ourselves and for others are not real choices. What can we do Ilan? We can try to recognize the present in the present. And we can ask ourselves, along with Zizek, Badiou and others: Is the past amenable to change as a result of new occurrences and solidarities in the present? Can we remake the past—that is, the inevitability of capitalist forces and relations of production—with our revolutionary praxis of the present? Can we alter the capitalist past with the supervention of socialism? Can we readjust the capitalist past and recognize that it was not the best of all possible ways of overcoming necessity but was a form of barbarism that can finally be uprooted in the twenty-first century? So far, such retroactive causality has worked in the interest of capital, since capitalism has created its socialist predecessors as inevitable totalitarian monsters. So I would ask: Can we reshape the conditions that shape us? Can we, in the frailty of our humanity, overdetermine the past that is set to determine us? Can we achieve some degree of control over the scope and nature of the causes that will determine us—that is, move us into oblivion perhaps, in terms as you say, of the total destruction of all life on earth? Can we, as Deleuze or Zizek might put it in their compendious accounts, rewrite the virtual eternal past, and transform retroactively the virtual fantasmatic coordinates of our existence and thus discover—and change—our preexisting fate? That is, can we learn from living in the future anterior, where contingency always appears as necessity? Can we make a difference that makes a difference?

IGZ: My dear friend Peter, you know how much I admire your genuine quest, your firmness against the truth of the historical moment, your determination, countering the realities of the day: insisting on *Utopia* in a post-metaphysical moment; in face of suffering, injustice and fear on the one hand, and dogmatism, hatred and favoring "effective violence" by some of our more enthusiastic students on the other. I see your personal attempt as a tragic attempt of unique worth because it signifies for me the essence of Critical Theory as invested in your devotion to transcendence, to refusal of injustice, to a genuine search for the genuine search. Your erotic devotion to the holy in light of the exile of holiness by an almost omnipotent anti-humanistic reality is of special importance for me because it actualizes holiness even if solely in a negative erotic manner. But as you remember from the Platonic Symposium, heavenly Eros by his nature cannot become an enduring-positive reality and he is more of an invitation to eternal-Diasporic life as a worthy Odyssey. I say this without necessarily accepting your philosophy and even with less common ground with the kind of acceptance realized by your disciples. At its best, for me Peter, your attempt and your personality signify devotion to the *refusal* to the suggestion of "homereturning" into the thingness, into the consensus, into the continuum of the *Same* even if the actual reception of your work enhances its transformation into its negative. I think too many students of Critical Pedagogy—revolutionary Critical Pedagogy included—gets the impression that Critical Pedagogy is less about self-responsibility, self-reflection and overcoming any self-evidence, as radical as one may be, and more about *an ecstatic devotion to the struggle against the self-evidence of the West*, its hierarchies and the suffering it inflicts. It is so unfortunate, Peter, that so many of our more passionate-critical students do not challenge self-evidence and normalizing education as such, in all their manifestations, surely not in our texts and in their conventions, fears, deliberations and practices. Instead they are concerned with negating the "bad" Western self-evidence as against the "good" self evidence—the self-evidence of the oppressed or the radical-emancipatory self-evidence of Peter McLaren and other Gurus of Critical Pedagogy, who offer them a sense of orientation, an unproblematic commitment to a quasi-holy aim; equipping them with false self-respect, granting them misleading psychological impetus and stability, deceptive intellectual fruitfulness and political rewards from other progressive movements, organizations and individuals, who are also overwhelmed by the *new anti-Semitism as the most powerful narrative under the new progressive sky* which safely leads them to the most rewarding self-forgetfulness in our era: Thanatos camouflaged as Eros, dressed with beauty and with the promise of the flags of "critique" and "resistance". It is a hymn to a new progressive education via the texts of the counter-Enlightenment heroes, proto-Nazi philosophers and their new neo Marxists (Badiou, Zizek) and their post-structuralist followers on the path toward a victory on the Jewish spirit and its realization in the form of white's racism and Western colonialism. It is so sad to see today many of the Critical Pedagogy thinkers dwelling in Nietzsche, Heidegger, Carl Schmitt, Blanchot, Deleuze and Zizek. This anti-Enlightenment ecstasies of the new progressive thinking is a reaction to the exile of holiness in "our" postmetaphysical moment; a quest to return back "home" into *thingness*, into the *Same*, in the form of rejoining the lost totality, returning into ecstasies in the absence of transcendence: "radicalism" as a counter-gift to the gift of meaninglessness which offers a return to the roots of sympathy with the cosmos of the kind that was possible before the constitution of self-conscious, alienation and exile of holiness via the gate of a totalistic-cathartic-quasi-holy emancipating praxis. Revolutionary pedagogy becomes the path *back to the primordial soup*. I have to say it. I have to say it loudly even if it is awfully painful even to begin thinking about it: my own work is very much in line with this tendency. It is part and parcel of the new anti-Semitism I refer to, and I think, Peter, it is important for us to seriously address the relevance of it to our work and to the work of other critical pedagogues. Yes, Peter, your work too. We should ask ourselves: what is it in our work which makes it such a fertile ground for *ecstatic self-forgetfulness* and such a dogmatic resistance to self-reflection within the framework of new anti-Semitism?

Let us begin with the first step: challenging as critical pedagogues our own work and its fruits. You mentioned the relevance of Critical Pedagogy to revolutionary Venezuela today. I will relate to it, and I will associate it to the reception of Critical Pedagogy in Israel, where I have been working very hard as a critical pedagogue for the last twenty years.

Please, Peter, let me refer to the dogmatism and self-forgetfulness initiated by the critical language in education within arenas where it is considered super-relevant for the freedom activists. Of course it is no less important to study the dogmatism and lack of courage among its opponents. Venezuela and Israel might serve as good examples, as the one is for you a focus of sympathy and fervent support and the other a manifestation of resistance to revolutionary praxis and represents white colonial terror.

In both examples, Peter, Critical Pedagogy is in service of an explicitly post-colonialist agenda that is committed to the wellbeing of the entire population, not of an oppressive elitist minority, be it a corrupt oligarchy in Venezuela or an advanced racist high-tech Zionist society in Israel. Critical Pedagogy, in these two examples, is committed to support anti-Western revolutions all over the globe and challenge the West's philosophical, psychological, political and economic foundations and practices while keeping silence or advocating other violent cultures and the essential challenges of human existence such as love. But at what price, dear Peter! What is the philosophical impetus which is here the womb, the engine and the represent-ational apparatus of the aims and practices of this critical language? Let us be more specific on this matter and focus on the case of revolutionary Venezuela and your support for this regime. Critical Pedagogy in this case serves a revolutionary regime that is corrupt no less, and maybe even more, than its oligarchic predecessors. The officers of Chavez who run the country not only receive an anti-Semitic education, they in parallel get very rich, build luxury villas and buy like crazy diamonds and real estate in face of 60% unemployment and record-high oil revenues. If you talked unofficially with these militaristic-oriented friends I would not be surprised if you heard not much about the importance of the truth, of responsibility or transparency in private and public affairs: you would hear much more that "Its our turn now! Don't you dare take it from us with deceptive language praising honesty or accountability". Maybe you would hear that "The poor are now to be enriched and that is us, so it is actually less about corruption and more about social justice".

Anti-transparency and disregard of responsibility in all levels of life are justified by the holiness of "the revolution" or "post-colonial emancipation". They certainly will not stress the importance of education for accurate analysis and true reporting to oneself and to others, and will not challenge machismo as a threat to a free society. For me, Peter, when *education to refusing responsibility and abandoning self-critique is actualized under the flag of "emancipation"* it is especially sad. And do not forget, dear friend, that never in recorded history was a revolutionary militaristic experiment actualized in such a privileged context, equipped with so many billions that keep on coming to the revolutionary government with very little work or danger. At the same time it is clearly a machoist-authoritative regime with a personality cult of Chavez as Leader Maximus. Critical Pedagogy does its best to enhance this personality cult and the ecstatic revolutionary dogmatism which it reproduces, forgetting the advice it could have on this topic from Antisthenes, Jesus, Montaigne, Freire or Adorno. Hardly ever in the current post-colonialist discourses is it possible to criticize Chavez, his regime and its Critical Pedagogy without being intimidated as a racist, a colonialist, or even worse as "a Zionist". Despite these rhetorical conventions of revolutionary Critical Pedagogy let us have a closer look at the Chavez regime and its educational agenda. I think we should go into it. We should also ask ourselves what is it in this version of critical education that draws to the Chavez regime and his Critical Pedagogy enthusiastic admirers to embrace personal and conceptual friendship with the most cruel, totalitarian and anti-Semitic people and regimes on earth: from the Hamas terrorist group that grabbed the Palestinian leadership in Gaza to "Dear leader" Kim Jong-Il, the dictator of North Korea, to Ahmadinejad in Iran. What is it in this critical language that leads it to a furious search for weapons in the Jewish school at Caracas and to intimate connections with traditional anti-Semites on the one hand and with the new anti-Semitism on the other? It is a Critical Pedagogy that sides with Ward Churchill in the USA and Mohamed Bachri and Teddy Katz in Israel. The theoretical dimension and the political dimensions are of utmost importance, Peter, of course; yet one should ask what is wrong with a revolutionary Critical Pedagogy which *enthusiastically*, not only strategically, sides with the most aggressive anti-humanists and anti-Semites one could meet in our time. To my mind, you cannot separate the post-colonial commitment to overcome the supposed immanent colonialism and oppression-drive of the Judeo-Christian civilization and supporting the pedagogical message of today's Iran which not only summons a world convention of Holocaust deniers but also officially threatens the Jewish state with another Holocaust while stoning to death women who went with an open heart to their lover or running cars back and forth over the hand of an eight-year old boy caught stealing bread in the streets of Tehran as a pedagogical lesson of great value. Something is *essentially* wrong with revolutionary Critical Pedagogy, my dear Peter, if these are the intimate friends of Critical Pedagogy and its Utopia. Of course, there are also political maneuvers, unsuccessful intrigues and rhetorical manipulations that you might find inevitable in light of the grand mission and the threat on the part of its enemies. But I think there is more to it. There is much more to it. Fundamentally, what here we refer to is not a strategic miscalculation or the price of building a diverse revolutionary coalition in face of the eschatological moment we are approaching in our struggle against "the West". It must be something much more *fundamental*. Something which concerns me, you, and our Critical Pedagogy friends more than it has to do with the personal character or even the nature of the politics of Sheikh Nasrallah, President Ahmadinejad or Leader Maximus Hugo Chavez. More broadly, it is *fundamental* to understanding the work of ideologies in a post-metaphysical era, and the paths by which the new progressivism initiates and recycles the greatest deliverers of the new anti-Semitism who prosper today in large parts of the radical progressive circles.

Even before going into the theoretical level, I must share with you one of the hardest experiences I have in my twenty years of actualizing Critical Pedagogy, challenging Zionism and working for the Palestinians. Maybe something similar happens in revolutionary Venezuela, where your work is respected so much and where it is so instrumental to the success of the revolutionary experience. As for me, Peter, I do reflect on the strange ways in which my critique of the State of Israel is taken up in service of neo-Nazi groups, Hamas terrorism, standard new anti-Semitism and even the most dogmatic tendencies among my own students. From here, I believe, we should further reexamine the roots of Critical Pedagogy and not only address the ways in which some of our work serves so well the KKK, the neo-Nazi groups, Hamas or the Iranian Islamic Republic. A personal note, dear Peter: one of my most embarrassing experiences is *facing the fruits of my own work* as a critical educator—a work that as you know caused me to be called the Jewish anti-Semite, caused me to be included in the list of the eight most dangerous academics in Israel, and so forth. Essential to this experience is that Critical Pedagogy in its post-colonialist prism, but also in other frames such as radical feminism, queer theories and revolutionary multiculturalism, ended up with students who "found" their voice by dogmatically recycling my work and turning it into a list of mantras, clichés and rhetorical rituals which are anything but authentic, reflective, edifying or emancipating. According to my personal experience, too many times *the struggle for political emancipation has become conditioned by self-deception*, intellectual cowardice and support for the victims' self-evidence and violence; current critical language in education, as it is actualized by my own Critical Pedagogy, too often does not insist on painful, demanding responsibility—only for rewarding and consensual-radical-rewarding "responsibility". No enhancement of self-reflection, empowering courage against the conventions of the self-satisfying "radicals" which have become a closed, self-referential dogma for myself and for so many of my students. It certainly did not open gates to responsible improvised existence of co-poiesis and eternal nomadism. In Israel there is not much *Love of Life* in this kind of successful critique that I meet among of the students who admire my work and the prospects of Critical Pedagogy. Many of my students end up not only in self-forgetfulness under the flag of "critique" and "radical" dogmas. They end up in support of explicit deception and effective manipulations, and favor brutal, direct violence under the banner of overcoming Judeo-Christian colonialism.

Dear Peter, as one can see in Uli Edel's 2008 film "der Baader Meinhof Complex" the opening of the gate for a sacred violence opens the heavens for violence itself as the supreme value. I cannot avoid acknowledging that in this context, and also in some other critical arenas, this support for the victims' counter-violence ends up by *celebrating violence as an aesthetic ideal and existential counter-drug-against-sleeping-to-death* in a post-metaphysical moment. Here Critical Pedagogy offers a celebration of violence against Love of Life, against responsibility and against the possibility of Diasporic dialogue. As one of my best Critical Pedagogy students said, after praising the importance of Critical Pedagogy in the service of the total liberation of Palestine and purifying it of all its Jewish presence, "If my son joins one of the terrorist groups here I will not try to stop him, I will salute him!" It is so sad not because it is so extreme, Peter, but because it is so genuine and typical; it is sad because it so illumines the other side of Critical Pedagogy and the ideology of praising difference, otherness and contingency in the service of self-forgetfulness or dogmatic collective struggle for the final victory over "colonialism", "the West" or **The Jew**.

It is my conviction that actual resistance to injustice and to the instrumentalization of the human spirit should be resisted and offered a creative alternative. Here I do agree with you. How unfortunate it is, however, that Critical Pedagogy more than once becomes an important manifestation of the enslavement of the free spirit and of normalizing our human fellows, manipulating their genuine suffering, fear and disorientation, to end in a dogmatic cult of "resistance" and "critique" as a way of "empowerment" which is, actually, a strong and specially effective route to *self-forgetfulness*. In light of my experience, Peter, we should face the truth that only too often current Critical Pedagogy is either irrelevant to many in certain arenas, or relevant in the wrong sense in other arenas. Either way, we, critical educators, should reflect on the kind of relevance and the fruits it bears as a challenge, as a danger— not solely as a gate to new beginnings or to comfortable, rewarding self-indulgence of the Guru and his leading friends with incomes of thousands of dollars for a lecture in an unending list of invitations or indentured disciples as partners in our "dialogues" and stable, enduring self-indulgence as the vanguard of present-day progressivism. It is hard to deny that the central figures of Critical Pedagogy are becoming closer to the position of Gurus than to the challenge of an ever-painful-challenging Socrates. Here I will mention only one point: the successful joining forces of Critical Pedagogy with the *attack against the essence of Western Spirit*—actually against Spirit as such; against the very drive for transcendence, individuality and freedom.

This success of Critical Pedagogy is fertilized by post-structuralist sources and it bears fruits that Plato, Descartes, Nietzsche, Marx and Adorno could not even imagine. Later in our conversation I will try to be more systematic in presenting the claim that today the commitment to overcome the essence of Western civilization finds its fertile arena in the framework of the new anti-Semitism as the Zeitgeist of "our" dull historical moment with special relevance for these very same circles, which until the last generation were the most progressive in the West. It is not so much that they stopped their commitment for progress: it is much more a change in the orientation of progressive activity in our time. I see much urgency in critically addressing these challenges. Such an attempt cannot be easy, conventional and without much pain and embarrassment, sometimes even self-destruction and re-constitution. It should begin, however. It should be begun at once, and by people like me and you. Peter, it is not a responsibility we can or should cast off and transfer to others, or avoid altogether. If our best students become dogmatic or surrender to hatred, to the "effective violence of the oppressed", to the celebration of the exile of Spirit or to the festivity of the End of Life, we cannot keep on avoiding a serious critique of the recycling of our rewarding rhetorical radicalism. We should rethink and challenge who we are, the grounds and routes of our routinely-recycled rhetoric and the reasons for our radicalism and sense of victimization as a gate to rewarding over-comfortable life as "radicals". At least, I know this is a challenge I should address. I try addressing it within my Diasporic philosophy and its collision with the triumph of new anti-Semitism.

PM: You have put many important challenges before us, and personalized them in a way that underlies their urgency for the left—not just in the United States and Israel, but internationally. Let me begin by addressing your concern about Venezuela. I have been to Venezuela numerous times at the invitation of Bolivarian educators, and continue to give talks and work with teachers and activists who support the revolution (which is not to say that they are not also critical of it, and express that criticism freely without fear or censure). One day at Miraflores Palace, during the days of the Bush administration, President Chavez told me that while we must work together to fight against unjust wars being wages on peoples in the name of democracy, we must remain in solidarity with the people of the United States who are working for social justice and liberation. After thanking me and a colleague of mine for the pedagogical work we have been doing, he never the less invited us to consider the Bolivarian revolution—and the work of Simon Rodriguez in particular—as an inspiration that can help us deepen our own project. There is no question in my mind that Chavez is sincere about his commitment to socialism and social justice. By enfranchising Venezuela's vast working-class through an attack on neoliberalism and a channeling of increased oil revenues into social projects aimed at increasing educational opportunities and medical treatment for the poor, he has not yet built a socialist state but rather is creating the conditions of possibility for a socialist alternative to capitalism—a socialism for the twenty-first century that is specifically Venezuelan. Now I am not saying Chavez is a Che Guevara redivivus. But I admire him, as I do Fidel Castro, but also, of course, I am not unqualified in my admiration. I have not witnessed dictatorial repression of those who speak out against the revolution. The opposition to Chavez in Venezuela (the ruling classes) is robust and the majority of the mainstream press and television is openly critical of Chavez. In fact, when I have feared for my safety the most has been in the presence of the fanatical opposition to Chavez—who loathe Chavez's commitment to the poor and the weak, and who deride him for his indigenous and African heritage (they frequently refer to him as a 'monkey'). When my colleague and I were invited to be present at Alo Presidente, Chavez's weekly television show, we found ourselves sitting close to Nicaragua's polemical poet and guerrilla/mystic of the revolution, Ernesto Cardenal. (Cardenal, by the way, left the FSLN in 1994 because he was harshly critical of the authoritarian turn of the Sandanistas led by Daniel Ortega, and he stated before the 2006 Nicaraguan General Elections that "I think it would be more desirable an authentic capitalism, as Montealegre's would be, than a false Revolution"). Cardenal stood up after Chavez remarked to the audience about imagining a new relationship of solidarity and anti-imperialist struggle between people of good will in the United States and those in Venezuela. Cardenal referred to Chavez a prophet who was proclaiming a desire for a mystical union among people from opposing nations based on love—and I think he was echoing Jose Marti, if I am correct on that:

> Mr. President, you have said some things that are very important and moreover are also prophetic... when I was a monk my teacher prophesized that one day the people of the United States and the people of Latin America were going to unite but not with an economic union, nor political, nor military, but a mystic union, of love, of two peoples (or nations) loving each other. I have now heard this from you and I want this to be revealed because it is something that hasn't been heard. I have heard it from my teacher and now you have made it a prophecy [translated by Nathalia Jaramillo].

Well, I don't want it to be said I am affirming Chavez as a prophet, but I am trying to counter the worldwide propaganda against Chavez by the transnational capitalist class. I think it is important to understand Chavez and his alliance with Iran in the context of imperialism's grand legacy and the role played by the United Sates. You know that ignoring the legacy of colonialism and imperialism only worsens its effects, Ilan. Do you remember when Pope Benedict XVI, who as Cardinal Joseph Ratzinger headed the Congregation for the Doctrine of the Faith (organized much the same way as when it was known as the Holy Inquisition), was a founding board member with "Neilsy" Bush of the Foundation for Interreligious and Intercultural Research and Dialogue that was created in Geneva Switzerland in 1999. It wasn't that long ago in Aperecida, Brazil that this Pope attacked grassroots Catholic activists who were still influenced by liberation theology, a theology he tried to crush when he was a cardinal. While in Brazil, he made the outrageous claim that indigenous populations had welcomed the European priests who had arrived with the conquistadores, claiming that they had been "silently longing" for Christianity. He also said that colonial-era evangelization involving the proclaiming of Jesus and his Gospel "did not at any point involve an alienation of the pre-Colombus cultures, nor was it the imposition of a foreign culture." I was pleased to see that Chavez joined indigenous groups in condemning the Pope's remarks, claiming that Benedict XVI has ignored the enslavement and genocide of indigenous peoples in Latin America and the destruction of their native cultures, and has also ignored what in some cases amounts to the complicity of the Catholic Church in such violence and destruction. Chavez proclaimed that "the bones of the indigenous martyrs of these lands are still burning." Now here I would like to echo some remarks by Arlo Kempf, who in his development of anti-colonial theory as a holistic response to oppression and exploitation underscores the importance of excavating the archaeology of the present in order to address and resist the intergenerational persistence of empire and the broad colonial trends linking past centuries to the present. He notes that in every inhabited region of the world, indigenous people are waging some form of anti-colonial struggle—they are resisting amputation, erasure, and genocide. He remarks that indigenous people throughout the world have no Israel to recover from their holocausts and have seen no end to their holocausts and that there has been no Treaty of Versailles because, as he puts it, the bad guys are still winning. We talk about modernity, Ilan. And Critical Theory, and the Frankfurt School and critical media literacy and radical democracy, and yet indigenous people, as Kempf notes, are doing battle with the European colonialism of the 17th, 18th, 19th and 20th centuries.

Clearly the legacy of colonial violence lives on, and not only in Latin America, but in North America as well. Racial hierarchies still spill across multiple dimensions of social life is not epiphenomenal to capitalism. That is, it is not derivative from or antecedent to capitalism but constructive of the very process of capitalist accumulation worldwide and the colonial and neo-colonial interaction of Western imperialist powers with non-Western peoples. Of course, these actions by Chavez in no way should cause us to be less critical of all revolutionary regimes, for we have seen many regimes that claim to be leftist revolutionary sin against their own values, preach wealth but produce the most grinding poverty, teach about love and solidarity and comradeship but inflict war and repression, salute democracy but egregiously violate human rights. Kafka wrote about the modern world in which the irrational has become the rational and where lies have become the new truth. So we must remain vigilante, and hold out for dialogue, for co-operation, for mutuality. Venezuela, in my view, is not proposing an ultimate horizon for naturalizing the anti-Semitism of the Iranian regime or of Hamas. The acts of the Venezuelan leadership, I believe, are conditioned by a set of circumstances tethered to recent attempts by the United States to bring down the socialist revolution in Venezuela and to continue historically its violent legacy of imperialist war—economic and military. Are reactionary ideologies encoded here, making this an unholy alliance? I don't believe that such an alliance makes it incapable for proponents of the Bolivarian revolution to examine or question their own revolutionary principles. I do not see this alliance as Chavez advocating the reprehensible values of the Iranian regime in terms of its repression of women, its execution of homosexuals, and the brutality of its religious fundamentalism and anti-Semitism. I am disappointed in Chavez embracing the leadership of Iran, especially so soon after a Holocaust denial conference in which Iran hosted the infamous former member of the Klu Klux Klan, David Duke. I think this is highly problematic in many ways. As far as Iran is concerned, Chavez might be thinking "the enemy of my enemy is my friend". But this is an insufficient reason for uncritically making such a gesture of solidarity. I find it hard to believe that Chavez himself is anti-Semitic. But yes, we have to question this alliance on more than geo-strategic grounds.

But the Bolivarian revolution has a momentum of its own. It is larger than every decision Chavez makes. Never the less, we need to exercise our best judgment, and not uncritically endorse everything the government does. We are criticalists, after all. Not contrarians, but criticalists.

But consider this, Ilan. Does not United States foreign policy constitute the greatest threat to world peace? The United States and Israel are considered to be— in fact, they are—imperialist allies that participate in crimes against humanity that are often disguised as self-defense or the defense of democracy. We don't need to rehearse Israel's oppression of the Palestinian people, or the United States' extermination of its indigenous peoples or its history of slavery, and racism and white supremacist patriarchal capitalism—our readers, I am sure are well aware of this history. But consider this. On June 4, 2009, President Obama admitted in a speech to the Middle East that the United States played a role in the overthrow of the democratically elected Iranian government (he was referring to the CIA overthrow of Prime Minister Mohammed Mossadegh), but we can now see the hypocrisy in US interference in the Iranian elections; Washington has been supporting Mousavi, the opponent of Ahmadinejad, because Ahmadinejad is, as Bill Blum reports, the Officially Designated Enemy of the United States, and that is why in the US media we didn't hear anything about Mousavi and his complicity in the attacks on the US embassy and military barracks in Beirut in 1983, which killed 200 Americans, or the 1988 truck bombing of a US Navy installation in Naples, Italy which killed five persons. (And do you really believe the US did not tacitly support the recent 'golpe' in Honduras and the kidnapping of President Zelaya? The US has intervened in a dramatic way in at least 30 elections around the world since World War II). But think about this—US warships are constantly patrolling the waters surrounding Iran; the US is constantly funding Iranian dissidents, and, as Bill Blum and Seymour Hirsch have reported, have used Iranian groups to carry out terrorists attacks inside Iran. They have kidnapped Iranian diplomats in Iraq, they have kidnapped Iranian military personnel in Iran and taken them to Iraq, they have manipulated Iran's currency and international financial transactions, and they have imposed political and economic sanctions against Iran. I am not a supporter of the current Iranian regime, again, let me make this clear. I am trying to articulate a context for understanding why two countries might join together to forge a strategic anti-imperialist alliance against the United States. Now let's look at Venezuela. In 2006, the US Army's 4th Psychological Operations Group (Airborne) arrived in Colombia and began implementing a strategy of pushing the FARC and the Colombian civil conflict into Venezuelan territory. This occurred at the moment when the US State Department and the Pentagon also started to publicly accuse Venezuela of collaborating with terrorism, specifically by referring to alleged dealings with the FARC. The United States House Foreign Affairs Subcommittee on International Terrorism and Nonproliferation, held a hearing titled "Venezuela: Terrorism Hub of South America?", and declared that "Venezuela, under President Hugo Chavez, has tolerated terrorists on its soil and has forged close relationships with officially designated state sponsors of terrorism: Cuba, Iran and North Korea. Colombian terrorist groups use Venezuelan territory for safe haven..." So this was coordinated with the transnational capitalist/imperialist press who began to associate Venezuela— in particular, the Chavez regime—with terrorism.

Recognize, please that the US Army's 4th Psychological Operations Group (Airborne) is the only active psychological operations unit. The official mission of the 4th Psychological Operations Group (Airborne) is to deploy internationally and conduct psychological operations and "Civil Affairs" (in other words, subversion) that support Washington's government agencies and its allies. As Eva Golinger has noted, the personnel of the 4th Group include regional experts and linguists and marketing and publicity specialists trained in the most powerful ways of influencing public opinion and who work in technical areas such as journalism, radio operations, graphic design, newspaper business, illustration, and long-range tactical communications. This group worked with the state owned petroleum industry in Venezuela to sabotage acts against the Venezuelan industry at the end of the year 2002, with the goal of forcing President Hugo Chávez out of power. The United States' most powerful team of psychological operations is working actively against Venezuela, classifying President Chavez as a "dictator" in international public opinion. As Golinger has noted, psychological operations are considered by the Pentagon to be their "most powerful weapon" to date. Do not the corporate media in the United State control traditional sources of information? Do they not serve the interests of the transnational capitalist class? So when, in 2007, Iranian President Mahmoud Ahmadinejad and President Chavez agreed to form a strategic alliance between their countries to defend common interests and signed four bilateral agreements in the areas of energy, finance, and industry—it is understandable that they would want to continue to work together to "defeat the empire." Chavez expressed gratitude towards the Iranians for their help in the recent installation of milk processing plants and corn processing plants in Venezuela, as well as the vehicle assembly plant "venirauto" and the joint tractor factory "Veniran Tractor." Clearly, Chavez wants to create a multipolar world, and is committed to fighting against a unipolar world dominated by the United States. Now I would hope, in time, that Chavez would challenge the Iranian regime on the repression of its people, its women, gays and lesbians and religious pluralists. But what about violence, and terrorism? A theologian friend of mine, Michael Rivage-Seul, in his excellent book, The Emperor's God, refers to the real God of the United States as violence. Let me summarize some of his ideas, ideas that I have written elsewhere.

Dom Helda Camera and Oscar Romero spoke of a "bloody trinity" of three levels of violence: structural violence or first-level violence or violence of the father (social, economic, political, and military systems and arrangements, codified in law and custom that are responsible for tens of thousands of innocent deaths throughout the world each day); revolutionary violence or second-level violence or violence of the son (responses to first-level, structural violence); and reactionary violence or third-level violence or violence of the evil spirit (the state's reply to acts of rebellion against structural violence). While structural violence (i.e., "the economic 'rules of the game' demanding that a world awash with food destroy or warehouse the excess produce rather than share it with the children starving" at the bottom of the economic ladder, the result being that "those children die as surely and predictably as if guns had been placed to their heads, and triggers pulled"), prevails in today's imperial regimes and their client states, revolutionary violence is the only violence condemned by such states. Yet according to Rivage-Seul, revolutionary violence is the only violence that can be theoretically justified, "as peasants and workers [seek] to defend their families from aggressions of the rich represented in the first and third levels". Jesus was likely an anti-imperialist, yet he, nonetheless, distanced himself from second-level violence, as well as from the

Roman Empire's first level of violence. Jesus, according to Rivage-Seul, understood that second-level violence would provoke a reactionary third-level violence and nothing would be changed (as his parable about the absentee landlord and his tenants illustrated). He ultimately rebuked the worship of a divinized violence. And while structural violence in and by the United States is often ignored, at least within the United States controlled as it is my the corporate media, it is common practice to reject revolutionary violence out of hand. And while the practice of Jesus clearly challenges us to implement the practice of non-violent resistance, Rivage-Seul asserts that it is inappropriate for those of us in the so-called First World to insist that resisters in underdeveloped (read as 'overexploited') nations adopt strategies and tactics of non-violent resistance in situations where they must actually defend the 'least of the brethren' in contexts shaped by extremely violent structures financed by U.S. tax dollars. In any case, we see the gross condemnation of second-level violence while excusing systematic aggression in service to U.S. corporate interests. Those who do not oppose the violence of the state have little moral authority to oppose the violence used by the poor. Having said this, I would have to agree with you, Ilan, that there is a clear and present danger of Critical Pedagogy being seen as a vehicle for direct violence. It is tragic to hear the words: "If my son will join one of the terrorist groups here I will not try to stop him. I will salute him!" I share your conviction that injustice and the instrumentalization of the human spirit should be resisted and such resistance should not lead to a blinding rage that is given shape by a simple "us-against-them" narrative. I agree that the Western Marxist discourse on totality has been in decline and we need to reinvigorate it but in a way that it becomes a truly liberating totalization that does not turn into its opposite— that does not become totalitarian! I am reminded of the words of Adorno, when he said: No universal history leads from savagery to humanitarianism but there is one leading from the slingshot to the megaton bomb. It ends in the total menace which organized mankind poses to organized men, in the epitome of discontinuity. It is the horror that verifies Hegel and stands him on his head." Adorno did believe that there is a Utopia that is "silently contained" in the image of the decline of the west. We must work to realize this Utopia. It is also my understanding that revolutionary Critical Pedagogy can be relevant in the wrong sense, as in the case of justifying a path devoid of dialogue where violence becomes sacralized for the wrong reasons. Thus, we need to undertake what Ramon Grosfoguel and Ana Margariata Cervantes- Rodriguez calls a "second decolonization" that can reveal how develop-mentalism, Eurocentric universalist knowledges and the myth of decolonization have served to conceal European/Euro-American responsibility in the fate of the world's peripheral regions. This means, of course, addressing the global class, gender, racial, sexual, and regional asymmetries produced by the hierarchical structures of the modern/ colonial capitalist world system. This also is our challenge.

IGZ: I share your pain, dear Peter. I can only hope that I also share in a worthy manner your openness to the Socratic Eros. I do not share, however, your understanding of the present political development, nor am I a partner to some of your theoretical pre-assumptions, the educational rhetoric of your pedagogy and its aims. To my mind, the educational dimension of the post-colonialist agenda needs a serious addressing. I think our conversation might give it a chance, but it might also, on the contrary, enhance dogmatism, fanatic reactions and radical self-indulgence among so many of our friends, regardless of the ideological camp they are swallowed by. I always have in mind that beyond, or, if you prefer, "underneath", the conscious, ideological and political differences and clashes, we, all humans, share the fundamental need for *love* regardless of its opposing paths as articulated by Socrates. We all share the invitation for *"homereturning" to nothingness* and the temptation to be given/ create/destroy total truth and impose total harmony; to be swallowed by, the justice of unchallenged beauty, and other manifestations of "homereturning" into the holiness of nothingness on the one hand, and eternal co-poiesis within an improvised Diasporic nomadic existence on the other. There is room for "critique" in each of these contradicting paths. One, however, leads to Thanatos-oriented self-indulgent ecstasy—all the more under the flags of "difference", anti-universalism and anti-hierarchal resistance to homogeneity and oppression inflicted by Jewish monotheism and its exclusivist moral telos as realized by the West. In contrast, the other longs for Diasporic co-poiesis and for openness to *hope* as a constitutive power of Love of Life. It is in eternal quest for a worthy address of the fundamental edges and tips of existence and thought: nomadism, which is very much in the infinity of the moment yet, is eternally focused on the specific and most concrete demands of the political dimensions of its situatedness. It strives *beyond critical education* via counter-education for the negative Utopia of dialectical empathy, for Diasporic revisiting of *the essence of "critique"* and its polar cultivation into opposing paths. One leads to responsibility toward Love of Life, its creativity, pain and hope. The other leads to surrendering to Will to Power and its victories in the form of self-realization and self-forgetfulness. One leads us to the new progressivism and anti-Enlightenment the other calls us to support the progressive tradition and edify Enlightenment. Diasporic counter-education calls us to go beyond these two rival critical agendas.

Today Diasporic counter-education calls us to address seriously the quest for victories and self-forgetfulness offered by the new anti-Semitism. It challenges the current rhetoric, practices and aims of Critical Pedagogy which tries so hard to be swallowed by the *Will to Power* under the flag of the destruction of its Jewish essence; to overcome the quest for exclusive worth and unique holiness which unavoidably victimizes the Others under moral, emotional, cultural, political and economic hierarchies it inflicts by its very existence. This is the reason why Critical Pedagogy, which is influenced by the new meta-narrative of the new anti-Semitism, is today totally devoted to de-colonization of the West and to the destruction of Israel, or at least to its "critique" and de-legitimation as represented even by "soft" American leftist such as Oliver Stone ("The Jews control the media") and Helen Thomas ("Get the hell out of Palestine back to Germany and Poland!") even if normally they do not use the language of the "peace activists" on the Gaza flotilla (in the radio of the *Marmara* in reply to the Israeli navy's call to stop their ship heading toward the zone of naval blockade): "Go back to Auschwitz!" In face of the new progressive thinking one cannot hope that critical educators will compare the Israeli blockade to the Egyptian blockade on Gaza. One should be very naïve to expect new progressive critique to relate to the reasons why both Egypt and Israel maintain a blockade on the Hamas controlled Gaza and surely one cannot expect present Critical Pedagogy to study what does this double standard critique show us about the Israeli situation, on the one hand and about the present stance of Critical Pedagogy on the other. The "Go back to Auschwitz!" ideology of present day peace activists is troubling, indeed, but the less dramatic articulations and the sophistication of the new progressive "critique" is here much more troubling, especially when it relates to genuine misdeeds and actual Israeli crimes. The new progressive course of "critique" is a symbolic journey for purification, a course of self-redemption by *holy sacrifice of the real Jew* as a vital part of the *holiest sacrifice of the spirit of Judaism*. It is a journey much more loaded and dangerous than the course of the *Marmara* to save the reign of the *Hamas* and the further debasement of the Palestinian people in Gaza under the rule of the Muslim Brotherhood and their anti-humanist educational agenda where the slogan "Death to freedom!" is among the most celebrated ideals. Its greatest mission is the overcoming of Judaism as universally actualized in the West and deconstructing its immanent colonialist-drive. This is the meeting point of the three new anti-Semitic powers in this context: 1. Hamas and Hezbollah whose policy, practice and principles lead to the unconditional destruction of Israel. 2. The Gaza flotilla activists who worked for the ending of the blockade on Gaza. 3. The new progressive supporters of the Gaza flotilla and the general project of not only destroying Israel but more importantly crucifying, again, **the Jew** this time as the Satanic root and soul of Western civilization, its devils and evils. Only typical is here the lecture that Nasrallah gave at Beirut last week telling his followers how happy he is that six million Jews live presently in Israel so that the Hezbollah does not have to chaise them all over the world and can kill the six million Jews all at one strike. The enthusiastic support of Hezbollah in Lebanon by Chavez, its arming with 50000 missiles (positioned intentionally in densely populated areas, preferably in schools, hospitals and Mosques) and the support of this kind of "resistance" by the new progressivists, including you, dear friend is but a local manifestation of the suggestive power of the new anti-Semitism.

So often do critical pedagogues devote their utmost educational efforts to the act of contributing rapturous violence and rhetorical suggestive magic to overcome the seductive gift of the rational and humanist-oriented "oppressive-colonial drive" of the West, which actualizes and universalizes the Jewish exclusive path in history and its unique moral standards and telos as manifested in the most brutal manner by the very existence of the State of Israel. Rarely, if at all, will the new progressive critique relate to the actual facts of the matter and normally it will be very quick to denounce Israeli oppression, state terror and Apartheid-oriented state policies and so forth. Within present Critical Pedagogy there is no much courage to address issues such as the actual standard of living of the Palestinian population in Israel compared to that of its neighboring countries (and, of course, compared to other sectors of Israeli society); the rights of homosexuals in Arab countries compared to the rights of Palestinian homosexuals in Israel; women's rights record in all Arab countries compared to Palestinian women's rights in Israel; rights and actual possibilities of disabled people in Arab countries compared to those of Palestinian disabled people in Israel; children's rights in the neighboring countries and the rights and actual possibilities of Palestinian children in Israel; social security actual and relative revenues of Palestinians in Israel compared to social security payments and policies in neighboring Arab countries; freedom of expression in Arab public spheres compared to the freedom of speech of Palestinians in Israel; political freedom in Arab countries compared to the political freedom of Palestinians in Israel and so on and so forth. And the question that reviles it all, dear Peter, the question that brings to light the truth of the matter when you so quick to delegitimate Israel: when the Palestinians in Israel are challenged with the question "would you prefer living in Israel as it is or, alternatively, in your village as part of a future greater Palestine, becoming a free and proud Palestinian citizen in your own free state?" 96% of them vote to stay Israeli citizens under the present conditions and they resist the possibility of their area becoming part of a greater Palestine in case of a future mutual agreement that will re-arrange and transform all dimensions and levels of Israeli-Palestinian co-existence (exchange of territories, return of refugees, economic, military and cultural agreements and so forth). We all know what would be the reply of the Catholic Irish people if offered such an offer or the reply of the people of south Sudan if offered such an offer. The Palestinians in Israel have a different reply that the progressive "critique" refuses to address while condemning Israeli Apartheid and working for a proper "resistance" to the very existence of a Jewish State in the Middle East. The hidden truth is silenced. It is silenced by the new progressive critique; but this silence, Peter, has a saying that we should address, like the hole in the center of the Romanian flag that was raised by the freedom fighters in Timisoara revolting in 1989 against the communist regime of Nicolae Ceauşescu. This truth and its silencing do not mean that there is no much work on the way for bettering Israeli democracy. Far form it. But it does reveal that the starting point of the new progressive critique is hiding a rich and terrible secret. A secret. Not a mistake. A silenced manifestation of an earnest devotion. A solemn acceptance of the redeeming promise of the new anti-Semitism. It is a commitment to compensate the West for the moral burden of acknowledging two thousand years of discrimination of the Jews as its ultimate Other by currently presenting the Jewish people not as a nation among all other nations but rather as one of its kind; in order to disinfect and purify itself as the ultimate oppressor it returns to **the Jew**. This time defining the uniqueness of **the Jew** as the source and as the cultivator of Western evil; a gift that contaminated the spirit of the West in the name of its exclusivism and its unique universal progressive mission. The renewed crucifixion of **the Jew**, however, is actualized under post-metaphysical sky and with the support of a Saint Peters' renaissance. The new sky deprives the Jews even from the potentials for worthy suffering that were incubated in their previous bonfires. The post-modern reality inflicts an additional burden on present day counter-education that should both enhance a new critical language that will challenge present new progressive "critique" and introduce new educational paths not only for the Love of Life even in face of the triumph of Luciferization of **the Jew**, but also in face of the actual evils inflicted by Israel and the challenge of searching for new universal paths for self-love and a mature solidarity with our Palestinian brothers and sisters; offering our hearts to the new progressivists who are presently so busy in our metaphorical Luciferization and actual extermination or "de-colonization". We are presently faced with a unique moral challenge: more than properly addressing the dullness of our latest crucifixion by the new anti-Semites our present challenge is the cultivation of a worthy addressing of the grand silenced secret of present day critical education to which the Israeli case is but a local manifestation of a universal condition. This is since **the Jew** is a metaphor for all humans, all Diasporic humans, not solely a local historical reality.

While praising the importance of heterogeneity, difference and legitimacy of *all* narratives and their epistemic, moral and political prisms, new progressive Critical Pedagogy is very busy de-legitimating exclusively the Jewish narrative, its uniqueness and its fruits. Gazing from the post-metaphysical moment in light of the desolation of the holiness of the monotheistic God and the holiness of the humanist killing-God-each-moment-anew, this postmodern narrative is unable to accept the legitimacy—certainly not the holiness—of the Jewish claim for exclusive-ness (as well as its Western universalized realization). This critical language is totally confused in face of the clash between the Being of holiness of opposing historical terrains (theocentric against homocentric as against post-homocentric arenas) and the essentially different clashes between the conflicting narratives they give birth to. The holiness of the *aporia* within the critique of conflicting narratives, and the quest to truly challenge the untruth of actual dogmas are beyond the reach of their courage. They educate for diversity and at the same time "resistance" to anything Western becomes the most sacred work of the new progressive educators. They do accept and many a times enhance ethnocentric contexts and exclusivist agendas within the framework of multicultural education, as long as the quest for homogeneity, exclusivity and colonialist uniqueness is anti-Judeo-Christian. The most microscopic manifestation of Judeo-Christian ethnocentrism is unbearable, while the most dreadful ethnocentric manifestations such as in the case of North Korea, Iran, Sudan or Gaza are acceptable or even celebrated by the new progressivists. The "old" progressivists sided with the humanists and democrats as against the anti-humanists and anti-democratic powers. The new progressivists support the most anti-democratic powers as long as they are anti-Western and if they are at the same time also harsh antisemites so much the better.

Many critical educators are swallowed by the common ground of the pantheistic ideology and the rhetoric of radical "difference" which *unites postcolonialism and neo-liberalism,* "the special rights of the victim" and "the special rights of the client", in face of the exile of the killer of the (monotheistic) God each-moment-anew-by-the-progress-of-humanism that is now crucified under the banner of Judeo-Christian colonialism. The new progressive educators are victimized ironically in such a rich manner by the untruth of the present post-metaphysical moment; and they become fanatic inquisitors; in search of a successful flight from the storm of the self-revelation of their being arch-oppressors. The new anti-Semitism will offer them a very promising narrative, suitable for the ultimate crucifixion which will give birth to "a genuine revolution", worthy "resistance" or a refuge from this awful threat in the post-homocentric era in which there is no God, no redeeming killing of God and no blaze of hope for purification but on the new anti-Semitic altar.

The West was instrumental in creating Utopia and educating for the realization of Utopia within fruitful Manichean frameworks. In the modern homocentric era it was extremely different from its specific characters in the theocentric era. Here I must acknowledge a major disagreement between us, Peter, which is rooted in our differences concerning the human condition and human telos in a post-homocentric historical moment. It is my understanding that the new critical language, the language of Diasporic counter-education, should transcend the limitations and overcome the telos as well as the impasses of humanistic education in the post-homocentric era. You apparently disagree.

It is a very costly mistake, Peter, to insist on *revolutionary humanist telos in a post- homocentric era*, an error that must lead to totalitarianism. Such confusion offers a desperate quest for alternatives which will keep the rhythm—in the absence of *holy* human meaning and telos—and the stability of self-deception in arenas characterized by this antinomy. The current progressive narrative of new anti-Semitism is very successful in camouflaging this abyss. It lucratively suspends the need for responsible addressing the transformation in the human condition. It offers a quasi-Utopian and revolutionary educational praxis that leads us to believe with Zizek that we can still make it after all: the genuine revolution, the revolution which is different from all wrong modern revolutions, is possible in a post-modern reality and in light of the truth of "our" post-metaphysical moment; promising that this time the revolution is not rooted in the quest for *homogeneity* but rather in the acknowledgement of the richness of *heterogeneity*, diversity, incommensurability and absence of truth. The passions, the holiness, the Eros striving toward the truth are called to the war of Gog and Magog, to the last day, the Day of the new Leninist Judgment, towards the promised grand victory and liberation on the seventh day, which is endangered by the spirit of Judaism as internalized and realized by Western colonial hierarchical-oppressive practice. I will go into it in a moment since it explains so much of current *false success* and the wrong relevance of hegemonic Critical Pedagogy.

But first I have to relate to a specific example which you introduced, and tell you, dear friend, that I do not share your enthusiasm concerning the incarnation of the post-colonial ideology in the Chavez regime which is synonym to his body and to his demand for eternal rule or the emancipatory potentials of the intimate collaboration of this regime with world powers such as the dictatorship of North Korea, Khomeinist Iran and terror groups such as Hamas, Hezbollah, South American guerilla groups—you name it. Here Peter, our disagreement concerns not so much questions such as whether a concrete deal with terrorists such as the Hamas movement or with revolutionary Iran is strategically justified or not. It concerns more fundamental questions: 1. *The revolutionary soul in a post-metaphysical moment*: the relations between the present socialist Venezuela and revolutionary Iran are fundamentally not pragmatically oriented. As Chavez articulated it himself, it is a matter of "soul brotherhood". And here I do agree with Chavez: he and Ahmadinejad are truly brothers in their souls. This brotherhood of souls is more than the unification of personal megalomania, quest for personality cult or the mere joining forces of two different authoritarian regimes in face of a common humanist enemy.

We should address its centrality in depth since it has to do with the possibilities and limitations of critical education that is so dear to the two of us. 2. *The fundamentals of "critique" in a post-colonial arena* and its implications for the possibilities of "old" and "new" Critical Pedagogy. So, I will try to elaborate on it while having in mind the characteristics of our historical moment. Here I would like to broaden the post-colonial picture. I will try to relate to the larger post-colonial agenda and not specifically to your work. We can return later to the relations between your revolutionary Critical Pedagogy and the larger post-colonialist educational project; but please, Peter, allow me to begin with the larger picture and question the fundamentals of the challenges of the present critical language in education.

Current Critical Pedagogy should address some fundamental changes in the human condition and their interrelations, if it is true to itself. Hegemonic Critical Pedagogy neither related to this transformation nor addressed its implications until this very day. So I will reintroduce this transformation since it is central to a set of assertions I would like us to treat in our conversation today. Here are the four major new developments Critical Pedagogy should address.

The first is the changes in all spheres and dimensions of life in face of *entering the edge of mega-speed reality*. Human existence and the question of political (re)structuring, emancipation and critical thinking are not only challenged by intensification in changes in all spheres of life and in the nature of the symbolic exchange while meeting ever faster movements of symbols, commodities, money and people: *a new human existence* is coming into being. We cannot disregard it Peter, and nor will Chavez, Ahmadinejad or even Marx, Che and Freire. Yes, not even Deleuze, since his thinking invites us to abandon the concept of an autonomous, responsible human subject and the possibility of transcendence, as well as the Utopia concerning the difference which makes a difference. Zizek and Badiou also fail to offer us a renewed Leninist violence in face of mega-speed realities even if they try so hard to articulate for the new progressive thinking an up-to-date revolutionary ethos. The second truth that critical education is too quick to disregard is *the probability of all life being brought to an end* by technological progress. This too, dear Peter is a major challenge for revolutionary Critical Pedagogy and it is so unfortunate that neither you nor other critical educators address this major challenge toward a new thinking, toward a new existence, toward the end. I have tried to address this open question in a more orderly manner on quite a few occasions, so here I will only mention briefly some of its implications for the possibility of free thinking and responsible improvising nomadic co-poiesis as a possible path beyond the limits of the present critical language in education.

1. Overcoming the postmodern *Sisyphean* continuum by entering the totality of the End of all Life on earth as a challenge to critical-progressive thinking. Humanistic-oriented Critical Theory and Critical Pedagogy are situated within a *linear* conception of time where it is self-evident that life is durable, that love and regeneration is logically guaranteed by the very concept of Life. The idea of progress is central to the critical act and to the possibility of dialectical praxis in critical education. *The current technological possibility of the end of progress*, and even more fundamentally the possibility of a historically close proximity to the end of Utopia, history and

Life itself, is of great importance, dear Peter. I think it is wrong to underestimate it or disregard it in present revolutionary Critical Pedagogy where a Pauline political theology faces a unique renaissance as part of the attempt to return to the origins of the concept of Love in St. Paul as against Judaism and the emphasis on the law and rationality, celebrating pantheism, diversity and kaleidoscopic anti-hierarchical identities and realities as against the phallocentrism and exclusivism of the Judeo-Christian civilization and its oppressive imperatives. It is today's most important yet unspoken philosophical challenge. Existentially, educationally—but also politically, it makes a difference which makes a difference if openness and the very endurance of life is no longer self-evident, and even more so if humanity works day and night to enhancing the probability of *the end* of all life on earth. Surely it makes a difference if the End might be treated as a physical speculation on the extinguishing of the sun in one billion years, or alternatively, if it stands as a reasonable chance of being the future that our children and grandchildren are bound to face. They will have to work harder and harder to prevent the (un)avoidable. What a grandiose Sisyphean imperative in the era of the end of mysterium and the rule of fabricated spectacles. It has lost even the self-evidence implicit in the classical Sisyphean work of life as a possible holiness in face of the Original Sin of the grant to humans of the fire of (inner) strength and the quest for truth. *The End* as an expected totality to unexpectedly at-any-moment-burst-in into the complexity of history contradicts the truth of post-metaphysical pragmatics. It actualizes **the totally other**. It reintroduces (even if only negatively) *holiness* and meaning—regardless of the suggestive rhetoric of Foucault, Deleuze, Zizek or Giroux.

It is an approaching objective reality that contradicts the conceptual and existential preconditions for the optimism of the critical-progressive legacy concerning the possibilities of thinking, of progressive politics, of the telos of homocentric education and of the essence of human life.

2. The End of all life has become technologically possible for the first time in human history, and it is not a mere logical possibility: it is politically highly probable, unless a total and universal change of consciousness and a Utopian catharsis are presently paving a new human path. At this very moment, Peter, because a moment from now it could be already too late. You, dear Peter, I, and our friends cannot hold on to old Marxian conceptions of progress or to traditional understanding of the relations between emancipating theory and praxis in face of such a transformation. Che as a paradigmatic educator or Marx and his lesson from the Paris commune, Gramschi and Adorno cannot help much here. Adorno should help us here in another sense, by insisting on negative dialectics and *negative Utopia*: refusing the naivety, negating the false optimism for total identity between the concept and its addressee, the quest for victory/reconciliation, final synthesis, emancipation and any other manifestations of positive Utopia of the kind that revolutionary Critical Pedagogy is founded on. Surely you remember that for Adorno the quest for tranquility, for a final, positive, solution to injustice or "peace", was a misleading education that was to be challenged. I consider Adorno a Diasporic philosopher who understood the dangerous mistake invested in the quest for positive, enduring "peace", "justice" or "emancipation", while insisting on refusing the victories of

dogmatism, injustice and self-forgetfulness. This is where we should add our contribution, Peter. Critical Pedagogy until today has failed to face the collision between the holiness and meaning of Jewish (and Western) uniqueness and the holiness of other grand unique creative powers and has forgotten Adorno's and Horkheimer's negative Utopia; right now it is racing faster and faster to the refuge of the new anti-Semitism. This refuge, however, will not save Critical Pedagogy and will not become a safe haven for the progressive movements in face of the other transformations in the human condition.

3. The third component is globalization and its fruits in a postmodern era. It integrates the objective anti-objectivism of the logic of the market and the reaction to the creative *void* left by the exile of the killer-of-God-each-moment-anew. Difference, multi-culturalism and the carnival of exchange, contingency and pantheism in all its forms celebrate the ongoing triumphant kaleidoscopic gala over "the father" and the Jewish spirit. They forget that the Jewish Diasporic spirit opens the gate to dialogue and genuine diversity, and that the Western Geist enabled (dialectical) freedom and the struggle against dogmatism, hierarchy and inequality, even the post-structuralist critique itself. This *anti-transcendental* run away from the humanist project and the realization of the Jewish spirit as universal Enlightenment, and the construction of a powerful anti-humanist project which is committed to overcome the colonialist nature of Enlightenment and its Jewish essence. It is enabled by the possibilities opened by the new anti-Semitism as the meta-narrative which celebrates simultaneously our "freedom" as free consumers in the market and as post-metaphysical new progressivists.

4. The fourth challenge I outlined for critical education was the challenge of *entering mega-speed arenas in a post-metaphysical era*, at a historical moment in which not only the inspiring *holiness* of God was deconstructed, but even the secular holiness of universal human progress toward liberty, critical understanding, greater justice and equality is ridiculed, deconstructed, and swallowed into the triumphant meaninglessness of "diversity". If immanence overwhelms transcendence, Peter, as it successfully does today, *no air remains for freedom* in the sense of actualizing responsibility, love, creativity and self-constituted telos. Not even for "meaning" or a difference which makes a difference. Later on I will try to elaborate more on this issue and make clearer our disagreement on this point. Here I will limit myself to relating to the post-colonial agenda in the broader sense and less to your project, to which we will return on the conclusion of my critique of this project and its intimate relations with new anti-Semitism. And still another personal remark: I ask the forgiveness of many friends of the critical education who might feel hurt by my articulation since they do not see themselves as anti-Semites. Actually, many of them are very proud to be anti-racist, and they understand anti-Semitism as a particular instance of racism and this is the starting point of their critique of Jewish and Israeli racism. Well, I will not only apologize here (and everywhere else); I will also say that there is a very important difference between "anti-Semitism" and the "new anti-Semitism", even if there are strong connections between the two. And still another personal remark, Peter: I see my own critical work as a part of the new anti-Semitism.

Critical educators should today acknowledge and courageously address these challenges: *what is it which gives birth to the post-metaphysical moment?* What are the fruits of this post-metaphysical moment? And how could we address them in a worthy manner (if it is indeed a post-metaphysical moment and there is no truth, meaning, love, togetherness or quest for justice which are not mere echoes and fruits of contingent power-relations and contextual fantasies, passions and reactions to reactions which manifest the triumph of Moira: meaninglessness as the spring of meaning)?

I will begin by asserting that the post-metaphysical moment is actualized by *the exile of the killer-of-God-each-moment-anew*. In other words, Peter, here I relate to the demolition of "the father" or the Jewish spirit of the humanist project and its fundamental preconditions by globalizing capitalism, the postmodern culture industry and other fruitful developments. The *void* caused by the exile of the killer of God and the demolition of the "Monotheistic" preconditions for progressive thinking and Utopian-oriented praxis was very creative indeed. Here I will relate to two of its most celebrated present-day offspring: the postmodern Pleasure Machine on the one hand, and the new anti-Semitism with its post-colonialist educational agenda on the other. The two are Siamese twins, inseparable children of the same tragic mother. Both are initiated not by Love of Life as eternally improvising co-poiesis but by its opposite: *fruitful anxiety*. 1. The postmodern Pleasure Machine is actualized by countless manifestations and contexts ranging from practical Kabala and Hinduism to new age literature, Yoga and spiritual training for ever more productive managers. 2. The other reaction is supposed to be a worthy negation of the temptations to surrender to the postmodern Pleasure Machine. It claims to become a new kind of political activism in face of the *exile of Spirit*, an exile which Adorno, Horkheimer and others acknowledged when criticizing the 1968 student revolution, the South American guerilla, and the uncritical support for North Vietnam. What are we addressing here, dear Peter? What we address here is *a quest for an alternative to transcendence*, to human progress and to mature happiness. Post-modernism is devoted to replying to this challenge: it produces both self-forgetfulness and quasi-spiritual alternatives, as well as alternative "emancipatory" politics ranging from cyberspace to post-colonial politics and revolutionary Critical Pedagogy as a fashionable spiritual commodity. Within the framework of this progressivism, in its new neo-Marxist as well as its post-modern frameworks *hate* becomes essential for the ecstasis of present "resistance" and "critique". The UN Durban anti-racist conference in 2001 could serve as a master example for the constructive dimension of hate for the new racism that is cultivated by current progressivism. The rhetorical flag of the Gaza flotilla ("Go back to Auschwitz!") is but another example. In various ways the new anti-Semitism becomes the ether for the new progressive thinking and for current Critical Pedagogy.

The realization in actuality of this *post-modern Geist* within the post-colonialist political framework is impractical unless it has an effective educational implement-ation. And postcolonialism does educate! It educates extremely lucratively for hate or neo-idealism, not for love. Postcolonialism tells itself that it educates fundamentally for "resistance" to the victimization drive which is so essential to Judeo-Christian monotheism/"the West"; contra any claim for objective-universal truths and values; especially it is directed against (Western) pretentiousness to deliver the word of "redemption" or "liberation" in a genuine, just and universally valid manner: whether it is in the form of authority/hierarchy of the symbolic father, phallocentric logos and its fruits, an almighty God and the missionaries that represent "him" or in the form of the humanist universal Utopia and the Enlightened pedagogues who are totally and genuinely devoted to its realization. "Resistance" as quasi-religiosity is actualized under different banners and in endless different arenas: resistance to "monotheism", resistance to "phallocentrism", resistance to "colonialism", activism in favor of "alternative sexual ideals and practices", and so many more. All these are united in their *commitment to overcome the essence of Judaism* as the root of Western metaphysics and its drive for truth/oppressing the Other: facing the truth of the post-metaphysical moment; the exile of the holiness of transcendence or progress in the form of a humanist killing of God.

In a hybridist, "plain" actuality, in which contingency, fashions and mere power-relations are established as the sole rulers, "resistance" to the West/Empire/Israel becomes an ecstatic quasi-holiness; part of the New-Age daily *spirituality* but also its grand alternative: "Israel" and sometimes "America" becomes an icon for all evil, but not unconditionally. "Judaism is in the root of all evil in the world", the celebrated post-colonialist Mikis Theodorakis tells us.

In all the diverse manifestations of the new anti-Semitism "Israel" is conceived and represented as the root and agent of "the West" and its immanent, multi-faceted, oppressive colonialist drive. It serves as an extreme, dense manifestation of a general phenomenon that the spirit of Judaism initiates and realizes universally, in countless arenas and on innumerable occasions. For the new anti-Semitism the critique of the West/phallocentrism/whiteness can without much difficulty replace the "resistance" to "Israel" or **The Jew**; yet there is a difference. While the West under the guidance of the Pauline-oriented redemption of Christianity or within the framework of Critical Pedagogy is invited to self de-colonization, and thereby might be saved, the State of Israel and the spirit of Judaism are to be totally destroyed. The USA or "America", when freed of its incarnation as the "Empire", has room on earth and Obama is a powerful icon that represents this possibility for America to redeem or to de-colonize itself. Not "Israel", according to the post-colonialist agenda. The State of Israel, as the incarnation of the Spirit of Judaism, must be utterly shattered.

Postmodernism, which is integrated so powerfully in the Critical Pedagogy of the last generation, challenges not only modernism but no less important, its "monotheistic" and "phallocentrist" foundations: the claim for an objective and universal validity of a certain set of values and assertions; a linear conception of time; binary logic; a telos whose aim is monolithic truth, ethnocentrist-oriented universal-peaceful order as the equivalent of orgasm, and so forth. The "pantheistic" character of the postmodern discourse, the St. Paul renaissance and its sensitivity and commitment to pre-structural "Love", "difference", "multi-culturalism", alternative to "phallocentrism", resistance to any hierarchy, to any stability, universalism and objectivism oppose existentially, philosophically, psychologically and politically the Jewishness of the Enlightenment's emancipatory project. It opposes the Jewish spirit which is the constitutive element and the philosophical impetus of Western cruel oppressive colonialism.

The post-colonialist momentum and Critical Pedagogy, which has become so relevant to some of those refusing the alternative of the postmodern Pleasure Machine, is a true *quasi-spiritual power*, not a merely political might. The "resistance" to "Israel" or the "critique" of "America" became a sacred work, certainly far from a kind of critical reasoning and argumentation within which one can resolve the disagreements between "the West and the rest" and between "Israel" and "the post-colonial alternative". Within it there is no room for the prospect of dialogue of the kind that Enlightenment has offered for the last two centuries, with so much enthusiastic optimism. Here Israel is irredeemably destined to become "the Jew among the nations", a demonic entity, not a concrete political reality which is essentially different from all other nations and political entities, even in light of the works of Hayden White, Benedict Anderson, Gilles Deleuze or Michel Foucault, to whom the new progressivists normally pay tribute as present-day high priests of the new religion. In the new anti-Semitism "resistance" to "Israel" has theological, philosophical, psychic and political meaning, which transcends specific disagreements such as the number of unnecessary road blocks imposed in the West Bank by the IDF or the exact borders of the future Palestinian state: there is no rational discussion that might satisfy the post-colonial agenda on these disagreements, and no room for a possible agreement—only total annihilation of the Jewish State of Israel, and this too solely as a first step toward "genuine decolonization". All possible agreements are conceived within this agenda as steps toward this aim.

There is a range of rhetorical differences between "resistance" to "Israel" and resistance" to **The Jew**, and between them important barriers are set: psychological, cultural, and politically correct. It is not (yet) politically correct to be explicitly anti-Jewish or a blunt anti-Semite in the traditional sense of the concept although as director Oliver Stone and others show us – the new progressivists are rapidly heading there ("The Jews control the media"). Presently, however, the old blunt anti-Semitism is conceived in normative critical discussions as obsolete, primitive, and unsuitable for present-day progressive activists. Even heroes such as President Assad of Syria, Hugo Chavez or Farouk Hosni deny their racism, rearticulate themselves or even apologize when caught in too blunt anti-Semitic expressions. Others, less politically correct, such as the post-colonialist novelist Jose Saramago, do not make these differences in their post-colonialist critique, when offering their "resistance" to "those experts in cruelty with doctorates in disdain, who look down on the world from the heights of the insolence which is the basis of their education. We can better understand their biblical god when we know his followers. Jehovah or Yahweh or whatever he is called, is a fierce and spiteful god, whom the Israelis always live up to".

According to this educational agenda, if the West is ever to purify itself of its impurities it must embark on genuine, courageous self-decolonization. The West, at its best, is presently struggling for the salvation of its soul by sacrificing its spirit. And the West is horrified. It is terrified by its present identity, by its past, as well as by the proposed remedy. So it gives birth neither to children nor to great new ideas. This anxious effort for salvation in conditions of fright, however, takes its toll: *hatred*. Ardent self-hatred. Its flame is thrown at the most essential of the Western spirit: its Jewish germ. This is the meeting point of Western post-colonial ideology, which affirms Western refusal to give birth to babies and grand new ideas and its celebration of the Palestinian practice of sending children as human bombs and burning the Zionist forests that were planted all over the deserted Land of Israel in the last 120 years of Jewish homereturning. The planting of the forests by the Israelis and the burning of the forests in Israel by the Palestinians are inseparable, as are the quest for redemption and the exile of the killer of God in a post-metaphysical moment. The new anti-Semitism offers an important gate for the path of salvation.

In a process of *projection* this threatening germ of Western civilization is enthusiastically extroverted by the new progressivism as its Other. **The Jew**, again, becomes the Other of Western civilization and the object of moral crucifixion and for actual annihilation, ranging from abasement to physical extermination. The re-declaration of **the Jew** as the paradigmatic *Other* is currently even more universal, and is enhanced by capitalist globalization and world opinion and the Islamist renaissance and not exclusively by Western progressivism. In the West what we are faced with is an attempt at purification of a terrible sin within the framework of the myth which triumphs in the Zeitgeist of the exile of Spirit. It is the last possible quasi-religiosity, which differs from everyday New-Age spirituality and still contains a connection to religiosity; the last possible holiness in the era of the exile of the killer of God and the deconstruction of the ethos of universal Utopian emancipation. *Self hatred* and the hatred of the *not-I* within the self, namely commitment to purification from the otherness of **the Jew** within Western culture as the most infamous dimension of Judeo-Christian civilization, join together not only psychologically but conceptually and spiritually. They give birth and re-present a new myth, a Zeitgeist, quasi- spirituality and rhetorical fashions, and even codes of the politically correct. These are not to be separated from global capitalism, massive immigration waves and the other manifestations of the present historical moment. In this sense the new anti- Semitism is the disease of our time as well as its constitutive myth and promise of a cure.

Within the historical change from arenas of ever faster changes, higher speed and humanist holiness in the killing-of-God-each-moment-anew to the exile of the killer of God, deconstruction of humanist holiness and entry into mega-speed realities, Western *self-hatred has replaced the spirit of reflection*. It has substituted the critical ethos and the spirit of homocentric "critique" which began its modern journey in Descartes' *cogito ergo sum*. Today it has reached its historical conclusion in deconstructing Spirit itself. The power of anxiety, frustration and fury which are incubated in the new anti-Semitism are fertilized by the downfall of modern Utopia, and more specifically, the dissolution of its last revolutionary experience in 1968. The post-1968 West is incompetent to face itself, its past and its telos in the era of mega-speed. No substitute has been created for the *metaphysical anchor* of the humanist revolt against monotheism. No alternative has been found or created for progressive education as a secular sacred work. No alternative exists to the lost humanistic Eros as an impetus for progress, as transcendence toward worthy life. It is not the end of vitality but rather its transformation from an Erotic one into a Thanatos-oriented vigor. The absence of erotic strength appears as *hospitality*; the hospitality of an invitation: an invitation to "homereturning" to nothingness. Within this hospitality the West cannot avoid facing its past and present, and the absence of a new *New Testament*, except by giving birth to quasi-spirituality, a return of the constitutive myth in the form of projection of its "Satanic" germ and its purification in the fire of the altar of self-decolonization. The theocentric era, in which humans submitted themselves to God, and the following homocentric era, in which humans devoted themselves to the deification of humanity by killing-God-each-moment-anew, are now *replaced* by a new era of the kind Marx, Nietzsche, Heidegger and Adorno could not even imagine. Two rival educational agendas flourish in this post-metaphysical era. They nourish each other and recycle a new myth, a new way of self-forgetfulness which enables human life even in the absence of holiness under the banners of the infinite right of the victim of the Judeo-Christian civilization on the one hand, and of the infinite right of the client in the McWorld on the other; life as an arena that initiates a kind of self-forgetfulness within ecstatic recycling of pleasures and symbols with no depth, telos or "meaning" beyond the affects of its recycling on the one hand, and life as ecstatic "resistance" which actualizes itself in feminist, multi-cultural, post-colonialist and queer prisms, on the other. Peter, to you, and to many other critical educators these seem antagonistic trends, yet to my mind they have so much in common. In my view these are two versions of anti-Diasporic existence: one path deconstructs Diasporic existence by enthusiastically being swallowed by the *Pleasure Machine*, the other by the *ecstasies of quasi-spiritualism* actualized in dogmatic "resistance" to genuine Diasporic existence and to eternal improvisation-transcendence as offered by Judaism.

The boundaries between these discourses are not always clear and stable. They all drink, however, from the well of the truth of the exile of holiness and from the de-construction of the preconditions for transcendence. They also produce partnership with the postmodern culture, which hails the local, partial, hybrid, contingent, and heterogeneous, and in the extreme also with the call for aimless-creative violence, for the triumph of the aesthetic demons, for the return of the Gnostic god. In arenas as depart as "the market" and "the practice of liberation and resistance" there is room for neither objective justice nor for universal human progress; alternatively, the victims'/clients' partial-rapid changing local and ethnocentric self-evidence is to be the substitute for the Utopian telos and its metaphysical anchor. The quasi-religious nature of the ecstatic "resistance" to the Jewish homogenization drive and to Western imposed hierarchies, to Western silencing, colonization and oppression, becomes an alternative to holiness and to Jewish insistence on Diasporic Love of Life. Anti-idealistic-oriented ideals become a substitute to actually living as a good human.

The absence of ground for an anchor—psychological, spiritual and political ground, in a post-metaphysical moment is a vivid birth-giving absence. It demands a response. A seemingly creative reply. A reaction whose grandeur will match the greatness of the exile of the pedagogy of killing God. The philosophical and psychological loss come together in quest of *compensation*: a quasi-transcendent aim or at least an explicit, visible, detectable enemy; so that the post-modern nomad might struggle against and indulge in self-forgetfulness, which offers an overwhelming illusion of ecstatic catharsis which will make bearable the loss of transcendence and the exile of holiness.

In the most fundamental manner, Critical Pedagogy is part and parcel of this ecstatic mission; therefore it is so common that it becomes part and parcel of the new anti-Semitism. At the same time, on a personal level and in light of its Marxist heritage it offers resistance to the new anti-Semitism both as the Zeitgeist of our historical moment and in its specific manifestations. Historically, however, as the Marxist dimensions are swallowed by the postmodern culture and the post-structuralist philosophical credo, Critical Pedagogy becomes of the new anti-Semitism, one of whose forefathers was Marx himself.

PM: Ilan, your criticisms of Marxism have also occupied the work of Raya Dunayevskya, Peter Hudis, Kevin Anderson and the Marxist humanist tradition, as well as Moishe Postone and others. Remember, Ilan, that the Marxist theory to which I ascribe is constantly attacked by Marxists from other schools of thought and traditions, and the point I am making is that there are many incarnations of Marxist theory, and are you not familiar with those that ask the same questions as you do—and which offer a very robust and important response? We wrestle with very similar issues. Again, you are offering important critiques of some Marxisms, but I hope you recognize that there is a strong history within the Marxist humanist tradition of engaging in similar critiques. I think you are projecting, here, my companero. Now let me try to engage in some of your other concerns. That there is a new anti-Semitism, Ilan, is undeniable. That Critical Pedagogy can-and often does-feed into this, needs to be taken seriously. In other words, in this era, this trembling era, in which we no longer give credence to metaphysical claims for knowledge, and in which we critique, and rightly so, the quest for absolute, apodictic trans-historical knowledge, we criticize logos and in doing so we regrettably destroy it—sometimes as sterile, dogmatic fundamentalists, and sometimes as postmodern deconstructionists—rather than reclaim logos for the nurturing of the transfor-mative subject, a subject that can become Other to itself either to resign itself to living in a social universe of exploitation by slumbering or suffering in the space between being and its Other, or to struggle protagonistically against it. Logos in this sense is deployed not in the service of the creation of new being and Other, but in the service of the worst ideals of the society one is attempting to remake. How do we create a society better than the one in which we were formed? To transcend phallocentrism, patriarchy, egoistic being, domination, and the coloniality of power—these are all struggles of the revolutionary critical educator. Those are the challenges I posed in my first response.

But to your challenge to the postcolonialism, I am reminded of remarks made by Hal Foster: "to call our own world postcolonial is to mask the persistence of colonial and neocolonial relations; it is also to ignore that, just as there was always a first world in every third world, there was always a third world in every first world." Is not postcolonialism the apogee of colonialism and not its end? A point I have tried to make in my work is that the cabaret avant-gardism of the postcolonial critic is not sufficient to dismantle the antagonisms of the present. It is important to reject a mutually exclusive transcendental ontology that is inhospitable to other ontologies or to observing our own acts of observation. Yet does not the human spirit strive towards the universal, for a universality of social justice for all—creating the conditions of possibility for freedom from necessity for all. This position, I argue, in no way rejects the pluriversity of knowledges. In fact, it affirms the legitimacy of knowledge disqualified by the imperiality of Eurocentered epistemology. We struggle here, Ilan, for the simultaneity of universal and particular rights.

In making the choice to struggle for a world in which being can be reconstituted creatively and freely, we should not make an idol of any master plan for socialism, including the socialism of the twenty-first century of the Bolivarian revolution in Venezuela, but we should take heed from the lessons learned, especially when there is a danger of revolutionary ideals turning into their opposite in the theater of social struggle. In this way I support the Bolivarian revolution, but not uncritically (but as Benjamin notes, the price of becoming more critical these days is to become more distracted). Just because the Bolivarian revolution is leftist does not mean it is spiritually just. Revolutionary ideals can become a prison house in which monstrous crimes can be committed in the name of truth and justice. I see a very worthwhile and powerful struggle in Venezuela on the part of the Chavistas, but as with all revolutions powered by a Utopian longing, we must be vigilant in the various ways you have been suggesting, Ilan. Just as imperialists can be pious and speak with a righteous indignation, revolutionary socialists can give themselves over to Egoistic being and dogmatism and megalomania. We must not fall into cynical reason of recognition and disavowal, and must not use our recognition of contradiction as a shield for remaining ambivalent when we should be engaging in protagonistic agency. Having said that I disagree that Chavez sees himself as some kind of soul-mate with Mahmoud Ahmadinejad. If this is the case, then it is a tragic situation. But I want to reiterate: A non-violent human agency must be our goal, and the means towards our goal must not partake of violence and destruction but rather be animated by the quest for a wholeness of being. And yes, we must be wary of the axial notions of linear history, the Cartesian dualism, the neo-orientalist and neo-primitivist endeavors of the poststructuralists, the modeling of the historical on the biological, and the grand narratives of progress and the tyranny of the logos that have driven Western nations to genocide and our struggle must be towards justice and equality—but please, Ilan, let's not forget the greatest totalizing force facing history—capitalism—which is anathema to the spirit, ecocidal and built on violent expropriation. The vile antagonism between capital and labor creates the conditions of possibility for so many other antagonisms, including anti-Semitism, racism, sexism, although these antagonisms can not be reduced to capital! Haven't our postcolonial savants failed to answer Fanon's demand for recognition? Do they not continue to project the Other as an outsider? Does not their tarrying with the Other constitute an exotic escape from Western rationality? Or an attempt to displace, defuse or sublimate the coloniality of power? Now it is important to understand, as Joel Kovel points out, that spirituality often entails violence, but non-violence is always more spiritual than violence. He contends that all spiritualities are in motion and to be motionless is to die, spiritually and corporeally. Sometimes the issue is whether on prefers life to death. Now Kovel is clear than the violence risked is never a good thing, but "its evil may be either tragic or nihilistic, depending upon its opening to further being, as against its closure of being." Does violence lead to an opening to further being, and to a less violent order? Kovel notes that sometimes so much violence has been historically sedimented (he uses the examples of the slave system or dictatorships in Latin America) that no motion may be possible without the expenditure of some violence. The question that I think is lacking in Critical Pedagogy is the ideologeme of distance. Fanon asked how to negotiate a correct distance from both the colonial power and the nativist past so as to avoid the triumphalism of Western master narratives and resistance motored by racialist separation? Here Hal Foster's model of deferred action is important. If subjectivity, as Lacan, notes is structured on a relay of anticipations and reconstructions of traumatic events, and if one event (disruptive) is only registered through another that recodes it (restorative) we come to be who were are only in what Foster calls deferred action. If the struggle of revolutionary Critical Pedagogy constitutes, therefore, a complex relay of anticipated futures and reconstructed pasts, as a form of deferred action, then we can see that this struggle acts on capitalist social relations as it is acted on by it. The repressed part of revolutionary Critical Pedagogy returns but it returns from the future. And, it is this delay, this deferral of action that allows us the space for dialogue, a dialogue that can serve as the conditions of possibility for a new beginning. So revolutionary Critical Pedagogy is a trauma that can be acted out hysterically—as in the case of your student's remark—or with the sufficient distance. It was Levi-Strauss, who as a Jew who left European fascism, was exploring the concept of distance (Foster writes that it was the ethnological equivalent of Lacan's mirror stage). Levi-Strass saw a danger in the fascist extreme dis-identification of the Other and also the extreme over-identification of the surrealists who would appropriate the Other. Early in the twentieth century, Levi-Strauss envisioned the Polynesian Islands being turned into aircraft carriers and Asia and Africa becoming slums. In our quest for the lost unity of our being, what is the necessary distance between the self and the Other, a distance that will produce neither dis-identification nor over-identification and appropriation—a distance that can result in relative equanimity? Of course, there are those critics who say that we cannot have critical distance today since the society of the spectacle necessarily subsumes criticality under distraction, given the nature of the new technologies and the media, where separations are concealed by an imaginary unity.

Now, back to the question of Israel. We are connected to and distanced by Israel by the same violence of the sacred that mandates a scapegoat for the transgressions of the West. Here, the question becomes: When does a legitimate criticism of Israel become legitimate and illegitimate? Have not we phallicized Israel as the demonic Other only to presuppose its castration from the body of the West? But when it is legitimate to criticize Israel, especially here in the United States when criticism of

Israeli politics towards the Palestinians is considered in all instances to be a form of virulent anti-Semitism, whether engaged in by Jewish professors or not? Here in the United States, you risk losing your job if you criticize Israel. Professors, rightly so, remain too terrified to critique Israel. The United States is very unique, perhaps, in this regard. This motivates a forced amnesia.

The danger of the new anti-Semitism is very real, but, again, we should not let this danger prevent us from criticizing Israel's legacy of extreme brutality against the Palestinians. And, in turn, we should be willing to criticize and take a stand against the violence against the Israeli people and challenge any government, socialist or capitalist, that refuses to engage the contextual and historical specificity of the struggle of the Jewish people, and simply engages in a rank demonization of Israel as the hellish Other who embodies the archetypal figure of the unrepentant Christ-killer. We must oppose those discourses and practices—and images—that concretely advance this new anti-Semitism, even—and perhaps especially—when advanced by critical educators. Ilan, I am concerned about the new anti-Semitism but of course, I am also trying to connect it to its historical roots. We must remember during the birth of the Jesus Movement and the Christ movement that these two movements were very different, not the just different incarnations of the same religion as we find in the Book of Acts. The Jesus Movement or the religion of Jesus was led by James, the brother of Jesus, and was very Torah-observant. The Jesus movement believed Jesus was the awaited Messiah. But the Messiah, we need to understand, was very different than the apostle Paul's concept of Jesus the Christ.

Paul's religion, the religion of the Christ, emphasized the mystical Jesus. In the days of the diaspora, in the time of the destruction of the temple in Jerusalem, Paul's Christ movement was much stronger than the Jesus movement, or Rabbinical Judaism, or the Gnostics. In fact, by the late fourth century, Proto-Orthodoxy, or the religion of Paul, was favored by Constantine and Theodosius even proclaimed it as the official imperial religion of the Roman Empire in 380. Barrie Wilson has written lucidly about this. Paul's writings, including the Book of Acts (which was loyal to Paul's interpretation of the development of the Christ movement, and was very deceptive) became the authoritative canon of scripture.

The rivalry between the Jesus Movement and the Christ movement and the ascendency of the Christ movement led to the deionization of Judaism. There was a tremendous devaluing of Jewish identity. We can trace this back to the rivalry between the very Hellenized mystical God-man of the Christ movement under Paul, and the Jewish Jesus of the Jesus movement under James. The Christ movement was much stronger and threatened rabbinical Judaism and the Jesus movement, including the Torah-observant followers of Jesus, the Ebionites. The Book of Acts, according to theologians such as Barrie Wilson, substituted the Jesus of History for the Christ of Paul's personal conversion experience.

The Book of Acts falsely and deceptively suggested that the Jesus Movement and Paul's Christ Movement were one and the same, with James finally in agreement with Paul to drop Torah observances and Jewish identity. But these movements were, as Wilson and others have noted, very separate. Acts privileged Paul's mystical Hellenized religion that was linked to death and resurrection theology. The Jesus movement did not engage in death and resurrection theology but focused on Jesus as the Messiah and maintained Jewish law and customs. But Paul won over the Gentiles by substituting the Jewish Jesus for the mystical Jesus as God-man. Paul's Hellenized religion or Proto-Orthodoxy, can be seen in the gospels of Luke and John—the Christifying gospels. But the Jesus movement is more reflected in the gospel of Mathew—and roundly rejected Paul's letters and the gospels of Luke and John. Jesus was concerned about how to keep Torah faithfully, and was concerned with Jewish law. But this was drummed out of Paul's Christ movement. So the roots of anti-Semitism can be traced to the differences of Paul's bringing Jesus into the orbit of a Hellenistic mystery religion which did away with Torah. He rejected Torah observance for all, and set his movement apart from Judaism and the Jesus movement. The prevailing view that all interpretations and understandings of Jesus and his mission except for those of Paul were false, helped to fuel a virulent anti-Semitism. The Christification process had anti-Semitic consequences and led to vicious attitudes towards the Jews that exist to this day. Critical Pedagogy, which is concerned with spiritual awareness and openness, needs to deal with this historically and materially.

But my adopted country is the United States, and I am now living here in las entranas de la bestia, and I must concern myself here with a history of violence and oppression. I have always appreciated the steadfastness in your criticisms of Zionism in the face of so much anger against you in Israel, you deserve our strongest ecomiums. I need to face the fact that I chose to live in the United States, a country whose leadership continues to engage in crimes against humanity. To what extent those crimes will continue under President Obama remains to be seen, since I am writing this very early in his presidency. But these are systematic, widespread, and officially and openly sanctioned crimes that are designed from the outset to kill and maim thousands of people in whatever theaters are deemed appropriate by the U.S. administration and it is unmistakably the most feared and powerful war machine that has ever been created. The use of remote controlled drone Predators that kill one enemy target for every 70 civilians killed, bunker busting bombs, cluster bombs, radioactive weapons such as depleted uranium shells, napalm, white phosphorous, weapons of mass destruction that have over the last fifty years left millions dead, the arming and funding of death squads in places such as East Timor, Argentina, Chile, Brazil, El Salvador, Guatemala, Honduras (especially the CIA- created "Battalion 316"), Colombia, Bolivia, Angola, and Mozambique, "Free-Fire Zones", the massacres of the infamous "Tiger Force" of U.S. Army's 101st Airborne Division, the American-style death squads of Iraq's "Salvador Option", the Chicago police dungeons, the practice of waterboarding by the U.S. that can be traced back to the U.S. conquest and occupation of the Philippines (1899–1902), the and to extra-legal operations such as the CIA's Operation Phoenix (that assassinated between 20,000–40,000 civilian Vietnamese "activists" between 1967–1971), and more recently, executive assassination rings under the aegis of the Joint Special Operations Command that engage in preemptive and proactive attacks on foreign nationals in their own countries—all of these actions taken by the United States over the last several centuries sends an unmistakable message to the world: The United States is ready and willing to employ vast arsenals of death to protect its geostrategic and financial interests around the world.

That the leading violator of international legality and prime perpetrator of international outlawry can view its own legacy with so few official admonishments is shocking to the rest of the world. As just one example, it would take 69 walls the size of the Vietnam memorial to list all the Vietnamese that were killed in that war.

The hooded figure standing on a stool at the U.S. Abu Ghraib prison in Iraq, wires to administer electric shocks dangling from underneath a blanket draped over his outstretched arms, on whose broken figure the imprint of the depraved brutality of the U.S. military was so dramatically augmented, haunts the blood-splotched corridors of our national memory. Sheikh Mohammed is waterboarded by CIA "interrogators" 183 times in one month in 2003—a torture technique so heinous that it provokes the human instinct to gasp for air when being suffocated (it is considered a war crime under U.S. law and illegal under international agreements signed by the U.S.). We will remember these crimes that were not labeled torture when they were undertaken by the U.S. military and intelligence agencies but were decried as torture when they were used by other countries such as Japan—the U.S. convicted Japanese torturers for waterboarding U.S. troops after WWII—and the Soviet Union. We will remember images of naked prisoners covered in feces forming a human pyramid for the amusement of U.S. guards. Or a naked prisoner on his hands and knees being led around on a leash by a female solider. We will remember the accounts of female interrogators wiping red ink disguised as menstrual blood on the faces of Muslim prisoners. Or a naked detainee lying on a wet floor, handcuffed, and having objects shoved up his rectum. Or the coffins where detainees were confined with insects described to them by their interrogators as venomous. We will remember these because they were not designed to extract information as much as they were created to strike fear into the hearts and minds of all those who would oppose U.S. interests, domestic and abroad. But we can have no memory of those who died during interrogations by the U.S. military, which whose alleged murders were left uninvestigated and prosecuted by the Bush Justice Department, even when the CIA inspector general referred a case. Of course, the top levels of government had given its imprimatur, and it is likely that this also involved key Democrats as well. While U.S. military personnel participating in the torture of detainees are required, when necessary, to apply sub-xyphoid thrusts or to undertake tracheotomy procedures during waterboarding, at least half of these deaths were likely to have been deliberate homicides.

Many pundits in the U.S. media, such as Thomas Friedman, justify the torturing of Al-Qaeda operatives because they represent a special cadre of fiends, whose martyrdom tactics require a special barbarism. When, after the release of four formerly secret torture memos, President Barack Obama announced— "[I]t is our intention to assure those who carried out their duties relying in good faith upon legal advice from the Department of Justice that they will not be subject to prosecution"—it set up a terrible precedent that haunts the legacy of WWII German soldiers who sought to be excused from prosecution for their participation in crimes against humanity because they were merely following orders and relying in good faith upon the advice of their superior officers—a defense clearly rejected during the trials of Nazi war criminals held at Nuremburg. Torture is clearly and plainly a crime against humanity. By granting immunity to torturers in the face of such crimes robs the U.S. government of its humanity as much as the prisoners whom it tortured.

But here we cannot divorce these acts from the ideology of imperialism and its link to capitalism, capitalism as a structural form of violence, the violence of the father, a form of state terrorism. For me, since the value form of labor (abstract labor) that has been transmogrified into the autonomous moment of dead labor, eating up everything that it is not, can be challenged by freely associated labor and concrete, human sensuousness we need to develop what I call a philosophy of revolutionary praxis. This involves envisioning a non-capitalist future that can be achieved by means of subjective self-movement through absolute negativity so that a new relation between theory and practice can connect us to the idea of freedom. This is decidedly not dogmatic blueprint, Ilan! It is a concrete Utopian struggle, as opposed to an abstract Utopian act. In other words, it is grounded in the living and tortured flesh of the oppressed and in their struggle. What does absolute negativity mean? As Peter Hudis argues, the abolition of private property does not necessarily lead to the abolition of capital so we need to push further, to examine the direct relation between the worker and production. Here, our sole emphasis should not be on the abolition of private property, which is the product of alienated labor; it must be on the abolition of alienated labor itself. As I have mentioned before, Marx gave us some clues as to how transcend alienation, ideas that he developed from Hegel's concept of second or absolute negativity, or 'the negation of the negation'. I've written about his, and it comes mainly from the work of the founder of Marxist humanism in the United States, Raya Dunayevskaya. In addition to this we need an approach to decolonizing pedagogy, and its not just a question of the epistemicide— the epistemological violence visited upon pedagogies (including pedagogies of liberation) via Eurocentric teaching philosophies and practices—but a question of pedagogies driven by neo-liberalization, involving themselves, both in tacit and manifest ways, in spreading market ideology. This is where I support movements in Latin America that are anti-neo-liberalization, including those associated with the Bolivarian revolution.

You mentioned, Ilan, the negative dialectics of Adorno. Hudis notes that the genius of Hegel was that he was fully aware that negation is dependent on the object of its critique. In other words, ideas of liberation are impacted, in one way or another, by the oppressive forms that one tries to reject, and that negation per se does not totally free one from the negated object. But unlike the postmodernists that centuries later followed him, Hegel believed that there was a way for negation to transcend the object of its critique. He therefore introduced the notion of "the negation of the negation." Hudis makes clear that the negation of the negation, or second negativity, does not refer simply to a continuous series of negations—that can potentially go on forever and still never free negation from the object of its critique. Hegel instead argues for a self-referential negation. By negating itself, negation establishes a relation with itself—and therefore frees itself from dependence on the external object. According to Hudis, this kind of negativity, second negativity is "absolute," insofar as it exists without relation to another outside itself. In other words, negation is no longer dependent on an external object; it negates such dependency through a self-referential act of negation.

According to Hudis, Marx did not dismiss the concept of the "negation of the negation" as an idealist illusion but instead appropriated the concept of the self-referential negation "to explain the path to a new society". Marx understood that simply to negate something is still leaves us dependent upon the object of critique, in other words, it merely affirms the alienated object of our critique on a different level. As Hudis and Dunayevskaya and other Marxist humanists have point out, that has been the problem with revolutions of the past, they remained dependent upon the object of their negation. The negation of the negation, however, creates the conditions for something truly positive to emerge in that absolute negativity is no longer dependent on the other. For instance, communism replaced private property with collective property but it did not negate this relationship. Communism in this instance still held onto the idea of ownership or having. This is what needed—and needs—to be negated.

According to Hudis, Marx believed that labor or human praxis can achieve the transcendence of alienation but what was need was a subjective praxis connected with a philosophy of liberation that is able to illuminate the content of a post-capitalist society and project a path to a totally new society by convincing humanity that it is possible to resolve the contradiction between alienation and freedom. We can't resolve such a contradiction within the social universe of capital and capital's value form of labor.

This understanding of absolute negativity as a seedbed for new beginnings, is the motor of a renewed critical/revolutionary pedagogy guided by the imperative of class struggle, and the development of a philosophy of praxis. But why Marx? For me, Marx provides a theory against capitalist society, and not just a theory of it. Class theory is therefore concerned with the abolition of class (Marx's position) and the opening up of human history from the desolation of its pre-history. The Marxist theory of class has largely been dismissed, around the globe and over the last several decades, supplanted by culturalist versions of class, what Deborah Kelsh here calls "cultureclass." Versions of cultureclass favor a focus on exploring the decentering seen to be an effect of systems of representation operating within apparatuses of power-knowledge delinked from class and the exploitation of labor power. As a consequence, cultural differences are understood in terms of hybrid and continually shifting "in-between-spaces" in culture, that is, as effects of culture. Dismissed is any understanding of cultural differences as differences that are sustained, exacerbated, and (re)produced by the totality of social relations of production, kept in play only as long as they are useful to capital in its thirsty search for more and more profit. Changing society means changing the social relations of production in their totality, and for this to occur, it is necessary for the proletariat to have knowledge of the totality of social relations; it is this knowledge that is central to the development of revolutionary class consciousness that enables universal liberation of all people from the capitalist regime of exploitation. And while it is important to recognize, with Gramsci, that consciousness can be "contradictory", the struggle for social justice cannot be successfully engaged through the perpetual and local parsing of the ambivalence inherent in power-knowledge relations, or through the repeated rupturing of a signifying chain, but through the revolutionary praxis of the oppressed, forged in sustained and principled class struggle, that aims to end class society. Knowledge workers can contribute to that revolutionary struggle by struggling at the level of knowledges to reveal the role dominant knowledges play in maintaining capitalism by hiding the social relations of production in their totality. It is important to emphasize this: historical materialist critique of the dominant knowledges is socially necessary labor for the abolition of capitalism.

In line with Marx, proponents of Critical Pedagogy hold that ideas must be situated in history and experience, as fallible generalizations that need to be ideologically unveiled by means of the praxis of historical materialist critique, which because it aims to develop knowledge of social totality, is a necessary (though not sufficient) praxis in the class struggle to transform existing social relations. The development of this praxis takes on a special urgency today, when obeisance to the capitalist class remains an unspoken given, when capitalism's capacity to integrate the working-class through their incorporation in financial markets and through the internation-alization of the neoliberal market economy remains steady, and when expectations that neoliberal capitalism can be superseded by a better form of organizing social and economic life—such as socialism (or even Keynesian capitalism)—have been repeatedly renounced and undermined by political elites who act as the agents for the capitalist class (and are handsomely rewarded for their ideological services).

The intensification of capitalism's two primal axes of reproduction—deregulation and privatization—has impacted the conditions of possibility for barbarism to appear and wreak havoc in new and horrific ways that do not escape the precincts of educa-tion and the politics of knowledge production. Sadly, in the academy, and especially in institutions of graduate education, the challenge to capitalism has not taken place in the realm of material life, but rather in the arena of discourse and the politics of representation. The reason-centered subject of colonial power that subjugates subaltern peoples of the periphery (semi-feudal peripheral social relations) is not challenged directly by revolutionary praxis but is now "decentered" as a text by way of a critique of Enlightenment humanism and by challenging the doxa of institutional disciplinary regimes. But does not such a stance too often end up as an official apologetics for neoliberal capital and imperial power?

While I advocate an epistemic relativism in arguing that there is no privileged access to the truth, and that there is no direct correspondence between an object and its representation, at the same time I am opposed to a judgmental relativism—that there are no grounds, rational grounds, for advocating some beliefs over others. We can't fall into the trap of assuming all beliefs or arguments are equally valid. We need some explanatory adequacy or judgemental rationality in making decisions about various theories, and we do this in relation to the material world, to things that exist independently of our attempts to explain them or account for them. How do we create new forms of sociality that constitute human subjects both in their heterogeneity and in their universality? Our particular struggle in this regard is to make sure such universality is not representative of the bourgeois male subject. All universalisms are dirty, claims Bruce Robbins, and by this he means that universal standards are arrived at in conditions of unequal power. But he also notes that it is only dirty universalisms that will help us against the powers and agents of still dirtier ones. Similarly, we can't abandon every and all notion of essence, of something that is beyond appearance, because if we do that—if we privilege the concept of difference—then the notion of appearance alone becomes evidence that there are different categories of humanity that have little or nothing in common—or that they are incommensurable. If we do that, we fall into the same logic as positivist racial theory—which deduces categories of races from mere appearances of skin, hair, and bone. Apprehension of formal difference then moves to an explanation for the existence of different ontological categories. This is a dangerous move, just as I think a rejection of all humanism is dangerous, a rejection that follows the notion that modernity itself leads to an annihilation of the other. And here is a point that many Marxists have made that has powerful validity, Ilan. Much of the barbarism of the 20th century is not so much a consequence of modernity as it was a product of specific capitalist social relations. Of course, we need to critique the false claim of universality inherent in the European particular, of course. But we must recognize, as you do Ilan that humanist principles can be coercive or liberating, depending on who is employing them and for what purpose. Here I am calling for a "nonabstract and nonhomogeneous" form of universalism as a political referent. We must be extremely cautious not to conflate universalism with uniformity, because universals can be both various and locally diverse. It is very evident, for instance, that colonialism has been intrinsic to the kind of universality that we have had in much of world history and that the only universal civilization that exists today is global capitalism. We need to distinguish between an abstract universalism that dissolves important differences among diverse phenomena and a concrete universalism that carefully draws such distinctions while upholding conditions that are binding for all. You talk, Ilan about the restricted and often dangerously destructive Western bourgeois character of Enlightenment universalism. I agree it is a worthy target of critique. But I do not feel we should jettison the term universal and cast it into the trash heap of epistemological history. The solution isn't getting rid of the concept of universalism but working towards a better universality—one conjoined with a pluriversality. Here, the work of Walter Mignolo and Ramon Grosfoguel on the idea of pluriversality is crucial. Terry Eagleton notes that what is holding back the realization of universal justice is the false universalism of Western man, who believes that this universal struggle for democracy and social justice can be achieved by extending his values and liberties to the entire globe. The universality we adhere to must not be a masked cultural particularity; yet at the same time we need to struggle in the name of everyone's right to negotiate their own differences—not at the philosophical metacultural level, but as real, living, breathing subjects of history sitting at the table of dialogue. This means committing to the objective truth of the values of other cultures, that is, not rejecting the nonsubjective character of their values. In other words, we need to recognize that all cultures have their own access to truth even though the values of other cultures might not be compatible with the values and conceptual schemes of my own culture. We cannot countenance the imposition of a Western subjectivism.

We need to respect other conceptual systems—other perspectives—because no single system can capture all truths. I have not given up on translability. Paulo Freire once told me to translate his work within the contextual specificity of where I was standing as a teacher. He told me that my job was one of translation—of translating his philosophical language into a language that impacted teachers in various pedagogical settings. That I should not simply impose his conception of knowing on my students—which would be a form of conceptual imperialism. Our misunderstandings with individuals from other cultures does not mean that these cultures are incommensurable. After all, our conceptual systems can be different—and we can find such systems to be incompatible or inconsistent or both—but there is always the possibility of translation, no matter how limited. I am not advancing a moral obligation for tolerating other cultures; I want to be clear on that. We need other grounds for taking a position against intolerance. We need to engage other cultures in order to better understand ourselves and the world as a totality. We engage in the values and belief systems of other cultures, not in a vulgar way by according them only subjective merit and by denying them any nonsubjective validity. We engage them by embracing a concept of truth. All cultures have access—their own access—to the truth. The rejection of the nonsubjective character of the values of other cultural beings (i.e., considering their views as just another position among many positions without any real truth value) is to fall prey to a Western ethnocentrism, imperialism and racism.

Anibal Quijano has warned us against the dualism and evolutionism situated the European subject as the most spiritually evolved while women and slaves were viewed as the most primitive, locked into their corporeality. Slavery, serfdom, wage labor, and reciprocity all functioned to produce commodities for the world market. What Quijano calls a "colonial power matrix" ("patrón de poder colonial") affecting all dimensions of social existence such as sexuality, authority, subjectivity and labor, Berkeley professor Ramon Grosfoguel conceptualizes as a historical-structural heterogeneous totality that by the late 19th century came to cover the whole planet.

Expanding on Quijano's work, Grosfoguel describes the coloniality of power as an entanglement of multiple and heterogeneous global hierarchies ("heterarchies") of sexual, political, epistemic, economic, spiritual, linguistic and racial forms of domination and exploitation where the racial/ethnic hierarchy of the European/non-European divide transversally reconfigures all of the other global power structures. As race and racism became the organizing principle that structured all of the multiple hierarchies of the world-system, Grosfoguel argues that the different forms of labor that were articulated to capitalist accumulation at a world-scale were assigned according to this racial hierarchy. Cheap, coercive labor was carried out by non-European people in the periphery and "free wage labor" was exercised in the core. Such has been the case up to the present day. Grosfoguel asserts that, contrary to the Eurocentric perspective, race, gender, sexuality, spirituality, and epistemology are not additive elements (epiphenomenal to) to the economic and political structures of the capitalist world-system, but a constitutive part of the broad entangled "package" called the European modern/colonial capitalist/patriarchal world-system. I agree with Grosfoguel on this point.

So what does this mean for revolutionary Critical Pedagogy? Those of us who are part of the project of Critical Pedagogy have attempted to create greater cultural space for the formerly excluded to have their voices heard (represented), at the same time we have to make sure that this does not unwittingly reinscribe a neo-liberal pluralist stance rooted in the ideology of individualism, of the possessive investment in white privilege, of free-market, neo-liberal capitalism. Why don't so-called multiculturalists recognize that the forces of diversity and difference are allowed to flourish provided that they remain within the prevailing forms of capitalist social arrangements? The neopluralism of a politics of difference (including those based on 'race') cannot adequately pose a substantive challenge to the productive system of capitalism—a system that is able to accommodate a vast pluralism of ideas and cultural practices. This politics of difference cannot capture adequately the ways in which various manifestations of oppression are intimately connected to the central dynamics of capitalist exploitation. But Marxist theory can help us in ways that other theories cannot. The language of Critical Pedagogy is indebted to this theory but is not restricted to it, in its search for a language connected to being and becoming and a validation of the Other in the self and the self in the Other. Self-love, not hatred, and a recognition of the Other in the spirit of mutuality and dialogue.

IGZ: It is very important, to my mind, dear Peter, that you too acknowledge the centrality of *love* for the act of critique and for the very possibility of a gate to dialogue. It is also important that you accept the unique significance of universalism while acknowledging the centrality of difference. Here we agree Peter, and I think we can also agree that much of the present attempts in the various trends of current critical education do not offer an unproblematic synthesis between the modern and the post-modern, between the language of difference and anti-universalism and the logos of emancipation and responsibility. This is an important starting point. This is, however, also where I face my uneasiness with current hegemonic versions of Critical Pedagogy as well as with your Manichaean Utopia.

A personal note, Peter, before articulating my uneasiness with the present stance of Critical Pedagogy. It is so embarrassing, but I will say it even if it is so hard to do so, since it relates to some of the dearest fortunes and hopes of some of my best revolutionary friends. 1. Many of my Critical Pedagogy friends dwell in the most privileged and expensive neighborhoods in America, within the most bourgeois dreams and demand record-breaking fees for lecturing on the topic of the suffering of the poor victims of the West. It is a cause for embarrassment, Peter, even if you could rightly say that it does not necessarily say anything substantial about my friends' concepts of revolutionary pedagogy or about their critical analysis of Western colonialism and so forth. One should separate the value of the theory from the embarrassing sides of the actual life and the personality of the thinker, you may say, having in mind Marx and others. 2. It is embarrassing for me to see the friends of some of the central representatives of critical education and the friends of their friends: Chavez and Norberto Rafael Ceresole, Ahmadidijad, Ward Churchill and Muhammad Bakri, Jose Saramago, Nasrallah, Kim Jong-Il, Assad Junior—the list is so long. These and their friends are the friends of the post-colonial agenda which made it only natural for a relatively "moderate" Arab country such as Egypt to invite for an official academic tour Holocaust deniers, to officially refuse to screen in Egyptian cinemas "Schindler's List" because it is sympathetic to Jews, to propagate in all cultural levels the most primitive anti-Semitic ideology on a daily basis as one could see even in the celebration of the renewed Alexandria Library. In the 2003 exhibition of the major monotheistic texts the Torah is positioned along with the notorious anti-Semitic *Protocols of the Elders of Zion*. But you do not have to search for the exceptions, only go into normal newspapers in Cairo or open any of the TV channels in Egypt and you will be overwhelmed with the most brutal anti-Semitic propaganda as part of daily normality, let alone if you listen to the Islamist theology and its political education. Only recently an Egyptian court ruled that any Egyptian citizen marrying an Israeli woman would automatically lose his Egyptian citizenship. Surely you are aware that in less moderate regimes, such as the Palestinian Authority in the West Bank, it is the law that any one who sells any land to an Israeli is to be executed, and that in the free Palestinian territory of Gaza anti-Semitism is the official ideology of the regime and terror against Jews is an explicit policy and central ideological commitment, neither a contingent reaction to any given "provocation" nor a temporary aim. 3. It is also embarrassing to see the dogmatism and the standardized language of many of the critical educators in relation to the (very important) critique of the West, "Monotheism", "phallocentric logos" and so forth, not to mention their "critique" of demonized "Israel". Without much study of the situation they readily take a list of accurate or fabricated citations or slogans and present their "critique" and judgment of "Israeli crimes" and so forth. In these "critiques" there is so much hubris and so little responsibility for *the essence of critique*; and there is not much self-respect either. Considering the sweeping generalizations, and considering the specifics of each of these accusations, it is frustrating to see some of my best friends draw into these rituals. And I present these claims as one who sees the importance of criticizing Israeli politics, and as one who does not consider himself a patriot. Quite the opposite. As you know, it is my firm conviction that Zionism is a very big mistake, a wrong path of the Jewish people, even if this mistake is at the same time also a powerful potential for a further edification of humanity. However, I just cannot cooperate with consensual anti-intellectualism and the new progressive "critiques" when they arc established on fraud, hatred and worship of an anti-humanistic quasi-holiness that I conceive as new anti-Semitism. The lists of "the crimes of the USA" or "the enduring brutality of Israel against the Palestinian people" and so forth are so unfounded, unbalanced and de-contextualized, Peter. They become more of a ritual, *a sacred work* of the devotees of the post-colonial quasi-religiosity—not a critique of the kind one can find in Marx or Horkheimer. Much of the critique of Israel is actually part of the agenda of the de-colonization of Western culture and challenging the Empire. As if Russia, China, Iran, North Korea or North Vietnam are any better and can offer an alternative to the Empire; assuming that if only

Syria under the rule of the Ba'ath party, Socialist Venezuela, Humeinist Iran, Liberated Zimbabwe or progressive Brazil will dominate the globe and not the Judeo-Christian ethos–the world will become a better place for becoming-human. I think it is important for us to remember, Peter, that it was only recently that Chavez was the first leader to congratulate Ahmadinejad, "his brother", for his important victory in the 2009 "elections" while the Iranian freedom activists are still being beaten to death in the streets of Tehran by the government's special units; or that with all the tens of billions of petrodollars that keep on coming, Caracas is today documented as the most criminal place on earth with 180 murder cases each weekend and with gigantic governmental corruption, while it actualizes Critical Pedagogy and post-colonial politics as its guiding educational path. Of course, Peter, there are also good things happening there for the poor, and one should not underestimate these either. But this is something one could say also about the Stalinist regime or the communist regime of Saloth Sar, widely known as Pol Pot, as he butchered one third of the Cambodian population sincerely believing that this was the imperative of the red flag, with the support of many of the radical socialists who currently support Chavez, Nasrallah, Ahmadinejad and their company. Peter, to my mind the context of the reforms and the general trend and its telos are of vital importance when evaluating educational developments in the current post-colonial arenas, which make revolutionary Critical Pedagogy so relevant in your view. But Peter, we should also ask ourselves *at what cost?* It is awkward for me to see my friends celebrating such authoritarian personalities and a politics of hatred and murder as the beginning of the genuine revolution, certainly their very concept of "a genuine revolution" that will correct the mistakes of previous revolutions and establish peaceful, post-capitalist human bloom. Let us refer to the critique and resistance to the crimes against humanity as realized by the USA and "Israel". Such crimes are allegedly manifested in Israel's bombardment of civilian homes in the Jenin battle in April 2002, in the Second Lebanese War (2006), or recently in the 2008 Gaza war. I would like to be more specific on this in order to enable a serious critique and a serious critique of the critique.

Knowledge and theoretization of the facts are so important—and dangerous here too, and the temptation to be swallowed by the struggle between the conflicting representation apparatuses and the struggling interpretational ecstasies, and to forget human suffering, happiness and hopes, is also so real. Either way the normal situation in the following examples is the enduring Palestinian and Hezbollah tactic of deliberately locating their rocket batteries, directed normally at civilian Israeli targets, in places such as their own schools, mosques and densely populated areas. As we speak, Peter, in a formally declared cease-fire the southern city of Ashkelon is attacked by Grad missiles and the Jordanian city of Akaba was mistakenly bombarded by Kasam rockets that were targeted from Gaza at the neighboring Israeli tourist city of Eilat. Now, Peter, in reference to the said "crimes against humanity", consider the dilemma of an Israeli pilot and Israeli society more generally: the pilot identifies a missile battery on the roof of such a house ready to be launched (normally) against an Israeli civilian target. He must decide *instantly*: should he fire a missile to destroy it (knowing that by that action he will also kill the family within this house)? Or should he save this family and sacrifice an Israeli family that will become the victim of such a decision in that it will make possible the successful launch of the Palestinian or Hezbollah missile? The decision must be immediate and uncompromising either way. It is an either-or situation. How should he act? What criteria should be the relevant guide, and what or who should be the supreme judge? Should the number of potential victims become a yardstick? The relative burden accumulated by each of the rival sides? Should he prefer, always and at any price, with no reservation, saving the Other at the cost of his own dear ones? Should he be guided by the commitment always and unconditionally to prefer the lives of his own dear ones? Should the normal behavior of armies in similar situations be of any relevance? Should he be guided by Jewish ethics, and what would be the right interpretation of it in this particular situation? Of course, one can say, as many critical pedagogues do: "*Your very existence is a crime against humanity*. Even if we postpone your scandalous historical existence as "the chosen people" and your self-imposed superior morality and unique Jewish mission in (negating) history, your very modern Zionist history in the last 120 years in Israel is responsible for initiating the existence of the Palestinian national identity and therefore their counter-violence, and you are responsible for both your crimes and the Palestinian reactions; it is, essentially, the *projection* of the Original Sin of the colonialist's violence boomeranging to him as counter-violence of his victim".

This is a serious argument which I will address later, because it is central to an understanding of current revolutionary Critical Pedagogy. But Peter, please, allow me to present you with another example of the normal disregard for the complexity of the moral dilemma and the problematic of the situation where an army targets civilian houses and the critics present this as crimes against humanity to be rightfully avenged.

The 2002 Jenin battle, as you surely know, is presented as a "massacre" and but another manifestation of the murderous nature of the Israeli existence. So here, against the fashionable rhetoric of my critical friends, I will remind you that this struggle was initiated as an Israeli response to a terrible series of terror attacks in 2002 when Israel decided to clear the West Bank of Palestinian terrorists who daily entered Israel and terrorized its population (this was before the building of the wall that reduced substantially the entry of human bombs and other "freedom fighters" into Israel). You might remember the letter I wrote to you at that time, sharing with you my friend that one of these "human bombs" decided the best thing to do is to kill as many Jewish children as possible and he exploded in the school bus no. 37 on Moria Boulevard at Haifa, only three houses away from our house, killing 16 children. The event, which followed three other attacks in Haifa alone and tens in other cities, was celebrated as an important victory over "Israeli colonialism", happened in the same bus stop where our dear Mae, then aged 13, normally gets off the bus on her way home from school. In Jenin, the Palestinian fighters were at the time offered a safe departure to Gaza (without their weapons) and the battle of Jenin could have been avoided. But no. They insisted on the battle. And they insisted fighting not in a remote hilltop or some other location that would not endanger the civilian population, but just the opposite: they insisted on having the battle at Jenin, specifically in the most populated part of the city. Not only that: they prepared 15000 explosive devices which were placed in the densely peopled Palestinian houses so that when the Israeli soldiers arrive these bombs would kill the Palestinian family and the Israeli soldiers all together. It is a grave moral decision to use your own civilian population in such a manner Peter, even if the population gladly cooperated with this cynical strategy. The Israeli army considering the situation had to decide between several fundamental possibilities: 1. To back off and avoid the battle, forsaking its mission to stop the terror wave which made life in Israel unbearable. 2. To bombard the Palestinian militants from afar by cannons or airplanes, accepting as unavoidable the civilian casualties—until the surrender or the destruction of the Palestinian military force at that location. 3. To engage in house-to-house combat, risking the lives of the Israeli soldiers but saving so many of the civilian Palestinian population that the Palestinian leadership cynically positioned as a propaganda tool. Please Peter, ask yourself honestly: what do you think the Chinese army would have done in such a situation? How would the North Korean army react in such a dilemma? And the Russian army? And the French, Peter, the French army? I can tell you what is my guess, without being able to verify it: Based on their military past I think each of these armies would have bombarded the militants from afar and would have avoided entering such a well prepared ambush. This is only a guess, of course. Well, let's return to the events of April 2 and 7 April in Jenin on the West Bank, which became the subject of the world famous film *Jenin Jenin* made by Muhammad Bakri, who described in it the so-called "massacre at Jenin" and the "Israeli crimes against humanity".

The Israeli army decided to put its soldiers at risk and to save as many Palestinian civilians as it could, and avoid a bombardment of the Palestinian force until its surrender or destruction. The Palestinian media claimed that thousands were massacred. Many NGOs, again, accused Israel of crimes against humanity, ethnic cleansing and you name it. The UN commission which investigated the events, far from being suspected as pro-Israeli, reported that Palestinian casualties numbered between 52, most of them militants, and that Israel lost 23 soldiers. In the public mind, however, the complexity of the situation and the moral dilemmas as well as the cynical Palestinian decision to sacrifice the civilian population as a propaganda trick was exchanged for a one-dimensional representation of the events in the progressive anti-colonialist media and apparatuses such as the film *Jenin Jenin*. In this self-styled documentary one can see Israeli tanks rolling over Palestinian girls and hear shocking testimony of eye witnesses that Palestinian kids were sent by the Israeli soldiers to disarm the Palestinian explosives, and after safely returning from their "mission" they were shot by the Israeli soldiers and replaced by another group of Palestinian children only to be shot after completing their terrible "mission" and so on and so forth. The editor and initiator of the film, a star in the Israeli cinema industry and a celebrated celebrity in Israeli intellectual salons, admitted that he fabricated the filmed "facts" using different techniques and tricks to create the illusion of a massacre in Jenin. As in the case of Dr. Ward Churchill in the USA, in the case of Bakri in Israel the left was divided in its response to the fraud. Some of our leftist friends in Israel, as in the USA, were firm in dissociating themselves from deliberate misleading representation and fraud, even in face of the good cause of resisting the Israeli politics. Others claimed that Bakri should not be condemned as a manipulative political activist and that *Jenin Jenin* should not be judged as a false documentary but as a work of art, a great work of art. In the name of art and free speech it is wrong to condemn Bakri and *Jenin Jenin*. Still others acknowledged the fraud, but from different and conflicting positions (Marxists and post-modern) and enthusiastically celebrated it as an important contribution to the liberation of Palestine. Are not some other members of the Bakri family actively involved in the terror attacks committed for the liberation of Palestine they would ask? And isn't he simply joining a family effort using the tools at his disposal to add his contribution to the same noble cause of freeing Palestine from colonialist oppression? Indeed, by deliberately falsifying the facts and misleading the viewer, *Jenin Jenin* in its essence represents the *true* stance of Palestine and Jenin as no "objective" documentary could offer a naïve viewer. This assertion, Peter, is vital for the understanding of current post-colonialist education and the mission of the new anti-Semitism, its run away from the truth and its disregard of the good, replacing it with quasi-idealist playfulness with narratives and "representations" that accepts Will to Power in its most vulgar versions as its new religiosity.

It reminds me of an MA thesis by one of my best Critical Pedagogy students, who writes in the introduction that in this research, under the enlightening inspiration of Spivak, she has no interest in the truth of the matter. Her primary interest in this MA thesis is to write in such a manner about Palestinian history that will ultimately empower Palestinian women of our day to serve ultimate national aims and requirements. But the Jenin battle, like the Second Lebanon War and its dilemmas, like the last Gaza conflict, do not stand unmediated and disconnected from the Zeitgeist. As one can see in the testimony and especially in the silencing reception of the testimony of Colonel Richard Kemp, former commander of UK forces in Afghanistan and a member in the UK intelligence committee. In his testimony he says:

> Based on my knowledge and experience I can say this: during the operation cast lead the Israeli Defense Forces did more to safeguard the civilian population in a combat zone than any other army in the history of warfare. Israel did so while facing an enemy which deliberately positioned its [military] capability behind the human shield of the civilian population. Hamas, like Hezbollah, are experts on driving the media agenda... the truth is that the IDF made extraordinary efforts to save the civilian population, dropping 2 million leaflets and making more than 100,000 telephone calls. Many missions were aborted to prevent civilian population casualties... More than anything the civilian casualties were the consequences of the Hamas way of fighting. Hamas deliberately try to scarify its own population...

This is the reason for the systematic misrepresentation of the conflict in Western media and for the quest for ever more terrible "facts" about the crimes against humanity perpetrated by the Israeli policies. This, of course, does not mean that Israeli policies and practices are so often wrong, unjust and terrible. Too frequently am I embarrassed by Critical Pedagogy educators who, in their post-colonial commitment to "resist" and "critique" the Israeli victimizer as an arch-representative of the Western, or the Judeo-Christian logos, are swallowed up by dogmatism and fail to face the richness, the complexity and the tragic nature of the situation where there are no Sons of Light and Sons of Darkness fighting each other, and certainly there are no easy solutions such as an Israeli withdrawal from the rest of the Palestinian territories (the total withdrawal from the Gaza Strip only made things worse; the Palestinian leadership did not conclude from it that peace was the proper response). It is embarrassing in Israel, as it is embarrassing in the USA, to see the support people like Ward Churchill enjoy, and I know how much you are involved in it, Peter, and how much you suffer from it personally, to the degree of becoming a number one enemy of the American people in some crazy right-wing lists of patriots and anti-patriots. I acknowledge also the benefits in academia and in progressive circles of being singled out by these right-wing patriots. I experience it myself in Israel as I am considered one of the most dangerous academics, a Jewish anti-Semite, and so forth. The benefits are psychological, academic, intellectual, political, and, yes Peter, also financial.

They open new possibilities for the language of critique in education but they are also a threat to a courageous addressing of the imperatives, limitations and open possibilities of critical language in education. And this brings me to the fourth cause of my unease with some critical educators who lack courage; they do not lack quasi-courage and cathartic energies: they lack *courage for self-reflection* and moral responsibility, especially in situations where their radical resistance is so well rewarded by progressive circles worldwide. 4. The post-colonialist prism of Critical Pedagogy in the case of Israel does not educate for courage and responsibility in face of rich moral dilemmas and theoretical aporias, or in the light of dialectal facts of history. If we continue to develop the Jenin example, what do we face if we broaden the picture and delve into its fundamentals to learn something about the current critical language in education and its limits, and about the possibility of a new critical language in education? We face two conflicting societies, two nation-building projects that clash with each other. The Palestinians and their post-colonialist supporters, and of course the wide range of the old and the new anti-Semites, see the very establishment of the State of Israel as a colonialist violence that has succeeded and goes in quest of more victories, oppression and victimization. Israeli society as a Zionist society conceives itself as a nation among all nations which has a right to self-determination, and that Israel is its legitimate home which deserves defending. The fundamental truism of Zionist existence is that the Jewish people and the Land of Israel are inseparable, and Zionism is about "homereturning" back to secular history and to the Land of Israel. As a critic of this Zionist decision to return to secular history, Peter, and as a person who faces also the reactions to Diasporic education, I suggest to Israelis (and to all humans everywhere) the alternative of Diasporic existence. At the same time I must also admit the genuine commitment of Israelis to return to normality, to what they and two thousand years of history considered their legitimate home—and the power of this love. It is not a colonial enslavement of a local population and its oppression, as far as the

Israeli narrative is concerned. Now Peter, what do we see when we study Critical Pedagogy and its post-colonial agenda in face of the clash of these two narratives? Critical Pedagogy accepts neither the rights that a Jew draws from the Torah or from the long Jewish history of commitment to return "home"— *"Lashana haba'a biyrushalayim"*—nor the actual enduring presence of the Jewish population in Israel throughout history till the very beginning of Zionist immigration in the last part of the 19th century. Critical educators rarely, embarrassing how very rarely, position themselves in between and against the two opposing nation-building projects as two narratives, neither of which is more authentic, genuine or rightful than the other. Critical pedagogues today normally insist that one, the Israeli project, is "colonialist" and the other, the Palestinian project, is genuine and authentic, or alternatively is an imagined, albeit genuine, community of victims. And it is so embarrassing for me to see Critical Pedagogy so far from making a courageous critique of *any* collectivism, of any nation-building project, be it Israeli, Palestinian, Italian or Argentinean. Still, on the personal level I have had so many conversations with many of my critical friends, and again and again they fail to see the *love* in the Zionist project: only its aggression and victimization. They search for drives to oppression and enslavement, and fail to see the self-sacrifice for the "homereturning" project, the high toll and anti-colonialist character of the Zionist decision to return to normality, to secular world history and to Israel. This is why they fail to recollect the tragedy of the situation. The gravity of the situation is far beyond their reach as the two opposing societies in this case are *struggling from different time fields*: the central social parts of the Israeli society are over-modernized and function according to the post-modern ideals, interests and yardsticks, while Palestinian society, like most of the Arab world, has not embarked on deep restructuring modernization dynamics and faces modernity already in crisis only to seek refuge in two alternatives which have formed a coalition against the Utopia of Enlightenment: Islamic fundamentalism and post-colonial counter-violence. Our critical friends, Peter, fail to offer a courageous critical education in face of Palestinian burning of the forests in Israel as part of the love of Palestine, which for them has become like a beloved woman who surrenders herself to her rapist. Their critical training is of no help to them either when faced with the facts that according to a serious study, for all the discrimination and suffering of Palestinians in Israel they strongly resist being liberated: *when offered the possibility of having their village part of greater Palestine in a future Israeli-Palestinian peace agreement, 96% would reject such an agreement if it made their village part of the Palestinian state*, while the same rate insist on the need to destroy Israel...

Dear Peter, these are the cracks through which the possibilities for worthy problematizations enable overcoming conventions and the invitation of a flight from courageous life. In too many cases, however, these potentials are instead used by Critical Pedagogy educators (they always come from the outside since Palestinian leaders are too fearful of Critical Pedagogy reflecting on Palestinian society, and they ban by law even the books of Edward Said) to educate the Palestinians, as the Canadian Howard Davidson and others do, for "resistance to oppression". No permission is granted even to critical philosophy of education in the West Bank, certainly not in Gaza under the control of Hamas, or for that matter in Iran, because of the potential of self-critique, dialogue and democratic deliberation. Instead, the call is for furthering unification, strengthening consensus and "resistance". In face of two opposing manifestations of patriotism and conflicting fields of legitimating the "homereturning" projects, Critical Pedagogy is silent—or worse, very active in the wrong direction, namely supporting the "counter-violence" of the Palestinian "victim" without understanding that *the two normalization projects victimize "their" citizens and each other* as part and parcel of the same logic, which has to be challenged, not enhanced, by critical education. Nietzsche was so clear on that in his *Schopenhauer as an Educator*: genuine education should liberate us from suggestive convention, identity and aims, even from the "I" as constituted by normalizing education and "our" collective. It is so hard for me to see some of my best friends failing here, in face of this challenge, educating for surrendering to the aims, conventions and interests of the anti-humanist powers, sometimes in coalition with fear of self-critique and friends in whose company I would not like my children or my students to be.

This brings me to a more speculative aspect of the possibility of a new critical language in education in face of its surrender to the new anti-Semitism, to self-forgetfulness and to the urge back to thingness in the form of "home". This "home", which Critical Pedagogy enhances, offers the hospitality of radical consensus or at least ecstatic sacred work of "critique" and "resistance" in a world where there is no longer room for transcendence, nor therefore for genuine progress of the kind Marx promised us. What Critical Pedagogy offers in these instances is an ecstatic "horizontal" self-forgetfulness in face of the deconstruction of humanistic holiness so that "pragmatic" approval of the victims' self-evidence will inherit and replace the Enlightenment's responsibility for universal progress towards justice, truth and freedom which is not in conflict with equality. The presence of the clash between freedom and justice, between love and the growing probability of the end of life as a manifestation of human progress and the rival anti-humanist invitations—to be completely swallowed by the postmodern Pleasure Machine, or alternatively by the new anti-Semitic spirituality—as it is today enhanced by so many of the better aspects of progressive and critical thinkers, is furthermore an impetus for *hope*.

The new critical language or that which is beyond the language of "critique" should address hope, courage, Love of Life, togetherness and responsibility in light of the new realities unforeseen by Heraclitus, Plato, Jesus, Buddha, Montaigne, Marx, Nietzsche, Einstein and Adorno. The philosophical, existential and political presence of the new anti-Semitism is too often manifested in different progressive prisms of radical multiculturalism, radical feminism, postcolonialism and queer theories. It should be addressed, Peter, in face of other developments such as the presence of mega-speeding of life. The tradition of "critique", for all its importance—and your work, Peter, is one of the better manifestations of its importance, is far from adequate for such a challenge, for such an attempt to justify *Life* under the new sky. I have tried to articulate the concepts of *derech-eretz*, *orcha* and *Diasporic life* as part of my response to the apparent limits to the language of "critique" and "resistance" in the historical moment governed by the quasi-spirituality of the new anti-Semitism.

In the Hebrew language *orcha* means a caravan of camels and humans with their belongings crossing the endless desert towards the destiny of this unique togetherness. *Orcha* is an improvised movement that is to find/create its own destiny. But *what is the essence of the destiny of orcha?* The essence of *orcha* turns, potentially, each "desert" and every moment anew into an oasis. This is the truth of the movement of *orcha* as an improvised co-poiesis. This is the truth of its destiny. The very rich existence of the caravan in the eternity of time and the endlessness of the "desert" is its genuine aim. It relates to a time when deserts were "endless" and had their own tempo, essence and telos, of which *orcha* is part and parcel. Strong ties connect *orcha* and *derech eretz*.

Orcha worthy of its name is a moral momentum. As such it is historically situated, influenced by social and cultural conditions. It has no meaning beyond specific material conditions and space-time relations. It transcends itself, however, at any particular time, and it is much more than what it is in any specific location each moment anew. It is *a living, improvised co-poiesis*: it is a unique, nomadic hospitality which overcomes the colonization drive and the quest for "homereturning" to thingness by eternally opening itself to the infinity of a mature improvisation each moment anew. This hospitality reclaims the good even in face of complex moments and deconstructed self-evidence that normally offers us totalitarian alternatives, sophisticated cynicism or blazes of self-indulgent radicalism as a replacement for the good deed.

Orcha is never totally determined by a quest for territorial sovereignty, not even by commanding knowledge and people. It is a kind of *togetherness-in-movement*, a moral momentum. It realizes the promise of togetherness of Diasporic existence and the *hope* of nomadism for transcendence, not for dwelling in the immanence. It is the specific manifestation of Diasporic dialogical morality. The maturity of the eternal improviser and co-poiesis join within it and become a *homeless hospitality*. Its nomadism is neither a punishment nor a mistake or an immature stage to be corrected tomorrow. What kind of hospitality is it if it does not represent the "home-returning" drive? It is the hospitality of the response. The response to an invitation for Diasporic life. It is dedicated to not being at "home" at all costs; refusing to become swallowed by the self-evidence, self-indulgence. The negation of the "I", the Other at "home" and the Other "there" is essential to Diasporic Philosophy. Refusing any identity thinking or any positive Utopia is here actualized ontologically, epistemologically, ethically, existentially, and politically within the co-poiesis of *orcha* as a dynamic togetherness which is simultaneously in the infinity of the moment which is very much within the framework of the historical moment and its material/political specific arenas and dynamics. This dwelling in the infinity of the moment enables it to reclaim the good in a historical reality of growing complexity and mega-speeds. Reclaiming good becomes a dimension of intimacy with the truth of Love of Life.

By reintroducing Love, *orcha* enables responsibility and strives for religious creativity. At the same time, *orcha* refuses all forms of positive Utopia in theory and practice. It overcomes any theoretical or political "home", self-evidence, truth, self-content, nirvana, and all other manifestations of Thanatos. In this sense it insists on consistent negativity as a form of Life. It is a negativity, however, which transforms itself and turns "deserts" into "oases" of togetherness that is so different than the ethnocentrism of the victims that is cultivated by the new anti-Semitism.

For me, Peter, Diasporic Philosophy represents *orcha* as a kind of hospitality in face of homelessness that is opposed to the self-forgetfulness manifested in the quest to be swallowed in the immanence and "homereturning" to the nothingness offered too often by "our" post-metaphysical moment even within critical education. This of course is only a first step Peter, but it already manifests *hope* and maybe even sensitivity to the need for counter-education which will enhance courage, yes, the courage to hope.

PM: The struggle for a new language, yes, Ilan. I am with you here. But before I discuss the implications for such a language, let me explain why the educational left here in the United States has been so harsh with Israel. And let me preface this, Ilan, with a final comment about President Chavez. I have told you that I am a supporter of the Bolivarian revolution but that does not mean I take an uncritical stance towards Chavez—or the Venezuelan government—as forging an alliance with Iran is concerned. I do not unqualifiedly support any position; I support or disagree with decisions in a dialectic mode. I have tried to make clear that revolutions are sites of struggle, where debates and dialogues should provide the launching pad for critique by the practice of absolute negativity (a term upon which I will elaborate later in my answer) as a striving for the seedbed for the new. Now let me proceed here to describe the context that I believe is responsible for powerful reactions against, and in many instances justified criticism of, the Israel state, not least of which is the powerful US/Israel axis of power and how it is perceived in various geopolitical locations around the world. But I am going to limit myself to the United States and Canada. Please understand, Ilan, that in the United States, and North America in general, I would say (as a Canadian-American, I lived the first thirty-five years of my life in Canada), it is patently clear that the media reports favor the Israelis as victims and demonize the Palestinians as terrorists. It is difficult, if not impossible, to contest this fact. This creates a great deal of anger and frustration, understandably, among critical scholars and activists in the United States. You risk being denied tenure (the case of Norman Finkelstein), or you have your professorship removed (the case of Joel Kovel) and you find yourself on the receiving end of pro-Zionist groups who launch vigorous public media attacks on you if you criticize Israeli attacks on the Palestinians (the case of William Robinson) from moral, political or diplomatic perspectives. Frequently these cases (and there are many more) involve a professor who is Jewish. I am saying this to try to unravel in very general terms the context here in the United States that accounts for leftist criticism of Israel. The Palestinian position is rarely, if ever, voiced. When, for instance, in the first few days of the Intifada, when Israel was using U.S. helicopters to destroy civilian complexes and apartments, and President Clinton responded by sending the largest shipment of military helicopters in years to Israel, the US press refused to publish this information, but the US left knew about it. We both know, Ilan, that the corporate media serve to legitimate the crimes of Zionism yet they never fail to describe the attacks by the Palestinians as acts of wanton barbarism. Those who wish to contest this one-sided treatment are accused of being anti-Semites. It is as if the one thing that unites the pro-Israeli media is anti-Semitism. So many university leftists try, at their own risk, to do what they can to give a response that challenges the pro-Israeli media. I think it is important to demythologize the Israel created by the US mainstream press—by criticizing Israel's militarized state, its expansion as an imperialist power, its building of ideological and real walls, its humiliation of Palestinian civilians who have to endure Israeli checkpoints (I've been through them myself on my way to Ramallah), its exceptionalism, its human rights abuses and its enduring institutionalized racism. Are not the Palestinians suffering from relentless Israeli settlement, are they not penned behind walls and barriers into isolated geographic spaces? Are not three Bantustans being created in the West Bank by the walls—in the north, central and south, separating these communities from East Jerusalem, which will sound the death-knell for these groups who depend upon East Jerusalem economically, culturally and politically? Is not much of this wall in violation of international humanitarian law? Is not this situation one that was designed by the Israelis to destroy the Palestinian people? As Joel Kovel notes, Zionists accept the destiny of the Jews as "a people apart" and the singular, ancient suffering of the Jews can be used to justify the subjection of the Palestinians to unspeakable suffering outside of the laws of humanity. Now this exceptionalism cuts the other way, too, as you have reminded us Ilan. It works to single out the Jews from the rest of humanity as objects of derision and hatred—that is, such exceptionalism fuels anti-Semitism. Many see, as do I, the cantonising and blockading of the territories Israel occupies—what some Israelis refer to as a snakepit or "Me'arat Nachashim"—as turning Gaza, for instance, into the kind of townships or Bantustans that existed under South African apartheid—a mega-prison where children have little or no future and where an entire people live in despair. And similarly, many Israelis see Palestinians who light the fuses of the rockets that are fired into Israel as sub-human terrorists. So some on the American left will respond to the pro-Israeli media with challenges such as: Didn't Chaim Weizmann, Israel's first president, call the Palestinians "the rocks of Judea...obstacles that had to be cleared on a difficult path"? On three occasions, hasn't the Israeli state has been led by a former terrorist: Menachem Begin (prime minister from 1977–83), Yitzhak Shamir (1983–92, with a break in 1984–6), and Ariel Sharon (2001–6)? Did not Benny Morris, in a January 2004 interview with the Ha'arez journalist Ari Shavit, claim that Ben-Gurion should have completed the project of the ethnic cleansing of Palestinians and did he not say as well that "the great American democracy could not have been created without the annihilation of the Indians." Isn't the balance of terror and violence overwhelmingly against the Palestinians? Didn't Moshe Dayan say: "We have no solution, you [the Palestinians] shall continue to live like dogs, and whoever wishes may leave, and we will see where this process leads." To what extent does Dayan's comment reflect the sentiment of the people of Israel today?

Why does Israeli law appear to supersede international law in east Jerusalem? This situation infuriates the radical left in North America, and understandably so, because we know that Israel is able to wreak havoc upon the West Bank, to tear apart the communities there, because the United States gives it an unparalleled amount of military, economic, and diplomatic aid, as Noam Chomsky and others have discussed. I have criticized the idea of the volkisch state—during talks in Israel when I criticized the Israeli state, and I have criticized the idea of an Islamic state in talks I gave in Pakistan. Can't we agree that the axis of US/Israel is one of the most powerful indirect causes of the rise of political Islam in its theocratic form? Isn't the refusal of Israel to give to the Palestinians the right of return, a factor that causes so much resentment by the revolutionary left in the United States against the Israeli leadership? Did not the Oslo Accords of 1993–1995 between Israel and the Palestine Liberation Organization signal the beginning of the most intensive expansion of Israeli settlements since 1967? Didn't the Palestinian Authority in the occupied territories, who began to enforce Israeli-American policies, lose much of the support of the Palestinian people? Is not the Arab League itself hostile to the Palestinian cause? Should not critical revolutionary educators try to unmask the myth that Israel is far from being egalitarian and democratic, but is lurching towards anti-socialism, quasi-fascisms and anti-egalitarianism? Isn't the very logic of Zionist discourse militate against a two-state solution? Or can Zionism be 're-signified' such that Israel can be forced to retreat to its 1967 borders? Was not the disengagement of Gaza really a cloak for the Israeli expansion into the West Bank? Did not the plan of disengagement call for Israel to take over on a permanent basis major population centers, cities, towns and villages, security areas and other places in the West Bank of strategic importance to Israel. So when revolutionary leftists notice that the U.S. supports these measures, they become, understandably, incensed. Are not these important questions to bring to the table? Should we, as the educational left, ignore them? When the left views Israel as a country founded on torture chambers, beatings, manipulation, and treachery are not many of us within the field of revolutionary Critical Pedagogy equally critical of the United States and its genocide against the indigenous population, its vicious history of slavery, and its continuing racism and economic exploitation under the wing of neo-liberal capitalism? Have not many of us denounced—and continue to denounce—the Holocaust, and the crimes against the Jewish people? One side of the Israeli/Palestinian conflict is an independent state backed by the unlimited resources of the world's leading superpower while the other side, who uses homemade rockets, is confined to a ghetto whose power, water, and food supplies are cut off at will. And so, yes, it is difficult for many of those in Critical Pedagogy to view the other narrative— "Bashana Habaha Birushalaim"—because this narrative has been drowned out by the media owned by the transnational capitalist class. It is very difficult, I agree, for critical educators to situate themselves critically within the two opposing nation-building projects. If there is a tendency to glorify the Palestinian nation-building cause, it is possible to see why this is the case and to work through this critically, in a spirit of mutuality and a striving for peace. The new language of Critical Pedagogy must be a pedagogy of peace-making. Once, during a talk in Israel, I was criticized by young people but some older Israelis, in their 80s, approached me and said they appreciated my talk about the struggle for socialism because it reminded them of why they immigrated to Israel in the first place—to create a socialist alternative to capitalism. So I agree with you that the new anti-Semitism is given nourishment, yes, and is sometimes sacralized, often by what is most critical in our pedagogies and, I agree, that this mandates the search for a new language. But the very practice of revolutionary Critical Pedagogy is at the same time a critique of the inadequacy of its own language, which is why the conceptual and discursive horizon of Critical Pedagogy continues to grow or, at least, it must continue to grow—after all, shouldn't Critical Pedagogy be always searching for a new language that helps to speak to the struggles of our times? Whether we speak as ghosts of the past, or inhabitants in the future anterior, we are always striving for a new language because language is the site in which history becomes conscious of itself in new ways. The new critical language may be beyond critique but it needs to include critique. I am not saying the language can be reduced to critique, but it must incorporate it—and, of course, it should anticipate the new, and that is why the concept of absolute negativity is so important. Here we have a lot to learn from the Hegelian approach to Absolute Knowledge. I disagree with critics who argue that this approach is a totalizing system that annuls difference and otherness (i.e., there is no outside) and hence cannot provide the ground for subaltern resistance to forms of domination, oppression. When Marx said that history does not begin until we reach a socialist society, that everything prior to that represents the "pre-history"—he was pointing to the fact that human alienation is pre-historical insofar as it represents an abstraction from our human condition. Consequently, absolute knowledge in Hegelian terms cannot be dismissed as subjective idealism; rather, it reveals how the opposition between self-consciousness and its object can be transcended in various stages of life's journey, with each stage revealing defects that nonetheless contain in them-selves the impulse to transcend their limitations, thus representing a movement through negation and negation of the negation. Negativity is thus posed as an absolute but not as an endpoint, as Peter Hudis and others have noted. There is a good sense in which this idea is a fertile one for Critical Pedagogy. The absolute in this case is a jumping off point for a new beginning. Thus, it is possible not only to know ourselves but also the negative of ourselves (what Hegel refers to as facing the "Golgotha" of Absolute Spirit) and from that experience we can learn which aspects of ourselves to sacrifice for us to achieve transcendence. Marx recognized that what Hegel regarded as the dialectic of self-consciousness and the alienation of thought from itself needed to be re-understood as the alienation of our actual corporeal capacities—thus placing actual corporeal human beings as the subject of the dialectic of negativity. In our dialectic of self-consciousness, in our struggle for a new language, we need to make sure that we do not slip into idealism, and we need to make sure that the subject is man and women in the flesh, the enfleshed, corporal subject. In looking at the idea of building a new language, we must not reduce this idea, this process, to thought externalizing itself in creating ideas and objects of thought and then transcending these objectified thoughts by returning to itself, that is, by knowing itself. I disagree with Hegel that history is the self-thinking thought that has transcended alienation by thinking itself. In our search for a new language, we must not confuse the subject of history with disembodied thought. We must ground our language—our new language of Critical Pedagogy—in human actuality, in sensuous human agency, because it is human sociality, social praxis, that produces thought and ideas. Our new language must envision the transcendence of alienated labor. We can't simply return thought to itself; this won't help us transcend the acute alienation of labor in capitalist society. Reconciling thought with itself will not abolish the alienated determinations of the external world. Yes, human creativity unfolds through labor, through the dialectical process of externalization and the transcendence of externalization, but alienation is not a product of thought that can only be transcended by thought, whether this is thought produced by a new language or existing languages. Only our sensuous human activity can transcend alienated labor, can transcend the reduction of human beings to value production. Because, if we are just looking for a new discourse of being and becoming, then our very search for a new language will be a product of the alienation we wish to transcend. So how are we going to transcend alienation? As Peter Hudis has noted, it is only by negating barriers to self-development that it becomes possible to transcend alienation. However, Hegel fully understood something that many previous philosophers (in both the Western and non-Western tradition) had long recognized: that negation is always dependent in some way on the object of its critique. The effort to negate something does not mean that you are free from it. Since negation involves a negation of something, the very act of negation always bears the stamp, in one way or another, of what has been negated. To say that x is different from y still defines x in terms of y, albeit negativity. Therefore, it is not so easy to free yourself from what you are against as it may appear at first sight; the very act of negation may posit a new form that bears the imprint of what you've negated!

The genius of Hegel was that he was fully aware that negation is dependent on the object of its critique. In other words, ideas of liberation are impacted, in one way or another, by the oppressive forms that one tries to reject, and that negation per se does not totally free one from the negated object. But unlike the postmodernists that centuries later followed him, Hegel believed that there was a way for negation to transcend the object of its critique. He therefore introduced the notion of "the negation of the negation." We are not talking about a continues series of negations here. Continually negating something will never free negation from the object of its critique. That's why Hegel's self-referential negation is "absolute," insofar as it exists without relation to another outside itself. Marx appropriated the concept of the self-referential negation "to explain the path to a new society". Marx understood that simply to negate something is still leaves us dependent upon the object of critique, in other words, as Hudis notes, it merely affirms the alienated object of our critique on a different level. That has been the problem with revolutions of the past; they remained dependent upon the object of their negation. The negation of the negation, however, creates the conditions for something truly positive to emerge in that absolute negativity is no longer dependent on the other. What is needed is a subjective praxis connected with a philosophy of liberation that is able to illuminate the content of a post-capitalist society and project a path to a totally new society by convincing humanity that it is possible to resolve the contradiction between alienation and freedom, by providing a language of possibility and hope, and by illuminating a vision of the a different future, a post-capitalist future. That's one reason, Ilan, why repeating the truths of an earlier era that no longer have the power to seize humanity's imagination won't necessarily help us. That's why we need a philosophy of praxis, powered by absolute negativity as a new beginning. Critical Pedagogy faces the test of "Golgotha"—of being reconstructed anew in the face of new phenomena and new contexts of being and becoming. And this reconstruction stipulates that we need to start to define the characteristics of a world outside of capital's value form—in other words, we need to start thinking about what a post- capitalist society could look like. In our struggle, we must be discouraged from sinking into an arid formalism or from becoming a transcendental leap into a hoary metaphysics, a mystical subjectivism or voluntarism, and we must not mistake this struggle for a new language as simply engaging in a polemical struggle. This is because what must be done in the real world demands that we forego an impotent millenarianism of transcendental ought that cries out for socialism while leaving the world precisely as it is.

Here we need to understand that the nationalization of property and state control of the economy is not "socialism" because socialism cannot be defined by public ownership of capital. Marx defined socialism as the abolition of capital. That remains an important part of our task, Ilan. As Peter Hudis notes, we must incorporate into Marxist theory the subjectivity of the forces of liberation that have arisen in our era—women, racial minorities, indigenous peoples, ecological struggles, and battles to extend the terrain of political democracy. We must also develop a philosophically grounded perspective of a genuine socialist society based on the abolition of capital and value production.

Of course, in our quest to universalize the struggle for socialism, we adopt a pluriversal approach which my friend Ramon Grosfoguel describes as a truly universal decolonial perspective that cannot be based on an abstract universal (one particular that raises itself as universal global design), but is the result of a critical dialogue between diverse critical epistemic/ethical/political projects towards a pluriversal as oppose to a universal world. Following Grosfoguel, and in keeping, Ilan, with your quest for a new language our decolonization of knowledge would require us to take seriously the epistemic perspective/cosmologies/insights of critical thinkers from the Global South thinking from and with subalternized racial/ethnic/sexual spaces and bodies.

So our language—our new language—must partake of the logic of interculturality, one that engages in the construction of new epistemological frameworks and that calls for a new geopolitical order of knowledge production that encourages an active "interculturalization."

The language of which you speak must assist up in transcending our constitutive contradictions. We are constituted by labor and capital and this contradiction plays itself out within the deep recesses of our psychologies (as the psycho-Marxists have shown us). As Glenn Rikowski has argued, we are constituted by the concrete, qualitative, use-value aspect; and secondly by the quantitative, abstract value-aspect of labor and we are produced, necessarily as 'living contradictions'. We are, assuredly, propelled by the movement inherent in this living contradiction in the direction of transforming ourselves by changing society (by the coincidence of changing circumstances and self-change, as Marx would put this notion we call revolutionary praxis), and through this by struggling to build a social universe outside of capital's value form. Ilan, we can't have real equality through exchange-value, but only on the basis of the equalization of labor power, or the equality of valorization of labor-powers. When we recognize this, we can work to create a post-capitalist future, and developing a new language of being and becoming is part of this struggle. As a collectivity of mutuality and respect for each other, we can begin to transcend every moment in each desert into an oasis, and develop that nomadic hospitality and Diasporic/dialogical morality of which you speak. We can develop a wandering pedagogy, not of the urbane flaneur, but of humanity as eternally homeless, living within the subjective mode, the mode of a free-standing hospice, but not only for the aged, but for the ageless. Here we are not returning home, to some geographic space that grounds our identity as a nation of peoples, because our home is now our way of being and becoming, because our journey is not to find ourselves through the appropriation of our space, our national, ethnic, or religious space, but to give ourselves over to the space of Otherness within ourselves. It has been my great pleasure to be able to reflect on such a journey with you.

7. THE POSSIBILITY OF A NEW CRITICAL LANGUAGE FROM THE SOURCES OF JEWISH NEGATIVE THEOLOGY

Ilan Gur-Ze'ev: Thank you Prof. Jonathan Boyarin for making this conversation possible. If we may begin on a personal note: do you consider yourself a Jew? And if so, in your view, why should one identify oneself as a Jew at this historical moment, when according to some texts we read, and according to some of the realities in the post-modern condition, there is no difference that makes a difference? Why insist at such a historical moment on being a Jew?

Jonathan Boyarin: It never strikes me… There is no moment I can recollect when I had the feeling that I was not a Jew. Or that I was something other than a Jew, that there are other primary identifications, besides human beings. For now I put brackets around "other than a Jew", which is more important. I mean, I will admit that on visits to friends, for example, it suddenly struck me that in some ways I am an American. But this was thinking, "Oh, I'm an American" when it never struck me before that it mattered that I am an American, and I don't think I ever thought like this before: I am an American and its more important than being a Jew. But what I have to get in first, before you say anything else, in response to your question is that for the last several years I have become more and more aware that by saying "I am a Jew" I know what that means, but I do not assume there is any particular objective correlative… It is a statement, but its more a performative kind of iteration than a description of some self that exist outside of the statement that I am a Jew.

IGZ: So you are not positioned, and you are not (re)positioning yourself like Franz Rosenzweig, who asks himself, should I continue to be a Jew? Should I become a Christian, and overcome my Jewishness?

JB: I never thought of becoming a Christian. There was a point in my adolescence that I saw American suburban Judaism as being so empty that I thought, "Oh, its a shame, after 3000 years it ends in this", but certainly it ends…

IGZ: You see "it" as an end?

JB: I saw it as an end. And then I was removed from that everyday contact, so I was still very Jewish although alienated. I was really in a place where there were not a lot of Jews around. Suddenly I started thinking of myself as being always-already more Jewish than the realm of my own self determination. So it became a question of what am I going to do with it? How do I make a Jew?

IGZ: As part of your refusal to further problematize your actual identity, or, as the realization of your philosophy?

JB: I wish my friend, Martin Lance, one of my dearest friends in the world— and part of the reason I am here in Jerusalem now is just to visit him, he lives in Baka

I. Gur-Ze'ev, The Possibility/Impossibility of a New Critical Language in Education, 165–185.
© *2010 Sense Publishers. All Rights Reserved.*

[neighborhood in Jerusalem] now—because he was together with me in college. We became very close partly because we felt the intellectual atmosphere in seminars, in a very demanding liberal arts college. I was very much troubled by seminars where I still felt that the assumption was that what was being discussed in the humanity seminars was something other than real life. That there is this realm of learning and it has its own value, but it is not to be confused with real life. And I had a feeling even then, as a 19-year-old, that this was not how I understood learning. And so I started to conceive of my own dissatisfaction as being Jewish. I called that "the origins of negative identification". There is something in the atmosphere, some element of a cultural atmosphere, that I need to breathe that I am not getting here. I associated that with Jewishness in a very general way, in saying, "OK, I sense a lack here, its a part of me that's not being nourished—how do I then go on to inform that?" But it was not a sudden religious inspiration in any traditional sense, and partly because it was associated with, I thought of myself as a Marxist in college. I wrote a senior thesis about Marxist anthropology, so sort of the Yiddish focused, and secular tradition was the easiest for me to begin with. And also a sense that my Jewishness was shaped by growing up in an intimate community of Jewish chicken farmers that was dissolving during my early childhood, so the sense of a sort of communal, familiar Yiddishkeit and its loss, as a very early experience, that might give a sense of what Jewishness was.

IGZ: You take the Critical Theory of the Frankfurt School so seriously in your writings, and Benjamin, Adorno and Horkheimer are so central for your thinking. In their last years Adorno and Horkheimer understood Critical Theory as Jewish negative knowledge, and they saw the importance of Judaism very much in the sense that Judaism was at the center of their philosophy, or at the center of the theological dimension of their thought. It was no longer the proletariat. Judaism for them was the actual manifestation of the claim for justice—through the consistent historical injustice that was inflicted on the Jews. And the anti-dogmatism of Judaism, of "ואלוהי מסכה לא תעשה לך": "thou shalt make thee molten gods" (Exodus 35: 17) which to my mind is the starting point of any Critical Theory that refuses dogmatism and ethnocentrism of any kind. This message of Jewish monotheism today terrifies many post-colonialists, who offer us a new anti-Semitism in the name of the lost Polytheism, hybridity and heterogeneity. But we'll certainly come to that later as a manifestation of current conflicting modes of criticism. In the meantime let us return to Horkheimer, who says in light of what he conceives as Critical Theory as Jewish negative theology: when a claim for justice acquires power, it can realize itself only at the cost of its transformation into its opposite and of self-destruction. Maybe this is the paradox of Zionism as a negation of exilic Jewish existence; perhaps this is the Original Sin of any Jewish state. How do you see this concept of the fundamentals of Judaism as a center for any genuine critical education and as a starting point for a possible rebirth of a critical language that is true to its mission, namely to its Diasporic origin and to its Diasporic telos?

JB: I can't give a global answer to the question. First of all I respond to the way you lay out this problem with one question of my own, which is naïve. So do not think it is obnoxious. The way you describe Horkheimer and Adorno on Jewishness as negative theology—how do you differentiate that from the way Herman Cohen identifies the essence of Jewishness with Kantian rational universal ethics as described by Derrida?

IGZ: In one sense, it is a continuation of the same trend, namely understanding Judaism as the impetus of negativism. Negativism that affirms Love of Life yet rejects positivism and institutionalized successful violence as part of this Enlightenment's tradition that Herman Cohen is so fundamental to. At the same time, Herman Cohen was still an optimist, not solely an Utopist. Following the Jewish Prophets and the Enlightenment's secularization of Jewish theology, he offered the idea of progress of rationality toward human universal redemption. The academic ideal of universal realization of academic freedom is a complementary vision of the realization of secularized Jewish theology in light of the vision of a successful "homereturning" project that will bring to its conclusion Diasporic existence. These two projects meet and integrate, and yet they are in conflict with each other, and each within itself, between the germ of eternal Diasporic life and the quest for ending Diasporic existence. As against these two modes of universal realization and overcoming of Judaism, Marx offered a third: capitalism as the realization of the essence of actual Judaism and the prospects of universal revolution and communist existence as an ultimate emancipation of humanity from the violence and oppression of Judaism. As I try to show in various places, present postcolonial philosophy further develops today this positive Utopianism within the framework of a new racism and a new anti-Semitism. In contrast, late Adorno and Horkheimer understood that rationality is instrumentalized and becomes irrational rationality. Instrumental rationality becomes implemented in ever more sophisticated manners; it enables and actually ensures efficient dehumanization, and even threatens the very existence of all life on the planet. Of course, it destroys the vision of Kant, Herman Cohen and Enlightenment in general, but at the same time it is part and parcel of the same secularized political theology, of the same world view and its material, social and cultural preconditions, symptoms and expressions. And from there they proceed to understand rationality very differently from the way Herman Cohen and Kant conceived it on the one hand, and Marx and present post-colonialists on the other. In what sense? In the sense that in opposition to Marx, who tried to overcome Judaism and its consistent Diasporic Love of Life and responsibility via universalism, and to present post-colonialists, who try to realize this very aim by turning to heterogeneity and "diversity" against the Judeo-Christian/whiteness colonialist-oriented homogeneity complex, the Frankfurt School thinkers insisted on a consistent Diasporic philosophy, on eternal, responsible co-poiesis and improvisation; in other words, on Diaspora as the worthiest form of human existence.

JB: I had as my dissertation advisor at the New School an anthropologist named Stanley Diamond, who was a very smart and a very difficult man; an important thinker in Marxism and anthropology. He published an article in late fifties called "Kibbutz and *shtetl*: The history of an idea". He actually did his first field work on an actual kibbutz in the late fifties, never published much, but in that article he talks about the social structure of the kibbutz as the reflection of the notion held by the *vatikim* [veterans of the Zionist settlement project] of the pathology of the social structure of the *shtetl* [a Jewish small town in eastern Europe before the

Holocaust), which for me was a very important idea in understanding that Israel is both a continuation and a concentration of the Jewish patterns and the fundamental rejection of Jewishness. Even today a lot of well educated Jews and people who care very much do not understand the extent to which the whole notion of Zionism was a rejection of Jewishness. But when I was working with Stanley Diamond and working on Yiddish and starting to wear a *kippa* [skullcap] around, he was very concerned that I should not become a Jewish chauvinist. Because, he said—in conversations, and you can also see it in his writings, for him the only positive value of Jewish identity is the marginal stance vis-à-vis civilization that it affords someone who is conscious of that identity; so that if you clothe it, it is not naked anymore and it is not as sensitive. Whereas I said—I don't know if I ever said it to him, but my response in my own head is that if you don't build any kind of structure around the marginal space, it collapses.

IGZ: Let us dare to rethink it; let us give it a second thought. Let us think again about the essence, the telos and the fortune of Jewishness as religiosity in the absence of the strong state and its institutions; Jewishness as religiosity, not solely as a religion. I will offer you an idea and you will tell me what you think about it. Jewishness as a religious, ecstatic co-poiesis: an experience of the absence of the presence of God. Education for a worthy facing of the absence of God, or—actually—of any positive absolute. Any dogma might give birth to responsibility and love (and there are complex and rich relations between these two) which is universal, global, existential; which precedes ethics and intellectual constructions, routines and safeguards. From *Yavne* onwards neither the sovereignty of the Jewish state nor the sacredness of the Temple represented Jewishness; nor did a certain religious dogma and its representatives. The Torah, text and textuality, as an object for overcoming and transcendence. It is an unrestrained imperative not to sanctify any interpretation or interpreter, but rather to overcome, to transcend while being responsible, living within the framework of the *Halacha* and the infinite horizons of interpretation, improvisation and Love of Life. Deciding to live outside secular history and its power-relations, refusing national sovereignty and devoting the self to prayer in the *Minyan*, Accepting the counter-rule of the Shabbat or the never-conclusive-interpretation-of-the-text, of living-toward-the-not-yet. For the Jew these, not the borders of the sovereign state, become the relevant realm. It is a Jewish, therefore a Diasporic, imperative, which is not merely pre-intellectual: as co-poiesis it precedes ethics and establishes a fundamental obligation to the otherness of the Other and to yourself as a promise, as a potential part of togetherness with the Other as a concrete challenge, abyss and focus of responsibility, and with the world as well as a concrete, bodily, historically situated human. Co-poiesis and being a partner to a *Minyan*, or Shabbat, offer so much more than loneliness on the one hand, and being swallowed by the bestiality of dogma, by the harmony of total surrendering oneself to constraints, or to the magmatic traces of ethnocentrism, on the other. Living as a responsible nomad in eternal exile in face of the absence of the absolute. Becoming a Diasporic human opens all ethnocentrist, dogmatic and ethical realms of self-evidence and closes, overcomes, at the same time, all temptations to "the worthy" project that offers "homereturning" and "peace" of all kinds. It is a great responsibility, a burden that does not offer compensation and rewards, only heavy, rich, Diasporic hospitality. So as a Diasporic human, on the one hand you are extremely aware of your being contextualized within political frameworks and specific power-relations that always come together with their limits and possibilities as enabled/inflicted by the historical moment; and on the other, you position yourself in face of these in light of your facing Diasporic religiosity. In this sense Critical Theory is so relevant today and not solely as an intellectual possibility: as a way of life of individuals, of committed people, who choose to experience the religious tension and responsibilities within, and in face of, globalizing capitalism, rising chauvinism, nationalism and ethnocentrism in all their versions. In this sense, would you agree that Jewish thought as a new form of Critical Theory is very much relevant for today's creative nomadic life possibilities?

JB: Absolutely. For me this is one of the key... but I would be hesitant myself of formulating it in even quite that assertive way. Because it is very easy to say, "We've been around so long and we've suffered so much—we know more than you do". I guess I understand the moral aesthetic that you are trying to articulate and I think you're right that sometimes I tried to follow it. In simple terms, it is very difficult to be assertive without being triumphant. I think also Heschel said, concerning the Sabbath, "The Jews live in time. They do not live in space". I don't claim that it is right, because I think first of all, that it means to focus only on the *Minyan* and not on the kitchen also. It is also to say that when we say **The Jew** we mean men.

IGZ: But "the kitchen" can actually be built anywhere—not solely nor first of all in Israel.

JB: Sure. But it means that everywhere you are there is a sense that you're fully shaped by that place, that you're not fully absorbed in it.

IGZ: Very much so. But is it so that it is fully...

JB: Maybe not, but it is not trivial.

IGZ: Okay, I'll share with you for a moment the poststructural concept...

JB: It is not trivial, because otherwise *kibbutz galuyot* [the return of all Jews around the globe to Israel] would be a much more straightforward matter but then everybody would come to Israel and basically get along and marry each other.

IGZ: Isn't it so that the *kibbutz galuyot* idea and the melting pot agenda, and the establishing of a strong Israel, are ultimately a barbarization of the essence of the idea of Judaism in the sense of destroying not only Jewish Diasporas but the very ideal of Diasporic existence?

JB: I don't like telling five or six million people that they're doing the wrong thing. I take a somewhat more modest view. I can understand why people like being in a place where most of the other people are like them. I don't share that, but I can understand why people would feel that way. I cannot sanction trying to guarantee the perpetuation of that majority through the structure of the state. That is a matter of practical politics and constitutionality and democracy.

IGZ: Isn't that what collectivism is all about? The constitutive idea of collectivism and surely of this dangerous ill health, of nationalism?

JB: No. The US is not a state based on an ethnic or religious definition of citizenship. In a fundamental respect, Israel is problematic in exactly the same way that all liberal democratic states are problematic. It has territorial boundaries, it is not fixed, but it is in principle a territorial state. And that in itself is highly problematic. The fact, the sensibility of whether it is a loss for everybody to be gathered in one place—I feel it is a loss; I feel that it is a part of the continuing disaster of the 20th century. Yet its the easiest and best way for me to explain why I like being Jewish. Being Jewish connects me to so many different people in so many different places over such a long period of time that it is the strongest thread that is available to me to allow me to be a specific person connected so much to humanity in general; to the extent that there is a concentration and a regularization of where and what and how Jewishness is—*that* is diminished. For the same reason, in this respect, I find *Habad Lubavitch* and their tactics very problematic. When my wife Alisa went to school here in Jerusalem in the seventies, she lived in *Katamon* [a neighborhood at Jerusalem] and worked with the neighborhood kids there, she was outraged that *Habad* disciples were going to children of religious Moroccan parents and telling them that their parent's home is not kosher, or telling them that the way they gathered was wrong. It really is a kind of cultural imperialism.

IGZ: Would you agree that the connectedness that is still important to you might become a soporific power that will put you asleep or that will lower your sensitivities intellectually, morally and aesthetically? Isn't it so that while you negate the concept of home, of homeland, of the negation of the negation of Diaspora by Zionism, you replace this "homereturning" project with an alternative "home-returning" project? Here I refer to another kind of "home" that I find you are committed to in your writings—longing for a "home" that is not territorial yet committed to the suggestive power of a deep human sleep, of human forgetfulness in the form of an alternative collectivism, while one of the worthiest trends in Judaism, which is especially important in my eyes, is the overcoming of the temptation of any kind of collectivism. Judaism offers togetherness as an alternative to collectivism and nationalism, which is committed to construct history and have the upper hand. It offers a commitment to another kind of togetherness—cosmopolitan togetherness, which you found, it seems to me, in radical feminism.

JB: Here I have to tell a story, I have to describe the situation. My brother started reading literary theory before I did, and in the summer of 1987 he went and spent the summer in the School of Criticism and Theory, which is in Dartmouth College, a summer institute every year. And he said, "You have to go, Jonathan". So I convinced Alisa to let me go the next year.

IGZ: How long was it?

JB: Six to seven weeks. And in that institute every year, at least then, there were four seminars that ran the whole time, and I took two of them. Edward Said was reading lectures that were the chapters of his book called Culture and Imperialism, and Nancy Miller was teaching the subject of feminist theory, you know. I am a critical anthropologist so I am very interested in cultural questions of anthropology, imperialism and colonialism, and I guess I had already found something in the Jewishness that I was trying to make. And through my reading of—especially my reading of *Dialectic of Enlightenment*, which, you are right, is a more important book for me than my writing reflects.... The critique of the enlightened imperial subject spoke to me very strongly as someone who wanted to be a radical graduate student in anthropology; and to try to think about the relations between philosophical imperialism and the Enlightenment and modern Jewish history in Europe predisposed me to finding very useful reading: Judith Butler and other feminist theorists, who were talking about the autonomist subject as a modern male, a European construction, and in my mind a Protestant construction. So really the piece I wrote called *The Impossible Internationalist*, which you are thinking of, grows out of being in the situation of being the host in seminars with very strong seminar leaders, and with certain people, women in the one case, people from the third world in the other case, who were empowered to speak there, and with me, appearing as an orthodox Jewish man with a *kippa*, not particularly authorized to speak in either seminar, and I did speak, of course. It was very frightening. I am not complaining about it, but that's what really pushed me to try to make those particular articulations. The other thing I wanted to say, in terms of the question of cosmopolitanism, which is not a term that I am opposed to, is that Diaspora is not only an intellectual state, not necessarily collective but communal, in the sense that I try to keep a very broad definition of Diaspora now that the business of deciding that certain groups of people are not diasporists... To me, one of the things that make the notion most vital is the possibility and the cultural technology of generational continuity in the absence of a majority. So yes—it is true that there is always a danger of sentimentalism, and what for me serves as a more or less effective check against over-indulgence in that sentimentalism—to the extent that I continue to participate, or participate more or promote the continuity of traditional forms like the synagogue—is that I am also aware that this is the only life I have. I do not want to be wasted, melting into a communalist. Because in some ways that is as much an abandonment of life as sitting around watching soap operas on TV. At the same time, I think it is also useful and defensible to say there are certain things we do because that is what Jews do. And you don't have to rationalize everything. I'm not saying "law"; I'm not saying "because that is what God told us to do". Its not a matter of faith necessarily. I think that a great deal of post-Enlightenment terror, both in the sense of individual terror, and eventually organized violence, has to do with the inability of an isolated organism that is aware of its own mortality to achieve some kind of equanimity with the fact of its own mortality. And I think that one of the key driving forces of the symbolic aspects of almost all human cultures until now has been to strengthen a real, not just a sentimental force, in structuring identificatory practices such that the organism does not, in the first instance, understand existence as starting with its birth and ending with its death, but almost in the first instance understands existence as being a continuity and a cycle, inflicted by its own mortality.

IGZ: But determined as well by both its hopelessness in effectively defending itself and its incompetence in colonizing the Other. While some trends in Judaism, also in your view as I understand it, as well as in certain trends in radical feminism, conceive women and Jews not only as one of the not very many manifestations of humans victimized by the *hegemon* or suffering from the phallocentristic-oriented history of the West, but also as committed in the first place to give birth to love, to solidarity, to responsible improvisation and co-poiesis, and less to the success, gains, victories and triumphs as offered by normal patriarchal history and current logic of the market. You see, in some respects Jews, women and other Others—and according to some of the feminist trends today, actually solely women of the right radical feminist politics and philosophy—continue where Jewish thought did not dare to proceed and elevate itself: insisting on the centrality of cosmopolitanism on the one hand, and on being very precise and concrete and very much in the totality of the moment on the other. How would you respond to the claim that the radical feminist philosophies and politics that you identify with are actually not offering only an agenda that Judaism today is short of offering us, but actually in a way are presenting an alternative to Judeo-Christian thinking, to Western colonialism and to phallocentristic-monotheistic-oriented love?—A commitment to negativity, a commitment on the one hand to resist power and success, which are patriarchal, colonialist, or committed to the absolute/homogeneity/universalist-frozen-oppressive ideas; or on the one hand to the idea of progress, and at the same time to being very much connected to the moment, to the concrete, to giving birth to the hybrid unexpected. Not as a mere idea: giving birth to a new child is actualizing genesis. It is realizing philosophy and being committed to **the totally other**, as a possibility. Of course, normalizing education and all the powers will at the same time begin their work and normalize the child and the mother and so on. But the very commitment to give birth, as well as the commitment of traditional Judaism to the transcendence, are two alternatives to the macho-ist or the colonialistic-oriented idea of overcoming, of victory, of the principle of ownership. In Hebrew you say בעלות [ownership] and בעילה [intercourse]: the man לבעול—makes-his—the woman, and בעלוּת signifies becoming that owner of a property, making the Other yours, your property, as the main road to negate the otherness of the Other. How do you see this rival-symbiotic relationship between radical feminism and Judaism?

JB: I won't pretend to answer that. Again, I find I am answering a lot of your questions with anecdotes. And I must say, the kinds of things I am starting to write now are different than the common themes, than what I've always done, so that conceptual questions bring to me anecdotes and bits. One bit is this last Shabbat I was in New York and I went to... I go to several different *schuls* in the neighborhood, and sometimes if I get up early on a Shabbat morning I go to the Shabbat *minyan* at 7:00. Why is there a Shabbat *minyan* on 7:00? Because when it was established 50–60 years ago it was for the guys who had to go to work. Now it is just because it is a quick *minyan*, there is no ceremonial speech and its very nice. But I see there sometimes one older man whom I like very much, and he picked me out a long time ago as somebody who he could tell stories about Jewishness to, but also about the world. And he said to me, almost a propos of nothing—he said, "The human is in God's image" האדם נעשה בצלם. This is a very important principle, which we forget about all the time now. So yes, there are hints that you have to listen very hard for. There are hints that what you are describing as a critical, almost a humane ideal was once a much more vigorous part of an integrated communal—not just a cosmopolitan and academic—Jewishness. I think also that some of the aspects of internal humor, internal critique, in Yiddish culture are resources for a kind of openness and sense of contingency. So that goes to one of your things, a sort of a vigorous pessimism, but the one I was thinking of was actually "*a klein folk, ober a baise*" [Yiddish]: "a small nation, but a nasty one". Now you can sentimentalize that too. Of course, you can say we can laugh at ourselves but we can also... I always have had a very hard time telling the difference, trying to interpret— Walter Benjamin thought he could tell the difference between political sense of history and nostalgia. And I have never been quite as confident. I think that there are places in the Jewish world where people are working very hard to address questions about women's rights, which are not questions that you ask me, but to address them without a sense of "Okay, we'll make it up in ways that are convenient to us". And this is not a redemptive moment, but I think it is creative. And that's at the margins of what we call orthodoxy.

IGZ: With your permission, Prof. Boyarin, I will go to another topic which is so central in your work: postcolonialism. How do you see the relation between Judaism and postcolonialism—on the one hand as two important manifestations of negativism, and on the other hand in relation to the possibility of postcolonialism as an alternative to the Jewish monotheistic and immanently colonialist-oriented moral and cultural telos?

JB: Well, first of all, I think of it as a kind of strategic coalition, in that if you understand that a notion of a disinterested social critique is not only a fiction, but a fiction that serves certain ends of powers and therefore it is important to situate critique, then it is obviously vitally important to situate critique in as many places as possible; and for that discussion to be based on as agile a notion of identity as possible. Jewish critical discourse, like the post-colonial discourse, is always working a balancing act to avoid on the one hand reifying itself in turn, which is also related to nostalgia, and on the other hand dissolving itself, cutting off its own legs from underneath it. For instance, when I addressed Jean Luc Nancy, who had a very appealing, but a very abstract—and I think he acknowledges it—explicitly post-Christian notion of community and strategy to addressing the desire for universality without engaging in imperial fantasies, I responded from a very particular situation, which leads to a more general suggestion of thinking about fragmentary communities rather than an aporia, rather than conceiving community as an aporia.

IGZ: Here I would like to challenge you a bit. In your writings you sound, to me at least, quite optimistic about the likelihood of establishing such a coalition between the marginalized: a prospect of going into a dialogue, a peaceful, inclusive dialogue between the marginalized and the oppressed as against the oppressor and its hegemonic narrative. I ask myself, isn't this optimism about the prospects of these coalitions and dialogues among the marginalized in fact anti-Diasporic? Anti-Diasporic in the sense that if we accept the postmodern delivery—and it is my understanding that you do in fact gladly accept it as anti-fundamentalism or as a refusal of fundamentalism, as resisting the concept and the longing for transcendence, as rebuffing the possibility of grand theories and universalistic-oriented values and so on, then actually, we are left with no valid yardsticks and with no erotic impetus to transcendence, to responsibility, to seriously committing ourselves in light of, within and between conflicting moral alternatives. Abandoning or being left without God, Torah, or a universally valid Critical Theory, are we not left to the

173

mercy of contingent symbolic violences, rival representation apparatuses and other manipulations? Would you agree that the deconstruction of the various realms of self-evidence, which include monotheism and the Utopian quest, has ended up in the exile of Spirit itself? If indeed we are left without either responsibility or poiesis, or seriousness about universalistic valid yardsticks to evaluate the conflicting sets of values and agendas, are we emancipated solely from "whiteness", "phallocentric Monotheism" and "humanist colonialism"? Or by the same token, are we also exiled from co-poiesis, transcendence and the very possibility of prayer, Eros and religiosity? The post-colonialist reply might be "Okay, we don't have a universally valid idea or yardstick, but we do have a principle to guide us: 'always side with the victimized, at all cost give more weight to the interests and to the self-evidence of the oppressed and not to that of the oppressor'. Professor Boyarin, what would be your response to the claim that what we end up with here is not emancipation from monotheism, Judeo-Christian colonialism or Western ethnocentrism—not at all, but unfortunately with nothing less than an alternative ethnocentristic world view, with just another triumph of the self-evidence, with victory over Diasporic existence and over critical-creative-erotic humanity?

JB: I think that's probably right. I think of myself probably as always having been very keen when I wrote what I wrote last year... and I also think that I only get older, I don't know if I get wiser. But I also think that things get worse and worse. I remember thinking, "Oh God, if Ronald Reagan gets elected to the presidency of the USA I'm leaving, that's it"—and it continues to get worse and worse. I don't have much of a notion now that I know who the oppressor is, in a collective sense, and I'm much more inclined toward an almost social-biological view or an anthropological view in the sense of viewing us as a species, which uses language as a particular adaptive mechanism, and say on the one hand, from a biological standpoint, that we are right now a very successful species because there are a lot of us, we are all over the place. It looks like we are creating a situation in which there would be not very many of us, because we are using it up. And so I tend more lately to think in terms of how well organized are we as a species? Not who has the power? Who doesn't have power? Who is the source of oppression and who is the source of liberation? Are we going to pull through? And the only way to pull through is to be organized much better. So to me its not an emancipatory project anymore. Its a project aimed at survival and rescue.

IGZ: If I proceed in light of your present articulation would you accept also my assertion that the present historical moment deconstructs not only the preconditions for emancipatory education, it even deconstructs the preconditions for Diasporic existence—in two conflicting ways: one is the enhancement of Instrumental Rationality which in a neo-liberal context contributes to the hegemony of the McWorld and to the McDonaldization of reality. In the present global market as well as in cyberspace there is no room for transcendence, there are no preconditions for a tragic or a heroic response to the exile of Spirit and to the deconstruction of the Absolute, be it God, human spirit or reason. The second is the counter-violence, the reaction of the oppressed and New Age spirituality, which offer a new educational vitality, new and renewed positive Utopias that contribute their share to the destruction of cultural, economic, technological and political conditions for Diasporic philosophy and for Diasporic education. These two conflicting trends are in conflict with Diasporic co-poiesis and responsible improvisation since they are united in enhancing the philosophy of life as the aim of life, mere life. Diasporic philosophy and counter-education as conceived by myself are conditioned by overcoming this narcissistic concept of the human. On the other hand I might reply that this impasse is the only genuine gate to a Diasporic philosophy which is true to itself.

JB: Yes and no. Because Diaspora does not come about as the result of... even if we do accept Diaspora to some extent as a chosen condition, not as a punishment. Historically it is accurate to say most voluntary diasporas are trading diasporas, they are commercial diasporas, and Diaspora is not an altruistic situation, it is also an alternative strategy of survival.

IGZ: For survival, or for worthier human life and mature responsibility?

JB: At this point, the most worthy project of survival in the global sense is survival itself. And that is why, as I was saying to you, I now pose this question of extinction and difference. Let us take seriously for half an hour the notion that it is rational to hypothesize what are we, all of us: we are using up our planet so quickly. Now, how does the discourse about human difference now seem? And I have to say that I have not really articulated an answer to that. But it does allow me to be even more vigorously anti-chauvinistic than I made myself be before.

IGZ: Because then even the "we" is different and it should be re-articulated. Who are the "we"? Who is included in the "we" and who or what is excluded? Should we include all citizens of the cosmos? Animals and plants too?

JB: "We" the Jews. Let us bring it back to that one. Here is I think a good hypothetical question that gets you to these issues, and I think you could debate this point either way. I have my notion about which side of the debate I prefer to take. But here is the question for the debate. Proposition: because one third of the Jewish people were annihilated in the middle of the 20th century, Jews have the right to have more children than other people do. I am not prepared to say right away the answer is "No, of course not". In other words, I am still interested in this tension between particular forms of humanity and in humanity in general because it is still the case, and it will always the case, that there is no "humanity" in general. And we will always have to figure out technologies and procedures and regulations for balancing sameness and difference. But we always face that project as long as we survive. So that is why in some sense it is survival and not emancipation that becomes the horizon of all cultural questions of politics, and politics of identity.

IGZ: Is it possible, in your view, to offer a concept of existence which is neutral, which is indifferent to conflicting values, truths and yardsticks for preferences and choosing alternative sets of values and conceptual apparatuses? According to what criteria or values or language game are we allowed to enact our responsibility or even respond to the call, to the invitation, to the imperative of going into action, and surely the right practices, that will guarantee the very existence of the world and our lives as citizens of the world? Is it rational, is it pre-rational yet unavoidable, to expect to face this global threat without seriously going into the challenge of philosophical, political and educational preconditions?

JB: I certainly do not think we can do that. I don't imagine that we could ever be able to do that in any sustained way. The reason that I propose we try doing it even for a little while is because I think that people are thinking for the future. I think that our thinking about identity now toward the future is hobbled. And I mean even someone like Homi Bhabha, by a taboo against failing ultimately to invoke hope. And that is why I said to you not just optimism, but hope, is a problem. That people feel it is not responsible to be realistic, or that if you won't say, "I'm going to think about what 50 years from now will be like, and I'm not going to do it with hope". And I think that since culture and language and projection are the way of human beings in the world, then we will only survive if we do it successfully. And there really is some measure of rationality, because as much as we shape the world through out consciousness of it, and our concepts of it, if we are not alive we do not have the chance to do that. And why did I become an anthropologist? Not just because I wanted to learn Yiddish, but because I'd love this thing that human beings have, which is—you asked me about feminism before, and in Donna Haraway's book *Primate Visions* she has an appendix to it—which is a song that my teacher, Rina Rapp, taught to her daughter Mira, when Mira was a little girl, and it ends with "Welcome to culture, my darling daughter, it is the greatest show on earth". I think human beings are the most interesting animal there is in the world. I can conceive that 50 years from now if there were no human beings, and the world would otherwise be as it is, there would be all the other animals, all the lions and tigers and bears, well I could live with that, but it is a shame. It really would be a loss. There is a sense in which the end of our being even able to have a discussion like this, or anybody having a speculation or argument—that is in the same category as the loss of a Native American language. Multiply it, because it is the whole typecast of the phenomenon, and as long as two people can keep doing it there is a possibility of further diversification and reinvention. But when that stops something is lost in the universe. Part of the value of the universe is a possibility of a consciousness other than God's to appreciate the Indians.

IGZ: You pose here again preconditions for Diasporic life in face of problematic economic, cultural, technological and political realities. These are very important, of course. I don't question it. I think, however, it is impossible to disconnect these from other preconditions for Diasporic existence. I mean preconditions for the possibility of doing good or resisting injustice, which are presently also preconditions for sustainability. In this sense Diasporic counter-education and the agenda of education for sustainability meet. The other Diasporic preconditions I refer to relate to the possibility of living within, in face of, and transcending the tension between existence in which the responsibility of the human as a citizen of this world is realized as a partner to the shared arena, community or (in)human conditions. And they also relate to the possibility or invitation to refuse to become at home in this present order of things, to overcoming the temptation to become part of any collective, dogma or self-forgetfulness. It is a tension between becoming of this world in specific realities that demand our response and responsibility, and being Diasporic within some or even most of its realities. This tension is dangerous and demanding, of course. However, where there is tension and conflict there is Life and air to breath for Eros. Where there is Life, human life as an eternal becoming, there is hope, which in opposition to optimism is beyond "our" present horizons and its realities. It is never to be explained or called upon by facts, realities and theoretical reductions. This is because it is a dimension of the possibility of the appearance of **the totally other**. It is a call we could, and one might say we should, respond to. To be awakened by and encouraged to become genuine Diasporic humans who dwell in co-poiesis and actualize each moment anew responsible improvisation. Because to be(come) an optimist is to refuse Diasporic life. Optimism is an invitation and part of the acceptance of the invitation to dwell within the reality as a "home" whose rules we could play by more efficiently and be successful more or less. To my mind it is actually a way to return to thingness, to the Same, to the mentioned-before; it is a manifestation of self-forgetfulness and a retreat back "home" to the continuum of meaninglessness, to the "home" of thingness. To be(come) Diasporic within this reality and in face of these preconditions is to be part of and at the same time to refuse to be part of this historical reality, to become a serious nomad, a responsible exile, a Diasporic human that as such has not abandoned the response-bility, togetherness and creativity in favor of the negativism of Diasporic life since she has an alternative; or maybe you would prefer to say genuine kinds of together-ness with herself, with the Other, with the world, togetherness that precedes ethics and intellectual constructions and transcends historical realities while acknowledging the specifics of historical, social and educational situatedness. In this sense, the very Diasporic existence is a call to overcome mere continuum and sustainable human life as the purpose of Life. This is what Diasporic co-poiesis is all about.

JB: And I think it is useful in terms of the predicament of the future that I've been talking about now, isn't it? Its not so new—to keep on going although you don't know what's going to happen in the long run.

IGZ: Would you agree that Diasporic existence is much more a call and an open possibility for the individual than for a collective? On the one hand it is the individual who is reconnecting herself or himself to the cosmos, to infinity and to the totality of the moment. Solely the individual, if it is possible at all. When it is a collective act, then, unavoidably, like in a discotheque or Fascist parades, it is a ceremony of de-humanization, of running back "home" to the Same, to the thingness. The Jewish *minyan*, in this sense, is its opposite, is a manifestation of Diasporic togetherness. But you don't agree, do you, Jonathan?

JB: That distinction never occurs in its pure form. So the answer—you know, we're talking for the *Journal of Philosophy of Education*. This is what I want to fill Jewishness with. What I want to be the resources of Jewishness...

IGZ: May I interrupt you with a short... I think that in our conversation we have now reached the turning point. In other words, we're facing the moment at which Judaism is a challenge for Diasporic existence. A challenge that counter-education, Diasporic counter-education, if true to itself, should transcend. In tradi-tional vocabulary it is possible to suggest here a more Spinozian attitude of relating to the world, to nature, to the cosmos as a totality and refusing all Diasporic narratives that are still connected to its ethnocentric birthsigns, or to cosmopolitanism that is still attached to the narrative of the fall from the Garden of Eden. So as a consistent Diasporic human, why should you personally and philosophically insist on Judaism? Don't you see that you have reached a point in your Odyssey at which you cannot run away from deciding which is dearer to you: Judaism or genuine Diasporic existence, and that it is impossible to prolong your present pleasant condition in which you can comfortably have them both?

JB: The only reasons, for me, are what I decided. I don't insist on anything. I decided, at a certain point I crystallized, but quite rapidly, so it felt like discovering the truth, that I had already been shaped more than I knew, by the name, in the sense of the name in Jewishness. That what I was in the world was already very much determined by this. And therefore, rather than try to transcend that, and make myself individual in some... I can be an individual in an abstract sense. How can each person be unique? There is a very serious demand in the Enlightenment that everybody has to be an individual. And again, a lot of terror and confusion comes from that. So already then it made sense to me to.... What this means, I will have to spend my life finding out. The more I know about what it has meant along the way—what other people in other situations have embroidered around that word, the stronger a combination of situatedness and autonomy I can have. And that is in a sense that how all of my writing is like the hard shell that a snail uses behind himself...

IGZ: But the very concept of autonomy is problematic for you.

JB: Freedom, call it something like freedom, yes, the ideal of autonomy...

IGZ: Is very problematic for you.

JB: Yes. So let me call it responsibility.

IGZ: But even if we think about responsibility and we give up for a moment the concept of autonomy or relative autonomy in the spirit of Enlightenment, in face of some of the concepts of post-structuralism, I would have to have to raise this question: is the concept of responsibility still defensible within your conceptual framework, if subjects are merely objects of manipulations and of subjectification processes of which humans are merely the products, effects, agents and echoes; and if these manipulations differ in kind from the monotheistic tradition, which Hegel or Marx explains to us in terms of the absolute, namely the objective and universal realization of historical laws, and subjects are essentially fragmentary, contextual and immanently contingent in the sense than you cannot seriously speak of the responsibility of the subject. This is because the subject you refer to does not have the preconditions for response-ability. The subject you describe and adore so much is not sovereign or autonomous. Not even potentially or as a constitutive ideal. Your subject is neither the owner of nor the rebel against his or her subjectivity: she has neither God nor the absence of God nor an erotic impetus, nor ecstatic co-poiesis, nor the freedom or a reason to actualize as part of her self-constitution and elevation. Even her narcissism and sophisticated cynicism are mere simulacra. As such, he or she cannot be Diasporic, of course. In this sense I would suggest that the concept of responsibility that you offer instead of freedom is part and parcel of the contingent effects/affects, an echo or reaction which is part of the immanence or mechanical continuum which is deterministic on the one hand and chaotic on the other; yet either way meaningless. Again, to your mind, in what sense is it possible to maintain the possibility of responsibility and Diasporic existence when there is no transcendence, not even as an open possibility? No part or glimpse of authentic otherness or any possible manifestation of **the totally other**; not even the Greek Moira playing with us, playing "us" in a way which talks itself to us/through "us" as if there were a genuine "I" who is invited to respond and enact responsibility.

JB: First of all, we are not an echo of mere contingency. But we are also structured as subjects. And in fact, no matter how much we understand that we are constructed as subjects, there are strict limits to the extent that we can deconstruct ourselves and still get around every day. So we certainly continue to live "as if", and in a very important sense live this paradox at the abstract level. It is perfectly analogous to the fact that while I have a very strong feeling that our whole world is falling apart, I'm putting away as much money as I can into a retirement account, you know. And also part of the answer is that it is the greatest show on earth.

IGZ: The show of whom? Whose show is it if we are permitted to pose such a question against the omnipotence of the meaninglessness which creates us, the question and the possible replies and reactions to it as different parts of its immanence? Is it a self-defeating—or even worse a self-ridiculing question? Maybe I can find a better articulation: is it possible to challenge the rules of the game and its very existence as the self-manifestation of the immanence? Or are we allowed to challenge, or to abandon our responsibility to challenge, this game and our preconstructed position/role in it, be it as dwellers, disciples or rebels? This nowhere land between immanence and transcendence, between the philosophy of the omnipotence of God/meaninglessness/the rules of the game or, alternatively, the supremacy of human free will and agency, this no-man's-land, this Diasporic de-territorialized yet specific arena is the locus of my question which I repeat now: whose game is it?

JB: I say it is the greatest game.

IGZ: But who or what is the creator? And who or what is the one or the dynamic multiplicity/chaos who is to make sense of this game and its fruits? Are we actually sovereign, or partially sovereign, autonomous players in this game? Or is it that we are merely a plaything, agents or media of a mechanism, continuum or immanence that is beyond our will, control or even our understanding, and we cannot make sense of this wholeness or of our existence solely as its product, echo and devoted-stupid agents?

JB: There is a thinking always going on, whether or not there is a self thinking it. There is a thinking always going on. And it works especially hard in dreams. I had dreams, so many dreams that I am traveling some place with a group of people. We're trying to establish a community somewhere, and often there are odd problems: you can't drive through the snow, all of a sudden you don't have a car, you're falling of a cliff, and sometimes I'm afraid to go to sleep. Because I know that I'm going to go to these weird places while I am asleep, and I have absolutely no control over it. Of course I'm going to fall asleep, I really... I'm losing control, I'm going to have these exhausting adventures and there's nothing I can do about it. And then—it happened to me a couple of nights ago—I said to myself, but that's what your life is, why should you be especially afraid when you go to sleep?

IGZ: Normalized life conventions are conceived mostly as self-evident projects. In terms of mental health, social stability and philosophical reasons they are set by the system as an aim of education and of human existence; the system reproduces reality, the apparatus of representing reality, and interpretation of reality, in a sense that makes people function more or less "successfully" and "efficiently". Of course there are sanctions and rewards and so on for successful/unconventional participation in organized social life within any collective. Would you agree, Prof. Boyarin, that this normality/success is nothing but the chains of the prisoners in the Platonic cave that normally are replaced by "emancipation", which offers nothing but another Platonic cave, alternative self-forgetfulness that the Diasporic counter-educator challenges less via the fruits of the plantations of "critique" and much more by crossing the normalities, awakening by and within responsible improvisation, co-poiesis and counter-education that is aware of its mission in a Godless world?

JB: Okay, so what I am saying is that up until now, the 20th century, you have a situation where most people can be doing that and some people may be more reflective, and Plato can say it is not worthwhile that way. And I can say, "But yes, there is a certain value. There is a great deal of value in human life in itself. Just as there is a value in any other creaturely life, and it is not as absolute as that". I'm saying that now we're reaching horizons where the combination of being able collectively to manipulate our environment, and to do that while being asleep at the wheel, has led to situations where we threaten to obviate the continued existence of whatever it is outside our consciousness that allows us to continue to breathe and to be conscious. Its almost like the old question: if a tree falls in the forest and there's no one there to hear it, did it really fall? So years ago I said, "Look, there are so many unemployed philosophers: go create a government program for them, we'll station them around the forest and we'll make sure that every time a tree falls in the forest someone will hear it, so we won't have that problem anymore." I am not saying that it doesn't matter whether you call it autonomy or responsibility or whatever you call it. Judith Butler is very clear on that and was helpful for me. She is saying in the book *Bodies that Matter*—she came back and she said, "Look, just because its constructive doesn't mean its not real". So she was talking about how gendered subjects get created, she was responding to people who said, "Well, if you say its all constructed, how can we have any feminist critique?" And she said, "Yes, it is constructed. But it is real". And I guess what I am saying now is, I'm not in a position to say whether or not unexamined life is or is not worth living. I'm inclined to say that unexamined lives are also very much worth living and examined lives maybe fundamentally neurotic, but in a collective sense, as a species, we have to examine better the ways we're organized in the various systems of the life-world or it will just stop. It will not be there anymore and the whole game ends.

IGZ: I have a problem with your articulation. Because I am not satisfied at all with the reply of Judith Butler that you find so helpful, according to which if it is constructed it does not mean that it is not real. An unavoidable question in this case will be: A. What kind of "reality"? and B. In what sense is it "real"? Here Judith Butler actually follows Michel Foucault, her teacher, and I have the same problem with Foucault. Following Foucault and Butler you still insist on emancipation, Prof. Boyarin, on the omnipotence of contingency by the same token. As I understand your work, you are still firm in refusing injustice. You seriously relate to the realization of concepts such as emancipation and peace. But on the other hand you emphasize the omnipotence of contingency and power relations. Here, you see, I have a problem with your work, as well as with Butler's and Foucault's. Because I would ask, who is the sovereign of this resistance? Who or what is the voice that talks itself through us to us and to others as if it is the self when we give a lecture about agency and resistance and categories such as freedom, peace or justice for the oppressed? Again, if there is no otherness of the Other or of myself in the sense of transcendence, if there is no potential transcendence, if there is no sacred or secularized holiness, if there is no room for co-poiesis and erotic creativity in the sense of the love of the subject that is not totally constructed—very much constructed yes, but not totally constructed—then with what are you left with? How do you establish seriousness toward responsibility?

JB: This is where I think Eric Santner in his recent work…he talks about… he doesn't know Hebrew so he doesn't do it very clearly, but he reads it through Rosenzweig. He's talking there about the difference between what he calls "law" and "מצווה", commandment, because there is a speaker…

IGZ: As in תפילת היחיד, the prayer of the individual, even without a text or any regulative ritual, and תפילת הציבור the public prayer, which is a defined, regulated public ritual.

JB: Yes. And again, an anecdote. That same older man who I like very much that said to me last week "זה האדם נעשה בצלם" ("the human was created in the image of God"): a couple of years ago I said to him, "I had a fantastic experience in *schul* last week". They sent me up to *daven Minha* [offer the Afternoon prayer], and I was *davening* [praying], and it just didn't matter where I was, when I was, the fact that I was born, the fact that I was going to die. I just was not worried about all that". And he said, "Don't you understand? A person *davens* for 40 years hoping to have an experience like that once". Well, what's funny, I can't give you a satisfactory answer. All I can think is that…

IGZ: Prayer in its best is actual transcendence. If your post-colonialist ideology leads you to the conclusion that there is no transcendence, then you have to accept also that this fashionable postmodern package you just received includes the ridiculing of, the impossibility of, *ontological Diaspora*. And in this sense while there might be many Diasporas in a globalized world there is no room for Diasporic humans. No genuine possibility for prayer that you just described as one of your more important experiences. Because if we understand prayer in the sense of Rosenzweig, according to which the essence of prayer is not its fulfillment but the possibility of prayer as transcendence, then you have to face otherness in the form of the face of the Other in the language of Levinas, or the totally other in the language of Adorno and Horkheimer. In any case, you cannot be satisfied with a declaration of the omnipotence of contingency, difference that does not make a difference, and mere contextual power relations. I think that facing this challenge is a starting point for Diasporic counter-education.

JB: I agree. I would say that for me, the stronger the awareness of contingency the less anxious I am about having to rationalize or authorize for myself a desire for justice. Because instead of standing up for justice in the name of what is written in the Torah or something like that, it feels more like a consciousness that happens to be in the world and senses justice as a good thing and welcomes justice. I do not have to grind it out of myself.

IGZ: But Adorno and Horkheimer that we spoke about in the fist part of the conversation understood justice in a negative way. Namely, facing injustice or using injustice is the possibility of doing good, the only possible manifestation of justice is its negation, injustice. Justice is not a positive category but rather a negative one, and this, to my mind, is a very important Diasporic consistent position. It is conditioned, however, by the possibility of reflection, or by the possibility of preparing ourselves for reflection, transcendence and overcoming our limits, as one might find in the example of a worthy prayer or in the case of the very few who risked their lives and their families' lives and saved Jews or Gypsies during the Holocaust.

JB: But I'm not talking about justice now. I'm talking about justice being sensed as a good in the same way that sunlight is sensed as a good, and I'm not talking about the impulse to self-sacrifice for activism. In terms of any conventional activism I think that we are so globally far gone that the best thing I can do, the most useful thing that I can do, is to say, "Stop hoping [for other] people. Think about how we can save ourselves". This sense in me is pushed further by the last lecture of George Bush. It is not just because a regime in an empire which is a dying empire—but as I was saying 20 years ago, a dying dragon could do a lot of damage if it waves its tale around. That is what we are doing now. But all of the people who would have energies directed toward saving ourselves collectively are now desperately trying to hold on to the bits of separate things, all of which are important, but none of which can happen by itself. Even then I said [leave] the impossible international, so there was negativity there. I was talking about an almost nostalgic longing for something, right? I almost have a sense that separate struggles dissipate our collective chances.

IGZ: What would be your new position towards postcolonialism, politics of identity and other struggles in the name of the marginalized and the hybridized and the deconstructed? In other words, what is your response to the shift from the quest and struggle for emancipation that was founded on unity, wholeness—or the quest for a renewed totality that will rebuild the Garden of Eden on earth, to the current emancipatory agendas which are founded on fragmentation and ever growing deconstruction, difference, relativism and hybridity which it seems go in quest of eternal Diaspora and nomadism and not of nirvana, total redemption and eternal-universal "peace"?

JB: I would say people should keep organizing. They should keep trying to articulate their collective interest. They should keep trying to articulate group interests with other group interests. But they should not kid themselves that if they shout loud enough it will help to form a great new world. The value of doing these things is not measured by whether or not the dreamed goal would be the outcome.

IGZ: In what sense does Judaism have a special role in this agenda?

JB: Given this concept of Diaspora, and what you are saying to me altogether, my answer is not any different from what I have worked from ever before. The human species is always characterized by difference, by blend of—not irreducible differences in the sense of eternal differences, of course, but irreducible differences in the sense of masses of differentiation among human beings; being an irreducible part of how human beings are in the world. Jews in the Diaspora have figured out one of the most durable ways of sustaining difference with relatively the least access to the monopoly of violence of any group I am aware of. And in that sense it is an extraordinarily successful model of sustaining difference within humanity.

IGZ: So in this sense, why not to offer a Judaization of culture more generally as the aim of (counter-)education in order to allow all humans Diasporic life as cosmopolitically oriented individuals? To be consistent with your understanding of the mission of Judaism I would ask: why should Judaism limit itself to its de-territorialized marginality, and not offer this nomadism and eternal-improvisational creative existence as a cosmopolitan human existence for all humans, for all potential fellow nomads? And as we are all united by our potential overcoming "home-returning" normalizing education and ethnocentrism, why should such counter-education enclose itself within the horizons of Judaism? I pose this question in light of the understanding that most people normally will insist on collectivism, ethno-centrism, fear, routine and dogmatism of various and sometimes rich kinds, and will resist the invitation to become great lovers: individuals, to live the dangerous life of a nomad who is in self-chosen eternal Diaspora as a manifestation of Life as holy when freed of Positive Utopia, on the one hand, and from flight back "home" to nothingness, on the other.

JB: I do not think it necessarily should be, otherwise I would respond to people like Lyotard and Nancy: you cannot allegorize the Jew. And I have said that. I have criticized the allegorizing, because I think in many cases, and I think of Lyotard particularly now, because he allegorizes the Jew in ways that not of necessity evacuate all of the specificity of Jewishness. But I am certainly not opposed to the notion of not generalizing, but diffusing, the notion of a textual existence: for example, the idea of a textual homeland. Part of the reason that I am very cautious about it is that, to the extent that we identify Jewishness with the textual homeland, it is to offer a very elitist and a very masculine notion of what Jewishness is. And I think another part of the reason why I am hesitating is that I am more used to thinking why do I valorize it at all than to thinking about why I don't generalize it further. So I am thinking about this anew. But one thing that I would have to think very hard that makes it interesting is that you are doing it in the context of otherness. There is an old story, I think it is in a collection of Yiddish stories called *Royte Pomeranzen*. A guy from a *shtetl* goes to America and he does very well. He makes a lot of money. And 20 years later, in the 1930s, he's so rich that he decides to take a trip back to Europe to see the old town. So he takes the ship, he gets off the ship, he gets on the train, and off the train, he hires the *Balegule* [coachman] to take him 15 miles to his town, and he talks to him and he says, "You know, I have been away for a long time. How many Jews are there in town?" The carter says, "About four thousand". And he says, "How many *goyim* [gentiles]?" "Two thousand".

And the coachman starts interviewing him: "You're from New York city. In your city how many Jews are there?" "About a million". "And how many *goyim*?" "Six million *goyim*!" There is a kind of ethnocentrism that is part of the technique of Jewishness, and it can be very ugly. I think it is not so much about should or should not. This is also part of the problem with a generalization or even diffusion: it means that people are going to want to know what it is and how you do it. And they are going to want an *Idiot's Guide to Jewishness*. And the problem with it is so complicated. It is so sophisticated that I can't simplify it. Part of it is that it is all of these things that we do. Part of it is about not just reducing to essences or what is more useful of thinking about a generalization per se... Take for example an issue in the Talmud the rabbis are talking about: if you see your neighbor's cow, רעך [your neighbor] means a Jew, no question. You see, its not just the 19th century chauvinism that you have to return it to the Jew. But if the cow is of a *goy* [gentile] you can keep it. There is clearly ethnocentrism there. But it is examined. And they tell stories about it and they have to justify it. And it is problematic.

IGZ: Would you agree that the generalization of some of the central ideas of Judaism should be universalized by overcoming this aspect of Judaism towards living Diasporically in face of the presence of the absence of the truth, the absolute or the Promised Land?

JB: Yes. And that is why I said that for me the possibility of doing it, the value of doing it, has to do with a sense of my being responsible for the Jew that I make of myself. Now you came at me and said, "How can you do that if things are so contingent?"

IGZ: If they are *totally* contingent, if we face meaning as the manifestation of a false totality or a totality which is beyond the dialectics of negation and its negation/affirmation.

JB: The best answer I have is: we have to act as if they are not, as if there is a projector that I am grasping and making work. A wonderful book by Derek Parfit called *Reasons and Persons* where he just really breaks down, and shows how artificial is, the notion that I was a child, I was that child, this happened to me when I was a child. Analytic philosophy cannot break that apart in a number of ways. But we cannot stop acting as if, and I do not think it is entirely necessary, but [better] the more we are aware that we're doing that, that we're acting as if, and that we're creating our world in a world which ultimately does resist that. When I say "transcend", the horizon that I am proposing is the limits of our collective species for its existence, and we bump up against that limit when we are so active on our life world to make it capable of supporting us. It is like in the movie *The Truman Show*: if he gets to the end he goes through, and there is a real world outside. What we're doing is we're reaching that painted horizon and when we burst through it we're going to find out that its just a bubble, and its going to collapse on us, there's nothing...

IGZ: What would be the mission, the commitment or the agenda of a Diasporic counter-education today in face of this situatedness of the human?

JB: In a crude sense—which is the best answer I can give for now, to provide young people with a sufficient sense of the tremendous excitement of what it has meant to be human; either in general or in specific ways. Specifically in the Jewish way, but understand that that it is also a way of being human, that they understand first of all that the greatest thing that we can do is to make it possible, to keep it going. And secondly, that it is enough and more than enough to make their own lives worthwhile and to be able to bear and accept and ultimately valorize their own mortality, that there is so much of a heritage of human consciousness and creativity that it can be explored for much more than one lifetime.

8. DIASPORA, PHILOSOPHY AND COUNTER-EDUCATION IN FACE OF POST-COLONIAL REALITY

IGZ: Thank you, Professor West for agreeing to enter this conversation. Especially as I asked for your permission to talk on some of the more difficult aspects of the critical mind and the critical language we love to love in a way that might problematize some of our most important habits of justifying our optimism concerning Critical Pedagogy. By the way, did you receive the book I sent you?

Cornel west: Oh, I did. I did. Its a lovely book.

IGZ: You did?

CW: Thank you; you had some interesting things about Adorno. I look at the Adorno every day; you see that picture over there?

IGZ: Oh...Adorno is a thinker who is of special interest for me. No, it is much more than having an interest in him. Even today I conceive him as a writer not to be very far away from; actually I did my PhD on Critical Theory and the history of pessimism.

CW: Yes, I saw that, the footnote there about 1996 on the problem of pessimism was fascinating. Adorno was somebody who ought to be a constant companion.

IGZ: Although, you know, unfortunately, most of the people that I meet normally relate to Adorno, Horkheimer and Marcuse only in their first period of critical thinking and they are very reluctant to approach the more mature, yes, even more sophisticated, and also more pessimistic and ambivalent texts of their later work.

CW: Absolutely

IGZ: After the *Dialectic of Enlightenment*, Prof. West, you are known in the world as a thinker who integrates different traditions, disciplines and practices in an improvisational-original way for a philosophy and practice which are critical. What for you are the educational implications of critical philosophy as an improvisational act which at the same time is the uttermost religious commitment?

CW: And its already... let me begin, that I thank you for letting me be a part of this conversation, and saluting your own work in this regard, because I think that my own thinking is close to what you call a second stage of Critical Theory and I say that because you see I view myself first and foremost a jazzman and a bluesman in the world of ideas. What that means is that going back to Plato and the traditional quarrel of philosophy and poetry, which is really a fight of education, a fight of paideia, what is going to be the fundamental means by which we engage and profound ways in which we form a tension cultivates souls and mature souls, those three levels of paideia, and as you know, that Plato, for dialectic argument and the critique of the poem, but it could be the minigrame poet, who talks about forms of persuasion and so forth. Now I believe that philosophers must go to school with the poets and poets must engage the philosophical reflection; that is why Benjamin is for me the great 20th century philosopher, because you know what Hannah Arendt said about him, he engaged in a poetic thinking that is philosophical, or he's a philosopher who has a poetic dimension and therefore he fuses the philosophic, the poetic and of course the political, which is always already shown through both. So I think when I resonate with you most as one who takes jazz and blues as a starting point is to acknowledge this fusion of the aesthetic, the poetic, the ethical, the political, the existential, the spiritual and the religious in a very special sense not in a institutional way of religion but in a sense of—as a subject matter of religion.

IGZ: Yes.

CW: Which is life and death, which is suffering, joy and so on. Now, at the same time I should say that 'The jazzman'/ 'The bluesman' means then that you have a tragic-comic disposition, I mean one of the things that you and I would probably have not disagreed on is—I would accent and I see it relatively silent in your work— which is the fundamental role of Chekhov and Beckett. Beckett says try, fail again, fail or better, at page 59 in the last poetic or prose work of Samuel Beckett, which is for me an echo of Chekhov (you know that for my own work Chekhov is the figure to turn to). I already see Chekhov then,1904, figuring the kind of insights that he peels out of Adorno, making the dialectics and thereafter, or all kinds of negative theology and thereafter, which is to say that it trumps and forecloses all solutions, anarchies and so forth. And really, talking about the Sisyphean process by which we engage in critique, live lives of compassion and project something beyond the self, knowing that it is unattainable still lures us. And that is for me always the key in the work of Chekhov. Now what does it have to do with education? Well, it has much to do with education because it means that first, all sentimental forms of education that posit all good on one side and all evil on the other is called into question. Its already called into question when you call [into question] positive Utopia even among our left wing comrades.

IGZ: This is the reason why when I read you, I told myself: here I have found a Diasporic philosopher. I am working now on articulating my own Diasporic Philosophy and on creating a Diasporic Philosophy collection which will also be an arena for a reconstruction of past Diasporic philosophies and philosophers. It is important for me to reconstruct this lost tradition from the pre-Socrates to present-day thinkers since we are entering the age of ambivalence and improvisation, of nomadism and deterritorializations, in which the presence of the absence of God and the transcendence become unavoidable to address and impossible for a worthy address. In other words, I think the history of Diasporic Philosophy has not yet written its last chapter and we have a responsibility to reply in a worthy manner to the Diasporic challenge. Already some of the pre-Socrates did…

CW: Euclides

IGZ: Heraclites is the foremost figure in this direction in my mind, and we should go into it presently. But even before that, please let me say that I consider you a genuine present-day Diasporic Philosopher. This is the reason why I would like to press you a little…

CW: Sure. Let me just add this before you go on. I think that where we also have a very deep agreement is the way we understand Pascal and Montaigne. Because my Pascal and sensibility, and my fundamental allegiance to Montaigne's aesthetical writing, but most importantly to his mature skeptical sensibility, require me sometimes to be skeptical about skepticism. He knows he has to live, he still has to love, he still has the doing and so forth, that when I see you for the second way of the Critical Theory invoking Pascal or Montaigne I say, this is someone of my spirit. So go right ahead. I just wanted to note those things to you, because you started with Heraclites and Adorno—well, there are those others in the middle.

IGZ: Yes, of course.

CW: ...So very important to both of us.

IGZ: Unfortunately there are not too many of them in the present day.

CW: That's true.

IGZ: Especially among our friends in the left who coat a positive Utopia with dogmatism and exclusion that they are committed to overcome. Now, this is exactly the reason why I would like to begin by challenging your own Diasporic Philosophy, because it is so important in my view. On the one hand, in your work, as I understand it, we all share a social responsibility and a moral commitment to resist injustice. I think your entire work might be understood as a contribution to this invitation, which is a moral imperative and an existential impetus like light for plants. At the same time, without having a direct voice from God, or a theoretical unquestionable foundation, what is the meaning and what are the preconditions of the morality of such a call for moral act in a multicultural reality and critical positioning of all inviting "voices", gods, and theoretical "unquestionable" foundations? Isn't the invitation to the moral act an existential impetus, a more sophisticated Platonic cave, that directs you and forces you and aims you? In light of your explicit anti-foundationalism, Professor West, and in the absence of absolute truths and objectivity, especially once you overcome the magic of the presence, and once you deconstruct the naivety of the "Platonic cave", who or what might ensure, create or promise a precondition for the moral act or for the kind of response that will be more than manipulative, meaningless or violent as a precondition for what Levinas calls the *Ehical I* and the very possibility of the moral that is more than, or different from the sum of its contingent conditions and productivity of its contextual power-relations? In the absence of God who is not yet exiled, deconstructed, or ridiculed, what besides the productivity of violence, could promise or enable an un-naive commitment to social justice, to resisting injustice and to Critical Pedagogy? Now, in my reading of your work I see three solutions: one solution would be to talk through the viewpoint of the victim. Let's elaborate more on your first solution.

In order to see the victim, to acknowledge victimhood, as against victimization, we need a representation apparatus and a theory that relates to it and to the world represented. We cannot make it directly, in an unmediated manner because the victim and the presence of victimization are also always enabled, constructed, represented and distributed as an object of the organization of our strives, as a cultural commodity, and as a political function, by conceptions, by organizations of lives and by the social power-relations in a specific historical moment and so forth.

Now, when you call us to identify the victim or accept as a yardstick for moral behavior the worldview/viewpoint of the victim you do not offer an alternative to the exile of God. One reason for this is that in most human complex situations how do you decide in an unproblematic manner who is the victim and who is the victimizer? And is it so that the victim is always solely a victim and the victimizer is solely a victimizer? What happens when each of the two sides sees in the other the victimizer and itself as the victim, like in the Israeli-Palestinian situation, and each of the sides is a victim and a victimizer, theoretically and politically and educationally? As a Diasporic philosopher, what would your educational message be in face of this ambivalent reality?

CW: I think that... first, I begin with that powerful moment beginning with Negative Dialectics. Adorno says that the condition of truth is to allow suffering to speak. If you are actually and fundamentally committed to truth and justice, you follow it wherever it goes. And there is no doubt that there is suffering that cuts across barriers, lines—class lines, gender lines, racial lines, cultural lines, national lines and so forth. So that if you keep track of the suffering maybe different forms of suffering, maybe existential suffering, political suffering, economic suffering, psychic suffering and so forth, if you keep track on suffering, therefore are concerned about true speaking, then you are always going to acknowledge that there is never a kind of simplistic binary opposition between victim and victimizer. Already you have multi-layers of suffering in varying historical contexts, which does not mean that there are not going to be any asymmetric relations of power, let's say [between] imperial power and colonies: but even there, it is still not as if there is no suffering on the imperial side. We know there is suffering on the colonized side but it is not as if the colonies are not agents that can in some sense bring power to bear on the imperial side and so forth. That is true of racialism, that is true of gender that is true of the Middle East context and so on and so forth. So, from the very beginning, if you are going to be historicist, you cannot historicize without contextualizing and what you contextualize you pluralize and once you pluralize you keep track of the various forms of suffering. Victimizing and being victimized [are connected] in a variety of different levels and registers. And if that is true it means that it is never the case that there is some kind of homogeneous linear victim versus victimizer, so that when I say I am in solidarity with those who suffer, I am actually saying I am in solidarity with suffering wherever you find it in various contexts that cross various kinds of lines.

IGZ: Could you say more about the various sufferings and the differences between them in light of the differences between various kinds of victimizers, and the too common presence of ambivalence between the victim and the victimizer and the truth of the victim who is at the same time also a victimizer? I present this ambivalence in order to face ambivalence, not to be swallowed by ambivalence, impasse and moral indifference. And we have not yet spoken even a word about the relation between the autopoiesis of the victimizer and the hospitality of Love as two opposing poles, two ecstatic alternatives that strive for co-poiesis: Life— Thanatos and Eros, or Christ and anti-Christ if you prefer that theological articulation. Ontologically, not solely existentially and historically, it is so difficult to differentiate the two. The difference is found, pronounced, distributed successfully normally only a posteriori, as part of the triumphal parade of the one who writes the history, the one who had the upper hand in establishing the hegemonic difference between the victim and the victimizer, who is strong or violent enough to establish the consensus or the false consciousness about the verdict on who is the true victim. Do you think we have something meaningful here to learn from the critical thinkers of the Frankfurt School?

I would say: Yes. Suffering. Worthy suffering and its relation to the quest for truth and worthier Life.

CW: Exactly. I mean, this part of... that is, again, what I love about Benjamin. Remember Adorno's essay on Benjamin when he talks about the specific gravity of the concrete? This is a distinctive benchmark of Benjamin's project, and I have always used it as a benchmark. Because if you take seriously the specific gravity of the concrete it means that all abstract narratives are called into question; because they are sentimental and they are ahistorical, they do not take context seriously enough. Now, you do not want to talk about this in such a way that just calls into question all talk of victimizing and victims, because on these different registers they are concrete. But if you lose sight of the concrete suffering you end up with these sentimental narratives that cast Victims all on one side (capital V), Victimizers on the other side (capital V), and you actually ahistorically make contention out of them.

IGZ: I think this is a very important point of departure to reflect on the new anti-Semitism, which unfortunately stems from the tradition of resisting racism and anti-humanism. But before we go into that I would like to ask you about the collision and the conflict between narratives: whether we do not have a theoretical home from where we can place our arguments or establish our lenses, or telescopes as moral, responsible people, as philosophers and educators; whether we are currently, and maybe eternally, in an historical moment that is fundamentally contingent. What is our existential, philosophical, educational position there, in face of conflicting narratives, within a contingent context? And how should we position ourselves in front of, facing, within conflicting narratives? And what are the educational implications of such homelessness?

CW: yes, I think that ...almost like Dante ...

IGZ: And, as you said before, most critical thinkers who talk about conflicting narratives have a narrative that is "their" home, or cave, a Platonic cave, of which they are its echo, its victim, and also at the same time its enthusiastic agent; which means that their seeing, their judgment and their praxis represents their blindness that is conceived as light, genuine revelation or courageous resistance to injustice.

CW: Absolutely. Like Dante's Inferno, which begins in the middle, in the midst, and sometimes in the darkness. Or even in the woods, in the sense that Sondheim talks about it. In the woods—you're in the middle and if you are always in the middle there is no home, or refuge or cave—a sure space that you have access to. That is what Rorty may call an Archimedes point...

IGZ: Heraclitus, you remember, after he writes, even if in his deliberately obscure manner, puts his writings in the temple and runs away from the company of humans to the wood. As in face of too easygoing interpretations of his words, so in the quest for a mature nomadism in the woods or mountains Heraclitus resists the temptation of "homereturning" or of establishing a paralyzing "home". He is in constant search, always in a state of awakening, never at home. But the mountains and the woods do not have to be physical and they are not necessarily "out there"; they might be part of us, within us, a kind of Diasporic autopoesis. Such sensitivity might become a starting point for a genuine Diasporic Educational Philosophy—especially for us today. Don't you agree?

CW: Yes. See, as a bluesman I recognize that we are always already in the middle, or how Beckett would call it—in the mass. Heidegger talks about being with mass. I agree with that, I would say the folk—like a bluesman. Now what does it mean? It means then that the best we can do is to somehow try to strengthen our armor on the Socratic level—which is we must have courage to engage in critical reflection on being in the middle, knowing that there is always a remainder for Adorno the stuff that theories can't catch. It is the blind spots the wasted material. Remember page 151 in the *Minima Moralia* of Adorno, where blind spots and wasted material that the dialectics cannot catch, which is the saying that there is a humility in being in the middle and to think you gain access to pure spaces intellectual arrogance, which is blinding all the time and misleading. So, if you have a humility, which is not so much to come to skepticism, it is simply to say you would resist, you would transgress, you would continually try to transcend, you will fail, you will fall on your face, you would be inadequate, you won't have the conceptual clarity and transparency associated with pure spaces—you are a bluesman. There is no way out. But it does not mean that you are not wrestling, it is more like Jacob in the 32nd chapter of genesis, you are wrestling in the midnight with angels of death, trying to emerge with something distinctive and new and novel—in that case that was a new name—god wrestler, Israel. But as human beings and subjects that are continually in process, in formation, we first must have the courage to engage in a Socratic reflection, but most importantly, we are trying to master the courage of love, the courage to be companionate, the courage to be empathetic and those are for me inseparable, but they are not identical. You see, the courage to think critically can be separate from the courage to love and this is a problem. They have to be intertwined, connected. You cannot be a bluesman and you got your mind working and your heart is cold and your soul is frozen.

IGZ: Unfortunately, it happens so much...

CW: you got to be able to unite them in such a way that you are... it is a way of life. The third moment is the tragic-comic one, that is the blue note, the Sisyphean—you never get there. You are always already in the middle. You want to die in the middle, not the exact same place. But you are still in the middle. There is no end point that is pure. There is no origin that is pure. There is no Alpha that is pure. There is no Omega that is pure. You are betwixt and between.

IGZ: But if we are not in the middle, but rather in nowhere place? What about living Diasporic life and being-toward-life as an enduring nomad? What about what I call living as an "eternal improviser"?

CW: Nowhere is where to be in exile—that is still a place. It is not as if you can go in exile in the semi-Platonic space above time and space or in some surreal space of Plotinus, away from body, away from culture, away from language and so forth, but what Mayson, and you talk about the Nomadic here, which echoes in some sense Deleuze, to be in space, both tied to and over again roots and you have to distinguish r-o-o-t-s and r-o-u-t-e-s. The nomadic is the interplay between the roots which are always already inadequate, but they are there. They are language that you have. It means the baggage that you carry. Carry some roots—your first language...

IGZ: Hebrew, for the Jewish mystic and it is still Hebrew for me as one who lost the Zionist negation of Diasporic life and its attempt to renew Hebrew as the language of concrete Life, genuine, concrete Life as if the Garden of Eden is not lost for us, embedded in secular history and power relations. This tension between Hebrew as the origin, the presence of God in immanence and Hebrew in modern, high speed progress and transcendence in face of the killing-of-God-each-moment-anew by modernist-oriented Utopia (which is nothing but secularized Jewish Theology) is an important gate for me: a path to sensitivity and responsibility toward "my" language that is neither "mine", nor the total prison of what I am as against what I could have become. This tension is part of the greatness of hope the originality of language always contains, even when the original language becomes the kind of Hebrew and Israeliness that surrounds, reacts to and enables the Israeli condition within which I am trying to realize my Diasporic responsibility, co-poiesis and improvisational nomadism.

CW: Hebrew. My first language is English. We can tell a story about Gur-Ze'ev's brother, Cornel, as for what our roots are, even that we are very critical of them and our routes—the routes that we have taken which are probably connected to our roots. You may have gone to study Heidegger, or to Paris to study the Louvre and so forth, but you carried your roots with you while you were involved in your routes— the routes that you have taken, and therefore ended up in the kind of an exiling sensibility: a nomadic sensibility, or as a Diasporic philosopher. I mean I rather call myself a bluesman, or a jazzman, rather than Diasporic. I have nothing against that category; I am a little suspicious of the categories of philosophers, because I have more of a poetic sensibility, I tend to trust you a bit more, because you have a blues sensibility and you talk about Diasporic. Usually in philosophy you talk about categories that get frozen and also petrify; they are no longer dynamic and fluid and protean, you see. While as a bluesman, improvisation is built into the very way in which you think and love and laugh and live.

IGZ: I think that in face of improvisation as an existential dimension it is not that you are detached from the responsibility to make a decision, to position yourself...

CW: You have to ...

IGZ: But without the guarantees, the fears, or the dogmas that enable you as well as mislead you to think in a naive way that makes it logically possible or psycho-logically easier for you to choose and to position yourself, as well as to decide in favor of self-forgetfulness. No genuine guarantees are preconditions for responsibility of the kind that enables genuine improvisation, which means to act, to make a decision, to live dangerously, to address the invitation of poetic life in the eternity of each moment anew, that are at the same time also contextual and have their history and their political fruits. And yet, I refuse to reduce the one to the other.

CW: Absolutely. The reason why you have to position yourself is that as a bluesman and a blueswoman of ideas—you still have to find your voice. You see, you cannot find your voice unless you have mastered the courage to think critically, the courage to empathize and love and the courage to wrestle the tragic-comic—which is to hope. So when you find your voice, why do you find your voice? In part, in order to try and be true to yourself and also because that voice might be empowering for others as they try to find their voice.

IGZ: When I read you, Professor West, and now as I listen to you meditating about finding your voice and about finding the voice of the silenced once, I feel that there is here also a danger we should be aware of. This is the danger of identifying with the marginalized, with the victims and in such a unique manner that might actually inflict on them injustice. Here I relate to a kind of response on our part that will thrust them into self-forgetfulness in the form of narrow-mindedness and dogmatism. When you do not invite them to challenge their own self-understood dimensions, you empower the normalizing education of the marginalized; and actually, the emancipation is nothing more than the replacement of a hegemonic normalizing education with a marginalized normalizing education. And so many times the marginalized, as they are people, as they are humans—their quest is to be in the middle, in the center, to be the hegemon, to replace a strive, a quest, a will to power with love, compassion, respond-ability that represents response-ability and not its negation in the form of surrender to the will to power which is also the manifestation of Thanatos and self-forgetfulness which is edified by self-indulgence, by surrendering to the self-evidence and normalizing education. As I see it, the normalizing education of the marginalized is by no means more compassionate than the normalizing education of the hegemony: it is only less effective, at least temporarily. It is important for us to face not only its violence but also the enduring vitality and the telos of its violence: it has its own victimization practices and limitations—not as an historical misstep or blunder to be easily corrected, but as part of human existence in the present historical moment in the West. So where are the gates, if any, to open for us on the path of moral commitment to struggle against injustice and to identify with the marginalized and the silenced, and at the same time respond in a mature manner to the awakening from the illusion that the marginalized are morally superior, do not actually victimize the less powerful whenever it is possible or prepare themselves for the oppression "that is genuinely justified" against their former oppressors or their rivals? It happens so much in Critical Pedagogy that actually you replace one dogmatism with another, one normalizing education with its alternative. Critical Pedagogy itself becomes dogmatized and transformed into an oppressive tool, even against those proclaimed to be emancipated by the critical educators.

CW: I would have to look at which passage did you have in mind, because my aim, my intention, is to keep the critical energy flowing, so that my critiques of the poor people, Puritanism, the provincialism of the black folk is pretty intense.

IGZ: And I know so many people criticize you for that.

CW: I am criticized within progressive groups and within the black community for being sometimes too critical of them. At the same time I do not want to lose sight of the parochialism and provincialism of the more powerful hegemonic discourses and practice and system that dominate the...

IGZ: Please, tell me more about the secret art of finding or creating the right balance and the correct relations between the two.

CW: I mean, it is a nomadic activity. You are moving to and from, continually trying to be true to yourself, which is the hegemonic element that is inside of us. There are a couple of hegemonic elements that we master, that we choose, and try to forever call into question—the kind of dogmatism, the kind of disposition, the kind of arrogant and condescending sensibleness that go hand in hand with the hegemonic process, so all those that are involved in this civil war that is inside of us, as well as the war of both positions and movement of ground you have talked about in larger society. That is why there are also passages that would give you an impression that that I am not as critical as I ought to be of those poor people, or oppressed people, or victims and so forth. But as you know, there are right wing discourses out there that we have to be cautious about, that trivialize the suffering of the poor people, of women and gays and lesbians and workers and the people of color. And therefore, in responding to those it might give the impression that you are over-compensating and therefore not being as critical as the very folk that you are trying to defend. You see what I mean?

IGZ: Yes. So now, as we see the problematic of being a nomadic moral human and a Diasporic person, I would like to present you with what I see in your work as three solutions, or three answers to this dilemma, and I would like you to help me to understand the tension between the three. One is that we do have a yardstick to choose a theory, ideology, or a tradition, or a way of life. We are not totally alone; we are accompanied by a possible theory, or meta-theory, that is capable of saving us from meaninglessness or naïve dwelling in "the genuine kingdom of truth and justice", or at least of offering us a modest, conditional, partial, temporary yardstick to decide in a meaningful manner within and among rival language games. And yet, this efficiency that enables us to side with the disabled or help the marginalized is in your work essentially contextual, instrumental and pragmatist. This prag-matism of yours enables emancipatory action and resistance to oppression and other manifestations of injustice, yet it does not come without the price tag of constant danger of replacing one normalizing education with another. The second path that I see in your work is the absence of God that speaks to us: there is no objective universal reason or human Spirit that can lead us actually in an unproblematic sense. We can only rely on rational critical argumentation of good hearts to ensure "disenchantment" and emancipation from illusions and oppressors. Getting your hands on the Maya Curtain is a possible emancipatory act that Critical Pedagogy should prepare us for. We cannot be content with the act of *alethea*; we cannot feast on the "body" and "spirit" of this *leviathan* of oppression and false consciousness. The essential pre-assumption here is that the rational "critique" is able to do the trick. In other words, ideology critique can do what only Baron Munchhausen succeeded in doing until now: to take us all out of the mud by hauling out our hair strongly enough with our own hands. This "disenchantment" trick is very problematic and extremely complicated because, again, if what we said about the absence of absolute truth is not valid solely about knowledge, but also about yardsticks for choosing and evaluating conflicting sets of values and argumentations, then the yardsticks too are constructed, manipulated and contingent. From what terra sacra, then, is it possible for us to offer a spring of rational decisions and critical theorists which are not victims or mere echoes of a specific set of effective manipulations, a resonance of a contingent code or dynamic in "our" contingent context?

The third path that I see in your work is that looking at argumentations, conflicts, theoretical discussions, ideologies and so on and so forth on a meta-level, or from the poetics, that as music Pythagoras understood that it is not only that two and two are four—the numbers have their relations and meaning also in a cosmological essential sense and manifest sacred harmony, the worthiest music. This is where he comes from, establishing a theory as a religious way of life. Religion here is a bonding of the ethical, the aesthetic, the bodily, the intellectual and the political dimensions, which integrate with each other in the absence of the original intimacy towards the cosmos. Actually, what you are suggesting here, Professor West is a Nietzschean way out from meaninglessness. A Nietzschean path in the sense that we will choose this or that, we will courageously create what might manifest our creative power while guided to make the right decision in the absence of God, or in the presence of the absence of all absolutes. In the absence of anything essential, absolute or transcendent we still have an impetus, a criterion, a telos, or an exclusive drive, and that is what vitalizes life more then anything else—the power of creativity, the power of overcoming narrowness and shallowness, dogmatism, anything freezing or encouraging fear. This principle is something very different from criteria such as revolutionary efficiency and so on and so forth. Now, how do you relate to the tensions between these very different solutions in your work? And are we called to understand this tension as a bridge—or as an abyss?

CW: Well, you got a lot on the table there. Let me begin with the point about ideology critique, because you see I accept the later Frankfurt School critique of ideology.

IGZ: And also its dogmatization and paralyzing sacred institutionalization by its dogmatic easygoing followers?

CW: That's right. I do not believe we ever have transparency or pure illusions versus pure reality. So the marks of a German ideology have got to go. Now that does not mean—here I am closer to Gordimer than Nietzsche though—I do believe in the need to overcome the perennial process of what we are becoming, and that might sound almost Sisyphean or Camusean—Albert Camus, or Nietzsche, but that is closer to Gadamer, that is to say, I do believe critical questioning matters—that is to say that because you reject transparency of ideology critique, it does not mean that every view is the same, every ideology is the same, every social system is the same and so forth. Fascism is different than a democratic project; authoritarianism is different that democratic law. But like democratic law it still has ideology, it still has various ways in which power operates and circulates and so on. Now, what I am saying is this—when I say I am closer to Gadamer than to Nietzsche it means that we are still always already in a historical context in which we do now have access to Archimedean points and pure spaces and so forth. All it means is, you have a thoroughgoing falliblism in which you're never going to get it right, ever. You see, that is very Jamesian, that is Dewey, and that comes from American pragmatism. That does not mean that all views are the same. Relativism, Nihilism—they are to be refused, rejected; at the same time you have falliblism, or historical contextualism, that in some ways calls into question a lot of the Nietzschean projects, in which it looks as if you are locked into a certain kind of relativism if not nihilism, passive or active, in this sense. So, I would not want my work or project to be associated with the first stage of ideology critique in the Marxian tradition at all, nor would I want it to be associated with some kind of dogmatism. Now, let me say this about dogmatism—a very important point to make and there is a sense in which I think that I detect in your own work. That reminds me—you know Robert Unger, you know Unger's work? You know his recent *self awakening*?

IGZ: No.

CW: Oh, it is a major stereotype, it is very popular. It is very similar to your work. This is very much about transcendent, transgression, a world of meaninglessness, relative to defining some plenitude of meaning of the various ways in which we are bound to a certain kind of failure; at the same time we must master the will to empathize, the Love of Life that you talk about—very close to Unger's work here. And he and I took a course at Harvard Law School and we fight over this, because, again, I am closer to Chekhov, that is... it is more of a... I remind you of certain late romantic tragic sensibility, where as Chekhov is in a different space, he is not either one of those; and what I mean by this is this—that there are ways in which an obsession would not be dogmatic itself before it becomes dogmatism. Why? Because what happens is that you begin to downplay the role of various narratives and philosophic maneuvers that you have already viewed as dogmatic, that might contribute to the Love of Life, that might contribute to the emancipation, contribute to the transgression, because they are dogmatic. Now, see if, we will say if you want to be skeptical about skepticism, or what John Dewey calls the difference between retail skepticism and wholesale skepticism. There is a retail dogmatism and wholesale dogmatism—if you are up for wholesale dogmatism you are just parasitic on foundationalism, you see what I mean.

IGZ: Well....

CW: There are moments I think in your text when you seem to be so preoccupied with not being dogmatic that it is not clear that you are willing to make wise judgment of how certain narratives that you think are dogmatic are actually promoting some of the similar things that you are after.

IGZ: Take for example the Israeli-Palestinian situation. When I am asked this question I say look, in one sense I am Diasporic and I understand Zionism as the barbarization of Judaism and its commitment to truth and challenging injustice in a cosmopolitan framework, in light of negative Utopia and the quest for love. On the other hand the Israeli state is a historical reality, real people live there, they have their happiness their hope, their, suffering, their responsibilities and so forth—and you might, and I would say, I feel I should become a Diasporic person and live as an eternal improviser in Israel too. And for certain reasons, in Israel, yes, even more than anywhere else! On the one hand I call on Israel, and it is not very easy you know, for self-inflicted immigration of the Jews and for educating our children to be honest and justice-striving persons, to prepare themselves for life in an eternal and endless Diaspora. I am trying to articulate an educational framework and a detailed program for inviting, preparing and training young people to live Diasporically and become nomads in the convoluted world of ambivalence, globalization, ethnocentrism and constant symbolic bombardments from rival Pleasure Machines which aim to seize their autonomy and rob them of their responsibility, happiness and fury. On the other hand, it is not only that practically such education is resisted by all and is very difficult to develop and to actualize there—it is so difficult a challenge also since my relation to Israel is far from one-dimensional. I do not hate Israel, and as you said, I am also connected and enabled by Israeliness, whatever that means. So when I offer counter-education, and I offer it both to Israelis and Palestinians, I articulate it not from the sources of hatred and scarcity. Too many of Israel's leftist critics do. And when relating to detailed and concrete historical controversies I do not agree Israel is the most anti-humanistic society, as it is so often represented by some of my best friends on the left; nor is it the agent and arch-manifestations of modern colonialism. As a Diasporic counter-educationalist I feel I should relate to the sources of the fear and hatred of Israel as the Jew among nations, especially among my friends in the left. This is the reason, as an example, for my resistance to the call to boycott Israeli universities, an activity which positioned me in confrontation with my friend Ilan Pappe. This is why no network is ready to recycle and distribute with much seriousness or interest my understanding of counter-education and the challenge I...

CW: A very courageous thing.

IGZ: Sometimes I am called the Jewish anti-Semite, don't ask... On the other hand, taking seriously the Diasporic position enables me to be a Diasporic person in Israel too. Being a Diasporic person in Israel, as a Jew and as an academic improviser, is quite a challenge in face of the crisis, suffering, ongoing trauma and quest for total "solutions". Therefore I call for the establishment of the new Yavne. You know the migration of Rabbi Yohanan Ben Zakay and his pupils from Jerusalem to Yavne, with only the Torah as a treasure worth saving from burning, defeated Jerusalem. It is of utmost importance that when the Romans captured the Temple, Rabbi Yochanan takes out, saves, one thing only, a book. Not weapons, not money, not a beautiful lady in the form of Helen who caused a clash of civilizations in another part of the globe: only a book. One book. He rescues the Torah and goes to Yavne, where he establishes a new beginning. In this new beginning Jews do not strive for political sovereignty but for life in the infinite horizons of the holy book, as a home. A geographical homeland and political sovereignty are not the actual homeland. Homeland is redefined as a self-positioning, as a becoming-toward-the-world-of-eternal-interpretation and moral action. This is because God doesn't tell us in an unproblematic manner what is the religious truth. In face of overcoming ethnocentrism and reification, interpretation too has a context, a concrete arena, and it is the absence of God and the presence of the law, the Halacha. So, I see the current reestablishment of Yavne in a globalized world and identifying with the victims and going against injustice, while understanding the shortcomings of every Critical Theory as a possible Diasporic position in Israel. This is one of my replies as to positioning yourself on different levels simultaneously, because we have ourselves as an "I" and as such we hospitalize also the "not-I" in ourselves; we have our beloved ones and co-poiesis while we know the victims are also enthusiastic candidates to become, or are already, actual victimizers; we have humanity and law, and we have the cosmos that we should reopen ourselves to, identify with, be responsible for, and respond to in manners that education for sustainability has not yet addressed....

CW: Now you see—I think what you have there though, and I appreciate that response, but I think what you just said now I totally agree with, because it is a highly new understanding of "home" versus "Diaspora", of the ways in which on the one hand you are very critical of any "home", but recognize that even the nomadic exilic Diasporic philosopher is engaged in a context. Now, when it comes to normalizing education versus second way Critical Pedagogy—the same kind of nuanced reading is required. The ways in which even a normalizing education, like the hegemony of the first stage of Critical Pedagogy, there are elements there that you can ascend in a positive way even if you bring critique to bear a basic assumption and presupposition. Now, if you in any way suggest a kind of an economy that becomes frozen, which does normalizing education and second way Critical Pedagogy, right. Then people begin to think—what god, are you really come here all on your own, are you reproducing? And replicating a certain pure marginality, opposition, transgression, quest for transcendence within a meaningless world—that is a danger! So that in the example you gave the Israeli thing, I said yes, that is new. I can go with this cause. That is Chekhovian. That is Beckett-like. Because you are in the mass. Whereas there are moments in the text where two elements become so oppositional that you lose that rich, concrete, existential entanglement. So that all of us have normalizing education right through us and at the same time here comes your courageous thing— loving an aesthetic way of life that is critical of the normalizing education inside of you, inside of me, inside of our students and so forth, and that is in part the point I...

IGZ: This is why I see, even in McLaren's work very important relevant elements for me. Even if I am critical of his understanding of Critical Pedagogy, not to mention his love affair with Hugo Chavez's postcolonialism that I understand as a manifestation of the new Anti-Semitism. Today you can see the streets of Caracas are full with slogans such as "Jews outside"; time and again the police burst into the Jewish school and Synagogue "in search of weapons" and kill demonstrating students on the campus, and so on and so forth. I ask my postcolonialist supporters of Chavez, Ahmadinejad, Nasrallah and Ward Churchill: you are for democracy, I know. So, how is it possible that these are your heroes and anti-Semitism-violence-and-silencing opposition is the flagship of your dearest friends?

CW: I think I ought to reply in terms of my own relations with Hugo Chavez; you let him know that you stand for, what I call a deep democracy. You let him know that you resound with his attempt to empower poor people economically and socially and you let him know that therefore you remain a nomadic bluesman, with your own distinctive voice of vision as you acknowledge that convergent, in terms of the oppositional American imperial court present, court manipulation and you let him know your opposition to his attempt to in any way to become an autocratic authoritarian. But you make that stance not just on the stage; I made that stance in Caracas, in my speech in front of thousands of people;

IGZ: It is very important.

CW: And with him. Absolutely. Because everywhere we go—in Israel, I am in an American empire, there in Venezuela where there is Oligarchic orientation of the economy, autocratic practicism when it comes to the political elite, or cross ideology.

IGZ: Yes. So, how do you approach from here toward dialogue, as an alternative to such autocratic manipulations? How do you understand the very ideal of dialogue? Maybe I should phrase it differently: How do you relate to the concept of dialogue, and how do you see the possibility to educate for dialogic attitude in a multicultural world, in a world where we understand that we have no universal, no meta-narrative to decide between conflicting narratives or language games, where the human subject is instrumentalized and manipulated and his/her voice is actually so many times the voice of something or someone that speaks for itself through her/him? How is it possible to educate for a dialogical way of life in the absence of a guiding God, or in face of successful deconstruction of all meta-narratives and the central values, symbols and criteria? What could be the building material of a possible dialogue that is not an alternative manipulation?

CW: It is a difficult question. First, let us just begin with this notion of dialogue, though. If you look at some of the great philosophers in the 20th century—Martin Buber, Gadamer, R.G. Collinwood, they are Socratic and dialogical, when you think of Bakhtin and the early criticism, but what they are really after—and this is where I think the jazzman metaphor cuts deeper—what they are really after is the polyphony of voices with improvisational style, but with body that carry history.

You see, the problem of dialogue is that taking it back to Socrates, the inimitable founding father, so much as the West, who we build on, but he has his limitations—he never cries. He never loves. Which means his body is subordinated. Whereas in jazz, dialogue is transfigured into voices that bounce up against one another, that are tied to their body and their histories and their cultures; but there is a mutual respect that mediates those voices. Well, you see, dialogue can become so tied to the cerebral, where bodies drop out. They are being on—body has been extended. So that as much as I like Dialogue, because I am a big democrat, as a jazzman I do not trust it, even my dear teacher, who just died, I remembered the other day, Richard Rorty—I used to tell him all the time: "Prof. Rorty, conversation and dialogue, especially for black people, whose bodies have been so debased that their voices are not what we are listening to at all. So he would say: "Let us just talk about polyphonic voices with bodies in spaces of equality and respect. So that we agree that we are never going to fully agree, but we can also agree that in disagreeing we do not dominate one another". And this is not how I am seeing historic and free communication—no, no, no, not at all—it is very different, you see. So that for me a starting point in talking, dialogue has to be transfigured with this jazz-like orientation.

IGZ: As a modernist I would say that dialogue is connected so much more to the concept of transcendence and jazz, as the logic of jazz demands, to eminence. The different preconditions for transcendence on the one hand, and immanence on the other, brings me to the tension between these two dimensions in your work. And someone critical of Enlightenment yet as someone who values so much Enlightenment's negative, I will tell you why I think it is so important to go there: because in your work one might find a different kind of dialogue, a Diasporic kind of dialogue, that has no truth, no defined, fixed and coherent truth awaiting somewhere for the Odyssey to come to its conclusion and grasp the truth as a worthy-way-for-self-annihilation. But your work is even more complex than that. On the one hand, you are in so many places against the transcendental dimension. On the other hand, in your understanding of the later thinking of Adorno and Horkheimer you do accept, and I do share your understanding of the importance of **the totally other**. And this is a very important point, because if there is no presence to **the totally other**, even if only in a manner we do not have any control of and we can never manipulate it, and we cannot predict if at all or when it will come, we cannot know what the true interpretation of it is, and so on and so forth. And sometimes what we see as **the totally other** is actually one of the manifestations of the *Same*. From a Shpinozist point of view this is since we are both part of the whole and a specific, eternally concrete particle that acknowledges its particularity. And yet, the category of **the totally other** enables a difference that makes a difference; enables, actually, Life. There is no Life without the presence (even in a negative manner) of **the totally other** and the preparation for it or the reaction to it or to its absence. Love is conditioned by **the totally other** and there are no fruits of love, no creativity, no children, no pupils, no artistic presentation without it.

CW: Or repetition without a difference.

IGZ: For having even a specific, particular, contextual 'Bereshit', you need 'Beria'. You need genesis for rebirth, because with no genesis or reappearance of genesis in the appearance of **the totally other** there is no Life, even if there is repetition, continuum and reaction. So we need that category of **the totally other** as a manifestation and precondition for transcendence. And here I come back to your work, Professor West. If we overemphasize the context, namely if we give prominence to immanence, we might lose homelessness, and this is too much of a loss. There is no room for the jazzman if he is overwhelmed and domesticated by the suggestions of the presence, and if he abandons his dialogue with the not-yet, with the unexpected, with the potential that is not yet awakened. There is no homeland and there are no transgressions without **the totally other**. If you give too much emphasis to the context, to our roots, to our countrymen, even to the present actual and truly important needs, you might end up in surrender, in granting the upper hand to contingency and violence, to meaninglessness—not to Love of Life. In order to genuinely challenge the facts of this world, really criticize them, actually clash with them, or in order to religiously address them as Diasporic humans, we ought to address **the totally other**; we must seriously tackle the possibility of transcendence without forgetting the facts of our world life and the presence of the context.

CW: These are very good questions. Two quick things though. One regards the distinction between a live immanence and a dead immanence. A live immanence is always predicated on some notion of transcendence. A dead immanence is just that recycling that you talked about. Now, I am always up for the former. The former has to do with acknowledging, no matter how much you talk about context. It never exhales the self, or the subject or the agent. There is always already some striving, that is what Unger would call "context transgressing" and "context transcending"—live immanence. Dead immanence, any such a philosophy, has nothing to do with it. Now, why is that so? Now, for me, again, as a jazzman, you begin with courage. Courage in the most enabling virtue for any human life, you have to start with the ways in which you fortify your energy in order to transact with environment, to live and love.

IGZ: Cornel, isn't it so that there are different kinds of courage? Because so many Nazi soldiers, Stalinist NKVD members or Khmer Rouge soldiers, as well as the American soldiers fighting the Nazi army were very courageous. The Muslim suicide bombers today are also very courageous. And surely you will agree that the courage for self-overcoming or self-awakening is essentially different from the one soldiers of various armies manifested in battle.

CW: But courage is not an ideologically promiscuous virtue. That is why it is an enabling one; it depends on what kind of moral content, political consequence, you apply that courage to. But at this point we are just talking about human life! That to live is to exercise courage. To have no courage is dead immanence. Now then: but that is why I call it enabling virtue—you need more than that. I mean for me it is compassion, love, right? And to love—the life of the mind—truth: Socratic. To love—conquers human beings: Judaic. Leviticus, 19: 18— "Love thy neighbor".

IGZ: So what would be the relations or the difference between vital immanence and transcendence?

CW: That you would have to acknowledge that there has to be some inseparability between a vital, live immanence and a transcendence that is never attained, never reached, never fully conformed to. Now, I want to comment about your remark about jazz though, because you see—jazz is the art form of vital immanence. That has a lot of love supreme, that is not in any way a dead immanence, at all. But it recognizes that you know—we got clay feet, that we are all human beings in space and time, or what Kafka calls The Death Sentence in space and time. That is what a bluesman is aware of, right? You carry around death with you every day. On the other hand, you are continually trying to transcend, knowing you are never going to get it right. That why in being in an improvisational art you know there is no such thing as de-defining of interpretation of this musical composition and so forth. So I think here, we are agreeing actually. This is one of my problems with Deleuze, that there are times that he talks about immanence as so anti-transcendent that it does not have the vital kind. I had a wonderful debate with a dear friend and brother— Badiou. We had a fascinating dialogue.

IGZ: About this?

CW: About this very issue. I brought him to Princeton and then we were having another one at the New-School, you know it would be nice to have you there. You know Simon Critchley's work?

IGZ: Yes.

CW: Because he has got a new book now and we were having—we were actually having a huge discussion for Simon and myself and—here… infinitely demanding, that the book that we are going to be talking about, but we are also reading these two as well. But I mention that because these same issues have been hammered out with these other two, and of course I have got my own distinctive twist on this thing, but I do think that there is a sense in which jazz as an art form, especially the great dead musicians, would be in full agreement with your conception of the Nomadic and Diasporic regarding vital or live immanence, or transcendence, the danger of altering one or the other to become severed, absolutely.

IGZ: You speak about the importance of one's enrollment in the struggle against elitism and injustice and the importance of education for courage. But what or who is the sovereign of such decisions even in pragmatic settings? I remind us of Foucault, who wrote so much about resistance as the manifestation of liberty. But when I ask his disciples today, 'So who is the sovereign of this decision of the "I"? Surely it is not the subject as such, because then you go into fundamentalism and essentialism. So is it an exterior master or the wrong central committee of the party?'—it turns out that the rules of the system are the sovereign since they constitute, determine and limit the resisting subject. So in this sense, how can we ensure, or what can we say about, a non-naïve, non-sentimental courage—not, again, in the language of authenticity? It turns out that we need another, a new critical language to talk about courage.

CW: Well, I mean I think that there is a way of using Shakespearian language of being "true to thyself", said by Polonius to his son, in Hamlet, without falling into the pitfall of authenticity. Because to be true to yourself is to engage in what Habermas would call "a critical self inventory", in which by examining yourself, you see history, society, culture deposited throughout. And therefore we are not talking about a pure subject, we are not talking about a pure identity, political orientation; we are talking about the stuff which you must come to terms with, critically wrestle with, and then decide to act in a fallible self-critical manner; that is what it means to be in the middle. That is what it means to be in Beckett's mass. Therefore, you ought to be constantly changing and maturing your hope, even though changing and maturation are not the same. So that you are going to be acknowledging the ways in which you fell on your face, but also acknowledging some of the insights you might have learnt, but there is no—I do not think there is any authenticity, or any authentic starting point here at all and when you see such gestures and vote, you ought to be highly suspicious, because they tend to be associated with autocratic authoritarian politics.

IGZ: When you insist on this self critique…

CW: Yes, self critical, yes.

IGZ: And it is so important for me, because so many of our critical friends do not wrestle with self-critique. Surely they are not ironic. So many times they are very far from self-critique, self-evaluation and a critical point of view. And here I have to say, Cornell, that I really appreciate your distance from the language of authenticity. At the same time, however, I would like to add something about one dimension of the language of authenticity. This dimension is vivid also in some other philosophical traditions and is of vital importance for Diasporic philosophy as I understand it. In other philosophical traditions, however, it is transformed, manipulated, deconstructed or silenced. I refer here to *religiositaet* as against *religion*. I use here *religiositaet* (*datiyut*—in Hebrew) in the sense that potentials of the human are connected to the understanding that we cannot completely overcome the conditions, facts, rules of the enabling language-game that we are prisoners in, the power-relations of "our" horizons. We never have a pure choice. We do have, however, hope, in the sense that we are hopeless, not only to the referent of hope— which of itself is normally exiled (sometimes even replaced and confused with optimism); the hope bursts in from the outside—the transcendent dimension. One example is taken from Plato. In the Platonic cave, when the people are there shackled in chains, chained to their impotence and false consciousness, suddenly, one of them awakes in the sense that he struggles his way out. Note that Plato's text says in Politea 7: 515: "suddenly". "Suddenly, one of them was freed of his chains". It was not so that this prisoner decides that it is wrong to be enslaved—mentally, intellect-ually, or physically, raised and forges his way "to the light". Why? I think I can tell you why. Because he did not choose freedom. Freedom chose him. So there is a sense of arbitrariness that enables the very possibility of struggle for freedom. At the same time, he could, like so many others before and after him, disregard this invitation or misinterpret it in the service of self-forgetfulness, and he did decide, he did enable self-awakening. It is not a simple either-or. Neither is it a simple "this— and that too". It is the combination of the two. This understanding is of special importance for me as a Diasporic thinker, in order to avoid the language of authen-ticity, that promises us that the self can free herself, that we are heirs to God, the actual God, the Nietzschean alternative to God. The understanding that the human situation is that each of us has a chance to emancipate, or to transcend, but that we cannot do it totally alone is here of vital importance. How do you see this dimension?

CW: You see, I have a big difference with you here though. I mean the difference, one fundamental difference, between Chekhov and Plato is that Plato is writing from the point of someone who is outside of the cave. He already conceives of himself as a lover of wisdom, the philosopher who has broken the chains, he is no longer a poet; he burns his poems, he followed Socrates. He has a clarity, so writing the text, he is not writing from the vanish point of those in the cave. Now, I am with Chekhov—I am in the cave, which is to say that I do not accept the binary position of the clarity outside and the darkness of the cave. We are in the mass, we are in the middle. But if we are stuck in the middle then there is going to be an element of choosiness, there is going to be an element of self-overcoming and a courageous attempt to break from various narrow assumptions, so that human effort and agency have to make a difference.

IGZ: But isn't it so that there are not two possibilities solely: "outside", and "inside"? There is a third possibility of acknowledging that there are infinite Platonic caves and that we are persuaded and obliged to replace one with another and so on and so forth, a recycling that might include waving the flags of emancipatory education or Critical Theory. The Diasporic person as I understand him is the one that is not freed from the Platonic Cave; neither is he the emancipated hero of rationalist critical thinking or the authentic act of liberation. He is not there in their naïve manifestations— "We are free!" "We are struggling for or on behalf of the right ideology, so we are permitted to do this or that!" He knows that there is no pure path out of any Platonic cave, there is no neutral or clean space to arrive to. He cannot simply go back into the naivety or the homeland he left behind. And yet, he struggles for transcendence and at best he is everywhere, as a nomad, and nowhere. He is in the middle as you say—and this is a third space, the nowhere place that is everywhere. Making up your mind, deciding, here, is very different from the possibilities of coming into terms with yourself and making a decision in the two extremes you referred too. Courage is of a very different kind in the third possibility, compared to the first two. Because if truth or God are not exiled and you are with the truth, or you believe you have the truth in your possession then, courage is something of one kind. It is more of the kind of courage manifested by brave soldiers in battle (even if here too it has its complications too). On the other hand, if you believe that you do not see the violence of Normalizing Education, because it is so effective that it enables the practice of camouflage that ensures its invisibility, then courage in the form of patriotism becomes a challenge to overcome. Diasporic courage is the courage of self-awakening, of addressing in a mature manner the temptation to nihilism and self-annihilation as well as the other kind of self-forgetfulness, that of enrollment in a ready made dogma, fashion, "inclusive" collectivism and easy-going emancipatory/critical alternatives that forget Love. We agree that we are able, in principle, to address these manipulations, to struggle for the possibilities for a mature addressing of them—while acknowledging that there is no escape or liberation that might offer in history *the totally other* as a continuous, factual reality. No pure space awaits us, and no courage, wisdom or critical education is capable of ensuring our entering the reworked Garden of Eden. Of special importance I see here is the courage to become an improvisational, and at the same time a moral, responsible, happy, solidarian person. I think that in your work, Cornell, the seeds of such a new language for critical education are already planted. And yet, I think you should give less emphasis to the context. Of course, we are always enabled, limited, players in a specific historical moment and in specific material conditions. I say here: Acknowledge and give honor to your body, but also to your needs and limitations, even to the suggestions and manipulations that urge you to surrender to self-forgetfulness. They are also part of the richness of the cosmos. And yet, I say: Do not give the context the last word!

CW: But I'm not, see—I never gave the context the last word that my conception of the tragic-comic that sits at the center of the blues sensitivity means. I mean can you imagine the bluesman ever giving context the last word? If you gave the context the last word there would be no voice, there would be no song, there would be no melody. In the end its like Capriccio, Strauss's Capriccio—his last big opera 1941. It is the human voice. It is like the Beethoven's ninth symphony—it is the human voice that has the last word in my project. Now, what do I mean by that? What I mean by that is that tragic-comic puts the premium on the radical incongruity, which is a little different than the ironic. You see, the ironic can actually perceive without compassion, whereas the comic, in its deeper sense, is always tied to compassion. That is Beckett. That is Chekhov. That is the blues, you see. There is no Chekhov without compassion. He is not ironic. No. He is deeper than that—he is comic. He is tragic-comic—the same is true about ... Gadoe, I mean this is not detached from feeling, emotion, passion, poesies, ecstasy and so forth; you see what I mean? So, I would want to argue that in fact my stress on the context is done precisely in order not to end up enervating the voice, the body, the resistance, the transgression, so they go hand in hand. Now, why is that important? I mean it is very important precisely because if you end up talking about the tragic-comic it means in the end that you cannot distinguish hope. All optimism goes, but hope and hope against hope is still out there.

IGZ: Yes. That is very important, this distinction between optimism and hope.

CW: Fundamental.

IGZ: So, in the absence of **the totally other** in a globalizing world, or in its a...

CW: I'm thinking, my brother, it might be on that hope–optimism thing, only because I have noticed three...

IGZ: So, in the world of globalization, and standardization, where on the one hand it seems as if there is no serious politically articulated opposition, humanist or spiritual, that is not part of the same system that it challenges, or is supposed to challenge, at times when on the one hand there is the fundamentalism as the totalistic alternative and on the other the post-colonialist, which would be sometimes problematic, in this context, love is so important in your work. Following actually Plato, in the symposium you acknowledge the multiphase and many natures of love in the present historical moment. Its not only that there is earthly versus heavenly love, but there is also patriotism, there is also love of lust, there is also love of self-hatred and there is also love in the Christian messianic tradition. Acknowledging the different preconditions and dynamics for distinction between the various kinds of love within this framework, how is it possible to sustain love and educate for edifying the kind of love that is concrete yet not of the kind of this world that your understanding of love should overcome or challenge?

CW: First, let me start with my own Christian baggage, that for me the breakthrough of Jerusalem, which is to say the break and the Judaic breakthrough, was one of the great moral moments in the history of the human race. Because— and I understand Christianity as a rich footnote to prophetic Judaism, so you really are talking about what it means to conceive of the prophetic, and here the great Rabbi Abraham Joshua Heschel, for me a talented figure in this regard, that what you really have is love for the concrete person. You see, Plato talks of the ladder of love in his Symposium; it is a love that ascends away from concreticity to the abstract, whereas the prophetic conception that comes out of Judaism has a transcendence of the *totally other* that breaks into time and space, but it lures us as it connects us to the concrete other and that is the quality of a different conception of love. So that Leviticus 19: 18, "Love thy neighbor as thyself" that the first generation of a Palestinian Jew named Jesus talks about and invokes—and of course that Jesus means much to me as a Christian. But he himself, he is not just Jewish, but he is part of this rich prophetic Judaic tradition that is talking about love in a very different way than Plato and Aristotle and the others. So that the prophetic, which is a Jewish creation, it is a Jewish invention, and therefore is to be understood as this grand heritage of humankind, rooted in the legacy of Jerusalem. Christianity will come, Islam will come and so much of the secular world would be a response to it, the Judaism and the Christianity and so forth. There is no Nietzsche without Christianity and Lutherism and so forth. So, why is it so important? It is important because it means, again, for a bluesman like myself, that the way of love is a kind of way of the cross, not a sadomasochistic way, but a way in which you never win in space and time, but you are willing to give your all in order to keep alive this legacy and because of your love to the concrete other, responding to **the totally other**. So, they are inseparable as horizontal in terms of the concrete Other, but it is transcendent with the immanent connection. **The totally other** telling you—you must embrace and you know Levinas' infinite responsibility whose Slavophilic love of Christ and the Christian tradition is all different versions of that Judaic revolution in the moral history of human kind. Now, that is my starting point. Now, there are secular versions of it—like the negative dialectic of Adorno, you see, and of course the later Horkheimer as you pointed out—is just more explicit about the Judaic roots of it, in his negative theology, but he has gone through some earlier moves that he begins to reject. I do not think you have to go to Schopenhauer, that you needed that...

IGZ: But isn't it so that on the one hand we are unavoidably positioned in a specific historical moment, in a specific body, overwhelmed by specific drives or dreams under certain and concrete material conditions, and at the same time we are eternal travelers; we are in face of the absence of God and the truth, we address the absence of the lost language of the builders of the Tower of Babel, which was destroyed by God's fear of a human race that was truly united in the quest for Love, which is not Godly or dogmatic?

CW: Or the absent god, the god that withdraws, who exiles himself.

IGZ: Globalization that sells love and passions and pseudo-erotic moments in speedy-dynamited life makes transcendent love impossible. As if there is so much of that in the market already, because in the market there are infinite differences that do not create/offer a difference. So how do you establish the exclusiveness and the uniqueness of the kind of love in such a market that levels down every alternative and reifies all differences and plurality?

CW: Now I think you are right. When Camus used to say that the future is the last transcendent, in a world without God, and one could say that the selling of love is the last structure of meaning. In a world without **the totally other**, impinging upon with creature—human creatures—in time and space. This is to say that it is precisely the radical insecurity of the market driven society that seduces people into love as a carrot, as a structure of meaning, given a pervasive meaninglessness, or the nihilistic conditions that are generated by this market bonbon—buying, selling, mending, promoting, advertising and so on. It is understandable. It is inexcusable—but it is understandable, you see. So, then the question becomes, Well then how do we stand the yearning for love? Now, you talk in the terms of the love of life.

In some ways I am more Jewish and Judaic than you. Because you got influenced by love in the 19th century, who talks about life, Love of Life. But that still had some Athens and Greek and Platonic elements to it. Whereas for me the Judaic one is not so much the love of life, but it is the love of the human beings who are living and dead. So it is a more concrete embodiment of love and that is part of the chance, you see.

IGZ: For me the love of life is important because the love of human beings is only part of love of other dimensions of life, like animals and even the mysterium and human beings are such an important part of *Sein*—of Being, human beings and Being. Being is so much richer than what is revealed and concealed in the human, and yet, it is wrong to overemphasize this separation from the very beginning.

CW: I think that is true.

IGZ: But, Cornell, you did not relate to the challenge in such an age of establishing the uniqueness and preserving the exclusiveness of the kind of love that is so important to you as against its alternatives. Could you, please, say more about competitive loves and struggling alternatives to Love in our era, alternatives that are so attractive to many of our children? I would go even further than that. Many of the progressive critical thinkers draw an abyss between the positive Utopia and the evil kingdom of capitalism, without distinguishing with enough sensitivity the promise and potentials that are opened by the same dehumanization process of the post-Fordist empire. The same historical moment enables in the cyberspace different kinds of Eros and different forms of creativity and maybe even new possibilities for love. To establish too sharp a differentiation between the two is so difficult if you are not dogmatic. But then how do you differentiate between the love on the internet, or in cyberspace more generally, which is supposed to be part of the kingdom of evil, and the Christian love that you talk about, the one that is part of the messianic tradition? Is it still possible to differentiate in a meaningful, or in a promising, manner between the two?

CW: Those are good questions. I mean, there is a certain irony here because first in relation to Love of Life and love of the concrete human beings, you are absolutely right that life is much broader and deeper than just human beings. But then, again, I am more Jewish and Judaic than you are. You have got Heidegger and others in the backdrop. When you actually get this Dasein and this embrace of all in which human beings are beings, but you have got other things going on. I am much more Judaic. Which is more homocentric, or humanist, in that way. And I think that I would have to learn more from you there. On the other hand when it comes to newness and novelty and new possibilities, you are more American than I am. Because America is the land of newness and novelty and innovation and invention. Whereas for me, I am a little suspicious of the talk about new loves, or new human beings. Following Chekhov and Beckett and the blues I tend to think there is not a whole lot of new under the sun, to invoke Ecclesiastes, and what I mean by that is that it does not mean, again, that we do not look for new possibilities and novel breakthroughs and so forth. But the language of newness and novelty, which America has colonized, is a very dangerous language, as we know that we ought to be in search of some form of newness, some forms of novelty. So when I hear new love—I mean I love your conception of "Pleasure Machine", I mean my God, its a wonderful formulation, but you know pleasure has been around long time.

IGZ: But this is exactly the reason why we should insist on it! Remembering that it is so easy to fall and to be swallowed by the jargon of the Bill Gates supporters and their associates. But, at the same time, still as people—and here we share I think a common ground, as people who share the importance of the messianic tradition and the Diasporic tradition. How do you search, or struggle, for the continuation of this tradition in the cyberspace, only to mention one arena as an example? In one of my books I study the hacker as a Diasporic human who continues this tradition. Of course there are many kinds of hacker communities and so on, but some do represent the kind of refusal and the kind of search for transcendence that is part of this Diasporic tradition where Love, happiness, and creativity are celebrated with religiously serious devotion as art, as an artistic, religious, way of life. Within this framework the religious impulse, not the institutional religion, is so much in the center, not as a gate for fanaticism and dogmatism, but, on the contrary, as a blooming of love of Life. Here, I think, critical thinkers should do much more.

CW: Oh, no I agree. What I affirm in your work, I mean even the essay on driving, and understanding the fluent traffic and so forth, that to me was just fascinating, because that is what thinking against the grain and thinking as an adventurer and taking a risk is all about. I agree. Its just that for me its going to be a matter of being very careful of trying to tease out the deeper forms of newness and novelty than the more superficial forms that the market is continually colonizing and recasting their sale and promoting. I know that you are very aware of that, because I would never want to engage in any analysis of an institution in a homogeneous way.

IGZ: But educationally... I saw you this afternoon with the kids here at the nearby school, with these young men and women, very young. They need guidance. They need the presence of the call. At the same time there are so many "guiding voices" struggling for relevance in imposing or reworking the youths' lives. How do you establish the exclusiveness of what you are saying? Of love, in face of creative violence and the actual de-humanizing powers of this culture industry?

CW: I had a conversation... maybe you were so kind to be a part of that. But I had that convention where I attempt to show that the Socratic energy and prophetic witness and tragic-comic blues like sensibility that I tried to represent was already in some ways immanent in their culture, so I joined them as a human who is involved in Socratic questions, all the songs, the common songs—who really loves you? And I was deeply involved, wasn't I? Not just your mom, but in your larger culture—what is your relation to them? Why is it that the most popular ones that they all acknowledge tend to be more superficial, market driven and so on? So that they began to see after I am gone that I am not just some isolated individual, or icon, who comes in from on high with all of these goodies. You see I am a big democrat. I reject that model. I come in, in the mass, in the middle along with them, but older, who thought longer and had more experiences, had more failures, maybe more breakthroughs, you see, and say: "Let us think together critically, democratically, religiously, but also hopefully". You want to leave them with another hope in that sense and I would say the same thing of the analysis of the cyberspace. If I knew as much as you do about cyberspace I would say—there's got to be some immanent possibilities there that are new and novel that we are to access, absolutely. Now, whether that is tied to new human beings, or new Love that is where I would say—well I am not sure about that, Ilan, I need to be maybe more open. I do not like "new human beings" talk at all, even though you and I talk regeneration and rebirth that are being part and possible in being humans. I talk with them about learning how to die in order to live, which is Montaigne. Which is Socrates and others. But the sense of new others, new love, that I am suspicious of... Because in the end, you know, the human condition in the beginning and when it comes to an end, as new and novel our circumstances and conditions may be, when it comes to love, when it comes to death bound creatures aware of it, I am probably more with Kafka than I am with you. Now, I could be wrong so I want to be fallibilistic about this. Okay, go right ahead.

IGZ: Let' address other new possibilities and vocabularies maybe you favor more. What are the benefits and the prospects of post-colonial education? And what are the dangers or the shortcomings of post-colonialist education? As I see it, some of it actually promotes reverse racism, ethnocentrism, dogmatism and new anti-Semitism. How do you articulate a kind of post-colonial education that will avoid these temptations towards new kinds of ethnocentrism, dogmatism and reversed racism?

CW: I mean, one, is that I never accepted the term post-colonial. Now my dear friend, comrade Spivak, 15–20 years ago we had a long discussion, I was telling her I do not accept the term. It is a backward-looking term and I tend to look forward. And secondly, I see so much of the persistence of the colonialism in various forms, but it is true to post-modern. I do not like this term because I think so much of the post-modern has a late-modern element shot through it, you see. So I do not really like the term post-colonial at all. Now, given the fact that we have a category where critiques write and so on, I don't think Said ever accepted the term either, because he is an old style humanist, but I say that because there is no doubt that narrow parochial versions of universalism went hand in hand with dominant versions of Enlightenment in Europe and Romanticism in Europe and so on. They needed to be demystified; they needed to be deconstructed, demythologized. The danger of course is that you simply re-inscribe new parochialism in the name of the critique of the proto versions of universalism, you see, and for me, because I think we are all in a continual quest for a certain kind of universalism that we will never attain, it behooves us to be both actually humble, but also to be much more historically contextual in the stories that we take. If you are humble it means that any self-righteous claims, any arrogant claims that you finally got it right, or somehow your universalism is better than someone else's by a rhetorical fiat—I just don't take seriously, you see. So I find a lot of the work under the rubric of postcolonialism. I'm just content to hold it at arm's length. Even though there are deep insights there, in terms of the demystifying side, the constructive side I just do not see too much energy. So there I think I do accept much of your critique of the post-colonial side. At the same time I never want to downplay the gravities of the white supremacies, the male supremacies, the imperial arrogance, the gentile-centered narrative that were told against marginal others: people of color, gays, lesbians, Jews, Arabs, whatever it is. So the question is: how do you walk this tightrope, because you do not want to fall into any of the parochial traps whatsoever, and unfortunately there is not a lot of space on that tightrope right now. Because things are so polarized in academy, and things are so Balkanized, the end of culture that you end up very nomadic and so on. These are the conditions under which us intellectuals work, who are committed to the kind of Diasporic vision. I do not think there is any escape from it.

IGZ: How do we proceed from here to your attitude towards the new anti-Semitism? More than once it is a label twisted by anti-critical or non-critical Israelis who search for escape in this formula for avoiding self-critique. At the same time there are, unfortunately, other reasons to use this term, reasons that make it much more relevant and more important for all of us today. The new anti-Semitism positions the State of Israel as **The Jew** among nations, similar to, yet essentially different from, traditional anti-Semitism that placed the Jew as the ultimate Other of Christian Western civilization. Some of the political articulations of this post-colonialist agenda present Israel as the Nazi state of our day, or as today's Apartheid-oriented South Africa, and actually target not Israel and its policies. It targets not the Other of Western culture but rather its essence and its most extreme and actual colonialist manifestation— "Israel". The category "Israel" manifests here at the first level the essence of colonialism, and sometimes it is replaced with "the American Spirit" or "whiteness". At the deeper level it treats "Israel" as the most extreme actualization of "Monotheism", "homogeneity" and "phallocentrism" that serve as the impetus and birthland of colonialism in all its varied forms and arenas. "Israel" therefore, should be overcome, exterminated: "we" should not only criticize or distance ourselves from it, nor is it enough to exterminate "Israel". Post-colonialist education directs us to purify ourselves of the "Israeliness" or "colonialist" dimensions of our identity; and what could be a better start than to begin this crusade by treating the facts about "Israel" according to our agenda of moral purification and emotional/political liberation from its colonialist manifestations within ourselves? This brings many responsible post-colonialists not only to side with anti-humanists, to dishonestly present the reality or offer vicious interpretations; it offers the wrong path for Westerners and third world intellectuals and educators in treating the history of their relations and the present moral obligations of each of us. What is your opinion?

CW: I read your last chapter in your book and it was a very powerful and challenging piece. Because you try to be fair to the persons who are trying to keep track of justice for the Palestinians' battle, even as you are aware, and ought to be, of the means for security of the Israelis, who include both Jewish and Israeli, Jewish and Arab citizens. At the same time the double standards are too often applied when it comes to the practice of Israel, recently the practice of other countries. It needs to be acknowledged and addressed and also the acknowledgement of the danger of engaging in characterizing critics as anti-Semites, as an excuse of not coming to terms with injustice in Israeli society, Jewish community and so on. All these are elements that need to be very delicately, but also firmly encountered.

That is what I liked about your essay. It is an unusual thing to find, because it requires a level of a kind of honesty, but is also painful, very painful, because sometimes we find it in our own souls. And you see my view is this—I think that anti-Jewish hatred, anti-Semitism itself, is somewhat of modern construct, because you've got anti-Judaic hatred coming out of Christianity, you've got anti-Jewish hatred that compounds that and those beyond it, what we call anti-Semitism linked to the pogroms and on to the Holocaust, or the Shoah. That it is one of the deepest and most visceral forms of bigotry. Certainly in Western civilizations and spills over beyond it. So it is one of the reasons why the point I am making about a Jewish brother who's sitting in America thinking—this is the promised land, the way Weimar Germany was, the way Alexander's Egypt was, it is just not true. Wherever there is Christianity you are going to find diverse anti-Semitic realities and potentialities, that is, in the West. Now whereas Islam—this is even more complicated and it is actually becoming more vicious in the Islamic world than before, it was more vicious in the Christian world than in the Islamic world. Things have changed. So the question becomes, how do we keep track of all those elements that are at work in your essay and still remain nomadic, still remain prophetic, self-critical? And I think that there is no formula, there is not even a general principle. It is going to be a matter of what Aristotle called practical wisdom. What kind of judgments are we making in a context that ensures that we will keep in track of anti-Jewish hatred, subtle or not so subtle? And of course that calls for hatred across the globe—anti-Arab hatred, anti-black and so forth. But on that issue of new anti-Semitism, it is a very complicated matter. Because you see here in the States, as you know, it is the conservative Jewish establishment that makes it difficult for talented Jewish intellectuals—Tony Jad, Anthony Grahft and we can go on and on, Michael Lareno, Sharlene Wallen, my own Thesis advisor and we've got a whole list, we can go on and on. These are just talented Jewish intellectuals, who are progressive, who are prophetic, some secular, some religious, self-haters and haters of other Jews. You have seen the same things yourself and you have got your own examples. Now we say, wait a minute—how can the conservative Jewish establishment so effectively cut these folks off, when that same conservative Jewish establishment played such a crucial role in the civil rights movement in the sixties and such a crucial role in highlighting forms of prejudice, but not all. It is a very very difficult… and I would include not just a *Commentary* magazine in this country, like you got *The New Republic*, they got electo-philism on all the democratic positions when it comes to domestic issues. But when it comes to this issue it is like Socratic reflection—just collapses. So you see, for me the question is of the next generation; to get them to see, you know what? That I am as committed to keeping track of anti-Semitism new and old, as I am of any other form of bigotry. But at the same time I am as committed to the quest for truth and justice and compassion as I always was before. It is tough, tough. But I think things are shifting, and in some ways the American Jewish intelligentsia in all of its variety are influenced by the discussion of yourself and others back in Israel, because you all are further ahead than we are on this issue new anti-Semitism, old anti-Semitism and so on, you see. I mean, a lot of it has to do with the kind of guilt that so many Jewish Americans have toward Israel, that all the hell that Israelis are catching from suicide bombers and so on. You can appeal to that as a way of supporting the state uncritically, narrowing the dialogue in the States. Because the Jewish suffering and Israeli suffering is real. But Israel knows the occupation is real, and it is ugly too. How do you keep both ideas in your head at the same time? It is a challenge for my Jewish brothers here in the States.

IGZ: Now let's go into something very similar. Critical Pedagogy, in order to be effective politically, more than once avoids going into self-critique and becomes dogmatic and canonizes an untouchable set of formulas and heroes, without naming them here in a list; we've got ... So how should Diasporic philosophy, in your mind, help reformulate Critical Pedagogy and enable a newer or reworked critical language in education?

CW: I think the first thing we have to do is take what you call the second stage, or what I call the second wave, of Critical Theory and Critical Pedagogy, and for me though that has to do with certainly late Adorno, Benjamin, Horkheimer, but it also means—and there is a wonderful sentence in your text, when you talk about those other Diasporic voices, which are non-Western, as well as those on the margins of the West, so that when you actually look at the kind of dialogue you have with feminist pedagogy and the way some of them move off to the private experience and identity claims and so forth, in ways others engage your issues, but also keep track of the misogyny and patriarchy. I would say the same thing about the white supereminence or realities and intellectual traditions that wrestle with that idea. That there has to be a polyphonic exchange of voices or dialogue between these pillars, but not to reach some kind of center and not to translate it in the praxis overnight and push up buttoning and you have got penance for all the suffering— *no, no, no!* But there has to be a process by which this polyphonic set of voices can come together and see where there is convergence and to see where there is divergence, but we are in the same progressive space.

IGZ: Yes.

CW: Where James is beginning to do that. I mean that you have got to help open up a space in terms of getting the second wave. But then, beyond that, I think that we have to engage publics, we cannot remain just in the academic public. The academic public is very important, but it has got to go to the popular publics; in a variety of places. From, you know, popular internet to popular music to popular arts and so forth and so on. See, once you democratize, you have got Socrates, who takes philosophy from heaven to earth and then Montaigne actually takes it to everyday life, in a more concrete existentialist, you know the self being and creation—Emerson and other great footnotes to Montaigne in that regard.

Whereas in William James you take it to the streets and he says that pragmatism is a philosophy that goes to the streets. And what I try to do, or Richard Rorty tries to do in democratizing philosophy and intellectual life, is you take it to the folk. You take it to the mud and the stink and the stench. Now, Beckett was already there. He is already there in the mass. But Beckett, as we know, he resists. When it comes to the traditional chord I would start it with Wordsworth and poetry; he has very little tolerance for philosophy. He reads it but he has not got the tolerance for it. I think you need to linger on it a bit more. You see what I mean? And doing that, the kind of discussion in the second wave, in the second stage of Critical Pedagogy, may generate some things that are unbeknownst to us.

IGZ: And you are doing so glowing, working in such a worthy manner towards this goal. I could see it clearly this afternoon, in your meeting at school with these young people that came from very diverse backgrounds and areas in America, and were so fascinated by your call—attracted, overwhelmed, actually. Attracted to what? What was it that invited them in such a rich presence? I think they were there in the infinity of that moment. They were there in such a rich manner, indeed, responding to an invitation to transcendence. They were there for love. They were there for addressing self-forgetfulness, namely for self-responsibility that you offered them. But at the same time I would like to ask you something little different yet connected to this fascinating educational meeting with the children, and we will conclude our conversation with that. At the same time that you were so meaningful for these girls and boys, more publicly, because you succeeded so much in offering respons-ibility and love and critique to much wider audience, you have also become an icon, a label, one of the products of the cultural industry. How do you, for your part, respond to this challenge of becoming an icon on the one hand and still insisting on seriousness and on the Diasporic position on the other? Is it so that the Diasporic human must become silenced, marginalized or undeciphered? Is it so that if he becomes very relevant and even acceptable, it must be only at the expense of his Diasporic stance and his integrity?

CW: It is a tough question, because it is a tension. And you have to live in the tension and it is either destructive of creativity and it is a stage-by-stage, moment-by-moment process. I mean in one sense, of course, my ending aim is to use what ever status, or form of intellectual political weapon, I have, to engage in a Socratic reflection bearing love and justice and preserving hope; or at least keeping some hope available to people. On the other hand, you easily get caught within the celebrity machine that reproduces a hierarchy and the seductions and the spectatorship or the spectacle. And you continually have to try and shatter that, even as you are always already put in it. Because you cannot just jump outside and say I am no longer a celebrity.

IGZ: And the very challenge of how can a critical Diasporic thinker be success-ful....?

CW: That's right.

IGZ: And I think as I saw you this afternoon, you do succeed, although it is most probably a very demanding position.

CW: Because on the one hand it gives you a platform, or stage, or certain kind of potential, but if it is for the wrong reasons and generates the wrong conse-quences, your critical voice is not heard. Now, in the end I think Rosenzweig is right and I want to end on him. Because Rosenzweig, as you know, he is not just one of the greatest philosophers of Dialogue, along with Buber and Gadamer.

IGZ: One of our most distinguished colleagues in the History of Diasporic philosophy.

CW: I think Rosenzweig is the greatest Jewish philosopher. I think Spinoza is a philosopher who happens to be Jewish; but for Rosenzweig it is witness, you see. And witness for him is not just praxis in the narrow secular Marxist sense. It is prayer as a species of both gift and yearning, but also of martyrdom. The text begins with death. Epistemology, neo-context—what are you going to do with death? And then he has read some Kierkegaard, but he has come to his own conclusion. And martyrdom is nothing but an intensified form of witness. And in the end the only way I ultimately shatter the celebrity status is to bear witness at the deepest level, which in the end means dying for what you believe in. And that witness is that which has fertilized the very soil, legacy, tradition and heritage that is Rosenzweig's bequest, not just for the Jews but to all of us, because—in terms of being part of the same effort to engage in what you call Diasporic thinking. But I do not think that my celebrity status could ever be used, applauded, mobilized in such a way that it is called into question and it points to something bigger than itself, in that quest for transcendence, transgression, responsibility, love, ecstasy and justice.

IGZ: Professor West, thank you very much for this unusual day.

9. CRITICAL THEORY AND DIASPORIC PHILOSOPHY IN HISTORICAL PERSPECTIVE

Ilan Gur-Ze'ev: Professor Jay, let me begin by thanking you for the opportunity to have this conversation. You are world wide known as one of the most important scholars of Critical Theory and you have written so much historically, sociologically and philosophically on the thinkers of Critical Theory of the Frankfurt School, on post structuralist and on the critical implications more or less from an Habermasian point of view, even if not without serious reservations and critiques of the Habermasian project. From within this very rich framework, what is according to your understanding, the reason that normally in the US scholars relate to Critical Theory of the Frankfurt School, fundamentally, basically, as if only the first, the positive-Utopian stage of its development exists and very rarely to the second, to the more mature part of the work of Adorno and Horkheimer and so unfortunately disregard the negativistic dimension of Benjamin and his friends in the Frankfurt School? Do you accept such a line of division between first phase and second phase, or, in other words optimist-positive stance in the first and pessimist-negative-Utopia in their second stance of development?

    Martin Jay: There are many ways to pluralize Critical Theory as one of the great virtues of the tradition has been its capacity to reinvent itself, while absorbing and learning from other traditions. Rather than a body of sacred texts that demand to be revered and reinterpreted, Critical Theory is a tradition that knows itself to be finite and imperfect; perpetually open to new ideas and challenges. As a result any periodization has to be temporary and provisional. One approach is to posit simple division between the first generation: Horkheimer, Marcuse, Adorno, Lowenthal, Fromm, and Benjamin and the second generation: Habermas, Albrecht Wellmer, perhaps Karl-Otto Apel, and more recently a third generation of people like Axel Honneth and Helmut Dubiel. That's one way to conceptualize the alternatives within the school, by distinguishing among three generations. The American reception of Critical Theory, which began tentatively when many of its members were here in exile, really didn't pick up steam until the sixties and seventies. It developed its own traditions and there are quite a number of people like Susan Buck-Morss, Jean Cohen, Andrew Arato, Paul Breines, Seyla Benhabib, Robert Hullot-Kentor, Richard Wolin, Russell Berman, Russell Jacoby, and Thomas McCarthy, many of whom wrote for the journal *Telos*, edited by Paul Piccone, before its lurch to the right. They interpreted the legacy of Critical Theory in too many ways to give you a quick, formulaic answer. The other factor to keep in mind concerns the history of the translation of Frankfurt School texts. The very important work that Habermas did at an early stage of his career, *The Structural Transformation of the Public Sphere*,

I. Gur-Ze'ev, The Possibility/Impossibility of a New Critical Language in Education, 217–231.
© *2010 Sense Publishers. All Rights Reserved.*

was delayed in translation to English. Until 1989, twenty-seven years after its original German edition. Then it had an enormous impact among historians, stimulating a new and intensified interest in Habermas's general project. The same thing happened with Adorno's *Aesthetic Theory*, a work that was published only posthumously in Germany after he died in 1969. It was first translated by Christian Leenhart with little impact. Then Robert Hullot-Kentor wrote a powerful critique of its accuracy in *Telos*. The translation was subsequently withdrawn by the publisher and Hullot-Kentor himself produced an entirely new version, which had an immense impact throughout the humanities, even in English Departments, where Adorno's work was previously not very influential *Aesthetic Theory* could now serve for some people as an antidote to the Habemasian positions that many had assumed were the only viable legacy of Critical Theory. A few others also have returned to the early Horkheimer or Marcuse for inspiration. Even figures who were relatively marginal in the Institute of Social Research's history, such as Franz Neumann and Otto Kircheimer, were given a new hearing because of their complex, mostly critical, relationship to the controversial political theorist Carl Schmitt, whose impact on Benjamin has also been a source of considerable discussion. In short, there are many different receptions rather than a single pattern Indeed, the reception history of Critical Theory is still unfolding in a far more vigorous way than is the currently case with other Western Marxist traditions, such as phenomenological or structuralist Marxism.

IGZ: How do you understand, or what is your relation to the educational implications, as they were developed by various people, here, in the US, within the framework of Critical Pedagogy? How do you understand, well, of course, there are various trends in Critical Pedagogy, but how do you understand the interpretation and the implications as developed within the American critical tradition?

MJ: I can't pretend to be a serious expert on this tradition. I know a little bit of Ivan Ilich, Paolo Freire, Henry Giroux, but not enough to have a truly informed opinion. I think you have to look at it at all levels of education and begin by asking what does it mean to have critical education at pre-school level? How do you train a toddler or a pre-schooler to have the skills that later stimulate their imagination and develop their critical resistance to authority without, however undermining their ability to learn from the authority that justifiably assumes that role? Then you obviously have to ask serious questions about various different educational environments, based on non-educational factors, such as socio-economic status. My mother taught math, for example, at a very tough junior high school in the south Bronx. I know from the scars that she earned how difficult it was to teach kids at that level, when they are going through all types of personal emotional changes and faced with real world dilemmas not of their own making...There the issue was how to channel the rebellious, anti-authoritarian instincts of the kids into ultimately constructive rather than destructive — mostly self-destructive — directions. In contrast, I was tracked early and spent my entire education surrounded by so-called "gifted" kids, so that even junior high school was relatively untroubled.. I was then privileged enough to go a selective high school, the Bronx High School of Science, where I had an enriched and challenging education. My own critical instincts, such as they are, were thus not a reaction to any experience of deprivation or discrimination, but rather were nurtured by rigorous and well-funded schools where I was surrounded other bright and motivated kids. As a teacher myself, I have been lucky enough to spend my entire career at a very competitive university, where I have had the luxury to focus almost entirely on the substance of my subject rather than the methods of teaching it. In short, I haven't really been sufficiently involved in debates over educational policy and pedagogy to provide an informed answer, nor would I want to generalize from my own limited experience as a student and teacher...

IGZ: Prof. Jay, how close do you see, or, what kind of similarities do you see between Critical Theory of Adorno and Horkheimer and that of Walter Benjamin? In light of the common ground between the various thinkers of Critical Theory maybe we could rethink the potential educational implications of some of the post-structuralists whom you study, from Foucault and De Man to Derrida, even if each of these thinkers has his/her own particular developments and contradictions. To be even more specific I mean here Adorno's negative dialectics and the concept of language that late Horkheimer developed in which he asserted that there is no way to differentiate between reality and conflicting apparatuses of representation and even the unavoidable reification of Critical Theory itself. Even in the *Dialectic of Enlightenment* we find the critical philosopher presented as a neurotic who refuses to be cured. To what extent, or, alternatively, in what sense is it possible to show similarities between this project and what we call today the post-structuralist's agenda?

MJ: Post-structuralism in itself is a problematic term, yoking together figures like and Lyotard, Deleuze and Lacan, who were very different, so one would have to be very careful before making generalizations. Foucault is perhaps the one to begin with. I had a discussion with him when he was at Berkley in the early eighties about his own relation to Critical Theory. Clearly, he did not know much about it when he was writing his own early works. But then when he did discover it, partly as a result of reading the French translation of my first book. (or so he told me, much to my obvious delight), he recognized many similarities. For example, stressing the relation between knowledge and power, which he explored from an essentially Nietzschean point of view, was something that they shared. The Frankfurt School denied that knowledge was ever, as an idealist might think, entirely independent of material influences, but rather rooted in structures, institutions and practices that themselves needed to be changed or at least challenged. Foucault was also fascinated by their interest in the body; their understanding that knowledge was refracted not only through discursive systems, but also grounded in what he would have called the disciplining and normalization of the body. He found in works such as *Dialectic of Enlightenment* a very strong understanding of that relation. He didn't, to be sure, share their interest in Freud's repression thesis, which Marcuse in particular developed... but he agreed on stressing the importance of the psychological internalization of social and cultural norms. In addition, in his later work, Foucault turned his attention to the question of human subjectivity, both in terms of self-fashioning and subjection, which raised the vexed question of agency and its limits, which was always a Frankfurt School concern. A recent book by Steven Pares called *Foucault 2.0*, shows the importance of his time in Berkeley, where he modified his earlier hostility to humanist notions of the individual subject, and began a dialogue with followers of the second generation of Critical Theory, who took seriously Habermas's work on communicative interaction. Indeed, before his death, Foucault wrote about Habermas and Habermas wrote about him, rather critically, but with increasing understanding and perhaps even mutual appreciation.

The relationship between Derrida and Critical Theory was perhaps even more complicated. Of all the figures associated with the Frankfurt School, it was Benjamin who attracted most of his attention, although when he received the Adorno Prize in Frankfurt, he turned his attention to the legacy of Adorno's work as well. Despite the criticisms launched against him by Habermas in *The Philosophical Discourse of Modernity*, the two of them put together a book a few years ago, which dealt mostly with political issues. Despite the different idioms in which their ideas were expressed, Adorno and Derrida were close in their recognition of the value of a negative rather than positive dialectics, a philosophy that decried coerced reconciliations. Although Derrida wouldn't have been as happy with dialectics per se, but nonetheless he shared Adorno's warning against the dangers of the identitarian overcoming of difference.

One can continue the comparison with the other figures in the two camps as well.

IGZ: You yourself compare Paul de Man and Adorno.

MJ: In certain respects, a comparison makes sense, for example concerning their common hostility to idealist aesthetics and appreciation of modernism. In America, it may be easier than in Europe to overcome labels and seek the productive cross fertilizations of different theories and different traditions,

IGZ: So, now, if we try to make the best of what we can from these similarities, from these fertilizing points of meeting in respect to their existential, philosophical and educational implications in the sense of the aim of philosophy, or the aim of progressive education, or the aim of Enlightenment, what should we make up of it in your mind?

MJ: There is no single imperative, no formula which will lead to progressive practical outcomes. One of the lessons that the twentieth century taught us, broadly speaking, is to be wary of the premature conflation of theory and practice, to believe you can move from a level of high theory to immediate action During the 1960's, Adorno of course was very critical of such attempts and wrote against Brecht and Sartre's fetish of commitment. Although there may well have been what was called a "political deficit" in Critical Theory as a result, he and his colleagues avoided endorsing ill-advised actions that hastily sought radical solutions to problems that were too complex to be resolved easily.

IGZ: But here was a difference, a great difference between him and Marcuse on this matter.

MJ: Marcuse was indeed far more involved with the student movement and for a while more optimistic about its chances to make a real difference, but even he, near the end of his life, recognized how difficult it would be to undermine what he called one-dimensional society and retreated into art as a placeholder for some future redemption...

Post-structuralism by large has also refused to legislate specific political positions Take for example, Foucault, who often talked about self-fashioning, There are commentators—James Miller for example—who try to stress the links between Foucault own life, transgressive and self destructive as it might have been, and his philosophy. But I think he was loath to allow himself to become an exemplary figure, who urged people to follow him. His own political investments were idiosyncratic and hard to turn into a pattern, for example, he supported gay rights and the Iranian revolution... We also know that virtually all the other figures that we have been talking about were unwilling to seek a smooth passage from theory to practice, even if they were at times politically active I suppose the lesson of all this is caution about seeking the immediate applicability of theory in that way that Marxists at times demanded. There is an articulated complexity between theory and practice, but not an immediate implication.

IGZ: I will try to press further on this point, with your permission. On the one hand, even if we suspend our rushing into the immediate and specific political implications of the shortcomings of language as such and of theory as a project, and even if we postpone our disillusion concerning the concept of the autonomous subject, surely, as responsible humans, we are called upon to say more about the existential, the philosophical, and, yes, the political implications of it. If we go into the other axis of the abyss, not only the shortcomings, not only the ambivalence on the edges, but the fundamental abyss between theory and the ability to unproblematically justify a call for concrete political action: even if we go into this modest implication, we can also derive from it very immodest implications, some of which are immensely violent, prima facie nihilistic and of various kinds. Maybe we will go into it later, but already in this point of our conversation I think we are called to say much more about implications and if you could say even something about the educational implications of this situation.

MJ: There is no single answer, as it is always historically variable. At certain moments, moments of crisis, moments of turmoil, moments of uncertainty, there is a great imperative not to remain on the sidelines as an imaginary witness, you are compelled to act one way of the other and you are always compelled to act on bad information, with effects that may go in other directions from your intentions. It is always the bad now rather than the good future, which is the moment of action. So there is no general formula that allows you to escape that uncertainty. However, there are other moments when for one reason or the other, when it may be wiser to devote one's activity to something else—to retreat into the study and write a difficult book, or to write some poetry that no one will read in a hundred years—to do something impractical without being forced to have a concrete instrumental and immediate effect. One of the things that the Frankfurt School always was very nervous about was the instrumentalization of theory, and I agree with their caution. Looking at the history of intellectuals and politics in the past 200 years, one can see that there are moments of engagement, moments of withdrawal, moments of engaging and producing good effects, moments of engaging and producing terrible effects. So, rather than following a simple rule that would be belied by circumstances, it is better to be open to opportunities when they arise, but never feel rushed into forcing them.

On the educational front, I think this is a very complex, even dangerous matter, because you want to educate people to think independently be autonomous, so you and you don't want therefore, to be overly directive and controlling. There is nothing worse than a well-meaning pedagogy that indoctrinates good ideas, producing the backlash we have seen against so-called political correctness. It made it difficult to think for yourself, because there was a preordained version of what was correct thinking, which was not the same as critical thinking, a large part of which is self-critique.

IGZ: Concerning your differentiating between different levels of language and your differentiation between normal history and moment of crisis. How do you justify this differentiation, between normal history, normal times and moments of crisis? Isn't it so that normality is, or, in other words, isn't it so that the possibility of stabilize the self or the system requires manipulation by different violences and effective apparatuses of manipulation that actually within "it", each moment anew, every moment that is produced as "normal" is a moment of crisis? Isn't it so that if we are normalized and overwhelmed by the system and its invisible violences unavoidably we do not see the crisis of each moment and we feel we can construct histories, reconstruct development, as if there is one trend, or two or three—those we are able to articulate by the theoretical and political means inflicted on us by the process of subjectification which is also a process of normalization. Isn't it so that this is the fundamental, invisible crisis that is kept silent by the system and so if we problematize it we come to the embarrassing gate for rearticulating the very unproblematic line of division between moments of crisis and normal times, between the "I" and "the context" of our upbringing/production/oppression?

MJ: That is an important point, an interesting point. I would say two things in response. One, that I like distinctions, so, distinction between the moment of normality and the moment of crisis helps me to understand some of the rhythms of history, or the changes that occur. In 1917, 1933, 1968, 1989, these are moments when systems, broadly speaking, were in a fragile state and in some cases—1917, 1933, 1989–they collapsed. In May 68 the system, of course, did not collapse but it could have gone either way, at least in Paris. So, one gets a sense of a kind of convergence of various strains within the system, which prevent those mechanisms of system's maintenance—call them ideological, call them functional, whatever you want to call them—from doing their job, and you get a basic challenge to the system at the most fundamental level. These are, to be sure, unusual moments and I would not say that we live in a permanent state of emergency, as. Benjamin once said in the desperate years before his suicide. But I would be reluctant to adopt that vocabulary, because then when the real crisis hits, when, say, a 1917 comes again, we will have no way to talk about it.

IGZ: But what if we live at the same time simultaneously in more then one existential, cultural, philosophical and political rapidly changing levels and nets?

MJ: It is a question who the "we" is. This is my second point. I've been lucky to have lived an enormously crisis-free life, a privileged existence without any major disruptions. My career, my family life, my earning power—I have lived a life which everyone deserves to enjoy, but of course most do not. As a result, I have been spared being confronted with a challenge of the sort that many people are forced to face in their lives. I of course know people whose lives were deeply disrupted by history, victims for example of the 9/11 attacks in New York. It has nothing to do with whether they were good people, bad people, or whether they deserved it or not. For these unlucky souls, life became a general crisis. In the US, which is basically a functional society, there are still many homeless people without medical insurance, who live on the margin of society. For them the crisis is as real as it is for people in Darfur or Baghdad, or Gaza In short, it really depends on who we are talking about and also whether or not the apparently distant crisis ultimately effects them We know in the history of Europe there were many people who thought that history would never effect them—and it did. So, I am not saying that I have entirely escaped its power, but rather that until it does it would be phony for me to say that I am living in a period of crisis and facing an existential challenge.

IGZ: Maybe before we pose the existence vs. non-existence of moments of crisis we should divide between two different things: individual/collective conscious experience of crisis which includes the individual/collective failing as well as the overcoming the experience of emergency that is immanent to the very possibility of a reflective "I", on the one hand, and the very possibility of an individual and collective historical "moment" on the other.

MJ: Before addressing that distinction, we have to acknowledge the sedimented meaning in the word "crisis." It originally denoted a certain moment of a medical trajectory, when either the fever breaks and the patient recovers or the patient dies. It implies a critical moment of decision, a moment of going in one direction or another. Perhaps it can happen at any moment, as I could die from a stroke right now, but by in large I do not think I am living through a kind of crisis on that level. Now, in retrospect you may say that I was unaware of the fact that there was a more general crisis, that for example an earthquake might hit right now and since I have not prepared my house I foolishly did not realize that a crisis could hit or that, say, anti-Semitism could rear its ugly head and I could find myself a victim, having been overly complacent. There, are, of course, many examples in history of people who were complacent about things that they should have recognized were potential threats... But at other times there was not really a crisis and alarmists were crying "wolf!"....

IGZ: Maybe we should relate to this moment of "crisis" also in a different sense. On the one sense the moment of crisis is the interruption of the continuum. The questioning, or, the cracking of the system or the realm of self-evidence, or an historical development such as the French Revolution or October 1917. On the other hand each moment anew, when we reassure the silencing of the tragedy, or when we restore confidence in the absurd of choosing one set of concepts or values and not its rival, making it a continuum, a part of a continuum, this silencing, this continues silencing is a silenced moment, a brink, maybe a false part of a stream or even an ocean of endless "moments", of crisis that we are not aware of. We fail to be aware of sometimes because we are so effectively caught by "our" platonic cave and sometimes because we are so much overwhelmed by the immanence, by the totality of the "moment", "context" or contingent net of power-relations. And then, of course, there is the refusal to face the crisis in the name of the totality or in light of the attempt, the hubris or the actual dwelling in the cosmos whether as God, a Deleuzian disciple or as a genuine Diasporic Nomad. How do you see it?

MJ: This is a very Sartrean position: that every moment we choose, every moment we are compelled to choose, every moment we are not in a way constrained by our past: and can choose something totally different. We also lack of principles by which we choose, there are no binding standards or norms by which we have to choose. We are basically alone and have to make radical choices, and moreover not only we are choosing for ourselves—we are choosing for all mankind. Following this logic of absolute freedom, I could suddenly give up my career, and become a religious worker in the slums of Calcutta, like Mother Teresa. But I am not going to do it because I am the cumulative effect of all my previous choices, which weigh on my present possibilities. I will never be a brain surgeon or a ballet dancer or a thousand other things that I at some point at my life I might have wanted to be, and I know that. The choices that I made give me a smaller menu every time I chose anew. Increasingly, my possibilities dwindle, and at a certain point in your life you recognize that you are the sum of the choices you have made and cannot undo, no matter how valiantly you strive to start anew.

IGZ: Prof. Jay, I hear you say "I have a modest choice" and I hear also that you did not say "I choose modest possibilities"…

MJ: There are many possible ways to exercise those modest choices. I may choose not to choose. I may be passive and accept the hand I've been dealt. I may be outraged at my fate and act for the sake of action. It depends on how functional the decision might be in shielding you from the kind of miseries that inevitably afflict us. Some philosophers and religious thinkers have tried to help us think about how we make choices, for example. Kierkegaard, who stressed how often we chose without criteria to help us, making leaps of faith. But not all decisions are heroic moments of existentialist choices, with momentous consequences for us or all of humankind.

IGZ: May I interrupt you here? I didn't articulate myself clear enough. My point was not that we are totally free to choose to avoid and so on and so forth. My point was that the system, the contingent historical moment and its regulating power-relations or the existential openness enables us, leads us or inflicts on us, some-time simultaneously drives and/or/vs. criteria, ideals, and conceptual apparatuses within which we choose or "choose" not only about the matter under consideration or the dilemma to morally respond to but even more fundamentally to choose or "choose" who we are/become or what are the ideals, drives, values or alternative horizons we should turn to or be redeemed by. And this is the tragic moment. This is the crisis that is normally avoided or silenced. This normally unveiled normality, this traceless silencing that enables normality, rational choice and political freedom is reassured every moment anew is the moment of emergency I relate to. It is an emergency and as such it contains also its negation and opens the gate for hope. It is an emergency in the most fundamental sense and as such in normal moments we are not aware of it. As long as we are the products of this contingent, as long as we are echoes or agents of "our" context". Tragedy in this sense, or the moment of crisis in this sense is not necessarily an individual, collective or historical outcry. It is not conditioned by conscious or historically dramatic grand crisis, dilemmas or decisions but rather much more the very silenced unaware possibilities and the routine/normality/productivity within which we are driven, or manipulated to go on or to become what the hegemonic dynamic expects us, calls us to become and celebrates with us, for us, and in a certain sense, against us, "us" in the sense of we, humans as an open possibility, as Diasporic, improvising, responsible nomads, as the realization of co-poiesis. In this light I would like to ask you: is it possible in your view to overcome the abyss between different sets of criteria, drives and telos? Is it possible in your view to respond in "a right way" or even "choose in a justifiable manner" between conflicting narratives? Is it possible to move from one to another, from the rhetorical level of language to the pragmatic one and onward to the just one in a justifiable manner that is not contingent, relative or fundamentally a manifestation of the productivity of dynamic meaninglessness? And still in other words, is it possible to overcome the abyss (or is it a crossing the bridge?) between the Levinasian "ethical I" to the "moral I", namely, to arrive safely to the political level? Is it an abyss that we talk about or is it a border or a bridge? Who is facing the promise, the bridge or the abyss? On the one hand stands the human, the individual. We can hope that she is in the stance of becoming-toward-the-otherness-of-Being, realizing co-poiesis as an eternal improviser which goes beyond the idea of a critical individual. This is since a Diasporic eternal improviser understands that there is no God, no objective reason, no emancipating theory nor historical laws that will offer safe way to an alternative Garden of Eden nor a worthy "homereturning" project to join. Not even a redeeming kind of universal pragmatics. No positive Utopia or worthy alternative to rivaling positive Utopias awaits us in the end of the road toward effective disenchantment/deconstruction. And on the other hand, this individual might find himself, might hope to face and as such should educate himself to be ready to meet a call, the presence of the totally other: the call to (re)position himself morally, to respond not solely intellectually but more fundamentally—and to act in response to the otherness, to the infinity of the moment, and "there" to communicate, to be part of and to enable Diasporic co-poiesis. Not to be a mere agent of the determinist dimension, not to return "back home" into the thingness, every moment anew. Neither to be a mere echo of the omnipotence of the contingent dimension in Life. The Diasporic human affirms this manifestation of Life and prepares herself in light of a moral decision to affirm Life. In this sense Diasporic education is an eternal, responsible improvised cultivation to transcend the human situation as a product, as a kingdom where various conflicting manipulations rule. It is an attempt to transcend the Hegelian smile of the deceiving power of history. Historical realities, the horizons of the Platonic cave, do not have the last word. Now, as I understand the thinkers of the Frankfurt School, they offered us three different solutions, well, not solutions, surely not solutions, but three different responses to this challenge. In its best this attempt does not offer the overcoming of pessimism, nor a final human victory over the omnipotence of the immanence, negativism or alienation. It does offer, however, the opening of a new door for co-poiesis, for realizing our responsibility and for political activism in face of disillusionment. Maybe Marcuse is a good example in this respect. Marcuse understands that he lives in a generation where in the West the proletariat is no longer the bearer of the revolution and does not represent the kind of historical awareness that enables in specific material conditions the possibility of a genuine revolution and emancipation. This was true in the sixties and seventies and surely in the age of globalization. Even if some will claim just the opposite, that the era of capitalist globalization finally opens the door for a genuine global emancipation from the terror of capitalism. In both cases, however, the next historical moment could embrace new potentials for emancipation. And if so, the very possibility, the very possibility for hoping for a new beginning or at list for fresh possibilities make the difference. It introduces hope and enables responsibility in face of cynicism, nihilism and relativism. It opens the way for educators, first and foremost for new kinds of dislearning and self-education in a way that questions, criticizes but does not disregard the ethos of resistance, critique and transcendence. The second response that I see among the Frankfurt School thinkers is an epistemological one. According to this kind of response from its very beginning the concept and the telos of Western philosophy cannot fulfill its aim. As much as the aim is truth, universal justice, freedom and a holistic or universal kind of stability. Not even in the pragmatic formal sense. There is no epistemological room for the pre-assumption and strive for universal equilibrium and stability, homogeneity, "peace" or unproblematic rational "consensus" in the sense that Marx strived for and today Habermas still represents. You remember that Marx strived for equilibrium in the future mature communist condition and discussed with Engels weather there will still be room for art as a dimension of critique in that future perfect society. Again, here the reply of Adorno and Horkheimer in *Negative Dialectic*, in *Dawn and Decline* and elsewhere is that we should overcome the drive for equilibrium/consensus/end of contradiction, dialectics and suffering. Conflict, dialectics, the absence of consensus or the presence of justice solely in the form of its negation are the manifestation of Life. The positive Utopia in all its forms represents existential and philosophical immaturity. The third response one can find among the writings of the Frankfurt School thinkers is an ontological one. As you can see in Benjamin's' concept of history, as an example, even the angel of history fails the overcome the immanent instability of Being, fragmentation, ambivalence or what I call ontological heteronomy. Heteronomy and conflict are here conceived not as a logical, historical or political failure to be fixed by the promise of emancipation or by the disciples of the genuine revolution. It is an unavoidable manifestation of Being itself. Now, what should be our reply? Our reply to it, again, as I can understand it, is to stress on the fertile similarities between post-structuralist and Critical Theory ways of problematizations. Maybe we should ask ourselves what can be saved in a modest way and what can be saved from the emancipatory project as a critical rational discourse within which we can elaborate, within which we can speak about dialogue between text and context. But at the same time you yourself take part in the critique of the preconditions to such a theory, you are so much aware of the fundamental levels of language and human existence and of its ambivalence, ambivalence that will never fade away, will never be silenced or overcome without a terrible human cost, and that too, only for a moment and never totally successful, unless we bring to an end the human Odyssey. Reading your works, Prof. Jay, I fail to see ultimately, how you justify in a non-merely-psychological level or not on a merely performative level performativity itself.

How do you justify the ideal/strive for psychological stability that plays immediately the role of a yardstick? How do you justify our ability and response-ability to become moral humans in light of your concept of the angel of contingency having always the upper hand? How is a Diasporic moral human possible in such a world?

MJ: I can't pretend to provide unproblematic justifications for any of the ethical commitments or political actions that either I would myself engage in or urge others to engage in. I think that the search for certainty or watertight guarantees or a universal transcendental principles, would be in vain. I have no faith that it is possible. It is more a question of following the great imperative the doctors always follow—do not do any harm. In other words: what you should do is to recognize that interventions, however well meaning, can also backfire and what we now call blowback producing unintended consequences often ensues from the most noble intended actions. You could argue, for example, that the Iraq war was the product of neo-conservatives who naively believed they were going to make the world safe for democracy (and maybe also were looking for a little bit of oil), You could say, if you give them benefit at that, they had good intentions, but still produced a total catastrophe. So, that would be my first imperative: be cautious and first recognize that you can do harm. Try to do as little bit of it as possible, and then also to be open to the possibility that your own values and methods can be challenged. When you enter new contexts you can always learn unexpected lessons that undermine your prior beliefs.

The last book I wrote, *Songs of Experience*, was on the concept of experience. It emphasized the importance of the knowledge of otherness produced by experiential openness to the world. Rather than coming from within, it follows from encountering something that is different, new, unexpected, something that happens to you—you do not produce it out of your own creativity or imagination. It is a willingness to be a little bit less autonomous, a bit more heteronymous, when it comes to relations to the external world. That seems to me a healthier imperative than believing I might ever come up with historical or transcendental normative justification for absolutes, either ethical or epistemological. Now, it does not mean that I do not believe in things deeply. It is not as if I am a total skeptic or want to change my clothes every time I see somebody wearing something else, or that I don't continue to embrace the various commitments that I have had in the past or regret. But I also value openness and the continued capacity to learn, which allows you to be less provincial and more understanding of other peoples' positions and values. It is a bit like Hannah Arendt's notion of enlarged consciousness, which is never universal, but is able to incorporate different perspectives, integrating them in ways that may not produce perfectly reconciled positions, but at least opens up a dialogue with others, rather than assumes eternal conflict of opinions.

IGZ: Again, we end up with a justification that is valid only concerning our body, our mental stability, health, or solely in light of specific local criteria within a specific system, solely within the horizons that dehumanize us by inflicting on us "our" limitations, strives and edification paths.

MJ: Well, system is an interesting concept. We need to situate the specific events, the specific life experiences that we have on a local level in something that is more global and systematic. This level may or may not be apparent to us, and as Marx argued, may work behind our backs and against our will. So, it is useful to have a conceptual understanding of that system, even though experientially we may only see it in terms of that which has manifest effects on us. This is an important task and there are many ambitious theories that have tried to do that. The problem, of course is, knowing exactly when you have got the system right, because the system itself may be too complex and incoherent to be easily amenable to conceptual organization. This is true even of the idea of capital, which is the one that we often think is most useful in making sense of the system under which we live. Years ago, scholars like Claus Offe challenged the idea of organized capital by coining the term "disorganized capital". It is hard to know exactly how it functions. Habermas was arguing something similar when he spoke of the "new unsurveyability" to describe the difficult of a totalizing gaze over the whole same thing.

The second point I would make is that I have very little confidence in the possibility of ever creating a totally different, new and better system in the manner of a positive Utopia. It is not as if there is somewhere out there lurking a system, which can be put into place like the changing of a lens, allowing us to see the world in a correct manner. Whatever system we have will be imperfect. We are always going to find ways to criticize; it may even be possible that system maintenance may be healthier than system subversion, because we do not know what is going to follow. So, I have, once again, no formulaic way to deal with these issues People are able to rise the level of system critique only when they are in enough pain to risk the unknown alternative... Otherwise you are undermining the system without sufficient motivation, with only the hope that you may produce something better. The suicide bombers who go into civilian areas and kill people are doing it because for them the system is so repellent it is worth the use of horrible means. But I have no sympathy with their reasoning, because they don't even bother to tell us what their alternative will look like or how they hope their actions will produce that outcome.

IGZ: What are the educational implications of such a conception of yours?

MJ: It is wise to operate on many different levels. To be able to articulate their own experiences and situate them in a larger context, students should be asked to think about their own histories their own family's history, and then they filter the answers through more general considerations about such issues as gender and class relations. But then they need to be urged to move beyond themselves and their own situation and be opened to otherness, difference etc. They need to be able to register and criticize both the good and bad effects of those encounters and then to leave the level of the personal and to think abstractly, to be able to think on a level that involves using difficult concepts, comparatively and systematically, and then to negotiate from one level to the next.

IGZ: I will share with you what are the reactions of most of my younger students when I offer them similar hopes. Either I am confronted by response of "it is a waste of our time", "you should be instrumental, you should be pragmatic, we should do as little as we can theoretically and emotionally so that we can save energy and time in order to be successful in specific targets that are represented to us by the latest fashion, normality or the hegemonic ideology". The second response that I am faced with is something of that kind: "what a stupid alternative you have chosen, this reflective, or critical way that you choose is radical: it is never to have the upper hand, never gives fruits, we should do better and go in a none-critical path, or, in critical ways, yes, but be should run away from your concept of critique. The alternative is not simply being critical or not being critical. The choice is not even between two different kinds of critique. Some Islamists offer us a specific belief and critique and some Jewish fundamentalism offer another kind of critique and positive Utopia, and still another one is offered by the logic of the market and some products of its culture industry develops very sophisticated and appealing manners and concepts of critique of which some versions of postmodernism are very appealing and tempting indeed. And still another one is the most dogmatic acceptance of the Critical Theory and Critical Pedagogy which I feel also very....

MJ: Estranged from.

IGZ: Prof. Jay, as an intellectual, how would you react to your student's expectations and disillusionment from hope, from the potential of the human mind and creativity and from the human heart? I will go even further and ask: in your mind, how is it possible to develop today, in face of globalizing capitalism, of the success of the Instrumental Rationality, how is it possible to defend and edify the critical education of the kind that you see as worthy?

MJ: I have had the privilege to teach at Berkeley, which has students who are often inclined towards thinking in more critical than instrumental or careerist terms. As a result, I do not feel I am swimming upstream when I introduce ideas which they may take home and have ridiculed by their parents. These kids are often ahead of me in terms of coming up with new reasons to feel outrage against injustice. Berkeley is a very diverse campus, we have a minority white students population; with many students of Asian and Hispanic background. Most of them are not complacent or elitist, so the environment is one in which it is easy to stimulate critical thinking.

When they will get older I imagine some will become more conventional, but at this point in their live, it is not an uphill battle. Of course, at some other institutions, a majority of students may be more conservative, interested in fraternities, football and partying. So, I do not know if there is a simple answer to that. Even these students can be radicalized or induced to challenge themselves, sometimes by one inspirational example in the classroom. Meeting students twenty or thirty years after their time at Berkeley, students, I often scarcely remember, will sometimes say: "this class was extraordinarily important to me and I had read a particular book, which really changed the way I think." You never know who that student going to be. One of the great things about teaching is that you can be like a benign virus that spreads throughout the environment; spreading throughout a body of people who then spread it again. Teaching can have a tremendous multiplier effect and one can be very surprised by the ways in which quiet students are the ones to catch the bug. So, if you introduce them to difficult and challenging ideas without demanding they take them on faith, they do not feel they are being indoctrinated I especially enjoy the opportunity to reason with smart students with conservative or conventional opinions, who can defend their ideas with gusto and ingenuity. It is refreshing to have a wide range of viewpoints in a class and you always learn from positions different from your own.

IGZ: In a sense, it is the faith of any version of non-dogmatic thinking, the faith of education at its best. Isn't it so that in another sense it is also a manifestation of our historical moment, where master signifiers of Enlightenment and modernity are being demolished, ridiculed or silenced, where ideals and values of humanism become overtaken, misused and de-constructed? And of course we still do not have alternative master signifiers to counter the loss of Utopia. The new critical language, the new improvisational language of the time that is in between the historical moments of any historical dynamic does not release us from our responsibility. Our in the strongest sense. And as such we are to position ourselves, to resist injustice, to do the good, to educate, or even to position ourselves in a worthy manner, while the criteria of the deconstructed humanistic self-evident is being ridiculed or deconst-ructed. Do you share this understanding of our historical, philosophical and educational situatedness? What are the implications of such an embarrassing, demanding situatedness as you understand it?

MJ: The vast majority of experiences that one has in which history impinges on our daily lives provide, I would suggest, a strong sense of being in a period of transition. We often feel we are either moving in a positive direction or in a period of decline, but somehow the story is still very much open-ended. There is a famous *New Yorker* cartoon in which Adam and Eve are leaving the Garden of Eden and Adam turns to Eve and says: "we are going through a period of transition." Of course, there are also moments of rupture, such as 9/11, which can be experienced as signaling an epochal shift, but these are infrequent and often seem in retrospect to be less radically a break than they appeared at the time.

There is also a very strong tendency for what might be called epigonal self-consciousness, the belief that there were giants before us and that we are merely midgets by comparison. Maybe, of course, to borrow the famous medieval metaphor, we're midgets is standing on the shoulders of the giants, or maybe we are standing tall on the ground after the giants have gone. Sometimes there are giants around us and we have not quite figured out who they are yet, and one day we will recognize that they have invented a new language that will sweep all before it. People talk about linguistic, cultural or visual turns, and you can be sure that there will be later turns in a totally different direction. I have little patience with talk about the exhaustion of ideas or creativity or the end of history, in the manner of Fukuyama's notorious claim of twenty years ago about the putative end of history with the triumph of liberal democracy. Even he has repudiated it now. Similar pronouncements about the end of theory, the end of art, etc all seem to me histrionic and premature. Nothing of cultural importance fully dies, but reemerges in a new form, a new idiom. At the end of Bush's miserable term it looks as if a progressive Democrat will win and it may be possible to reinvigorate a political world that has seemed so dreary for so long. And Critical Theory will still have a role to play. I think I have mentioned Russell Jacoby's book *The Last Intellectuals*, which talks of the passing of a certain kind of independent, critical intellectual. Well, there are still intellectuals today, still people who are doing good work, even in the academy, still people who are willing to challenge conventional wisdom and prepare future generations for the challenges to come.

IGZ: Prof. Jay Toda Raba, Thank you.

MJ: Thank you very much, I enjoyed talking to you.

NIGEL TUBBS

10. TOWARD A NEW CRITICAL LANGUAGE IN EDUCATION[1]

There is a new myth of the heterogeneous that is reducing the political to a sinful Enlightenment.

If the book *Critical Theory and Critical Pedagogy: Towards a New Critical Language in Education* (Gur-Ze'ev, 2005) can be thought to crystallize anything it must be the question of whether Critical Pedagogy can sustain an emancipatory *telos*. In this, it therein reflects a theme that engages far beyond Critical Pedagogy, one that sees the emancipatory tradition of Hegelian-Marxism challenged by the post-Enlightenment perspectives of much recent European philosophy. In addition, perhaps, if the book fails in anything, it must be the all too frequent avoidance of totality by its authors not engaging with each other's papers in any real way, despite this being Ilan's avowed aim in bringing us together. If the book *is* the new critical language then it is not yet able to speak itself.

What, then, has the book brought together? Peter McLaren sees Critical Pedagogy taken to 'just about every transdisciplinary tradition imaginable' (Gur-Ze'ev, 2005, p. 81), which has, he says, compromised 'an earlier, more radical commitment to anti-imperialist struggle' (Gur-Ze'ev, 2005, p. 78). He seeks to re-establish pedago-gical struggle as 'class struggle' (Gur-Ze'ev, 2005, p. 90) for without an 'interpretive framework that can unpack the labour/capital relationship in all its capillary detail, Critical Pedagogy is doomed to remain trapped in domestic currents and vulgarized formations' (Gur-Ze'ev, 2005, p. 84). This leads to the kind of perspective that is held in most suspicion by critics of the emancipatory model of critique, namely where 'the oppressed under capitalism are always circumscribed by a determined totality' (Gur-Ze'ev, 2005, p. 91) and have 'no point of reference with which to articulate a counter-praxis to capital' (Gur-Ze'ev, 2005, p. 91). The critical pedagogue is seen here as privileging his own revolutionary standpoint, representing counter-praxis on behalf of the oppressed until such time as they can see things clearly for themselves.

There are contributions to the book which highlight this sense of privilege. Douglas Kellner cautions that some philosophers of education work with 'questionable conc-eptions of reason, subjectivity, and democracy, and neglect the importance of the body, gender, race, sexuality, the natural environment' (Gur-Ze'ev, 2005, p. 57). He therefore concludes that 'the poststructuralist critique of modern theory provides important tools for a Critical Theory of education in the present age' (Gur-Ze'ev, 2005, p. 57). Gert Biesta goes further. Those who decry the ethical postmodern agenda 'seem unable to let go of their epistemological and metaphysical certainties'

I. Gur-Ze'ev, The Possibility/Impossibility of a New Critical Language in Education, 233–245.
© *2010 Sense Publishers. All Rights Reserved.*

(Gur-Ze'ev, 2005, p. 149). They are still tied to the use of education 'as an instrument for emancipation' (Gur-Ze'ev', 2005, p. 149) which will, he says, ultimately and inevitably lead to 'a form of totalitarianism that is foreign to what Critical Pedagogy stands for' (Gur-Ze'ev, 2005, p. 152). Against education for emancipation Biesta advocates the impossibility and undecideability of education, and argues for Critical Pedagogy to challenge itself according to a 'fundamental ignorance... that makes room for the possibility of disclosure' (Gur-Ze'ev, 2005, p. 152).

The issue of privilege is also addressed in a different way by Michael Apple and Anat Rimon-Or. Apple provides a different kind of critique to McLaren and in particular to the shadow of the (vulgar) conception of false consciousness that might accompany the privileged and enlightened standpoint of the emancipator. He notes that certain elements of conservative modernization gain popularity and support not because the oppressed are duped, or are puppets, but rather because some of its themes 'are connected to aspects of the realities that people experience' (Gur-Ze'ev', 2005, p. 95). Indeed, these themes 'resonate deeply with the experiences, fears, hopes and dreams of people as they go about their daily lives' (Gur-Ze'ev, 2005, p. 95). In other words, the conservative right has asserted the validity of civil society and transmitted this validity through colonizing the territory of cultural values. It is not so much Apple's suggestion that, in the face of this conservative success 'we need to continue to build on more progressive alliances between our core constituencies around issues such as class, race, gender, sexuality, ability, globalization and economic exploitation, and the environment' (Gur-Ze'ev, 2005, p. 109) that is significant here. Indeed, in the context of the book, if I may use a shorthand here, this falls contra McLaren but pro Kellner. I think that what is really significant in Apple's article is that he returns to the priority of subjectivity in civil society and, again in the context of the book, this puts him contra McLaren but also contra Biesta's themes of impossibility and undecideability which, at their core, decry the illusory status and fixed identity of the epistemologically presupposed subject.

In this respect alone, in the focusing on subjectivity within civil society as real and non-deconstructable, Apple reminds Critical Pedagogy of the most difficult of all aspects of Critical Theory, put by Adorno in 'Why Philosophy' like this: 'politics aimed at the formation of a reasonable and mature mankind remain under an evil spell, as long as they lack a theory that takes account of the totality that is false' (Adorno, 1991b, p. 28). Or, more directly, one cannot claim a serious political critique of modern social relations without recognizing that the totality of bourgeois social relations is true.

I want now to suggest that such an insight can be found in the book most clearly in Anat's chapter. I don't think, for example, that a theory of the totality that is false can be found in Ilan's chapter. Ilan, I think, does not take seriously enough the fact that negative dialectics must acknowledge the truth of its dependence upon existing social forms or, if you like, the totality of its complicity and the complicity of its totality. I will return to Ilan's notion of diasporic philosophy presently.

I draw attention now to Anat's chapter and in particular to her treatment of the totality, the objectivity, of social relations. If I have understood her correctly she is arguing not only that 'we cannot eliminate the effects of power relations that construct our discourses' (Gur-Ze'ev, 2005, p. 329) but also, with McLaren, that 'material conditions determine consciousness' (Gur-Ze'ev, 2005, p. 334). Her argument here, at face value, appears to side with the vulgar conceptions of false consciousness of the oppressed who 'can suspend neither the practices in which they are involved nor their needs' (Gur-Ze'ev, 2005, p. 334). It is the case for Marx, she says, that 'material conditions have to change for these subjects before they will be able to think critically' (Gur-Ze'ev, 2005, p. 334). Yet here, through Plato and the concept of reason, she sees philosophy as the stance of critique, one in which both the power relations of discourse *and* the material consciousness of the proletariat 'are already deferred' (Gur-Ze'ev, 2005, p. 334). She notes here that the 'educational act' (Gur-Ze'ev, 2005, p. 334) of critical education 'is revolutionary in itself' (Gur-Ze'ev', 2005, p. 334), because in critique the proletariat become 'future philosophers' (Gur-Ze'ev, 2005, p. 333). Nevertheless, 'it doesn't cultivate revolutionists in the Marxist sense' (Gur-Ze'ev, 2005, p. 334). 'Critical education stems from critical thinking; hence it must postpone social needs, including those of the revolution' (Gur-Ze'ev, 2005, p. 334). She concludes that 'the sphere in which liberating transformation occurs is the sphere of critique, not of revolution' (Gur-Ze'ev, 2005, p. 337).

Anat draws out two implications here. First, that counter-education will only be critical and transformative if it suspends the ideological determination of 'human' needs in order to criticize them. Conjoining Plato, Nietzsche and Marx she argues for the implicit morality of reason and desire as 'the perpetual desire to maintain the ability to criticize' (Gur-Ze'ev, 2005, p. 336). No Marxist educator can or should 'predict what our students will do with the abilities that we develop in them' (Gur-Ze'ev, 2005, p. 336). As such, she says, 'there is no Marxist education, only Marxist educators' (Gur-Ze'ev, 2005, p. 336–7).

The second implication is that in critique 'the conjunction of the reasonable and the moral is a function of the ability to resist compulsions' (Gur-Ze'ev, 2005, p. 338), ability that normalizing education can remove in such a way as to leave 'no trace of its absence' (Gur-Ze'ev, 2005, p. 338). Put together, then, I think that Anat finds here that first, power relations can insist on certain desires; second, that the desire to refuse these desires reproduces those power relations; and third, that wisdom, therefore, 'is the privilege of the oppressor only, and that the oppressor alone holds the key to the liberating acts and solutions' (Gur-Ze'ev, 2005, p. 338).

I single her chapter out from the others in the book for its interweaving of some of Critical Theory's most important themes. The sphere of needs, of civil society, is a totality that can mask itself as a totality. This can be unmasked by the vengeance of the oppressed or the wisdom of the emancipator who uses his 'influential speaker position' (Gur-Ze'ev, 2005, p. 340) to begin to end the predetermined course of the suffering of the other. If unmasking *is* a vengeance then it is still a reproduction of civil society and of the realm of needs—the route to terror. Critique, however, is wisdom when it educates for the suspension or the deferral of civil society or desire, for it alone is (and Anat doesn't say as much, but this is my reading of what she might intend) the totality of civil society and, whilst being privileged in being able to speak, speaks nevertheless against this totality and this privilege.

Is there here, a curious and bold mix of philosopher king as radical critique whose suspension of desires created by the totality speaks therein of a desire for justice from a position of wisdom, a kind of Platonic and Zarathustrian dialectic of Enlightenment? Anat accepts false consciousness not from the position of the revolutionary vanguard but from the point of view of the philosophical educator who knows totality but does not overcome it. As with Apple, so now with Anat, subjectivity in all its forms of misrecognition has to be taken seriously, has to be recognized as true, else the terror of the arbitrary will be unleashed against 'wrong' consciousness. Anat has opened up here an attempt to think the totality critically, yet without new forms of terror. Without saying so, I think she is working with the truth of the dialectic of Enlightenment in a way that Critical Pedagogy has rarely done.

I want now to spend a little time reflecting on Ilan's notion of diasporic Jewish philosophy. Its negativity is appealing, but it's yearning for the absent other can, I think, be seen to imply a determination other than just Jewish, one that is perhaps Protestant and even baroque. I therefore offer this critique in the spirit of Judaism *and* Modernity, in the spirit of Adorno *and* Hegel, and in the spirit of Ilan *and* me. The engagement may have significance deeper than the parts that constitute it.

It is clear why the notion of diasporic philosophy is attractive at this current juncture. If Critical Theory's realization is correct that the power of the totality of social relations has inscribed itself even into critical thought, then it is the dialectic of Enlightenment that at once both realizes this and repeats it. Despite the passing of forty years since *Negative Dialectics* and sixty years since *Dialectic of Enlightenment*, can we claim to have moved on from the notion of totality that Adorno in particular propounded? If not, then as a modern phenomenon the post-Enlightenment approaches to the totality of contingency which call for 'new' ways of thinking, 'new' languages, 'new' ethics, and even for avoiding earthly contingency by invoking the absolutely absent and the heterogeneous other, fail to maintain the integrity of the position they expose. Modernity, since Rousseau and Kant, has always worked within the difficulties that are posed by reason as contingent. This notion of philosophy as the self-conscious work of contingency is, for example, entirely missed by Michael Peters in his chapter when he states that 'nowhere in the *Critique [of Pure Reason]* does Kant address the question of how such critical enquiry, itself, is possible' (Gur-Ze'ev, 2005, p. 38). This is, in short, to misunderstand modernity entirely.

Nevertheless, it is one thing to work with and as contingency, it is quite another to call for the overcoming of reason's or modernity's aporias; something, for example, Rousseau, Kant, Hegel, Kierkegaard and Adorno never did. We could all drown in the number of papers written that are seeking paths 'towards' something else, something 'new' or 'beyond' the current. Against this, Anat's insight is significant. She does not call for absolute others, or for new ethical paradigms, or for new ways of speaking; only for a firm recognition of the dialectic of Enlightenment and the condition of the possibility of critique, for the understanding that totality determines both critique and the critique of critique, and for wisdom in the philosophical consciousness that recognizes this. It is, in my opinion, one of only two chapters in the book to remain within the limits of the objective, and thus to speak truly in the spirit of Critical Theory.

So, to Ilan's notion of Diaspora. It is the case, I think, that Ilan's notion of diasporic philosophy as portrayed in his Introduction is a major contribution to the new language in education that he desires from the contributors. Building upon the idea of negative Utopia in 'mature Critical Theory' (Gur-Ze'ev, 2005, p. 13) Ilan seeks to reject the dogmas within Critical Pedagogy of 'emancipation' (Gur-Ze'ev, 2005, p. 14), 'solution' (Gur-Ze'ev, 2005, p. 15) or 'salvation' (Gur-Ze'ev, 2005, p. 15). These dogmas that 'Critical Pedagogy educators normally are so quick to promise us in so many voices and agendas' (Gur-Ze'ev, 2005, p. 14) have lost not only the idea of negative Utopia but also an attachment to 'worthy suffering' (Gur-Ze'ev, 2005, p. 16). He accuses the voices of the former of only being able to make a 'return into thingness' (Gur-Ze'ev, 2005, p. 16). This is to highlight the dialectic of Enlightenment as ubiquitous in all forms of rationality including revolutionary critique. Yet, and against the totality of the dialectic here which Ilan calls 'a reconciling "homeret-urning"' (Gur-Ze'ev, 2005, p. 16), he offers the 'transcending potential' (Gur-Ze'ev, 2005, p. 16) of realizing 'homelessness in a Godless world' (Gur-Ze'ev, 2005, p. 16), or the diasporic philosophy that refuses 'all calls for escape in self-protection and pleasure/truth as the ultimate goal of Life' (Gur-Ze'ev, 2005, p. 17). As a version of negative dialectics this diasporic philosophy 'maintains both dualism and dialectics, yet insists on love and intimacy in a Godless world, where human rationality cannot establish any alternative Garden of Eden, meaning, aim, or an authentic "I"' (Gur-Ze'ev, 2005, p. 17).

Yet, from a more critical perspective, I note that the notion of diasporic philosophy seems to be constituted from a conglomeration of various critical perspectives. It is, I think, a mix that, taken together, threatens to avoid totality and to avoid objective relations. For example, from Heidegger Ilan takes the 'existential situate-dness' (Gur-Ze'ev, 2005, p. 9) of being-thrown-into-the-world and, combining it with the 'exile-Redemptive narrative' (Gur-Ze'ev, 2005, p. 9) of 'late Adorno and Horkheimer' (Gur-Ze'ev, 2005, p. 9), offers a 'concept of living-toward-the-not-yet-in-a-Godless-world' (Gur-Ze'ev, 2005, p. 9). Indeed, the term 'totally other' Ilan takes from Heidegger's *Letter on Humanism*.[2] But does this combination take seriously enough Adorno's deep concern over Heideggerian 'jargon'? Ilan might respond that it is not a jargon of authenticity that he is defending here but rather a notion of the inauthenticity of home and of roots. Indeed, he is clear that the Frankfurt School thinkers 'along with Heidegger and existentialism' (Gur-Ze'ev, 2005, p. 8) refused any metaphysics that could offer such a home. But I am not clear what 'refusal' means here. Did Heidegger refuse metaphysics when he stated in *What is Metaphysics* that metaphysics is *Dasein* itself?[3] Does Adorno 'reject' metaphysics when, for example, decrying resignation, he states that 'Enlightenment must examine itself'? This becomes the call to education previously framed by Plato in the cave and by Kant in public reason. However, the dialectic of Enlightenment is seldom seen to be a philosophical education into the antinomy of theory (metaphysics, universality) and practice (the will, the particular) that constitutes resignation, and is more often seen merely as one repeating resignation. Adorno and Horkheimer seem to sum up this resignation, this lack of philosophical education, when they state that 'it is characteristic [of the totality] that even the best-intentioned reformer who uses an impoverished and debased language to recommend renewal, by his adoption of the insidious mode of categorization of the bad philosophy it conceals, strengthens the very power of the established order he is trying to break' (Adorno and Horkheimer, 1979, p. xiv). Indeed, Habermas praises Adorno in particular as being the only philosopher 'to develop remorselessly and spell out the paradoxes of... the dialectic of Enlightenment that unfolds the whole as untrue' (Dews, 1992, p. 99). But, Habermas adds, this insight into the fallibility of subjective knowledge 'should be trivial by now' (Dews, 1992, p. 199). His own view is that we have to learn from the dialectic of Enlightenment the negativity which Hegel first expressed some two hundred years before, and move on. His own work has therefore been based upon the conviction that 'one cannot live with the paradoxes of a self-negating philosophy' (Dews, 1992, p. 99).

Nevertheless, Adorno and Horkheimer are not resigned to failure, nor do they abandon the critical project. They hold to the idea that at the very least, dialectical and negative thinking will enable the more overtly totalitarian and positivistic representations of Enlightenment to be subjected to criticism, and thereby lose the power they currently enjoy. The dilemma is summed up by them in the following way: 'there is no longer any available form of linguistic expression which has not tended toward accommodation to dominant currents of thought' (Adorno and Horkheimer, 1979, p. xii). Nevertheless, they say, 'we are wholly convinced... that social freedom in inseparable from enlightened thought' (Adorno and Horkheimer, 1979, p. xiii). Critique is necessary, because 'if Enlightenment does not accommodate reflection on [its] recidivist element... if consideration of the destructive aspect of its progress is left to its enemies, [then] blindly pragmatized thought loses its transcending quality and its relation to truth' (Adorno and Horkheimer, 1979, p. xiii). This is no refusal of metaphysics. It is, if anything, an avoiding of avoiding metaphysics as part of the totality (and this is what I find in Anat's paper).

Nor am I clear about the relationship that Ilan's notion of diasporic philosophy has with metaphysics. Consider his description of the 'totally other' that bursts into reality by not appearing at all, and that is therefore 'beyond determinism, contingency and predictability' (Gur-Ze'ev, 2005, p. 11).[4] Where Adorno finds totality and objectivity of categorization to be the condition of and the conditioning of critique, Ilan says that the totally other produces 'untouched horizons, fresh master-signifiers, and fruitful, dynamic, new creations' (Gur-Ze'ev, 2005, p. 11) offering 'newly born possibilities' (Gur-Ze'ev, 2005, p. 11) for 'transcendence' (Gur-Ze'ev, 2005, p. 12). These possibilities are not 'conditioned by laws of freedom, determinism, or representation' (Gur-Ze'ev, 2005, p. 11). Ilan, my friend, can you really mean this? Have you found a way beyond the totality and objectivity of bourgeois social relations, a totality with which Adorno knew he could not but be totally complicit?

I think the attractiveness of this idea of diasporic philosophy for Ilan lies in four related characteristics. First, it offers a critique of imperialism in all its forms, including that found within Critical Pedagogy, without abstractly reproducing imperialism in doing so. Second, this means it can reach out to the many cultural struggles that have been assimilated into Critical Pedagogy by offering them recognition of the significance of difference and of suppression at the margins, without falling into the forms of totalitarianism that Biesta warns about. Third, it stands as a concrete critique of those in the state of Israel for whom relations to the other are determined by fixed geopolitical notions of home and homeland. Indeed, this observation invites us to explore some of Ilan's other work, which we do in a moment. Fourth, Ilan sees the notion of the totally other that diasporic philosophy speaks of as a way of inviting emancipatory Critical Pedagogy to continue its renunciations of 'the temptations, imperatives, and fashions of the world of facts' (Gur-Ze'ev, 2005, p. 20) because 'even when it collapses into dogmatic, non-creative, and ethnocentrist practices of "emancipation" and "critique," [it] still symbolizes the quest for **the totally other**' (Gur-Ze'ev, 2005, p. 20, author's emphasis).

Together then these characteristics of diasporic philosophy offer a new critical language in education. They offer 'an alternative to being swallowed by all "home-coming" appeals and all salvation/emancipation agendas and educational projects that offer to constitute the "I" in the "we"' (Gur-Ze'ev, 2005, p. 18); and Ilan acknowledges that this is 'the kind of religiosity that Adorno and Horkheimer praised in Judaism' (Gur-Ze'ev, 2005, p. 19).

I am mindful here of Ilan's writing on the significance of diasporic philosophy for the impasse between Israel and the Palestinians. This gives the case for diasporic philosophy a concrete political substance that could appear to make philosophical critiques of diasporic philosophy seem somewhat abstract, even decadent, in comparison. It is surely right never to forget the violent objectivity that Ilan works within and against. *Nevertheless*, the case study of diasporic philosophy in Israel raises important issues endemic to the very notion of diasporic philosophy. In *Beyond the Modern-Postmodern Struggle* (and from a paper originally titled 'Can't you see that the time has come in Israel for a counter-education that will prepare for a self- initiated Jewish displacement') Ilan makes important and moving observations. It is an essay written in pain about pain, not least that in an 'unreserved siding against injustice' (Gur-Ze'ev, 2007, p. 3) one is also forced to admit that 'there is no room even for a just State of Israel' (Gur-Ze'ev, 2007, p. 2). This is because, 'from its very beginning Zionist education failed in its major mission' (Gur-Ze'ev, 2007, p. 4), that is, to purify the Israeli, the *Sabra*, of the Ghetto mentality. It was, he says, 'not sufficiently potent to constitute a non-patronizing Jewish generosity that would extend its hand to the Arab world' (Gur-Ze'ev, 2007, p. 5). It was unable to move out from its Zionist notion of 'homecoming' and, as such, eschewed Jewish life as diasporic. Ilan argues here for a diasporic philosophy, one that will make possible 'the second Israeli exodus' (Gur-Ze'ev, 2007, p. 6), an 'Israeli self-initiated evacuation of Israel' (Gur-Ze'ev, 2007, p. 6) which will have homelessness as its home and will realize therein the individual who is willing 'to open the gates to the nomadic existence of a brave lover of life and creativity' (Gur-Ze'ev, 2007, p. 6). This nomadic life 'signifies the abyss of existence, meaninglessness, suffering, and the absence of God' (Gur-Ze'ev, 2007, p. 7); in sum, the 'Spiritless post-modern world' (Gur-Ze'ev, 2007, p. 7). It is therefore a call to 'individuals of all nations' (Gur-Ze'ev, 2007, p. 7) to the very condition of the philosophical, namely, 'Being as Diasporic becoming' (Gur-Ze'ev, 2007, p. 9).

But here too Ilan seems prepared to call upon a remarkably wide range of intellectual support. We have seen that diasporic philosophy refers to late Adorno and Horkheimer and contains elements of Heidegger. Now we see a Levinasian theme in the 'totally other' (Gur-Ze'ev, 2009, p. 8); a 'poiesis' (Gur-Ze'ev, 2007, p. 51); a Derridean theme in the undecideability, the 'open possibility' (Gur-Ze'ev, 2007, p. 6) of diasporic philosophy; and Deleuzian 'rhizomatic' (Gur-Ze'ev, 2007, p. 8) creativity, suggesting that diasporic philosophy is not dialectical, yet also stressing that the 'self-initiated displacement of the Jews from Israel is a dialectical project' (Gur-Ze'ev, 2007, p. 6), a dialectic of 'collective counter-educational effort' (Gur-Ze'ev, 2007, p. 6) and an open possibility for the individual alone. Ilan concludes that he is offering 'a dialectical reconstruction of our historical moment' (Gur-Ze'ev, 2007, p. 61). It is by no means clear how the emancipatory tradition and recent French post-structuralist thought can be reconstructed in this way. Indeed, this remarkable attempt to synthesize in diasporic philosophy Frankfurt School Critical Theory, French post-foundational thought and Heideggerian *unheimlich* is also represented by Ilan as 'the precondition of philosophical life as presented by Plato' (Gur-Ze'ev, 2007, p. 8).[5]

Ilan brings post-foundational insight regarding dogma to Adorno's negative dialectics in arguing that whilst for Adorno 'dialectics is the consistent sense of non-identity, it also assures the impossibility of *any* stable ground for "standpoint"— not only the "wrong standpoint"' (Gur-Ze'ev, 2007, p. 46). It is in this way that the post-foundational and the critical share an anti-dogmatic stance. As such, it is in the appearance of the result of their respective theorizing rather than in their method-ologies, their theory and practice, that Critical Theory, Critical Pedagogy and non-foundationalism have been cast together in Ilan's net of a new critical language for education. The dialectical and non-dialectical may appear to arrive at a shared critique regarding identity, dogma and foundation, but the political determination of this common ground shows it not to be common at all. Indeed, the 'home' that the book offers for all these voices masks the different political insights that ground these different perspectives. The politics of the project will not itself become part of the project until and unless the contributors lose this home to the wilderness of civil society.

As second theme also emerges from the third chapter of Ilan's *Beyond the Modern-Postmodern Struggle*. Counter-education sets its aim at 'the present absence of the quest for transcendence and meaning' (Gur-Ze'ev, 2007, p. 42) and reintroduces the seriousness of 'redemption' (Gur-Ze'ev, 2007, p. 42) in Christian theology (the theme of subjective reformation will be seen to be crucial for Ilan). Yet at the same time it also aims to open 'an alternative thinking' (Gur-Ze'ev, 2007, p. 43) from the 'all-celebrated triumph of "Sprit" and its cannibalistic-oriented offspring such as Instrumental Rationality' (Gur-Ze'ev, 2007, p. 43). I imagine Ilan has Hegelian *Geist* in mind here, even though he finishes the chapter with the call for counter-education 'against the exile of Spirit' (Gur-Ze'ev, 2007, p. 61). Losing and retrieving spirit at one and the same time is not explored by Ilan as a spiritual theme or as philosophy. A call to retrieve spirit by an alternative to spirit is unphilo-sophical and its fate is misrecognition of its reproduction (if one might use this term from old Critical Pedagogy) of political relations. Avoiding *Geist*, avoiding its determinate character, means that Ilan's negative theology of diasporic philosophy will always refuse its own political determination. We come full circle here, for it is this misrecognition that has form and content as 'the present absence of the quest for transcendence and meaning' (Gur-Ze'ev, 2007, p. 42). In other words, Ilan's negative theology is a (baroque) form of social and political misrecognition. Indeed, Ilan sees absolute spirit or reason as concepts of 'homecoming' (Gur-Ze'ev, 2007, p. 56). This misses the antinomical phenomenological structure of modern abstract philosophical consciousness which is already a failure to arrive home. The time of philosophy has not yet come, but that does not equate to saying that philosophy cannot know its truth in this experience of its arrival and non-arrival (and which therefore contradicts Zizek whom Ilan quotes in relation to the impossibility of self-consciousness knowing itself. Hegel's response, as always, to such an interpretation is that the fear of error is itself the error).

Ilan also notes that 'a philosopher worthy of the name must become what I call "a diasporic human being"' (Gur-Ze'ev, 2007, p. 44). Two points here. First, this homelessness already 'belongs' to anyone wishing to retrieve the absolute, the philosophy of history and modern *Geist*. He or she is homeless within the community of scholars that accepts the impossibility of knowing the absolute. Second, noted above, is the diasporic human being recognized when we—philosophers and theorists—make the book a home for our work? This is not say that the book should not be written. Quite the contrary. It should be written *and* it should be comprehended as objective. 'We' cannot be at home in the book if the book is to be treated seriously as an objective form of social relations. The book will only be truly political in this sense, that is, when it too is both home and exile, or is re-formed as a culture of opposition within the dialectic of Enlightenment.

It is perhaps the 'end' of this idea of culture as political formation and re-formation, an end that itself has cultural form as the new heterogeneity of the absolutely other, that really explains the form and content of Ilan's diasporic philosophy. Bluntly, I see in this end of culture the fetishism of philosophical education—the negative—as without substance and therefore as not even the negative. In Marx, commodity fetishism meant giving a life to objects. But the same can happen in reverse, and here it is the negative that is assumed not to have a life of its own, which is, in effect, to fetishize the nothing as heterogeneity, as other than the negative. The end of culture here is the end of objectivity for it is the end of the idea that nothing is also something. Looking sometimes as a protection of the negative from its being objectified, it is in fact the reduction of negativity from negativity to nothing. The negative has become stripped of any determination at all and is now only a shell—no, not even a shell—but posited rather as 'open possibility.' This is not what the negative has meant in the Hegelian tradition, nor is it what Adorno meant by it, particularly in relation to knowing the totality of the false within the totality of the false. There are clear signs, I fear, that Ilan's notion of negative dialectics as open possibility is absolutely not the significance of non-identity. I am saying here that Ilan threatens to join the end of culture by eschewing negation as of philosophical significance even in asserting diasporic philosophy. It renders diasporic philosophy an ideology without political re-formative philosophical experience, or as the end of culture.

An example of this one sided reading of the negative can be found in Ilan's privileging of process over determination. He argues that Adorno's (and Benjamin's) Messianism without Messiah is important for the '*quest* for the Messiah or human emancipation' (Gur-Ze'ev, 2007, p. 48, my emphasis) rather than 'its "successful" fulfillment' (Gur-Ze'ev, 2007, p. 48). This is, from Adorno, to think redemption but not to objectify it. Here is precisely the point of difficulty for Ilan's diasporic philosophy. It must think transcendence, meaning and emancipation 'as they would present themselves from the standpoint of redemption' (Adorno, 1991a, p. 247; Gur-Ze'ev, 2007, p. 48). This quotation is from the last paragraph of Adorno's *Minima Moralia*, published in 1951. It states, 'the only philosophy which can be responsibly practiced in the face of despair is the attempt to contemplate things as they would present themselves from the standpoint of redemption: all else is reconstruction, mere technique. Perspectives must be fashioned that displace and estrange the world, reveal it to be, with its rifts and crevices, as indigent and distorted as it will appear one day in the messianic light' (Adorno, 1991a, p. 247; Gur-Ze'ev, 2007, p. 48).

Ilan then says that 'this is why Judaism was so important for Horkheimer' (Gur-Ze'ev, 2007, p. 48). However, Adorno puts this messianic light back into the objectivity of social relations. He says that negativity, of course, can always delineate 'the mirror-image of its opposite' (Adorno, 1991a, p. 247) and as such philosophy can always know the absence of God and redemption. But, and this is why the paragraph from Minima Moralia has to be read and quoted as a whole, Adorno then immediately negates the knowing of this absence. 'It is also the utterly impossible thing, because it presupposes a standpoint removed, even though by a hair's breadth, from the scope of existence, whereas we well know that any possible knowledge must not only be first wrested from what it is, if it shall hold good, but is also marked, for this very reason, by the same distortion and indigence that it seeks to escape' (Adorno, 1991a, p. 247).

But Adorno does not stop here, in this restating of the dialectic of Enlightenment. He goes on to make a statement that I think stands in opposition to all recent work that fetishizes despair as the heterogeneous and absolutely other. He says, 'the more passionately thought denies its conditionality for the sake of the unconditional, the more unconsciously, and so calamitously, it is delivered up to the world' (Adorno, 1991a, p. 247). Such thought becomes the new myth of the heterogeneous that is reducing the political to a sinful enlightenment. Adorno concludes *Minima Moralia* by stating that in comparison to the work that thinking is called upon here to perform—to comprehend the impossibility of its being unconditional in order that the thought of 'the totality that is false' (Adorno, 199b, p. 28) remains possible—'the question of the reality or unreality of redemption itself hardly matters' (Adorno, 1991a, p. 247). This is to think and to comprehend the possibility of the impossible in a very different way, I think, from Ilan's diasporic philosophy.

The negative, then, is not all possibility. It is the knowing of impossibility, a knowing that does not furnish an undecideability. On the contrary, it is a knowing that sees the negative become known according to itself—negative *and* negated. This contains the half-truth of diasporic philosophy, that it is essentially negative, but diasporic philosophy does not then lend itself to be comprehended as negated.

The latter is negation's philosophical self-education. If Ilan moves diasporic philosophy into this re-formation, this *culture* of diasporic philosophy, then the negativity of homelessness is retained but is also, and contradictorily, unavoidably at home as well in this homelessness. Otherwise critique as diasporic philosophy has no social import and is not of its own political and social conditions of possibility.

I am arguing here that when Ilan misses this second characteristic, the 'at home' of homelessness, he avoids the totality of modernity and the unavoidable predetermination of all homelessness within the state. This is not to put an argument for the state against diaspora. It is an argument for recognition of the totality against posited elusiveness. Indeed, is Ilan's Jewish theology here not also at odds with Buber's claim that even though the statutes cannot be merely accepted, nevertheless revelation must still become legislation and still requires 'builders' (Buber, 1967, p. 54)? Is it not also at odds with Rosenzweig's observation of the exiled Jews being led forth as 'a nation from the midst of another nation' (Deut. 4:43)? This Jewish being, in exile, is not an infinite possibility, it is an identity, albeit a difficult and contradictory one, or in Rosenzweig's phrase, a 'naturally grown freedom' (Rosenzweig, 1955, p. 84). Even though Rosenzweig says here that it is not 'the negative but the positive [that] will be dominant' (Rosenzweig, 1955, p. 84), it is still a relation of Yea, Nay *and* Nought. *The Star of Redemption* (Rosenzweig, 1971) has a speculative significance that the open possibility of diasporic philosophy, I fear, does not. I do not see the 'humanisms' of Buber and Rosenzweig lending support to Ilan's diasporic philosophy. In the end, what diasporic philosophy is missing is its actual relation to Law—Oral, Written, and bourgeois—with all the consequent dangers of the aestheticization of the political in the 'erotic endeavour that opens for us the possibility on non-repressive creation, happiness, responsibility and worthy suffering' (Gur-Ze'ev, 2007, p. 39). Ilan, my friend, I wonder if, in pulling up 'the tent pegs of the Torah' (Rosenzweig, 1955, p. 87) in the cause of nomadism, you risk losing the reason for exile?

Therefore, and against diasporic philosophy, I am suggesting that Judaism in modernity is not homeless; it is aporetic. It is at home and not at home at the same time. This is the Jewish question (Marx). But it is also the modern political question of Kant and Hegel. Which of us, Jew and Gentile, is *not* at home in civil society, in the formal recognition of the private life of the person? And which of us, Jew and Gentile, *is* at home in the state which cannot reconcile persons into an I that is We? Spirit in Hegel is this homelessness that belongs to the social relations that determine it. In this sense I find Anat's recognition of the role of philosophy within the experience of power relations much closer to actual political experience than Ilan's placing of political philosophical experience as only homeless, and never also at home. In Anat's account, philosophy and wisdom are at home in homelessness and homeless even at home. I believe this is much more the political significance of the dialectic of Enlightenment as negative *and* as philosophical critique.

Lastly here, I wonder again if there is in Ilan's Judaism in fact an elective affinity with Protestantism and with modernity that passes unnoticed. When Benjamin described Baroque allegory was he not showing how the Mourning Play represented the (unrecognized) spiritual misrecognition of subjectivity, and how it represented both the crisis of Lutheran subjective inwardness that salvation is unrelated to the idolatry of good works, and the crisis of modern Jewish subjectivity that Benjamin saw as 'the decay of aura' where God deserts the Written and Oral Law? One response to the Protestant crisis is an aesthetic of inward piety, 'the beautiful soul' in Goethe and Hegel who pines or yearns for an impossible redemption of the unbearable desertion of God in the state. Might it be said then that in Ilan's notion of worthy suffering, this pious heart clings to itself, yearning in its negativity for a reconciliation of inner and outer that fuels only their continued real political separation? Ilan addresses this element of yearning in *Beyond the Modern-Postmodern Struggle*, grounding the possibility for transcendence in the praxis of prayer. Following Rosenzweig ere Ilan argues that the ability to pray, to open a dialogue between earthly human conditions and present absent God, already speaks of something higher than the content of prayer. But, and again here, if prayer is a yearning for what is unreachable, it also speaks of the bad absolute of modern political freedom or, more accurately, it speaks already of the home that homelessness requires. The longing for the presence of the absolute is really the political misrecognition of the presence and the absence of the absolute within modern bourgeois social relations. What Ilan calls 'yearning' is in fact a determinate form of the relation between state and religion, and not, as in diasporic philosophy, of the relation of the religious to exile. Ilan's gnosticism is actually a modern political misrecognition of the relation of state and religion.

Perhaps neither Christianity nor Judaism in general have really learned how to recognize political and therefore spiritual actuality. Critical Theory has reached towards this theme through Benjamin and the dialectic of Enlightenment, a trajectory that is already Hegelian. Critical Pedagogy has never done this and I see no sign in the book that it is about to. Nor, sadly, does the book reveal much interest in the political actuality of subjectivity as a real experience. Is it too strong to suggest that the aestheticizing of despair at the unbearable desertion of God, be it past or future Messiah, as the totally other, or as transcendent homelessness, betrays real political subjectivity just as much as does the fetishism of aporia as open possibility and undecideability?

One last observation. Diaspora is a relevant notion in the critique of modernity, but not necessarily for the reason that Ilan extols. Modern reason is itself diasporic. The dialectic of Enlightenment has always represented this character. When myth becomes Enlightenment, reason is at home in its sovereignty. When Enlightenment returns to myth reason is homeless again and once more seeking its roots in the unknown. To know reason as this totality, which the dialectic of Enlightenment does, is to know the activity of reason itself to be both family and stranger, and to know modernity as the aporia of otherness, i.e. otherness as state *and* religion, religion *and* state. It is to Ilan's Judaism and Modernity that we should look, not for a new critical language in education, but for a retrieval of the educational and philosophical significance of Critical Theory in particular and, more widely, of the Hegelian-Marxist tradition.

NOTES

[1] I have retained the original title of the paper, written for Ilan's meeting in 2006 in Oxford.
[2] Ilan does distance his diasporic philosophy from Heidegger around the concept of nature (see Gur-Ze'ev, 2005, p. 15).

[3]   The extent to which the *Letter on Humanism*, for example, revokes this, raises questions that are explored in Derrida's *Of Spirit*.
[4]   The original here says 'unpredictability,' which I take to be a typographical error.
[5]   I am dubious as to whether this range of perspectives can be reconstructed within Ilan's notion of diasporic philosophy in any meaningful way, and I am more inclined to see any such question addressed within the speculative relation of philosophy's Higher education; see Tubbs, 2005.

REFERENCES

Adorno, T. W. (1991a). *Minima moralia*. London: Verso.

Adorno, T. W. (199b). Why philosophy. In D. Ingram & J. Simon-Ingram (Eds.), *Critical theory: The essential readings*. New York: Paragram House.

Adorno, T. W., & Horkheimer, M. (1979). *Dialectic of enlightenment*. London: Verso.

Buber, M. (1967). *On judaism*. New York: Schocken Books.

Dews, P. (1992). *Autonomy and solidarity*. London: Verso.

Gur-Ze'ev, I. (Ed.). (2005). *Critical theory and critical theory today: Toward a new critical language in education*. Haifa: university of Haifa.

Gur-Ze'ev, I. (2007). *Beyond the modern—postmodern struggle in education*. Rotterdam: Sense Publishers.

Hegel, G. W. F. (1977). *Phenomenology of spirit*. Oxford: Oxford university Press.

Rosenzweig, F. (1955). *On jewish learning*. New York: Schocken Books.

Rosenzweig, F. (1971). *The star of redemption*. London: RKP.

Tubbs, N. (2005). *Philosophy's higher education*. Dordrecht: Springer.

ZYGMUNT BAUMAN

11. EDUCATION IN THE WORLD OF DIASPORAS

Cities, and particularly mega-cities like London or Barcelona, are nowadays dustbins into which problems produced by globalization are dumped. They are also laboratories in which the art of living with those problems (though not of resolving them) is experimented with, put to the test, and (hopefully, hopefully…) developed. Most seminal impacts of globalization (above all, the divorce of power from politics, and the shifting of functions once undertaken by political authorities sideways, to the markets, and downward, to individual life-politics) have been by now thoroughly investigated and described in great detail. I will confine myself therefore to one aspect of the globalization process—too seldom considered in connection with the paradigmatic change in the study and theory of culture: namely, the changing patterns of global migration.

There were three different phases in the history of modern-era migration.

The first wave of migration followed the logic of the tri-partite syndrome: territoriality of sovereignty, 'rooted' identity, gardening posture (subsequently referred to, for the sake of brevity, as TRG). That was the emigration from the 'modernized' centre (read: the site of order-building and economic-progress—the two main industries turning out, and off, the growing numbers of 'wasted humans'), partly exportation and partly eviction of up to 60 million people, a huge amount by nineteenth century standards, to 'empty lands' (read: lands whose native population could be struck off the 'modernized' calculations; be literally uncounted and unaccounted for, presumed either non-existent or irrelevant). Native residues still alive after massive slaughters and massive epidemics, have been proclaimed by the settlers the objects of 'white man's civilizing mission'.

The second wave of migration could be best modeled as an 'Empire emigrates back' case. With dismantling of colonial empires, a number of indigenous people in various stages of their 'cultural advancement' followed their colonial superiors to the metropolis. Upon arrival, they were cast in the only worldview-strategic mould available: one constructed and practiced earlier in the nation-building era to deal with the categories earmarked for 'assimilation'—a process aimed at the annihilation of cultural difference, casting the 'minorities' at the receiving end of crusades, *Kulturkämpfe* and proselytizing missions (currently renamed, in the name of 'political correctness', as 'citizenship education' aimed at 'integration'). This story is not yet finished: time and again, its echoes reverberate in the declarations of intent of the politicians who notoriously tend to follow the habits of Minerva's Owl known to spread its wings by the end of the day. As the first phase of migration, the drama of the 'empire migrating back' is tried, though in vain, to be squeezed into the frame of the now outdated TRG syndrome.

I. Gur-Ze'ev, The Possibility/Impossibility of a New Critical Language in Education, 247–259.
© *2010 Sense Publishers. All Rights Reserved.*

The third wave of modern migration, now in full force and still gathering momentum, leads into the age of *diasporas*: a world-wide archipelago of ethnic/religious/linguistic settlements—oblivious to the trails blazed and paved by the imperialist-colonial episode and following instead the globalization-induced logic of the planetary redistribution of life resources. Diasporas are scattered, diffused, extend over many nominally sovereign territories, ignore territorial claims to the supremacy of local demands and obligation, are locked in the double (or multiple) bind of 'dual (or multiple) nationality' and dual (or multiple) loyalty. The present-day migration differs from the two previous phases by moving both ways (virtually all countries, including Britain, are nowadays both 'immigrant' or 'emigrant'), and privileging no routes (routes are no longer determined by the imperial/colonial links of the past). It differs also in exploding the old TRG syndrome and replacing it with a EAH one (extraterritoriality, 'anchors' displacing the 'roots' as primary tools of identification, hunting strategy).

The new migration casts a question mark upon the bond between identity and citizenship, individual and place, neighborhood and belonging. Jonathan Rutherford, acute and insightful observer of the fast changing frames of human togetherness, notes[1] that the residents of the London street on which he lives form a neighborhood of different communities, some with networks extending only to the next street, others which stretch across the world. It is a neighborhood of porous boundaries in which it is difficult to identify who belongs and who is an outsider. What is it we belong to in this locality? What is it that each of us calls home and, when we think back and remember how we arrived here, what stories do we share?

Living like the rest of us (or most of that rest) in a diaspora (how far stretching, and in what direction(s)?) among diasporas (how far stretching and in what direction(s)?) has for the first time forced on the agenda the issue of 'art of living with *a* difference'—which may appear on the agenda only once the difference is no longer seen as a merely temporary irritant, and so unlike in the past urgently requiring arts, skills, teaching and learning. The idea of 'human rights', promoted in the EAH setting to replace/complement the TRG institution of territorially determined citizenship, translates today as the 'right to remain different'. By fits and starts, that new rendition of the human-rights idea sediments, at best, *tolerance*; it has as yet to start in earnest to sediment *solidarity*. And it is a moot question whether it is fit to conceive group solidarity in any other form than that of the fickle and fray, predominantly virtual 'networks', galvanized and continually re-modeled by the interplay of individual connecting and disconnecting, making calls and declining to reply them.

The new rendition of the human-rights idea disassembles hierarchies and tears apart the imagery of upward ('progressive') 'cultural evolution'. Forms of life float, meet, clash, crash, catch hold of each other, merge and hive off with (to paraphrase Georg Simmel) equal specific gravity. Steady and solid hierarchies and evolutionary lines are replaced with interminable and endemically inconclusive battles of recognition; at the utmost, with eminently re-negotiable pecking orders. Imitating Archimedes, reputed to insist (probably with a kind of desperation which only an utter nebulousness of the project might cause) that he would turn the world upside down if only given a solid enough support for the lever, we may say that we would be able to tell who is to assimilate to whom, whose dissimilarity/idiosyncrasy is destined for a chop and whose is to emerge on top, if we only were given a hierarchy of cultures. Well, we are not given it, and are unlikely to be given it soon.

CULTURE IN THE DIASPORIC SETTING

We may say that culture is in its liquid-modern phase made to the measure of (willingly pursued, or endured as obligatory) *individual* freedom of choice. And that it is *meant* to service such freedom. And that it is meant to see to it that the choice remains *unavoidable*: a life necessity, and a *duty*. And that responsibility, the inalienable companion of free choice, stays where liquid-modern condition forced it: on the shoulders of the *individual*, now appointed the sole manager of 'life politics'.

Today's culture consists of *offerings*, not *norms*. As already noted by Pierre Bourdieu, culture lives by seduction, not normative regulation; PR, not policing; creating new needs/desires/wants, not coercion. This society of ours is a society of consumers, and just as the rest of the world as-seen-and-lived by consumers, culture turns into a warehouse of meant-for-consumption products—each vying for the shifting/drifting attention of prospective consumers in the hope to attract it and hold it for a bit longer than a fleeting moment. Abandoning stiff standards, indulging indiscrimination, serving all tastes while privileging none, encouraging fitfulness and 'flexibility' (politically correct name of spinelessness) and romanticizing unsteadiness and inconsistency is therefore the 'right' (the only reasonable?) strategy to follow; fastidiousness, raising brows, stiffening upper lips are not recommended. The TV reviewer/critic of a pattern-and-style setting daily praised the New Year's Eve 2007/8 broadcast for promising 'to provide an array of musical entertainment guaranteed to sate everyone's appetite'. 'The good thing' about it, he explained, 'is that its universal appeal means you can dip in and out of the show depending on your preferences'.[2] A commendable and indeed a seemly quality in a society in which networks replace structures, whereas the attachment/detachment game and an unending procession of connections and disconnections replace 'determining' and 'fixing'.

The current phase of the graduated transformation of the idea of 'culture' from its original Enlightenment-inspired form to its liquid-modern reincarnation is prompted and operated by the same forces that promote emancipation of the markets from the remaining constraints of non-economic nature —the social, political, and ethical constraints among them. In pursuing its own emancipation, the liquid-modern consumer-focused economy relies on the excess of offers, their accelerated ageing, and quick dissipation of their seductive power—which, by the way, makes it an economy of profligacy and waste. Since there is no knowing in advance which of the offers may prove tempting enough to stimulate consuming desire, the only way to find out leads through trials and costly errors. Continuous supply of new offers, and a constantly growing volume of goods on offer, are also necessary to keep circulation of goods rapid and the desire to replace them with 'new and improved' goods constantly refreshed—as well as to prevent the consumer dissatisfaction with individual products from condensing into general disaffection with consumerist mode of life as such.

Culture is turning now into one of the departments in the 'all you need and might dream off' department store in which the world inhabited by consumers has turned. Like in other departments of that store, the shelves are tightly packed with daily restocked commodities, while the counters are adorned with the commercials of latest offers destined to disappear soon together with the attractions they advertise. Commodities and commercials alike are calculated to arouse desires and trigger wishes (as George Steiner famously put it—'for maximum impact and instant obsolescence'). Their merchants and copywriters count on the wedding of the seductive power of offers with the ingrained 'oneupmanship' and 'getting an edge' urges of their prospective customers.

Liquid-modern culture, unlike the culture of the nation-building era, has no 'people' to 'cultivate'. It has instead the clients to seduce. And unlike its 'solid modern' predecessor, it no longer wishes to work itself, eventually but the sooner the better, out of job. Its job is now to render its own survival permanent—through temporalizing all aspects of life of its former wards, now reborn as its clients.

The solid-modern policy of dealing with difference, the policy of assimilation to the dominant culture and stripping the strangers of other strangehood, is no longer feasible, even if considered by some as desirable. But neither are the old strategies of resisting the interaction and merger of cultures likely to be effective, even if considered preferable for people fond of strict separation and isolation of 'communities of belonging' (more precisely, communities-of-belonging-by-birth).

'Belonging', as Jean-Claude Kaufmann suggests,[3] is today 'used primarily as a resource of the ego'. He warns against thinking of 'collectivities of belonging' as necessarily 'integrating communities'. They are better conceived of, he suggests, as a necessary accompaniment of the progress of individualization; we may say— as a series of stations or road inns marking the trajectory of the self-forming and self-reforming ego.

François de Singly rightly suggest[4] that in theorizing the present-day identities the metaphors of 'roots' and 'uprooting' (or, let me add, the related trope of 'disembedding'), all implying one-off nature of the individual's emancipation from the tutelage of the community of birth as well as the finality and irrevocability of the act, are better abandoned and replaced by the tropes of casting and drawing of anchors.

Indeed, unlike in the case of 'uprooting' and 'disembedding', there is nothing irrevocable, let alone ultimate, in drawing the anchor. If having been torn out of the soil in which they grew, roots are likely to desiccate and die out so that their (very unlikely) reviving will be verging on miraculous—anchors are drawn hoping to be safely cast again elsewhere; and they can be cast with similar ease at many different and distant ports of calling. Besides, the roots design and determine in advance the shape which the plants growing out of them will assume, while excluding the possibility of any other shape; but anchors are only auxiliary facilities of the mobile vessel that do not define the ship's qualities and resourcefulness. The time-stretches separating the casting of anchor from drawing it again are but episodes in the ship's trajectory. The choice of haven in which the anchor will be cast next is most probably determined by the kind of load which the ship is currently carrying; a haven good for one kind of cargo may be entirely inappropriate for another.

All in all, the metaphor of anchors captures what the metaphor of 'uprooting' misses or keeps silent about: the intertwining of *continuity* and *discontinuity* in the history of all or at least a growing number of contemporary identities. Just like ships anchoring successively or intermittently in various ports of call, so the selves in the 'communities of reference' to which they seek admission during their life-long search for recognition and confirmation have their credentials checked and approved at every successive stop; each 'community of reference' sets its own requirements for the kind of papers to be submitted. The ship's record and/or the captain's log are more often than not among the documents on which the approval depends, and with every next stop, the past (constantly swelled by the records of preceding stops) is re-examined and re-valued.

AN INSIGHT INTO POSSIBLE FUTURE

Just to make it somewhat clearer what the postulated re-shaping of our commonly used cognitive frames would need to involve and what obstacles it is likely to face on its way, let's have a closer look at the recent intellectual adventure of a group of researchers from the Zoological Society of London who went to Panama to invest-igate social life of local wasps. The group was equipped with the cutting-edge technology, which it used over 6000 hours to track and monitor the movements of 422 wasps coming from 33 nests.[5] What the researchers found out, has turned upside down their and ours centuries-old stereotypes of the social insect's habits.

Indeed, ever since the concept of 'social insects' (embracing bees, termites, ants and wasps) was coined and popularized, a firm and hardly ever questioned belief was shared by the learned zoologists and the lay public: that the 'sociability' of insects is confined to the nest to which they belong—the place in which they have been hatched and to which they return every day of their life, bringing the spoils of their foraging ventures to be shared with the rest of the hive's natives. The possibility that some working bees or wasps would cross the boundaries between nests, abandon the hive of *birth* and join another one, a hive of *choice*, was seen (if it was ever contemplated) as an incongruous idea. It was axiomatically assumed instead that the 'natives', the born and therefore 'legitimate' members of the nest, would promptly chase the maverick newcomers away and destroy them in case they refuse to run.

As all axioms, that belief was neither questioned nor tested. The thought of tracing the traffic between nests or hives did not occur either to ordinary folks or to the learned experts. For the scholars, the assumption that the socializing instincts are limited to the kith and kin, in other words to the community of birth and *therefore* of belonging, 'stood to reason'. For the ordinary folks, 'it made sense'. Admittedly, the technical means to answer the question of inter-nest migration (electronic tagging of individual wasps) were not available—but they were not sought either since the question as such was not considered worthy of being asked. Instead, a lot of research energy and funds were dedicated to the question how social insects spot a stranger in their midst: do they distinguish it by sight? By sound? By smell? By subtle nuances of conduct? The intriguing question was how the insects manage what we, the humans, with all our smart and sophisticated technology, only half succeed to achieve. That is, how they succeed in keeping the borders of 'community' watertight and to protect the separation of 'natives' from 'aliens'—that is, of 'us' from 'them'.

What passes for 'reason', as much as what is taken to make 'good sense', tends however to change over time. It changes together with the human condition and with the challenges it posits. It tends to be *praxeomorphic*. What is seen as 'standing to reason' or 'making sense' takes shape from the realities 'out there' seen through the prism of human practices—of what humans currently do, know how to do, are trained, groomed and inclined to be doing. Scholarly agendas are derivatives of mundane human practices. Problems encountered in daily human cohabitation decide the 'topical relevance' of issues and suggests the hypotheses which the research projects seek subsequently to confirm or disprove. If no effort is made to test the received popular wisdom, it is not as much for the lack of research tools, as for the fact that common sense of the time does not suggest that such a test is needed. The research escapade of the London Zoological Society team hints, if such a hint is needed, that this may not be a case any longer. Something happened to common human experience that cast doubt on the 'naturalness' and universality of the 'inborn' limitations to sociality...

Contrary to everything known (or rather believed to be known) for centuries, the London team found in Panama an impressive majority, 56% of 'working wasps', to change their nests in their life time; and not just move to other nests as temporary, unwelcome, discriminated against and marginalized visitors, sometimes actively persecuted but always suspected and resented—but as full and 'rightful' (one is almost tempted to say 'ID card carrying') members of the adoptive 'community', collecting food and like them feeding and grooming the native brood just like the 'native' workers did. The inevitable conclusion was that the nests they researched were *as a rule* 'mixed populations', inside which the native-born and the immigrant wasps lived and worked cheek-to-cheek and shoulder-to-shoulder—becoming, at least for the human outsiders, indistinguishable from each other except with the help of electronic tags...

What the news brought from Panama reveal is above anything else the asto- nishing reversal of perspective: beliefs that not so long ago were imagined to be reflections of the 'state of nature', have been revealed now, retrospectively, to have been but a projection upon the insects of the scholars' own human, all-too-human preoccupations and practices (though the kind of practices that are now dwindling and receding into past). Once the somewhat younger generation of scholars brought to the forest of Panama their own (and ours own) experience of the emergent life practices acquired and absorbed in the now cosmopolitan London, that 'multi- cultured' home of interlocked diasporas, they have duly 'discovered' the fluidity of membership and perpetual mixing of populations to be the *norm* also among social insects: and a norm apparently implemented in 'natural' ways, with no help of royal commissions, hastily introduced bills of law, high courts and asylum-seekers' camps... In this case, like in so many others, the praxeomorphic nature of human perception prompted them to find 'out there, in the world' what they have learned to do and are doing 'here, at home', and what we all carry in our heads or in our subconscious as an image of 'how things truly are'...

How could that be?!—asked the Londoners baffled by what they found, hardly believing at first the facts so different from what their teachers told them to expect. When they sought a convincing explanation of the wasps' of Panama bizarre ways and means, they found it expectedly in the warehouse of tested and familiar notions. Wishing to accommodate the unfamiliar in the familiar worldview, they decided that the newcomers allowed to settle 'could not be truly aliens'—strangers no doubt they were, but not as strange as the other, *genuine* strangers: 'they joined the nests of closely related wasps—cousins, maybe...' Such explanation put anxiety to rest: after all, the right of 'close relatives' to visit and to settle in the family home was always a birthright. But how do you know that the alien wasps were 'close relatives' of the native? Well, they must have been, mustn't they, otherwise the insiders would've forced them to leave or killed them on the spot—QED.

What the London researchers clearly forgot or failed to mention, is that it took a century or more of hard work, sometimes sword-brandishing and some other times brain-washing, to convince the Prussians, the Bavarians, Badenians, Würtenbergians or Saxons (just as it takes now to convince the 'Ossis' and 'Wessis' or Calabrians and Lombardians...) that they were all close relatives of each other, cousins or even brothers, descendants of the same ancient German stock animated by the same German spirit, and that for those reasons they should behave like close relatives do: be hospitable to each other and cooperate in protecting and increasing shared welfare... Or that on the way to the modern centralized nation-state and to the identification of nationhood with citizenship, the revolutionary France had to include the slogan of *fraternité* in its call addressed to all sorts of 'locals' now appointed *les citoyens*—to people who seldom looked (let alone moved) heretofore beyond the frontiers of Languedoc, Poitou, Limousin, Burgundy, Brittany, Guyenne or Franche-Comte... *Fraternité*, brotherhood: all Frenchmen are brothers, so please behave as brothers do, love each other, help each other, make the whole of France your common home, and the land of France your shared homeland... Or that since the time of French Revolution all movements bent on proselytizing, recruiting, expanding and integrating the populations of heretofore separate and mutually suspicious kingdoms and princedoms, have the habit of addressing their current and prospective converts as 'brothers and sisters'...

But to cut a long story short: the difference between 'cognitive maps' carried in their heads by the older generations of entomologists, and that acquired/adopted by the youngest, reflects the passage from the 'nation-building' stage in the history of modern states to the 'multicultural' phase in their history; more generally, from 'solid' modernity, bent on entrenching and fortifying the principle of territorial, exclusive and indivisible sovereignty, and on surrounding the sovereign territories with impermeable borders—to 'liquid' modernity, with its fuzzy and eminently permeable borderlines, the unstoppable (even if bewailed, resented and resisted) devaluation of spatial distances and the defensive capacity of the territory, and an intense human traffic across all and any frontiers.

Indeed, human traffic... It goes both ways, frontiers are crossed from both sides. Britain, for instance, is today a country of *immigration* (even if the successive home secretaries go out of their way to be seen as trying hard to erect new barriers and stem the influx of foreigners); but also, according to the latest calculations, almost million and a half born Britons are currently settled in Australia, almost a million in Spain, several hundred thousand in Nigeria, even a dozen in the North Korea. The same applies to France, Germany, Poland, Ireland, Italy, Spain; in one measure or another, it applies to any bordered-off territory of the planet except a few remaining totalitarian enclaves that still deploy the anachronistic Panopticon-style techniques designed more to hold the inmates (state subjects) *inside* the walls (state borders) than to keep the aliens *outside*.

Population of almost *every* country is nowadays a collection of diasporas. Population of almost every sizeable city is nowadays an aggregate of ethnic, religious, lifestyle enclaves in which the line dividing 'insiders' and 'outsiders' is a hotly contested issue; while the right to draw that line, to keep it intact and make it unassailable, is the prime stake in the skirmishes for influence and battles for recognition that follow. Most of the *states* have passed by now and left behind their nation-building stage and so are no longer interested in 'assimilating' the incoming strangers (that is, forcing them to shake off and forfeit their separate identities and to 'dissolve' in the uniform mass of 'the natives'); and so the settings of contemporary lives and the yarn of which life experience is woven are likely to remain protean, variegated and kaleidoscopic for a long time to come. For all that matters and all we know, they may keep as well changing forever.

We are all now, or fast become, like the wasps of Panama. But more exactly, it has been by chance the lot of the wasps of Panama to 'make history', as the first 'social entity' to which the emergent, precocious and waiting-to-be-recognized-and-endorsed cognitive frame was applied; a frame derived from our novel experience of increasingly (and probably permanently) variegated setting of human cohabitation, the fuzziness of the line separating the 'inside' from the 'outside', and the daily practice of mixing and elbow-rubbing with difference. What had been predicted more than two centuries ago by Immanuel Kant (that designing, elaborating and putting in operation rules of mutual hospitality must at some point become a necessity for the human species since we all inhabit the surface of a *spherical* planet) now turns into reality. Or it becomes rather the most seminal challenge of our time, one that calls for the most urgent and most thoroughly considered response.

The composition of the over two hundred 'sovereign units' on the political map of the planet is increasingly reminiscent of that of the thirty-three wasps' nests investigated by the research expedition of the London Zoological Society. When trying to make sense of the present state of our planetary human cohabitation, we could do worse than borrowing the models and the categories that the researchers in Panama were obliged to deploy in order to make sense of their findings. Indeed, none of the nests they explored had the means to keep their borders watertight, and each had to accept the perpetual exchange of its population. On the other hand, each seemed to manage quite well under the circumstances: to absorb the newcomers without friction and suffer no malfunction because of the departure of some older residents. Furthermore, there was nothing in sight remotely reminiscent of an 'insect centre' able to regulate the insect traffic—or, for that matter, anything else amenable to regulating. Each nest had to cope with the life-tasks more or less on its own, though the high rate of 'personnel turnover' probably assured that the know-how gained by any one nest could and did travel freely and contributed to the survival success of all other nests.

Moreover, London researchers seem, firstly, not to have found much evidence of inter-nest wars. Secondly, they found that the inter-nest flow of 'cadres' appeared to compensate for the locally produced excesses or deficits of nest populations. Thirdly, they realized that the coordination and indirect cooperation among social insects of Panama have been, it seems, sustained without either coercion or propaganda; without commanding officers and headquarters in sight; indeed, without *centre*... And whether we admit it or not, and whether we relish it or fear—we, the humans scattered among more than two hundred 'sovereign units' known under the name of 'the states', also manage for some time now to live *without a centre*—even if the absence of a clear, all-powerful, unquestionably authoritative and uncontested global centre is a constant temptations for the mighty and the arrogant to fill that void or at least to try to fill it.

'Centrality' of the 'centre' has been decomposed and the link between previously intimately connected and coordinated spheres of authority has been (perhaps irreparably) broken. Local condensations of economic, military, intellectual or artistic powers and influences are no longer (if they ever were) coinciding. Maps of the world on which colors of political entities mark their relative share and importance in—respectively—global industry, trade, investment, military power, scientific achievements or artistic creation, would not overlap. And to make such maps serviceable for any length of time, the paints we use would need be applied sparingly and easy to wash off, since the current rank of any land in the pecking order of influence and impact is by no means assured to last.

And so in our desperate effort to grasp the dynamics of planetary affairs, the old and hard dying habit of organizing the mental image of global power balance with the help of such conceptual tools as centre and periphery, hierarchy, superiority and inferiority, looks ever more as a handicap rather than, as before, an asset; as blinders rather than search lights. The tools developed and applied in the research of Panama wasps may well prove much more suitable for this task.

TEACHER-STUDENT RELATIONS IN THE LIQUID-MODERN SETTING

On the origins of one of his remarkable short stories, 'Averroes' Search', the great Argentinean writer Jorge Luis Borges said that in it he has tried "to narrate the process of failure", of "defeat"—like those of a theologian seeking the final proof of God's existence, an alchemist seeking philosophical stone, a technology buff seeking a perpetuum mobile or a mathematicians seeking the way to square the circle... But then he decided that "a more poetic case" would be one "of a man who sets himself a goal that is not forbidden to others, but is to him". That was the case of Averroes, the great Muslim philosopher, who set to translate Aristotle's *Poetics*, but "bounded within the circle of Islam, could never know the meaning of the words *tragedy* and *comedy*". Indeed, "without ever having suspected what theatre is", Averroes would have to fail when trying "to imagine what a play is".

As a topic for a wonderful story told by great writer, the case finally selected by Borges proves indeed "more poetic". But looked from the less inspired, mundane and humdrum sociological perspective, it also looks more prosaic. Only few intrepid souls try to construct a perpetuum mobile or find a philosophical stone; but trying in vain to understand what others have no difficulty in understanding is an experience we all know only too well from autopsy, and learn daily anew. Now, in the 21st century, more than our ancestors did in the times past… Look at just one example: communicating with your children if you are a parent. Or with your parents, if you still can…

Mutual incomprehension between generations, "old" and "young", and the suspicion that follows it, have a long history. One can easily trace symptoms of suspicion in quite ancient times. But inter-generational suspicion has become much more salient in the *modern* era, marked by the permanent, rapid and profound changes of life conditions. The radical acceleration of the pace of change characteristic of modern times allowed the fact of 'things changing' and 'being no longer as they used to be' to be noted in the course of a single human life: the fact that implied an association (or even a causal link) between the changes in human condition and the departure and arrival of generations.

Since the beginning of modernity and through its duration, age cohorts entering the world at different stages of continuous transformation tend to *differ* sharply in the evaluation of life conditions they *share*. Children as a rule enter a world drastically different from the one which their parents were trained and learned to take as a standard of 'normality'; and they will never visit that other, now vanished world of their parents' youth. What by some age-cohorts may be seen as 'natural', as 'the way things *are*', 'the way things are *normally done*' or '*ought* be done', can be viewed by other as an aberration: as a departure from the norm, bizarre and perhaps also illegitimate and unreasonable state of affairs, unfair and abominable. What to some age cohorts may seem a comfortable and cozy condition, allowing to deploy the learned and mastered skills and routines, might appear odd and off-putting to some others; whereas some people might feel like fish in the water in situations which made others feel ill at ease, baffled and at a loss.

The differences of perception have by now become so multidimensional that unlike in the pre-modern times the younger people no longer are cast by the older generations as 'miniature adults' or 'would be adults'—not as the 'beings-not-yet-fully-mature-but-bound-to-mature' ('mature into being like us'). The youngsters are not hoped or supposed to be 'on the way to becoming adult *like us*', but viewed as a rather *different* kind of people, bound to *remain* different 'from us' throughout their lives. The differences between 'us' (the older) and 'them' (the younger) no longer feel as temporary irritants destined to dissolve and evaporate as the youngsters (inevitably) wise up to realities of life.

In the result, the older and the younger age cohorts tend to eye each other with a mixture of miscomprehension and misapprehension. The older would fear that the newcomers to the world are about to spoil and destroy that cozy, comfortable, decent 'normality' which they, their elders, have laboriously build and preserved with loving care; the younger, on the contrary, would feel an acute urge to put right what the ageing veterans have botched and made a mess of. Both would be unsatisfied (or at least not-fully-satisfied) with the current state of affairs and the direction in which their world seems to be moving—and blame the other side for their discomfort. In two consecutive issues of a widely respected British weekly two jarringly different charges were made public: a columnist accused 'the young people' to be 'bovine, lazy-arsed, chlamydia stuffed and good for nothing', to which a reader angrily responded that the allegedly slothful and uncaring youngsters are in fact 'academically high-achieving' and 'concerned about the mess that adults have created'.[6] Here, as in uncountable other similar disagreements, the difference was clearly between *evaluations* and subjectively-coloured *viewpoints*. In cases like this, the resulting controversy can hardly be 'objectively' resolved.

Ann-Sophie, a 20-years old student of the Copenhagen Business School, said in response to the questions set by Flemming Wisler:[7] 'I don't want my life to control me too much. I don't want to sacrifice everything to my career...The most important thing is to be comfortable...Nobody wants to be stuck in the same job for long'. In other words: keep your options wide open. Don't swear loyalty of a 'till death do us part' kind—to anything or anybody. The world is full of wondrous, seductive and promising chances; it would be a folly to miss any of them by tying your feet and hands with irrevocable commitments...

No wonder that on the list of basic life skills which the young are prompted and eager to master, *surfing* towers high above the increasingly old-fashioned 'sounding' and 'fathoming'. As Katie Baldo, guidance counselor of the Cooperstown Middle School in the New York state[8] has noted, 'teens are missing some major social cues because they are too engrossed in their iPods, cell phones, or video games. I see it all the time in the halls when they can't voice a hello or make eye contact'. Making an eye contact and acknowledging the physical proximity of another human spells waste: dedication of precious and scarce time to 'going in depth'—a decision that would interrupt or pre-empt surfing of so many other inviting surfaces. In the life of continuous emergency, *virtual* relations beat easily the '*real* stuff'. The off-line world prompts young men and women to be constantly on the move; such pressures would be however to no avail were it not for the electronically based capacity of multiplying inter-individual encounters by making them brief, shallow and disposable. Virtual relations are equipped with 'delete' and 'spam' keys that protect against cumbersome (above all, time-consuming) consequences of in-depth interactions. One can't help recalling Chance (a character played by Peter Sellers in 1979 Hal Ashby's film *Being there*), who having emerged into the busy town street from his protracted *tête à tête* with the world-as-seen-on-TV, tries in vain to remove a discomforting bevy of nuns from his vision with the help of his hand-held pilot...

For the young, the main attraction of the virtual world derives from the absence of contradictions and cross-purposes that haunt the off-line life. Unlike its off-line alternative, the on-line world renders the infinite multiplication of contacts conceivable—both plausible and feasible. It does it through the *weakening* of bonds—in a stark opposition to its off-line counterpart, known to find its bearings in the continuous effort to *strengthen* the bonds by severely limiting the number of contacts while deepening each one of them. This is a genuine advantage to men and women whom a thought that a step taken might (just might) have been a mistake, and that it might (just might) be too late to cut the losses it caused would never stop tormenting. Hence the resentment towards everything 'long term'—be it planning of one's life, or commitments to other living beings evidently appealing to the young generation's values, a recent commercial announced the arrival of a new mascara that 'vows to stay pretty for 24 hours', and commented: 'Talk about a committed relationship. One stroke and these pretty lashes last through rain, sweat, humidity, tears. Yet the formula removes easily with warm water': 24 hours feels as already a 'committed relationship', but even such 'commitment' won't be an attractive choice if not for its traces being easy to remove...

Whatever choice will eventually be made, shall be reminiscent of Max Weber's, one of the founders of modern sociology, 'light cloak' which one could shake off one's shoulder at will and without notice, rather than of Max Weber's 'steel casing', offering effective and lasting protection against turbulence but also cramping the movements of the protected and severely tapering the space of free will. What matters most for the young is the retention of the ability to *re-shape* 'identity' and the 'network' whenever a need to reshape arrives or is suspected to have arrived. The ancestors' worry about *identification* is increasingly elbowed out by the worry of *re-identification*. Identities must be *disposable*; an unsatisfying or not-sufficiently-satisfying identity, or an identity betraying its advanced age, needs to be *easy to abandon*; perhaps bio-degradability would be the ideal attribute of the identity most strongly desired.

Interactive capacity of the internet is made to the measure of this new need. It is the quantity of connections rather than their quality that makes the difference between chances of success or failure. It helps to stay *au courant* of the latest talk of the town—the hits currently most listened to, the latest T-shirt designs, the most recent and most hotly talked about parties, festivals, celebrity events. Simultaneously, it helps updating the contents and redistributes the emphases in the portrayal of one's self; it also helps to efface promptly the traces of the past, now shamefully outdated contents and emphases. All in all, it greatly facilitates, prompts and even necessitates the perpetual labours of *re-invention*—to the extent unachievable in the off-line life. This is arguably one of the most important reasons for the time spent by the 'electronic generation' in the virtual universe: time steadily growing at the expense of the time lived in the 'real world'.

The referents of main concepts known to frame and map the *Lebenswelt*, the lived and lived-through, the personally experienced world of the young, are gradually, yet steadily transplanted from the off-line to the online world. Concepts like 'contacts', 'dates', 'meeting', 'communicating', 'community' or 'friendship'—all referring to inter-personal relations and social bonds—are most prominent among them. One of the foremost effects of the new location of referents is the perception of current social bonds and commitments as momentary snapshots in the on-going process of renegotiation, rather than as steady states bound to last indefinitely. But let me note that 'momentary snapshot' is not a wholly felicitous metaphor: though 'momentary', snapshots may still imply more durability than the electronically mediated bonds and commitments possess. The word 'snapshots' belongs to the vocabulary of photographic prints and photographic paper, which can accept but one image—whereas in the case of electronic ties *effacing* and *re*-writing or *over*-writing, inconceivable in the case of celluloid negatives and photographic papers, are most important and most resorted to options; indeed, the only indelible attribute of electronically-mediated ties…

But let's also remember that the bulk of the presently young generation never experienced real hardship, long and prospect-less economic depression and mass unemployment. They were born and grew in the world in which there could shelter under socially produced and serviced water-and wind-proof umbrella that seemed to be there forever to protect them against inclement whether, cold rains and freezing winds—and in a world in which every next morning promised a day sunnier than the last and more lavishly sprinkled with pleasant adventures. When I write these words, clouds gather however over that world. The happy, sanguine and full of promises condition, which the young came to believe to be the 'natural' state of the world, may not last much longer. An economic depression (threatening, as some observers insinuate, to be as deep if not deeper than the crisis experienced in their own youth by the parents' generation) may linger just after the next corner. So it is too early to decide how the ingrained worldviews and attitudes of the present-day young will eventually fit the world to come, and how that world would fit their ingrained expectations.

NOTES

[1] Jonathan Rutherford, *After Identity*, London: Laurence & Wishart 2007, pp. 59–60.

[2] See Philip French, 'A Hootenanny New Year to All', *The Observer Television 30 December 2007–5 January 2008*, p. 6.

[3] See Jean-Claude Kaufmann, *L'invention de soi: Une théorie d'identité*, Hachette 2004, p. 214.

[4] *Les uns avec les autres*, p. 108.

[5] As reported on 25 January 2007 by Richard Jones, in 'Why insects get such a buzz out of socializing', http://www.guardian.co.uk/g2/story/0,,1997821,00.htm/

[6] See *The Guardian Weekend* of 4 and 11 August 2007.

[7] See 'The Thoughtful', in *fo*, January 2008, p. 11.

[8] http://www.wxii12.com/health/16172076/detail.html

MICHAEL A. PETERS AND TINA A. C. BESLEY

12. THE NARRATIVE TURN AND THE POETICS OF RESISTANCE—TOWARD A NEW LANGUAGE FOR CRITICAL EDUCATIONAL STUDIES

Who someone is or was can only be said if we know his or her story, that is his or her biography.

> Hannah Arendt, *The Human Condition*, 1958, p. 5.

[M]an is in his actions and practice, as well as in his fictions, essentially a story-telling animal. He is not essentially, but becomes through his history, a teller of stories that aspire to truth. But the key question for men is not about their own authorship; I can only answer the question "What am I to do?" if I can answer the prior question "Of what story or stories do I find myself a part?"

> Alastair MacIntyre, *After Virtue*, 1981, p. 216.

INTRODUCTION[1]

In the landmark text *The Landscape of Qualitative Research*, Denzin and Lincoln (2003: 3) claim that qualitative research as a field of inquiry in its own right has traversed a complex historical territory defined in terms of seven historical moments which they define as: traditional (1900–1950); the modernist or golden age (1950–1970); blurred genres (1970–1986); the crisis of representation (1986–1990); the postmodern, a period of experimental and new ethnographies (1990–1995); postexperimental inquiry (1995–2000); and the future, moral discourse and the development of scared textualities (2000–). Denzin and Lincoln's (2003) history is, of course, also a *narrative* that charts an ideal and primitive chronology and tells a story of the development of a discipline and field of inquiry, that magically begins in 1990 and entertains seven stages of development, maturing epistemologically and ethically as a discipline. This staged narrative—a modernist history with a strong telos—is the basis for entertaining a story about the development of a discipline. It is curious then that the notion of narrative does not figure more centrally in the landscape they paint for narrative inquiry is contemporaneous with qualitative research, intimately involved with its various incantations and periods, probably just as old in terms of its modern developments and could be given a similar history in terms of its unfolding moments. This chapter provides a brief introduction to an understanding of the literary history of the narrative form and its adoption as the model for understanding (*verstehen*) and the philosophical basis for the Geisteswissenschaften that began with Dilthey and included some of the most innovative thinkers of the late twentieth century including Ricoeur, Foucault and the historian Haden White. It is argued

I. Gur-Ze'ev, The Possibility/Impossibility of a New Critical Language in Education, 261–274.
© *2010 Sense Publishers. All Rights Reserved.*

that following the discursive turn narrative and narratology (the study of narrative) provide a model for a new critical language in education. It is also argued that resistance often first registers in a form of poetics that expresses the emotions and feelings associated with exploitation and other forms of oppression. The chapter begins by discussion the poetics of early narrative forms before reviewing the role of narrative and narratology in the human sciences; next by reference to Lyotard it discusses the crisis of narratives in the postmodern condition, the notion of narrative identities and the 'narrated nation' before restating the general argument concerning the ways that narrative and the narrative turn provide a potential 'new critical language' for education. Education and pedagogy are fundamentally narratively-centered and narrative and its poetics provide a suitable model for analyzing and understanding the relation of education to themes of power and ideology.

THE POETICS OF EARLY NARRATIVE FORMS

The narrative form is perhaps the earliest genre to capture human experience, recorded orally and in written form as the Homeric epics, Orphic Hymns, lyrical Greek poetry and, later, fables and ballads which were fictional and poetical accounts of mythical and sometimes historical events and heroes. The epic, in particular, as a narrative genre of poetry that retells in a continuous narrative the life and works of a heroic or mythological person, is the basis of the Western canon in the form of the *Iliad, Odyssey* (with elements reaching back to 1500BC) and *Nibelungenlied* (a Middle High German epic poem written in the early 13th century and based on the legends of Siegfried and of the Burgundian kings). These epics constitute a narrativizing of experience, often read or performed musically, distinguished by its scale and style, and dealing with events and persons deemed to be historically real. They date from the 8th century; epic was an exhausted form by the 6th century until its Hellenistic revival. Before Herodotus' histories the epic served as a form of recorded historical experience and reconstruction for the tribe. The transmission, learning and performance of the epic (sometimes over several days) formed the basis of tribal 'education' that depicted the typical epic hero cycle that constituted a predictable cycle of events. Thus, narrative poetry as epic and allegory, poeticized heroes and events, and became the memory of an essential temporal experience— an original reconstruction of events and persons.

Both the *Iliad* and *Odyssey* had elements of tragedy that prefigured the great Greek dramas or *staged narratives* such as Sophocles' *Oedipus* that typify the golden age of Greek drama. The Greek tragedy was characterized by an absence of a narrator and signaled experimentation with multiple voices which are all equally authoritative. The tragedy as a narrative 5th century experimentation with modes of speech combined elements of epic, lyric, elegiac, and epinician poetry along with speech belonging to oracles, prayer, and lament. James Barrett (2002) in his Preface *Staged Narrative Poetics and the Messenger in Greek Tragedy* notes that

> This multiplicity of generic forms and voices thus conspicuously reproduces what occurs in other avenues of public discourse at Athens, perhaps most of all in the political arena, where debate among "equals" ... was a fundamental

premise of democratic systems as they evolved throughout the fifth century…
(http://www.ucpress.edu/books/pages/9601.html)

The narrative poem in the form of epic and folk ballad (dating from the 12th century; and later, the literary ballad of the 18th century), were early forms of the mythological, historical and folk tale, prefiguring the rise of the novel and other short prose forms, particularly, fairy tales, fables, biographies and autobiographies, short stories, fantasy, legend, mystery, trvelogues, and science fiction. The period 1200–1750 saw the rise of the novel and marked the beginning of a new form of fictional narrative described by the word in English, Spanish (*novela*) and Italian (*novella*). It was predated by the romantic fiction (*romans*) that developed in 12th century France and consisted in a series of adventures, such as the Arthurian legends, before what we know as the 'novelistic' work of Boccaccio, Chaucer, Machiavelli, and Cervantes. The origins of the English novel in the period 1600–1740 marked a new stage in narrative reflexivity and encouraged a new set of theorizations by the likes of Georg Lukacs, Gerard Genette, M. M. Bakhtin, and Roland Barthes, among others. The novel as a new literary form begun by Fielding, Richardson and Defoe in eighteenth century England and Furetière, Scarron and Lesage in France, indicated a new realism about life and placed new value on originality, freedom from traditionalism in literature and particularly the epic romance, and individualism (Watt, 1957). It is during this period (the 'long eighteenth century') that most of the major innovations in narrative technique take shape with fiction, in the early stages, involving the close imitation of true narratives and, at the end, competing with and contributing to the writing of historical narrative. The hard and fast distinction between fictional and historical narratives is, therefore, useful as a basis for intellectual discernment and not as a rigid separator. It is interesting to speculate that fictional and historical narrative forms long borrowed from one another before scholars first took this as a formal problem and then began experimenting with various combinations. Indeed, it is part of the argument of this paper that early forms of social science qualitative research, including introspection, took its inspiration historically from literary forms, although it is difficult to separate off historical from fictional narratives. The confession, the memoir, letters, the diary and fictional forms like the novel—along with the portrait and sculptural bust as its visual artistic counterpart—developed a set of rhetorical, authorial and reader conventions that led later to personal histories, to the biography and autobiography, and to life histories, all of which serialized the temporal form of experience as a systematic reflective form of re-search.

NARRATIVE, NARRATOLOGY AND THE HUMAN SCIENCES

In our culture, as Paul Ricoeur (1984, 1985, 1988) remarks in his landmark three volume study *Time and Narrative*, there are two main forms of narrative: narratives as 'fiction' that even if based in real events and characters, depart from reality as an exercise of imagination; and, historical narratives which while unable to do without composition seeks methodologically to attain a degree of objectivity as form of social inquiry. It is with Riceour that narrative attains its centrality to understanding the connections between narrativity, identity and time. Narrative is the discourse that frames the agent's experience and gives expression to the complex historical present that represents the agent's actions in a sequence and context and thus becomes a condition of temporal existence. It also is a mode for transforming historical time into human time understood as a public time in which generations and lives can be located and predecessors can be determined. Narrative also thus forms the basis for a narrative conception of identity, drawing actions into a 'plot' with a temporal span, emplotting actions and providing a story-like unity to give characters depth as persons who can initiate action in response to events, actions that have an ethical dimension in so far as they involve mutual recognition and responsiveness to others, and therefore can be morally evaluated.

Riceour's work on personal identity through narrative is path-breaking and it reminds us that it is only in the last fifty years that narrative has emerged as an autonomous object of inquiry and now has invaded ethnography, medicine, law, and psychoanalysis. Indeed, it has been argued that the humanities are to be distinguished by their narrative form of understanding. Marie-Laure Ryan in *The Routledge Encyclopedia of Narrative* emphasizes the fundamental significance of narrative by noting its descriptive uses:

> narrative is a fundamental way of organizing human experience and a tool for constructing models of reality (Herman ....); narrative allows human beings to come to terms with the temporality of their existence (Ricoeur....); narrative is a particular mode of thinking, the mode that relates to the concrete and particular as opposed to the abstract and general (Bruner...); narrative creates and transmits cultural traditions, and builds the values and beliefs that define cultural identities; narrative is a vehicle of dominant ideologies and an instrument of power (Foucault....); narrative is an instrument of self-creation; narrative is a repository of practical knowledge, especially in oral cultures ...; narrative is a mold in which we shape and preserve memories; narrative, in its fictional form, widens our mental universe beyond the actual and the familiar and provides a playfield for thought experiments (Schaeffer); narrative is an inexhaustible and varied source of education and entertainment; narrative is a mirror in which we discover what it means to be human.

http://lamar.colostate.edu/~pwryan/narrentry.htm (accessed 4 August, 2005)

This list is comprehensive and wide ranging in noting the uses of narrative in relation to philosophy, cognition, history, cultural studies, studies of power and 'ideology', anthropology, fiction and, even, education itself. Prima facie it sets up the case for considering narrative and the study of narrative 'a new critical language of education'. Strictly speaking, of course, narrative per se is not a 'new language,' even if by this term we mean a new critical vocabulary or perspective. It is a *genre* which is both pervasive and powerful across the gamut of human existence and endeavour running across disciplines and fields (and even sub-genres, like poetry and prose), but still nevertheless a genre.[2] Narratives not only take a variety of forms in spoken, written, kinesthetic, pictorial, and musical modes of representation but also can be incorporated within other language activities (e.g., a prayer), and can also incorporate other activities (e.g. an argument). Its pervasiveness and power makes it a suitable object of theoretical study in education, especially given that pedagogy itself and pedagogical styles are themselves narratively structured or styled; and narratology—the modern structural study of narrative—provides a ready set of theories, analytical tools and a critical vocabulary that lends itself to consideration as a 'new critical language of education.' Not only is it critical in the sense that it deals with questions of power, of ideology, of representation and signification, but also it provides a means of consistent analysis across a range of related fields that take on increasing importance in a media-saturated society—media studies, film theory and has strong application to digital communication per se.[3]

The beginning of modern genre studies under the influence of German Roman-ticism began with the recognition that genres altered their form over time, that they are indeed dynamic social categories that change and mutate, often establishing new forms by breaking literary conventions. In terms of the development of the study of narrative, its genesis and analytical refinement both theoretically and methodo-logically has been relatively recent, as Herman et al (2005) indicate:

> The 'narrative turn,' as it might be called, gained impetus from the develop-ment of structuralist theories of narrative in France in the mid to late 1960s. Tzvetan Todorov coined the term 'la narratologie' in 1969 to designate what he and other Francophone structuralists (e.g., Roland Barthes, Claude Bremond, Gérard Genette, and A.-J. Greimas) conceived of as a science of narrative modeled after the 'pilot-science' of Saussure's structural linguistics. Noting that narratives can be presented in a variety of formats and genres, structuralists such as Barthes argued explicitly for a cross-disciplinary approach to the analysis of stories—an approach in which stories can be viewed as support-ing a variety of cognitive and communicative activities, from spontaneous conversations and courtroom testimony to visual art, dance, and mythic and literary traditions.[4] http://people.cohums.ohio-state.edu/herman145/RENT.html (accesssed 7 March, 2006)

Certainly this now standard history of narratology that nods to the French struc-turalists and finds its beginnings in the movement of Russian formalism (see Peters, 1996, especially Chapter 1). David Darby (2001: 830) plots the genesis of narratology beginning with the 1966 publication of an issue of *Communications* containing a collection of essays by members of the Poétique group. He goes on to write:

> Along with Gérard Genette's more analytically comprehensive codification of narrative forms in his 1972 book Figures III, this work constitutes the immediate ancestry of the formalist tradition that established itself in North America around 1980 under the ambitiously scientific name of narratology. The catechism of narratology's more remote prehistory is equally well rehearsed, with its reverential acknowledgment of the contributions and influences of Russian Formalism, structuralist anthropology and linguistics, French struct-uralist literary theory, and so on.

Yet we have to be careful with standard histories and competing traditions also need recognition. Darby (2001) himself takes of 'a tale of two formalisms'

265

mentioning a German tradition initiated by the work of Eberhard Lämmert and Franz Stanzel (1984) dating from 1955 and issuing in a series of important texts. Also a more nuanced understanding of contemporary lines of development would recognize not only the Russian formalists but also the work of Georg Lukács (1885–1975) on the novel who adopted Marxist categories under the inspiration of Hegel (and under the spell of Dilthey, Simmel and Weber) to problematize the naturalism of the european novel and outline the historicization of aesthetic forms (see Lukács, 1962). In the same Hegelian vein we might also mention Bakhtin.

Bakhtin (1895–1975) and his circle (including Kagan, Medvedev, Voloshinov, among others) focused centrally on the question of signification in cultural life, maintaining linguistic production is dialogic and proposing in essence a philosophy of culture. Bakhtin theory of the novel in particular, strongly indebted to German idealism (Goethe, Schlegel) and the growing influence of Hegel thought on him, grants a new centrality to the novel and he traces its essence through history in a series of works including his book of the *Bildungsroman* and its significance to establishing a new realism. His theory of dialogue and *speech genres*—a form of oral utterance governed by recognizable conventions or 'codes' (e.g., greetings, interviews, committee meetings, conference speeches) is especially fertile ground for critical educational researchers (see Bakhtin, 1981; 1986).

Modern genre studies are strongly influenced by movements in North America and Australia (the Sydney school) which draw on the one hand on the 'new rhetoric' paradigm based large on the speech act theories of Austin and Searle and sociolinguistics of Michael Halliday (who introduced the synonymous term 'register'), on the other.[5]

This is not to argue that these development and theoretical threads are all of a piece or even can be woven into a fabric that encompasses its disparate elements but only that it provides *theoretical resources* for establishing a new critical language. We now focus on the question of power in relation to narrative as the *critical* ingredient as it surfaces in the work on Lyotard (1984), a feature of his work that has not been fully explored or worked through.

THE CRISIS OF NARRATIVE IN THE POSTMODERN CONDITION

In the postmodern condition, Jean-François Lyotard (1984) argues that grand narratives (or master narratives or meta-narratives) functioned in the past to legitimate institutional and ideological forms of knowledge and are no longer credible have now given way to little personal narratives (*petit récits*).

Lyotard (1984) in *The Postmodern Condition* champions Wittgenstein's language games as the basis of his analysis of the crisis of narratives. He emphasizes the pluralistic nature of language-games to advance an attack on the conception of universal reason and of the unity of both language and the subject. There is no one reason, only reasons, he argues, where no one form of reason takes precedence over others. The traumatic aspect of *The Postmodern Condition* here points to the tearing apart of old organic bodies that regulate thinking. Where Habermas and Critical Theory emphasizes the burfication of reason into its instrumental (positivistic) and moral-practical forms, Lyotard (following Wittgenstein) and Foucault emphasize the (postmodern) multiplicity and proliferation of forms of reason, defined by the rules of particular discourses or language-games. Each of the various types of utterance—denotative, prescriptive, performative etc.—comprises a language-game, with its own body of rules. The rules are irreducible and there exists incommensurability among different games. Lyotard makes three observations concerning language games. First, he argues in true Wittgensteinian fashion that the rules do not have a bedrock justification, nor do they carry with them their own legitimation. Where Wittgenstein might say they are constituted in practice, Lyotard claims they are the object of a contract, explicit or not, between players which gives rise to an "agonistics" of language. Second, "if there are no rules, there is no game"; and, third, "every utterance should be thought of as a 'move' in the game" (Lyotard, 1984: 10). Indeed, the social bond is comprised of such moves.

This is the basis of Lyotard's "innovation" for he emphasizes a notion of language-games which is based upon the idea of struggle and conflict. In one deft stroke Lyotard politicizes Wittgenstein's conception of language. Two principles underlie Lyotard's adopted method as a whole: "To speak is to fight, in the sense of playing, and speech acts fall within the domain of a general agonistics" (Lyotard, 1984: 10). As Jameson explains in his Foreword, utterances are not conceived of either as a process of transmission of information or messages, or a network of signs, or even in terms of a semiotics as a signifying system: rather they are seen as an agonistics of language— "an unstable exchange between communicational adversaries" (p. xi). This elevates the conflictual view of language as a model for understanding the nature of the social bond: "each of us lives at the intersection of many of these [language games]. However, we do not necessarily establish stable language combinations, and the properties of the ones we do establish are not necessarily communicable" (Lyotard, 1984: xxiv). Against both the functionalist view (Talcott Parsons) which represents society as a function whole and the Marxist view which represents society as a duality based on the principle of class struggle, Lyotard advances a "postmodern" conception of the social bond based squarely upon the notion of language games. Each one of us is located at "nodal points" in circuits of communication or at "posts" through which messages pass. The social is thus "atomized" into flexible networks of language games. Yet "No one, not even the least privileged among us, is ever entirely powerless over the messages that traverse and position him at the post of sender, addressee, or referent" (Lyotard, 1984: 21).[6]

It is not our intention to provide a full analysis of Lyotard on narrative but rather to excavate and make obvious his political reading and also how it aided the shift away from grand narratives to *petit récits* and paved the way for narratives of race, class and gender and 'narratives of identity' that characterizes cultural studies and post-colonial studies. There is now many studies which use the apparatus of narrative in educational studies to carry out qualitative research, most of which do not reflect on the nature of narrative or its methodological or theoretical perspectives.[7] We want to focus on one relatively recent application of narrative that has great promise for educational discourses concerning multiculturalism, ethnicity and nationalism (and, not quite so obviously, also internationalization and globalization).

NARRATIVE IDENTITIES: NARRATING THE NATION

Benedict Anderson (1983) in *Imagined Communities* commented that 'since WWII every successful revolution has defined itself in *national* terms….and, in doing so, grounded itself firmly in a territory and social space inherited from a pre-Revolutionary past' (p. 2). Even Marxist movements have tended to define themselves in this way. While the end of nationalism has been pronounced and prophesized, especially in discourses of globalization, it is clear that the end is not remotely in sight. When we turn to Marxist historiography many agree that Marx conspicuously failed to offer a viable account of nationalism. Anderson's starting point and his aim in *Imagined Communities* is to argue that nationalism and, as he says, 'nation-ness' is a 'cultural artifact of a particular kind' (p. 4). Having reviewed theories of nationalism (their objective historical modernity, their formal universality as a socio-cultural concept in the sense of everyone having a 'nationality', and the 'political' power of nationalism versus their philosophical incoherence), Anderson introduces his own anthropology definition of the nation: 'it is an imagined political community-and imagined as inherently limited and sovereign' (p. 6). This definition then counter poses Gellner's formulation of the nation as 'invention' and fabrication' to emphasize 'imagining' and 'creation'; and the upshot is that 'communities are to be distinguished… by the style in which they are imagined' (p. 6). As he argues,

1) The nation is *imagined* because the members never know their fellow-members. In a real sense nationalism invents the nation.

2) The nation is imagined as *limited* because it has finite territorial boundaries.

3) The nation is imagined as sovereign because this is an age of post-Enlightenment and Revolution, i.e., an age of freedom of individuals.

4) It is imagined as a community because the nation is conceived as'deep, horizontal-comradeship.'

Anderson's now well-known and path-breaking analysis is to maintain that nationalism has to be understood not in relation to self-consciously held political ideologies, but the large cultural systems that preceded it. The origins of national consciousness as a new form of awareness took root in the explosive, interaction between a system of production and productive relations (capitalism), a technology of communications (print), and the fatality of human linguistic diversity.

What is explicit in Anderson's analysis is the emphasis he places on narrative and the novel and on the development of print culture.[8] Of course, it also offers a compelling account of why nationalism became such a potent force during the nineteenth century and come to dominate literary and cultural studies leading to a more considered interpretation of national literary histories and their power to project a narrative image of the nation.

There is now so much literature that deals with the meta-question of how cultures provide the resources to narrative craft and construct the image of the nation and the way in which these functioned to arrive at and prescribe western modernity as a new moral order that became filtered, canonized and curricularized to serve as the meta-narrative for the cultural system as a whole. The educational implications here are so obvious as to bear little direct comment. Rather than analyze them here we wish to briefly mention two other landmark texts that have advance the discussion by theorizing the links between nation, narration and imagination.

Clearly, Anderson's analysis was fundamental, though in different ways to both Homi Bhabha's (1990) *Nation and Narration* (and his subsequent *The Location of Culture*) and Charles Taylor's (2004) *Modern Social Imaginaries*. Bhabha begins his account with an acknowledgement of Anderson:

> Nations, like narratives, lose their origins in the myths of time and only fully realize their horizons in the mind's eye. Such an image of the nation—or narration—might seem impossibly romantic and excessively metaphorical, but it is from those traditions of political thought and literary language that the nation emerges as a powerful historical idea in the west.

Benedict Anderson, who's *Imagined Communities* significantly paved the way for this book, expresses the nation's ambivalent emergence with great clarity:

> The century of the Enlightenment, of rationalist secularism, brought with it its own modern darkness.... [Few] things were (are) suited to this end better than the idea of nation. If nation states are widely considered to be 'new' and 'historical', the nation states to which they give political expression always loom out of an immemorial past and... glide into a limitless future. What I am proposing is that Nationalism has to be understood, by aligning it not with self-consciously held political ideologies, but with large cultural systems that preceded it, out of which—as well as against which—it came into being.

> The nation's 'corning into being' as a system of cultural signification, as the representation of social life rather than the discipline of social polity, emphasizes this instability of knowledge.

Bhabha (1990) goes on to talk about "implicit relationship between narration at the center of nations (stories of national origins, myths of founding fathers, genealogies of heroes) and narratives that seek to name the land and organize the space in which people live." He notes that alongside "'the cult of nationality in the european nineteenth century,' it was especially the novel as a composite but clearly bordered work of art that was crucial in defining the nation as an 'imagined community.'"... Nations, then, are imaginary constructs that depend for their existence on an apparatus of cultural fictions in which imaginative literature plays a decisive role." His work, together with a host of leading scholars including those strongly influenced by Foucault and Derrida such as Edward Said also led to explorations of what we might call "place, race and space" within the framing rhyming couplet nation and narration—not only the narration of the nation-state but also its colonizing and post-colonizing narratives (see, for example, Said 1979; Chatterjee, 1993).

Charles Taylor's (2004) *Modern Social Imaginaries* also sits within this framing of narrative even though his canvas is most ostensibly 'philosophical' and aimed at western modernity more generally. Taylor's sources for narrative are extensive beginning with his own theory of narrative identity and his assessment of narratives as a central form of self-interpretation that he has written about in a series of works beginning with the anti-naturalism of 'Interpretation and the sciences of man' (1971/1985) and developed in *Sources of the Self* (1989) and *Ethics of Authenticity* (1991). Where Riceour develops his analysis directly through the structure of narration as emplotment, Taylor tends to eschew technical questions of narrativity to locate narrative on the side of 'character' directly at the ethical level focusing on the 'thematic unity of life' where narratives serve as the basis for self-interpretation and 'strong evaluations' (which refer to the 'worth' of different desires, feelings, actions or modes of life). For Taylor narratives make explicit our conceptions of the good life and our lives as wholes. Selfhood can be captured in a 'moral topography of self' (Taylor, 1988) where narrative helps us to navigate such moral spaces in relation to the pursuit of goods but also to change our moral maps.[9]

In *Modern Social Imaginaries* Taylor acknowledges his debt to Anderson and to Jameson and Habermas to propose a grand historical narrative on 'modernity' which he describes as a

> [h]istorically unprecedented amalgam of new practices and institutional forms (science, technology, industrial production urbanization), of new ways of living (individualism, secularization, Instrumental Rationality); and of new forms of malaise (alienation, meaninglessness, a sense of impending social dissolution).

The social imaginary that Taylor sketches is one based on a network of beliefs that emerged the late seventeenth and early eighteenth centuries: a belief in individuals which rejects premodern Aristotelian views of the subject in relation to the society and anchors an understanding of political institutions in terms of rights of individuals as free agents.

Political society is organized to defend individual rights and individuals are understood primarily as autonomous bearers of rights, free to exercise their agency in shaping both their own lives and the social order where rights, freedom, and mutual benefit are to be secured to all individuals equally. This is not the place to engage with Taylor's conception but only to emphasize the link between narrative self-understandings, imagination, the role of the narrative arts in shaping our political life.

NARRATIVE AS A NEW CRITICAL LANGUAGE IN EDUCATION

We have tried to demonstrate that narrative and the narrative turn provides a potential 'new critical language' for education by focusing on its media, its theorization and its methodologies. What renders it particularly appropriate for a critical educational studies is the emphasis on education and pedagogy through narrative—education as fundamentally narratively-centered, both as a study and as an activity—and the way in which narrative forms a bridge between the humanities and the social sciences where there is room enough for an understanding of all kinds of narrative, including its poetics, and its relations to themes of power and ideology.[10] In common with the turn to subjectivity that took place with the displacement of structuralism as a metaparadigm for the social science, poststructuralism has begun to retheorize narratology to understand hermeneutically and analyze the narrative construction of identity both individual and collective (as in the 'neighborhood', the 'school', the 'classroom', the 'nation', 'culture'). New narrative approaches are emerging including autobiography, autoethnography, biography, personal narrative, life history, oral history, memoir, and literary journalism which combine various literary and social scientific forms and question the authority of social scientists to tell other people's stories (Casey, 1995; Polkinghorne, 1997; Smith, 1997; Alvermann, 2002). Educational scholars apprising themselves of narrative as a new critical language and basis for research need to understand the genealogy of narrative as a basis for understanding the recent interest in the subject.

Herman, Jahn and Ryan (2005) documents the shift to focus on the narratives of ordinary people where it has come to be seen as 'as a basic human strategy for coming to terms with time, process, and change—a strategy that contrasts with, but is in no way inferior to, 'scientific' modes of explanation that characterize phenomena as mere instances of general covering laws.' She proceeds to mention aspects of a new interdisciplinary and international form of research that includes, for example, the book series *Frontiers of Narrative*, (university of Nebraska Press), *Studies in Narrative*, (John Benjamins), and *Theory and Interpretation of Narrative*, (Ohio State University Press) as well as the following journals: *Image (&) Narrative, Journal of Narrative Theory, Language and Literature, Narrative, Narrative Inquiry, New Literary History, Poetics, Poetics Today, Style.*

The study of narrative has come a long way since Tzvetan Todorov invented the term 'narratology' in 1969 and Roland Barthes and Claude Bremond emancipated narrative from literature and from fiction to initiate its understanding as a semiotic phenomenon that transcends disciplines and forms thought, subjectivity and culture in their relation to the representation of time, agency and history. Narrative also has a strong connection to politics and what we have called the 'poetics of resistance' that first registers freedom narratives and revolutionary subjectivities including the 'poetry of witness' as in Holocaust poetry, the 'reclaiming of history', the 'decolonization of the mind' and the 'rewriting of culture'.

NOTES

1 A version of this paper was delivered at 'Toward a New Critical Language in Education a symposium organized by Ilan Gur-Ze'ev at PESGB, Oxford University, 2006.
2 Genre is originally a French word meaning 'kind, 'sort', 'style' (OED) derived from the Latin *'genus'* and Greek *'genos'*, referring to grammatical identity as masculine or feminine in the French language the use of which became extended in literary studies to indicate setting, mood and format applied also to art forms in music, painting, sculpture, as well as literature. The concept was strongly adopted by both Mikhail Bakhtin and Georg Lukas during the 1920s and has origins in Aristotle's *The Poetics* where he talks of the mode of imitation in poetry through narration thus distinguishing epic, lyric and drama (and comedy and tragedy).
3 See, for instance, Leen Breure's 'The Development of the Genre Concept' at http://www.cs.uu.nl/people/leen/GenreDev/GenreDevelopment.htm#The%20Origin%20of%20Genre.

4   They editors also usefully note: "International in scope—encompassing Continental europe, Scandinavia, Israel, the united Kingdom, North and South America, and Asian, African, and other nations—this activity [of interdisciplinary study of narrative] has also spawned interdisciplinary book series (e.g., *Frontiers of Narrative*, published by the university of Nebraska Press, *Studies in Narrative*, published by John Benjamins, and *Theory and Interpretation of Narrative*, published by Ohio State University Press). Scholarship in the field has given rise, as well, to a number of internationally recognized journals in which articles about narrative figure importantly (e.g., *Image (&) Narrative*, *Journal of Narrative Theory, Language and Literature, Narrative, Narrative Inquiry, New Literary History, Poetics, Poetics Today, Style*)."
5   Breure (2001) provides the following description of genre at the turn of the century in terms of: *pattern of communication* (interaction between writer and reader, speaker and audience); *situatedness* (genre as communicative action); *dynamism* (not static forms); *content, form and function*.
6   For a fuller account of Lyotard see Peters (1995), in relation to emancipation and cultural difference see Peters (2000), in relation to Marxism and the knowledge economy see Peters (2004), and in relation to the question of nihilism, from which the preceding two paragraphs are drawn see Peters (2006).
7   See, for example, as well as standard references such as Bruner (1987), Polkinghorne (1988), Witherell & Noddings (1991), Hopkins (1994): the bibliography from narrative psychology at http://web. lemoyne.edu/~hevern/nr-educ.html; the annotated bibliography on 'narrative inquiry and text' at http:// www.positivepractices.com/RuralEducation/NarrativeInquiryandText20.html; Gudmundsdottir, S. (1995) The Narrative Nature of Pedagogical Content Knowledge In Mcewan, H. and egan, K., *Narrative in Teaching, Learning and Research.*, 24-38. New York: Teachers College. http://www.ipt. unit.no/~jsg/ sigrun/publikasjoner/PCKNARR.html Rossiter, Marsha (2003) 'Narrative and Stories in Adult Teaching and Learning,' *ERIC Digest*, http://www.ericdigests.org/2003-4/adult-teaching.html; Heather J. Richmond (2002) 'Learners' Lives: A Narrative Analysis' *The Qualitative Report*, volume 7, Number 3 September, at http://www.nova.edu/ssss/QR/QR7-3/richmond.html.
8   Note Anderson's remark: 'there is a special kind of contemporaneous community which language alone suggests—above all in the form of poetry and songs. Take national anthems, for example, sung on national holidays. No matter how banal the words and mediocre the tunes, there is in this singing an experience of simultaneity. At precisely such moments, people wholly unknown to each other utterthe same verses to the same melody. The image: unisonance' (p. 145).
9   As Arto Laitinen argues in 'Charles Taylor and Paul Ricoeur on Self-Interpretations and Narrative Identity' : 'narrativity has five functions in Charles Taylor's theory. Narratives are (i) an optional medium for articulating some of our implicit self-interpretations and strong evaluations. Narratives alone enable us to (ii) care about our lives as wholes and to (iii) interpret our movements in a moral space. Further, narrative thinking provides a way of providing concordance to (iv) diachronous and (v) synchronous dissonances in our strong evaluations' at http://www.jyu.fi/yhtfil/fil/armala/texts/ 2002a.pdf.
10 Tina Besley taught an advanced seminar at the University of Illinois based on narrative which was divided into three sections: writing the self; writing cultures; and, writing research which is the basis for our reconceptualization of narrative in relation to the theme of this conference.

REFERENCES

Arendt, H. (1958) *The human condition*. Chicago, University of Chicago Press.
Alvermann, D. E. (2002). Narrative approaches. In M. Kamil, P. Mosenthal, P. D. Pearson, & R. Barr, (Eds.), Methods of literacy research: The methodology chapters from the handbook of reading research (Vol. 3, pp. 47–64). Mahwah, NJ: Erlbaum.
Anderson, B. (1991) [1983]. *Imagined communities: Reflections on the origin and spread of nationalism* (2nd ed.). London: Verso.
Bakhtin, M. (1981). *The dialogic imagination: Four essays* (M. Holquist, Ed., C. Emerson & M. Holquist, Trans.). University of Texas Press.

Bakhtin, M. (1986). *Speech genres and other late essays* (V. W. McGee, Trans., C. Emerson & M. Holquist, Eds.). University of Texas.

Barrett, J. (2002). *Staged narrative: Poetics and the messenger in Greek tragedy.* Berkeley, CA: University of California Press.

Bhabha, H. (Ed.). (1990). *Nation and narration.* London: Routledge.

Bruner, J. (1986). *Actual minds, possible worlds.* Cambridge: Harvard University Press.

Bruner, J. (1987). Life as narrative. *Social Research, 54*(1), 11–32.

Casey, K. (1995). The new narrative research in education. *Review of Research in Education, 21,* 211–253.

Chatterjee, p. (1993). *The nation and its fragments: Colonial and postcolonial histories.* Princeton, NJ: Princeton University Press.

Darby, D. (2001). Form and context: An essay in the history of narratology. *Poetics Today, 22*(4), 829–852. Retrieved March 7, 2006, from http://muse.jhu.edu/journals/poetics_today/v022/22.4darby.html

Denzin, N. K., & Lincoln, Y. S. (Eds.). (2004). *The landscape of qualitative research: theories and issues.* Thousand Oaks, CA: Sage.

Foucault, M. (1978). *The history of sexuality* (R. Hurley, Trans.). New York: Random House.

Herman, D. (2002). *Story logic: Problems and possibilities of narrative.* Lincoln, NE: University of Nebraska Press.

Herman, D., Jahn, M., & Ryan, M. L. (Eds.). (2005). *The Routledge encyclopedia of narrative theory.* London: Routledge. An excerpt of 'Introduction & Rationale' available at http://people.cohums.ohio-state.edu/herman145/RENT.html

Hopkins, R. L. (1994). *Narrative schooling: Experiential learning and the transformation of American education.* New York: Teachers College Press.

Lukács, G. (1962). *The theory of the novel. A historico-philosophical essay on the forms of great epic literature* (A. Bostock, Trans.). Merlin Press.

Lyotard, J. F. (1984[1979]). The postmodern condition: A report on knowledge (G. Bennington & B. Massumi, Trans.). Minneapolis, MN: University of Minnesota Press.

MacIntyre, A. (1981) After Virtue: A Study in Moral Theory. Notre Dame, University of Notre Dame Press.

Peters, M. A. (Ed.). (1995). Education and the postmodern condition (Foreword by Jean-François Lyotard). Westport, CT & London: Bergin & Garvey. Paperback edition, 1997.

Peters, M. A. (2000). Emancipation, education and philosophies of history: Jean-François Lyotard and cultural difference. In P. Pradeep & P. Standish (Eds.), *Lyotard: Just education* (pp. 23–35). London: Routledge.

Peters, M. A. (2004). Lyotard, marxism and education: The Problem of knowledge capitalism. In J. Marshall (Ed.), *Poststructuralism and education* (pp. 43–56). Dordrecht: Kluwer.

Peters, M. A. (2006). Lyotard, Nihilism and education. *Studies in Philosophy and Education,* forthcoming.

Polkinghorne, D. (1988). *Narrative knowing and the human sciences.* Albany, NY: State University of New York Press.

Polkinghorne, D. E. (1997). Reporting qualitative research as practice. In W. G. Tierney & Y. S. Lincoln (Eds.), *Representation and the text: Re-framing the narrative voice* (pp. 3–21). Albany, NY: State University of New York Press.

Ricoeur, P. (1984, 1985, 1988). *Time and narrative* (Vol. 3, K. McLaughlin & D. Pellauer, Trans.). Chicago: University of Chicago Press.

Rousseau, J.-J. (1953). *Confessions* (J. M. Cohen, Trans.). New York: Penguin Classics.

Said, E. (1979). *Orientalism.* New York: Vintage.

Schaeffer, J.-M. (1999). *Pourquoi la fiction?* Paris: Seuil.

Smith, J. K. (1997). The stories educational researchers tell about themselves. *Educational Researcher, 26*(5), 4–11.

Stanzel, F. (1984). *A theory of narrative* (C. Goedsche, Trans.). Cambridge: Cambridge University Press.

Taylor, C. (1985) [1971]. Interpretation and the sciences of man. In *Philosophy and the human sciences* (Chapter 10). Philosophical papers (Vol. 2, pp. 15–57). Cambridge: Cambridge University Press, 1985. (*The Review of Metaphysics, 25,* 1, 1971)

Taylor, C. (1988) 'The moral topography of self'. In S. B Messer, L. Sass, R. L. Woolfork (Eds.) *Hermeneutics and psychological theory* (pp. 298–320). New Brunswick, NJ: Rutgers University Press.

Taylor, C. (1989). *Sources of the self*. Cambridge: Cambridge University Press.

Taylor, C. (1991). *Ethics of authenticity*. Cambridge, MA: Harvard University Press.

Taylor, C. (2004). *Modern social imaginaries*. Durham, SC: Duke University Press.

Watt, I. (1957). *The rise of the novel: Studies in Defoe, Richardson and Fielding*. Berkeley, CA: University of California Press.

White, H. (1981). The value of Narrativity in the Representation of History. In W. J. T. Mitchell (Ed.), *On narrative*. Chicago: University of Chicago Press.

Witherell, C., & Noddings, N. (Eds.). (1991). *Stories lives tell: Narrative and dialogue in education*. New York: Teacher's College Press.

JAN MASSCHELEIN

13. THE IDEA OF CRITICAL E-DUCATIONAL RESEARCH—E-DUCATING THE GAZE AND INVITING TO GO WALKING

We walk, not in order to arrive at a promised land, but because walking itself is the revolution

(Subcommandante Marcos)

[For Foucault] to think always meant to think about the limits of a situation. But it also meant to see

(Deleuze)

INTRODUCTION

Thinking about educating the gaze as a proposal for critical educational research we are easily coming to the idea that it should be about the way in which we could help students to arrive at a more open, better, more critical, emancipated or liberated view. We should help them to open their eyes i.e. to become (more) *conscious* about what is 'really' happening in the world and to become aware of the way their gaze is itself bound to a perspective and a particular position (e.g. a gendered, western, … position). We should look for another more adequate, critical perspective which in fact takes also into account the perspective of others. Educating the gaze, then, would be about becoming conscious and becoming aware, it would be about getting at a better understanding.

In this line one could say that *modern* education has been concerned to (re-)present the world in a 'critical' way. The questions about how we (re)present our world to newcomers—something which involves selection, choice, justification and judgment concerning what is worthwhile to be transmitted or to be given to the new generation—are apparently still the one's we have to ask today. One could state indeed that (modern) education is about the world 'once more', the world explained and (re)presented in a 'right order' in response to a reigning confusion. However, in the last century this idea of (re)presenting the world has been strongly complicated by the increasing awareness of the implied problem: How is the representation related to what it represents? The Belgian painter René Magritte offered maybe one of the strongest and most famous images of this problem. He made a painting of a pipe with the caption 'Ceci n'est pas une pipe'. This is not a pipe, but a painted pipe and one cannot decide whether the painted pipe represents the 'real' pipe. This means that when we let children 'see the world', we don't show them the world, but what we see as the world, and what we consider to be important, valuable and

I. Gur-Ze'ev, The Possibility/Impossibility of a New Critical Language in Education, 275–291.
© 2010 Sense Publishers. All Rights Reserved.

useful about it. Therefore, educators do not only have to think about the 'right' representation but should be aware that they are not showing the world, but representing it: 'ceci n'est pas le monde'. And then the question seems to appear again: What do we have to represent and how to represent it?

However, my hypothesis is that the problem of critical education in our (postmodern) times is changing. Not in the first place because we moved from education to learning and to 'learning to learn' as the main aim (thereby seemingly solving the problem of 'what to learn'), but because our condition has changed (related partly to the omni-presence of images). Indeed, in contrast to the very common idea in educational theory and philosophy that one of our main endeavors in education should be to raise a critical awareness with students that every 'world' is but a view on the world, just one vision, one perspective, each and every person having her own perspective so that we have a plurality of perspectives and that everything is an interpretation (a reading)—'ceci n'est pas le monde', but a vision on the world, 'a window', 'a frame'—I would maintain that today this awareness is very widely spread and indeed has become the basic stance. And I would maintain that it confronts education with a problem which is, so to say, opposite to the modern one. Not: How to represent the world and how to make students aware that this representation is not the 'real world'? This awareness is present enough. But: How to turn the world into something 'real', how to make the world 'present', to give again the real and discard the shields or mirrors that seem to have locked us up increasingly into self-reflections and interpretations, into endless returns upon 'standpoints', 'perspectives' and 'opinions'. This problem, I think, is neither an epistemological one (about true representations) nor a normative one (regarding what to value, what to select, how to judge), but is precisely about the (dis-)stance i.e. the way we relate to the world, it is about the right distance which opens up an existential space. This problem does not concern images, symbols or signs (related to stories and interpretations), but concerns the gaze and the ethos of looking itself. "… to give again the real to realize it is genuinely to look at it" (Nancy, 2001, p. 34) It is not about the problematic of representation. Indeed this problematic has been debated in all (im)possible ways (its relation to the real and to illusion, its subjectivity or objectivity, its historical, social, cultural determinations, etc.). It is rather about a look at the world as a regard for the world and its truth. This movement is not a movement beyond what is visible, but a movement towards its work or power, not only to make it known, but to make it 'real' or 'present'. The given must be given again in order to become really given: it must be received and recreated to be what it is. To give again the given is to 'realize' it, to make it impress, to insist on its present and presence. Which is not a mere matter of vision or the symbolical representation of a cognitive or cultural content (or a story or a frame). The present is not what appears as such and before us (as an object of knowledge or an issue of interpretation), but what is experienced when we are *attentive* or when we are 'present in the present'.

The proposal for critical education and critical educational research that I will sketch is related to this idea of being 'present in the present'. It is related to an understanding of education not in the sense of 'educare' (teaching) but of 'e-ducere' as leading out, reaching out. E-ducating the gaze is not about getting at a liberated or critical view, but about liberating or displacing our view. It is not about becoming *conscious* or *aware*, but about becoming attentive, about paying *attention*. Consciousness is the state of mind of a subject that has or constitutes an object(ive) and aims at (critical) knowledge. Attention is the state of mind in which the subject and the object are into play. It is a state of mind which opens up to the world in a way that it can present itself to me (that I can 'come' to see) and that I can be transformed. Attention opens up an atopical (and not an utopical) space: a space of possible self transformation and self-displacement i.e. a space of practical freedom. In my idea e-ducating the gaze requires a critical research practice which effects a practical change of ourselves and of the present we live in, not an escape from it (towards a vision of a better state from where we could judge the present). Such a critical research practice is not depending on method, but relying on discipline; it does not require a rich methodology, but asks for a poor pedagogy i.e. for practices which allow to expose ourselves, practices which bring us on the street, so to say, displace us. I want to elaborate what such a critical e-ducational research practice is about starting from an example: the example of walking (and copying). Consequently e-ducating the gaze could be about an invitation to go walking.

Of course, walking invokes implicitly the idea of travel ('voyage') and the idea of travel "conjures up the image of an innovative mind that explores new ways of looking at things or which opens up new horizons. That mind is a critical one to the extent that its moving beyond a given set of preconceptions or values also undermines those assumptions" (Van Den Abbeele 1992, xiii). One could thus easily recognize a very familiar and classical topos of western thought—and of western educational thought (how could we forget for example Rousseau's invitation of Emile)—when critical educational research is connected to an invitation to go walking.[1] However, I think it is worthwhile to reconsider, once more, this invitation—which is nothing less or more then an invitation to engage in e-ducative practices i.e. practices which bring us out, help us out (e-ducere)—trying to see whether we could recover a bit of its radical critical power.[2] In the following pages I don't want to develop an argument or to define and justify the project and program of a critical educational practice or theory, but I want to explore a bit the terrain of critique and critical research, not in order to mark and demarcate or circumscribe it, nor to measure it and to install beacons. There is nothing here to be demarcated. It is just an attempt to pave a way, to cut through a way and to see where it could lead hoping this can make the invitation (which is also a presentation) to go walking attractive in the litteral sense i.e. makes us moving. Or to put it differently, I am not interested here in the examination of the epistemological or methodological claims of critical educational research and their validity, but precisely in an exploration of its e-ducational aspects i.e. the way in which it involves transformations of the relations to ourselves, to others and to the world.

I will explore this idea along a comment on two quotations. One is a small remark by Foucault, the second a short but beautiful passage by Walter Benjamin. I start with the last one.

WALKING: LEARNING THE POWER THE ROAD COMMANDS

In 'One Way Street' Benjamin writes:

"The power of a country road is different when one is walking along it from when one is flying over it by airplane. In the same way, the power of a text is different when it is read from when it is copied out. The airplane passenger sees only how the road pushes through the landscape, how it unfolds according to the same laws as the terrain surrounding it. Only he who walks the road on foot learns the power it commands, and of how, from the very scenery that for the flier is only the unfurled plain, it calls forth distances, belvederes, clearings, prospects at each of its turns like a commander deploying soldiers at a front. Only the copied text thus commands the soul of him who is occupied with it, whereas the mere reader never discovers the new aspects of his inner self that are opened by the text, that road cut through the interior jungle forever closing behind it: because the reader follows the movement of his mind in the free flight of daydreaming, whereas the copier submits it to command" (Walter Benjamin, 1927b/1979, p. 51).[3]

I want to read this passage as an extremely precise indication of what critical educational research could be about,[4] revealing also why revolution lies in the walking and is not depending on the Promised Land it would allow to enter, as Sub-commandante Marcos tells us. Benjamin indicates clearly what this walking has to do with seeing, with opening one's eyes, with getting a new view or look (in German: 'Ansicht'), which is not about arriving at a certain perspective or vision, but about displacing one's gaze so that 'we' are '(t)here' and that the '(t)here' can present itself to 'us' in its evidence and command 'us'. Displacing one's gaze so that one can see differently, can see what is visible (since the "distances, belvederes, clearings, prospects" are not hidden, are no reality beyond) *and* be transformed (that is why we have to put the 'we' and 'us' between brackets). That is exactly what walking is about. In this sense we could say that walking is a displacement of the gaze that enables experience, experience which is not just a passive undergoing (being commanded or cutted, one could say) but also a kind of cutting the road through.

The issue about walking is not that it would offer us a better view (and we could replace view also by reading or interpretation) or a more true view, a more adequate, more complete view, that it would allow us to attain a different perspective, to transgress the limits of one's perspective and getting to a new perspective by confronting it with other perspectives, but that it allows us a view beyond every perspective, a view that transforms us (and therefore is experience) while its evidence commands us. It allows for a view beyond every perspective since a perspective is bound to a standpoint in the sense of a subjective position, which is exactly also the position of a subject in relation to an object or objective. Walking is about putting this position at stake; it is about ex-position, being out-of-position.

The first thing which Benjamin makes clear is that there is a difference between walking a road and flying over it so that we get a certain view of it. A difference which is similar to the difference between the copying of text by hand and the reading of a text—one could say the interpretation or understanding of a text.

The difference being that it works differently, that its power is different. Walking the street or the road makes that the road imposes itself upon us with a certain authority, that it commands our gaze and presents us with a striking reality in its differences, with an evidence that commands. It should be clear that Benjamin is not saying that the gaze we have on the road is different according to a different viewpoint or perspective (the viewpoint down in the street, or up in the air), which would be the idea that we should not only take the perspective from above, but also from below, in fact, taking into account different viewpoints and perspectives, every viewpoint or standpoint offering its own perspective (and maybe implying that the one from below is better, more human, true, or whatever). So it is not about different visions or views or perspectives (which would be offered by a different standpoint or *subjective position—indeed the position of a subject*), although the difference between walking and flying has an effect on the view, on what we see. And Benjamin is not referring to the difference between a view from nowhere, or an objective viewpoint on the one hand and a subjective, lived and engaged viewpoint or perspective on the other hand. No, he is referring to a difference in the activity itself, a difference between walking and flying, copying and reading, being different ways of relating to the world, *relating to the present, to what is present.* This difference is a difference in power, in the effect of that activity on ourselves and on what is revealed, what appears. The one who flies, Benjamin says, only sees, but the one who walks the road "learns of the power it commands" ("erfährt von ihrer Herrschaft") i.e. *experiences* how some given comes to appear, is commanded to appear, how it presents itself to us, *becomes evident* and "commands our soul", inscribes itself, "cuts through". (Of course there is no doubt that one, but as I believe only to a certain extent, could walk like one is flying).

Flying over a road (and reading it) makes this road to be part of a plane surface, a plain which appears from the perspective of the flyer revealing it to be situated against a horizon. The road appears as an object which obeys the same laws as all the other objects appearing before a subject against a horizon in and on that plane i.e. as objects which can be explained, defined, ordered, identified, codified (in relation to the subject) just like the whole reality (or present) around it. Objects behave according to laws (or reasons) imposed or supposed by the subject (that is its intentionality). The road then is subjugated under the laws of the perspective of the flyer and has no power on the flyer ("it is only the unfurled plain", "nur die aufgerollte Ebene"), it cannot touch him or her, or better it cannot cut through him or her. He or she gets a certain knowledge, knowledge as an interpretation, as a reading as a way of grasping reality, as offering an objectivity for a subjectivity. An object(ivity) is something which appears from a certain perspective, which is read from a position related to an intention of a subject (a grasping of an object against the horizon which is an obeying to ones I: "the movement of his mind in the free flight of daydreaming").

Walking then is not about changing the perspective or getting to a certain perspective (that for example of the promised land), but, like copying by hand, it is about a totally different relation to the present, it is about physically delivering oneself, embarking to follow an arbitrary line i.e. the road and the text, as "a road cut through" the intentions, and ex-posing oneself to its command. This command opens a new look ("neue Ansichten") upon ourselves, but also "calls forth distances, belvederes, clearings, prospects" i.e. it presents us with an evidence beyond visions and perspectives.

Benjamin is thus suggesting that walking, just like copying, liberates our gaze, *opens our eyes*—which is itself of course also a very old and familiar topos in educational and philosophical thought—displaces our gaze, which is not the same as offering us a (new) perspective or vision or reading.[5] It is not a kind of consciousness raising or the revelation of a truth beyond what we (are used to) see. To open our eyes is to get a look at what is evident; it is, as I would like to say, about being or getting attentive or to expose oneself. Walking the road, like copying the text, are ways of exploring and relating to the present which are in the first place e-ducative. They are forms of critical educational research. They constitute a kind of research practice (a kind of mapping as I would say) which is about being attentive, that is open to the world, exposed (to the text) so that it can present itself to us in a way which commands us. This command is not the command of a tribunal, it is not the imposition of a law or principle (which we would be supposed to recognize or impose ourselves), but the manifestation ("learning") of a power which makes us move and thus paves the way. It is not directing us, not leading us to the Promised Land, but pushing us. It does not tells us where to go, but pushes us to move from where (who) we are. The copying of the text is then not just a representation but a cutting through of the road. It is a paradoxical activity: to be commanded by something which is not yet given, but on the way to be given, something which is exactly presenting itself, along the way that one is following. Copying a text as concrete activity is reproducing or recasting the text which is not representing it (it is not its representation or its reading), but presenting it. In the same line we could see walking a road as a mapping of the present which does not give us an overview (and therefore mapping is not about representing a totality) but cuts the road through (paves the way). Walking is at the same time going a way and paving a way which *commands the soul*. Walking one could say is a physical activity of displacing one's gaze (that is as displacement a leaving of one's position, an ex-position) along an arbitrary line, a traject that at the same time exists (and is recaptured) and is paved for new, the way for new looks (so not leading somewhere given before i.e. without a destination or orientation).

Walking is to gain a critical distance, which is not to get at a meta-standpoint, but at a distance in which one's 'soul' is dissolved from inside. It is a practice "to risk one's very formation as a subject" (Butler 2001)[6] through a different relation towards the present—that is also why Foucault considers critique to be 'an issue of attitude' ("une question d'attitude"). In this attitude towards the present that present is not judged (interpreted) i.e. not brought before a tribunal, for example the tribunal of reason or interpreted from a certain perspective; it is not evaluated against a vision of the promised land, but we expose our selves to that present, implying a suspension of judgment and a physical embarkment or delivering which can dissolve us and, thus, liberate us, liberate our gaze.

In this idea critical e-ducational research is neither aiming primarily at insight and knowledge, nor at increasing awareness or raising consciousness, but it is a research which opens up an existential space, a concrete space of practical freedom i.e. a space of possible self-transformation[7] which entails a liberation (i.e. an e-ducation) of the gaze and in that sense enlightens. In this research knowledge is not meant for understanding (to improve our understanding), but for cutting i.e. concrete bodily inscription and transformation of who we are and how we live.[8] This research is therefore characterized by a concern for the present and for ourselves in relation to that present, a concern to be present in the present which is another way of indicating that the first concern of this research is to be attentive i.e. precisely to be present in the present. To be attentive is a limit-attitude which is not directed at limiting the present (by judging), but at exposing one's limits and at exposing at the limits. Walking, then, is a critical practice involving a limit-attitude that transforms us, not by making us conscious, but by making us pay attention. This brings us to a little remark of Foucault concerning the practice of critique.

But let me first make a brief note.

I cannot elaborate it here, but the kind of walking the road and/as copying the text as suggested by Benjamin could be related to the ideas of mapping and cartography which have been popular for some time and are now again attracting increasing attention.[9] What is interesting in this 'cartographic turn', says Bosteels, is neither the increased interest in maps appearing in literary and artistic works, nor the tiresome use of the term 'mapping' as a mere synonym for 'describing', but rather the explicit interpretation of cartography as an exemplary cultural activity with a seemingly intrinsinc critical and often Utopian—I would prefer to say atopian—potential. I think that approaching the idea of mapping starting from the activity of walking and of copying and *not of reading* (or flying over) could be very helpful to get beyond a rather sterile discussion on the issue of representation (and its validity) related to this idea of mapping as critical activity. Mapping is then not about reading and ordering or re-presenting, but about simultaneously recapturing and inventing, about copying and "cutting a road through". It should be clear that what I suggest here is referring to a totally different idea of mapping then the one which is apparently getting popular also in educational contexts. A good example is a study by Lambeir which presents itself explicitly as a mapping which should help to educate our gaze.[10] It is a study which attempts to map 'cyberspace' as being our present. Lambeir states that wherever people face a confused and perhaps dangerous landscape, something is needed to enable them to make their way through it. Today we seem "to lack a map that guides people through the foreign world … through the jungle.. of the ongoing technological revolution" (Lambeir 2004, p. 1). The map would offer conceptual schemes or sets of ideas that frame the problems. In fact mapping then is first of all to make an overview of the landscape, to mark it and demarcate it, to take care that one is not getting lost and not disturbed. And making maps, as he says, implies to remain with two feet on the ground—which is obviously not the movement of walking—avoiding ways which would lead us nowhere. I cannot develop it in detail here, but, as I noted, looking at mapping from what Benjamin says about copying and walking, would offer a totally different idea of mapping. Starting from that idea the proposal of Lambeir would make us into bad viewers and in fact it would make us blind for the present and immune for transformations. It would make us inattentive.

TO GO WALKING AND TO BECOME ATTENTIVE

In a very short reply to a letter which appeared in the French Newsletter 'Le Matin' regarding his attitude towards Iran Michel Foucault approved Maurice Blanchots remark "que la critique commence par l'attention, la présence et la générosité [that critique starts with attention, presence and generosity]" (Foucault, 1979a, p. 762, my translation). I would like to see this remark, like the one by Benjamin, as a very fruit-ful and promising indication to elaborate a different idea of critical educational research which would consist in the invitation to be attentive, present and generous.[11] As I suggested already such a critical research practice could be described, in a particular way, as the *art* of bringing in touch, of opening the eyes—liberating the gaze and mobilizing the gaze i.e. the art of presenting, of making present.[12] That means that it is not the art of representing (implying the questions of selection, judgment, false or true, see my introduction), of raising consciousness, of critical reflection, of transferring or mediating knowledge or insights or overviews. What is at stake is leaving behind the sovereignty of the judgment (of bringing the present before a court and its laws, of relating it to a vision, of projecting it against a horizon) and regaining, one could say, the sovereignty of the gaze which gives something to see, makes it, so to say, evident. Critical research is then about e-ducating the gaze as becoming attentive.

Critical e-ducational research is not about making conscious or *being conscious* (Freire 1972/1986), but about attention and *being attentive*. Attention instead of consciousness. To be attentive is to open oneself to the world. Attention is exactly to be present in the present, to be there—in the present—in such a way that the present can present itself to me (that it becomes visible, that it can come to me and I can come to see) and that I am exposed to it in such a way that I can be changed, that I can be touched or 'cut' or contaminated, that my gaze can be liberated (through the 'command' of that present). As such attention makes experience possible.[13]

Being attentive is the opposite of being absent (in English attention also relates to 'attend', with is a different connotations of care—attend a patient, the lamps, a customer, of being at—attend the church, of being present, of listening to, of going along). Being absent means that we are not there, that we are captivated by the horizon of expectations, projections, perspectives, visions, views, images, dreams which are ours, i.e. our intentionality—which constitutes us as a subject in relation to an object or to an objective (or orientation); we could say that the state of mind of someone who has an orientation, an object or an objective is the state of mind of a subject (a subject of knowledge). To be attentive is not to be captivated by an intention or a project or a vision or perspective or imagination (which always give us an object and catches or imprisons the present in a re-presentation), attention does not offers me a vision or a perspective, it opens for what presents itself as evidence. Attention is lack of intention. Attention entails the suspension of judgment and implies a kind of waiting—critique as the art of waiting (Foucault)—in French attention relates to 'attendre' = to wait (see also: Artières 2000).

Being attentive, according to Simone Weil, means that the will to subject under a regime of truth is neutralized and that the supplementary energy with which the subject (of knowledge) projects itself in the objects is exhausted. This particular kind of attention implies and enables a being-present which brings the subject into play and defers the expectation for a benefit and in that sense it is generous.[14]

THE NEED FOR A POOR PEDAGOGY (AS AN ART OF WAITING, PRESENTING AND MOBILIZING)

Critical educational research i.e. research that opens the eyes, that puts us at a distance of ourselves, that opens the space of a possible transformation, is not depending on the subjugation to a method or the abeyance to rules and procedures which would be shared by a certain community (for example the scientific community, or the community of rational beings, the community of those who subjugate to the claims of communicative reason). It does not require a rich methodology, but asks for a poor pedagogy, a pedagogy which helps us to be attentive, which offers us the *exercises of an ethos or attitude*, not the rules of a profession, the codes of an institution, the laws of a kingdom, the stories and dreams of a "mind in the free flight of day-dreaming" (Benjamin). And therefore sending an invitation to go walking is not the same as requiring to submit under some laws or rules—for example of a method functioning as a tribunal or as guarantee to get to valid answers; or, in the words of Habermas: the conditions of communicative reason or the laws of dialogue.

Critical educational research requires a poor pedagogy, a poor art: the art of waiting and of presenting. Such a poor art is in a certain sense blind (she has no destination, no end, is not going anywhere, not concerned with the beyond, has no sight on a promised land and is not concerned with it), she is deaf (she hears no interpellation, is not obeying 'laws') and speechless (she has nothing to teach, no teachings to give). She offers no possibility of identification (the subject position—the positions of the teacher and the student—is, so to say, empty), no comfort.

A poor pedagogy is inviting to go outside into the world (not into the parks, homes and kingdoms), to expose oneself i.e. to put oneself in an uncomfortable, weak 'position' and offering means and support to do so. I think that she offers means for experience (instead of explanations, interpretations, justifications, representations, stories, criteria, etc.), means to become attentive. These are poor means, means which are insufficient, defective, which lack meaning, which lack signification, which are not referring to a goal or an end, pure means, tracks leading nowhere, which means which can lead everywhere: as a 'passe-partout'. As Bataille writes: " … les moyens pauvres (les plus pauvres) ont seuls la vertu d'opérer la rupture (les moyens riches on trop de sens, s'interposent entre nous et l'inconnu, comme des objets recherchés pour eux-mêmes)." (Bataille 1954, p. 29)

A poor pedagogy offers means which can make us attentive, which eliminate or suspend the will to submit oneself to a regime of truth[15] or to submit oneself to an advantage or a profit. A poor pedagogy does not promise profits. There is nothing to win (no return), no lessons to be learned. However, such a pedagogy is generous: she gives time and space, the time and space of experience.

A poor pedagogy is not putting under surveillance, she is not monitoring, she is not guarding over a kingdom (the kingdom of science, of rationality, of morality, etc.), she does not impose entrance conditions, but she invites to go and walk the roads, to go into the world, to copy the text that is to expose oneself. Walking the roads, the streets, means literally to leave the comfort of the home to go into the world. The world is the place which belongs to no-one, which has no entrance gate which has to be put under surveillance. To go into the world it suffices to make an effort (to go walking, copying). What is needed is the will to move and to exhaust the energy of projection and appropriation (which time and again establishes its own order), what is needed is a concrete effort as a kind of disciplining of the body and the mind which is not normalizing, but in a sense weakens our position. Walking and copying are such physical disciplining activities. Walking and copying are the names for al kinds of e-ducative practices which allow for experience and exposition. They imply giving up the comfort of a position (of an orientation, of a good intention, the comfort of the awareness, the explanation or the stories).[16]

A poor pedagogy is a pedagogy which says: "look, I won't let your attention become distracted, look! Instead of waiting for thrills and a denouement, for stories and explanations, Look!". It impresses the gaze by offering trajects, like arbitrary lines (roads, the lines of the text). It offers cuts, incisions as lines that mobilize the gaze, take the gaze away, attract it, take it along.[17] But the line does not define the gaze and does not offer a perspective. This pedagogy creates no scene, depicts no horizon, offers no tradition, offers no representation, it draws a line as cutting an opening, which is attraction for a look (a gaze). This line is a traction of the gaze all along its movement, while it is also defining a side of the space as the side of the gaze, its framing and carrying distance, its focus and adjustment. But this line is no scene, no theater (it does not display scenes of a theater, is in itself no story or narrative and demonstrates nothing, is not suggesting an explanation or an interpretation or a reading of the world—it is not the flightline of Benjamin's flyer, but the road), it is a line which makes a cut, through which pictures can offer themselves, a 'passe-partout'. So the cutting is no representation or no reflection. And what is revealed, then, what appears along the line, is not a defigurated, chaotic world, which would need the right viewpoint (or an overview) or explanation, the right vision. Walking along the line is not getting lost in Plato's cave where what we see would attest to a different world. No, the line is an opening cut in the world onto this very world. So the walking (the movement) does not need a destination or orientation which would give it its (true) meaning, whereby the ideal of course would be the arrival (even if we would know that we will never arrive). What the line offers is not a distorted, incomprehensible, false or chaotic reflection of the world, it does not offer a vision on the world, but it opens up to the world. Walking along that line is walking without a program, without an end but with a burden, a charge: what is there to see and to hear?

A poor pedagogy offers means that helps us to get in the position of the vulnerable, the uncomfortable position, the exposition. As soon as one leaves this exposition, the gaze changes and we get objects (and objectives) appearing to subjects, we get knowledge instead of experience. (I don't doubt the importance of knowledge but I state that critical educational research is not about knowledge, or better it is about knowledge which is not about understanding, but about cutting, about a possible self transformation—see above). A poor pedagogy offers means for getting out of position, so that the soul can be commanded by the road, also the road paved by the text at the moment that I copy the text. Copying like mapping is following a traject which is not directed by leading ideas or by (hypo)theses of the copier (as in the case of reading as interpretation).

This pedagogy presents the world, offers it 'evidence'. "Evidence always comprises a blind spot within its very obviousness: in this way it leans on the eye. The 'blind spot' does not deprive the eye of its sight: on the contrary, it makes an opening for a gaze and it presses upon it to look." (Nancy 2001, p. 12) It is this pressure which the pedagogy exerts: it presses. And the blind spot could be seen as the (arbitrary) line—the road cut through, the text as a road—which opens for a gaze. A poor pedagogy spells out a need to look and to make use of one's eyes: the evidence and the certainty of a gaze which is mobilized, a gaze as regard for the world and its truth (ibid. p. 14).

Pedagogy as eye-opener as mobilizer and animator of the look, making it vigilant and attentive for a reality that impresses. This pedagogy is not offering a mirror, a reflection or representation. It is not about vision or sight (insight, imaginary vision, etc), but about looking: opening the seeing to something real, which imposes itself as evidence.— "not what is evident in what is simply given (plainly or empirically, …), but what is evident in what shows up when one does take a look …[which] is quite far from a vision that is merely sighting (that looks in order merely "to see"): what is evident imposes itself as the setting up of a look ("elle s'impose comme la mise en puissance d'un regard"). If this look regards that upon which it casts itself and cares for it, it will have taken care of the real: of that which resists, precisely, being absorbed in any vision (visions of the world, representations, imaginations)" (ibid. p. 18). Pedagogy, thus, as art of looking made possible and of experience made possible implies a movement and mobilization in the sense of 'to bring out…' (e-ducere): an education in looking at the world: "a look taken by the hand and led away on a journey that is not an initiation, that does not drive to any secret, but that amounts to making the gaze move, stirring it up, or even shaking it up, in order to make it carry further, closer, more accurately …. Motion is … presence insofar as it is truly present, that is to say coming forward, introducing itself, offered, available, a site for waiting and thinking, presence itself becoming a passage toward or inside presence" (ibid. p. 26, 30) And presence is not a matter of vision: it offers itself in encounters, worries or concerns. So it follows that the questions which go along with walking a road (Where do you come from? What are you doing? What do you think about…?) make up a way of looking, questions which are not intrusive, but show a 'regard' for the other.

A poor pedagogy does offer exercises as the art of sharpening our attention, stretching our gaze toward the real and its truth. Which is not the truth about the real, but the truth that comes out of the real—the truth lies not in a thesis or representation, but in the experience. It is to give again the real (which is not simply given) to 'realize' it (see Benjamin) i.e. to look at it and to regard it.

The energy of the movement is "the energy of a mobilized, activated or animated look: that is to say the power of *regard* (égard) with respect to what presents itself to a look. In French *regard* (look) and *égard* (regard) are more or less the same word: *re-gard* indicates a propitious distance for an intensified guard (*garde*), for looking after (*prise en garde*) (it is a Germanic root, wardon/warten, that yields all this words). Guarding calls for watching and waiting, for observing, for tending attentively and overseeing. We look after what is ahead and after the way it presents itself: we let it present itself" .... "looking is regarding and consequently respecting The word respect also has to do with regard (and look) (respicere): it watches for..., turned toward..., guided by attention, by observance or consideration. A rightful look is respectful of the real that it beholds, that is to say it is attentive and openly attending to the very power of the real and its absolute exteriority: looking will not tap this power but will allow it to communicate itself or will communicate with it itself. In the end, looking just amounts to thinking the real, to test oneself with regard to a meaning one is not mastering" (ibid.38)

A pedagogy which would open the eyes is not a pedagogy which would offer the true view on the present (thereby always already devaluating that present and judging upon it), which would introduce in what is really going on and what there is really to see. It is not a pedagogy which would imply a reversal of the gaze (from the dark cave to the bright sun, from the messy world to the order of reason, etc.) and the teaching of a (more) true, or human or just view (a world view) or vision. It is not offering a representation or a vision (and therefore it offers no possibility of identification) which brings the present in an order (see mapping as ordering). To open the eyes is not to develop or elaborate a vision (an intuitive, an ideative, or fantasmatic vision). To offer representations, visions, interpretations is a way to capture the gaze, to discipline it in the sense of normalize it. A Critical Pedagogy does not capture the gaze, but requires it, mobilizes it, animates it, makes it going-along so that the gaze is not imprisoned but can be seduced and taken away by what is evident. And the evidence is not what is simply given, but what *comes* to appear when the gaze cares for the present instead of bringing it before a tribunal.

To walk along a road implies a possible transformation ("the command of the soul"), the 'subject' of that walk is the subject of experience (which is not the subject of knowledge or consciousness) and therefore is in a certain way no subject (that has an object and an orientation). To say it differently: the subjects of experience and the subjects of attention i.e. the subjects of critical educational research are particular kinds of subjects, it are subjects that are in between, under the way, without orientation, without object(ive). These subjects do not subjugate to the tribunal of (qualitative, quantitative) scientific research, or to tribunal of communicative reason, or the requirements of dialogue, but are under the command of the present that is coming. And we know from Benjamin that the walker like the copier is not listening to the "the movement of his mind in the free flight of daydreaming" (that is what the reader is doing, the one who understands and interprets: listening to the commands of his 'I' i.e. the commands which make him a subject and let appear what he's reading as objects against his horizon—or tradition). In this sense the gaze is also liberated of the 'I' and not subjective or private although it is certainly personal (and attached to the body), involving us, involving "our soul". And that is precisely what is at stake in critical educational research as the opening of an existential space, a space for practical freedom: our soul.

Note: An invitation to go walking is an invitation to share an (limit) experience. Now, of course, referring to experience is a tricky business (see a more detailed discussion in Masschelein 2006). In her paper 'The evidence of Experience' Joan Scott criticized in a clear way the assumption that experience would offer an evidence in which something would become visible (what has hitherto been hidden like by "documenting the lives of those omitted or overlooked in accounts of the past" p. 776). So, we have to be careful here when we refer to 'evidence' and certainly to 'evidence of experience': "When experience is taken as the origin of knowledge, the vision of the individual subject (the person who had the experience or the historian who recounts it) becomes the bedrock of evidence on which explanation is built. Questions about the constructed nature of experience, about how subjects are constituted as different in the first place, about how one's vision is structured— about language (or discourse) and history—are left aside ....To put it another way, the evidence of experience, whether conceived through a metaphor of visibility or in any other way that takes meaning as transparent, reproduces rather than contests given ideological systems—those that assume that the facts of history speak for themselves and those that rest on notions of natural or established opposition between, say, sexual practices and social conventions...the project of making experience visible precludes critical examination of the workings of the ideological system itself, its categories of representation ...., its premises about what these categories mean and how they operate, and of its notions of subjects, origin, and cause. ...". In fact, inspired by Foucault, we should acknowledge that 'experience' is produced. "It is not individuals who have experience, but subjects who are constituted through experience. Experience in this definition then becomes not the origin of our explanation, not the authoritative (because seen or felt) evidence that grounds what is known, but rather that which we week to explain, that about which knowledge is produced. To think about experience in this way is to historicize it as well as to historicize the identities it produces" (ibid. p. 779–780). "Experience is not a word we can do without, although, given its usage to essentialize identity and reify the subject, it is tempting to abandon it altogether. But experience is so much part of everyday language, so imbricated in our narratives that it seems futile to argue for its expulsion. It serves as a way of talking about what happened, of establishing difference and similarity, of claiming knowledge that is 'unassailable'. Given the ubiquity of the term, it seems to me more useful to work with it, to analyze its operations and to redefine its meaning. This entails focusing on processes of identity production, insisting in the discursive nature of 'experience' and on the politics of its construction. Experience is at once always already an interpretation and something that needs to be interpreted". (ibid. p. 797)

As will have become clear, hopefully, the way in which I use 'experience' and 'evidence' here, equally inspired by Foucault (and Nancy) is displacing these terms in an other register, an existential one and not an epistemological or methodological one. It is not about addressing a scientific community, but about sending an invitation to everybody i.e. to nobody in particular.[18]

NOTES

[1] Referring to Gauny, Jacque Rancíere once noted that one of the essential budget costs of the emancipated individual was the cost of shoes, since: "lémancipé est un homme qui marche sans cesse, circulé et converse, pait circuler du sens et communique le mouvement de l'émancipation" (Rancíere, J. [1998] *Aux Bords du Politique.* Paris: La Fabrique, 70).

[2] During the last years I travelled with post-graduate students in a course on 'world-forming education' ("éducation mondiale") for 10 to 14 days to post-conflict cities (Sarajevo, Belgrade, Tirana, Bucharest, Kinshasa) and non-tourist megapoles in China (Shenzhen, Chongqing). Students were asked to walk day and night along arbitrary lines drawn on city maps. Lines starting and leading nowhere particularly, lines without plan, crossing at random neighborhoods, buildings, areas. Everyday, during long talks, I asked each of them very simple questions: What have you seen? What have you heard? What do you think about it? What do you make of it? At the end of the travel they had to present somewhere in the city their 'look at the city'. What is at stake in this travels and walks is neither discovering far countries and exotic habits nor visiting 'the poor', but making the (slight) move which shapes the mapping of a 'there' to a 'here'. It is these walks that offer the background for what I try to say in this essay.

[3] The original German text is: "Die Kraft der Landstrasse ist eine andere, ob einer sie geht oder im Aeroplan drüber hinfliegt. So ist auch die Kraft eines Textes eine andere, ob einer ihn liest oder abschreibt. Wer fliegt, sieht nur, wie sich die Strasse durch die Landschaft schiebt, ihm rollt sie nach den gleichen Gesetzen ab wie das Terrain, das herum liegt. Nur wer die Strasse geht, erfährt von ihrer Herrschaft und wie aus eben jenem Gelände, das für den Flieger nur die aufgerollte Ebene ist, sie Fernen, Belvederes, Lichtungen, Prospekte mit jeder ihrer Wendungen so herauskommandiert, wie der Ruf des Befehlshabers Soldaten aus einer Front. So kommandiert allein der abgeschriebene Text die Seele dessen, der mit ihm beschäftigt ist, während der blosse Leser die neue Ansichten seines Inneren nie kennen lernt, wie der Text, jene Strasse durch den immer wieder sich verdichtenden inneren Urwald, sie bahnt: weil der Leser der Bewegung seines Ich im freien Luftbereich der Träumerei gehorcht, der Abschreiber aber sie kommandieren lässt." (Walter Benjamin, 1927a, p. 90)

[4] I believe that other readings are possible and I am aware of the very ambiguous character of what I am doing here in 'reading' this text. However, I cannot go into these issues here.

[5] There is of course a whole literature on walking as research tool, as a ritual, as performance, as intervention, as tool for sharing insights and as embodiment of the critical process. (See for example: *Walking as knowing as making. A peripatetic investigation of place* (2005) www.Walking inplace.org/converge/home.htm; Le Breton, D. (2000) *Eloge de la marche.* Paris: Métailié; Solnit, R. (2002) *Wanderlust. A History of Walking.* London/New York: Verso). Walking straight, arbitrary lines is a practice also well known in art (See for example: R.Long, *Walking a Line in Peru* in 1970, or the work *JFK* of D. Adams & L. Malone in 1997; see also: Franco Carreri. (2002) Walkscapes. Walking as aesthetic experience. Barcelona: Gil; Davila, Th. (2002) *Marcher, Créer. Déplacements, flâneries, dérives dans l'art de la fin du XXe siècle.* Paris: Regard).

[6] In this context it would have been interesting to have a look at: Thoreau, H.D. 'Walking' in: *The Natural History Essays* (1980) Salt Lake City: Peregrine Smith Books and more particular at some idea's developed by Cavell in: Cavell, S. (1999) *Conditions Handsome and Unhandsome. The constitution of Emersonian Perfectionism.* Chicago/London: The University of Chicago Press (for example regarding he idea of "what the soul's 'attraction' is to its journey ...; of how to picture such journeying (Emerson's word for it is taking steps, say walking, a kind of success(ion), in which the direction is not up but on, and in which the goal is decided not by anything picturable like the sun, by nothing beyond the way of the journey itself—this is the

subject of Emerson's 'Experience'" (p. 10) "... rather that 'having' 'a' self is a process of moving to, and from, nexts" (p. 12).

[7] It opens up a space of freedom, not of abstract but of very concrete freedom i.e. a space of possible (self) transformation, which is also the space of thought as intellectual and not as logic activity. Cfr. Foucault: "ouvrir une espace de liberté, entendu comme espace de liberté concrète, c'est-à-dire de transformation possible" (1983, 1268).

[8] "This is because knowledge is not made for understanding; it is made for cutting" (Foucault 1997). In French: "C'est que le savoir n'est pas fait pour comprendre, il est fait pour trancher" (Foucault 1971, p. 1016).

[9] See for example: Bruno Bosteels, "A misreading of maps: the politics of cartography in Marxism and Poststructuralism," in *Signs of change: Premodern—modern—postmodern*, ed. St. Barker (Albany: State university of New York Press, 1996), 109–138; Thomas Flynn, Sartre, *Foucault and historical reason. A poststructuralist mapping of history* (Chicago/London: The University of Chicago Press, 2005).

[10] Bert Lambeir, *The educational cyberspace affaire. A philosophical reading of the relevance of information and communications technology for educational theory.* (Leuven: Unpublished doctoral dissertation. K.U. Leuven, 2004). But see also for a similar idea of mapping: Crampton, J.W. (2004) *The political mapping of cyberspace.* Edinburgh: University Press.

[11] Freire also invokes a generosity introducing his pedagogy of the oppressed, but it remains very unclear what he means by this generosity. (Freire 1972, 1986, p. 20–23, 30). He distinguishes between false and true, authentic, humanist generosity, the first being a generosity which does not alter the situation of injustice in which the generosity is needed and therefore perpetuates the dependence of generosity, the second being the one which erases dependency and thus finally erases the need for generosity itself. The generosity which is meant by Foucault/Blanchot has to be situated in a totally different register as I try to indicate elsewhere (see Masschelein 2006)

[12] Of course, classical critical educational research was also interested in the present. However, it always was/is an interest in limiting it i.e.judging upon it. (See: Masschelein/Simons/Quaghebeur 2005). It consists in indicating to what limits the present (acting, speaking, thinking) should hold in order to be 'right' or 'just' (or 'human', or 'reasonable'). Therefore critique starts by looking for and asking for (justification or foundation of) the principles upon which it could rest or in whose name it could operate. It starts therefore by subjugation under a tribunal (of reason, tradition, humanity...) and requires of its subjects such subjugation. For McLaren, to indicate just one very influential example, a transformative practice and a Critical Pedagogy seem to be impossible without "a regulative principle" (McLaren 1995, 252), without criteria: "certain normative options (that) are necessary for an emancipatory educative praxis" (ibid.:256). Critique is for him about judgment. "But to judge we must have a criterion of judgment—a criterion that will justify us not only in refusing colonizing relations between the plural cultures of modernity, but will allow those cultures to speak to, to argues with, and to understand each other, however gropingly. This criterion is the idea of freedom. Freedom is the common measure of all discourses of modernity" (ibid. 250).

[13] In Dutch the word for attention is 'aandacht' which is composed by 'aan', which is the pronoun that expresses to be near, close, in touch, and 'dacht', which comes from the verb 'denken' i.e. thought. So one could translate attention as 'to think near'. The second word for attention is 'to be present' ('aanwezig zijn') and therefore not to be attentive is to be absent (afwezig zijn), not to be there. In German you have a similar word 'Andacht', which however seems to have different connotations which are more explicitly religious. The usual word for attention being 'Aufmerksamkeit' (See also: Waldensfels 2004)

[14] See: Weil, Simone (1962) *La pesanteur et la grace.* Paris: Plon. See also: Waldenfels, B. (2004) *Phänomenologie der Aufmerksamkeit.* Frankfurt: Suhrkamp.

[15] Fabian, talking about anthropological research 'looking' at the other, suggests that maybe our best research is done while we are 'out of our minds', that is while we relax our inner controls, forget our purposes, let ourselves go. It is the ecstatic side, which is no 'method' he says, but the need of passion—"as drive and suffering, terror and torture"—being a condition to really see.

(Cfr. J. Fabian, *Anthropology with an attitude. Critical essays* (Stanford: Stanford University Press, 2001)

[16] For Foucault arriving at an attentive attitude asks for a labor of askēsis, an exercise or work on the self in order to leave behind the judgmental attitude. In this context it is worthwhile to point at some concrete features of this askēsis (or 'philosophy') in the case of Foucault and maybe first of all at to the fact that it includes not only a certain *practice of the mind* (a disciplined and sustained reading, studying, ...—Foucault spoke about 'une transformation studieuse, une modification lente et ardue par souci constant de la vérité' which he distinguished from 'une illumination soudaine') but explicitly also a certain *practice of the body* since the work on the self is beyond a merely cognitive relation (it is not about 'knowing oneself'). It involves a particular physical relation towards one's 'present' i.e. a *physical* encounter with texts, events, places, archives, ... (implying sometimes bodily abhorrence or exhaustion encountering these archives or copying them; or physical pleasure and excitement visiting locations, etc.). The body is not on a distance, but appears as an instrument to diagnose that present (and in that sense experience it). It could be at once an instrument to measure the intolerable, painful character of the present, and an instrument of investigation and of thought. This practice of the body had different forms but one was precisely the voyage or travel, involving not only visiting different places, but walking for long hours and long distances, which Foucault estimated to be necessary for his work, one reason being that it implied always in a certain way a 'face-à-face'. The deplacement as a physical experience (in its various forms) belonged to the work and contributed to produce the *attention*, so crucial for Foucault in many ways (See also: Masschelein, J. & Simons, M. (2008). Do historians (of education) need philosophy? The enlightening potential of a philosophical ethos. *Paedagogica historica, 44*(6), 647–660. Artières, Philippe. "Dire l'actualité. Le travail de diagnostic chez Michel Foucault." In Foucault. *Le courage de la vérité*, edited by Frédéric Gros. Paris: Puf, 2002.

[17] Offering a line as a cut is what, according to Nancy, is happening in the films of Abbas Kiarostami. See: Nancy 2001. Nancy's ideas regarding Kiarostami's films have been inspiring for my presentation of a poor pedagogy and for the concrete educational research experiments that lay at the basis of this essay (see footnote one). Offering a line as a cut and passe-partout (opening an existential space) was what I tried to do when carrying out these experiments where students walked cities along totally arbitrary lines.

[18] This paper is an extended and elaborated version of the article "E-educating the gaze: the idea of a poor pedagogy" published in *Ethics and Education* (2010) (in press). It includes also some elements from: Masschelein, J. (2009). *The World 'once More': Walking Lines*. Teachers College Record [online post], retrieved December 9, 2009, from http://www.tcrecord.org

REFERENCES

Artières, P. (2000). Dire l'actualité. Le travail de diagnostic chez Michel Foucault. In F. Gros (Ed.), Foucault. *Le courage de la vérité* (pp. 11–34). Paris: Presses universitaires de France.

Bataille, G. (1954). L'expérience intérieure. In *Œuvres Complètes. V* (pp. 6–190). Paris: Gallimard.

Benjamin, W. (1927a). einbahnstrasse. In W. Benjamin (Ed.), (1991). *Gesammelte Schriften* (pp. 83–148). Bd. Iv.1. T. Rexroth (Ed.). Frankfurt am Main: Suhrkamp.

Benjamin, W. (1927b). One-way street. In W. Benjamin (1979). *One-way street and other writings* (E. Jephcott & K. Shorter, Trans.). London: NLB.

Benjamin, W. (1927c/1994). *Eenrichtingstraat* (P. Koopman, Trans.). Groningen: Historische Uitgeverij.

Bosteels, B. (1996). A misreading of maps: The politics of cartography in marxism and post-structuralism. In St. Barker (Ed.), *Signs of change: Premodern—modern—postmodern* (pp. 109–138). Albany, NY: State University of New York Press.

Butler, J. (2001). What is critique? An essay on Foucault's virtue. In S. Salih (Ed.), *The Judith Butler reader*. Malden/Oxford/Victoria: Blackwell Publishing. Or In D. Ingram (Ed.). (2000). *The political*. Oxford: Blackwell.

Comenius, J. A. (1623, s.d.). *Het labyrinth der wereld en Het paradijs des harten*. Amsterdam: Schors.

Foucault, M. (1971). Nietzsche, la généalogie, l'histoire. In D. Defert, F. Ewald, & J. Lagrange (Eds.), *Dits et écrits II 1976–1988* (pp. 1004–1024). Paris: Gallimard, edition Quarto.

Foucault, M. (1983). Structuralisme et poststructuralisme. In D. Defert, F. Ewald, & J. Lagrange (Eds.), *Dits et écrits II 1976–1988* (pp. 1250–1276). Paris: Gallimard, edition Quarto. (English: Structuralism and post-structuralisme. *Telos*, XvI, n° 55, pp. 195–211)

Foucault, M. (1997). Nietzsche, genealogy and history. In M. Foucault (1997–2000), P. Rabinow (Ed.), *Essential works of Foucault, 1954–1984*. New York: New Press.

Freire, P. (1972, 1986). *Pedagogy of the oppressed*. New York: Penguin.

Flynn, Th. R. (2005). *Sartre, Foucault and historical reason. A poststructuralist mapping of history*. Chicago/London: The University of Chicago Press.

Lambeir, B. (2004). *The educational cyberspace affaire. A philosophical reading of the relevance of information and communciations technology for educational theory*. Unpublished Doctoral Dissertation. K.U. Leuven.

Masschelein, J. (2004), How to conceive of critical educational theory today? *Journal of Philosophy of Education, 38*(3), 351–367.

Masschelein, J. (2006). Experience and the limits of governmentality. *Educational Philosophy and Theory, 38*, 561–575.

Masschelein, J., & Simons, M. (2008). Do historians (of education) need philosophy? The enlightening potential of a philosophical ethos. *Paedagogica historica, 44*(6), 647–660.

McLaren, P. (1995). *Critical pedagogy and predatory culture*. London/New York: Routledge.

Mollenhauer, K. (1986). *Vergeten samenhang*. Meppel/Amsterdam: Boom (Vertaling Van: Vergessene Zusammenhänge.)

Nancy, J. L., & Kiarostami, A. (2001). *L'évidence du film/the evidence of film*. Brussels: Yves Gevaert.

Ranciére, J. (1998). *Aux Bords du Politique*. Paris: La Fabrique.

Simons, M., Masschelein, J., & Quaghebeur, K. (2005). The ethos of critical research and the idea of a coming research community. *Educational Philosophy and Theory, 37*(6), 817–832.

van Den Abbeele (1992). *Travel as metaphor. From Montaigne to Rousseau*. Minneapolis/Oxford: University of Minnesota Press.

Waldenfels, B. (2004). *Phänomenologie der Aufmerksamkeit*. Frankfurt am Main: Suhrkamp.

GERT BIESTA

14. D IS FOR DEMOCRACY—CRITICAL EDUCATION BETWEEN INCLUSION AND INTERRUPTION

In exploring the im/possibilities of a new critical language in and for education, it is important to include a discussion about the idea of democracy. After all, one of the main ambitions of the critical 'project' has been to overcome authoritarian power structures, and the idea of democracy precisely points at a situation in which *all* are involved in the ruling of society and are so on equal terms. Democracy, as Abraham Lincoln has put it, is the government of the people, by the people, and for the people, and thus entails "the twin principles of *popular control* over collective decision-making and *equality of rights* in the exercise of that control" (Beetham & Boyle 1995, p. 1; emph,. in original). Although many would agree with such a definition at a general level, there have been ongoing discussions about the more precise meanings of the democratic idea of popular rule. Such discussions not only focus on the different forms of ruling (e.g., direct participation or indirect representation) and on questions about who should be included in the definition of 'the people' (e.g., free men; landowners; women; children; all human beings; all living beings; everyone and everything). They are also concerned with different *justifications* of the idea of democracy, ranging from democracy as the optimal context for human flourishing to democracy as 'the worst form of government except all those other forms that have been tried' (Winston Churchill).

In this chapter I discuss two different ways in which the idea of democracy can be articulated. One sees democracy as a particular 'order' and conceives of democratization as the *inclusion* of as many as possible into this order. The other starts from the observation that no order can ever be totally inclusive, and thus identifies democratization with *interruptions* of the order in the name of democracy. Whereas the first sees democracy as something that can become 'normal,' the second sees democracy as essentially 'sporadic.' While the first approaches democratization from the 'inside out,' reaching out from the centre to the margins, the second approaches democratization from the 'outside in,' moving from the margins to the centre. The main interest of the first therefore list in extending the scope of the democratic order, while the focus of the second is on the ongoing renegotiation of the borders of the democratic order. Whereas the first would see the main task of democratic education as that of making 'newcomers'—children, immigrants—ready for their inclusion into the democratic order, the second would align democratic education more closely with learning processes that are at stake in the (re)negotiation of the borders of the democratic order.

In exploring these two different ways of understanding democracy and democratization I am not suggesting that 'traditional' forms of Critical Pedagogy would

I. Gur-Ze'ev, The Possibility/Impossibility of a New Critical Language in Education, 293–303.
© *2010 Sense Publishers. All Rights Reserved.*

map neatly onto the first approach, while the second approach would represents the building blocks for a radically 'new' critical language in and for education. This is not only because the distinction between the 'old' or 'traditional' and the 'new' is always in a sense artificial in that what is 'old' or 'traditional' only becomes so in the light of a claim to the 'new.' It is also because Critical Pedagogy in itself is a multi-faceted phenomenon which includes Marxist, neo-Marxist, feminist, post-modern and post-structural articulations and these differ significantly in their theoretical orientation and practical outlook (see, e.g., Gur Ze'ev 2005). This means that if there is a dividing line, it is more likely to run through the different versions and varieties of Critical Pedagogy than that it would inaugurate something that is radically new and different. The main ambition of this chapter, therefore, is to highlight the fact that there are different options available within the discourse and practice of democracy, without wanting to prescribe how one should orientate oneself in relation to them. This is not to suggest that there are no differences between the strategy of inclusion and the strategy of interruption. As I will argue below, one of the main differences between the two is that there is an in-built contradiction within the strategy of inclusion which has to do with the existence of a power differential between those who are on the 'inside' of the democratic order and those who are on the 'outside.' The strategy of interruption can be read as attempt to overcome this contradiction (see also Biesta, in press).

This chapter is organised in the following way. I begin with a discussion of inclusive approaches to democracy and democratization. For this I focus on the idea of deliberative democracy, not only because it is a good example of inclusive thinking within democratic theory but also because I consider it to be one of the more significant recent developments within democratic theory. I confine the discussion to the ideas of Elster, Dryzek and Young. I show how within the development of deliberative democracy particular issues about inclusion have arisen and how these issues have been addressed. I argue that this reveals a strong tendency within deliberative democracy to aim for the inclusion of as many as possible within the democratic order. I then present the case for understanding democratization in terms of interruption and democracy as sporadic rather than normal. Here my main source of inspiration is the work of Jacques Rancière. Rancière provides us with a way of understanding democratization that does not emanate from the centre of the demo-cratic order but rather occurs through the redrawing of the borders of that order. Rancière's views not only lead to a different appreciation of the political significance of order and interruption, but also articulate different power relationships and different political identities and subjectivities within those relationships. In the final section of this chapter I highlight some implications for the theory and practice of critical education.

THE STRATEGY OF INCLUSION

In contemporary political theory a distinction is made between two models of demo-cratic decision-making: the *aggregative* model and the *deliberative* model. The first sees democracy as a process of aggregating the preferences of individuals. A central assumption is that the preferences of individuals should be seen as given and that politics is only concerned with the aggregation of preferences, often, but not exclusively, on the basis of majority rule. Where these preferences come from, whether they are valid or not, and whether they are held for egoistic or altruistic reasons, is considered to be irrelevant. The *aggregative* model assumes, in other words, "that ends and values are subjective, non-rational, and exogenous to the political process" and that democratic politics is basically "a competition between private interests and preferences" (Young, 2000, p. 22).

Over the past two decades an increasing number of political theorists have argued that democracy should not be confined to the simple aggregation of preferences but should involve the *deliberative transformation* of preferences. Under the deliberative model democratic decision-making is seen as a process which involves "decision making by means of arguments offered *by* and *to* participants" (Elster, 1998, p. 8) about the means and the ends of collective action. Deliberative democracy is not about "determining what preferences have greatest numerical support, but [about] determining which proposals the collective agrees are supported by the best reasons" (Young, 2000, p. 23). The reference to 'best reasons' indicates that deliberative democracy is based upon a particular conception of deliberation. Dryzek, for example, acknowledges that deliberation can cover a rather broad spectrum of activities but argues that for *authentic* deliberation to happen the requirement is that the reflection on preferences should take place in a *non-coercive* manner (Dryzek, 2000, p. 2). This requirement "rules out domination via the exercise of power, manipulation, indoctrination, propaganda, deception, expression of mere self-interest, threats... and attempts to impose ideological conformity" (ibid.). This resonates with Elster's claim that deliberative democracy is about the giving and taking of arguments by participants "who are committed to the values of rationality and impartiality" (Elster, 1998, p. 8) and with his suggestion that deliberation must take place between "free, equal and rational agents" (ibid., p. 5).

The 'deliberative turn' (or re-turn; see Dryzek, 2000, pp. 1–2) is an important step in the development of democratic theory and democratic practice. Firstly, it represents a more full expression of the basic values of democracy, particularly the idea that democracy is about actual participation in collective decision-making. In the aggregative model there is, after all, little participation, and decision-making is mainly algorithmic. Also, the deliberative approach has a stronger educational potential because in the deliberative model "political actors not only express preferences and interest, but they engage with one another about how to balance these under circumstances of inclusive equality" (Young, 2000, p. 26). Because such interaction "requires participants to be open and attentive to one another, to justify their claims and proposals in terms of [being] acceptable to all, the orientation of participants moves from self-regard to an orientation to what is publicly assertable" (ibid.). Thus "people often gain new information, learn different experiences of their collective problems, or find that their own initial opinions are founded on prejudice and ignorance, or that they have misunderstood the relation of their own interests to others" (ibid.). As Warren has argued, participation in deliberation can make individuals "more public-spirited, more tolerant, more knowledgeable, more attentive to the interests of others, and more probing of their own interests" (Warren, 1992, p. 8).

Deliberative democracy, so its proponents argue, is therefore not only more *democratic* but also more *educative*. A third asset of deliberative democracy lies in its potential impact on the *motivation* of political actors in that participation in democratic decision-making is more likely to commit participants to its outcomes. This suggests that deliberative democracy is not only an intrinsically desirable way of social problem-solving but probably also an effective way of doing this (see Dryzek, 2000, p. 172).

The deliberative turn can be seen as an attempt to bring democracy closer to its core values and in this respect represents an important correction to the individualism and 'disconnected pluralism' of the aggregative model and of liberal democracy more generally (see also Biesta, 2006). However, by raising the stakes of democracy, deliberative democracy has also brought the difficulty of democratic inclusion into much sharper focus, and thus has generated—ironically but not surprisingly—a series of problems around the question of inclusion. The main issue here centers on the *entry conditions for participation* in deliberation. The authors quoted above all seem to suggest that participation in democratic deliberation should be regulated and that it should be confined to those who commit themselves to a particular set of values and behaviours. Young, for example, argues that the deliberative model "entails several normative ideas for the relationships and dispositions of deliberating parties, among them inclusion, equality, reasonableness, and publicity" which, so she claims, "are all logically related in the deliberative model" (Young, 2000, p. 23). Most of the proponents of (versions of) deliberative democracy specify a set of entry conditions for participation, although what is interesting about the discussion is that most go at great pains to delineate a *minimum* set of conditions necessary for democratic deliberation rather than an ideal set (see, e.g., the contributions in Elster, 1998). Young provides an interesting example with her distinction between reasonableness (which she sees as a necessary entry condition) and rationality (which she doesn't see as a necessary condition). For Young being reasonable doesn't entail being rational. Reasonableness refers to "a set of *dispositions* that discussion participants have [rather] than to the substance of people's contributions to debate" (Young, 2000, p. 24; emph. added). She concedes that reasonable people "often have crazy ideas," yet "what makes them reasonable is their willingness to listen to others who want to explain to them why their ideas are incorrect or inappropriate" (ibid.). In Young's hands reasonableness thus emerges as a communicative *virtue*, and not as a criterion for the logical quality of people's preferences and convictions.

This example not only shows why the issue of inclusion is so prominent in the deliberative model. It also explains why the deliberative turn has generated a whole new set of issues around inclusion. The reason for this is that deliberation is not simply a form of political decision-making but first and foremost a form of political *communication*. The inclusion question in deliberative democracy is therefore not so much a question about who should be included—although this question should be asked always as well. It is first and foremost a question about who is able to participate effectively in deliberation. As Dryzek aptly summarises, the suspicion about deliberative democracy is "that its focus on a particular kind of reasonable political interaction is not in fact neutral, but systematically excludes a variety of voices from effective participation in democratic politics" (Dryzek, 2000, p. 58). In this regard Young makes a helpful distinction between two forms of exclusion: *external exclusion*, which is about "how people are [actually] kept outside the process of discussion and decision-making," and *internal exclusion* where people are formally included in decision-making processes but where they may find, for example, "that their claims are not taken seriously and may believe that they are not treated with equal respect" (Young, 2000, p. 55). Internal exclusion, in other words, refers to those situations in which people "lack effective opportunity to influence the thinking of others even when they have access to procedures of decision-making" (ibid.) which can particularly be the outcome of the emphasis of some proponents of deliberative democracy on "dispassionate, unsituated, neutral reason" (ibid., p. 63).

To counteract the internal exclusion that is the product of a too narrow focus on argument, Young has suggested several other modes of political communication which should be added to the deliberative process not only to remedy "exclusionary tendencies in deliberative practices" but also to promote "respect and trust" and to make possible "understanding across structural and cultural difference" (ibid., p. 57). The first of these is *greeting* or *public acknowledgement*. This is about "communicative political gestures through which those who have conflicts... *recognize* others as included in the discussion, especially those with whom they differ in opinion, interest, or social location" (ibid., p. 61; emph. in original). Young emphasises that greeting should be thought of as a starting-point for political interaction. It "*precedes* the giving and evaluating of reasons" (ibid., p. 79) and does so through the recognition of the other parties in the deliberation. The second mode of political communication is *rhetoric* and more specifically the affirmative use of rhetoric (ibid., p. 63). Although one could say that rhetoric only concerns the form of political communication and not its content, the point Young makes is that inclusive political communication should pay attention to and be inclusive about the different forms of expression and should not try to purify rational argument from rhetoric. Rhetoric is not only important because it can help to get particular issues on the agenda for deliberation. Rhetoric can also help to articulate claims and arguments "*in ways appropriate to a particular public in a particular situation*" (ibid., p. 67; emph. in original). Rhetoric always accompanies an argument by situating it "for a particular audience and giving it embodied style and tone" (ibid., p. 79). Young's third mode of political communication is *narrative* or *storytelling*. The main function of narrative in democratic communication lies in its potential "to foster understanding among members of a polity with very different experience or assumptions about what is important" (ibid., p. 71). Young emphasises the role of narrative in the teaching and learning dimension of political communication. "Inclusive democratic communication," so she argues, "assumes that all participants have something to teach the public about the society in which they dwell together" and also assumes "that all participants are ignorant of some aspects of the social or natural world, and that everyone comes to a political conflict with some biases, prejudices, blind spots, or stereo-types" (ibid., p. 77).

It is important to emphasise that greeting, rhetoric and narrative are not meant to *replace* argumentation. Young stresses again and again that deliberative democracy entails "that participants require reasons of one another and critically evaluate them" (ibid., p. 79). Other proponents of the deliberative model take a much more narrow approach and see deliberation exclusively as a form of *rational* argumentation (e.g., Benhabib, 1996) where the only legitimate force should be the "forceless force of the better argument" (Habermas). Similarly, Dryzek, after a discussion of Young's ideas,[1] concludes that argument always has to be central to deliberative democracy" (Dryzek, 2000, p. 71). Although he acknowledges that other modes of communication can be present and that there are good reasons to welcome them, their status is different "because they do not *have* to be present" (ibid., emph added). For Dryzek at the end of the day all modes of political communication must live up to the standards of rationality. This does not mean that they must be subordinated to rational argument "but their deployment only makes sense in a context where argument about what is to be done remains central" (ibid., p. 168).

THE STRATEGY OF INTERRUPTION

I have focused on deliberative democracy for two reasons: First of all because I consider it to be one of the more significant developments within the field of democratic theory, and secondly because it is a paradigm case of what I have referred to as the strategy of inclusion. Deliberative democracy clearly represents the sphere of democracy as a particular 'order' and delineates this order as an order or reasoned or rational deliberation. The ambition of the idea of deliberative democracy is that this order should become the 'normal' situation. This is why the question of inclusion is mainly understood as a practical question, i.e., as the question how we can make our democratic practices even more inclusive (internal inclusion) and how we can include even more people into the sphere of democratic deliberation (external inclusion). The assumption here is that if we can become even more attention to otherness and difference we might eventually reach a situation of total democratic inclusion. Democratization is therefore understood as the process through which those who are outside of the sphere of democracy are brought into this sphere. Young's work is a good example of an attempt to make the sphere of democracy itself more accessible and inclusive. It is, however, not too difficult to see how the 'logic' of inclusive democratization brings with it a particular educational agenda, one which focuses on developing the skills and dispositions of 'newcomers'—children, immigrants—so that they can become effective participants in the democratic deliberation.

Although attempts to make democracy more inclusive and accessible are laudable and although deliberative democracy has some clear advantages over aggregative models of democratic decision making, the strategy of inclusion of which deliberative democracy is a paradigm example is not without problems. The main problem, so I wish to suggest, has to do with the power differential between those who are on the 'inside' of the democratic order—those who, in the case of deliberative democracy, represent the 'standard' of reasonableness and rationality—and those who are on the 'outside' of the democratic order. The very language of inclusion not only suggests that someone is including someone else. It also suggests that those on the 'inside' are settings the terms for inclusion and that it is for those on the 'outside' to meet those terms which makes those on the 'outside' dependent upon those on the 'inside' for their inclusion. This shows that the 'logic' of democratization within the strategy of inclusion is basically a colonial logic. The question this raises is whether it is possible to think democracy and democratization differently and, more importantly, whether it is possible to overcome the contradiction built into the strategy of inclusion. To explore this possibility I now turn to the work of Jacques Rancière.

Whereas in the discourse of inclusion democracy is seen as something that can be permanent and normal, Rancière has argued for an understanding of democracy as essentially *sporadic*, that is, as something that only 'happens' from time to time and in very particular situations (see Rancière, 1995, p. 41; p. 61). Rancière's argument relies on a distinction between politics—which for Rancière always means *democratic* politics (democracy as "the institution of politics itself"—Rancière, 1999, p. 101)—and what he refers to as *police* or *police order*. Rancière defines the police as "an order of bodies that defines the allocation of ways of doing, ways of being, and ways of saying, and that sees that those bodies are assigned by name to a particular place and task" (Rancière, 1999, p. 29). It as an order "of the visible and the sayable that sees that a particular activity is visible and another is not, that this speech is understood as discourse and another as noise" (ibid.). Police should not be understood as the way in which the state structures the life of society. It is not, in Habermasian terms, the 'grip' of the system on the lifeworld, but includes *both*. As Rancière explains, "(t) he distribution of places and roles that defines a police regime stems as much from the assumed spontaneity of social relations as from the rigidity of state functions" (ibid.). One way to read this definition of police is to think of it as an order that is *all-inclusive* in that everyone has a particular identity and position in it. This is not to say that everyone is included in the running of the order. The point simply is that everyone has an identity within the order—everyone is visible in a particular way—although some are included with an identity that excludes them from the running of the order. Women, children, slaves and immigrants all had a clear place in the democracy of Athens, viz., as those who were *not* allowed to participate in political decision making.

Against this background Rancière then defines *politics* as the disruption of the police order in the name of equality. Rancière explains that he reserves the term 'politics' "for an extremely determined activity antagonistic to policing: whatever breaks with the tangible configuration whereby parties and parts or lack of them are defined by a presupposition that, by definition, has no place in that configuration" (ibid., pp. 30–31). This break is manifest is a series of actions "that reconfigure the space where parties, parts, or lack of parts have been defined." (ibid., p. 31). Political activity so conceived is "whatever shifts a body from the place assigned to it" (ibid.). "It makes visible what had no business being seen, and makes heard [and understood; G.B.] a discourse where once there was only place for noise." (ibid.)

> (P)olitical activity is always a mode of expression that undoes the perceptible divisions of the police order by implementing a basically heterogeneous assumption, that of a part of those who have no part, an assumption that, at the end of the day, itself demonstrates the sheer contingency of the order [and] the equality of any speaking being with any other speaking being. (ibid)

Politics thus refers to the event when two 'heterogeneous processes' meet: the police process and the process of *equality* (see ibid.). For Rancière, as I have already mentioned, politics is always democratic politics. Democracy, however, "is not a regime or a social way of life"—it is not and cannot be, in other words, part of the police order—but should rather be understood "as the institution of politics itself" (ibid., p. 101). Every politics is democratic *not* in the sense of a set of institutions, but in the sense of forms of expression "that confront the logic of equality with the logic of the police order" (ibid.). Democracy, so we might say, is a 'claim' for equality.

This does raise a further question, however, which is who it is that makes this claim. Who, in other words, 'does' politics or 'performs' democracy? [2] The point of asking the question in this way is not to suggest that there is no subject of politics, that there are no democratic actors involved in democracy. The point is that political actors—or subjects—do not exist *before* the 'act' of democracy, or to be more precise: their political identity, their identity as democratic subjects only comes into being in and through the interruption of the police order. This is why Rancière argues that politics is itself a process of *subjectification*. It is a process in and through which political subjects are constituted. Subjectification is "the production through a series of actions of a body and a capacity for enunciation not previously identifiable within a given field of experience, whose identification is thus part of the reconfiguration of the field of experience" (ibid., p. 35).

Democracy—or to be more precise: the appearance of democracy—is therefore not simply the situation in which a group who has previously been excluded from the realm of politics steps forward to claim its membership of the existing order. It rather is a redefinition of that order so that different identities become possible. Democratization, so we might say, is no longer seen as just a *quantitative* change— adding more 'elements' to the existing order—but refers to a *qualitative* change in which the order itself, and the available subject-positions and identities within that order, become changed. Democratic activity is, for example, to be found in the activity of nineteenth-century workers "who established a collective basis for work relations" that were previously seen as "the product of an infinite number of relationships between private individuals" (ibid., p. 30). Democracy thus establishes new, *political* identities. Or as Rancière puts it: "Democracy is the designation of subjects that do not coincide with the parties of the state or of society" (ibid., pp. 99–100). This means that "the place where the people appear" is the place "where a dispute is conducted" (ibid., p. 100). The political dispute is distinct from all conflicts of interest between constituted parties of the population, for it is a conflict "over the very count of those parties." (ibid.) It is a dispute between "the police logic of the distribution of places and the political logic of the egalitarian act" (ibid.). Politics is therefore "primarily a conflict over the existence of a common stage and over the existence and status of those present on it" (ibid., pp. 26–27).

This shows that for Rancière democratization is *not* a process that emanates from the 'centre' and extends to the 'margins.' It is not a process in which those who are already democratic—an impossible position from Rancière's point of view anyway—include others into their sphere. Rather democracy appears as a claim from the 'outside,' a claim based upon the perception of injustice, or of what Rancière refers to as a 'wrong,' a claim made in the name of equality. Those who make the claim do not simply want to be included in the existing order; they want to *redefine* the order in such a way that *new* identities, new ways of doing and being become possible and can be 'counted.' This means that for Rancière democratization is not a process of the inclusion of excluded parties into the existing order; it rather is a transformation of that order in the name of equality so that different ways of being, saying and seeing become possible, both for those who were originally not part of the order and for those who were. The impetus for this transformation does not come from the 'inside' but rather from the 'outside.' But it is important to see that, unlike in the prevailing discourse about democratic inclusion, this outside is not a 'known' outside. For Rancière democratization is not a process that happens *within* the police order. It is not a modification of that order but rather an interruption of it; an interruption from a place that could not be expressed or articulated from within this order.

All this is not to suggest that Rancière would prefer anarchy over order. Although Rancière would maintain that democratization is basically a good thing, this does not mean that the police order is necessarily bad. Although this may not be very prominent in Rancière's work—which means that it is easily overlooked—he does argue that democratization can have a positive effect on the police order. Democratic disputes can produce what Rancière refers to as "inscriptions of equality" (Rancière, 1999, p. 100); they can leave traces behind in the (transformed) police order. This is why Rancière emphasises that "(t)here is a worse and a better police" (ibid., pp. 30–31). The better one is, however, not the one "that adheres to the supposedly natural order of society or the science of legislators"—it is the one "that all the breaking and entering perpetrated by egalitarian logic has most jolted out of its 'natural' logic" (ibid., p. 31). Rancière thus acknowledges that the police "can produce all sorts of good, and one kind of police may be infinitely preferable to another" (ibid., p. 31). But, so he concludes, whether the police is 'sweet and kind' does not make it any less the opposite of politics (see ibid.).

DISCUSSION

In this chapter I have presented two different conceptions of democracy. One sees democracy as a particular order and conceives of democratization as the process of including those who are on the 'outside' of this order into the order. This is done, on the one hand, by making the order of democracy itself more inclusive and, on other hand, by making those on the 'outside' of the democratic order 'ready' for their inclusion, and it is here that education is supposed to play a crucial role. The other sees democracy as essentially sporadic and conceives of democratization as the interruption of a particular police order. It is, however, not any interruption that constitutes democratization, but only those interruptions that occur with a claim to equality. Such interruptions result in a reconfiguration of the police order and thus imply a redrawing of the borders of the order. On this account democratization is not about the inclusion of those who are known to be excluded. Democratization rather leads to a reconfiguration of the police order in which different identities and subjectivities become possible—where 'noise' becomes 'voice.' This is the reason why Rancière sees democratization as a process of subjectification.

We could see these different ways of understanding democracy and democratization simply as two options—two options, moreover, that are available to choose from. There is, however, an important difference between the two options. As I have argued in this chapter, the strategy of inclusion has an in-built contradiction which has to do with the power differential between those who are on the 'inside' of the democratic order and those who are on the 'outside.' The strategy of inclusion, so we might say, starts from the assumption of inequality and sees inclusion as the way in which a more equal situation can be achieved. Yet it can only do this within a colonial framework where those who are on the 'outside' of the democratic order are added to and included in the existing order. The order itself, however, is beyond question. This is where Rancière provides us with a radically different conception of democratization, one which focuses on the transformation of the existing order. Such transformations only exist as interruptions from the 'outside;' interruptions, moreover, that not simply ask for inclusion in terms of the existing order, but for the reconfiguration of the order so that new and different identities and subjectivities become possible, so that a different equality can be instated. These interruptions are not dependent upon the 'permission' of those on the inside and it is precisely for this reason that this understanding of democratization no longer relies on a colonial 'logic.' It also shows that the basic premise of this conception of democratization is that of equality rather than inequality.

While I do think that there are important differences between the two conceptions of democracy and democratization, I do not simply wish to position them as 'old' and 'new,' as 'colonial' and 'post-colonial,' or even less as 'bad' and 'good.' The reason for this is that I take Rancière's point that there is a worse and a better police seriously. I do not think that we should read Rancière as a plea for anarchy. I am more inclined to read him in the way in which Derrida makes a distinction between justice and the law (Derrida 1990). The law, so we might say, represents justice but always does so in an imperfect manner. That is why laws are deconstructible and why the deconstructability of the law is a good thing. To think that the law can become just, to think that we can reach a situation of total justice, is a dangerous mistake because we should always remain open to the possibility that what appears as justice turns out to be less than just. This possibility is not a possibility we can oversee. It is a possibility we have to live with in the very name of justice, and this is why we should always be open to the possible deconstruction of the law in the name of justice. From this angle justice remains something that is always to come, something that never will be fully present. If we read Rancière from this angle we can perhaps appreciate more fully why his views do not simply want to overcome the police order, but rather want to remind us that democratization necessarily has to be understood as the interruption of this order, rather than that it is expressed through this order. But this is not to say that any existing order cannot carry 'inscriptions of equality.' This not only means that from the perspective of equality there can be worse and better police orders—which means why it is also important to 'invest' in orders and ordering. It also means that critical education can work both in relation to the policy order *and* in relation to its interruption. Problems arise when critical education would work only in one of these modes and would forget the wider picture. In this regard I am inclined to believe that both 'archic' and 'anarchic' modes of critical education are in themselves problematic. If there is anything 'new,' therefore, that follows from the discussion in this chapter it is a call for the development of a critical language and a critical educational practice that locates itself in the tension between the archic and the anarchic, between order and border, between inclusion and interruption.

NOTES

[1] Dryzek refers to work published by Young before her *Inclusion and Democracy* (Young 2000). Several of the issues Dryzek raises about Young's position seem no longer to be part of the position she takes in *Inclusion and Democracy.*

[2] This is a rather awkward way of putting the question, but it is consistent with Rancière's line of thinking. Rancière, for example, writes at some point about "(t)he people through which democracy occurs" (Rancière, 1999, p. 99).

REFERENCES

Beetham, D., & Boyle, K. (1995). *Introducing democracy. 80 Questions and answers.* Cambridge: Polity Press.

Biesta, G. J. J. (2006). *Beyond learning. Democratic education for a human future.* Boulder, CO: Paradigm Publishers.

Biesta, G. J. J. (in press). A new 'logic' of emancipation: The methodology of Jacques Rancière. *Educational Theory.*

Derrida, J. (1990). Force of law: The mystical foundation of authority. *Cardozo Law Review: Deconstruction and the Possibility of Justice, 11*(5–6), 920–1045.

Dryzek, J. S. (2000). *Deliberative democracy and beyond. Liberals, critics, contestations.* Oxford: Oxford university Press.

Elster, J. (Ed.). (1998). *Deliberative democracy.* Cambridge: Cambridge university Press.

Gur Ze'ev, I. (Ed.). (2005). *Critical theory and critical pedagogy today. Toward a new critical language in education.* Haifa: Studies in education (university of Haifa).

Rancière, J. (1995). *On the shores of politics.* London/New York: Verso.

Rancière, J. (1999). *Dis-agreement. Politics and philosophy.* Minneapolis/London: University of Minnesota Press.

Warren, M. (1992). Democratic theory and self-transformation. *American Political Science Review, 86,* 8–23.

Young, I. M. (2000). *Inclusion and democracy.* Oxford: Oxford university Press.

ANAT RIMON-OR

15. CRITICAL EDUCATION AND THE INQUIRY INTO THE FACULTY OF CONSCIOUSNESS[1]

Common to Nietzsche, Marx's critique of Hegel and Adorno's late writing is the notion that the failures of philosophical insights reflect some neglected social activity that was left out of philosophical consideration. This forgetfulness is what has constituted the philosophic perception, and, in its turn, it deconstructs it. Awareness of the margins which signify its failures guides the philosopher to new perceptions, to a new temporal stability (Adorno, 1973, pp. 17–18, 202; Nietzsche, 2001, §58, 307, 345; 1886, chapters 1–2);[2] disavowing them would cause the philosophical insights to participate in social exclusion and suffering (Adorno, Ibid.).[3] This is the connection between awareness of suffering (and/or its elimination) and critical thinking which Adorno and Lyotard delineate in different ways, under the influence of Marx. According to this idea, a search into the dismantlement of one's own field and perceptions is a significant-critique's point of departure, and the emergence of social knowledge. Philosophy is not different, according to this notion, from all other fields of social praxis — it creates its own victims and subjected subjects. The power that makes it so crucial to the social institutes structured by the influence of Enlightenment is the power of critique — the everlasting constitution of the subject of knowledge as the process of extracting oneself from dogmatism and heteronomy made by its own tools. That is the way Foucault positions Critique in the age of Enlightenment.[4]

Critical education fails in two levels, which, I think, are intermingled. One is the failure that Gur-Ze'ev describes in the topic of the forthcoming meeting;[5] the other is its failure to found itself as a significant field in Critical Thinking and in the development of knowledge. Below I will try to show the connection between these two problems of Critical Education, according to the lines of critique delineated above. I will do so from within the Marxist field. According to this discussion, the separation between postmodern notions and Marxist ones is misleading. In this way I will encounter two topics of the meeting.

As critical thinkers, influenced by the Frankfurt School, we naturally engage in the question of the faulty consciousness of the proletariat, or of the individuals in democracy, as our point of departure. I would like to suggest that the notion of faulty consciousness should be reconsidered and that this reconsideration might enlighten for us the reasons for our failures in classrooms as well as in the academy. The discussion of terror will accompany my argument so as to support my contention that the demarcation of lines separating postmodern notions and Marxist ones is misleading.

In the last century we have dealt with the faulty consciousness of the individual as our goal as critical educators. When we tried to reconstruct our systems of values, following the postmodern critique, we inclined to position the terror of fundamentalist

I. Gur-Ze'ev, The Possibility/Impossibility of a New Critical Language in Education, 305–314.
© *2010 Sense Publishers. All Rights Reserved.*

Islam as a signifier of the unacceptable in plural societies. In doing that — in positioning these questions as our topics — we dismiss the fact that the severest crisis of western societies, including this daunting list: the collapsing of the welfare state; the powerlessness in front of, and the legitimation of, child employment; international trade in women; the press' cooperation with the government in Israel and the U.S during the last wars in which these countries were involved; the commercialization of the press; the cooperation of judges, teachers and social workers with illegitimate regimes and with social harms inflicted upon the margins by unleashed capitalism; the willingness of judges to judge politicians occupied by their governments by the terms of their own government's laws: the helplessness of the law systems against the overcoming of capitalists in the political sphere, etc. These are all performed or condoned by intellectuals and/or middle class clergy who accomplished in their life time a course of Higher Education.

When we think of the failures of Critical Education we must, first of all, think of it in this contest. Below I will explain that the reasons are immanent to critical thinking.

I do not have any argument with McLaren that the whole issue, in the last instance, is economic. But from this point I want to emphasize the break between the critic's perception of the 'whole' and the critic's performance as an educator as well as of transformator. The lesson of Lyotard (see esp. 1998, pp. 12–13 (§21), [6] and, in some aspects, that of Derrida (See, for example 1997, pp. 10–18, or 165–171) is not relativism or the multiplicity of conflicts, but the irreducibility of genres and practices.

Two comments before I go on:

1) If I may continue the direction that I started in the last conference, the long dynasty of critical theories started with Plato through Kant, Marx, Nietzsche, the Frankfurt school early and late, Dewey, Lyotard, and postcolonial writing is characterized by a manner of writing that emerges out of awareness of suffering, distractions, exclusions, ignorance and/or misperceptions, and aims towards changing them (Rimon-Or, 2005). Some of the notions mentioned above position awareness of suffering and destructions as references on which the scholar writes as witness; some position this awareness as the point of departure of thinking, like the late Adorno, Dewey, or Lyotard.

2) From this point of view, it is not the question of what is an unacceptable evil, which should constitute critical discourse after the postmodern critique. What extracts postmodern and postcolonial critique from relativism is that it is constituted out of the awareness of unuttered suffering, scientific mistakes and discursive limitations. Hence, its break with Marxism is less severe than it looks at first glance as I will show bellow. To delineate lines of unacceptable deeds would lead critical thinking nowhere. For example: if we ask whether the 9.11 events are more unacceptable than the massive harm and destruction caused by the West, with the support of its leaders, economics and law systems, to the Islamic world and Africa, the answer is always meaningless. But the question opens a fertile critique of the dominant world's conceptions in the West. Only when the focus of the gaze turns to the dominant side, by critics who share its discourses, the question gains the potential to expose some truth. From this perspective the

critical philosopher cannot be 'humanistic'. Wittgenstein' remark: "the philosopher is not a citizen of any community of ideas" (Fann, 2002, p. 290) should be taken seriously in the form of critique suggested by Adorno and Lyotard.

More than that, rating the explosions on the scales of humanity built by conceptions of humanity structured on the background, and in opposite to, and at the expense of, the culture of the one who turns his body into a living bomb, closes the discourse in itself. We can only ask what kind of suffering, exclusion and distress is expressed by the revolt. But by the same token we also should ask what kind of suffering, exclusion and distress is expressed by the absence of revolt. The latter is the question that necessitates a revising of the notion of faulty consciousness. Spivak's essay "Can the Subalterns Speak?" (1988) is relevant here.

Critical Theory can search only for the signifiers of scientific failures, which are contingent in theory's structure (as Marx did in his critique of political economist, as well in his critique of Young Hegelians), or of suffering, which the critic exposes as contingent in social/economical/political structures (as Marx did in his early writings, as well as, though in a different way, in *Capital*). Critical education can only train the minds to search for those signifiers. For doing this one should develop forces of resistance: to norms, to prevalent notions, to stimuli of easy promotion and financial success. One must be trained to work 'against the current'. In Lyotard's terms we would say that the role of the critical thinker is to give voice to *Differends*. This means, first of all, to learn to listen to what cannot be uttered in accepted arbitrations; second, it means acquiring an ability, as well as readiness, to give voice to what was silenced; third, to take responsibility for what was said (Lyotard, 1988, §22,23,165,166. Adorno formulates a similar idea in this way:

> Every step thought takes comes up against society, and no step can pin it down as such, as one thing among other things... The stance adopted by thought as such, regardless of its content, is a confrontation with nature that has become habitual and has been internalized; an intervention and not a mere reception. (Adorno, 1973, p. 21)

And here I return to the problem I posed in the beginning. If this is the task of Critical Pedagogy, and critique in general, at whom does it aim? Does it really aim towards the proletariat as such? For the proletariats these topics become irrelevant as long as they are excluded from Higher Education. Acquiring critical thinking is exactly the luxury they are deprived of (see Rimon Or, ibid). That is the crucial loss of the proletariat, and I will come to that immediately. Even if we ignore the exclusion of proletariats from Higher Education, according to what I said before critical thinking's role restricts it to the critique of bourgeois' society, institutes and structures of knowledge. This is also a lesson we should learn from poststructuralist writings. What I said above is not an undermining of Marxist analysis; it is the demarcation of its discursive limitations. And we cannot shrug it off as a discursive problem. When it comes to the critical discourse it turns, in a non-reducible manner, to an ontological problem.

Two different questions thence follow: one is practical: keeping in mind that the greatest damage to democracy is being made by scholars and professionals, what are the aims of critique in Academic Institutes? It has to do with questions like: "Who are the candidates?"; "What should they learn, or what are the indispensable abilities without which judges, teachers, social workers, economics, philosophers, could not be graduated?" And in total opposition to what we have learned to recognize as postmodern relativism, it posits for us a strict criterion: it is the ability to criticize one's own dominant values and presuppositions through the awareness of the destructions, eliminations, suffering, limitations, they cause due to their structure. Critical Education must engage with these questions if it wants to confer meaning on its work in classrooms. Below I will give more reasons for that.

The other question is how can we know something about the damaged consciousness of the tremendously expanded economic margins? What can we say about them? How can we deal with it? There is no question about its destructive role, which, unfortunately, is not subversive in capitalist democracy, as we can see now in a most horrifying way in Israel and in a less horrifying mode, but nonetheless frightening, in the legitimation of the enforcement of all social spheres to economic discourse in the western world.

As Adorno poses it in *Negative Dialectics* we must recognize that the object of knowledge is eternally detached from us (1973, p. 31). And in order to produce some relevant knowledge we mast recognize its limitations. In the end we can only question knowledge about ourselves, in the form of deconstruction.

Adorno doesn't apply this acknowledgement to the perception of the proletariat, or the individual in late capitalism. Nevertheless, we can accomplish this move. First of all we must acknowledge the fact that our tools of understanding are very limited: What leads a mother, today, in Israel, who cannot feed her sons, to vote for a government which will send her older son to function as a war criminal in the Palestinian areas, when she knows that she will pay by the continuance of the hunger, and by endangering the life, both of her sons and of her self? Can we base her willingness to kill her own sons, and the children of other mothers, on her faulty consciousness? Are parents who sell their daughters in order to feed their boys unaware of their abuse by their leaders? I think that every superficial conversation will reveal the fact that they know it perfectly well. They know it perfectly well long before they have to starve them, sell them and send them to be killed as murderers. To reduce these massive phenomena to Marx's perception of faulty consciousness or to the Frankfurt School notions of the dissolution of the individual is to degrade human being too far.

I think that we should take into account the calls that came, in the last two conferences of Critical Education and INPE, from the South African scholars. If I understood them correctly, the critical thinkers were all united behind the impression that our structures of knowledge, and our discourse as a whole, lose their meaning in the face of massive and severe poverty in their state. The same helplessness is shared by Israeli critics today.

I want to suggest that this breakdown of knowledge in the face of society does not originate in the collapse of the South African or the Israeli societies. It emerged with critical philosophy in Plato and it lingers there today since it hasn't been solved.[7] That philosophy and sociology in the West were formed in the image of the affluent sectors of society is the point of departure of Marxist and neo Marxist thought and it is not a topic for discussion in this context. But the fact that we still think that we have a reliable explanation (and sometimes even a remedy) for the collapsing of the subject in situations of sever deficiency, and the collapsing of the democratic institutes, should be reconsidered. More then that, the fact that we think that as scholars, who belong to the bourgeois — class and institutes —, radicals as we are or may be, we can face the collapsing subjects as the bearers of the answer instead of as questioners (if I may paraphrase Homi Bhabha), should teach us something about our failures.

While posing the collapsing of the individual at the center of the investigation, we must presuppose some criteria for recognizing the subject or the individual. This move prevents us from investigating these presumptions. In other words, it prevents us from investigating the gap between the subject of investigation and reality. It is precisely the closing of this gap that brings thinking to a halt, according to Adorno.

> For the difference between the so called subjective part of mental experience and its object will not vanish by any means, as witness the necessary and painful exertions of the knowing subject. In the unreconciled condition, nonidentity is experienced as negativity. From the negative, the subject withdraws to itself and to the abundance of its ways to react. Critical self-refection alone will keep it from a construction of this abundance, from building walls between itself and the object, from the supposition that its being-for itself is an in-and-for-itself. The less identity can be assumed between subject and object, the more contradictory are the demands made upon the cognitive subject, upon its unfettered strength and candid self-reflection. (Adorno, 1973, p. 31)

When Homi Bhabha (1998) suggests inquiring into the notion of 'whiteness' instead of into the 'problems of the blacks', he repeats the same idea. Bhabha suggests that the sense of 'whiteness' was created through the encounter with the 'black'. Hence, reflections on the notion of 'whiteness' will create knowledge of society, which will also dismantle racial perspectives. This dismantling will free human beings who are perceived as black from the identity enforced on them by the notion of whiteness. When Lyotard places the problem of *differends* at the center of his analysis he poses the limits of accepted genres at the center of investigations. Despite all the differences, these two ways of inquiry share a similar principle: they produce knowledge about accepted theories and ways of thinking and at the same time give ways to other voices and forms of subjectivities. As we can understand from the citation from Adorno above, this deconstruction of dominant truths should continue as long as critical thinking continues, since the object of perception creates its nonidentity in a non-reducible manner.

I said at the beginning of this paper that Marx's method of inquiry fits with the principles of critical thinking presented above: Marx pointed at scientific failures contingent on political economy's presuppositions, as well as at proletariat's suffering, as contingent on a capitalist system. This move enabled him to present the capitalist system, which was perceived as natural and developed, as historical and 'prehistoric'. In the same way it allowed him to present the social order, which was perceived as progressive, as a source of exploitation and misery (though, dialectically, progressive). New objects of investigation were created as the 'familiar and the natural' was examined from a perspective that focused on its margins.

From this point one can continue the Marxist way of thinking in two ways. The first is by identifying the concept of the 'proletariat' with proletariats. This way, although it is Marxist, is not critical. The other way is to continue Marxist thought by deconstructing the concept of the proletariats. This means to inquire into what the concept of the proletariats miss, due to their exclusion from academic discourse.

This transformation of critical discourse means first of all a struggle in the academy for massive participation of students from the margins of society — economic margins, as well cultural ones. It continues Marx's critique of Hegel, as Adorno formulates it in the first chapter of *Hegel: Three Studies* (1994). In this chapter Adorno argues that Hegel's forgetfulness of the suffering of labor reveals the truth of society in Hegel's days. But as Adorno formulates the work of the philosopher "in the face of Hegel" he forgets labor again. He forgets the exclusion of labor from the thinking of labor. In this way he reveals the truth of his days, at list in the academy of the 60th.[8] My argument is that deconstruction of the notion of proletariats should start from this point. In this way it will continue Marxist thought adequately.

If we accept the idea that the gap between the subject and his object will never disappear, we can conclude that deconstructing the division of labor between scholars and proletariats is a way to produce knowledge about proletariats. It is worth recalling here Laclau and Mouffe's *Hegemony & Socialist Strategy* (1985), in which they argue that participating in discourse is the only way to constitute a class, although a class that will always surpass its definitions. We should recall here also the revolutionary role that women and scholars from the colonized parts of the world have played in western social sciences since they entered it, as well as Hegel's forgetfulness of labor, to understand how far mistakes of perceptions can go, even when they are critical. In the social sciences we must talk to our subjects, if we want to open our presuppositions to the procedures of refuting. And the opening of the doors of the Academies to subjects from the social margins changes the structures of society. This is the transformative power of critical thinking. I want to suggest that there is no other.

The experience of the influence of de Beauvoir, Gilligan, Fannon, Said and others teaches us that essentialism is not always an immanent feature of human beings. Sometimes it is created on the line of social encounter structured in the form of power relations. It is created when the dominant group fixes the others to its structures of understanding and develops a total opacity to the fact that they do not speak the same language. As Bhabha taught us (1994),[9] by doing that, the dominant group closes the doors to a large spectrum of its own experience. It is the opacity to the experience of oneself which creates the question of essentialism during the encounter with the subjected Other, at least sometimes.

I want to suggest that this is what happens to us in the case of the faulty consciousness of the proletariat. We haven't talked to them in the last 150 years; they don't come to our universities. When they come to their age, most of the time they don't answer the requirements; sometimes they cannot afford it. In the Marxist critique both reasons appear as side effects of faulty consciousness or of capitalism, but the phenomenon does not appear as a cause for a detachment of knowledge from social reality. The meaning of that is that the exclusion of the proletariats does not come up as a problem of knowledge in the social sciences and in philosophy. Had it happened, segregation in schools would have arisen as an urgent problem in the universities. And if they don't acquire our own knowledge and way of thinking in numbers big enough to found a discourse about their experience, we cannot talk with them.

Thus, we excluded the experience of the subjectivity's dismantlement from the focuses of our investigations, having signified it as a transparent occurrence, which does not occur to us as critical thinkers. As Bhabha shows, this attitude is a crucial cause for cultural self-destruction. That is why we should turn to the destruction in our own field if we want to open the discourse of faulty consciousness to discussion. And this is what we should do as critics.

Forgetting that experience is mediated and gain meaning through language, hence, that common genres constitute a precondition to communicate experiences, is first of all a suspension: of the familiar, of needs, of time; it is to forget that education is an encounter with other perspectives by *means of mediation* (and hence the immensely important role of the mediator); it is to forget that education is a possession of different languages and attitudes; an investment of time and money — not for the sake of having more of the same, but for the sake of acquiring a new language for dealing with our own faulty consciousness. This notion of education is shared by Marx and Dewey (see this argument in Colapierto, 1988, pp. 11–36). We forgot that this is what we have to give the subjected in order to talk with them, and we forgot that talk with them is what we need in order to educate ourselves, to supply knowledge back to society, and to become a social area of social transformation.[10]

In this point the two tasks of Critical Pedagogy converge. May it be that the universities produce faulty consciousness scholars and professionals, in big numbers enough to destroy democracy, and education, *because* scholars have forgotten to position themselves in front of faulty consciousness as questioners?

Raising these questions is not a merely optional for critical thinking. The forgetfulness of knowledge's dismantlement at its margins leads to destruction since it produces opacity to suffering and in its turn causes knowledge to be irrelevant as long as it adheres to its own terms. This is the connection between sensitivity to suffering and the truth of knowledge upon which Adorno insists in the Introduction to *Negative Dialectics*. Paulo Freire deals with a similar problem when he demarcates the gap created between the scholar and the illiterates while experience is translated into perceptions of reality. In *Pedagogy of the Oppressed* Freire argues that the meaning of experience given by the oppressed is the subject matter of the transformative educator. Dialogue in Freire terms means that the scholar poses his/her perception of the illiterates as a question while he/she inquires into the meaning assigned by the oppressed to terms and experience. The absence of dialogue is destructive since it enforces the implementation of wrong and blind perceptions of reality. It destroys its objects of knowledge, which are, in The Arts and Social Sciences, real human beings, and it destroys its own relevance as a source of knowledge for democracy, as the postcolonial and feminist writing have taught us. I think that we can see it today in the collapsing of the welfare state, in its legitimation, and in our own help-lessness in the face of poverty, evil's justifications and the degradation and the decrease of Humanities and Education in the Universities. Both courses of destruction cause the detachment of critique and knowledge, of critique as knowledge, from its objects, and at the same time expel expanded circles of human beings out of the reach of knowledge.

If Critical Pedagogy seeks to criticize itself I suggest starting with the notion of faulty consciousness. Whether we like it or not, this is our point of departure in all the conflicting notions of Critical Thinking, and I think that we have enough evidence to show that we miss our object of instruction. Marxist thought in education, due to its subject matter, cannot maintain its relevance if it does not linger a while in front of this failure.

I want to suggest, very briefly, that if we turn to our own failure to protect our own field, the term faulty consciousness is not good enough. I think that we are facing a situation in which a more or less conscious and defined activity of scholars encounters a powerful environment which reacts to its deeds and phrases in a way that obliterates its meaning. Hence, consciousness itself becomes irrelevant in a way that does not depend on the scholars. In this situation the term 'resisting' misses the point. What the subjects really need is a protection, a protected social area in which their activity could have some meaning. The latter appears as a precondition for resisting. The fact that we could not resist the decrease of our own field should signify for us, among other things, that the lessons of resistance in times in which external forces destroy subjectivity, still have to be learned. This experience stands in the center of Marx's critique of labor in *Early Writings*.

What we took from Marx with no question is the supposition that when human beings have nothing to lose they revolt, or at least react in a way that enables scholars or the political party to link it to a revolutionary move. The assumption that external conditions of equilibrium are preconditions for resisting changes the perception of the role and praxis of critique, and the analysis of its absence. Instead of transforming the notion of resistance, we confuse ourselves among plural perspectives of the social conflicts, trying to define them according to Marxist terms, asking if they reveal the need to break with Marx, or if they can still be defined in economic terms. These questions enclose us 'within the walls of presumed definitions' in Adorno's terms. I think that, had we talked more to the social margins, we would have understood that acts and phrases change their meaning in the social encounter, and we could have protected our own field, and society, in a much more effective way. But this is for another discussion.

Praxis in the field of Critical Education must have two directions — both of them deal with the awareness of suffering and destruction. One is educational praxis in the classroom, which I mentioned above: the training of students to work against norms and perceptions in order to recognize their limitations, and to resist them. The other is to question, in the academic world, the detachment from the margins, the possibility that a veil of ignorance separates dominant structures of knowledge from social reality, and hence, between praxis of scholars and their intentions.

In Critical Education we should raise these questions as a question of the responsibility of scholars to communicate with the margins and as a question of the responsibility of scholars for knowledge.

These two courses are not reducible. The one positions the subjected, or its disappearance, as referent while the critique addresses his interlocutors (students) as speakers of the dominant sectors of society. In the other the referent is oneself. Both extend and continue Marx, albeit they practice the Marxist's conception as it should be done by scholars as political agents restricted to the affluent parts of society.

NOTES

[1] This paper was prepared for the International Critical Pedagogy Workshop, in Madrid, August, 2004.

[2] See also Eric L. Krakauer's explanation about Adorno's way of thinking (1998, p. 77).

[3] See Laclau and Mouffe's argument in this matter (1985, p. 125).

[4] I.e. in the assay that bears that name: "What is enlightenment" (1984).

[5] "The apparent failure in the educational reality at schools, universities, youth movements, community centers, and other cultural and social fields where Critical Theory in education is being seriously tested in actual life situations".

[6] The whole discussion of *The Differend* deals with the idea that the meaning of experience takes form in discourse and by discursive means.

[7] See in this matter two different essays, each deal with different subjected group. The first presents a research of James Scott (1992) about peasantry in middle age. Scott presents a history of resistance, which reveals the peasants as incline to overestimate their power to avert power relations. His finding stand in odd with Marxist and other notions that see peasantry as more or less stable class, influenced by religious faith of accepting one's place on earth. He argues that historians, as well as other scholars and dominant elites do not have access to the social areas in which the activity of resistance takes form, and when claims are made openly they appear in disguise. Scholars cannot recognize occasions of resistance as such, since their elitist affiliation prevent them from acquiring the relevant knowledge of interpretation (1992, pp. 222–223). The other essay (Boyarin, 1997) presents a similar claim regarding knowledge about political-cultural subjected group.

[8] It is interesting, in this case, to see Merleau-Ponty critique of Bergson: "... it is a generalized perception, it is in actual and present perception... that it is necessary to search for the relationship of our being with things: "we are of it" thus means that these colors, these objects which we see, decorate and inhabit even our dreams, that these animals are humorous variants of ourselves, that all beings are symbolic of our life, and that this is what we see in them" (Merleau-Ponty, 1970, p. 16–17).

[9] See esp. "Mimicry and Man", "Articulating the Archaic" (Bhabha, 1994) and "The White Stuff" (1998). Nigel Pleasant's (2002, pp. 172–174) critique of Winch might also be relevant here.

[10] I am not talking here about dialogue between students and teachers but about the mobility into the critical discourse of researchers from the margins.

REFERENCES

Adorno, T. W. (1994). *Hegel: Three studies*. London & Massachusetts: The MIT Press.

Adorno, T. W. (1973). *Negative dialectics*. London: Routledge & Kegan Poul.

Bhabha, H. (1998). The white stuff (Political aspect of whiteness). *Artforum, 36*(9), 21–24.

Bhabha, H. (1994). *The location of culture*. London & New York: Rouledge.

Boyarin, D. (1997). Trickster, martyrs, and appearance: 'Hidden Transcripts' and the diaspora art of resistance. *Theory and Criticism, 10*(Summer 1997), 145–162.

Colapietro, Vincent, M. (1998). From 'individual' to 'Subject': Marx and Dewey on the person. In W. J. Gavin (Ed.), *Context over foundation* (pp. 11–36). Boston & Tokyo: D Reidel Publishing Company.

Fann, K. T. (2002). Beyond Marx and Wittgenstein. In G. Kitching & N. Pleasants (Eds.), *Marx and Wittgenstein*. London & New York: Routledge.

Foucault, M. (1984). What is enlightenment? In P. Rabinow (Ed.), *The foucault reader* (pp. 32–50). New York: Pantheon Books.

Freire, P. (2005). *Pedagogy of the oppressed*. New York: Continuum.

Jacques, D. (1997). *Of grammatology*. Baltimore & London: Johns Hopkins University Press.

Krakauer, E. L. (1998). *The disposition of the subject: Reading Adorno's dialectic of technology*. Evanston, IL: Northwestern University Press.

Laclau, E., & Chantle, M. (1985). *Hegemony & socialist strategy*. London: Verso.

Lyotard, J.-F. (1988). *The differend*. Minneapolis, MN: University of Minneapolis.

Merleau-Ponty, M. (1970). *In praise of philosophy*. Northwestern University Press.

Nietzsche, F. (2001). *The gay science*. Cambridge: Cambridge University Press.

Nietzsche, F. (1886). *Beyond good and evil: Prelude to a philosophy of the future*. Harmondsworth, Penguin.

Pleasants, N. (2002). Marx and Wittgenstein. In G. Kitching & N. Pleasants (Eds.), *Marx and Wittgenstein* (pp. 160–182). London & New York: Routledge.

Rimon or, A. (2005). Power relation and liberation. In I. Gur-Ze'ev (Ed.), *Critical theory and critical pedagogy today* (pp. 329–340). Hifa: Haifa University Press.

Spivak, G. (1988). Can the subaltern speak? In G. Nelson & L. Grossberg (Eds.), *Marxism and the interpretation of culture* (pp. 271–313). Urbana, IL: University of Illinois.

Scott, J. (1992). False consciousness, or laying it on thick. In R. M. Merelman (Ed.), *Languege, symbolism, & politics* (pp. 209–246). Boulder, San Francisco, & Oxford: Westview Press.

HEINZ SÜNKER

16. GLOBALIZATION, DEMOCRATIC EDUCATION (BILDUNG), AND THE CRISIS OF DEMOCRACY

What is must be changeable if it is not to be all

(Th. W. Adorno, *Negative Dialectics*)

1.

The last big crisis in capitalism—in the late 20's/early 30's of the last century—became in some nations a crisis of democracy with murderous consequences for many human beings. With respect to contemporary conditions it has to be stated that there is a strong connection between social analysis and educational answers to the type of social crisis.[1]

Under the conditions of the still existing neo-liberal regulation strategies, in late capitalism there was and is an attempt to enforce homogenization processes in the form of globalization[2] that scorn the official deregulation policy as well as the dispersed difference thinking. For what goes by the official name of deregulation policy by all means also in the form of various strategies of social policy (cf. Clarke 2004) on a world scale is really nothing more than an attempt to enforce global social relations that follow unrestrained market logics, or profit orientation, and the turning of potential citizens into customers.[3] This is in the interests of securing power in the context of hegemonic disputes (cf. for example Altvater/Mahnkopf, 1996; Dixon 2000; Jessop, 2002; Altvater 2005).[4]

What C. Boggs (2000) subtitles as "Corporate Power and the Decline of the Public Sphere" behaves complementary to this and conveys the national as well as international standard. Bringing together classical social analytical topics such as capitalism, politics, democracy, political conscience and political involvement, with reference to today's US American reality but by all means able to be generalized, to a historically concrete relationship, he reaches a devastating conclusion about the state and perspective of democratization in his study that is titled "End of Politics". In particular he points out against those who (still) opt for the "taming" or "civilizing" of capitalism, the support of democracy in the form of "civil society", as an result of empirical research: "The reality is that civil society, with the end of the cold war, has come to embrace a turn toward privatization, toward a neo-liberal emphasis on market capitalism that is fully compatible with the growth of corporate colonization and economic globalization" (2000, p. 276). This is an extension of the understanding that earlier lead Bowles/Gintis (1987, p. 3; cf. Meiksins Wood 1995) to the conclusion that no capitalist society nowadays is able to be properly seen as democratic because this must go hand in hand with the securing of personal freedom

I. Gur-Ze'ev, The Possibility/Impossibility of a New Critical Language in Education, 315–331.
© *2010 Sense Publishers. All Rights Reserved.*

and socially responsible and made responsible dealing with power. When looking at 'politics' and its constitutional conditions, in the USA and elsewhere, this basic deficiency has not only not been remedied, rather it even gained strength after the collapse of the state capitalist systems of Central and Eastern Europe. This leads Chossudovsky—in his study "The Globalization of Poverty. Impacts of IMF and World Bank Reforms"—(2002, p. 310) to the challenging conclusion: "Marked by conflicts of interest and as a consequence of its ambivalent relationship towards private economical and financial interests, the state system in the West is experiencing a crisis. Under these conditions parliamentary democracy has become a mere ritual. There are no alternatives available for the voters. Neo-liberalism has become an integral part of the political program of all the great political parties. Like in a one party state election outcomes today have practically no effect on the actual path of state economic and social politics".

The decline of 'politics' and 'democracy', which seems to be even more advanced in the USA in light of the rule of the 'thief in the president's position' (Kellner, 2001; cf. Palast, 2003)—and is connected with many crimes (Mandel, 2004)—, has been a deciding qualitative problem of the topics "democratic education", "achieving democracy", "education for democracy" and its mediation with the background of social relations for both political structures and political conscience.[5] The obvious enforcing and strengthening of an oligarchic rule in today's class structured capitalist societies, the colonization of the every day life of adults and children through consumerism (classically: Lefebvre, 1972; Marcuse, 1987), the oppression of potential alternatives (Berman, 2000; Steinberg/Kincheloe, 1997), the colonization of the conscience of those ruled by indoctrination, manipulation and disinformation (Chomsky, 2000, p. 173 onwards; 2001, p. 99 onwards), the myth of the classless society; all this has always belonged to the known inventory in hegemonic struggles.[6]

Against a reductionist judgment of the situation one could and can maintain, owing to the importance of the differentiation of strategies and institutions, "Even with the necessary criticisms of the unequal power relations surrounding education and the larger society, we need to remember that schooling was never simply an imposition on supposedly culturally/politically inept people. Rather, educational practices were and are the result of struggles and compromises over what should count as legitimate knowledge, pedagogy, goals and criteria for determining effectiveness" (Carlson/Apple, 1998, p. 11). The involved problems of forming opinions and judgment as a basis for 'political ability' are also referred to by Bourdieu's views when he confirms that it is valid to recognize the contradiction that exists in the fact that everyone "is granted an equal right to personal opinion, but not everyone is given the means by which to carry out this formal, universal right" (Bourdieu, 2001, p. 89; cf. Bourdieu, 1984, p. 639, 686 onwards).

First of all the task of "reformulating the concept of democracy" comes into view with its differently formulated attributes, but pointing in the identical direction (Hirsch, 1995, p. 198, cf. p. 187), or the clarification of the question of possibilities for a "rediscovery of politics", as Boggs (2000, p. 278) calls it, as a base for hopes for processes of "re-politicization": "Political renewal depends on recovery of precisely those concerns that a depoliticized society so thoroughly devalues, namely, collective consumption, social planning, citizen involvement, and the imposition of public controls over capital".[7] This shows very clearly the challenges and tasks in dealing with our topic: mediating a concept of democracy with concepts of autonomy and self-determination, and therefore making use of the German concept of 'Bildung'.[8]

With this conceptualization the necessity to account for the fundaments and content of 'participation' is linked in the context of theory and practice of democracy in a way that is appropriate for the present. Pateman remarked here: "Davis (1964) has said that the 'classical theory (i.e. the theory of participatory democracy) had an ambitious purpose, 'the education of an entire people to the point where their intellectual, emotional and moral capacities have reached their full potential and they are joined, freely and actively in a genuine community', and that the strategy for reaching this end is through the use of 'political activity and government for the purpose of public education'. However, he goes on to say that the 'unfinished business' of democratic theory is 'the elaboration of plans of action and specific prescriptions which offer hope of progress towards a genuinely democratic polity' (pp. 40 and 41). It is exactly this last that can be found in the theories of the writers on participatory democracy; a set of specific prescriptions and plans of action necessary for the attainment of political democracy. This does take place through 'public education' but the latter depends on participation in many spheres of society on 'political activity' in a very wide sense of the term" (1970, p. 21; cf. Széll, 1988).

Especially as education and politics are part of the bulwark of bourgeois society, one must remember on the other hand that, spoken by the Marx of *Grundrisse*, "the great historical side of capital" or "the great civilizing influence of capital" (Marx no date: p. 313; cf. Berman, 1988, p. 90 onwards) has, to a great extent, fallen down in these areas, although within systematic borders that, as in the beginnings of the history of education (Heydorn, 1979) clearly let the opposite to partial, utilizable talent and to the overlapping freedom orientated perspective of education emerge.

In light of the possibilities of generalizing education today, which are particularly based on historical/social developments as well as changes in the labour process (cf. Heydorn, 1980, p. 290), in the interests of securing humanity and the ability to survive (cf. Bloch, 1959: chapter 55) at least essential elements of the debate about 'education' and 'democracy' are portrayed as renewable.[9]

2.

Here Adorno's thoughts on a "democratic education theory" (Adorno, 1998b) are given fundamental importance and are to be linked to his formulated starting point in his text "Education after Auschwitz": "The premier demand upon all education is that Auschwitz not happen again" (Adorno, 1998a, p. 191; see also 1973, p. 361 onwards).

Adorno's concept suggestion and postulate could assume the function of a clamp because through them relationship regulations become possible in the context of social constitution, political culture and education processes, which are fundamental for our topic.

Against the background of the often devastating experiences of our century - especially with respect to the German experiences -it may seem bold to deal in a text with Democracy, Education, and Ethics in the Post-Auschwitz World, i.e., asking for a democratic pedagogy and democratic education today. So I would like to declare at the outset that my concern here is simply to recall a number of ideas from the history and present of the discipline of pedagogy, from the tradition of democratic ideas, if possible to rethink them -with a social-theoretical and social policy interest - and to examine their consequences for a democratic education.

The focus of my deliberations are—as I said—Adorno's (1903–69) thoughts on democratic pedagogy (Adorno, 1998b) and the starting point of his very famous text *Erziehung nach Auschwitz* (Education after Auschwitz). This shows: Auschwitz is the salient sign of the decline of civilization. Adorno's categories and postulate can serve as a focal point because they enable understanding of the relationships between social conditions, political culture, ethics and educational processes which are decisive for our topic.

We can see what is most significant about the relationship between political culture, democratic politics and subjectivity in the radio debate, which has since become famous, between Theodor W. Adorno, the outstanding intellectual in post-fascist Germany, and Arnold Gehlen, his counterpart - a conservative 'mandarin', on 3 February 1965:

> **Gehlen** Yes, the child, who hides behind the mother's skirt, it has both anxiety and the minimum or optimum of security that the situation produces. Mr. Adorno, you of course again see here the problem of autonomy. Do you really believe that we should expect everyone to bear this burden of a concern with principles, with excessive reflection, with the on-going after-effects of the confusions of life, because we have sought to swim free? That is what I would very much like to know.[10]

> **Adorno** To that I can very simply say: Yes! I have a conception of objective happiness and objective despair, and I would say that as long as we unburden people [with authoritarian institutions, H.S.] and do not grant them full respons-ibility and self-determination, so long too will their well-being and their happiness in this world be a sham. And a sham which will one day burst. And when it bursts, it will have terrible consequences. (Grenz, 1974, p. 294f.)

The core of this dispute is the meaning of maturity and responsibility.[11] Adorno responded to Gehlen's statement with the remark, I mean, the need which drives people to this unburdening is precisely the burden imposed by institutions, that is, the world's agencies which stand outside and over them. It is thus to a certain extent so: first they are chased out, sent out by the mother, into the cold, and are under terrible pressure; and then, afterwards, they flee into the lap of precisely the same mother, namely society, which chased them out. In the context of his view of the conditions of the constitution of subjectivity and its (in)capacity for action, he is here clearly speaking of the relation between autonomy—self-determination – account-ability.[12] This triad can be illuminated by an exploration of both individual and social history. In defending Adorno's position, intellectuals are the keepers of political culture in a democratic tradition and meaning (cf. Sünker, 1994). This means that, against the (neo-) Aristotelian tradition—which is concerned with 'elites'—not only a few people are able to reflect, to carry the burden of reflection and responsibility, but all are able to do so. It includes, today, the task to (re-)construct the public and, therefore, the political culture in a participatory model. Within this approach, 'the public sentiment which is encouraged is not reconciliation and harmony, but rather political agency and efficacy, namely the sense that we have a say in the economic, political and civic arrangements which define our lives together, and that what one does makes a difference' (Benhabib, 1989, p. 389). This is the basic assumption to defend concepts of resistance.

Reflections on historical experience, which contains more than any gathering of knowledge, can lead to a socio-historical consciousness accompanied by a capacity for judgment which provides a capacity for action. Thus it can help serve this democratic, participatory goal.

Education - precisely in the ways it differs from 'knowledge' - has to derive its present from the past, to make history the content of educational processes (Benjamin, 1969; Flacks, 1988; Wehler, 1988). For a democratic pedagogy this means, *inter alia*: learning from the history of this country or its regions, and - in my case - the history of German political culture. This requires, firstly, engaging with the question 'What does it mean to deal with the past?' (Adorno, 1998b). And, secondly, posing the question, what form can be taken by an alternative to domination in individual action and social structures in democratic social conditions and an accompanying political culture in Europe—and beyond.

In view of the frequently unsuccessful engagement, dominated by political majorities, with recent German history, and the accompanying consequences for the quality of political culture in Germany up to the present day (Mitscherlich and Mitscherlich, 1967; Brunkhorst, 1987; Stern, 1991), for the moment we can only say that this question, as a question for everyone interested in a substantial democratization of all areas of life, must stay on the agenda.

The second question which follows from this is related to a problem which is decisive for the future of a European society: that which currently appears as right-extremism and hostility to foreigners, as well as a re-activation of politically motivated violence in this society, and in its adoption by a majority of the dominant political class exposes the latter, relates to traditions in the European and German history and the history of the political culture which many overwhelmingly believed in (Lepsius, 1988).[13]

In this situation it becomes clear that the question of democracy once again reappears on the agenda. Adorno maintained that the delay in German democracy also resulted in crucial problems in the way the past was dealt with: "But democracy has not become naturalized to the point where people truly experience it as their own and see themselves as subjects of the political process". This is why, continued Adorno, democracy was evaluated according to the success or failure it brought with it (Adorno, 1998b, p. 93).

Speaking about the necessity of "a return to the subject," Adorno put forward his thesis that education only makes any sense as critical self-reflection. And he concluded: "The single genuine power standing against the principle of Auschwitz is autonomy, if I might use the Kantian expression: the power of reflection, of self-determination, of not-cooperating (Adorno, 1998a, pp. 195). This indicates the relationship between a democratic education and an education for democracy with which we should engage.

An initial formulation of this foundational question can be found in classical pedagogic conceptions, as they appeared in the reflective and wide-ranging early bourgeois theoretical debates. At the end of the eighteenth century Kant (1724–1804), in his lecture *'Über Pädagogik' (On Pedagogy)*, wrote perhaps education constantly improves, and every successive generation takes another step towards the full realization of humanity; for behind education lies the great secret of the realization of human nature (Kant, 1964, p. 700). He also tied this to a positive anthropology which placed social conditions, and thus the social conditionality of humans, in the foreground: "Good education is precisely that which produces everything that is good in the world. The seeds which lie within people must be constantly developed. For the basis of evil cannot be found in the natural constitution of people. The only cause of evil is that nature is not brought under control. People contain only the seeds of good" (Kant, 1964, p. 704f.). If, as Kant stresses, education constituted the most important and difficult question posed to humanity, it thus also led to this requirement: "Children must be raised not towards the current, but the future possibly improved state of the human race, that is, the idea of humanity, and everything appropriate to its destiny. This principle is of great importance. Parents generally raise their children only so that they fit into the existing world, even though it may be ruined. They should, however, better raise them so that a future, better state is brought about" (Kant, 1964, p. 704).[14]

In the first third of the nineteenth century Schleiermacher (1768–1834) - one of the discipline's founding fathers - also in a lecture titled *'Über Pädagogik'* said that education should be based on the intergenerational relationship, from which derives the task that the younger generation should be delivered to the main communities in which they have to become self-sufficiently active (Schleiermacher, 1983, p. 94). Because he was concerned with the category fundamental to the educational relationship, the future - thus the capacity for construction - he binds the perspective of the socially-based action of the rising generation to the dual task of conservation and change. At the same time this premise leads him to a crucial principle concerning the relationship between pedagogy and politics: Both theories, pedagogy and politics, strive towards what is most complete; both are ethical disciplines and require the same treatment. Politics will not reach its goal if pedagogy is not an integral part of it, or if a similarly developed discipline does not stand beside it. The more communal life within the state is practically disrupted - theoretically seen, misunderstood - the less it is possible for a correct approach to exist in relation to the influence of the older generation on the younger (Schleiermacher, 1983, p. 12; cf. Mollenhauer, 1980, p. 103).

3.

The positions of Kant and Schleiermacher constitute a critique of the instrumentalization of people - foundational for all approaches to a critical theory of society - to which Adorno's frosty conclusion, which in a certain sense describes a final stage in social relations, relates in a complementary way.[15]

This leads us to the task of examining social relations in their consequences for the relations between individuals and society. For the present this means to deal with the contradictory results of the capitalist framework of societalization for people, to dissect their conditions of existence. The relations between society and individual are constituted by a contradiction between a production and a destruction of the social, of sociality, which can be understood as a result of the capitalist framework of societalization, as inherent to it from the outset (Bowles and Gintis, 1987; Berman, 1988). This contradiction can be seen as both a general and a particular social problem, because it is generation-specific, too. What is interesting here in terms of ethics, education and pedagogy is that when one takes up this contradiction between the production and destruction of sociality, one can speak of a caesura or break in the development of the social potential for both control and communication.

This finding is relevant within the framework of educational and pedagogic reflections if one poses the question, firstly, of possible determinations of the relationship between education and society,[16] and secondly of the consequences for possible foundations and practices of democratic education.

What is of interest here is, of course, the question of the possibilities of a development of communicative potential within and opposed to social contexts which cannot free themselves of their hegemonic form. The issue then becomes one of the analysis of societalization and individualization, of democratic theory and its 'praxis' in the form of political culture, of the question of the constitutive conditions of subjectivity as a basis for the development of self-sufficient life orientations, and finally of a theory of educational processes, the social-theoretical and sociopolitical challenge which still lies in the classical conception of every individual's capacity for education and reason.[17]

This task becomes relevant precisely when one acknowledges Theunissen's comment, his reflection on social reality, that autonomy is complicated or even hindered, undermined to the same degree that the social deformation of individuals increases (Theunissen, 1989, p. 86). For in connection with classical and still contemporary positions, which precisely in this way indicate their modernity, it is important to pose the problem of a contract based on the principle of communalization (Theunissen, 1989, p. 87) and thus the construction and principles of a relational reason (Geyer-Ryan and Lethen, 1987, p. 68). It seems to me to be crucial to establish a mediation between what Benjamin brought forward on the basis of his conception of the relevance of mutual recognition for processes of identity formation, that there is a coercion-free sphere of human agreement which is completely inaccessible to domination: the actual sphere of agreement, speech (Benjamin, 1966, p. 55), and the problem, how power can be criticized from a perspective which appears to profit from and out of it. The question is how reason in itself can establish that murder is worse than non-murder, if it is to one's advantage. In the light of a relational reason, murder becomes suicide; this is already the response of the Odyssey (Geyer-Ryan and Lethen, 1987, p. 69).

The systematic significance of these positions for the constitution of subjectivity and its consequences, is whether the issue is still the difference between a construction of knowledge which remains external to the individual, and the development of the individual themselves in constellations of educational processes (Sünker, 1989), so that it can become clear how education, Enlightenment and experience are inter-woven with each other.

The thesis put forward by Adorno, quoted and discussed earlier, that people must experience democracy as their own affair, understand themselves as the actors in political processes, is complementary to the task of taking this up and spelling it out for institutionally-formed educational processes.[18] Opposed to one-dimensional, linear interpretations of the working possibilities in the institution of the school, we must insist that the contradiction contained within the dialectic of the institut-ionalization of education, between education and domination (Heydorn, 1979), indicates that the institution of the school in its diversely-determined structures, dimensions, levels of action encompasses possibilities for the promotion of emancip-ation and autonomy for all who work in these institutions. This raises the question, firstly of professionalization, the self-understanding of pupils and the consequences contained therein for praxis, that is, the initiation or promotion of educational processes.[19] Secondly that of the relationship between the individual being educated and the inner structures of educational processes and their objects (cf. Holzkamp, 1993; Tomasello, 1999; Kincheloe/Steinberg/Hinchey 1999).

This requires a pedagogy of recognition which, as Heydorn - taking up the Socratic maieutic - made clear in his emphasis on the significance of the 'other' in educational processes (Heydorn, 1979), lies in the promotion of the formation of subjectivity—on the basis of intersubjectivity (cf. Sünker, 1989). This demands at the same time the conceptualization of the relationship between democratic education and the education of democracy in the context of a social formation that recognizes 'problems of justice' to be a political problem and approaches solutions analytically and practically. A main line of this positioning, that overlaps the relationship of the individual and society and defines it as political, can be found in the Marxist problem with which both the problem of identity and difference between normality and normativity becomes a central theme as a 'question of measure' in order to evaluate historically concrete relations: "Here the old view where people, in whatever narrow minded national, religious or political determination they appear to be as the purpose of production, seems to be very raised above the modern world, where production seems to be the purpose of human beings and wealth appears to be the purpose of production. In fact, however, when the narrow minded bourgeois form is stripped away, how is *wealth different to the universality, produced by universal exchange, of needs, abilities, pleasures, productive powers etc. of individuals*? The complete development of human control over the powers of nature, that of so-called nature as well as one's own nature? *The absolute exhaustion of one's creative resources with no other requirement than that of past historical development, that makes this totality of development, that is to say, of the development of all human power as such, not measured by a given scale, an end in itself*? Where one does not reproduce oneself with certainty, rather produces one's totality? Does not try to remain an achievement, rather exists in the absolute movement of becoming?" (Marx no date, p. 387, remark H.S.)

To remove from pedagogical processes - as far as is possible in society and history - the existing formation of subject and object also means making it possible for the rising generation to live and experience democracy in everyday life and in institutions such as family, school, work (Bowles and Gintis, 1987, pp. 204, 208). This holds fast to the possibilities for dealing with individuals and associations of individuals - against the pedagogization of socially produced problems within social relations, that is within social relations of power. This understanding certainly depends on a culture of hope (Benjamin, 1966), an ideal of education, as Kant formulated it; but it also refers to the necessity of building up new social movements to confront the experiences of domination in the various areas of life with experiences and life-forms orientated towards mutual understanding.[20, 21]

In the interests of defending or supporting democracy this perspective gains in importance when one socially theoretically and socially politically assumes a finding for the present social situation and its processing, as Vester et al. (2001, p. 103) depicted in their study "Social milieus in social structural change": "According to theories by Giddens and Beck it is not the milieus that are in decline today. The class cultures of every day life are to a greater extent extraordinarily stable particularly *because* of their ability to be altered and differentiated. What collapses to a certain degree are the hegemonies of certain parties (and fractions of intellectuals) over the followers in ideological positions. Therefore we do not have today a *crisis of milieus* (as a result of the change in values), rather a *crisis of political representation* (as a result of a growing distance between the elite and the milieu)".

Dangerous for civilizing progress it is therefore today a mixture that consists of this crisis of representation, which can partly be said for Continental Europe in the sinking quotas of election participation in the "annoyance" at parties, but not at politics, and problems of the state's ability to take action that can reach the "powerlessness of politics in industrial societies" (Jänicke, 1986).

In this situation we face the 'depoliticisation' of politics by dominating powers. But in the interest of the survival of our planet we should be interested in what Castell calls "a responsible, educated society" (1998, p. 353; cf. Flacks, 1988, p. 68 onwards), i.e. a society based on the reflexivity and competencies of educated citizens (citoyens) who are interested in public discourse on public issues and democracy.[22]

Therefore principles of universalization and reciprocity are on the agenda. As Heller (1984) concluded the perspective is 'To create a society in which alienation is a thing of the past: a society in which every man has access to the social "gifts of fortune" which can enable him to lead a meaningful life... True "history" is pregnant with conflict and continually transcending its own given state. It is history—consciously chosen by men and molded to their design—that can enable all men to make their everyday lives "being-for-them" and that will make the earth a true home for all men' (1984, p. 269).

This shows again the necessity to discuss the problem of regulating the social in a reasonable way—especially in a time when the "extraordinary gap between our technological overdevelopment and our social underdevelopment" (Castells, 1998, p. 359) is threatening comparable to the situations in the first half of the twentieth century. Therefore we have to bring the topic "democratic education—education for democracy" to bring to the fore.

Thereby once again in a new form the task of reformulating the relation of education and democracy comes to light, whose practical formation depends on the interests and competences of educated citizens whose 'educated' and 'stubborn' (therefore different yet able to be generalized) "capacity for expression and to distinguish" (Negt/Kluge, 1993, p. 289) forms the basis for the mediation of the power of judgment and reasoning that is historically socially necessary in general as well as in particular interest.

This perspective is strongly connected with the political project of the "abolition of all education restriction" (Heydorn, 1994/95, IV, p. 138). Here one must adhere to the fact that a) "Education is no independent revolutionary movement, not even indirectly, it can only be so in connection with the entire historical movement" (IV, p. 62), but it b) is essentially about realizing that education "makes its own unchanged contribution which is irreplaceable. This contribution must not be withdrawn from the institution; it cannot be made in the same way in any other place" (IV, p. 141).

A real democratization of our societies has to be seen as a problem of our planet's ability to survive. We have to perceive it as a task for various policies tied to the power of judgment and competence of action of all citizens.[23] The demand for education for everyone and everywhere remains in this context on the agenda as a central challenge for the real existing social inequalities and overcoming it in a democratic way.

As Heinrich Heine put it 160 years ago: the problem is about the understanding of 'contemporary conditions', if everyone understands the present time, i.e. has the competence of analyzing her/his society, "peace, welfare and freedom" can be realized as a general perspective (Heine 1972: 368f.).[24]

NOTES

[1] This murderous outcome was especially the case in Germany as it is to be remembered (cf. Sünker/ Otto, 1997).

[2] With respect to the history of globalization see the works of Wallerstein on modern world system analysis (1974, 1980, 1989), Sassen (1998) is dealing with questions of the political economy of globalization when more or less everyone believed that this process would never end.

[3] S. Benhabib therefore deals with the topic 'the emergence of citizenship as a political problem in an era of globalization' (2006); G. Whitty (1998) deals with processes of marketisation and commodification of education and its consequences of turning citizens in customers, cf. Sünker (2007: chap. 2).

[4] Duchrow's view (1997, p. 102) refers to the fact that it concerns here by all means a conscious struggle for power, above all from the side of the often violent possessors of power: "Correspondingly in secret documents it is also demanded that in this conflict about the ownership of and sharing out of powers that try to alter the status quo, one must fight 'on all levels of power', namely military, political, economical and socio-psychological.

The interesting thing is, however, that in 1987 secret services and Supreme Commanders of the North and Latin American Armed Forces present at the conference in which the documents were presented seemed to be quite stable and superior in military, political and economic matters. Most of their attention is aimed towards what they call the 'socio-psychological' or cultural level of power, people's 'hearts and thoughts'. Practically this means for them that the main struggle against the 'international communist movement' henceforth must be introduced to churches, schools, universities and, above all, to the media. Correspondingly the main opponents become: the basis church, release theology and human rights' groups as well as solidarity networks like Amnesty International and development organizations like 'Brot für die Welt', who work with the poor. The head of the Philippine security authorities once expressed his broad view of the enemy at a torture trial of Edicio de la Torre, a release theologian with the sentence: 'We are suspicious those who do good deeds and do not get rich'. Social movements are defamed through disinformation campaigns; their activists are disabled or even murdered by death commands like the Jesuits in El Salvador or, at the moment, in the hottest war of low intensity in South Africa. Of course this strategy includes the old methods of equipment and of military and death squadron training that pose as representatives of the USA, as well as economical destabilization programs. Nicaragua and El Salvador as well as other Central American countries are the best known examples of recent history".

This view makes clear how different power strategies can be used, whereby the first "area" of the shaping of power refers to the fact that Foucault has obviously been received even in these circles.

[5] "The decline of American power" (Wallerstein, 2003; cf. Berman, 2006) is becoming a more and more common topic which ends in the topic "failed states" (Chomsky 2006; cf. Jänicke, 1986).

[6] The emphasis on the importance of competence for regulating social relationships by means of subjects makes it even more clear how important it is to break down the basis for opposite action, which Siemsen (1948, p. 5) labeled "the blind subjection to a state leadership, a party or a fuehrer". The analysis of media politics, media culture and the control of behavior by the media also belong to this context (cf. Kellner, 1995).

[7] In this context confer with Meiksins Wood (1995, p. 290f.): "I have suggested throughout this book that the capitalist market is a *political* as well as an economic space, a terrain not simply of freedom and choice but of domination and coercion. I now want to suggest that *democracy* needs to be reconceived not simply as a political category but as an economic one. What I mean is not simply 'economic democracy' as a greater equality of distribution. I have in mind democracy as an economic regulator, the *driving mechanism* of the economy.

Here Marx's free association of direct producers (which does not, even in Marx's terms, include only manual workers or people directly involved in material production) is a good place to start. It stands to reason that the likeliest place to begin the search for a new economic mechanism is at the very base of the economy, in the organization of labour itself. But the issue is not simply the internal organization of enterprises; and even the reappropriation of the means of production by the producers, while a necessary condition, would not be sufficient, as long as possession remains market dependent and subject to the old imperatives. The freedom of the free association implies not only democratic organization but emancipation from 'economic' coercions of this kind".

[8] The German language allows to distinct between "Erziehung" (education 1) and "Bildung" (education 2). While education 1 is aiming at affirmation, accommodation, conformity, education 2 is aiming at maturity and responsibility, reflexivity, social judgment, aesthetics, human development without forgetting society—or better: processes of societalization (cf. for a conceptual analysis Sünker, 2007: chap. 7).

[9] Here the deciding factor is to keep an eye on how fundamentalism and perspective are determined by processes of change; cf. Bloch's thoughts on this: "Change is possible in the false meaning to a great extent; the Huns also caused change, there is also change through Caesar mania, through anarchy, even through the mental illness of blather, which Hegel calls a 'perfect picture of chaos'. But *dignified* change, even that of the *Kingdom of Freedom* only occurs through dignified under-standing; with more and more precisely controlled necessity" (1959, p. 326).

[10] With these 'nice' words Mr. Gehlen is trying to hide his collaboration with National Socialists.

[11] See with respect to Adorno's approach and concept of "Mündigkeit", translated as "maturity and responsibility" French/Thomas (1999).

[12] See for a mediation of concepts of autonomy, modernity and democracy Arnason (1990).

[13] An initial thread to this discussion is today the theme 'Youth and Violence', which reveals this in its various facets and brings forwards very diverse findings in relation to the question of the conditions

(Otto and Merten, 1993; Heitmeyer, Möller and Sünker, 1992). A second thread relates to the theme 'The 68ers and Youth Violence Today' and value education, in which the thesis itself is not very interesting, but rather the question of the role which can be played in hegemonic struggles by such a nonsensical proposition such as the responsibility of the 68ers for today's youth violence.

Otherwise it seems to me to be worth referring to a conception of the problem of education similar to that of S. Bernfeld (1892–1953) over seventy years ago: "The educative role of the family is now everywhere in question, and the old pedagogical remedies on which our grandparents still relied have ceased to be effective, or at least have lost most of their authority. With regard to moral and social questions, a general insecurity prevails, robbing parents of the courage to enforce their will and lay down the law. Beset by a host of feelings, which include guilt and hostility to family and children, parents are caught in a situation of psychic stress and reach out for whatever help tested educational doctrines may give them. Even if these should not quite bring the desired results, they would at least permit the parents to justify themselves: they could say that they had done what was possible. This situation indeed creates a considerable interest in education, but not necessarily a high appreciation of it. On the contrary, there are indications that predict an early fatigue and disappointment in the parts of the parents. For the plain fact is that educational theory does not meet the expectations people set on it" (Bernfeld 1973, p. 3f.).

[14] Interesting too is Kant's observation that not only parents but authorities, too, are to be considered as obstacles to the road to an improvement of the human condition:

"Monarchs regard their subjects only as instruments for their goals. Parents care for the house, monarchs for the state. Both do not have as their aim the welfare and the completeness for which humanity is destined and for which it is capable (Kant, 1964, p. 704).

Marcuse (1987, p. 34) compared Kant's position with the reality of capitalism and reached the following conclusion: "The monopoly capitalistic manipulation of the population, the inflationary economy, the 'defense' policy of 'kill and overkill', the training for genocide, war crimes that become normal, the brutal treatment of the great number of prisoners have lead to a frightening increase in violence in every day life. ... The whole complex of aggression and its victims indicates a proto-fascist potential *par excellence*".

[15] This diagnosis of the frost also throws a characteristic light on the question of the preconditions of National Socialism, as the German form of Fascism, in people themselves: "A barbaric experiment in state control of industrial society, it [the Hitler period, H.S.] violently anticipated the crisis management policies of today. The often cited 'integration,' the organizational tightening of the weave in the societal net that encompassed everything, also afforded protection from the universal fear of falling through the mesh and disappearing. For countless people it seemed that the coldness of social alienation had been done away with thanks to the warmth of togetherness, no matter how manipulated and contrived; the völkisch community of the unfree and unequal was a lie and at the same time also the fulfillment of an old, indeed long familiar, evil bourgeois dream. The system that offered such gratification certainly concealed within itself the potential for its own downfall" (Adorno, 1998b, p. 95; cf. Adorno, 1998a, p. 201; Sünker/Otto, 1997).

[16] Socio-historical and socio-political analyses of the relationship between education and society can be found in an extremely interesting Anglo-Saxon discussion, which revolves—following very often the work of B. Bernstein—around the concept 'new sociology of education' and 'Critical Pedagogy' (Giroux and McLaren, 1989; Wexler, 1990; McLaren, 1993; Farnen/Sünker, 1997; Whitty, 2002; Ball, 2003; Apple 2003; Kincheloe 2004). On the German-language discussion see Heydorn, 1979; Lenhart, 1987 and von Friedeburg, 1989, Sünker/Krüger, 1999. Both approaches meet in emphasizing the relevance of 'consciousness rising'.

[17] With clear words Heydorn makes it obvious that neither violence nor liberation have automatisms: "It concerns the production of what is efficient, obedient, exchangeable and moronic, technical rationality is separated from human rationality according to system. Relying upon previous history this is considered possible, revolution of technology and the deformation of humans. In schizophrenia

not only the mental asylum and collective suicide lie in wait, but also the possible uprising of people to produce themselves" (Heydorn, 1979, p. 289).

[18] It is understandable that this emancipatory perspective is far more difficult to represent in the framework of school socialization process (cf. Wexler, 1999) than in the context of educational work which is not based in the school context as youth work (cf. Peter, Sünker and Willigmann, 1982). In view of debates on global society and interculturalism, such an approach to the task of schooling seems even more relevant (Steinberg, 2001; Richter, 2006).

[19] Here it should be considered that—following the famous phrase from Marx' 'Theses on Feuerbach" (1969, p. 5f.)—"conditions have to be changed by men and the educator himself has to be educated".

[20] Here the systematic place of a justification of "communicative freedom" is also named (Theunissen, 1978, p. 45 onwards), a conception which, unlike that of Habermas, does not limit itself only to the area of interaction.

[21] As opposed to the worship of technology, streams of money and their power, the logics of the market, social movements are presently opting for alternatives, as Castells (1998, p. 351) writes: "What is characteristic of social movements and cultural projects built around identities in the Information Age is that they do not originate within the institutions of civil society. They introduce, from the outset, an alternative social logic, distinct from the principles of performance around which dominant institutions of society are built". This opting for alternative social logics qualifiedly distinguishes the present situation from the beginnings of capitalism, as Braudel (1994, p. 164) describes: 'In short there are many poor people, many are miserable—a large proletariat for which the science of history is gradually providing a place according to the requirements of difficult research. A proletariat that burdens the entire activity of the century and whose weight is becoming more and more pressing in the course of the years. On this ground a persistent so-called *Brigantentum* is flourishing—a real social revolution which is taking an endless, unproductive course. For at the end the general misery settles the conflict: it mercilessly throws the poor and destitute back to the starting point. In Spain it is down to two factors: the survival of the old wealth and a stronger decline in population that both produce a strange social class, a proletariat that is similar to the plebs of Ancient Rome. Poor people who have always lived in poverty, no hopers from the cities as they have become famous through picaresque novels, muggers, real and fake beggars, all the gente del hampa and the hampones, the vagabonds—all these people have stopped work, admittedly only after the other side, that of work and employment, did not want to have anything to do with them".

[22] This is one reason why Heydorn (1980, p. 301) ends his "Survival through education" with the sentence: "Consciousness is all".

[23] This includes the question of aesthetics: "Indelible from the resistance to the fungible world of barteris the resistance of the eye that does not want the colors of the world to fade. Semblance is a promise of nonsemblance" (Adorno, 1973, p. 405).

[24] Flacks links democratization and special welfare entitlements: its the question of "the growth in public investment in education and the production and distribution of culture. Public education was one of the first demands of the nascent labor movement in the early decades of the nineteenth century; the extension and improvement of public education, including mass Higher Education, has been a fundamental issue for all of the great social movements ever since" (1988: 250).

REFERENCES

Adorno, T. W. (1973). *Negative dialectics*. New York/London: Continuum.

Adorno, T. W. (1998a). Education after Auschwitz. In Th. W. Adorno (Ed.), *Critical models. interventions and catchwords* (pp. 191–204). New York: Columbia University Press.

Adorno, T. W. (1998b). The meaning of working through the past. In Th. W. Adorno (Ed.), *Critical models* (pp. 89–104). ibid.

Altvater, E. (2005). *Das Ende des Kapitalismus, wie wir ihn kennen. Eine radikale Kapitalismuskritik.* Münster: Westfälisches Dampfboot.

Altvater, E., & Mahnkopf, B. (1996). *Grenzen der Globalisierung. Ökonomie, Ökologie und Politik in der Weltgesellschaft*. Münster: Westfälisches Dampfboot.

Apple, M. W. (2003). *The state and the politics of knowledge*. New York/London: RoutledgeFalmer.

Arnason, J. P. (1990). The theory of modernity and the problematic of democracy. In *Thesis Eleven* No. 29, 20–45.

Ball, St. (2003). *Class strategies and the education market. The middle class and social advantage*. London/New York: RoutledgeFalmer.

Benhabib, S. (1989). Autonomy, Modernity, and Community. In A. Honneth et al. (Hrsg.), *Zwischenbetrachtungen. Im Prozess der Aufklärung*, (pp. 373—394). Frankfurt/M.

Benhabib, S. (2006). Citiensip als politisches Problem in Zeiten der Globalisierung. *Sozialwissenschaftliche Literatur Rundschau, 29*(H. 52), 97–10.

Benjamin, W. (1966). Zur Kritik der Gewalt. In W. Benjamin & A. Novus (Eds.), *Ausgewählte Schriften* II. Frankfurt/M.: Suhrkamp.

Benjamin, W. (1969). Geschichtsphilosophische thesen. In W. Benjamin (Ed.), *Illuminationens* (pp. 268–279). Frankfurt/M.: Suhrkamp.

Berman, M. (1988). *All that is solid melts into air. The experience of modernity*. New York: Penguin.

Berman, M. (2000). *The twilight of American culture*. New York: Norton & Norton.

Berman, M. (2006). *Dark ages America*. Noton & Norton.

Bernfeld, S. (1973). *Sisyphus, or the limits of education*. Berkeley et al., CA: University of California Press.

Bloch, E. (1959). *Das prinzip Hoffnung*. Frankfurt/M.: Suhrkamp.

Boggs, C. (2000). *The end of politics. Corporate power and the decline of the public sphere*. New York/London: The Guilford Press.

Bourdieu, P. (1984). *Die feinen Unterschiede. Kritik der gesellschaftlichen Urteilskraft*. Frankfurt/M.: Suhrkamp.

Bourdieu, P. (2001). Meditationen. *Zur Kritik der scholastischen Vernunft*. Frankfurt/M.: Suhrkamp.

Bowles, S., & Gintis, H. (1987). *Democracy and capitalism. Property, community, and the contradictions of modern social thought*. New York: Basic Books.

Braudel, F. (1994). *Das Mittelmeer und die mediterrane Welt in der Epoche Phillips II*. 2. Bd. Frankfurt/M.: Suhrkamp.

Brunkhorst, H. (1987). *Der Intellektuelle im Land der Mandarine*. Frankfurt/M.: Suhrkamp.

Carlson, D., & Apple, M (1998). Introduction: Critical educational theory in unsettling times. In Carlson/Apple (Eds.), *Power/Knowledge/Pedagogy. The meaning of democratic education in unsettling times* (pp. 1–38). Boulder, CO: Westview.

Castells, M. (1998). *The information age* (Vol. III: End of Millennium). Malden, MA: Blackwell.

Chomsky, N. (2000). *Chomsky on miseducation*. In D. Macedo (Ed. and introd.). Lanham, MD: Rowman & Littlefield.

Chomsky, N. (2001). *War against people. Menschenrechte und Schurkenstaaten*. Hamburg/Wien: Europa verlag.

Chomsky, N. (2006). *Failed states. The abuse of power and the assault on democracy*. New York: Metropolis.

Chossudovsky, M. (2002). Global Brutal. *Der entfesselte Welthandel, die Armut, der Krieg*. Frankfurt: Zweitausendeins.

Clarke, J. (2004). *Changing welfare, changing states. New directions in social policy*. London: Sage.

Dixon, K. (2000). *Die Evangelisten des Marktes*. Konstanz: UVK.

Duchrow, U. (1997). *Alternativen zur kapitalistischen Weltwirtschaft*. Gütersloh: Güthersloher. Verlagshaus.

Farnen, R., & Sünker, H. (Eds.). (1997). *The politics, sociology and economics of education*. Interdisciplinary and comparative perspectives. Houndmills: MacMillan; New York: St. Martin's.

Flacks, R. (1988). *Making history. The American left and the American mind*. New York: Columbia University Press.

French, R., & Thomas, J. (1999). Maturity and education, citizenship and enlightenment: An introduction to Theodor Adorno and Hellmut Becker, education for maturity and responsibility. In *History of the Human Sciences, 12*(3), 1–19.

Friedeburg, L. von (1989). *Bildungsreform in Deutschland*. Frankfurt/M.: Suhrkamp.

Geyer-Ryan, H., & Lethen, H. (1987). *Von der Dialektik der Gewalt zur Dialektik der Aufklärung*. Eine Re-vision der Odyssee. In W. Reijen & G. Schmid-Noerr (Hrsg.), *Vierzig Jahre Flaschenpost: "Die Dialektik der Aufklärung" 1947–1987* (pp. 41–72). Frankfurt/M.: Fischer.

Giroux, H., & McLaren, P. (Hrsg.). (1989). *Critical pedagogy, the state and cultural struggle*. Albany, NY: Suny Press.

Grenz, F. (1974). *Adornos Philosophie in Grundbegriffen*. Auflösung einiger Deutungsprobleme. Mit einem Anhang: Theodor W. Adorno und Arnold Gehlen: Ist die Soziologie eine Wissenschaft vom Menschen? Ein Streitgespräch (pp. 225–251). Frankfurt/M.: Suhrkamp.

Heine, H. (1972). Französische Zustände. In *Werke und Briefe*. Bd. 4, hg. Berlin/Weimar: V. H. Kaufmann.

Heitmeyer, W., Möller, K., & Sünker, H. (Hrsg.). (1992). *Jugend—Staat—Gewalt. Politische Sozialisation von Jugendlichen, Jugendpolitik und politische Bildung*, 2. Aufl. Weinheim/München: Juventa.

Heller, A. (1984). *Everyday life*. London et al.: Routledge & Kegan Paul.

Heydorn, H.-J. (1979). *Über den Widerspruch von Bildung und Herrschaft*. Frankfurt/M.: Syndikat.

Heydorn, H.-J. (1980). überleben durch Bildung. umriss einer Aussicht. In ders.: *Ungleichheit für alle. Bildungstheoretische Schriften* 3, (pp. 282—301). Frankfurt/M.: Syndikat.

Heydorn, H. J. (1994/1995). *Werke. Bd. IV*. Liechtenstein: Topos.

Hirsch, J. (1995). *Der nationale Wettbewerbsstaat. Staat, Demokratie und Politik im globalen Kapitalismus*. Berlin/Amsterdam: Ed. ID-Archiv.

Holzkamp, K. (1993). *Lernen. Subjektwissenschaftliche Grundlegung*. Frankfurt/M.: Campus.

Jänicke, M. (1986). *Staatsversagen. Die Ohnmacht der Politik in der Industriegesellschaft*. München/ Zürich: Piper.

Jessop, B. (2002). *The future of the capitalist state*. Cambridge: Polity.

Kant, I. (1964). Über Pädagogik. In I. Kant (Ed.), Band 10. *Werken in 10 Bänden*. Darmstadt: WBG.

Kellner, D. (1995). *Media culture. Cultural studies, identity and politics between the modern and the postmodern*. London/New York: Routledge.

Kellner, D. (2001). *Grand Theft 2000. Media spectacle and a stolen election*. Lanham, MD: Rowman & Littlefield.

Kincheloe, J. (2004). *Critical pedagogy*. New York et al.: Peter Lang.

Kincheloe, J., Steinberg, Sh., & Hinchey, P. (Eds.). (1999). *The post-formal reader. Cognition and education*. New York/London: Falmer.

Lefebvre, H. (1972). *Das Alltagsleben in der modernen Welt*. Frankfurt/M.: Suhrkamp.

Lenhart, v. (1987). *Die Evolution erzieherischen Handelns*. Frankfurt/M.: Peter Lang.

Lepsius, M. R. (1990). *Interessen, Ideen und Institutionen*. Opladen: Leske & Budrich.

Mandel, M. (2004). *How America gets away with murder. Illegal wars, collateral damage, and crimes against humanity*. London/Ann Arbor, MI: Pluto.

Marcuse, H. (1987). Konterrevolution und Revolte. In ders.: *Schriften* (pp. 7–128). Bd.9. Frankfurt/M.: Suhrkamp.

Marx, K. (n.d.). *Grundrisse der Kritik der politischen Ökonomie*. Frankfurt/M.: EVA.

Marx, K. (1969). Thesen über Feuerbach. In K. Marx (Ed.), *Werke* (pp. 5–7). Bd. 3. Berlin: Dietz.

McLaren, P. (1993). *Schooling as a ritual performance. Towards a political economy of educational symbols & gestures*. London/New York: Routledge.

Meiksins Wood, E. (1995). *Democracy against capitalism*. Cambridge: Cambridge University Press.

Mitscherlich, A., & Mitscherlich, M. (1967). *Die Unfähigkeit zu trauern. Grundlagen kollektiven Verhaltens*. München: Piper.

Mollenhauer, K. (1980). einige erziehungswissenschaftliche Probleme im Zusammenhang der erforschung von "Allatagswelten Jugendlicher". In D. Lenzen (Hrsg.): *Pädagogik und Alltag. Stuttgart* (pp. 97–111). Klett-Cotta.

Negt, O., & Kluge, A. (1993). *Maßverhältnisses des Politischen.* Frankfurt/M.: Fischer.

Otto, H.-U., & Merten, R. (Hrsg.). (1993). *Rechtsradikale Gewalt im vereinigten Deutschland. Jugend im gesellschaftlichen Umbruch.* Opladen: Leske & Budrich.

Palast, G. (2003). *The best democracy money can buy. An investigative reporter exposes the truth about globalization, corporate cons, and the high-finance fraudsters.* Plume.

Pateman, C. (1970). *Participation and democratic theory.* Cambridge: Cambridge University Press.

Peter, H., Sünker, H., & Willigmann, S. (Hrsg.) (1982). *Politische Jugendbildungsarbeit.* Frankfurt/ M.: Diesterweg.

Richter, E. (2006). Intercultural education: A contribution to peace in the developing global society? In Fischman, G., McLaren, p., Sünker, H., & Lankshear, C. (Eds.), *Critical theories, radical pedagogies, and global conflicts.* (pp. 307–316). Lanham et al., MD: Rowman & Littlefield.

Sassen, S. (1998). *Globalization and its discontents.* New York: The New Press.

Schleiermacher, F. (1983). *Pädagogische Schriften I. Die vorlesungen aus dem Jahre 1826.* Frankfurt a. Main: ullstein.

Siemsen, A. (1948). *Die gesellschaftlichen Grundlagen der Erziehung.* Hamburg: Oetinger.

Steinberg, S. (Ed.). (2001). *Multi/Intercultural conversations.* New York et al.: Peter Lang.

Steinberg, S., & Kincheloe, J. (Eds.) (1997). *Kinderculture. The corporate construction of childhood.* Boulder, CO: Westview.

Stern, F. (1991). *Im Anfang war Auschwitz. Antisemitismus und Philosemitismus im deutschen Nachkrieg.* Gerlingen: Bleicher.

Sünker, H. (1989). *Bildung, Alltag und Subjektivität.* Weinheim: Deutscher Studien verlag.

Sünker, H. (1994). Are intellectuals the keepers of political culture? Some reflections on politics, morality, and reason. In R. Farnen (Ed.). *Nationalism, ethnicity, and identity,* (pp. 193–204, 486–488). New Brunswick/London: Transaction.

Sünker, H. (2007). *Politics, bildung and social justice. Perspectives for a democratic society.* Rotterdam: Sense.

Sünker, H., & Otto, H.-U. (Eds.). (1997). *Education and fascism. Political identity and social education in Nazi Germany.* London/Washington: Falmer.

Sünker, H., & Krüger, H.-H. (Hg.). (1999). *Kritische Erziehungswissenschaft am Neubeginn ?!* Frankfurt/ M. Suhrkamp.

Széll, G. (1988). Participation, worker's control and self-management. *Current Sociology, 36*(3).

Theunissen, M. (1978). *Sein und Schein. Die kritische Funktion der Hegelschen Logik.* Frankfurt: Suhrkamp.

Theunissen, M. (1989). *Möglichkeiten des Philosophierens heute, in: Sozialwissenschaftliche Literatur Rundschau, 12,* 77–89.

Tomasello, M. (1999). *The cultural origin of human cognition.* Cambridge/London: Harvard University Press.

Vester, M., et al. (2001). *Soziale Milieus im gesellschaftlichen Strukturwandel.* Frankfurt/M.: Suhrkamp.

Wallerstein, M. (1974). *The modern world-system: Capitalist agriculture and the origins of the european world-economy in the sixteenth century.* New York: Academic Press.

Wallerstein, M. (1980). *The modern world-system II. Mercantilism and the consolidation of the European world-economy, 1600–1750.* New York: Academic Press.

Wallerstein, M. (1989). *The modern world-system III. The second era of great expansion of the capitalist world-economy, 1730–1840s.* New York: Academic Press.

Wallerstein, I. (2003). *The decline of American power. The U.S. in a Chaotic world.* New York: The New Press.

Wehler, H.-U. (1988). *Aus der Geschichte lernen?* München: Beck.

Wexler, Ph. (1990). *Social analysis of education. After the new sociology*. New York/London: Routledge.

Wexler, Ph. (1999). *Die Toyota-Schule. Ökonomisierung von Bildung und postmodernes Selbst* (pp. 35–57). Sünker/Krüger.

Whitty, G. (1998). *Citizens or consumers? continuity and change in contemporary education policy*. In D. Carlson & M. Apple (Eds.), *Power/Knowledge/Pedagoy* (pp. 92–109).

Whitty, G. (2002). *Making sense of education policy*. London: Paul Chapman.

KLAS ROTH

17. EDUCATION FOR THE MARKET AND
DEMOCRACY—AN INDISSOLUBLE TENSION?

> Between capitalism and democracy there is an *indissoluble* tension; in them
> two opposed principles of societal integration compete for primacy
>
> (Habermas, 1987, p. 345)

The classical—the instrumental—model of rationality and rational decision-making, which dominates the language of modern economics and capitalism, serves not only to explain, understanding or inquiring into human agency and rational decision-making; it also serves to transform and co-ordinate the beliefs and values of those concerned within the European Union, so that these beliefs and values become reasons for taking action that leads to the desired end. I will show that the restructuring of education at EU policy level is conditioned and affected by the classical model. I argue that the weaknesses of the dominant way of thinking about rational decision-making and the narrowness of the language of market economy and capitalism offer merely a simplistic account of human agency, and that a more fully-fledged view of rationality—an *un*conditional one—has to be taken into account. Such a view offers a richer view of the triangular relation between education, the market and democracy and serves to challenge the 'marketization' of education in the EU. I submit that the conditioned and instrumental mode of rationality and the language of market economy and capitalism need to be challenged and altered; we need a more enriched, balanced and mature notion of human agency, for a better understanding of education in this triangular relation.

I first outline ideas for the classical model and argue that the restructuring of education within the EU is affected by the instrumental mode of rationality and the language of capitalism. I also discuss some problems concerning the classical model. Secondly, I discuss particularly the narrow account of human agency underlying the 'marketization' of education in the EU, and suggest an alternative. I argue that the "new" view of education, which I advocate, is practical and serves as a more balanced view of "principles of societal integration", reflecting the possibility of a "new" critical language of education.

THE CLASSICAL MODEL OF RATIONALITY AND
THE MARKETIZATION OF EDUCATION IN THE EU

If rational decision-making is about selecting means that enable those concerned to achieve their ends, and the cause of their action is their reasons, then they must know what they desire and use the means that enable them to achieve their ends. They must also elicit their reasons and act upon them to achieve these ends. Such a model

I. Gur-Ze'ev, The Possibility/Impossibility of a New Critical Language in Education, 333–349.
© *2010 Sense Publishers. All Rights Reserved.*

of rational decision-making illustrates how it is believed to be possible to maximize people's interests, preferences and/or desires, and influences the "dominant school of thought in modern economics" (Sen, 2002, p. 23; see also Elster, 2000 for a discussion on the standard model of rationality influencing modern economics, and Friedman, 2002 for a defense of capitalism). The capitalist mode of rational decision-making exhibits a strong focus on *privatization* and on private property. This is understood either as a natural right as asserted by John Locke in the European tradition or as an inevitable political and legal right as in the American tradition. There is also a focus on *efficiency* in producing and distributing the goods and services needed for the satisfaction and fulfillment of desires. Thus it is believed by many people that the market, which has always existed, ought to be free and unconstrained as far as possible, that its goods and services should not be constrained by anything but the (lowest possible) price and valued only insofar as they satisfy the desires of its actors. Moreover, there is a concentration on *competition*: those who participate in producing and distributing goods and services compete with each other. This usually means minimizing the costs of production and distribution, but also the costs of wages, advertising, materials, machinery, technology and so on. Christopher Green, for example, says: "a competitive market encourages enterprise and ideas, self-reliance and independence, initiative and entrepreneurship, the very qualities in fact required for individuals and nations to be successful. Competition is a natural phenomenon. It relates to the 'survival of the fittest', the state of affairs that organizes our biological and economic worlds." (Green, 2005, p. 2–3) The ideology of capitalism also focuses on *mobility* and *flexibility*: goods are produced where costs are lowest. This suggests that the production of goods is or should be moved from one area to another in order to reduce costs. This in turn means that production should be flexible and mobile. It also suggests that labour too needs to be flexible and mobile: move to where the production is or risk being unemployed!

Thus it seems that rational decision-making in the ideology of capitalism serves to help those who participate in producing the goods and services to compete with each other to satisfy the desires of consumers by producing and distributing goods and services at the lowest possible cost. However, the competitors on the market do not inevitably act only for the benefit of citizens and their interests. In many cases they act in their own interests more than in those of others. They also act either to increase or to retain their power; it also happens that those in power deceive those concerned—the workforce and others—to believe, erroneously, that they are acting (mostly or solely) in the interest of the latter more than in their own interest. There is also a tendency in the classical model of rationality to consider that the meaning or understanding of relevant notions such as 'self-interest', 'desire', 'preference' is determined by what they designate, representing the "real" interests of those concerned.

However, it has been shown by, for example, Davidson (2001a; 2001b; 2005) that even though utterances may designate objects and events in the physical world, the explanation of meaning is not exhausted by the reference of an utterance; he argues that, to explain the meaning of an utterance, we need to take into account usage, people's beliefs and intentions, and their reactions to objects and events in the world (see also Roth, 2009 for a discussion on whether the meaning of an utterance can be explained only in terms of its relation to its reference).

The foregoing suggests that the classical model rests on presuppositions concerning the meaning of utterances that are ill-founded. It also suggests that the beliefs and values of those concerned as well as their reactions to objects and events have to be considered in any account of rational decision-making. Moreover, if the meaning of an utterance including notions such as 'interests', 'desires' and/or 'preferences' cannot be decided easily, then it cannot be decided with certainty how we can come to know what goods or services best satisfy those concerned. It also implies the difficulty or impossibility of knowing or learning how to satisfy the desires and the like of those concerned in the most efficient way possible, because there is no way that we can ascertain the meaning of 'the real desires' and the like.

The classical model may appear a simple one of human rationality and agency, for use not only to explain rational decision-making but also to prescribe how those concerned may find out how best to achieve their ends and to inquire into why they fail to achieve their ends and satisfy their desires. The model is not new (see for example Habermas, 1987, Kant, 1785/2006 and Searle, 2001 for discussions on the classical model and its weaknesses). Aristotle, for example, wrote around 400 BC that: "the cause of action (the efficient, not the final cause) is choice, and the cause of choice is desire and reasoning directed to some end." (Aristotle, 1996, p. 146) David Hume wrote in 1739–40, more than 2000 years later, that "Reason is, and ought only to be the slave of the passions, and can never pretend to any other office than to serve and obey them." (Hume, 1978/1739–40, p. 415) Moreover, Donald Davidson writing in 1963, about 220 years later, states that:

> A reason rationalizes an action only if it leads us to see something the agent saw, or thought he saw, in his action—some feature, consequence, or aspect of the action the agent wanted, desired, prized, held dear, thought dutiful, beneficial, obligatory, or agreeable [and that] Whenever someone does something for a reason, therefore, he can be characterized as (*a*) having some sort of pro attitude toward actions of a certain kind, and (*b*) believing (or knowing, perceiving, noticing, remembering) that his action is of that kind. Under (*a*) are to be included desires, wantings, urges, promptings, and a great variety of moral views, aesthetic principles, economic prejudices, social conventions, and public and private goals and values in so far as these can be interpreted as attitudes of an agent directed toward actions of a certain kind. (Davidson, 2001c, p. 3–4)

These authors, however, focus on different issues. Hume, for example, claims that it is only the passions that motivate the agent to act, and that reason only functions as an instrument for finding out what means one has to use to satisfy one's passions; in other words, it is only our passions that ultimately determine what we do. Aristotle and in particular Davidson on the other hand emphasize the connection of desire and beliefs more than Hume does as valuable not only for motivating human action, but also for making action rational or rationalized. It seem then that, according to this more elaborate classical model, we must consider not only our passions but also our beliefs and pro attitude when we give an account of human agency; it is not only our passions that motivate or causes our actions, but our reason(s) as well, and that our reason, too, can determine what we do. But as has been hinted above and from what will be seen later, the classical model is far from providing the only or even the best account of rational agency; it does not necessarily take the unconditional character of our practical identities into account, nor therefore the value of our reflexive and deliberative potential (more on this in Part two).

It appears that this model—the instrumental one—enables those concerned to give an account of rational decision-making and human agency. It could, for example, be used to explain the conditions for rational human agency as well as the notion of human agency, and also to inquire into whether: 1) the actions agents perform are rational; 2) those concerned are acting for one or several reasons; 3) the expressed reason(s) serve as a cause of their action; 4) the reason(s) serve as a part of what they want to realize; 5) what they want to realize serves as an end or goal for their action; 6) they have the competences necessary for achieving their ends or goals; 7) they have "the right kind" of knowledge and values to achieve specific ends or goals; 8) they have other means or resources necessary for achieving such ends or goals; 9) "the right kind" of ends or goals are a part of what they want to, or do actually, realize; 10) they direct and perform the necessary actions leading to achievement of desired ends; 11) they have the same or similar enough ends, and 12) they achieve the ends they desire.

The model could then function as a tool for eliciting why education fails to coordinate and direct the actions of those concerned. This suggests that knowledge of why education fails, for example, to prepare young people for work in the market economy and for democratic citizenship enables us to know how to make education function better. The model could, for example, be used to explain that education is not caused by "the right" desire(s) or that those concerned in education lack the right desires or motives and that they therefore cannot achieve what is or should be expected of education. If, for example, the market desires certain skills while pupils and students want to be educated for something else, not necessarily the kind of work required, disagreement arises between "the market" and those being educated. The market, for example, may need more scientists and engineers, as in the case of China, who will embrace the cherished knowledge and values and act to achieve desired end(s). It could also mean that those educated are trained to become flexible, mobile, effective, competitive, creative and innovative and so on in order to achieve a desired end, as in the case of the European Union (see below).

The model could also be used to explain that education does not transfer or manage the right kind of knowledge effectively. If this is why education fails, then it could be a matter of either changing the kind of knowledge imparted or managed, and instead imparting or managing what is considered "the right kind of knowledge"; or, alternatively, of changing the methods of teaching or learning so that "the right kind of knowledge" could be acquired or managed successfully. Other reasons why education is believed to fail are when it is directed to achieving the wrong end(s), or uses the wrong means for achieving the "right ends"; or that it does not have "the right or sufficient means" for achieving "the right ends". This is closely related to the idea of imparting "the right kind of knowledge" but focuses more on the ends or the transformation of the ends and requires a change in the kind of knowledge being managed or imparted through education.

The model could also serve to explain why education fails to handle or manage "the right kind of values" and to adapt to changes in society at large. Thus if the focus is on shaping the loyalty and moral commitment of members of a certain society and/or culture so that they become, for example, patriotic, then one aim of education could be to cultivate patriotism vis-à-vis the nation-state (see Roth, 2007 for a discussion on this). This suggests that all those who are or want to be citizens of a nation-state that furthers loyalty and moral commitment in terms of patriotism or nationalism have to be assimilated or integrated into it; alternatively they could be deported or exterminated if not accepted as members of that society (as happened in, for example, Nazi Germany). If, on the other hand, there is increased recognition of difference and diversity concerning, for example, life-styles and identities such as gender, ethnicity and religious affiliation, then the aim of education could be not the cultivation of patriotism or nationalism but the recognition of pluralism and of respect and tolerance of others with beliefs and values different from one's own.

The above also suggests that education can be, and is used for shaping and directing the beliefs, values and desires of those being educated to achieve desired ends. Bauman says: "The secret of every durable (that is, successfully self-reproducing) social system is the recasting of its 'functional prerequisites' into behavioral motives of actors. To put it in a different way, the secret of all successful 'socialization' is making individuals *wish to do* what *is needed* to enable the system to reproduce itself." (2007, p. 68) Hence, if there is a change in what, for example, the system desires, then beliefs and values have to change so that people want to do "what is needed".

And this is what is happening today within the European Union. The overall aim is: "*To become the most competitive and dynamic knowledge-based economy in the world, capable of sustainable economic growth with more and better jobs and greater social cohesion.*" (European Commission, 2002, p. 7) The Commission of the European Union expresses the belief that the desires, knowledge and values of all the people within the member states need to be transformed so that they too want to do what is considered needed and achieve the overall aim of the Union. The conditions for changing people's desires, beliefs and values in the European Union are therefore created so that desires and the like are shaped and co-ordinated in such a way that they function as reasons for action leading to the desired end. One tool for doing this is education. The European Union promotes the mobility of students/learners and teachers through Erasmus and Comenius projects, the development of cooperation between schools, universities and working life, and the stimulation of language learning; it also promotes the improvement of the recognition of degrees, qualifications and competences for educational and professional purposes as well as for the co-ordination of activities in Higher Education through the Bologna process and the development of open and distance learning. Moreover, the Union also focuses on the need to develop the necessary "skills for [building] the knowledge society" (ibid. p. 16) through education (see below), and on the need for more people to gain "access to internet and multimedia resources" (ibid. p. 18). The EU also wants to increase "recruitment to scientific and technological disciplines" (ibid. p. 19), and to educate citizens so that they use the resources in the best possible way. Moreover, the European Commission wants those concerned to create "an open learning environment" (ibid. p. 23), in, for example, educational settings, and to make "learning more attractive" (ibid. p. 24) within and outside these. The Commission also supports "[education for] active citizenship, equal opportunities and social cohesion" (ibid. p. 25). Further, it also promotes the strengthening of the links between "working life and research, and society at large" (ibid. p. 27), meaning, inter alia, that partnerships "between all types of education and training institutions, firms and research facilities for their mutual benefit" (ibid. p. 27) should be promoted, and that "the spirit of enterprise [or 'entrepreneurship']" (ibid. p. 28) should be furthered as well. The Commission also wants to support and improve "foreign language learning" (ibid. p. 29) and increase "mobility and exchange" (ibid. p. 30) as well as encouraging the strengthening of cooperation in general within the Union.

To accomplish all this, the European Parliament and the Council of the European Union recommend that member states "develop the provision of [eight] key competences for all as part of their lifelong learning strategies, including their strategies for achieving universal literacy" (Official Journal of the European Union, 2006, 394/11) through education. These competences "are defined … as a combination of knowledge, skills and attitudes appropriate to the context" (ibid. 394/13) and claimed to be needed by all individuals "for personal fulfillment and development, active citizenship, social inclusion and employment" (ibid. 394/13), and for the achievement of the strategic target of the European Union for 2010, namely to "become the most competitive and dynamic knowledge-based economy in the world".

The first key competence concerns the trained ability to communicate in the mother tongue and the second the ability to communicate in foreign languages. The third key competence concerns the ability to develop and apply "mathematical thinking" (ibid. 394/15), and to use "the body of knowledge and methodology employed to explain the natural world, in order to identify questions and to draw evidence-based conclusions" (ibid. 394/15). Moreover, it concerns the ability to apply "that knowledge and methodology in response to perceived human wants and needs" (ibid. 394/15). The fourth key competence concerns the ability to use information technology "for work, leisure and communication" (ibid. 394/15). The fifth concerns the ability of 'learning to learn', that is, "to pursue and persist in learning, to organize one's own learning, … through effective management of time and information, both individually and in groups" (ibid. 394/16). Moreover, the Parliament and the Council claim that "[l]earning to learn engages learners to build on prior learning and life experiences in order to use and apply knowledge and skills in a variety of contexts: at home, at work, in education and training" (ibid. 394/16). The sixth key competence concerns the development of social and civic competence, that is, the ability to "participate in an effective and constructive way in social and working life [and resolve conflict where necessary] … in increasingly diverse societies" (ibid. 394/16) such as those within the European Union. It also concerns the development of the ability to "show tolerance, express and understand different viewpoints" (ibid. 394/17). The seventh key competence concerns the development of the ability to take initiative, and includes the idea of entrepreneurship, that is, the ability "to turn ideas into action" (ibid. 394/17). The latter includes the ability to be creative, innovative and take risks, which is needed for individuals "in their everyday lives at home and in society, but also in the workplace" (ibid. 394/17). The eighth and final key competence concerns the cultivation of cultural awareness and a "solid understanding of one's own culture" (ibid. 394/18); it also concerns the ability to express "ideas, experiences and emotions in a range of media, including music, performing arts, literature, and the visual arts" (ibid. 394/18), and to gain cultural knowledge of the "local, national and European cultural heritage and their place in the world" (ibid. 394/18). The latter is asserted to be essential for understanding "the cultural and linguistic diversity in Europe and other regions of the world [and] the need to preserve it" (ibid. 394/18).

We see that the European Union creates conditions for shaping, directing and co-ordinating the desires, knowledge, values and actions of those concerned within member states so that they can aim at achieving the desired goal and strategic target for 2010 mentioned above. We also see that the subordinated aim is to prepare young people through education for active citizenship, in civil society. The primary aim is partly motivated by the changed character of work and new conditions for communication through information technology, but also by changed conditions for shaping and directing the loyalty and moral commitment of EU members with their dual citizenship (see Soysal, 1994 and Habermas, 2001 on the changed character of citizenship, and Roth and Burbules, 2007 on changing notions of citizenship education in contemporary nation-states within, inter alia, the European Union). The character of work is changing as well as conditions for it: work has shifted from agricultural to industrial, to the production of knowledge in what is called interchangeably *knowledge capitalism* (Burton-Jones, 1999; Peters & Besley, 2006), the *knowledge economy* (Dolfsma & Soete, 2006; Peters, 2007), the *knowledge society* (Hargreaves, 2003), and the *learning society* (OECD, 2000). The above suggests that since the character of work is changing and the knowledge needed for specific kinds of work is changing as well, then the aim of education has to be changed too. Thus if the aim of education is to prepare young people for work in agriculture, it has to provide the kind of knowledge needed for this. If, on the other hand, education is to prepare young people for work in industry, then education has to provide the kind of knowledge needed for this. The same applies to the preparation of young people for the production and management of knowledge and services. Now this is what is happening today in our world, not only in the developing countries in Asia, Africa, South America or India, but also in the USA and in the European Union. The world's economies are becoming increasingly dependent upon knowledge-driven production more than on the production, distribution and profit from goods or services. Knowledge has become a "product" which can be sold and improve profits, a commodity. This suggests that knowledge is used as a means to some end; that those concerned use the knowledge that optimizes their possibilities to realize their desires and achieve their ends. The Internet and information technology permit one to increase the speed of exchange of information and knowledge and reach customers and possible clients to a degree never possible before. They may also improve profits. Knowledge has become capital, and perhaps even the most important form, to be sold like any other goods or services on the open free market. Hence, capitalism as an ideology formerly concerning goods and services nowadays also concerns knowledge and the management of knowledge for improving its own profits in our post-industrial societies.

The role or function of education is being transformed in our post-industrial societies and there is an increased cry to adapt it to rapid social change, particularly in its new role in the developed countries, for building and servicing a "knowledge-based society" (OECD, 2000, p. 11) and/or a "knowledge-driven economy" (European Commission, 2002, p. 7). Hence the relationship between education, the market and learning is changing, with an increased focus on developing the competences of individuals for lifelong learning so that they are able to manage knowledge as efficiently as possible, and in order to increase profit. And since knowledge has become capital, a commodity among other capital/commodities, the cry for developing the competences of individuals to use knowledge is greater than ever.

The above are, however, disputed claims. As we shall see, I criticize the overall aim of the European Union for focusing too heavily on the needs of the market, and on the closely related issues of competition, efficiency, mobility, usability, results and continuous improvement motivated by the desire to achieve the end(s) in the best possible way(s) and at the lowest possible costs. It is also under fire for overstressing the development of, inter alia, creativeness, ingenuity, flexibility, competitiveness, risk-taking and the like, leading to the increased 'marketization' of new capital and life-worlds, and of education.

I dispute the 'marketization' of education here because it suggests that the classical mode of rationality comes to affect the social regulation of behavior among people and the conditions for co-ordinating beliefs and values more than the unconditional view of rationality. The result is not only that goods or services are being handled instrumentally or used for strategic purposes, but also that people themselves and their competences have become valued and used as commodities on the market in our post-industrial societies of consumers (see Bauman, 2007 on this and similar issues). Thus people and their competences are seen as yet another category of goods or services and are consumed and valued only as long as they and their competences are considered useful and valuable for some specific aim: serving to achieve society's aims or to gratify the desires of other consumers. Bauman says:

> *Members of the society of consumers are themselves consumer commodities*, and it is the quality of being a consumer commodity that makes them bona fide members of that society. Becoming and remaining a sellable commodity is the most potent motive of consumer concerns, even if it is usually latent and seldom conscious, let alone explicitly declared. ... 'Making oneself a sellable commodity' is a DIY job, and individual duty. (Bauman, 2007, p. 57)

We have also seen that the European Union creates conditions for shaping and directing, through education, the values of its citizens so that their loyalty and moral commitment, while basically to the nation-state, are also to the European Union.

This suggests that education has to handle "the right kind of values", and adapt to changes in society at large, shaping the loyalty and moral commitment of members of a society and/or culture within a Union member state so that they both understand "the cultural and linguistic diversity in Europe and other regions of the world", and preserve (!) their own national culture.

This suggests that presumptive citizens of the European Union have to desire the declared overall aim and strategic goal of the Union, acquire "the right kinds of beliefs and values" and have them serve as reasons for their actions and as parts of what they desire so that they *wish to do* what *is needed* to enable the system to reproduce itself". They must also develop "the right kind" of competences to achieve desired goal(s) and have the means to perform "the right kinds" of action leading to these goals.

Moreover, we have seen that the restructuring of education in the European Union is heavily permeated by the language of competition, efficiency, mobility and flexibility. We shall also see that the unconditional character of a citizen's practical identity is not reflected at policy level in the EU. Further, the restructuring of education in the EU is most likely a response to economic globalization, that is, to the "processes that enables the free flow of goods, services, investments, labour and information across national borders in order to maximize capital accumulation [and that] global capitalism involves the commodification of all kinds of human endeavour in order to produce surplus value and profit." (Olssen, Codd, O'Neill, 2004, p. 5) It seems too that educational policy "is increasingly in response to international developments, and increasingly involves international agreements and collaboration, as can be seen in the rise to prominence and power of quasi-regional or supranational organizations such as the World Trade Organization (WTO), the North Atlantic Treaty Organization (NATO), the European Community (EEC), the World Bank (WB), or the International Monetary Fund (IMF) ..." (ibid. 2004, p. 7). Michael Peters says:

> At the level of public policy 'knowledge economy' and 'learning economy' are twin terms that can be traced to a series of reports that emerged in the mid 1990s by the OECD (1996a, 1996b, 1997) and the World Bank (1998, 2002), before they were taken up as a policy template by world governments in the late 1999s (see Peters, 2001a, 2001b). In terms of these reports, education is reconfigured as a massively undervalued form of knowledge capital that increasingly will determine the direction of the world economy, the organization of firms and knowledge institutions, and the future structure and delivery mode of public services in health and education. (Peters, 2004, p. 165)

In times of systematic reform of education, involving the decentralization of state control over it, privatization and reinforcement of choice, the strengthening and promotion of partnerships "between all types of education and training institutions, firms and research facilities" as well as of the links between "working life and research, and society at large"; the furthering of "the spirit of enterprise [or 'entrepreneurship']", and the stress on increasing "mobility and exchange", it is not surprising that people's beliefs and values within the European Union are shaped and directed so that they wish to do what is considered necessary for achieving the desired end.

Nor is it surprising that the restructuring of education at EU policy level is thus permeated by the language of market economy and capitalism.

The above can be seen as an effect of an economic system, here a capitalist mode of rational decision-making, which regulates not only the production and distribution of goods and services but also the conditions under which citizens come to realize their own ends and under which their own personal and practical identities are constructed; since their actions are affected by the language of capitalism, it seems that they basically constitute themselves (or are constituted) as market commodities, not as active democratic citizens reflecting their unconditioned rationality in practice.

I argue below that the identity of citizens, and in particular education for active citizenship, do not necessarily have to be characterized by or reduced to capitalistic or economic terms leading to the 'marketization' of education and the 'commodification' of citizens and their competences within the European Union. If my analysis is correct, we need a much richer view of rationality and identity, including a more balanced view of "opposed principles of societal integration", as well as of the triangular relation between the market, democracy and education for active citizenship in Europe; one which is unconditional and reflects the potential of human beings as reflective and deliberating citizens. Now let us discuss such an alternative.

IDEAS FOR A FULLY-FLEDGED VIEW OF RATIONALITY AND DEMOCRATIC CITIZENSHIP IN THE EU

As human beings we are, according to Korsgaard (1996a, p. 92), "essentially reflective". We act not only upon our perceptions, desires or impulses as animals usually do; we can also act upon reason(s), and we have beliefs and values that affect our agency. These pervade our lives, yet we can also choose not to act upon them, or to challenge and change them. This is possible because the "human mind is [according to Korsgaard] self-conscious" (ibid. 1996a, p. 92). Hence we—as human beings—can attend to, inter alia, our impulses, desires and perceptions as reasons; we can reflect upon them and challenge them, and decide whether they are legitimate reasons for our actions.

However, people not only give or can give reasons of various kinds for their actions, they can also endorse them as well as the beliefs and values related to them; otherwise they would not be believed to act upon them; and since freedom is "the capacity to do otherwise" (Korsgaard, 1996a, p. 96), people can both act and think that they can act otherwise. And since human beings can be aware of their reasons and their particular identities and are able to challenge and change them, they can also construct them differently and think that they can act differently; their act of self-determination is therefore unavoidable. People can ask themselves: "Should I act upon a particular inclination, desire or perception or should I act upon another reason given?" This suggests that human beings can distance themselves from their desires and the like and reflect upon whether they should function as legitimate reasons for their actions. And, since our identities not only supply us with theoretical knowledge of who we are (Korsgaard, 1996a) but are also practical, they serve to guide us in relation to others, the world and ourselves; depending on how we understand each other and ourselves, we act upon our specific web of beliefs and related values. If, for example, two persons view themselves as man and wife, they regulate their relations with one another accordingly. If they view themselves instead as teacher and student, they regulate their relations in accordance with the beliefs and values associated therewith. If, on the other hand, these persons see themselves as professors and think that research should be basically empirical, and if they understand the notion of empirical research in a specific way and do not similarly value conceptual development or philosophical research, then perhaps they do not even understand or value the reflective or deliberative character of philosophical research. They may even believe that conceptual schemes organize, fit or explain unorganized experience. If this is what empirical social-sciences researchers believe, then they will embrace what Davidson calls the third dogma of empiricism, that is, the dualism between scheme and content, between "organizing system and something waiting to be organized." (Davidson, 2001d, p. 189) He argues that such a dualism "cannot be made intelligible and defensible. It is itself a dogma of empiricism, the third dogma. The third, and perhaps the last, for if we give it up it is not clear that there is anything distinctive left to call empiricism" (ibid. 2001d, p. 189). Davidson thinks that it is the holistic character of our web of beliefs that constitutes our understanding of the world, others and ourselves and that a person's reason rationalizes his action, and "leads us to see something the agent saw, or though he saw, in his action … [and that] Whenever someone does something for a reason, therefore, he can be characterized as (*a*) having some pro attitude toward actions of a certain kind, and (*b*) believing (or knowing, perceiving, noticing, remembering) that this action is of that kind." (Davidson, 2001c, p. 3) And Korsgaard too seems to think that reasons and in particular beliefs and pro attitudes as parts of one's practical identity also serve as a description "under which you value yourself, a description under which you find your life to be worth living and your actions to be worth undertaking." (Korsgaard, 1996a, p. 101) You need, according to her, to have at least "*some* conception of your practical identity, for without it you cannot have reasons to act" (ibid. 1996a, p. 120), and this conception serves not only to define, but also to regulate, our actions in the world and in relation to other people. Hence, our practical identity has normative force. This means, on the one hand, that when someone wills an end, which to some extent is dependent upon the web of beliefs of which it is a part, then that person also wills the means to that end. And since this works as a description or an explanation of what someone wills (and it is usually the case that when people will some end, they use the means available to achieve it), and also as a self-imposed imperative, it guides that person's action both vis-à-vis others and himself. However, before those concerned decide to accept their specific practical identity, they have to inquire into the quality of the maxims upon which it rests. A dogmatic person can believe that he must act without inquiring into the quality of the maxims upon which his practical identity rests; a more open-minded person may see no necessity to act without at least one convincing reason, and may also think he can change his mind if other and more convincing reasons appear. That is, if his practical identity is understood as contingent, dependent upon specific needs, then it appears as an instrument for the achievement of some end, no matter whether the person felt guided by it. Thus if his practical identity were understood primarily as contingent and dependent upon the needs of, for example, the market or of other people's desires, inclinations or lusts, then the person and his practical identity would be reified and recognized as usable for specific interests. However, Korsgaard argues (1996a; 1996b) that someone's practical identity must not be understood only as conditioned, that is, as a means to some end; his practical identity can also be understood as *un*conditional, that is as an end in itself.

The conditioned identity can be seen as a means to some end, but the unconditional identity is an end in itself, that is, being a father, a clerk or a fireman is usually a means to some end, and if someone understands themselves and their identity as conditioned, they view themselves basically as a means to some, or someone's, end(s) and are therefore always also liable to other people's recognition of themselves as valued or disvalued means to some end. One's identity can then also be susceptible to one's *own* recognition and value of oneself. And if, as Bauman (2007, p. 57) claims, people today have come to view others and themselves basically as market commodities, have incorporated an image of themselves as members of a consumer society to be treated similarly to other objects of desire and valued to the extent they are usable for the interest of others, then they have both become the object of other people's desire(s) and recognized themselves as commodities valued solely to the corresponding extent. The above may explain the interest in such TV programs as Extreme Makeover, in which people transform their appearance to please others, even undergoing plastic surgery, believing and hoping they will be more attractive to the other. It also explains why knowledge, particularly theoretical knowledge, has become a market commodity valued to the degree to which it is usable for the achievement of some end. It follows that there is a need for people able to produce such knowledge and to apply it efficiently in real-life situations. Now this ability is encouraged both by the OECD and by the European Union. There is, for example, a strong demand for the development of people's competences to manage theoretical knowledge, that is, produce, communicate and apply knowledge in the best way possible way (OECD 2000). As we saw above, the European Union supports the development of key competences for, and as an expression of, lifelong learning strategies in order to achieve the overall aim: to "become the most competitive and dynamic knowledge-based economy in the world…".

So, if persons basically understand themselves and their practical identities as conditioned, in for example the above-mentioned sense, they will most likely view themselves and others, their theoretical knowledge and abilities, basically as means to some further end. Hence they will not necessarily understand their practical identities as *un*conditioned, nor view themselves as reflective beings able to deliberate, challenge and change whatever concerns them. Their practical identity may then instead be valued as a means to some end and dependent upon contingent ends, and persons will strive to act efficiently and be successful as means to some further end. They will then probably not actualize their potential as human beings, that is, their ability to reflect upon themselves and the way(s) their identities are constructed;

nor necessarily take responsibility for their actions vis-à-vis others or change their actions and their constructed identities.

Korsgaard says that to "hold someone responsible is to regard her as a *person*—that is to say, as a free and equal person, capable of acting both rationally and morally. It is therefore to regard her as someone with whom you can enter the kind of relation that is possible only among free and equal rational people: a relation of reciprocity." (Korsgaard, 1996b, p. 189) If people basically view themselves merely as a means to some end, they will probably *not* value deliberation as a specific mode of communication—an intersubjective, critical and reflective reason-giving mode of communication, which calls attention to reason and virtuous behaviour. Moreover, people viewing themselves merely as means to ends will probably not view *each other* as equal in communicative procedures that is, equally entitled to express judgments and give reasons. Consequently, they may be intolerant of other people's possibilities and right to express themselves and give reasons to a satisfactory degree; they will most likely not reflect upon their inability and/or unwillingness to express and explain their beliefs and values and respond with respect to other people's reasoning; neither will they be sincere and willing to inquiry into the legitimacy of judgments expressed and reasons given. Instead, such people will probably view themselves and others as beings seeking the satisfaction of their desires. They will instead and most likely preserve the necessary and valuable identities and use the theoretical knowledge they have and the competences they have developed to satisfy the needs and desires they are believed to encompass.

In the classical instrumental model, people's identities need to be preserved and stable if the capitalist ideology is to function effectively and if the European Union is to become "the most competitive and dynamic knowledge-based economy in the world"; otherwise it would be difficult to know what needs to satisfy and what goods, services or knowledge need to be produced in order to satisfy the desires of such identities.

Such beliefs are disputed and ill-founded, as shown above. Moreover, if a person understands him-or herself basically as human, he has to understand himself as an end in himself and not merely as a means to something else. This implies being aware of one's potential as a human being and taking responsibility to actualize this as stemming from a reflective being capable of acting for at least one reason and deliberating upon it, together with others whenever needed. It also means that viewing oneself as a human being involves valuing one's unconditional, rational nature above any other, conditioned end as part of one's practical identity. This suggests that having some sort of identity means that we hold each other responsible and answerable for our actions and our identities. This suggests in turn that your movement will not be an action unless it is attributable to you, and something that you are the author of. And to violate your identity or conception of yourself as a human being "is to lose your integrity and so your identity, and to no longer be who you are. That is, it is to no longer be able to think of yourself under the description under which you value yourself and find your life to be worth living and your actions to be worth undertaking. It is to be for all practical purposes dead or worse than dead. When an action cannot be performed without loss of some fundamental part of one's identity, and an agent could just as well be dead, then the obligation not to do it is unconditional and complete." (Korsgaard, 1996a, p. 102) Hence, if we as human beings do not actualize the reflective structure of our consciousness in our everyday practice, or if our practical identity is not constructed in such a way that the reflective structure is a part of it, then it is or will become incomplete, simplistic and expresses narrowness; and we will not be cultivating ourselves as autonomous persons. The full function of deliberation is, then, to unify ourselves as autonomous, and not merely to determine how we should act efficiently and become successful. This suggests that when we as human beings actualize and cultivate our human potential, we strive to unite ourselves as autonomous and do not accept the use of ourselves or others merely as a means to some end; we act when we have at least one (convincing) reason for our action(s) and value ourselves as humans worthy of pursuing the action, while remembering the rights of other people and the possibility to become aware of the reasons of other people, to seek reasons, to reflect on them and even to challenge the meaning and legitimacy of expressed utterances. It also suggests that with a practical identity, a person will not lack reasons to act, nor will anyone else understand that person as not acting rationally in the world or in relation to others. An action, then, must be performed by an agent who can be seen as the author of that action, rather than as a product of some external or internal force. If the latter is the case, the person will not be considered the author of the action or free to act differently; nor will she actualize her human potential as an autonomous being. However, since human beings are free to choose in many cases between different actions and objects of desire, they are also free to refrain from acting, either towards others or towards themselves; hence freedom, as well as the potential to act upon reason, is a human predicament. This does not suggest that there is someone—an I—who exists prior to the act, some mysterious essence or entity behind or before the act which cannot be seen or grasped but has to be assumed. One's identity and in particular one's practical identity is constituted by one's actions and choices, according to Korsgaard (1996a). And since a person is in principle free to choose, he can also, with varying success, construct his identity differently. This construction is then always a matter of degree, as are its unification and integration. Hence, if the identity is poorly constructed, the scope for valued action is also poor. Thus a burglar may think that the only valued action is stealing, and that reading poetry or studying philosophy are not valued actions. Someone else with a differently constructed identity may believe that poetry and philosophy are worth-while activities. And it is obvious that people not only have different identities but engage in constructing them more or less actively. This suggests that it is a form of work to have a certain identity, and that a specific practical identity sets normative standards for what is considered valued action. It also suggests that the possibility to construct our identity puts us in challenging or problematic situations: Korsgaard again: "The reflective structure of human consciousness [however] sets us a problem. Reflective distance from our impulses makes it both possible and necessary to decide which ones we will act on: it forces us to act for reasons." (Korsgaard, 1996a, p. 113) And conditioned identities, which are contingent and dependent upon actual conditions, are mostly valued as means to some or someone's end(s). However, it is only our humanity that is unconditioned and an end in itself and rational in a fully-fledged sense. This means that a human being "necessarily represents his own existence in this way; so far it is thus a *subjective* principle of human actions" (Kant, 1785/2006, 4: 429), and that if and when "you view yourself as having a value-conferring status in virtue of your power of rational choice, you must view anyone who has the power of rational choice as having, in virtue of that power, a value-conferring status." (Korsgaard, 1996b, p. 123) It also means that anyone "must treat rational nature wherever you find it (in your own person or in that of another) as an end" (ibid. 1996b, p. 123), and not merely as a means to something else. Hence, it is the power of rational choice that characterizes our humanity: we cultivate our humanity insofar as we actualize and cultivate our reflective and deliberative skills together and unite our self-understanding as autonomous and not only as efficient persons. This suggests, on the one hand, that we as human beings can realize our humanity as well as unite our identities and our self-understanding more or less well. It also suggests, on the other hand, that the creation of citizenship through, for example, education within the European Union or elsewhere *can* reflect the reflective structure of our humanity.

To sum up, it seems that the construction of citizenship or education for citizenship at EU policy level reflects the simplistic mode of instrumental thinking or rationality as expressed in modern economics and capitalism rather than the potential of its members as reflective and deliberative citizens. I have argued that we need to reconsider the relation of the conditional with the unconditional identity of people's identities, and view the latter as the primary one, and understand education for democracy as an end in itself. If we can do this, we no longer necessarily need to consider the tension between capitalism and democracy as indissoluble. This tension stems from the fact that conditional identity is viewed as paramount, and merely as a means to some end. Were the unconditional identity primary, the reflective and deliberative character and potential would be considered unavoidable and valued for its own sake in human agency. We would also gain a better understanding of education in the triangular relation between education, the market and democracy; an education which would reflect the reflective and deliberative potential of its future citizens and encourage the unification of their self-understanding, rather than the reification of their practical identities. It seems then that if citizenship education can be understood as unconditional and not only as conditioned, it will reflect the possibility of a "new" critical language of education; one which acknowledges not only an instrumental mode of rational decision-making and human agency, but also people's potential as deliberative human beings and as ends in themselves, not merely as means for something else or for someone else's desired ends.

REFERENCES

Aristotle. (1996). *The nicomachean ethics*. Hertfordshire: Wordsworth editions limited, cop.
Bauman, Z. (2007). *Consuming life*. Cambridge: Polity.
Burton-Jones, A. (1999). *Knowledge capitalism: Business, work, and learning in the new economy*. Oxford: Oxford University Press.

Davidson, D. (2001a). *Epistemology externalized. Subjective, intersubjective, objective* (pp. 193–204). Oxford: Oxford University Press.

Davidson, D. (2001b). *Three varieties of knowledge. Subjective, intersubjective, objective* (pp. 205–220). Oxford: Oxford University Press.

Davidson, D. (2001c). *Actions, reasons, and causes. Essays on actions and events* (pp. 3–19). Oxford: Oxford University Press.

Davidson, D. (2001d). *On the very idea of a conceptual scheme. Inquiries into truth and interpretation* (pp. 183–198). Oxford: Clarendon Press.

Davidson, D. (2005). *Truth and predication.* Cambridge, MA: Belknapp Press.

Dolfsma, W., & Soete, L. (2006). *Understanding the dynamics of a knowledge economy.* Cheltenham, UK, Northampton, MA, USA: Edward Elgar.

Elster, J. (2000). Rationality, economy, and society. In S. Turner (Ed.), *The Cambridge companion to weber* (pp. 21–41). Cambridge: Cambridge University Press.

European Commission. (2002). *Education and training in Europe: Diverse systems, shared goals for 2010.* Luxembourg: Office for Official Publications of the European Communities.

Friedman, M. (2002). *Capitalism and freedom* (40th anniversary ed.). Chicago: Chicago University Press.

Green, C. (2005). *The privatization of state education: Public partners, private dealings.* London, New York: Routledge.

Habermas, J. (1987). *The theory of communicative action. The critique of functionalist reason* (Vol. 2). Cambridge: Polity Press.

Habermas, J. (2001). *The postnational constellation. Political essays.* Cambridge, MA: The MIT Press.

Hargreaves, A. (2003). *Teaching in the knowledge society. Education in the age of insecurity.* New York, London: Teacher College Press.

Hume, D. (1978/1739–40). *A treatise of human nature* (2nd ed.). Oxford: Clarendon Press.

Kant, I. (1785/2006). *Groundwork of the metaphysics of morals. Cambridge texts in the history of philosophy* (M. Gregor, Ed. & Trans.). With an Introduction by Christine M. Korsgaard. Cambridge: Cambridge University Press.

Korsgaard, C. (1996a). *The sources of normativity.* Cambridge: Cambridge University Press.

Korsgaard, C. (1996b). *Creating the kingdom of ends.* Cambridge: Cambridge University Press.

OeCD. (1996a). *The Knowledge-based economy.* Paris: The Organization.

OeCD. (1996b). *Measuring what people know: Human capital accounting for the knowledge economy.* Paris: The Organization.

OeCD. (1997). *Industrial competiveness in the knowledge-based economy: The new role of governments.* OeCD Conference Proceedings, Paris: The Organization.

OeCD. (2000). *Knowledge management in the learning society,* Paris: OeCD Publications Service.

Official Journal of the European Union. (2006). *Recommendation of the European Parliament and of the Council of 18 December 2006 on key competences for lifelong learning* (2006/962/EC).

Olssen, M. Codd, J., & O'Neill, A.-M. (2004). *Education policy: Globalization, citizenship & democracy.* London, Thousand Oaks, New Delhi: Sage Publications.

Peters, M. A., & Besley, A. C. (2006). *Building knowledge cultures. Education and development in the age of knowledge capitalism.* Lanham, Boulder, New York, Toronto, Oxford: Rowman & Littlefield Publishers, Inc.

Peters, M. A. (2001a) *Globalization and the knowledge economy: Implications for education policy.* Paper presented at the Eight International Literacy & Education Research Network conference on Learning, Dimotiko Skolio of Spetses, Spetses, Greece, 4–8 July 2001. In B. Cope & M. Kalantzis (Eds.), *Learning for the Future,* Proceedings of the Learning Conference 2001, Common Ground. http://MichaelPeters.Author-Site.com/.

Peters, M. A. (2001b, May). National education policy constructions of the 'Knowledge economy': Towards a critique. *Journal of Educational Inquiry, 2*(1). http://www.education.unisa.edu.au/JEE/.

Peters, M. A. (2004). Education and ideologies of the knowledge economy: Europe and the politics of emulation. *Social Work & Society, 2*(2), 160–172.

Peters, M. A. (2007). *Knowledge economy, development and the future of higher education*. Rotterdam: Sense Publishers.

Roth, K. (2007). Cosmopolitan learning. In K. Roth & N. C. Burbules (Eds.), *Changing notions of citizenship education in contemporary nation-states* (pp. 10–29). Rotterdam: Sense Publishers.

Roth, K., & Burbules N. C. (2007). *Changing notions of citizenship education in contemporary nation-states*. Rotterdam: Sense Publishers.

Roth, K. (2009). Some thoughts for a new critical language of education: Truth, justification and deliberation. *Philosophy & Social Criticism* (in press).

Searle, J. R. (2001). *Rationality in action*. Cambridge, MA, London: MIT Press.

Sen, A. (2002). *Rationality and freedom*. Cambridge, MA, London: Belknap Press of Harvard University Press.

Soysal, Y. (1994). *Limits of citizenship. Migrants and postnational membership in Europe*. Chicago: University of Chicago Press.

World Bank. (1998). *World development report: Knowledge for development*. Oxford: Oxford University Press.

World Bank. (2002). *China and the knowledge economy: Seizing the 21st century* (C. Dahlman & J.-E. Aubert, Eds.). Washington: The World Bank.

BOB BRECHER

18. IS CRITICAL EDUCATION STILL POSSIBLE IN UK UNIVERSITIES?

What, if anything, can be done to further critical university education in the United Kingdom today, subjected as the universities have been and doubtless will continue to be to the global neo-liberal revolution? I shall approach the question by considering at a general level what universities might be for (section I). Then I shall say something about their present situation in light of that (section II), before going on to offer some practical suggestions about how the universities' critical function might none-theless be furthered, even if in the teeth of the neo-liberal hurricane (section III).

I WHAT ARE UNIVERSITIES FOR?

In the context of what might very broadly be termed the western intellectual and political tradition, what is the point of a university education?[1] I mean, not for the individuals who attain such an education, but for the polity that either institutes and organizes it, or in the case of private universities, permits and/or encourages it.

Here is one view, a view that until quite recently would have been relatively uncontroversial across a whole range of polities: with appropriate adjustment regarding nomenclature, structure and institutional nature, from ancient Athens, to medieval Bologna, to seventeenth century Prague, to nineteenth century Harvard to the new universities of 1960s Britain. One of its clearest expressions was offered by John Stuart Mill, and it is worth quoting at length, if only in order clearly to lay out what we are at the point of losing altogether:

> The proper function of a University in national education is tolerably well understood. At least there is a tolerably general agreement about what a University is not. It is not a place of professional education. Universities are not intended to teach the knowledge required to fit men for some special mode of gaining their livelihood. Their object is not to make skilful lawyers, or physi-cians, or engineers, but capable and cultivated human beings. It is very right that there should be public facilities for the study of professions. It is well that there should be Schools of Law, and of Medicine, and it would be well if there were schools of Engineering, and the industrial arts. ... But these things are no part of what every generation owes to the next, as that on which its civilization and worth will principally depend. ... What professional men should carry away with them from an University, is not professional knowledge, but that which should direct the use of their professional knowledge, and bring the light of general culture to illuminate the technicalities of a special pursuit. Men may be competent lawyers without general education, but it depends on

I. Gur-Ze'ev, The Possibility/Impossibility of a New Critical Language in Education, 351–366.
© 2010 Sense Publishers. All Rights Reserved.

general education to make them philosophic lawyers — who demand, and are capable of apprehending—principles, instead of merely cramming their memory with details. And so of all other useful pursuits, mechanical included. Education makes a man a more intelligent shoemaker, if that be his occupation, but not by teaching him how to make shoes; it does so by the mental exercise it gives, and the habits it impresses (Mill, 1867).[2]

For Mill, then, the point of universities is 'the mental exercise' and 'the habits' they inculcate; and of course those he has in mind are exactly the same ones that both Socrates and Kant, among many others, would have endorsed: independent and critical thought; skepticism of authority; and the ability to weigh argument and to distinguish it from rhetoric (Mill, 1989). Furthermore, and for all that he writes elsewhere, we should note that in this passage at least Mill's position is not an élitist one: he is speaking of shoemakers no less than of lawyers, offering no ammunition for those who would dispatch the former to erstwhile polytechnics, conceived of as places of vocational training, and admit only the latter to universities, understood as vehicles of something very different, namely Higher education.

But that is of course no longer the accepted view. The neo-liberal revolution of the last third of the twentieth century demands something very different from universities. However, since it is in the nature of the case that the neo-liberal view has not been enunciated with the elegance of expression associated with Mill, we shall have to make do here with Mike Campbell, director of development at the Sector Skills Development Agency (SSDA)—since closed—which was 'responsible for funding, supporting and monitoring' twenty-five Sector Skills Councils which go to make up 'The Skills for Business network [which in turn] aims to boost the productivity and profitability of the UK'. After all, it is only because '[G]lobal economic forces are driving the UK's skills requirements' that '[B]y 2020 we'll need far more graduates than today', and that is why business has to '[T]ake the higher ground' (SSDA, 2007). Here then is Campbell's view of what universities are for. Again, it is worth quoting at length so as properly to appreciate its depth and richness:

> Our prosperity depends on how many people are in work and how productive they are. ... The country needs more highly qualified people to compete in a globalized economy, and the labour market is likely to need at least 4.5 million more graduates by 2020. Higher standards of living require higher standards of learning. ... That's why the Government has accepted ... new public service agreement targets and delivery agreements. ... This expansion cannot, and will not, be achieved by the expansion of full-time undergraduate provision for two reasons. First, the number of 18-year olds will decline by more than 100,000 up to 2020. Second, 70 per cent of our 2020 work force is in employment now, so to improve the skills of the adult workforce we have to focus much more on part-time provision and on working with mature students. This means more engagement with the world of work, collaborating with employers; it means a greater focus on the vocational relevance of qualifications; a greater emphasis on continuous professional development; and more emphasis on employability skills, including literacy, numeracy and communication skills. ... It means more

of a focus on 'economically valuable skills'. This makes sound business sense, but it is also government policy. For example, the Higher Education Funding Council for England's 2007–08 grant letter made clear that most growth should be targeted at higher-level skills development of the existing workforce. ... Higher Education has to give employers more power in the university world. ... Higher Education can make a major contribution to building better businesses, a better paid and more employable workforce, and a more successful economy. As a nation, we need to upskill big time and in quick time (Campbell, 2007).[3]

For Campbell, then, the function of universities is as "upskiller" of the national workforce in the drive to compete economically with those of other nations in the global labour market. It is hard to imagine a more different conception from Mill's; or, unhappily, one that more accurately expresses British 'government policy', as Campbell rightly notes.[4] Unsurprisingly, his view echoes that of Mao Zedong, writing in 1942:

A man studies through from grade school to university, graduates, and is then considered learned. Yet, in the first place, he cannot till the land; second, he has no trade; third, he cannot fight; fourth, he cannot manage a job. ... What he possesses is only book knowledge. ... Books cannot walk, and you can open and close a book at will... (in His-en Chen, 1981, p. xxx).

That echo should come as no surprise: for we should note in passing that the neo-liberal revolutionaries, no less than varieties of allegedly Marxist revolutionaries, seek quite explicitly to fashion human beings to fit their ideology.[5] In a time of the mass Higher Education that the "free market" requires to ensure continuously rising consumption and continuing corporate control of increasingly competitive production by, broadly, western interests, it is inevitable that the universities should come to be a major ideological site of that revolutionary effort; along, of course, with education more generally, healthcare provision and other elements whose place is to play a supporting role for corporate and/or state economic interests. In this respect, it is only the neo-liberal pretence of seeking merely to give human nature its head that distinguishes its revolutionary nature from, for example, Marxian or socialist attempts to fashion human beings anew. Of course, none of that is to say anything one way or the other about the desirability or advisability of such a commitment.

There is, however, something that both these views of the point of universities have in common: both are concerned with a certain disciplining of people, as of course education always requires, whether we are considering potty training, literacy or pure mathematics. But while Mill's view requires the inculcation at once of the intellectual discipline required to think critically ('the mental exercise it gives, and the habits it impresses') and what might be termed the social discipline required of a citizen ('capable and cultivated human beings'), what Campbell's requires explicitly is labour discipline ('new public service agreement targets and delivery agreements'; 'to improve the skills of the adult workforce'; 'a focus on 'economically valuable skills'). But how is such a discipline to be instituted and maintained? Only by ensuring compliance, complaisance and obedience—that is to say, by stifling any genuine 'mental exercise' so as to ensure that human beings, while becoming 'capable' workers, do not become 'cultivated', lest they cease to comply, learn to think for themselves and, in acting on such thinking, become disobedient. It is implicit in Campbell's view, then, that universities should seek to achieve the exact opposite of what Mill thinks they should be aiming at: where Mill's concern is with making 'a man a more intelligent shoemaker, if that be his occupation', Campbell's is with the 'need to upskill big time and in quick time'. In short, Mill's aim is to encourage thought, Campbell's to minimize it.

Now of course education—whether we are thinking of formal schooling or the matter of 'bringing up' children—has always had a dual function: at once to ensure cultural reproduction and to encourage criticism, at the very least, of that cultural reproduction. That is why Bob Jones University, for example, on whose website 'You can experience God's gift of salvation today' (www.bju.edu)—the American institution which honoured Ian Paisley, erstwhile figurehead of Protestant bigotry in Northern Ireland, with a "doctorate"—is no more a university than, again for example, the Yeshivas of Jerusalem or the Madrassas of northern Pakistan. Thus there is always a tension in education between, to put it briefly, ensuring conformity and encouraging non-conformity; or, to put it more starkly, between controlling and promoting thought; or, to put it even more starkly, between making people stupid and making people think. Socrates is the founding figure here, reflected first in Plato's *Republic* and then throughout the entire history of western education. In fact, one way of thinking about the rise of universities from the medieval period onwards is to see them as performing these two functions together through a (patriarchal) paternalism. The cultural renewal required to avoid stagnation would be achieved through entrusting it to a small and politically reliable élite which would at once push at the frontiers of thought and occupy positions—in the Church, the Court and so on—from which it would ensure that everyone else continued to do as they were told. Certainly that seems to be the model in terms of which Oxbridge continues both to think of itself and to function: consider, for example, the continuing composition of both Cabinet and Shadow Cabinet in the UK—the great majority, today as fifty or a hundred years ago, are Oxbridge (and largely Oxford) graduates.

The story of why neo-liberalism requires at once conformity and risk-taking, stupidity and intellectual advance, anti-individualistic social and moral conservatism and the highly individualistic *homo economicus* bestriding the free market is a long and interesting one; and, as we have already seen, one whose internal contradictions have instructive parallels with those of the so-called communism—more accurately described as state capitalism—of the Soviet era. However that may be, what is not in question is the fact that the current situation of the universities in the UK is the result of some twenty-five years of revolutionary neo-liberalism's direct diktat and indirect pressure. We are where we are because that is where neo-liberalism has put us— assisted all too often by our own complicity.[6] The pendulum has moved a very long way from Mill in the direction that Campbell and his ilk would have us go. What, then, are the salient features of our present position? For if there is anything that can be done to promote a critical university education of the sort broadly envisaged by Mill, it has to be done from that starting-point.

II UNIVERSITIES IN THE UK TODAY

Campbell's insistence that universities adopt the function of skills-trainers delivering a service to global capital is entirely typical of the thinking of New Labour: in the notorious words of the then Secretary of State for education and Skills, Charles Clarke, 'The medieval concept of scholars seeking truth is not in itself a justification for the state to put money into that. We might ... support them as an adornment to our society' (Clarke, 2003). All too many—though by no means all—Vice-Chancellors would agree with Campbell, if not, or not openly, with Clarke; so would an increasing proportion of first-year undergraduates; and of course so would a good deal of public opinion. There are endless calls like Campbell's that UK universities should become the servants of business, and the process of commodification has come a very long way since 'entrepreneurship' first reared its head on the university scene in the late 1980s. The effect of turning universities into (largely second-rate) businesses and university education into a commodity to be provided to customers is all too familiar.

In summary, students have become customers or clients; academics are fast becoming short-term contractual "facilitators"; administration is now management; and business interests have all too often replaced academic disinterest. At the same time, tax-funded grants and tuition fees have been replaced with variable tuition fees to be individually, i.e., privately, repaid; both the curricular independence of the "old" universities and the genuinely peer-run system of review in the then polytechnics (the Council for National Academic Awards) have been replaced by the Quality Assurance Agency ("owned", naturally, by the universities), subject "benchmarks" and the so-called Higher Education Academy. Learning, as academics continue to bemoan, is no longer a process demanding sustained engagement, at once induction into and critique of a culture, but rather a process—emulating the demands of the national curriculum that has been imposed on state, but not on public (i.e., private) schools—which requires a lack of interest and an absence of intellectual effort. The very idea of knowledge is increasingly understood as information, and thus as an unconnected series of fragments, familiarity with which is of solely instrumental value. Thus the assessment of students' intellectual abilities has become a matter of "measuring" their (apparent) knowledge, with external examiners becoming mere ciphers, whose only role is to confirm mathematical rectitude.[7] As George Steiner eloquently puts it:

> Anti-teaching is statistically close to being the norm. Good teachers, fire-raisers in their pupils' nascent souls may well be rarer than virtuoso artists or sages (Steiner, 2003, p. 18).

As in our schools, so in our universities.

To get a flavour of what this actually means in the everyday life of universities, it is worth dipping into the UK universities' trade paper, the *Times Higher Education Supplement*, or *THES*, for 2007. We should also note in passing that it rebranded itself as a magazine to make it 'much more accessible and attractive' at the beginning of 2008, now including more about 'promotions and staff achievements'

('"Higher" unveils new look', 2008) as well as the 'Who got that cash?' column introduced in 2007. In its apparent acceptance of a conception of universities as no less beholden to the forms and structures of entertainment than as having the function of "upskillers" for the owners of labour, this is a paradigmatic ideological package, at once marketing and representing skills training as entertainment-cum-leisure.

One of Brown's first actions when he replaced Blair as Prime Minister in May 2007 was to split ministerial responsibility for schools and universities: the former were put under Department of Children, Schools and Families; and the one point of contact between this structure of infantilism and the Department of Innovation, universities and Skills—where the universities now tellingly found themselves—was the National Council for Educational Excellence, naturally comprising two Vice Chancellors, the Chief Executives of Tesco and Rolls Royce, the Director General of the CBI, the Chair of a financial management group and a hedgefund partner. Two years later, even that was deemed insufficient: in 2009, the universities were subsumed under the Department of Business, Innovation and Skills. In 2007, we were told that 'marketing and public relations professionals must get involved in academic planning at the highest level' ('Allow PR in course design', 2007). In 2009 such a régime was imposed: even our own earlier collusion in the devaluation and irresponsible misuse of terms like "élite", "world-class" and, above all, "excellent"' ('"Damaging overuse" of hype', 2007)—one of the most damaging features of our current estate—was similarly deemed insufficient.[8] Doubtless the same terms will soon be used to describe the supermarkets', banks' and others' in-house training programmes, 'already accredited by the QCA [Qualifications and Curriculum Authority—the regulatory body for public examinations and publicly funded qualifications below university level]' ('In-house training', 2007) as they burgeon into fully-fledged undergraduate, and even postgraduate, qualifications. The 2007 decision of the gruesomely eponymous Qualifications and Curriculum Authority, acting of course on Brown's cue, to give Flybe, Network Rail and—naturally— McDonald's permission to offer 'A-level-style qualifications' ('Learning on the job', 2008) was only the first step. Two years later, the reality is taken for granted.

At the same time, the substitution of knowledge-acquisition for learning and "facilitation" for teaching—for mass Higher Education must on no account be a critical education, and so education has to be conceptualized as something that is to be "delivered"—means that the 'small-group teaching' ('Ill-equipped staff', 2007) which is a necessary condition of encouraging people to think is sacrificed and the notion of academic expertise jettisoned 'as customer-led culture prevails' ('Class sizes', 2007). It is no bar to the academic credibility of a course that an academic admits that 'I have sometimes gone into seminars crossing my fingers, hoping that the students have prepared a good presentation, because I know sod-all myself' ('A lecturer', 2007). But perhaps knowing 'sod-all' no longer matters very much, since '[T]he quality of academics' research will be judged according to the number of times their published papers are cited by their peers under a key part of the system that will replace the [current] research assessment exercise'; and (although this farce is at present intended to cover only the natural sciences and mathematics) it hardly takes the insight of an Einstein to imagine the likely 'potential threats to the credibility of a citations system, including likely changes in researchers' behaviour to maximize their performance' ('New RAE', 2007). Again, what may be thought truly bizarre is academic complicity in this farrago of intellectual corruption: a particularly appalling example is Eric Thomas, Vice Chancellor of Bristol University: 'It is,' he informs us, 'essential that the sector fully engage with this important consultation with the aim of ensuring that the new arrangements maintain the excellence of the UK research base ('Add input', 2007).

Still, why not corrupt academics' research, given that the standards of student assessment are continually being massaged, starting at school and continuing into university? Here is Tim Birkhead, Professor of Behavioral Ecology:

> Much of the assessment in university science departments relies on project work in which students undertake a research project, collect their own data and analyze it. It has become increasingly obvious that much of the data in these reports is fabricated, made up, faked. Remarkably, in discussion about this students are often extremely sanguine, pointing out that this is what they did in school. In the desperate race to meet assessment targets teachers happily give credit when their pupils obtain the 'right' results, because without them, they won't get the right marks and teachers won't get the right marks either when they are assessed ('Let's face it', 2007).

Not that there is anything remarkable about this, though: it is simply a rational response, both on the part of students—who are in fact customers paying for their qualifications, and thus their grades—and of their schoolteachers, who need to pay the mortgage. Increasingly, the same is true of their lecturers. It is not every day that a professor resigns 'in disgust after senior managers overruled his decision to fail 13 of his students' because he is 'not prepared to continue working in an institution where examination boards are merely a formality that can be overturned by a head of school without any consultation' ('Marks U-turn', 2007). For many others, however, material necessity dictates silence, especially as—and this is something those who have an academic career are prone to overlook—already six years ago 'nearly half of all Higher Education staff work on a casual basis' ('Will full-timers?', 2008) and actualization continues apace. In the university as elsewhere, '[S]taff will need to be more aware of and aligned to the strategic needs of the Higher Education institution' ('Staff Loyalty', 2007)—even if not for rather different reasons than those proposed by the Leadership, Governance and Management Strategic Committee of the Higher Education Funding Council for England. Ironically as ever, even our Members of Parliament have managed recently to catch up with the reality they themselves insisted on imposing: 'Universities were yesterday embroiled in a furious row over dumping down after a parliamentary inquiry revealed the number of first-class degrees had almost double in a decade' (Hinsliff, 2009).

Where does all that leave us in the UK today? An élite system (some 5% of the population went to university fifty years ago) has changed into a mass system, with around 45% now obtaining a university qualification. Loyalty to one's discipline or area is under constant pressure, while loyalty to one's institution is all too rarely either deserved or possible. Both teaching and research have become quantified and commodified, and the importance placed on students' learning by government, a good deal of management and very often students themselves is in inverse proportion to the lip-service paid to it. Morale has all but disappeared.

III WHAT IS TO BE DONE?

On the basis of the perhaps mistaken conviction that the worse things are—up to a point—the greater the opportunity to change them, and that crisis can sometimes lead to welcome change rather than greater disaster, let me offer an optimistic view about the prospects for critical education. A condition of such optimism's being other than uselessly Utopian is that we—academics—are actually convinced that a critical education is an end worth pursuing and that we are responsible for pursuing it.[9] First, then, I shall say a little more about that end, before, second, thinking about the structural means whereby we might attain it. Then, third, I shall briefly explore the implications of that for how we teach. Finally I shall touch on the issue of solidarity that stands in the background whenever action is contemplated.

A Critical Education

At the outset of this piece I characterized a critical education as fostering independent and critical thought; skepticism of authority; and the ability to weigh argument and to distinguish it from rhetoric. It is not a matter of acquiring information, important though that may be as a means to some of such an education's specific instances. Nor is it a matter of acquiring professionally useful skills, or skills that may be useful to an employer, even though the sort of skills that such an education does have to foster—in brief, the transferable intellectual skills[10] of analysis and synthesis, of distinguishing what is relevant from what is not, of communicating and developing ideas—may happen to be useful in certain job settings. Or not: in my experience, for all that many employers like to speak of wishing that their graduate entrants possessed these skills, their exercise, unsurprisingly, is only rarely encouraged, or even tolerated. As Newman put it in his classic *The Idea of a University*, 'the true and adequate end of intellectual training and of a University is not Learning or Acquirement, but rather, is Thought or Reason exercised upon Knowledge, or what may be called Philosophy' (Newman, 1907, p. 139): the 'real cultivation of the mind' which such an education aims at is a matter of fostering 'the force, the steadiness, the comprehensiveness and the versatility of intellect, the command over our own powers, the instinctive just estimate of things as they pass before us, which sometimes indeed is a natural gift, but commonly is not gained without much effort and the exercise of years' (Newman, 1907, p. xvi).[11]

Such an education, however, is not in my view—and *pace* Newman—a matter of pursuing knowledge "for its own sake" (on which see Newman, 1907, p. 99 ff, Discourse 5, 'Knowledge its own end'). Rather, and putting it briefly and starkly, all knowledge is fundamentally practical, in that it is a necessary condition of action. While some knowledge, clearly, is directly practically and some not, the point of knowledge, so to speak, is that it enables us to do things. It is for the sake of action that knowledge is a human pursuit at all, which is what I take Plato's argument in the *Republic* in part to be when he has Socrates explain that the 'Idea of good ... is the cause of science and of truth ... apprehended by knowledge, and yet, fair as both truth and knowledge are, ... different from these and even fairer ...' (Plato, 508e). That is one reason why the notion of a critical education is not one that it is particularly helpful to contrast with a practical, or vocational, education. For while there are differences between, say, the philosophy of mathematics on the one hand and systems software or pharmacy on the other—and both are important—they are not well marked by the "academic/vocational" distinction. That is Mill's point when he says, as we have seen, that 'Education makes a man a more intelligent shoemaker, if that be his occupation, but not by teaching him how to make shoes; it does so by the mental exercise it gives, and the habits it impresses' (Mill, 1867). It is *education* that is the point: and whatever the benefit to particular individuals of education, that citizens be thus educated is a social good. For without critique, a culture stagnates.

The purpose of a critical education, then, can be summed up as helping students think.[12] To do that, however, demands a genuine recognition of and commitment to teaching on the part of the teacher. Obvious though it is, the point deserves under-lining: if a critical education is to be on offer in our universities, then we, the teachers, have actively, and indeed urgently, to commit ourselves to such an education, and thus to our students. For as Steiner insists,

> Authentic teaching is a vocation. It is a calling. The wealth, the exactions of meaning which relate to such terms as 'ministry', 'clerisy', 'priesthood' modulate into secular teaching both morally and historically. Hebrew rabbi simply signifies 'teacher'. But it reminds us of an immemorial dignity. At its most elementary levels—which are, in fact, never 'elementary'—in the teaching, for example, of young children, of the deaf-mute, of the mentally impaired, or at the pinnacles of privilege, in the high places of the arts, of science, of thought, authentic teaching results from a summons (Steiner, 2003, pp. 16–17).[13]

Teaching is thus inevitably a political activity. First, it is political because '[T]he pulse of teaching is persuasion. The teacher solicits attention, agreement, and, optimally, collaborative dissent' (Steiner, 2003, p. 26). Second, it is political because whether one teaches many or few, all who can benefit or an élite, has far-reaching political consequences: that, after all, is why neo-liberals (in contrast to Mill) are so averse to critical education as opposed to "upskilling".

So if we in the universities are to try to help our students to think, and to enable as many people as possible to become 'our students', we need to be clear that we are engaged in political activity.

Exploit the Contradictions

If such political activity is to succeed, then it needs to be clear about the conditions of that politics—of that sort of teaching. As I have argued, neo-liberalism needs at once a trained ("educated") workforce and thus mass, rather than élite, entry to the university system (if not to certain universities, of course) and to ensure so far as it can that that workforce be indeed trained rather than educated. And that, in reflecting fundamental contradictions in the neo-liberal project, offers at least one opportunity. Needless to say, this is not at all to reject other tactics. My point is, rather, that neo-liberalism's internal contradictions open up a specific possibility.

The general contradictions in the neo-liberal project are clear: between economic "freedom" and the social and moral authoritarianism required if *homo economicus* is not to move from economic to the sort of personal-political libertarianism which would undermine market disciplines; between rampant individualism and the sort of social cohesion required for there even to be a market; between the rich in their "gated communities" and the poor who have to be kept away from the gates lest they break in; between private and public, lest the state dissolves altogether, thereby removing the subsidies and the safety net on which the corporations rely.[14] These large-scale contradictions are reflected in the tensions, to say the least, that characterize public life and public institutions such as the National Health Service, education, immigration and the law.

Thus, to turn specifically to the universities. We defer to their customers or clients, while serving them ever less well; student-centered learning aims, goals, outcomes, timetabling and all the rest of the "give them what they want" apparatus disguises the fact that students are increasingly patronized, infantilized and subordinated to the demands of research as the amount and quality of teaching they are buying diminishes; and average marks increase as standards fall. And the same is of course happening in schools—which is why levels of literacy and numeracy continue to deteriorate, plagiarism is encouraged and schoolchildren are bored out of their heads by the rote learning, multiple-choice fiddling and never-ending testing that has replaced education. At the same time, an increasing minority of these embryonic customers are reacting positively and not just negatively: over the past four years or so, Philosophy has been the fastest-growing secondary school subject in the UK. That sort of reaction surely has a lesson for us in the universities: it may just be possible that if we take our "customers" seriously as students, so they will come to do the same. So why not use both the structure and the language of course review, course validation, student satisfaction surveys and so on to move away from bite-sized, modularized and fragmented structures to coherent degree programmes that instantiate a critical education? The rhetoric is all about empowerment, challenge, learning to think and being able to apply knowledge and understanding to novel situations. It has to be, since the neo-liberals' real goals would not survive honest articulation: just as oppression is always ideologically articulated as freedom, authoritarianism as democracy, mindlessness as realism and wrong as right, so believing whatever you are told, lack of curiosity, interest or imagination, inability or unwillingness to think clearly cannot be cited as what we are trying to encourage. So why not subvert the ideology as it is in fact presented by taking it seriously and insisting that students are indeed taught in ways and structures which encourage these abilities?

Nor should we imagine that we would be alone in attempting such a task. Not every Vice Chancellor or policy-maker is a born-again neo-liberal; not every manager or administrator shares the government's agenda of imposing idiocy on the population. Thus Lord Dearing, for example, erstwhile Post Office CEO and latterly lead author of an influential Report which heralded many of the neo-liberal "reforms" of the 1990s,[15] has more recently, and quite remarkably, argued that '[U]niversities must "hold a mirror up to society" in the drive to sustain it as democratic, civilized and inclusive'; that 'Higher Education must take the lead in mending society's "fault lines"'; and that, in his own words, 'the wellbeing of our civilization is (also) at hazard' ('Dearing looks', 2007). Nor is the entire academic profession complaisant or silent. Early in 2007, for example, staff in the University of Central Lancashire's Business School—responding to their managers' initiative in setting up an online forum 'to allow staff to debate the school's future strategic direction'— 'delivered a damning indictment of the quality of their own students' ('Immature students', 2007). (Whether this response was an example of exploiting contradictions—in this case the need for a democratic veil—or whether the managers' initiative was genuine I do not know.) Or consider Stephen Rowland's call to reject 'narrow-minded and patronizing' government attitudes to mass Higher Education:

> Protesting the excellence of their own institutions, they [their leaders] have said little about their purposes or those of the sector as a whole and how these relate to the needs of society. Mission statements and straplines have come to replace serious thinking about what universities are for, rather than be a distillation of that thinking (Now then', 2007).

In the universities as elsewhere, people are rejecting philistine neo-liberal ideology as its contradictions rise to the surface. My own university, as it happens, and on the basis of a year-long discussion among all its members, 'is committed to delivering socially purposeful Higher Education that serves and strengthens society and underpins the economy; contributes critically to the public good; enriches those who participate; and equips our graduates to contribute effectively as citizens...' ('University of Brighton', 2007). While that is hardly typical, it is a commitment that many others would share. Situation is by no means hopeless—provided that we really do think that a critical education is worth the effort required.

Challenging Students

As Mary Warnock, another figure in the liberal tradition from whose view of university education the Left would do well to learn, already put it some twenty-five years ago:

> The aim of the universities can never be to follow the market, in the sense of offering whatever it is that students want. Prospective students often do not know what they want, and certainly do not know what, in order to achieve academic goals, they ought to be given. On the contrary, universities must try to remedy the inability to make intelligent choices, forced upon people by their position in the market economy (Warnock, 1985, p. 25).

There are of course many ways in which that might be done, and there will be differences among disciplines and fields of study, as well as differences in the detailed situations of colleagues in different universities. Nonetheless, it may be helpful to suggest a few pointers, which others will perhaps develop and extend.

We might start by thinking about what it is that we think students taking a particular degree (whether single-disciplinary, multidisciplinary or interdisciplinary) be able to do by the time they finish; and that might lead us to consider how to operationalise in particular contexts the notion of a critical education adumbrated above. That done, what are the implications of the relevant objectives for the priorities required in respect of the students who come to us in an era of mass Higher Education and in most cases through the school system? What reasonable standards of literacy and/or numeracy should we insist upon by the end of, say, the first year? And what do we need to do to ensure they are met? Given that more and more students come to university academically, and often functionally, at best semi-literate, what should we do about it? Merely to insist that it is not our job to do what should have been done at school will change nothing.

In that context, what do we need to do by way of showing—and I mean showing, not just explaining—what the demands of a university education are? If we have to start from where our students are—and we do—then we need, I suggest, to be explicit about where we intend them eventually to be and why. We need also to be clear about the sort of expertise we are offering, about the differences between the intellectual authority of, say, an engineer, an anaesthetist and a historian.[16] And we need to be clear about the standards expected, no less than about the need to fail students who do not meet them. Nor should these be thought of as impossibly Utopian, as if we did not really believe most people to be capable of being critically educated and benefiting from it. As numerous empirical studies have long shown, how well people do is in part dependent on how well, or badly, they are expected to do.[17] In connection with the matter of our own expectations of students and the need to show rather than merely explain, and especially in circumstances where on-line and distance "learning" is insidiously replacing face-to-face teaching, and (badly paid) graduate students are increasingly being wheeled in "to do the teaching" while full-time and experienced academics write articles which hardly anyone reads, two things need urgently to be done. First, we need to remember the centrality of talking with our students. For, to go back to Steiner again, 'before writing, during the history of writing and in challenge to it, the spoken word is integral to the act of teaching. The Master speaks to the disciple. From Plato to Wittgenstein, the ideal of lived truth is one of orality, of face-to-face address and responses' (Steiner, 2003, p. 8)'.[18] For (and notwithstanding Steiner's masculinism) '[T]he written word does not listen to its reader. It takes no account of his questions and objections. A speaker can correct himself at every point; he can amend his message. The book sets its main morte on our attention' (Steiner, 2003, p. 32).[19] Second, we need ourselves to conduct the requisite conversations at the earliest stage possible, and thus to set the expectations students need to have both of us and of themselves. That is to say, first-year teaching needs to be a priority: get that right, I would venture to suggest, and much of the rest will more easily follow.

One more thing before my final point. Critical education is something that, if it is worth pursuing at all, has to be pursued across the entire university, across all its disciplines. One of the besetting problems that the UK's notorious and disastrous "arts/ science" divide has bequeathed the university sector is that all too many colleagues who are otherwise committed to some version, at least, of a critical education seem to think it is something largely or wholly limited to the arts and humanities, and perhaps some of the social sciences. That is nonsense: the natural sciences, technology, mathematics and anything else that is properly a subject of university research and study needs to be critically taught and learnt; and we in the humanities should not make the arrogant assumption that the concerns of a critical education are somehow more "ours" than those of our colleagues, either practically or theoretically. Indeed, a reasonable test of what is or is not a proper object of university study is its capacity to demand a critical approach and response: thus there is no good reason why the much derided media studies should necessarily be excluded; whereas hairdressing appears rather more hard-put to establish its credibility.[20]

Solidarity

Trying to turn the university tanker away from neo-liberal indoctrination towards critical education, let alone beginning to succeed, may of course turn out to be welcomed as—and if—the neo-liberal revolution is overturned. If the winds of the neo-liberal revolution continue unabated, however, then any attempt to institute such an education is likely to be firmly resisted by government and by their allies in our universities. At that point, the virtue of solidarity will be required: solidarity between immediate colleagues; between the academics, managers, administrators and of course students working in a particular university; between universities; and, perhaps above all, between university and public, a public which will of course include more and more university graduates. Undue optimism being uncalled for, we had better start building these solidarities now; and at the same time take on the role of public intellectual in a serious engagement with our fellow citizens to build a new political consensus that rejects the neo-liberal normalization of all our lives.

NOTES

[1]   I do not intend to imply that other traditions—for instance those of the Arab world, India and central Asia or China—are very different from the European in respect of their conceptualization and institutionalization of what in the latter has for nearly a thousand years been described as a university.

[2]   An early and perspicuous analysis of what might be termed the strange death of western liberal education was John Passmore (1989).

[3]   See also the *THES*'s account of the British government's World Class Skills: Implementing the Leitch Review of Skills in England, its response to a review of skills with which Campbell was closely concerned ('Take a "business-facing" approach', 2007).

[4]   Although the present, New Labour, administration has done more to destroy critical education at every level than the Conservatives ever managed, this is not a party political matter: on this, as on every aspect of economic and social policy, the UK's two parties, each a paragon of neo-liberal ideology, differ only on the details of how to ensure "efficient delivery".

[5]   For a brilliant and detailed study of the (literal) violence in which this consists where neo-liberalism requires to be exported, see Naomi Klein, 2007.

[6]   I explore certain facets of this in Brecher, 2005.

7   Some of the material in this paragraph is taken from Brecher, 2005.
8   The first speaker is Tim O'Brien, international development director at Nottingham Trent University; the second is Sir David Watson, Professor of Higher Education Management at the Institute of Education, University of London, and formerly Vice Chancellor of the University of Brighton.
9   I say something about academics' responsibilities more generally in Brecher, (2004).
10 As contrasted with the 'transferable skills', or the so-called personal skills, so beloved of neo-liberal propaganda, which allegedly make their possessors more employable, but which are neither personal, transferable nor skills, but rather non-educational competencies—whether or not desirable ones—necessary to perform whatever jobs might be available. With thanks to Patrick Ainley for insisting on the distinction; and for his other comments on an earlier draft.
11 Compare p. 101, where Newman describes a liberal education as one in the course of which '[A]habit of mind is formed which lasts through life, of which the attributes are, freedom, equitableness, calmness, moderation, and wisdom.' For a stimulating contemporary discussion inspired by Newman, see Graham (2002).
12 In this connection at pre-university level, see Allen and Ainley, 2007.
13 Cf. Steiner, 2003, pp. 183–4: 'There is no craft more privileged (than teaching). To awaken in another human being powers, dreams beyond one's own; to induce in others a love for that which one loves; to make of one's inward present their future: this is a threefold adventure like no other.'
14 For example, since Britain's railways were privatized, public subsidy for the now private companies greatly exceeds that to the nationalized system, even allowing for inflation. Just recently, the UK government had to underwrite Northern Rock, a private bank/building society, to the tune of some £25 billion to avert its imminent collapse.
15 See the Report of The National Committee of Inquiry Into Higher Education (1997), known as the *Dearing Report*: accessible at www.leeds.ac.uk/educol/ncihe/
16 For an attempt to work through some of these issues in the context of early neo-liberal attempts to attack critical education, see Brecher and Hickey, 1990.
17 See for instance the classic discussion in R. Rosenthal & L.F.Jacobsen, *Pygmalion in the Classroom: Teacher Expectation and Pupils' Intellectual Development* (New York: Holt, 1968), cited in P. Zimbardo, *The Lucifer Effect* (New York: Random House, 2007). For more on how 'beliefs create expectations', see Zimbardo, 2007, pp. 221–228 and 262–296, esp. 283–284.
18 This is one reason why Steiner insists that '[E]roticism, covert or declared, fantasized or enacted, is inwoven in teaching, in the phenomenology of mastery and discipleship'—Steiner, 2003, p. 26; see also pp. 140 ff.
19 See in this context 'Security limits tutor access', an article about how a swipe-card system in a new building at the University of Manchester excludes students from having access to their tutors. One notes that, while as a student reports, '[E]ven my tutor noted the security doors and restricted access was "ridiculous"', it appears not to have occurred to tutors to refuse to work under such conditions; and that the tutor whose comments are the most prominent 'wished to remain anonymous'.— ('Security limits', 2008). *THES*, 4 January 2008.
20 Not, of course, that that has dissuaded at least one university from 'doing hairdressing': see 'Restyling pays off at Southampton Solent', *THES*, ibid.

REFERENCES

A 'lecturer in media ... who asked The Times Higher not to use her real name', quoted as 'Abigail Smith'. (2007, May 4). *THES*. Available at <http://www.timeshighereducation.co.uk/>
Allen, M., & Ainley, P. (2007). *Education make you fick, innit?: What's gone wrong with England's schools, colleges and universities and how to start putting it right.* London: Tufnell Press.
Allow PR in course design, official says (2007, November 9). *THES*. Available at <http://www.timeshighereducation.co.uk/>
Birkhead, T. (2007, November 23). Let's face it, in terms of real education the school experiment of the past 20 years or so has been a disaster. *THES*. Available at <http://www.timeshighereducation.co.uk/>

Bob Jones University website: <http://www.bju.edu>

Brecher, B. (2005). Complicity and modularization: How universities were made safe for the market. *Critical Quarterly, 47*, 72–82.

Brecher, B. (2004). Do intellectuals have a special public responsibility? In W. Aiken & J. Haldane (Eds.), *Philosophy and its public role* (pp. 25–38). Exeter: Imprint Academic: St Andrews Studies in Philosophy and Public Affairs.

Brecher, B., & Hickey, T. (1990). In defence of bias. *Studies in Higher Education, 15*, 299–312. Available at <http://www.share.co.uk/publications.she/asp/>

Campbell, M. (2007, December 14). Help everyone get the skills to compete. *Times Higher Education Supplement.* Available at <http://www.timeshighereducation.co.uk/>

Clarke, C. (2003, December 19/26). The Medieval concept. [In Quotes of the year]. *THES.* Available at <http://www.timeshighereducation.co.uk/>

Class sizes spark fears over quality (2007, May 4). *THES.* Available at <http://www.timeshighereducation.co.uk/>

'Damaging overuse' of hype criticized (2007, July 6). *THES.* Available at <http://www.timeshighereducation.co.uk/>

Dearing looks beyond skills (2007, December 14). *THES.* Available at <http://www.timeshighereducation.co.uk/>

Graham, G. (2002). *Universities: The recovery of an idea.* Exeter: Imprint Academic.

'Higher' unveils new look (2008, January 4). *THES.* Available at <http://www.timeshighereducation.co.uk/>

Hinsliff, G. (2009, August 2). Dumbing down row over value of degrees. *Observer.* Available at <http://observer.co.uk>

His-en Chen, T. (1981). *Chinese education since 1949: Academic and revolutionary models.* New York: Pergamon Press.

Ill-equipped staff forced to fill in for absent colleagues (2007, May 4). *THES.* Available at <http://www.timeshighereducation.co.uk/>

Immature students without basic english enrage uclan staff. (2007, March 30). *THES.* Available at <http://www.timeshighereducation.co.uk/>.

In-house training goes national. (2007, May 1). *Education Guardian.* Available at <http://guardian.co.uk>

Klein, N. (2007). *The shock doctrine: The rise of disaster capitalism.* London: Allen Lane.

Learning on the job. (2008, January 29). *Guardian.* Available at <http://guardian.co.uk>

"Marks u-Turn is 'mockery of exam process'". (2007, March 30). *THES.* Available at <http://www.timeshighereducation.co.uk/>

Mill, J. S. (1867). *Inaugural address delivered to the University of St Andrews, February 1st 1867.* London: Longmans, Green, Reader & Dyer. Available at <http://cdl.library.cornell.edu/cgi-bin/moa/page viewer?root=%2Fmoa%2Flivn%2Flivn0092%2F&tif=00654.TIF&cite=http%3A%2F%2Fcdl.library.cornell.edu%2Fcgi-bin%2Fmoa%2Fmoa-cgi%3Fnotisid%3DABR0102-0092-13&coll=moa&frames=1&view=text>

Mill, J. S. (1989 [1869]). *On liberty.* Cambridge: Cambridge university Press.

New Rae based on citations. (2007, November 9). *THES.* Available at <http://www.timeshighereducation.co.uk/>

Newman, J. (1907 [1854]). *The idea of a university.* London: Longmans, Green & Co.

Now then, what am I meant to be doing here? (2007, June 1). *THES.* Available at <http://www.timeshighereducation.co.uk/>

Passmore, J. (1989, May 26–June 1). Hearing voices, *Times Literary Supplement*, 567–568. Plato, *Republic*, Various editions.

Report of the National Committee of Inquiry into Higher Education, known as the *Dearing Report.* (1997). Available at <http://www.leeds.ac.uk/educol/ncihe/>

Restyling pays off at Southampton Solent. (2008, January 4). *THES.* Available at <http://www.timeshighereducation.co.uk/>

Rosenthal, R., & Jacobsen, L. F. (1968). *Pygmalion in the classroom: Teacher expectation and pupils' intellectual development*. New York: Holt.

Sector Skills Development Agency website: <http://www.ssda.org.uk>

Security Limits Tutor Access. (2008, January 4). *THES*. Available at <http://www.timeshighereducation.co.uk/>

Staff loyalty key to Hefce report. (2007, November 30). *THES*. Available at <http://www.timeshighereducation.co.uk/>

Steiner, G. (2003). *Lessons of the masters*. Cambridge, MA: Harvard university Press.

Take a 'business-facing' approach, ministers say. (2007, July 27). *THES*. Available at <http://www.timeshighereducation.co.uk/>

Thomas, E. (2007, November 9). Add input to make metrics count. *THES*. Available at <http://www.timeshighereducation.co.uk/>

University of Brighton. (2007). University of Brighton's Corporate Plan 2007–12, Vice-Chancellor's Introduction. Available at <http://www.brighton.ac.uk/aboutus/corporateinfo/corporateplan.php?PageId=403>

Warnock, M. (1989). *Universities: Knowing our minds*. London: Chatto & Windus.

Will full-times please spare a thought for us? (2008, January 4) *THES*. Available at <http://timeshighereducation.co.uk>

Zimbardo, P. (2007). *The Lucifer effect*. New York: Random House.

DOUGLAS KELLNER

19. SCHOOL SHOOTINGS, VIOLENCE, AND THE RECONSTRUCTION OF EDUCATION—SOME PROPOSALS

In my book *Guys and Guns Amok: Domestic Terrorism and School Shootings from the Oklahoma City Bombings to the Virginia Tech Massacre* (Kellner 2008), I have argued that there are many causes to the rise of school violence and events like the Columbine and Virginia Tech school shootings. Complex historical events like the Iraq invasion or the Virginia Tech and Columbine shootings require a multiperspectivist vision and interpretation of key factors that constitute the constellation from which events can be interpreted, explained, and better understood. Thus addressing the causes of problems like societal violence and school shootings involves a range of apparently disparate things such as critique of male socialization and construction of ultramasculine male identities, the prevalence of gun culture and militarism, and a media culture that promotes violence and retribution, while circulating and sensationalizing media spectacle and a culture of celebrity. Such a constellation helps construct the identities, values, and behaviour that helps incite individuals to use violence to resolve their crisis of masculinity through creation of an ultra-masculine identity and media spectacle, producing guys and guns amok.

Accordingly, solutions that I suggest to the problems of school violence and shootings in *Guys and Guns Amok* range from more robust and rational gun laws, to better school and workplace security with stronger mental health institutions and better communication between legal, medical, and school administrations, to the reconstruction of masculinity and the reconstruction of education for democracy. In addition, we must consider examining better ways of addressing crime and violence than prisons and capital punishment, draconian measures aimed increasingly today at youth and people of color. Today our schools are like prisons, while in a better society schools would become centers of learning and self-developing, while prisons could also be centers of learning, rehabilitation, and job-training and not punitive and dangerous schools for crime and violence.

Escalating violence in schools and other sectors of society today in the United States is a national scandal and serious social problem. Deaths in the U.S. caused by firearms run to about 30,000 per year in which around 12,000 are murders and 17,000 are suicides with the rest accidents.[1] Of the 105,000 guns shops in the U.S., only about 1% are the origins of 60% of the guns that are seized in crimes. As David Olinger notes: "Collectively, U.S. citizens are the most heavily armed in the world. Americans own about 250 million rifles, shotguns and handguns, nearly one per person and at least one-third of the guns in the world.... From

I. Gur-Ze'ev, The Possibility/Impossibility of a New Critical Language in Education, 367–378.
© *2010 Sense Publishers. All Rights Reserved.*

1999 through 2004, according to the U.S. Centers for Disease Control and Prevention, guns killed an average of 80 people a day. Gun homicides averaged 31 a day."[2]

The massacre at Virginia Tech in 2007 was the 25th school shooting on an American campus since the Columbine school shootings in 1999. That figure represents more than half the number of shootings at schools across in the world in the same time span.[3] Deadly school shootings at a wide range of schools have claimed over four hundred student and faculty lives since Columbine. As publicists for a new edition of Lieberman's *The Shooting Game* indicates (2007): "In March and April of 2006, 16 deadly Columbine-style plots were hatched by over 25 students arrested across the U.S.A. from the heartland up to North Pole, Alaska. As the fall semester began, there were more deadly shootings in Montreal, Colorado, Wisconsin and even a tiny Amish school in Pennsylvania."

In this article, I will suggest some proposals to deal with the escalating problem of school violence and school shooting and will argue for the importance of radical pedagogy that proposes new modes of conflict resolution and ways of dealing with bullying, hatred, and violence that emerges in schools.

BEYOND THE CULTURE OF MALE VIOLENCE AND RAGE

Dealing with problems of school and societal violence will require reconstruction of male identities and critique of masculinist socialization and identities. Unfortunately, the media and some gang culture, gun cultures, sports, and military culture produce ultramacho men as an ideal, producing societal problems from violence against women to gang murder (see Katz 2006). As Jackson Katz urges, young men have to renounce these ideals and behavior and construct alternative notions of masculinity. As Katz concludes, reconstructing masculinity and overcoming aggressive and violent macho behavior and values provides "a vision of manhood that does not depend on putting down others in order to lift itself up. When a man stands up for social justice, non-violence, and basic human rights—for women as much as for men—he is acting in the best traditions of our civilization. That makes him not only a better man, but a better human being" (2006, p. 270).

Major sources of violence in U.S. society include cultures of violence caused by poverty; masculinist military, sports, and gun culture; ultramasculine behavior in the corporate and political world; high school bullying and fighting; general societal violence reproduced by media and in the family and everyday life, and in prisons, which are schools for violence. In any of these cases, an ultraviolent masculinity can explode and produce societal violence, and until we have new conceptions of what it means to be a man that include intelligence, independence, sensitivity, and the renunciation of bullying and violence, societal violence will no doubt increase.

As I was concluding this study in July 2007, a striking example of men and guns running amok circulated through the media in stories of how former Virginia Tech football player and NFL star Michael Vick was indicted on dog-fighting charges. It was alleged that vick and three associates had been actively participating in the illegal sport of dog-fighting for at least six years. The indictment states that Vick's associates executed eight dogs for performing poorly in the month of April, utilizing methods such as hanging, electrocution, shooting, and physical beatings. The outrage led 90 year old Sen. Robert Byrd to denounce the practice from the Senate floor, declaring it "barbaric, barbaric, barbaric!"[4]

Throughout late July, network newcasts were showing dog-fighting culture all around the US, with claims that there are at least 40,000 sites where dog fights regularly take place. A July 29, 2007 episode of *60 Minutes* indicated that a form of extreme fighting that combines boxing, wrestling, street fighting, and martial arts has become one of the most popular sports in the US, and the accompanying montage showed groups of men cheering the most bloody fights and beatings.

Sports culture is thus also a major part of the construction of American masculinity that can take violent forms. In most of the high school shootings of the 1990s, jocks tormented young teenage boys who took revenge in asserting a hyperviolent masculinity and went on shooting rampages. Larkin (Larkin, 2007, 205ff) provides a detailed analysis of "Football and Toxic High School Environments," focusing on Columbine. He describes how sports played a primary role in the school environment, how jocks were celebrities, and how they systematically abused outsiders and marginals like Columbine shooters Eric Harris and Dylan Klebold.

The "pattern of sports domination of high schools," Larkin suggests, "is apparently the norm in America" (206). Larkin notes how football "has become incorporated into a hyper-masculinized subculture that emphasizes physical aggression, domination, sexism, and the celebration of victory. He notes that more "than in any other sport, defeat in football is associated with being physically dominated and humiliated" (208). Further, it is associated with militarism as George Carlin, among others, has noted in his comedy routine:

In football the object is for the quarterback, also known as the field general, to be on target with his aerial assault, riddling the defense by hitting his receivers with deadly accuracy in spite of the blitz, even if he has to use the shotgun. With short bullet passes and long bombs, he marches his troops into enemy territory, balancing this aerial assault with a sustained ground attack that punches holes in the forward wall of the enemy's defensive line.

In baseball the object is to go home! And to be safe! (Carlin, cited in Larkin 208).

Larkin argues that football culture has "corrupted many high schools," including Columbine where "the culture of hypermasculinity reigned supreme" (209). Hence, Larkin concludes that: "If we wish to reduce violence in high schools, we have to de-emphasize the power of sports and change the culture of hypermasculinity. Football players cannot be lords of the hallways, bullying their peers with impunity, sometimes encouraged by coaches with adolescent mentalities" (210).

Hypermasculinity in sports is often a cauldron of homophobia and many of the school shooters were taunted about their sexuality and responded ultimately with a berserk affirmation of compensatory violence. Yet hypermasculinity is found throughout sports, military, gun, gang, and other male subcultures, as well as the corporate and political world, often starting in the family with male socialization by the father, and is reproduced and validated constantly in films, television programs, and other forms of media culture.

There have been educational interventions that address hypermasculinity, violence against women, homophobia, and which provide alternatives to a hegemonic violent masculinity. For example, since 1993 author and activist Jackson Katz and his colleagues have been implementing the Mentors in Violence Prevention (MVP) program, which trains high school, college and professional athletes and other student leaders to speak out and oppose violence against women, gay-bashing, and other forms of domestic and sexual violence. Featuring interactive workshops and training sessions in single-sex and mixed-gender settings, as well as public lectures, MVP has been expanded throughout North America to deal with men's violence in many arenas, from the corporation to politics, police and intelligence agencies, and other institutional arenas where men's violence is a problem.[5]

This is not to say that masculinity per se, or the traits associated with it, are all bad. There are times when being strong, independent, self-reliant, and even aggressive can serve positive goals and resist oppression and injustice. A post-gendered human being would share traits now associated with women and men, so that women could exhibit the traits listed above and men could be more loving, caring, emotional, vulnerable and other traits associated with women. Gender itself should be deconstructed and while we should fight gender oppression and inequality there are reasons to question gender itself in a more emancipated and democratic world in which individuals create their own personalities and lives out of the potential found traditionally in men and women.

Obviously, media culture is full of violence and of the case studies in Chapter 3 in *Guys and Guns Amok* of violent masculinity, Timothy McVeigh, the two Columbine shooters, and many other school shooters were allegedly deeply influenced by violent media culture. Yet, while media images of violence and specific books, films, TV shows, or artifacts of media culture may provide scripts for violent masculinity that young men act out, it is the broader culture of militarism, gun culture, extreme sports, ultraviolent video and computer games, subcultures of bullying and violence, and the rewarding of ultramasculinity in the corporate and political worlds that are major factors in constructing a hegemonic violent masculinities. Media culture itself obviously contributes to this ideal of macho masculinity but it is, however, a contested terrain between different conceptions of masculinity and femininity, and between liberal, conservative, and more radical representations and discourses (Kellner, 1995).

After dramatic school shootings and incidents of youth violence, there are usually attempts to scapegoat media culture. After the Virginia Tech shootings, the Federal Communication Commission (FCC) issued a report in late April, 2007 on "violent television programming and its impact on children" that call for expanding governmental oversight on broadcast television, but also extending content regulation to cable and satellite channels for the first time and banning some shows from time-slots where children might be watching. FCC Commissioner Jonathan S. Adelstein, who is in favour of the measures, did not hesitate to evoke the Virginia Tech shootings: "particularly in sight of the spasm of unconscionable violence at Virginia Tech, but just as importantly in light of the excessive violent crime that daily affects our nation, there is a basis for appropriate federal action to curb violence in the media."[6]

In a *Los Angeles Times* op-ed piece, Nick Gillespie, editor of *Reason*, noted that the report itself indicated that there was no causal relation between watching TV violence and committing violent acts. Further, Gillespie argued that given the steady drop in incidents of juvenile violence over the last twelve years, reaching a low not seen since at least the 1970s, it is inappropriate to demonize media culture for acts of societal violence. Yet, in my view, the proliferation of media culture and spectacle requires renewed calls for critical media literacy so that people can intelligently analyze and interpret the media and see how they are vehicles for representations of race, class, gender, sexuality, power, and violence.

In the wake of the Columbine shootings, fierce criticism and scapegoating of media and youth culture erupted. Oddly, there was less finger pointing at these targets after the Virginia Tech Massacre—perhaps because the Korean and Asian films upon which Cho modeled his photos and videos were largely unknown in the United States, and perhaps because conservatives prefer to target jihadists or liberals as nefarious influences on Cho, as I point out in Chapter 1. I want to avoid, however, the extremes of demonizing media and youth culture contrasted to asserting that it is mere entertainment without serious social influence. There is no question but that the media nurture fantasies and influence behaviour, sometimes sick and vile ones, and to survive in our culture requires that we are able to critically analyze and dissect media culture and not let it gain power over us. Critical media literacy empowers individuals over media so that they can produce critical and analytical distance from media messages and images. This provides protection from media manipulation and avoids letting the most destructive images of media gain power over one. It also enables more critical, healthy, and active relations with our culture. Media culture will not disappear and it is simply a question of how we will deal with it and if we can develop an adequate pedagogy of critical media literacy to empower our youth.

Unfortunately, there are few media literacy courses offered in schools in the United States from kindergarten through high school. Many other countries such as Canada, Australia, and England have such programs (Kellner & Share, 2007). In the next section, I will suggest that to design schools for the new millennium that meet the challenges posed by student alienation and violence and provide skills that students need for a high-tech economy requires a democratic reconstruction of education. But to address problems of societal violence raised in these studies requires a reconstruction of education and society, and what Herbert Marcuse referred to as "a revolution in values" and a "new sensibility."[7] The revolution in values involves breaking with values of competition, aggression, greed, and self-interest and cultivating values of equality, peace, harmony, and community. Such a revolution of values "would also make for a new morality, for new relations between the sexes and generations, for a new relation between man and nature" (2001: 198). Harbingers of the revolution in values, Marcuse argued, are found in "a widespread rebellion against the domineering values, of virility, heroism and force, invoking the images of society which may bring about the end of violence" (ibid).

The "new sensibility" in turn would cultivate needs for beauty, love, connections with nature and other people, and more democratic and egalitarian social relations.

Marcuse believes that without a change in the sensibility, there can be no real social change, and that education, art, and the humanities can help cultivate the conditions for a new sensibility. Underlying the theory of the new sensibility is a concept of the active role of the senses in the constitution of experience that rejects the Kantian and other philosophical devaluations of the senses as passive, merely receptive. For Marcuse, our senses are shaped and molded by society, yet constitute in turn our primary experience of the world and provide both imagination and reason with its material. He believes that the senses are currently socially constrained and mutilated and argues that only an emancipation of the senses and a new sensibility can produce liberating social change.

Ultimately, addressing the problem of societal violence requires a democratic reconstruction of education and society, new pedagogical practices, new social relations, values, and forms of learning. In the following section, I want to sketch out aspects of a democratic reconstruction grounded in key ideas of John Dewey, Paulo Freire, Ivan Illich, and Herbert Marcuse.

NEW LITERACIES, DEMOCRATIZATION, AND THE RECONSTRUCTION OF EDUCATION

To begin, we need to recognize a systemic crisis of education in the United States in which there is a disconnect between youth's lives and what they are taught in school. Already in 1964, Marshall McLuhan recognized the discrepancy between kids raised on a fast-paced and multimodal media culture and the linear, book and test-oriented education of the time, where kids sit in a classroom all day. Since then there has been a proliferation of new media and technologies, but education has been retreating to ever more conservative and pedantic goals, most egregiously during the Bush era and its phony "No Child Left Behind" program which is really a front for "teaching for testing." In this policy, strongly resisted by many states and local school districts, incredible amounts of time are wasted preparing students for tests and teachers, and schools are basically rated according to their test results.[8]

Reconstructing education will involve an expansion of print literacy to a multiplicity of literacies. An expanded multimedia literacy and pedagogy should teach how to read and critically dissect newspapers, film, TV, radio, popular music, the Internet, and other media of news, information, and culture to enable students to become active and engaged democratic citizens. While 1960s cultural studies by the Birmingham school in England included a focus on critically reading newspapers, TV news and information programs, and the images of politics, much cultural studies of the past decades has focused on media entertainment, consumption, and audience response to specific media programs (Kellner, 1995). This enterprise is valuable and important, but it should not replace or marginalize taking on the system of media news and information as well. A comprehensive cultural studies will interrogate news and entertainment, journalism and information sourcing, and should include media studies as well as textual studies and audience reception studies in part of a reconstruction of education in which critical media literacy is taught from kindergarten through college (Kellner,1995, 1998 and Kellner & Share, 2007).

Critical media literacy needs to engage the "politics of representation" that subjects images and discourses of race, gender, sexuality, class, and other features to scrutiny and analysis, involving critique of violent masculinities, sexism, racism, classism, homophobia, and other hurtful forms of representation. A critical media also positively valorizes more progressive representations of gender, race, class, and sexuality, and notes how many cultural texts are ambiguous and contradictory in their representations.

The Internet and multimedia computer technologies and cultural forms are dramatically transforming the circulation of information, images, and various modes of culture, and the younger generation needs to gain multifaceted technological skills to survive in the high-tech information society. In this situation, students should learn both how to use media and computer culture to do research and gather information, as well as to perceive it as a cultural terrain which contains texts, spectacles, games, and interactive media which require a form of critical computer literacy. Youth subcultural forms range from 'zines or web-sites that feature an ever-expanding range of video, music, or multimedia texts to sites of political information and organization.[9]

Moreover, since the 1999 Seattle anti-corporate globalization demonstrations, youth have been using the Internet to inform and debate each other, organize oppositional movements, and generate alternative forms of politics and culture.[10] Consequently, at present, computer literacy involves not merely technical skills and knowledge, but the ability to scan information, to interact with a variety of cultural forms and groups, and to intervene in a creative manner within the emergent computer and political culture.

Whereas youth is excluded for the most part from the dominant media culture, computer and new multimedia culture is a discursive and political location in which youth can intervene, producing their own web-sites and personal pages, engaging in discussion groups, linking with others who share their interests, generating multimedia for cultural dissemination and a diversity of cultural and political projects. Computer culture enables individuals to actively participate in the production of culture, ranging from discussion of public issues to creation of their own cultural forms, enabling those who had been previously excluded from cultural production and mainstream politics to participate in the creation of culture and socio-political activism.

After using the Internet to successfully organize a wide range of anti-corporate globalization demonstrations in Seattle, Washington, Prague, Toronto, and elsewhere, young people played an active role in organizing massive demonstrations against the Bush administration threats against Iraq, creating the basis for a oppositional anti-war and peace movement as the Bush administration threatens an era of perpetual war in the new millennium. Obviously, it is youth that fights and dies in wars that often primarily serve the interests of corrupt economic and political elites. Today's youth is becoming aware that its survival is at stake and that thus it is necessary to become informed and organized on the crucial issues of war, peace, and the future of democracy and the global economy.

Likewise, groups are organizing to save endangered species, to fight genetically-engineered food, to debate cloning and stem cell research, to advance animal rights, to join struggles over environmental causes like climate change and global warming, and to work for creating a healthier diet and alternative medical systems. The Internet is a virtual treasury of alternative information and cultural forms with young people playing key roles in developing the technology and oppositional culture and using it for creative pedagogical and political purposes. Alternative sites of information and discussion on every conceivable topic can be found on the Internet, including important topics like human rights or environmental education that are often neglected in public schools.

Thus, a postmodern pedagogy requires developing critical forms of print, media, computer, and multiple forms of technoliteracy, all of which are of crucial importance in the technoculture of the present and fast-approaching future (Kahn & Kellner, 2006 and Kellner & Share, 2007). Indeed, contemporary culture is marked by a proliferation of image machines that generate a panoply of print, sound, environmental, and diverse aesthetic artifacts within which we wander, trying to make our way through this forest of symbols. And so we need to begin learning how to read these images, these fascinating and seductive cultural forms whose massive impact on our lives we have only begun to understand. Surely, education should attend to the multimedia culture and teach how to read images and narratives as part of media/computer/technoculture literacy.

Such an effort would be linked to a revitalized Critical Pedagogy that attempts to empower individuals so that they can analyze and criticize the emerging technoculture, as well as participate in producing its cultural and political forums and sites. More than ever, we need philosophical reflection on the ends and purposes of educational technology, and on what we are doing and trying to achieve with it in our educational practices and institutions. In this situation, it may be instructive to return to John Dewey and see the connections between education, technology, and democracy, the need for the reconstruction of education and society, and the value of experimental pedagogy to seek solutions to the problems of education in the present day. A progressive reconstruction of education will urge that it be done in the interests of democratization, ensuring access to information and communication technologies for all, thereby helping to overcome the so-called digital divide and divisions of the haves and have-nots so that education is placed in the service of democracy and social justice (Dewey, 1997 [1916]; Freire (1972, 1978) in light of Ivan Illich's (1970, 1971, 1973) critiques of the limitations and challenges of education in postindustrial societies. Yet, we should be more aware than Dewey, Freire, and Illich of the obduracy of the divisions of class, gender, and race, and so work self-consciously for multicultural democracy and education. This task suggests that we valorize difference and cultural specificity, as well as equality and shared universal Deweyean values such as freedom, equality, individualism, and participation.

A major challenge for education today is thus to promote computer and media literacy to empower students and citizens to use a wide range of technologies to enhance their lives and create a better culture and society. In particular, this involves developing Internet projects that articulate with important cultural and political struggles in the contemporary world, developing pedagogies whereby students work together transmitting their technical knowledge to other students and their teachers, and teachers and students work together in developing relevant educational material, projects, and pedagogies in the experimental Deweyean and Freirean mode.

Teachers and students, then, need to develop new pedagogies and modes of learning for new information and multimedia environments. This should involve a democratization and reconstruction of education such as was envisaged by Dewey, Freire, Illich, and Marcuse, in which education is seen as a dialogical, democrat-icizing, and experimental practice. New information technologies acting along the lines of Illich's conceptions of "webs of learning" and "tools for conviviality" (1971; 1973) encourage the sort of experimental and collaborative projects proposed by Dewey, and can also involve the more dialogical and non-authoritarian relations between students and teachers that Freire envisaged. In this respect, the re-visioning of education involves the recognition that teachers can learn from students and that often students are ahead of their teachers in a variety of technological literacies and technical abilities. Many of us have learned much of what we know of computers and new media and technologies from our students. We should also recognize the extent to which young people helped to invent the Internet and have grown up in a culture in which they may have readily cultivated technological skills from an early age.[11] Peer-to-peer communication among young people is thus often a highly sophisticated development and democratic pedagogies should build upon and enhance these resources and practices.

One of the challenges of contemporary education is to overcome the separation between students experiences, subjectivities, and interests rooted in the new multimedia technoculture, and the classroom situations grounded in print culture, traditional learning methods and disciplines (Luke & Luke, 2002). The disconnect can be addressed, however, by more actively and collaboratively bringing students into interactive classrooms, or learning situations, in which they are able to transmit their skills and knowledges to fellow students and teachers alike. Such a democratic and interactive reconstruction of education thus provides the resources for a democratic social reconstruction, as well as cultivates the new skills and literacies needed for the global media economy. So far, arguments for restructuring education mostly come from the hi-tech and corporate sectors who are primarily interested in new media and literacies for the workforce and capitalist profit. But reconstruction can serve the interests of democratization as well as the elite corporate few. Following Dewey, we should accordingly militate for education that aims at producing democ-ratic citizens, even as it provides skills for the work place, social and cultural life.

Both Paulo Freire and Ivan Illich saw that a glaring problem with contemporary educational institutions was that they have become fixed in monomodal instruction, with homogenized lesson plans, curricula, and pedagogy, and that they neglect to address challenging political, cultural, and ecological problems. The development of convivial tools and radically democratic pedagogies can enable teachers and students to break with these models and engage in a form of Deweyean experimental education. The reconstruction of education can help to create subjects better able to negotiate the complexities of emergent modes of everyday life, labour, and culture, as contemporary life becomes ever more multi-faceted and dangerous. Supportive, dialogical and interactive social relations in critical learning situations can promote cooperation, democracy, and positive social values, as well as fulfill needs for communication, esteem, and politicized learning. Whereas modern mass education has tended to see life in a linear fashion based on print models and has developed pedagogies which have divided experience into discrete moments and behavioural bits, critical pedagogies produce skills that enable individuals to better navigate and synthesize the multiple realms and challenges of contemporary life. Deweyean education focused on problem solving, goal-seeking projects, and the courage to be experimental, while Freire developed critical problem-posing pedagogies of the oppressed aiming at social justice and progressive social transformation, while Illich offered oppositional conceptions of education and alternatives to oppressive institutions. It is exactly this sort of critical spirit and vision, which calls for the reconstruction of education along with society, that can help produce more radicalized pedagogies, tools for social and ecological justice, and Utopian possibilities for a better world.

A democratic reconstruction of education will involve producing democratic citizens and empowering the next generation for democracy should be a major goal of the reconstruction of education in the present age. Moreover, as Freire reminds us (1972 and 1998), Critical Pedagogy comprises the skills of both reading the word and reading the world. Hence, multiple literacies include not only media and computer literacies, but a diverse range of social and cultural literacies, ranging from ecoliteracy (e.g. understanding the body and environment), to economic and financial literacy to a variety of other competencies that enable us to live well in our social worlds. Education, at its best, provides the symbolic and cultural capital that empowers people to survive and prosper in an increasingly complex and changing world and the resources to produce a more cooperative, democratic, egalitarian, and just society.[12]

NOTES

[1] For U.S. gun statistics, see http://www.haciendapub.com/edcor12.html (accessed on June 4, 2007).

[2] David Olinger, *The Denver Post*, April 23, 2007 at http://www.denverpost.com/portlet/article/html/ fragments/print_article.jsp?articleId=5728141&siteId=36. (accessed on June 4, 2007).

[3] See "A Time Line of Recent Worldwide School Shootings" at http://www.infoplease.com/ipa/ A0777958.html; see also a site "Number of children and adults killed and wounded in school shootings around the world since 1996" at http://www.iansa.org/women/documents/Schoolshootings 1996-2006_000.doc. (accessed on June 2, 2007).

[4] See "Vick dogfighting charges stir stinging reaction," CNN News, July 20, 2007 at http://www.cnn. com/2007/U.S./07/20/vick.dogfighting/index.html?iref=mpstoryview (accessed on July 21, 2007).

[5] Information, publications, films, and other material on the Mentors in Violence Program can be found at http://www.jacksonkatz.com/ (accessed September 26, 2007).
I refer to Katz's work elsewhere in these studies and thank him for material and ideas that have been valuable for these studies. There is also a book *Violence Goes to College: The Authoritative Guide to Prevention and Intervention*, (Nicoletti, Spencer-Thomas and Bollinger, 2001) assembled by a group that has yearly conferences on university violence in a multiplicity of forms and develops violence prevention strategies. See their website at http://www.violencegoestocollege.com/ (accessed September 27, 2007).

[6] Cited in Nick Gillespie, "The FCC's not mommy and daddy," *Los Angeles Times*, May 2, 2007: A23.

[7] See Herbert Marcuse, "A Revolution in Values" in Marcuse 2001, and on the new sensibility see my introduction to the volume of collected papers of Marcuse on *Art and Liberation* (2006).

[8] This misplaced pedagogy of teaching for testing did not just originate with the Bush administration, but has long been a feature of pedagogically-challenged schools; see Janet Ewell, "Test-takers, not students," *Los Angeles Times*, May 26, 2007: A19. For some compelling criticism of Bush Administration "No Child Left Behind" policies, see the dossier "Correcting Schools," *The Nation*, May 21, 2007: 11–21.

[9] See Jones 2002 and Kahn and Kellner 2005. Some good sites that exhibit youth voices, participation, and politics include http://www.moveon.org; http://www. raisethefist.com; http://www.tao.com; the youth blog site at http://www.Bloghop.com/topics.htm?numblogs=14566&cacheid=1044419966.35 69 (accessed on May 14, 2007).

[10] See Best and Kellner 2001 and Kahn and Kellner 2005.

[11] For instance, Mosaic, Netscape and the first browsers were invented by young computer users, as were many of the first Websites, list-serves, chat rooms, and so on. A hacker culture emerged that was initially conceptualized as a reconfiguring and improving of computer systems, related to design, system and use, before the term became synonymous with theft and mischief, such as setting loose worms and viruses. On youth and Internet subcultures, see Kahn & Kellner (2003).

[12] For my further perspectives on developing at Critical Theory of education and reconstructing education, see Kellner 2004 and 2006; Kahn and Kellner 2006; and Kellner and Share 2007.

REFERENCES

Best, S., & Kellner, D. (2001). *The postmodern adventure: Science, technology, and cultural studies at the Third Millennium*. New York: Guilford.

Dewey, J. (1997 [1916]). *Democracy and education*. New York: Free Press.

Freire, P. (1972). *Pedagogy of the oppressed*. New York: Herder and Herder.

Freire, P. (1998). *A Paulo Freire reader*. New York: Herder and Herder.

Illich, I. (1970). *Deschooling society*. New York: Marion Boyers Press.

Illich, I. (1971). *Celebration of awareness*. London: Marion Boyars.

Illich, I. (1973). *Tools for conviviality*. New York: Harper and Row.

Jones, S. (2002). *The internet goes to college: How students are living in the future with today's technology*.

Kahn, R., & Kellner, D. (2003). Internet subcultures and oppositional politics. In M. David (Ed.), *The post-subcultures reader* (pp. 299–314). Oxford and New York: Berg.

Kahn, R., & Kellner, D. (2005). Oppositional politics and the internet: A critical/reconstructive approach. *Cultural politics*, *1*(1), 75–100.

Kahn, R., & Kellner, D. (2006). Reconstructing technoliteracy: A multiple literacies approach. In J. R. Dakers (Ed.), *Defining technological literacy* (pp. 253–274). New York and England: Palgrave Macmillan.

Katz, J. (2006). *The macho paradox*. Naperville, IL: Sourcebook.

Kellner, D. (1995). *Media culture*. London and New York: Routledge.

Kellner, D. (2004). Technological transformation, multiple literacies, and the re-visioning of education. *E-Learning*, *1*(1), 9–37.

Kellner, D. (2006). Toward a critical theory of education. Critical theory and critical pedagogy today. In I. Gur-Ze'ev (Ed.), *Toward a new critical language in education* (pp. 49–69). University of Haifa: Studies in Education.

Kellner, D., & Share, J. (2007). Critical media literacy, democracy, and the reconstruction of education. In D. Macedo & S. R. Steinberg (Eds.), *Media literacy. A reader* (pp. 3–23). New York: Peter Lang.

Larkin, R. W. (2007). *Comprehending columbine*. Philadelphia: Temple University Press.

Luke, A., & Luke, C. (2002). Adolescence lost/childhood regained: On early intervention and the emergence of the techno-subject. *Journal of Early Childhood Literacy*, *1*(1), 91–120.

Marcuse, H. (2001). *Toward a critical theory of society. Collected papers of Herbert Marcuse* (Vol. 2, D. Kellner, Ed.). London and New York: Routledge.

Marcuse, H. (2006, 2001). *Art and liberation. collected papers of Herbert Marcuse* (Vol. 4, D. Kellner, Ed.). London and New York: Routledge.

McLuhan, M. (1964). *Understanding media: The extensions of man.* New York: Signet Books.

BEATRICE DIKE AND JOHN COLBECK

20. CRITICISM OF CRITICAL PEDAGOGY—ON THE NEAR-IMPOSSIBILITY OF SELF-CRITICISM

HOW DO WE SEE CRITICAL PEDAGOGY? STARTING ASSUMPTIONS AND HYPOTHESES

We see Critical Pedagogy as a way of continuous, interactive, dialogical learning designed to interrupt and deconstruct historically positioned, static, conditioned and conditioning systems of domination (power over others)—systems of oppression and empowerment. By empowering some—the power-full organizers of the systems— the systems enable the oppression of others, the power-less classes. Some aspects of this oppression, in language, for instance occur unseen, subliminally, unawares when we first learn to use words 'properly' = like our adult minders do.

A socialist-Marx-ist interpretation of empowerment requires deconstruction of artificial (false, conditioned and conditioning) consciousness. This deconstruction opens up opportunities for people to bring about changes which are in their own, the oppressed's, interests. Some of the democratic deficit can be remedied when the oppression is seen and identified.

Such learning is a process through which people gain access to participation in management of their own affairs, once the disenfranchised (voteless and voiceless) become aware of their oppression.

Our account here owes much to McLaren (2003), Freire (1970) and to Gramsci (1977) to whom we now turn.

THREE RECENT PERSPECTIVES ON CRITICAL PEDAGOGY

In his perspective McLaren (2003) argues for collective liberation from domination, through developing new senses of the value of co-operation, humility, trust and hope in order to resist the power over others exerted by economic and social 'capital' in everyday life. It is a practice based on critical multiculturalism, which allows students to recognize and explore the complex interconnections and gaps that occur between their own and other cultural and social identities. It is a proposed learning method which will raise the level of students' consciousness. McLaren's idea requires making space within the context of the classroom to engage in revolutionary Critical Pedagogy. This approach might have met students' needs in terms of negating repressive influences. The aim was to break down capitalist subordination in everyday life and in the curriculum. It was intended to provide the voteless and largely voiceless 'oppressed' with tools to challenge the status quo social relationships and to chall-enge the power of economic and social capital.

I. Gur-Ze'ev, The Possibility/Impossibility of a New Critical Language in Education, 379–389.
© 2010 Sense Publishers. All Rights Reserved.

We conclude regretfully that, when considering the heavily prescribed nature of the curriculum among European nations, McLaren's (2003) method will be difficult to practice in the classroom.

In Freire's (1970) perspective, he argues for educational theory and teaching/ learning practices based on the use of dialogue and collaboration. Within the classroom he envisages a culture circle approach for people to share ideas using popular culture— newspapers, media. Students are shown an image to generate themes for discussion; then they make a list of themes and, based on this list, the teacher prepares the sources and feeds the sources back to the learners. While they are discussing it those who cannot read are developing an interest in words and, most importantly, the oppressed might start to recognize their internalized oppression and the nature of the social conditions which form and shape their cultural environment. However, it is also difficult to practice this mode in the classroom, taking into account the heavily loaded and prescribed nature of most nation states' school curricula.

Gramsci, with his concept of counter-hegemonic education, believes in the Marxist philosophy that man is not merely a puppet, controlled by some naturalistic law. Man, in his view, is an active thinking and doing agent who must not only try to understand his own reality, but also rise above it. (Roger, 1991). His argument is that school, church, media and family all tend to present the ideology of the ruling classes' 'world view.' The ruling, power-full classes not only provide a (their own) 'world view', but they also tend to identify their 'seen' world with the 'common sense' of the people. A classic example is the moral panic concerning youths' poor primary socialization in the home; this led to the conclusion that secondary socialization was required—a reason for citizenship education in schools. This supports Gramsci's argument that the dominance of the bourgeoisie stands on two similar pillars of power—economic domination, intellectual and moral leadership—economic capital and social capital.

Regarding the government's agenda for citizenship education, Gramsci would argue that it is direct domination, legally imposed on the young in compulsory schooling. Gramsci, (1977, p. 42) said a learner does not have to be a "passive and mechanical recipient." The relationship between the pupil's psychology and forms of education must always be "active (we would stress 'two-way, *inter*-active') and creative, just as the relation of the worker to his tools is active and creative" (Burke, 1999, p. 7). A carpenter chooses the tools; his tools (partly) identify him as a carpenter.

Gramsci further argues that hegemony can be challenged through informal education (community education). Hegemony is seen as "…the practices of a capitalist class or its representatives to gain state power and maintain it." (Roger 1991, p. 28). Hegemony can be referred to as something that comes out of societal and class struggles and serves to contour and manipulate peoples' minds.

In summary, all three forms of Critical Pedagogy described focus on the idea that student opposition to the experience of institutionalized schooling can be stimulated by awareness of contradictions perceived between the dominant discussions of school knowledge on the one hand, and students' own lived experiences of subordination and of being oppressed on the other.

Advocates of Critical Pedagogy adopted as premises their beliefs that children should be allowed to develop their own inner potential rather than have ideas and techniques from the adult world imposed on them. One criticism of this stance is that it makes naive assumptions about social structure and language. None of us can completely escape the influence, embedded in language, of our ancestors. This stance neglects the possibility that the same children, even if encouraged to develop their true potential, might still be discriminated against in wider structural and linguistic terms. This means that the so-called freedom of the individual exists only within the limitations of a given structure, social group and linguistic community to which she belongs.

Notably it would seem that critical pedagogies could themselves be considered political theories, since their arguments and ideas contain value assumptions and often imply (internal) visions of an ideal society.

We conclude, as our assumption informing the next section, that if the participants in education, including adult learners, are to develop an attitude towards the social structure which is neither passive acceptance nor idealistic in its formulation, trainee teachers and learners need both the skill of dialogue and the skill, or attitude, of self-criticism.

SELF-CRITICISM: STARTING HYPOTHESIS

In this section, we started from the hypothesis that John Stuart Mill was right. We have, for the most part, only partial truths His statement is both subversive and cautious. It is, we claim, self-critical in spirit or attitude We stress, at the outset, the cautious aspect in the phrase 'for the most part'. Mill is not an absolutist or a singular thinker adopting an Either/Or logic in which statements are absolutely or completely true or false, black or white, good or evil. We stress this because, in discussions, we have met miss-understandings implying that we suggest a "rhetoric of the total impossibility of self-criticism." Not so. In the positive part of our work we suggest several constructive approaches towards overcoming the *difficulties* of trying to criticize oneself. We do suggest, in the section on 'Difficulties' that these difficulties are greater than advocates of critical thinking usually think.

Class-room teaching-instruction is not a one-way, neutral, objective, non- personal process, detached from its traditional 'roots'. All teachers'interventions are, unavoidably, experience-biased, two-way interactions set within traditional power relations in social and historical contexts. Those power relations have been established and maintained for millennia, starting with property rights. "Property is theft." (Proudhon, 1840) They—property rights, for instance, and uses of the word 'proper' to mean 'correct'—are now deeply embedded in our uses of words. They will not be easily changed unless or until we expose their oppressive influence. That influence-power works mainly in favour of authority-powers, in favour of the middle-power classes (owners of 'property' and 'capital') who organize everything (largely) in their own favour.

If Mill is right, statements can be, *and usually are*, only partially, partly or half-true.

This moves us from the banal statement that, since we are all human and fallible, we all make mistakes *some of the time*, (almost all general statements are falsifiable: there are exceptions) to the radical suggestion that we all make miss-takes *most of the time*—*not*, we have to stress again, *all* of the time. "All men are liars—*sometimes*, mostly by mistake."

Once we began to entertain this radical hypothesis, we began to find more and more examples supporting it. No relativistic disaster befalls. On the contrary, liberation of thinking ensues. Many ancient, and a few modern, or post-modern philosophers have said the same, in different ways.

In the section on 'Difficulties' we bring historical support for the thesis of *near* impossibility, from the history of ideas. We find logical or conceptual support from careful consideration of pervasive ambiguities in language (plural meanings of words). We find empirical support from examples of current uses of words. We suggest aesthetic considerations—that our world looks better this way—with this attitude towards truths.

Finally, we make suggestions as to the consequences of our conclusions for educating practices.

THE DIFFICULTIES, AMOUNTING TO NEAR IMPOSSIBILITY

We think the logical-conceptual difficulties, stemming from current uses of words, are the most powerful arguments in favour of radical changes in those uses of words.

There are interdependent logical and psychological reasons why thorough criticism, and particularly thorough *self*-criticism, is *almost* impossible. It requires self-contra-diction, speaking against my self. I can speak against my *yesterday's* self, but not against my now, here self.

The catch (of self-reference) is this: when, today, I am detecting and criticizing my mistakes of yesterday, my judgment of those mistakes is dependent on my criteria for judgment which I am taking for granted, however temporarily, today. However far we pursue this chain, or regress, the criteria for the 'last' (or first?) premise (criterion) have to be taken for granted.

Self-criticism is the most important kind of criticism; it is almost never done. A critic's work is therefore, it seems, never done—never complete. The criteria for the last criticism have to be taken for granted. Gödel's incompleteness theorem applies.

Why is it (almost) impossible? Who is the self, doing the criticizing, when I criticize my self? Meno's paradox of self-reference suggests one reason: if I am to re-cognize wisdom, I must already have it. As above, any criticism depends on criteria which are not, for the moment, being criticized but taken for granted.

Psychologically, inertia is massive. It is very difficult to change a mind-set embedded in us unconsciously from early childhood, when we began to learn to use words 'properly' like our adult minders (those who gave us our word-minds) use them. Along with language, we absorbed, subliminally, a multitude of assumptions, beliefs and values of which we often remain unaware until we die. Many of those assumptions have been embedded in our language for thousands of years. Until we are aware of those invisible, *mythical* tyrants (Gyges, Procrustes, Cyclops, Daedalus and, above all, Narcissus) we cannot expect to escape their influence-power. You cannot escape from a prison if you are not aware that you are in one.

This point is empirically important. At this crucial and malleable stage of a child's up-bringing, the 'democratic deficit' is almost total.

When a two or three-year-old is learning how to use words for the first time, she has virtually no choice but to learn to talk, and so to think and act, like her parents or her (significant word) 'mind-ers'. The situation of the child is exactly one of a 'differend' as described by Lyotard (1988). A child has no alternative language in which to protest against the language she is being obliged, effectively under compulsion and subliminally, unawares, to adopt. It can be argued that this language is, in many respects, one of oppression doing 'wrongs' to those who have no vote and little voice in its production.

It would be naïve to assume that what parents do, and how they use words, is always for the benefit of children. When adults teach children to use words 'properly' they are teaching them to use words like they, adults do. ('Proper' = 'My own'.) But the meaning of 'talk properly' (use words like I use them) has been shifted to mean 'talk correctly'. It is years before children become aware, if they ever do, of this slide of meaning in favour of authorities and their adult 'correctnesses'.

We cannot *blame* adults for this, which is probably the most powerful kind of subliminal indoctrination under virtual compulsion. We are all 'victims' of it, in Lyotard's (1988) special sense of 'victim'. We have no alternative language in which to protest against wrongs done to us—mistakes—in language itself.

Rorty (1989) puts it well: "The trouble with arguments against the use of a familiar and time-honoured vocabulary is that they are expected to be phrased in that very vocabulary." He later goes on "Such arguments are always parasitic upon, and abbreviations for, claims that a better vocabulary is available." For scholars, perhaps, different word uses in other languages (Greek, Latin, French ...) cast a critical light on our uses of words: use of 'proper', above, is a good example where etymology exposes self-promoting shifts of uses of words in favour of their users.

Two important examples where another language offers a criticism of our own language, are the words 'mean' and the word 'understand'.

In French, the verb 'to mean' translates (carries across, meta-fers) as '*vouloir dire*' = 'to want (wish, will) to say'. This means that words themselves, not being people— intending or wanting agents—do not 'mean': they cannot 'want to say' anything. It is always *people*—word-*users*—whose 'meanings' we are trying to transmit, ex-press, interpret and understand or com-prehend (grasp with). The French '*comprendre*' also suggests a translation from 'understand' to 'com-prehend' (with-grasp).

This suggests a modification of Wittgenstein: "The meanings of words, always plural, are the meanings (wanting to say) of their users, senders and receiver-interpreters." We are putting *our* meanings into these words. You are taking *your* meanings out of them. It would be no small miracle if those two meanings, in two different sets of minds or mind-sets, *completely*, perfectly co-incided, matched or corresponded, one-to-one. It is already no small miracle that events occurring among *our* neurons and cells can cause events among yours. That these events do have *some* similarities is supported by the fact that we can, often, agree together well enough for many practical purposes. We call it comm-uni-cating—coming Together As One.

The point here, for our purposes, is that criticism of one language (position, perspective, mind-set) can be mounted only from another. Another, possibly more important example is use of the word 'sin'.

Historically, in the practice of archery, when a bowman missed his target, it was called a 'sin'. Etymologically, the word 'sin', as it occurs in English bibles is a translation of the Greek word '*hamartia*'. That Greek word also meant 'mistake of aim' or 'missing the mark' as in archery.

This suggests, we think, that a *huge* shift of meaning has occurred leading to a modern concept of 'sin' which is associated by certain kinds of religious people and 'moral' people (people who are knowing, certain about good and evil) with judgments of good and evil, disobedience to God, and the 'original sin' of Adam and Eve.

The metaphor of archery, aiming at a target suggests that there are at least *two kinds* of miss-take of aim: the first, and most obvious kind is that we aim at a target, aim badly and miss. But the second kind is more important and relevant to self-criticism: we may discover, when we succeed in *hitting* the target, even scoring a 'bull's eye', that we have been aiming at a 'wrong', miss-taken *target*—that our own 'good' intentions were not 'good' in their consequences. Our intentions were, and still are perhaps, paving roads to hell while we 'mean well'.

Typical expressions of this experience are "We are shooting ourselves in the foot," and he (the engineer-organizer) was hoist with his own petard." (Blown up by his own bomb like modern terrorists and those equally, oppositely mistaken fundamental-ists who retaliate against them.) When George Bush retaliates, he copies and so becomes his own worst enemies, on a bigger scale. His 'peace-loving' cruise missiles are bigger. He doubles the violence which he opposes.

Becoming aware of this miss-translation of *hamartia* took us straight back to Mill. Instead of saying "We are all miserable sinners," we can say, with Mill, we all make (partial) mistakes, mistakes of partiality, *most* (not all) of the time.

Instead of calling it 'original sin' we can see Adam and eve as making the original (very early) miss-take of aim and identity—aspiring to knowledge of good and evil—eating the poisonous fruit from that tree, aping God. Or we can see them as 'falling' for the tempting advice of a talking snake: "Ye shall not die (God told a lie). Ye shall be as Gods, knowing good and evil." (Genesis 2 and 3). Translation: "Ye shall become righteous, religious people, or moral philosophers!"

Historically, again, it was all said long before the Authors Of The New Testament said it. In the Tao Te Ching, Lao Tse (~ 500 BCE) or the unknown author of the collection of wisdom sayings, probably from earlier still, advocates 'not knowing', least of all about 'morality' and 'good and evil'. That wisdom-advice is given no less than twenty times in eighty one short, one-page chapters. He also starts, as we do (along with Nietzsche, Wittgenstein and post-modern writers), from skepticism about the reliability of *words*.

"The tao (small 't') which can be told (expressed in words) is not the eternal Tao. (Chapter 1, first sentence.)

If uses of words themselves are unreliable—unavoidably biased (partial) in favour of the values and beliefs of their users—then few, if any, statements can be verified as *completely, absolutely or universally* 'true'.

Even Karl Popper, arch-objectivist, insisted that a universal claim can never be verified unless or until *the end* of time comes along. We would have to go everywhere, become everyone and live for ever to verify it.

POSITIVELY, THE POSSIBILITIES

It is impossible to be aware of our own miss-take of aim at the time we aim. If we were aware of this mistake we would not be aiming like that. In that case, self-criticism cannot be done alone. Our last criterion cannot be criticized. We have no 'mirror' with which to 'see' our own mind's eyes; they are what we see with. Compare: "We cannot expect to see a photon; it is what we see *with*."

That leaves at least two possibilities of criticizing ourselves.

We may use other people as our 'mirrors' (reflexivity). They have little difficulty in seeing *our* mistakes, albeit still fallibly, with their own mind's eyes.

We can see their mistakes, albeit with our still fallible 'eyes'. That suggests a method like that of Socrates' dialogues. When we find our selves detecting someone else's mistake, we will usually find, in reflection (reflexivity), that we have a similar mistake in our own 'eye'. (The motes and beams story). My enemy-opponent shows me what I am like. We are making the same kind of mistake as Hitler made, only our 'beam-holocaust' is *bigger*—ours is a global holocaust. We have already annihilated millions of species of our own Family Of Life-Kind, by mistake. If we go on like that, we are likely to annihilate our selves by failing to recognize a very ancient, Africa-Egyptian wisdom expressed as *ubuntu* (interdependence) and *umoja* (Together As One).

If we adopt another very ancient, often repeated wisdom of 'not knowing' or "Nobody knows" (awareness of human fallibility) we can begin to be aware of, and expose to critical examination, the many invisible tyrants (Gyges) embedded in language. We become *free* to make up our own minds. Indeed, we are *forced* to become *aware* that we do, and have to, make up our own minds, every time we choose a word to serve our purposes, in pursuit of our values, in accordance with our (Procrustes) framework of beliefs. We tend to fit all new experiences into our own framework, or iron bed of fixed concepts and words. Procrustes is (a joke against) us.

We become aware of treading in a minefield in which every word is a 'mine' in at least three senses: (i) it is rich in potential for exploring its many meanings and connections; (ii) it is rich in possibilities for blowing up in our own faces—hoisting us with our own petard; (iii) it is always a 'mine'—someone's own (= 'proper') meaning has been put into it by a sender or (another) meaning, taken out of it by a receiver (interpreter-trans-late-er, meta-fer-er, carrier across).

If we become *aware* that "We all make miss-takes of aim and identity *most of the time*," (because words are miss-leading, miss-trans-lated, miss-carried-across) we will become *aware* that, if we speak or write for 45 minutes at a time (mono-logue), we will have made about 45 miss-takes needing correcting. A dialogue may avoid that miss-take.

A second method of enabling and expressing self-criticism is to speak or write in ironic, self-mocking or self-satirical style. Lewis Carroll, A Milne, Nietzsche and the Gospel writers (scribes and probably Pharisees) are important examples of such satirical 'jokers'. Taking them literally is a disastrous mistake. If we have no sense of humour, we get exactly the wrong end of the stick with which they are trying to beat us. If we laugh at the emperor with no clothes on, we miss the point: he is a caricature of us—of all authorities and power people.

A joke is an unexpected truth. Ability to see a joke against my self is called 'having a sense of humour'. Authorities and powers *tend* to lack this. For nearly two thousand years, Christ-ian authorities have insisted on literal interpretations of 'our' bibles. A-the-ists also often base their opposition on the same miss-taken, literal interpret-ations. Christ-ians call their Bible 'the' word of God. It was written down and translated by men—male scribes (academics) and (probably) Pharisees. Those groups are self-critically caricatured by the authors of The (our) New Testament. A-the-ists tend to see it as irrelevant myth or, taken literally, nonsense.

It *is indeed* myth-stories (from much earlier, Pagan wisdom literature). Much of it is non-sense, if you make the *miss*-take of taking the stories literally as historically true. Snakes do not talk. But the *metaphorical, satirical* truths in those 'stories' are still relevant now, and ahead of our time, as of theirs, *about our human nature*. The roots of the myth-stories (mysteries) are much earlier wisdoms from Egypt, Africa, Greece, Persia, India and China.

More than the symbolic 'three wise men from the East' brought the gifts of their wisdoms to Jesus at his spiritual 'birth'. The connection of the gospel stories with those roots was almost ob-literated in the witch-hunts and burnings of people and books at Alexandria and elsewhere, perpetrated in the name of a loving God. Most of the Tao Te Ching and much of the Bhagavad Gita, for instance, reappears in The (our) New Testament, but in (probably fictional) *story* form—of jokes against our selves. Modern counterparts of the 'types' satirized in both Old and New Testaments are still easily identifiable—they are *us*—power-full people in all walks of life.

"Power *tends* to corrupt" (Acton 1897, our italics). It need not be so, but it *generally* does. Power over others makes corruption *possible* and so, given human nature as it now is, it makes corruption (abuse of power) *probable*, *predict-able*, not always, but often.

Uses of words are systematically distorted in favour of their users—US. It must be so (we invent and use words for our purposes) but becoming aware of that might set us more nearly free to laugh, self-critically at our pompous, Narcissistic selves—emperors with no real clothes on, only the symbolic 'moral' 'fig-leaves' of deception adopted by Adam and Eve when they (thought they) knew about good and evil.

"If we can learn to laugh at our selves, we will never be short of things to laugh at." (Source forgotten. Does it matter who said it? We say it again now, in our own names and no-one else's, in 2007.)

CONCLUSIONS SO FAR

Before proceeding to discussion of the consequences of our conclusions, it may be helpful to summarize them here.

1. If critical thinking is desireable, then there seems no good reason to avoid including *self*-criticism.
2. If that is right, then it is desire-able that we, as educators and teachers in positions of authority and power as responsible adults, parents or 'mind-ers' and *exemplars*, will *exemplify in practice* the value of self-criticism.
3. The many advocates of 'not knowing' in the history of ideas from Lao Tse, Socrates, the authors of the (our) Old and New Testaments through to Mill, Nietzsche, post-modern writers and Pooh Bear suggest that attitude, or spirit of 'not knowing' as a first principle, or premise of a self-critical thinking attitude. It can also be described as 'awareness of fallibility', in a radical sense of awareness that we are *likely* to be mistaken *more often than wise*. Natural selection, applied to ideas, might lead us to expect that there will always be more foolishnesses around, destined to die, than there are wisdoms destined to survive for long, let alone for ever.

Although there is no space to discuss it adequately here, we draw attention to George Soros' (2000) book *Open Society: Reforming Global Capitalism*. Soros develops three central ideas in his book: 'Fallibility', 'Reflexivity' and 'Democratic Deficit'. Those three interdependent principles have been influential in much of what we have written.

PRACTICAL CONSEQUENCES FOR A PEDAGOGY OF TOMORROW

1. One simple step would help us to exemplify a self-critical attitude to children. We should avoid almost all uses of 'know' (in the sense of knowing 'that' some 'thing' is *completely* 'true' or *completely* 'good'). We should honestly admit to children, so that they can trust *us as honest persons*, that "Nobody knows (anything much of importance)."

We should, in almost all cases, use the word 'belief'. The justifications of beliefs lie along a continuum, or spectrum, of different degrees and kinds of reasons in justification. These lead to different degrees and kinds of confidence, or assessment of reliability. With a small number of exceptions, the extremes at either end of that continuum (completely justified, certainty, at one end, or with zero justification at the other) are neither attainable nor desire-able. The word 'belief' clearly implies the possibility of being wrong, whereas it is difficult for a child to challenge a teacher in authority who claims to know, especially when the knowledge is called 'objective' implying that it is independent of fallible people.

We should also clean up the Augean Stables of our language by avoiding nearly all uses of 'the' in the singular: the faith, the bible, the one God, the world, the sun, the universe, the human species, the truth, the good, the concept, the meaning of a word. In all those cases 'my' or 'our' would be more accurate, honest and modest. It would also draw attention to our responsibility for those words, non-words and things.

Even, or perhaps especially, science, is most honestly and modestly described as a belief system which depends, like all systematic constructions, on foundations which cannot, themselves, be verified or justified with further reasons: they are what we justify (everything else) *with*.

2. A second, more general step will be to establish courses in language awareness to make, first ourselves and then children, aware of the systematic unreliability of language, particularly of 'common sense', consensus and authority uses of words, like 'proper' sliding to mean 'correct', like *hamartia* being miss-trans-lated as 'sin' when it means 'mistake' or 'missing the mark. This points towards use of a dialogical, two-way *exchange* of perspectives (hearts and minds) in an *interactive model of two-way learning*, rather than (or mixed with) one-way, top-down teaching.

EXAMPLES FOR A CLASS-ROOM

In physics, for instance, we could start secondary school science by suggesting *mistaken,* but plausible ideas for the children to *falsify* for themselves. One of us (John) regularly 'taught' children at age 11, that the sun and moon both go round us in very nearly the same path. It is an obvious fact of simple observation. It requires an attitude towards adopting more than one perspective (Galilean relativity) to resolve the puzzle. The discussion often became heated. When I asked one 11-year old boy "Why on earth do you think our earth goes round our sun?" he almost shouted at me "Its a scientific fact." It is not. No-one has ever travelled outside the solar system to see what Galileo imagined. Children were provoked into criticizing teacher.

It was also more fun to tell children what Aristotle believed, that constant force produces constant speed. It was obvious to him, from observing a donkey pulling a cart. Why ever not? It is not easy to prove either idea wrong but evidence and theories can be produced to persuade us otherwise.

More generally, by admitting fallibility—that "Nobody knows" (much, if anything) including teacher, we motivate children to *participate* in their own learning processes. 'Not knowing' (puzzlement) is a necessary condition for inquiring or wanting to learn.

When we confront children with a huge, fortress-like construction of science called 'knowledge' they are effectively 'forbidden', at worst, or severely discouraged, at best, from criticizing an apparently impregnable authority of orthodox correctnesses of all kinds. We need to give children the opportunity to argue against us on more nearly equal terms as people who are equally valued, however unequal and different they may be in any or every other respect.

Of course, children do have to learn about the currently fashionable set of beliefs before they are in a position from which to criticize. But the word 'belief' makes explicit a self-critical attitude—awareness of fallibility "I believe" 'implies' "But I may be wrong. I am fallible."

This attitude, exemplifying a self-critical attitude has the advantage of generalis-ability: it can be applied in every subject and, indeed, in every dialogical conversation, interaction or two-way intercourse in which we exchange perspectives with children. It needs no extra time in the curriculum.

Perhaps Michael Polanyi's (1958) attitude is a good encapsulation of the attitude we commend: Science "comprises everything in which we may be totally mistaken." Alternatively: "We (probably) have (almost) everything about half wrong." The status of our truths is never firmer than 'not yet falsified'. That attitude towards our truths is, like John Stuart Mill's, an invitation, or challenge, to criticize our own most precious assumptions.

REFERENCES

Acton, L. (1897). Letter to Bishop Mandell Creighton, quoted in *Oxford dictionary of quotations* (p. 1). Oxford: Oxford University Press.

Burke, B. (1999). Antonio Gramsci and informal education, the encyclopaedia of informal education, http://www.infed.org/thinkers/et-grm.htm. (5/04/2005)

Freire, P. (1971). *Pedagogy of the oppressed.* Harmondworth: Penguin.

Lao Tse. (2000). *The Tao Te Ching.* (M. Stephen, Trans.). London: Kyle Cathie.

Lyotard, J. F. (1988). *The differend: Phrases in dispute* Minneapolis, MN: Minnesota Press.

McLaren, P. (2003). *Journal of Transformative Education, 1*(2), 117–134.

Mill, J. S. (1859). *On liberty and other essays.* Oxford: Oxford University Press.

Polanyi, M. (1958). *Personal knowledge.* London: Routledge and Kegan Paul.

Proudhon, P. J. (1840). *Property is theft.* Oxford Dictionary of Quotations, Oxford University Press, 1992.

Roger, S. (1991). *Gramsci's political thought: An introduction.* London: Lawrence and Wishart.

Rorty, R. (1989). *Contingency, irony, solidarity.* Cambridge: Cambridge University Press.

Soros, G. (2000). *Open society: Reformiong global capitalism.* London: Little, Brown.

OLLI-PEKKA MOISIO

21. AS HEARD IN SILENCE—ERICH FROMM, LISTENING AND TO-BE-HEARD IN EDUCATION

What I liked in anthropology was its inexhaustible faculty of negation, its relentless definition of man, as though he were no better than God, in terms of what he is not.

—Samuel Beckett 1955, 52

People learn nothing and have succeeded in nothing unless they think this is the most important thing to do.

—Erich Fromm 1994, 76

The Talmud tells us how God told Moses, when Hebrews were trying to get across the red sea, that he should raise his staff, and after that the waters would open. Moses did raise his staff but the waters did not open. The sea was silent and the Hebrews had no way to go. Not until the first person jumped to the water, on that very moment waters gave way for the Hebrews to go. This story tells us at least two things. On the other hand nothing will happen if we are not ready to work together (i.e. to jump) for the goals that each of us sees the most important thing to do in the current situation. We have to have faith and fortitude in order to succeed. But on the other hand I think that this is also the source of the substantial pessimism that the real critic must face. In fact this pessimism should be a part and parcel of the criticism and evaluation of the real possibilities. The point would be to learn to listen for the call of the moment, to hope in face of despair. But how exactly we might learn this in a world that has almost lost the ability for this? What kind of education might give room for the existence of hope that discloses how "the world itself, just as it is in a mess, is also in a state of unfinishedness and in experimental process out of that mess" (Bloch 1986, 221).

Fear has made us stop while facing the sea of time and opportunity, our given historical moment. African-American Nobel Prize-winning author, editor, and professor Toni Morrison described our time with two traits in 2004. She said that our time is characterized by fear and melancholy. She has grown to fear her country— the United States of America. Millions share her fear but they also fear for their own concrete and personal lives. This fear, which springs all around the world, especially in the countries that form the so called axis of evil, show where Morrison's melancholy springs. Its fountain is the knowledge about what United States of America has become. Fear and melancholy are very much a part of everyone's' lives, if not consciously, then at least subconsciously.

But we can also claim that in addition to Morrison's two characteristics there are at least four other characteristics to describe our historical moment: risk, uncertainty, human invisibility and instrumentality of human self-relation and the relations

I. Gur-Ze'ev, The Possibility/Impossibility of a New Critical Language in Education, 391–408.
© *2010 Sense Publishers. All Rights Reserved.*

to others. Taken together these six characteristics are the constellation that forms the individual, ordinary human beings view point to the globalization as they are the effects of and reactions to this same process. This is why we need to listen more carefully the experiential dimension of globalization in everyday life world and this also should mean something in the field of education. These characteristics might help us to understand the role of emotional processes in the process of learning and teaching.

Famous social critic and psychoanalyst Erich Fromm (1900–1980) wrote about therapy as an art of listening. But this art of listening was connected as a central part to a larger idea of change from having orientation to a productive orientation—to be as a full human being. This is as I see the fundamental question that we must face today as we face the global ecological, economical and human catastrophe. In the 1960s Fromm began to deepen his idea of the orientations present in western societies that he had already found in the 1930's and 40's. He was able to articulate the fundamental and macabre fascination with death and things that we have in Western-world. Fromm believed that the central driving force behind this was the desire to make up for a lack of authentic being and selfhood. This was done in identifying with the lifeless when enjoying things as long as they are reified and without life.

To describe this orientation toward death Fromm used the concept of necrophilia. He was concerned to go beyond the popular usage of the term that made reference to a sexual contact with the dead; and/or the desire to be near bodily or visually to corpses. Fromm wanted to open up necrophilia as a character-rooted passion: the passion to transform and to see living as something non-living (Fromm 1973, 332). He writes that "Man is biologically endowed with the capacity for biophilia, but psychologically he has the potential for necrophilia as an alternative solution" (Ibid., 366). As Sigmund Freud did earlier in individual level, Fromm set this passion to "tear apart living structures" within a proper social and political contexts.

> With the increasing production an division of labor, the formation of a large surplus, and the building of states with hierarchies and elites [...] large-scale human destructiveness and cruelty came into existence and grew as civilization and the role of power grew. (Fromm 1973, 435.)

In his famous book *To Have or To Be* (1976) Fromm argues that two ways of existence were competing for "the spirit of mankind". The having mode looks to things and material possessions and is based on aggression and greed. The being mode is rooted in love and is concerned with shared experience and productive activity. Fromm (1976, 165) argued that only a fundamental change in human character "from a preponderance of the having mode to a preponderance of the being mode of existence can save us from a psychological and economic catastrophe" and set out some ways forward.

In this article I want to ask can we use Fromm's (1994) writings about therapy as an art of listening, as a way to articulate more carefully the usually hidden dimensions of the relationship between student and teacher—the scream and whisper. With these texts in mind among others, I want to probe little bit the question how are listening, to-be-heard, trust, responsibility and obligation connected together in a teaching environment and educational counseling sessions in the era of globalizing capitalism. Especially I am interested in the theoretical and practical dimensions of the concept of active listening, and the connection of it to the education aimed to change. Active listening is the vessel of hope, which is the fundamental dimension of every human act directed at change.

If we would practically adopt the idea in the previously told Talmudic story then we would have to ask quite frankly, what would be the starting point of learning that would make it possible for the students to see the common goal and interest within their individuality? I think that this goal cannot be brought outside but has to been developed from the shared historically situated life experiences. By posing this question we see how difficult it would be to formulate such a starting point. Unless we would be able to formulate a kind of norm that every person has a right to full birth as an individual, full growth to her individual potentialities, full aliveness regardless her actual personality.

ACTIVE LISTENING AS A MODEL OF RADICAL COUNSELLING/TEACHING

I think that the best way to start to understand what Fromm meant with his idea of active listening is to open the discussion with a quote from interview that was done by R. I. Evans in the 1960's. In this part of the interview that was published as a book *Dialogue with Erich Fromm* in 1966 Fromm is describing his work as a practicing therapist. Fromm (Evans 1966, 35) says "now I listen you, and while *I'm listening, I have responses* which are the responses of a trained instrument. [...] I'll tell you what I hear. This will often be quite different from what you are telling me or intended to tell me. Then you tell me how you feel about my interpretation [...] We move along this way freely. I am not claiming that what *I hear* is necessarily correct, but it deserves attention because of the fact that your words produce this reaction in me".[1]

Fromm (1994, 98) argued that the fundamental point in this relationship is to listen and to say what is heard and not to interpret. Only this way the relationship can be formed as an active interaction between two human beings where different responses are the key element. With these different responses the practical goal of therapy can be reached. Fromm sees that the main practical goal of therapist is to seek a way to penetrate behind the patient's "official goals". This is imperative if it is intended that the therapeutic relationship should produce real improvement or change in the patient's behaviour. Behind these official goals Fromm sees a "secret plot" that is motivating self-defeating behaviour. With this idea it is intended to activate dialectic between these two aspects of patient's personality as they bear upon an issue that has an immediate significance in the patient's life.

It is easy to see the importance of these ideas within educational philosophy if we want to promote radical learning and change. Quite many recent developments in the field are pointing to same kind of understanding of the teacher-pupil relationship but they lack the idea that what education is primary interested in doing is not so much to make persons more suited to the social environment, than to make them radically self-aware of their situation and their own resources to act in these situations.

What is quite unique in Fromm's ideas, and in fact was unique in the field of therapy also, is an idea, that the person that produces the dialectic—be it teacher of therapist— does not stay outside the dialectic. Once the process has begun teacher is inevitably part and parcel of the same process and must act accordingly.

But it is obvious that we do not have to encourage or force teachers in a full autobiographical self-disclosure but we do not have to necessary deny it either. Actually there is nothing harmful doing just that, but at the same time it is not actually quite clear what we can gain from full self-disclosure. But what is needed is a certain kind of self-revelation that is fundamental part of the radical learning. What I have in mind is that this self-revelation requires teacher to expose their own strengths and limitations of understanding and their own value systems far more openly and directly than occurs in usual, teacher centered neutrality. The reading of Fromm's texts on therapy reveals us that this was something that he saw also fundamental for therapeutical cure.

LaPlanche and Potanlis (1973, 93) famously described that there are three ways to understand counter transference in psychoanalysis. In fact they saw a term as a cross-road where therapist should decide which of the three roads she should follow. First road is the classical road of striving neutrality so that the possible treatment can be "structured exclusively by the patient's transference". Second road is the road of therapeutics private scrutiny of their counter transference reactions. From these personal reactions they can "interpret utterances of the unconsciousness in other people". Third road is for the analyst to disclose to the patient "the actual emotions felt"—i.e. the personal emotions. LaPlanche and Potanlis add that "this approach is on the tenet that, resonance from the unconscious to the unconscious constitutes the only authentically psychoanalytic form of communication".

Fromm took LaPlanche's and Potanlis's third road even further than they have expected because he saw that this form of therapeutic communication was intended to convey not only a message but a model. It was a vehicle for the patient to experience what Fromm called "authenticity" in human relationship. This kind of "authenticity" should be seen not as in a strict sense of the word, i.e. as something that we truly in a fundamental sense are but as an attitude to be there and actually listen what other human being is saying to us—to be open to other and let her words reach us as a whole human being. In a sense we might argue that in this kind of relationship teacher is taught by the pupil given that they do not treat each other as an object; i.e. teachers have to try to see her as taking part in a same process as her pupil. As Karl Marx (1844, 326) wrote in his so called Paris-manuscripts from the 1844 describing the same experience that Fromm called authentic human relationship:

> Assume man to be man and his relationship to the world to be a human one: then you can exchange love only for love, trust for trust, etc. If you want to enjoy art, you must be an artistically cultivated person; if you want to exercise influence over other people, you must be a person with a stimulating and encouraging effect on other people. Every one of your relations to man and to nature must be a specific expression, corresponding to the object of your will, of your real individual life. If you love without evoking love

in return — that is, if your loving as loving does not produce reciprocal love; if through a living expression of yourself as a loving person you do not make yourself a beloved one, then your love is impotent — a misfortune.

I think that some sort of authentic human relationship is also necessary in educational settings. I mean that there must be a way to articulate what it means that we could have an authentic human relationship also to the themes and issues that are in the centre of particular educational situation. This re-articulation may be done from the perspectives of both teacher and pupil as a new shared sensibility. Fromm (1955, 347–352) wrote about "collective art" as a way to rearticulate meaningful relationship with the issues at hand. In Fromm's mind it means for art to be collective that we "*respond to the world with our senses in a meaningful, skilled, productive, active, shared way*". I think that this formulation can be transported to education and learning in general without enormous difficulties. In this kind of activity teacher and learner can together be one with others in "a meaningful, rich and productive way" (Fromm 1955, 348).

The need to this kind of shared sensibility may be seen when we start by pointing out that in fact all learning or acquisition of knowledge is based on fear. With this idea we gain access to the emotional work that is going on all the time in the different stages of educational process in general. This fear may be seen from two different angles. Firstly, it is the minimal structuring dimension of all knowledge acquisition as stated above. All not known is something that we are afraid of. As Max Horkheimer and Theodor W. Adorno (2002, 11) write in *Dialectic of Enlightenment,* "nothing is allowed to remain outside, since the mere idea of 'outside' is the real source of fear". But at the same time fear is also the fundamental dimension of knowledge thus grown out of fear. By this I mean that when we have certain knowledge we might be afraid if something or someone is threatening this knowledge and identity that we have formed from and for it (cf. ibid. 23–24).

Is it too much to hope for that for example regular teacher in her teaching environment with its normal hardships and problematic could form an authentic human relationship that Fromm envisioned? Can we say that this kind of relationship could be taught or is it more the case that it can only be learnt, or more clearly stated, mimetically acquired from the social environment? The premise for this relationship to actualize is that the whole person has a productive character orientation towards others and the world. What if our character orientation is non-authentic, sadomasochistic, non-productive, having-orientation that Fromm diagnosed? Can this kind of person—as teachers are after all human beings—stimulate the needed creative and productive relationship? Can she ever serve as an example of authentic human relationship? The answer is obvious: no.

There is something strange going on when we look at the teacher education in general. The same strange process where the original goal of education vanishes to thin air happens in the education of physicians. What happens is that these students gradually loose from their sights the fact that they are in contact with human beings while practicing medicine. When these doctoral candidates are asked in the beginning of their education that why they want to become doctors the answer is that they want to help other human beings. The reason for this altruist impulse to vanish might be that the education on doctors is long and the problems that they tackle with are enormously difficult so that they have to develop a technical rationality.[2] This way they can solve the problems without any distracting emotional elements. But what is strange is that this same process goes through in every level of occupations where other human beings are trying to help others in need of help be it teachers, social workers etc.[3]

The most debatable and problematic dimension of this method be it in education or in therapy lies here. But I think it is safe to say that the same problems are lurking behind the other roads that can be followed in the field of education because the fruitful interaction is based on the idea that teacher or analyst "is not afraid of his *own* unconscious for then he will not be afraid or embarrassed by opening up the patient's unconscious" (Evans 1966, 55).

AM I DRIVEN OR PUSHED TOWARDS SOMETHING?

Fromm (1932) articulated in his work how capitalism fosters anal character with all their special pathologies. He unified social and individual characteristics with his concepts of authoritarian character, hoaring character and marketing character (Fromm 1941; 1945). Fromm (1973, 349) then understood sadistic character and the necrophilious character as a progressively more malignant forms of a "normal anal character". These extreme forms are produced by any conditions that increase the force that underlay normal banality: narcissism, unrelatedness and destructiveness.

Fromm distinguishes between benign aggression, which mainly take place in self-defense, and malignant aggression, as the urge to be cruel, to exercise power over others, or simply to destroy. This arises, according to Fromm, when person finds it impossible to satisfy his existential needs, i.e. roughly his need to do something significant, in a way that is creative and constructive; and so tries to fulfill him by destroying rather than creating. This may come about of person's own character, or family relationships; but it may also be caused or encouraged by social conditions. "There are specific environmental conditions conductive to... the development of the life-furthering syndrome... to the extent these conditions are lacking; he will become... characterized by the presence of the life-thwarting syndrome." (Fromm 1973, Chapter 10, section 4, part 2.)

These conditions are named as "freedom, activating stimuli, the absence of exploitative control, and the presence of 'man-cantered' modes of production" (Ibid.). "Activating stimuli" such as "a novel, a poem, an idea, a landscape, music, a loved person" invite a response of active interest and mental or psychical activity, and do not produce satiation or boredom when repeated. Passive stimuli produces immediate thrill, followed by release of tension, followed by boredom and the need for a new stimulus of different kind, since there is no novelty created by response. Hence in the society in which passive rather than active stimuli are the most easily available, there will be a growing tendency to gain easy excitement by arousing malice and destructiveness: "It is much easier to get excited by anger, rage, cruelty or the passion to destroy than by love and productive and active interest." (Fromm 1973, 10, 3, 4.) This is not determined inevitably by social circumstances, but is heavily influenced by them: "man is never so determined that a basic change... is not possible... environment inclines, but does not determine" (Fromm 1973, 10, 4, 5).

We might see teacher in an ideal sense as "the activating stimuli"—she produces a strive towards something. This striving is something more than a mere being-driven-towards something that simple stimulus produces. But the teacher needs some intervention or mediation to do just this. In Fromm's eyes activating stimuli "requires a 'touchable' stimuli in order to have an effect—touchable not in the sense of being educated, but of being humanly responsive. On the other hand, the person who is fully alive does not necessarily need any particular outside stimulus to be activated; in fact, he creates his own stimuli." (Fromm 1973, 270.)

What Fromm was articulating in the previous paragraphs from the psychological viewpoint might be re-articulated in the concrete educational setting by using the concept of "experiential learning" that John Dewey has famously developed in his *Democracy and Education.* Dewey (1916, 141) argues that

> To "learn from experience" is to make a backward and forward connection between what we do to things and what we enjoy or suffer from things in consequence. Under such conditions, doing becomes a trying; an experiment with the world to find out what it is like; the undergoing becomes instruction—discovery of the connection of things.

Learning by *doing* becomes in this sense learning by *trying*. Students become active agents of their learning process. This does not mean that the teacher's role diminishes but even though teachers still has a definite role in this process their role is fundamentally changed. It is obvious that teacher cannot be seen as a sole actor of the situation anymore. Knowledge is not given above but seen as shared in some specific context.

> Through dialogue, the teacher-of-the-students and the students-of-the-teacher cease to exist and a new term emerges: teacher-students and student-teachers. The teacher is no longer merely the-one-who-teaches, but one who is himself taught in dialogue with the students, who in turn while being taught also teach. They become jointly responsible for a process in which all grow. [...] Men teach each other, mediated by the world, by the cognizable objects which in banking education are "owned" by the teacher. (Freire 2003, 67)

Freire (2004, 74) argued that these frame of references are "generative themes" and the role of teacher is to see and articulate those themes together with students. These themes are usually scattered and not fully articulated and it is left to teacher to reframe them into meaningful wholes. But teacher does not do this alone as students will give in this reframing and reorganization work important experiential impulses to serve as a material index.

> Does it require deep intuition to comprehend that man's ideas, views, and conception, in one word, man's consciousness, changes with every change in the conditions of his material existence, in his social relations and in his social life? (Marx & Engels 1848, 73.)

Dewey (ibid. 160) saw that "no thought, no idea, can possibly be conveyed as an idea from one person to another". The only way to do just this is through practice of testing and experiencing. This can be too easily be read as promoting self-centered narcissism but Dewey connected to his idea of experience the must to develop communicative, collaborative and deliberative skills. As Myles Horton[4] (1990, 57) writes:

> I knew that it was necessary [...] to draw out of people their experience, and help them value group experiences and learn from them. It was essential that people learned to make decisions on the basis of analyzing and trusting their own experience, and learning from what was good and bad. [...] I believed then and still believe that you learn from your experience of doing something and from your analysis of that experience.

This collaboration within learning practices should be seen not as collectivization of individuals. We might argue that in an inescapable climate of neoliberalism, that "removing ourselves from the influence of others is a revolutionary act" (Brookfield 2005, p. 196). But this kind of removement of oneself should not be seen as an identity political act of self-articulation. Like Peter McLaren put it in his opening lecture of the Paulo Freire Research Center-Finland in the University of Tampere (20.11.2007): in the dark times of neoliberal terror, it is not important to ask, as researchers in "cultural" Critical Pedagogy and other domesticated forms of Critical Pedagogy, Who am I (identity political positioning). But instead to ask the fundamental question, where are you—and to reply: I am here! Even though I have certain reservations of specific ideas of McLaren (i.e. the leader role of teachers, straightforward use of Marxian economical theory) I find it very useful this idea of the need for ethical and real political positioning within educational practices (McLaren & Farahmandpur 2005; McLaren & Jaramillo 2007). This positioning might help students to form better picture of the times where they are living and also help them to develop insight to the role of information production and consumption.

As we have seen in previous paragraphs, the decisions and goals that the specific teaching situation should address are based not only on tacit knowledge of the students but on knowledge gained from shared experience via discussions and collaborative reflection and active doing. For example as a teacher Horton "realized for the first time that he could lead a discussion without knowing all the answers. He sharpened their questions, got them to talk about their own experiences, and found that they already had many answers" (Parker & Parker, 1991, p. 2). I think that such experience plays a central role in education.

We might want to argue that group collaboration and problem solving involve people's shared experiences that are often solutions that may have already existed in some sense. These solutions were unseen or were pieced together through reflection from the apparent synergy of engaging one others ideas, experiences and knowledge in discussions (Peters & Bell, 2001). Participants "get much more out of what they didn't come for than what they came for, because they start exchanging experiences" (Kennedy, 1981, p. 107). As Dewey, Horton believed that the best way of learning is by actually doing, which provides substance for reflection and growth. This is something that Hegel already understood while articulating the development of self-consciousness in *Phenomenology of Spirit* as a necessary self-objectification and return and I think that it might have a productive impact even in different fields of theoretical subjects. This brings about the dichotomy of learning that Dewey brought up in his *Democracy and Education*.

> On the one hand, learning is the sum total of what is known, as that is handed down by books and learned men. It is something external, an accumulation of cognitions as one might store material commodities in a warehouse. Truth exists ready-made somewhere. Study is then the process by which an individual draws on what is in storage. On the other hand, learning means something which the individual does when he studies. It is an active, personally conducted affair. The dualism here is between knowledge as something external, or, as it is often called, objective, and knowing as something purely internal, subjective, psychical. There is, on one side, a body of truth, ready-made, and, on the other, a ready-made mind equipped with a faculty of knowing—if it only wills to exercise it, which it is often strangely loath to do. The separation, often touched upon, between subject matter and method is the educational equivalent of this dualism. Socially the distinction has to do with the part of life which is dependent upon authority and that where individuals are free to advance. (Dewey 1916, 389–390.)

HOW TO MOTIVATE LEARNERS TO LEARN AND TO CHANGE

Adam Smith wrote in his magisterial *Wealth of Nations* in 1776 about a not welcomed side effects of the division of labour which he saw fundamental dimension of the well organized and productive societies. The most devastating side-effect was that the division of labour produced stupidity or more generally we might argue that it produced one-dimensionality persons. Smith (1776, 987–994) saw that since the common people are engaged in simple and uniform tasks in the productive system in order to maintain their lives, it is necessary to provoke their minds with mental stimuli which would encourage them to speculate about their own otherwise dull occupations. With this they can gain much wider and richer viewpoint to the world, themselves and the relationship that they have to each other. Smith thought that this overcoming of one dimensionality is needed because otherwise people would start to act socially rebellious and plan upheavals. This was something that Smith despised.

But what drives human being to get used to one-dimensionality? I think that Smith was wrong in that he thought that if living becomes enough estranged, one-dimensional and improvised then people would almost automatically start to do something to improve their lives. Marx shared this optimism in some elementary form. With this problem in mind it might be useful to have a look on Fromm's argument in his book *Escape from Freedom*. We might want to redirect the central thesis of the book towards our question and argue that fear is one of the central motivators that have taught human beings to learn to love their particular fate. Fromm thought that this fear was specific fear of taking charge of one's life. As Dewey (1989, 44) once argued "the serious threat to our democracy is not the existence of foreign totalitarian states. It is the existence within our own personal attitudes and within our own institutions of conditions which have given a victory to external authority. The battlefield is also accordingly here—within ourselves and our institutions." Thus it is imperative that education starts by acknowledging the shared social and experiential world and tries to meaningfully incorporate this into topics at hand in schools and education in general.

Social and economical conditions shape emotionally and psychologically conditioned needs. As Marx (1859, 28–29) argued in his *Grundrisse*:

> Hunger is hunger, but the hunger gratified by cooked meat eaten with a knife and fork is a different hunger from that which bolts down raw meat with the aid of hand, nail and tooth. Production thus produces not only the object but also the manner of consumption, not only objectively but also subjectively. Production thus creates the consumer. (3) Production not only supplies a material for the need, but it also supplies a need for the material. As soon as consumption emerges from its initial state of natural crudity and immediacy— and, if it remained at that stage, this would be because production itself had been arrested there—it becomes itself mediated as a drive by the object. The need which consumption feels for the object is created by the perception of it. The object of art—like every other product—creates a public which is sensitive to art and enjoys beauty. Production thus not only creates an object for the subject, but also a subject for the object. Thus production produces consumption (1) by creating the material for it; (2) by determining the manner of consumption; and (3) by creating the products, initially posited by it as objects, in the form of a need felt by the consumer. It thus produces the object of consumption, the manner of consumption and the motive of consumption.

Fromm (1941, 15) argued that within different needs there is also a strong and fundamental human need "to be related to the world outside oneself, the need to avoid aloneness". If human being is forced to be without experience of belonging, it will have an effect of psychical disintegration. In a sense you can live among human beings and have in this sense physical communion with them but still be deprived from psychical communion with them or ideas, symbols and social patterns. This kind of spiritual aloneness Fromm (ibid.) called moral aloneness.

> The more man gains freedom in the sense of emerging from the original oneness with man and nature and the more he becomes an 'individual', he has no choice but to unite himself with the world in the spontaneity of love and productive work or else to seek a kind of integrity of his individual self. (Fromm 1941, 18.)

In education it is imperative that this kind of possibility for spontaneity and productive work is maintained even though it is a brute fact that in schools many different structural and personal dimensions work against this goal. One way to see the problematic is to make a distinction between different authorities that are present in educational situations: rational, irrational, and anonymous authority.

Fromm (1941, 225) thought that *"self is as strong as it is active"*. Different authorities promote or hinder this activity. Irrational authority is working to promote the actualization of the interest of authority in question. It does not see any particular use or need for the activity of the subjected person if not the active self-repression of that particular individual or groups of individuals. Whereas irrational authority is working for the authority, rational authority works to promote the actualization of the developmental potentials of the person in question. As Fromm (1957, 176–177) argues "by irrational authority I mean authority which is based on force, either physical or emotional, and the function which is the exploitation of other person, materially, emotionally, or otherwise. Rational authority is authority which is based on competence, and the function which is to help another person accomplish a certain task".

Rational authority is part and parcel of the real education because in real education educational activity is concerned in nurturing the developmental goals of the persons who are educated. In this sense real education is up-bringing in some fundamental sense while education which is based in irrational authority is not education at all but more handling of the things—the total instrumentality of delicate educational relationship between two persons. Education is "identical with helping the child realize his potentialities" (Fromm 1947, 207). But this kind of real education does not mean that this educational relationship is in some sense biologically based natural relationship and does not need rational control. This would lead to a certain kind of *laissez-faire* where we could not recognize any principle, would not state any value and would obscure hierarchy. This would lead to a much more thorough intervention from society and its regulative imperatives it would give foothold to anonymous authority.

By anonymous authority Fromm (1955, 99) understood "the authority of public opinion and the market". This kind of authority fosters the need to adjust and to be approved by the some commonly approved value. It produces always present unconscious sense of fundamental powerlessness. As Fromm (ibid, 102) states "there is no overt authority [i.e. irrational and rational authority] which intimidates us, but we are governed by fear of the anonymous authority of conformity. We do not submit to anyone personally; we do not go through conflicts with authority, but we have also no convictions of our own, almost no individuality, almost no sense of self."

It is obvious that education that is based on rational authority would need much more rational evaluation and control from teachers part than handling of thing which is much more non-rational and based on impulses and regulations coming outside of human relationship in this sense. The critical question in this is, that how can we find out what could be the most productive course of development for the person that is being educated. In face of this question it is imperative that we focus not so much on the positive, regulative principles than on the minimal terms and try to picture what might be most harmful for the growth of individual person.

Education should aim to the goal where human being is able to "give birth to himself, to become what he potentially is" (Fromm 1945, 237). With this idea Fromm is moving quite near what Theodor W. Adorno meant while he used the concept of non-identity. In Fromm's mind the education is in some fundamental sense self-education. Only individual person is able to actualize the potentials if the surrounding settings do not hinder that effort. In education we usually think that we are able to form a clear picture of all the aspects of educational situation via mostly empirical research.

Adorno tried to articulate with his concept of non-identity that we are unable to disclose reality fully. We have a strong drive for identifying or even reducing educational reality. This is done nowadays for example in evidence-based educational research that is strongly determined by a causal perspective linking professional intervention and educational outcome (Biesta 2007, pp. 6–8). This has furthered the process that has taken place in western countries where the focus in education (among many other fields of human activity) has fundamentally shifted from the process of creative activity to the end result of that process.

Immanuel Kant famously wrote about legislation of reason most notably in his *Critique of Pure Reason*. Adorno argued in *Negative Dialectics* that this legislation of reason is bound to a separation of mental and physical labor. After Kant all human existence was judged in relation to the mental realm. Enlightened thought tried to show that this realm was the sphere of universal reason, i.e. it is detached from the concrete conditions of social existence.

> The transcendental generality is no mere narcissist self-exaltation of the I, not the hubris of an autonomy of the I. Its reality lies in the domination that prevails and perpetuates itself by means of the principle of equivalence. The process of abstraction—which philosophy transfigures, and which it ascribes to the knowing subject alone—is taking place in the factual barter society (Adorno 1973, 178.)

Individuals learn to abstract from their social conditions when judging their specific situations. This is done possible with transcendental subject and the realm of pure reason. Alfred Sohn-Rethel (1985) argued in this connection that the reference to a general subject and pure reason is an objectification that works as a complement to the capitalist principle of exchange.

> Beyond the magic circle of identitarian philosophy, the transcendental subject can be deciphered as a society unaware of itself. Such unawareness is deducible. Ever since mental and physical labor were separated in the sign of the dominant mind, the sign of justified privilege, the separated mind has been obliged, with the exaggeration due to a bad conscience, to vindicate the very claim to dominate which it derives from the thesis that it is primary and original—and to make every effort to forget the source of its claim, lest the claim lapse. (Adorno 1973, 177.)

But Adorno's concept says more than only criticize the methods of educational sciences. It tries to articulate to us that the technologically based educational science and some of us who believe in the products of these sciences forget that in education we are dealing with human beings who are trying to articulate what they are experiencing and what they are doing in particular situations (Thompson 2005).

EDUCATION IS NOT THERAPY BUT BECAUSE IT IS NOT THERAPY IT CAN PROVIDE THERAPEUTIC EFFECT

It is obvious that we need to keep in mind that education or counseling is not a form or practice of therapy—its main function is *Vergesellschaftlichung* i.e. preparing people to a life in *a specific society*. The goal of therapy in general is also socialization to the given society. Mostly this is done by restoring the work ability of a human being. And with this function we see also one of the main problems that beset education, i.e. what if the whole society is sick, what then is the role of education, in the process where this socially structured sickness is moved into the individual level? But still we might argue that even though they are not therapy they still can produce a therapeutic effect in student i.e. the need to find a new way of being and acting in the world more responsible way. This is possible when we articulate the process and goal of education from the radical point of view. Then we are able to withstand the goal of therapies in whatever form as fundamentally oriented to cure a person only so that she can function normally within the "pathology of normalcy".

"Pathology of normalcy" means that we see as normal behaviour the statistically normal ways of being and acting in the world. Education as radical education is oriented in curing human beings from the "pathology of normalcy". The real cure is outlined as a realization of possibility to gain self-knowledge as becoming aware of myself as part of "pathology of normalcy". In the age of globalizing capitalism we need this therapeutic effect that education at best can produce. With it we can face the ever increasing division of the world into a well off part and the part that is pushed into evermore deeper poverty driven by the promise of the increase of prosperity. With it we might be able to make counter effect to fear, melancholy, risk, uncertainty, and human invisibility.

> The closer I am to reality the more am I capable to live my life adequately.
> The less close am I to reality, the more illusions I have, the am I capable
> to deal with life in an adequate way. (Fromm 1994, 168.)

To be invisible is when people refuse to recognize that you are a human being. To be invisible is when you lose your sense of human dignity. To be invisible is to realize that people no longer recognize your existence and your struggle to live in harmony inside the social world. As Ralph Ellison (1980, 3) wrote in his novel *Invisible Man*: "I am invisible, understand, simply because people refuse to see me." And this invisibility has become a sad fact of life for millions of inhabitants across the globe. When we look at the global situation, we can write without hesitation that today families are invisible, children are invisible, women are invisible and men are invisible. As we awake each morning to a consumer ideology, what is not invisible is the commodity itself. We have become a commodity of flesh and bone— a commodity to be bought and sold on the open market.

Within this objectified commodity fetish, there is uncertainty and life risk. When the human being becomes an objectified form, she becomes a disembodied commodity and as such, becomes a 'person' without substance. No longer possessing a human body we become unseen and unfelt not only in the workplace but also inside the social. And here lies the risk and uncertainty. Every commodity relationship runs the risk of being discarded or being placed in a pile of garbage. A commodity has an uncertain future. It value is determined by its usefulness. When the human being has a commodity form, her usefulness always comes into question and hence, the uncertainty of life and risk.

But what this means for the thinking and acting in the world? This kind of commodification runs through the whole culture. It leaves nothing untouched. We might still criticize the school system same as we can criticize the whole society because it emphasizes too much the issues of knowledge and intelligence. In fact when the new capitalism production has taken hold of the production and selling of knowledge in the large scale this process will accelerate even more. Fromm (1973, 30) saw that this kind of culture where even the acquiring the knowledge about the surrounding world is seen as a commodity production produces a kind of brain-human-being. This kind of being is in touch with her environment, be it natural or social in nature, only with his intellect. Emotional reactions are missing from her intellectual operations which gradually become one dimensional and dull.

It is obvious that in critical attitude we need certain amount of critical distance from what is given but this does not mean that we have to detach ourselves from issues involved in order to for critical attitude. Like Marcuse once wrote while describing Bertolt Brecht's answer to the problem how theatre could in the present situation bring forth truth:

> To teach what the contemporary world really is behind the ideological and material veil, and how it can be changed, the theater must break the spectator's identification with the events on the stage. Not empathy and feeling, but distance and reflection are required. The "estrangement-effect" (*Verfremdungseffekt*) is to produce this dissociation in which the world can be recognized as what it is. "The things of everyday life are lifted out of the realm of the self-evident... That which is 'natural' must assume the features of the extraordinary. Only in this manner can the laws of cause and effect reveal themselves" (Brecht, 1957). (Marcuse, 1964, p. 67.)

Marcuse is talking here about *artistic alienation*. Artistic alienation is a conscious alienation of the alienated existence and hence its meaning is different than Marx's use of the concept of alienation. Marx is pointing out the relationship that human beings have towards themselves, others and the things that they produce in the scheme of capitalistic production. Practical human activity is seen as the formation of the self-conscious humanity. The purpose of which is for the collective assertion in social development on behalf of individual and humanity.

The problematic of artistic alienation brings us to the question concerning the aspects of reason, reasoning, intelligence and experience. To be educated in a fundamental sense human beings have to be in contact with the world as a whole human being i.e. with all of their senses and potentials as Hegel described in his *Phenomenology of Spirit*. Learning seen as a creative process is very important in this connection as then we are able to shift our focus back to the "only satisfaction that can give [...] real happiness—the experience of the activity of the present moment" (Fromm 1941, 226). Without this viewpoint we are only chasing phantoms in a constant dissatisfaction.

There is something fundamentally right when Fromm criticized the division between intellect, emotions and the will. This division highlights the difference between reason and intelligence. Intelligence is connected with the immediate goals and it searches the tools of acquiring these goals. It is something that Horkheimer (1938) called instrumental reason or subjective aspect of reason. Here reason takes the form of tool and it operates with the already given set of rules, regulations, and identitarian thought. There is no way to see beyond what is given as all that is recognized is the already familiar. It is as if the world is something that we know as same and everything that lays beyond it is not recognizable at all. This kind of reason "proves to be the ability to [...] co-ordinate the right means with a given end" (Horkheimer 1947, 5). Horkheimer asserts moreover that "however naive or super-ficial this definition of reasoning may seem," it springs from the "profound change of outlook that has taken place in Western thinking in the course of the last centuries" (ibid. 4).

We need upbringing and education that is versatile in the nurturing of the feeling, willing, creativity and experiencing. It seems that this kind of support is diminishing while the greater part of education is connected with streamlining the intellectual operations of the students to fulfill the regulation and goals of the educational system. Reason in proper sense goes beyond the immediate needs and goals, be it that they are set by the system or individual.

A SCREAM HEARD IN SILENCE

There is the fundamental need to be silent while others talk—to let the silence be heard. Without this silence we are not able to get a hint from the non-identitical in the given. But at the same time this silence must be seen as a hidden scream that is written to the very texture of modern life as it articulates the desperation of the individual human being. This is a dialectical nature of silence. As Samuel Beckett (1952, 32) once wrote, in his *Waiting for Godot*, when we "stopped crying. You have replaced him as it were. The tears of the world are a constant quantity. For each one who begins to weep somewhere else another stops. The same is true of the laugh." This is horrifyingly true in global capitalism. This experiential dimension should be brought up in education against the language of profit and personal gain because it is the only way to be able to reach the inner workings of globalized capitalism. Like Holloway once wrote: "When we talk or write, it is all too easy to forget that the beginning was not the word, but the scream. Faced with the destruction of human lives by capitalism, a scream of sadness, a scream of horror, above all a scream of anger, of refusal: NO." (Holloway 2003, 15.)

Finnish novelist and critic Christer Kihlman (1971) introduced the vertical and horizontal screams that articulate out positioning towards the world in the capital-istic society. The vertical scream comes from inside us. It is "a lonely scream of individualism, a scream that stems from the wealth of the unbearable riot of the market and scam, a helpless scream in front of the facade of conflicts, a scream through the superficial" (Kihlman 1971, 17). Kihlman calls this vertical scream of individualism also 'bourgeois scream'.

The horizontal scream is a 'proletarian scream'. It is heard as a distress "from the depths of desperation, poverty and sadness, from the endlessly painful reality of the people who have been cheated, trampled, and humiliated, from the bottom of the well of the final defeat." The horizontal scream of unprecedented human misery refers to the growth of global injustice and the polarization between the rich and the poor, and wounds also those who try to maintain a decent living in the midst of terrible economic over-development.

The screams of refusal are ethically demanding. Yet the power of the horizontal scream is about how to drown the vertical, for, as Kihlman (ibid.) writes, the horizontal scream "is a scream, which we must listen to, for it is getting louder around us all the time, all over the world, from the throats of millions of starving people, listen, it comes behind the horizon, it is here so close, it goes horizontally into the very ground in which we stand, and hits us at a right angle, challenging like the sound of a storm bell, the scream of an unfulfilled promise, the scream of anger of those from whom both a robe and a rice cup have been stolen, a scream that demands solidarity and justice, the only scream, which really judges." (Ibid. 18)

It is very important to attain the ability of people to come together to reshape and remold the world in their own image and collective interest in teaching environments. In this sense radical pedagogy is shot through with the firm belief that as human beings, we can change the world into a more humane place for the majority, and not just for the privilege minority. In this the ethically demanding screams are important because with them it might be possible to open up theoretical discussions to the experiential registry of each human being involved.

We are afraid of letting out a scream of sadness, a scream of horror, above all a scream of anger, of refusal because it opens up the possibility that we lose the struggle of self-preservation both intellectually and physically. Grown ups and children alike might be seen as a rope dancers, like those in Friedrich Nietzsche's *Thus spoke Zarathustra*. We are afraid of falling down, but not only because we might get hurt, or that it might be fatal to us, but because we long for this fall. In connection to learning, the mass that swells beneath us is seen as opposite to autonomous thinking, and the force of our own experiences. It is a merge of us into something bigger than us, renunciation of adulthood or the aloofness that development has brought about, our integrity.

NOTES

[1] Italics mine.

[2] There are obviously exceptions in this: for example doctors working in the *Medecins Sans Frontieres* and a like. There is quite interesting article by Glannon & Ross (2002) where they argue that when seen from the global scale the real altruists in medicine are still the patients.

[3] I have developed this theme more systematically in connection to moral sentiments (especially pity, compassion, empathy, sympathy) in Moisio 2004.

[4] Myles Horton (1905–1990) was an American educator, socialist and cofounder of the Highlander Folk School, famous for its role in the Civil Rights Movement.

REFERENCES

Adorno, T. W. (1973). *Negative dialectics.* New York: Routledge.

Beckett, S. (1952). *Waiting for godot.* New York: Grove Press.

Beckett, S. (1955). *Molloy.* New York: Grove Press.

Biesta, G. (2007) "Why 'What Works' Won't Work: Evidence-Based practice and the democratic deficit in educational research", In *Educational Theory, 57*(1), 1–22.

Bloch, E. (1995). *The principle of hope* (Vol. 1). Cambridge: MIT.

Brookfield, S. (2005). *The power of critical theory.* San Francisco: Jossey-Bass.

Ellison, R. (1980). *The invisible man.* New York: Random House.

Evans, R. I. (1966). *Dialogue with Erich Fromm.*

Dewey, J. (1916). *Democracy and education: An introduction to the philosophy of education.* New York: Cosmo.

Dewey, J. (1989). *Freedom and culture.* New York: Prometheus Books.

Freire, P. (2003). *Pedagogy of the oppressed.* New York: Continuum.

Freire, P. (2004). *Pedagogy of indignation.* Boulder and London: Paradigm.

Fromm, E. (1932). Psychoanalytic charaterology and its relevance for social psychology. In *The crisis of psychoanalysis* (pp. 164–187). New York: Henry Holt.

Fromm, E. (1941). *Escape from freedom.* New York: Henry Holt.

Fromm, E. (1945). *Man for himself.* New York: Henry Holt.

Fromm, E. (1955). *The sane society.* New York: Henry Holt.

Fromm, E. (1957). Medicine and the ethical problem of modern man. In *The Dogma of Christ* (pp. 169–187). New York: Henry Holt.

Fromm, E. (1973). *The anatomy of human destructivness.* New York: Holt, Rinehart & Winston.

Fromm, E. (1976). *To have or to be?* New York: Continuum.

Fromm, E. (1994). *The art of listening.* New York: Continuum.

Glannon, W., & Ross, L. F. (2002). "Are doctors altruistic?" In *Journal of Medical Ethics, 28*, 68–69.

Holloway, J. (2003). In the beginning was the scream. In W. Bonefeld (Ed.), *Revolutionary writing.* New York: Autonomedia.

Horkheimer, M. (1938). The end of reason. In A. Arato & E. Gebhardt (Eds.), *The essential Frankfurt school reader.*

Horkheimer, M. (1947). *Eclipse of reason.* New York: Continuum.

Horkheimer, M., & Adorno, T. W. (2002). *Dialectic of enlightenment* (E. Jephcott, Trans.). California: Standford university Press.

Horton, M. (1990). *The long haul.* New York: Doubleday.

Kennedy, W. B. (1981). Highlander Praxis: Learning with Myles Horton. *Teachers College Record, 83*, 105–119.

Kihlman, C. (1971). *Ihminen joka järkkyi.* [The Human who Trembled] Helsinki: Tammi.

LaPlace, J., & Pontalis, J. B. (1988). *The langue of psychoanalysis.* New York: Norton.

Marcuse, H. (1964). *One dimensional man: Studies in the ideology of advanced industrial society.* London: Routledge & Kegan Paul.

Marx, K. (1844). Economic and philosophical manuscripts of 1844. In K. Marx & F. Engels (Eds.), *Collected works* (Vol. 3). Moscow: Progress.

Marx, K. (1859). Grundrisse. In K. Marx & F. engels (Eds.), *Collected works* (Vol. 28). Moscow: Progress.

Marx, K., & Engels, F. (1948). *The communist manifesto* (A Norton Critical ed.). New York: W. W. Norton.

McLaren, P., & Farahmandpur, R. (2005). *Teaching against global capitalism and the new imperialism.* Boulder, CO: Rowman and Littlefield.

McLaren, P., & Jaramillo, N. (2007). *Pedagogy and praxis in the age of empire.* Rotterdam: Sense Publishers.

Moisio, O.-P. (2004). Sääli sosiaalisena siteenä—uudesta solidaarisuudesta. [Pity as a Social bond—notes on a new solidarity]. In T. Helne, S. Hänninen & J. Karjalainen (Eds.), *Seis yhteiskunta—tahdon sisään.* Jyväskylä: SoPhi.

Parker, F., & B. J. (1991). *Myles Horton (1905–90) of highlander: Adult educator and southern activist.* (ERIC Document Reproduction No. eD 336615).

Peters, J., & Belle, B. (2001). Horton of highlander. In P. Jarvis (Ed.), *Twentieth century thinkers in adult and continuing education* (2nd ed.). Sterling: vaistyldus Publishing.

Smith, A. (1776). *The wealth of nations.* New York: Bentham.

Sohn-Rethel, A. (1985). *Soziologische theorie der Erkenntnis.* Frankfurt am Main: Suhrkamp.

Thompson, C. (2005). The Non-transparency of self and the ethical value of Bildung. *Journal of Philosophy of Education, 39*(3), 519–533. Horton (1905–90) of Highlander.

ARIE KIZEL

22. TOWARD A NEW DIALOGICAL LANGUAGE IN EDUCATION

In searching for a new language that will rescue Critical Pedagogy from besiege, Ilan Gur-Ze'ev wrote: "What is regrettable, however is that so much of Critical Pedagogy has become dogmatic, and sometimes anti-intellectual, while on the other hand losing its relevance for the people it conceived as victims to be emancipated" (Gur-Ze'ev, 2005, p. 10). Gur-Ze'ev argued, further, that today many critical pedagogues are ready for or actually searching for a new critical language in education that will reach beyond the achievements and limitations of Critical Pedagogy. However, various current versions of Critical Pedagogy do not pursue the attempt of Critical Theory to propose a holistic Utopia. Furthermore, the absence of love, creativity, and a human vista have led Critical Pedagogy into a blind alley.

In this regard, a critical perspective that incorporates the possibility of loosening the chains, as envisaged by Plato, is merely one aspect of Critical Theory, a fundamentally theoretical one, however rich and manifold. This option has the potential to have an emancipatory effect on teachers and educators who feel attracted ideologically to the principles of Critical Pedagogy, and can provide them with a home base in their shunning of normalizing education. However, many feel increasingly more despondent in such endeavors, as described by Elizabeth E. Heilman: "Critical Pedagogy fails to offer stories in which ordinary active citizens and teachers work for positive social change as part of their ordinary lives" (Heliman, 2005, p. 129). Heilman diagnosed the problems of Critical Pedagogy claiming that it is "still very much [a] victim of [...] textualization, loss of the subject, and excessive suspicion of the functioning of power in micro contexts" (Ibid., p. 121). And, further, that the results of these problems are "the absence of immediacy in the move from macro level critique to micro level classroom work" (Ibid).

RETURNING TO DIALOGIC PEDAGOGY

In order to enable Critical Pedagogy to be relevant today, it must—among other things—also be reconnected to the domain of schooling, not abandon or ignore it. Declining to enter this domain may reinforce alienation that will increase delegitimization. It must see itself once again obligated to developing tools and techniques that enable the teacher and pupil to escape, immediately, the extant discourse that resides in the heart of the confusion that abounds and to rejuvenate the language that makes liberation and emancipation possible. In doing so, it would not be, as Nicholas C. Burbules argued, a "truism to say that Critical Pedagogy must be fundamentally dialogical" (Burbules, 2005, p. 193). Indeed, as this essay will argue,

I. Gur-Ze'ev, The Possibility/Impossibility of a New Critical Language in Education, 409–416.
© 2010 Sense Publishers. All Rights Reserved.

a return today to the dialogic insights in the philosophy of Martin Buber, as well as that of Immanuel Levinas, can enrich Critical Theory and enable it to renew itself through a non-naïve philosophy and even consider itself as secular grace as described by Dana Freibach-Heifetz (Freibach-Heifetz, 2009). Such an endeavor would attempt to integrate the dialogic into an all-encompassing Critical Pedagogy that has strong roots in intra-school practice and that is especially capable of withstanding environmental forces that seek to transform the school into another economic institution.

Such practice must oppose the often violent propulsion by vested economic forces of neo-liberal-commercial discourse into the heart of pedagogical activity; an initiative that seeks through manipulation to build upon its successful transformation of the charge given schools—to prepare pupils for life as producer-consumer. This trend has come to dominate educational discourse through application of a variety of strategies, including communication techniques that have induced fear and obedience into teachers and transformed the task of the principal into a demand to satisfy changing, temporary, temperamental, capricious, and often neurotic desires that lack parental authority and, principally, the capacity to establish clear goals for ongoing educational practice. The school system lacks the tools to defend itself from such omnipotent assault and hence many sectors have transformed themselves and now cooperate and manage the subservient, smooth running, and efficient operations sought by neo-liberal forces, albeit an educational atmosphere antithetical to very nature of education and learning. Thus, pedagogy of fear and apprehension drives and paralyzes the educational system, causing the best to leave while chasing others away.

Such operations are maintained and condoned through silent collaboration by non-professional forces involved in the schools operations, such as non-government agencies and parents. However, frequently, the involvement of the latter evolves into intervention that includes, for example, threats issued to principals by parental groups. The most popular threat is to close down the educational institution. In response, principals capitulate for fear of harming the good name of their school.

This neo-liberal assault has come to infuse an academic academy that has already surrendered, in part, to the ratings-driven culture. And, in accordance with this market mentality, ideas such as excellence and oppositional resistance are reduced to being, at the least, irrelevant and expendable, if not damaging and subversive. Evidence of the consumer discourse between student and university has been present for some time; including rude statements directed by students at lecturers, retribution by means of the teaching assessment survey, as well as internalization of self-serving defense mechanisms. Thus, it is not surprising that one head of a college in Israel wrote in an internal newsletter to his faculty: "Students are above all else clients. This is how they see themselves and this is their perception. As clients, they do not request, they demand service. They have come here to purchase an education [...] and they expect to receive service from us just as they would receive it in any shop when they purchase a product [...] These are the rules of the game today, and they are intensifying".

The inevitable result, and crisis, it should be noted, is recognizable in student recruitment through marketing of enticements, similar to those offered by credit card companies; for example, changing course names, adapting contents to utilitarian economic purposes, as well as pedagogy and research to the logic of the market place.

According to the logic of this cultural thrust, efficiency will replace political freedom, courage, and the capability to oppose accepted and rigid ideas. From here, the path to groveling and superficiality is short. Indeed, we can expect that within a short time students will organize themselves to sue lecturers. In fact attorneys of Higher education institutions are dealing at present with legal suits lodged by students, primarily by the disappointed—those disappointed by the high demands, the difficulties they have to confront, the investment required, and with low marks they received. The client is disappointed.

This attack, primarily against the public school system, has become the national hobby in many countries and the results are: paralysis of internal forces, severe exhaustion of administrators who seek solace in retirement, increasing pressure to internalize market-driven, neo-liberal discourse. For example, the demand that educators to be aware of and adapt to market forces, or in other words to surrender to them. Living, surviving, amidst such an impossible conundrum, composed of opposing interests, has become a mechanism that repetitively produces a weakening of the self.

Alexander M. Sidorkin argued that the educational community has fallen into a false belief that policy-making is the way to change education (Sidorkin, 1999, pp. 2–3). According to Sidorkin, an educational discourse full of talk about charter schools, uniforms, inclusion, and site-based management is a rhetoric that resembles the language of a sales representative.

Given the weakening of voices from the academy and the nature of such discourse, it is imperative today to re-connect Critical Theory and Critical Pedagogy to the educational enterprise through, among other initiatives, renewal of the philosophy of Martin Buber and its extension as dialogic pedagogy. Doing so will demonstrate its uniqueness and recruit administrators and educators in the school systems to view it as a tool that can renew faith in the mission and necessity of dialogic pedagogy. In this regard, Sidorkin claimed that this is necessary because what is presently claimed to be "dialogic" in the classroom is not necessarily dialogic; for example, when opposition to monologic discourse is presented in a monologic manner. Elizabeth Heilman captured the essence of this claim when she stated: "We need to explore how intersections among power, knowledge, and identity can be understood in different contexts, and we need to wrestle productively with active, lived contexts of classrooms and communities" (Heliman, 2005, p. 121).

FROM THE DIAGNOSTIC TO THE DIALOGICAL

Buber's approach makes it possible to see the passage of events through the prism of "dialogic power." His critical dialogic approach to history is especially important in light of modern man's crisis. Such importance is not only due to its dialogic potential but primarily because it is essential for its "treatment" (Barzelai, 2000, p. 129). Indeed, Buber did not see his method as an abstract philosophy but rather as a fundamental and valuable aspect of reality: He claimed that in pointing to the concrete, he is pointing to something that has not been seen at all or only insufficiently. Buber suggested that such a "discovery" can be compared to being open to listening to what one hears, to grasp it, and to go directly to the window. And, upon raising the window, to enjoying the view.

Buber's most famous work, I and Thou (*ICH und Du,* 1923), was first translated into English in 1937 by Ronald Gregory Smith, and since has been considered to have initiated a Copernican revolution against the scientific-realistic attitude (Sidorkin, 1999, p. 11). Buber discussed the nature of the all-important human encounter and focused on the dialogic dimension in concrete situations. He called for the presence of the whole-being. It is his *I and Thou Dialogical Principle* that gives us hope today that we can proceed beyond the perception that critique is a dead end and that gives direction to educators, teachers and especially intellectuals. Sidorkin wrote that in the dialogical, Buber, like Bakhtin and Copernicus, re-discovered the center of the human universe: "It is the center in a sense that the very fact of human existence is contingent upon engagement in dialogical relations." (Ibid). Indeed, as stated by Buber, "All real living is meeting" (Buber, 1957, p. 11).

Buber's anthropological thought is founded on the dialogic approach that views the human being as essentially a dialogic creature. The core purpose of his thinking, in which the "dialogic man" is central, is not to hone consciousness and enrich knowledge. Rather, Buber aspires to strengthen human cooperation which is, in his view, existential, faith-driven, and inter-personal. Buber sought to shift the issue of human existence into one that seeks to be inclusive of human experience.

He opposed the anthropological reduction eluded to in Kant's question that was assumed by Heidegger. Juxtaposed to them, Buber sought to expand the boundaries of human thought and called for a transition from knowledge-based understanding, which is by nature partial and assumes that human beings are creatures of under-standing, to dialogical knowledge that is by nature complete and comprehends human beings fully. Buber's existential thought is one of involvement in life, the starting point for which is the idea that existence is fundamentally co-existence. The essence of Buber's thought resides in his dialogical-based perception that human essence is relational. Neither perception nor understanding is what determines the core of human existence, rather *being-in-relation to* (Erziehung) and the *encounter* (Begegnung). Thus, while Heidegger emphasized the fatality of human existence and Kant consciousness, relationality is the existential fact of existence for Buber (Meir, 2004, p. 71; Kepnes, 1992).

Buber called for implementation of a "method of dialogism" (Barzelai, 2000, p. 145) that requires *entry* from a person's inner knowledge and so assigns a secondary place to external perception. The dialogic method bridges the chasm between experience and consciousness; that is, it joins facilitation of experience with postfacto knowledge of an experience. Furthermore, by means of human attach-ment, dialogic thought establishes a bridge with reality and in doing so the encounter with the Other (Buber, [1938] 1962, pp. 430–431). According to Buber, only reflective introspection—not empirical impression—is capable of perceiving human essence and thus "consciousness is not gained by means of parsing a concrete entity rather through deep penetration into essence of a concrete entity; such penetration reveals the essence-within of such an entity" (Ibid, p. 97).

Buber, like Bakhtin, assumed that in order for there to be complete human existence, a person must not only enter into the dialogic situation but must know and value the fact that one is making such an entry. Nicholas Burbules captured the essence of this stance, as follows: "Dialogue is not something we do or use; it is a relation into which we enter" (Burbules, 1993, p. xii). And, as Buber stated: "Benevolence touches us when we approach it, are open to, and perhaps expect it. But benevolence cannot be a concern ... it comes without searching, as in "don't touch—and it appears" (Buber, 1959, pp. 58, 61).

Buber always insisted that the dialogic principle, the duality of primal relations that he called the I-Thou and the I-It, was not a philosophical conception but a reality beyond the reach of discursive language. Buber argued that productivity is only true existence when it takes root in the immediacy of a lived life. It is the dominant belief of our time that production is the primary criterion of human worth. But illegitimate production, production without immediacy, is no criterion, for it is not reality but delusion.

LOVE OF LIFE WITH RESPONSIBILITY

Buber's major claim was that human existence can be defined by the way in which we engage in dialogue with each other, with the world, and with the divine. According to Buber, human beings may adopt two attitudes toward the world: I-Thou or I-It. *I-Thou* is a relation of subject-to-subject, while *I-It* is a relation of subject-to-object. In *I-Thou* relations, human beings are aware of each other as having a unity of being. Accordingly, human beings do not perceive each other as consisting of specific, isolated qualities, but engage in a dialogue involving each other's whole being.

In *I-It* relationships, on the other hand, human beings perceive each other as consisting of specific, isolated qualities, and view themselves as part of a world that consists of things (Buber, 1957). This is a relationship of separateness and detachment, but not in the sense that Gur Ze'ev views the Diasporic-nomadic person. Buber explained that human beings may try to convert the subject-to-subject relation to a subject-to-object relation, or vice versa. However, the *being* of a subject is a unity that cannot be fragmented and analyzed as an object. To attempt to analyze a subject as an object involves assuming that the subject is no longer a subject. However, *a priori*, it is impossible according to Buber for a subject, a human being, to be, or to be treated, as an object. In contrast, love, as a relation between I and Thou, is a subject-to-subject relation and shares a sense of caring, respect, commitment, and responsibility. These points are similar to Gur-Ze'ev's call to life-with-Love and Love-of-Life with responsibility.

Diasporic Philosophy, in which Critical Theory is considered by Gur-Ze'ev to be part of its second stage of development, has no starting point, telos or territory, and it undoubtedly distances itself from all manner *returning-home projects*. Still, above all else, Diasporic Philosophy emphasizes the erotic essence of Being: *Love of life*—not as "critique," as a claim for justice for the oppressed or revenge is essential to it. Buber and Levinas's ideas, as well as the philosophy of personal dialogue may be an instructive method for such ethical inquiry as well as for defining the nature of personal responsibility. It is not a naïve approach, but rather an existential, Diasporic, counter-educative engagement in an era of disaffection, terror, and unfamiliarity.

For Buber, *encounter* (*Begegnung*) has significance beyond co-presence and individual growth. He looked for ways in which people could engage with one another fully—to meet themselves. The basic fact of human existence was not the individual or the collective as such, but rather for Buber—"Man with Man".

Principles of the dialogic method and dialogic encounters are especially relevant today, in regard to the possibilities of counter-education, and can become—if developed—an avenue for enriching a new language of Critical Pedagogy. For example: (*a*) The relation to the Thou is immediate; (*b*) Between I and Thou there is no terminology, no politically-correct language or pseudo-police, no preconception and no imagination, and memory itself changes, since it plunges from singularity into the whole; (*c*) between I and Thou there is no purpose, no greed, and no expectations; (*d*) longing itself changes since it changes from dream into appearance; (*e*) only where all means and objectifications do not exist can encounter happen.

According to Buber, the authentic solution to existential loneliness is misframed as being dependent on the choice between collectivism and individualism (Buber, [1938] 1962, p. 110). In Buber's view, we should be liberated from this Kierkegaardian belief in favor of a third option—the interpersonal path residing in the bond between one person and another. This alternative lies "beyond the subjective, out of the domicile of the objective, on a path along a narrow ridge along which you and I meet, in the in-between (Ibid., p. 112).

Buber argued that the real in these thoughts is an extension of the notion of relation beyond interhuman relations to the whole of existence. In his opinion, the whole of existence is determined by the kind of relations I develop with both human and material entities. I can live through I-It relations if I imagine life to be a destiny imposed upon me or an aimless accident. But, I can also live through dialogical relations and conceive of life as a search for answers. This means that I have to respond, genuinely, to the actualities in the situation, not through plans to realize other aims. Doing so assumes self-responsibility, instead of self-realization; or in short, response. Gur-Ze'ev could call this—enduring improvisation.

For Buber encounter (*Begegnung*) has significance beyond co-presence and individual growth. He looked for ways in which people could engage with each other fully, including meeting with themselves. Again, the basic fact of human existence is not the individual or the collective as such, but rather "man with man". Significantly, for Buber, dialogue involves all manner of relations: with self, other(s) and all manner of creation. Recognizing this principle enables us to see that it is the conceptual linchpin of his teachings. The life of dialogue involves the turning towards the other. It is not found by seeking, but by grace. In a very real sense we are *called* to, as opposed to actively searching for, genuine dialogue. Accordingly, silence, for Buber, plays a crucial part in dialogue. Indeed, it could be argued that *attentive silence* is the basis of dialogue. This idea may seem strange at first sight, but is fundamental in the practices and experiences of groups such as the Quakers.

Thus, Buber offered us a vision that projects vitality and a nomadic approach that is not based on collective sociality, but rather on love of life and responsibility. As such, it is a dimension of a pedagogy of Hope.

The dialogic dimension relates, as well, to the principle of responsibility, as enunciated by Emanuel Levinas. His view is based on the idea that, as a speaking subject, a person does not place oneself in the center, but turns to the Other. This attitude of commitment to the Other must also be expressed in action; for example, in clothing the naked, feeding the hungry. Such an understanding can be combined with the Diasporic option proposed by Gur-Ze'ev, as expressed in his statement: "Responsibility, within the framework of Diasporic Philosophy, is part of and enables *The Good*, yet it is a Diasporic Good, not a domesticated good" (Gur-Ze'ev, 2005, p. 29).

In summary, Critical Pedagogy can be enriched by dialogic elements, as understood by Martin Buber, among others, because the fundamental fact of human existence is "man with man". The dialogic stance toward the world and the Other demands a person's entire essence as a human being. It makes possible removal of the wall of alienation that persons often build around themselves. Further, the dialogic stance allows a person to realize the fullness of an experience, something impossible in the Kantian stance of consciousness due to its partial nature. Thus, while the stance of consciousness is one in relation to life, the dialogic stance is one in relation to essence. Consciousness alone is insufficient to understand such quality; rather it is only within the essence of the relational that consciousness and essence of life reside for persons.

The possibilities that such thought makes possible for critical school practice are expansive and have the potential to be a cultural breakthrough that will enable a person to create an authentic connection with the world in which he or she is living and, as well, create a shared ground among all persons in which a person's capabilities are rooted.

In relying on relations and connections, on obligations, and on linkages that could be employed in an instrumental and unauthentic manner, Buber could be criticized for relying on naïve optimism—on negative Utopia. It should be noted that he does not rely on naïve, *returning-home* projects that produce violence and hatred.

The responsibility of dialogic education in the Diasporic sense can be actualized in educational procedures in the field, combining theory and practice. Being attentive and discovering the richness in Buber's words and thoughts can open a door to creative inter-relationships between people, on the one hand; and to elude naïve Utopia, on the other hand. The overvaluation of productivity is so great in our age that even truly productive men give up the roots of a genuinely lived life and wear themselves out turning all experience into value as public communication. As Buber said one who meets men with a double glance, one open and inviting fellowship, the other a secret one that conceals the conscious aim of the observer, cannot be delivered from his sickness by any talent that he brings to his work, for he has poisoned the springs of his life.

REFERENCES

Barzelai, D. (2000). *The dialogic person: The contribution of Martin Buber to philosophy.* Jerusalem: Magnes Press. (Hebrew)

Buber, M. (1957). *I and Thou.* New York: Collier Books.

Buber, M. (1959). *In the secret of dialogue: On man and confronting experience.* Jerusalem: Mosad Bialik. (Hebrew)

Buber, M. ([1938] 1962). *The problem of man: A philosophical anthropological investigation.* Jerusalem: Mosad Bialik. (Hebrew)

Burbules, N. C. (1993). *Dialogue in teaching: Theory and practice.* New York: Teachers College Press.

Burbules, N. C. (2005). Dialogue and critical pedagogy. In I. Gur Ze'ev (Ed). *Critical theory and critical pedagogy today—toward a new language in education.* Haifa: University of Haifa.

Freibach-Heifetz, D. (2009). *Secular grace.* Tel Aviv: Resling. (Hebrew)

Gur Ze'ev, I. (2005). Critical theory, critical pedagogy and diaspora today. In: I. Gur Ze'ev. (Ed.), *Critical theory and critical pedagogy today—toward a new language in education.* Haifa: University of Haifa.

Heliman, E. E. (2005). Escaping the blind between Utopia and dystopia. In I. Gur Ze'ev. (Ed.), *Critical theory and critical pedagogy today—toward a new language in education.* Haifa: University of Haifa.

Kepnes, S. (1992). *The text as thou: Martin Buber's dialogical hermeneutics and narrative theology.* Bloomington, IN: Indiana university Press.

Meir, E. (2004). *Dialogue between existential Jewish philosophers.* Jerusalem: Magnes. (Hebrew)

Sidorkin, A. M. (1999). *Beyond discourse: Education, the self and dialogue.* New York: State University of New York Press.

RAQUEL DE ALMEIDA MORAES

23. IS A NEW CRITICAL LANGUAGE IN EDUCATION STILL POSSIBLE NOWADAYS?

INTRODUCTION

In opposition to a typical banking instruction practiced by the cultural and educational capitalistic industry "which uses a simplified language for the use of the masses" (Tognolli), with "fixed invariables, prompt *clichés*, and a stereotypical translation of everything" (Adorno), we think that it is possible to discuss with "nonviolent intersubjectivities"—which involves recognizing the difference, the total difference (Gur-Ze'ev), aiming to awaken the consciousness of how "men are deceived in a permanent way " (Adorno). *This requires the usage of critical language in poetic* (Bakhtin) *and dialogic* (Freire) *way.* Alternatively, when the critical language is authoritarian and violent, it will be used in the same domination sense, consequently hindering emancipation.

With the premise of developing a counter-hegemony against the authoritarian and seductive language of banking instruction, where knowledge is considered a trade object and the students are passive individuals, reduced to clients in the globalization phase of Capital, we presume that critical language in education must be a poetic and dialogical mediator in cultural circles (Freire, 1986), including cyberspace (Moraes, 2006a), generating a counter reaction to the hegemonic predominant trend.

In order to develop this assertion, the conceptions of language of Bakhtin and Freire and their significance in Cultural studies and Critical Theory's perspectives will be elucidated so that we may finally determine the inferences through the general premise of human emancipation, democracy and nonviolence, the Utopia that leads the present proposition. According to Geoghegan (1987, p. 135): "Marxism without a future orientation is blind".

LANGUAGE IN MIKHAIL BAKHTIN AND PAULO FREIRE

Modern philosophy of the nature of signs and their role in social commu-nication has a tradition in the Graeco-Roman civilization embracing both Platonic and Aristotelian reasoning on the relation "between language sounds, and the human mind. It involves the Stoics and their dialectical approach to the opposition between the signifying and the signified". (Matejka, 1973, p. 161)

From Saussure's perspective, the concept of sign is viewed as the very pivot of verbal communication and of any communication of meaning in general. According to him, language "is a system of signs that express ideas". [...] "Since language is only one among several systems, Saussure considers linguistics a branch of the general science of signs" (Matejka, 1973, p. 162).

I. Gur-Ze'ev, The Possibility/Impossibility of a New Critical Language in Education, 417–426.
© *2010 Sense Publishers. All Rights Reserved.*

Following the spirit of Cartesian dualism, Matejka states that Saussure insists on a "clear-cut separation between the actual speech act and the abstract system of norms internalized by the linguistic competence of the speakers" (*Op cit.*, p. 163). "In separating language from speaking," he says, "we are at the same time separating what is social from what is individual, and what is essential from what is accessory and more or less accidental" (Ibid.).

Within such a complex analytic model, "not only the opposition between language and speech has to be taken into account, but also the opposition between the speaker and the hearer." [...] "Neither the speaker's nor the hearer's role is favored" (*Op cit.*, p. 164).

In opposition, Mikhail Bakhtin (1986) and Paulo Freire (1987) regard language as essentially dialogical. Their ideas about man and life are marked by the belief that the interaction among individuals is the basic principle of language as well as consciousness. The meaning and significations of signs (widely comprehended as sounds, gestures, images, words and silence) depend on the relationship between individuals and are built on the interpretation of statements. Through this perspective, the center of interlocution is no longer polarized between the "I" and the "You", the speaker and the hearer, the sender and the receiver, inserted now in a dialogical movement in the communication surrounding meaning.

According to Lima (2001), this means overcoming visions of a restrictive model marked by one-sided directivity, which places the sender as the originator of closed messages and the receiver as a passive individual before them. It suggests giving a new dimension to the space of reception transforming it into an interaction and conversion space and also, modifying the roles of senders and receivers, speaker and hearer, to a dynamic co-author/creator relationship.

In a final analysis, it means recognizing that inter-acting is more than purely sending and answering messages; it entails perceiving emission and reception as repercussive spaces, given that the sender and receiver become part of dialogical interconnected cord relations. Such relations are always in progression, that is, they are always confronting each other, being built and deconstructed simultaneously in a dynamic and dialogical relationship (Moraes; Dias; Fiorentini, 2006b).

Taking on this view in education begets challenges. Traditionally, communication has presented a linear, imperative and unilateral character in the educational realm. On a practical basis, we can observe that dialogue is restricted to a lower level of detailing or elucidation of molded one-sided speeches, derived from a sender, whose interactive space for building is virtually inexistent, and the language turns into a reproduction tool for the contemporary system. In Freire's perception (2001), two individuals have to share a meaning domain so that the dialogue can take place. "Regarding the communicative-dialogic relation, interlocutors express themselves through a common linguistic sign system" (Freire, 2001, p. 67).

Moreover, Freire (1987) condemns the communicative monologue affirming that teaching is not transferring knowledge, but generating the possibilities for its production or construction. To him, teaching requires criticism and respect regarding the pupils' character autonomy. Otherwise, official reports, extension and cultural invasion will take place instead of true communication. To Freire, man is an associative being who, through his work, transforms nature into a cultural world when defied by it. By creating the world of labor and culture, he realizes himself historically immersed in the oppressors/oppressed contradiction, arising the need of its overcoming.

It is impossible to understand thought outside its double function: a cognitive and communicative act. As a result, education is conceived as a political, communicational act, and not an act of extension, since communication "implies a reciprocity that cannot be corrupted" (Freire, 2001, p. 69). Communication is education and dialogue "to the extent which there is no knowledge transfer, but an encounter of interlocutors that seek the significations of meanings" (Ibid.).

From Freire's viewpoint, education is inserted in the society, as opposed to being detached and reduced to a capitalistic function of training for mere labor adjustment. Capitalism delivers a "banking" kind of education that represents "the educator/pupil non-conciliation". From this perspective, education would serve as an auxiliary to the transformation and change process. In the book "*Medo e Ousadia*", Freire and Shor state that social change is "the establishment of a different relationship with knowledge and with society" (Freire; Shor, 1993, p. 48).

Thus, the change also occurs through the consciousness and more precisely, through the language domain. In the book the "*Pedagogy of the Oppressed*", Freire states that: "Existing, humanly, is naming the world, changing it. And once it has been named, the world reappears to the names as a problem and requires of them a new *naming*" (Freire, 1987, p. 78).

Naming the word—which is also labor, is praxis; it is the transformation of the world—not a privilege of few, but A RIGHT ENTITLED TO ALL. It is through an authentic loving, thoughtful and critical dialogue that the process of consciousness and humanization takes place. This is the ultimate purpose of education, and that, according to Freire, occurs when man rediscovers himself as a founder of the world and his experience by detaching himself from his world of experience.

However, the process of consciousness does not mean discoursing about subjects and donating knowledge that have absolutely any correlation with the people's yearnings, needs, hopes, aspirations and fears. The subjects that will be approached (generating themes) must be decided on in an agreement so that non-alienating truthful communication between educator and pupil can take place. This process implies a new methodology that cannot contradict the dialogicity of a liberating education.

Discovering generating themes entails the recognition of one's humanity, being at the same time products and producers of history, therefore unfinished individuals. In contrast, it is also recognizing what Vieira Pinto (Freire, 1987, p. 90) calls "limit-acts": those directed to overcoming and denying, rather than passively accepting, a given circumstance.

Through this perception, Freire considers it essential that the dialogical educator, acting as an interdisciplinary team member, contribute to question this universe of themes withdrawn in investigation, rather than simply returning it as a thesis to the men from whom he/she received it.

Bakhtin (1986) deepened a theoretical gap that permeates the relationship between base (the economic structure of society) and superstructure (the State and social consciousness)—through the study of the *language*. According to him, alongside natural phenomena, technological material and consumer goods, "there is a particular universe, the sign universe" (Bakhtin, 1986, p. 32).

Under this premise, we can only ask: Where does the ideological, or sign, come from? To Bakhtin (1986, p. 32): "the individual awareness is not an architect of this ideological superstructure, but only one more tenant in the social building of the ideological signs".

In Bakhtin's view, the word is conceived as a sign, and as such, it must be perceived as an originator of social relations; it is present in every comprehension and interpretation act. Thus, since signs mediate the relation of man and his reality— as semiotic material of his conscience—all of the individual's mental activity can be conveyed under the form of signs, externalizing itself through words, gestures, or other means resulting from the previous speech. Speech is not individual, it occurs between speakers. Language is not spoken in emptiness; on the contrary, it is uttered in a concrete historical situation in which enunciation, communication circumstances and social structures are interpenetrated—in which its meaning is accomplished— through and in the interactions between the individuals. This attempt to under-stand the relations between language and society in a complex dialogue between existence and language, world and mind, what is given and what is created, between the world of experience in action and the representation in the world of speech, allows us to understand the impossibility of an individual formation without other-ness, therefore manifesting the presence of the other within the boundaries of the inner world.

Though Bakhtin considers all speeches or texts as dialogical, "not every text shows the various voices of speech" (Barros *Apud* Faraco et *alli*, 2001, p. 36). In the mono-glossia speeches, these voices are concealed, disguised, dissimulated, as if they were one voice, one speech. But in the heteroglossia speeches, the coexistence of distinct varieties within a single linguistic code is possible. As for authoritarian speeches, the voices are overwhelmed by each other, the dialogues are hidden and speech turns into the speech of one sole truth. Heteroglossia or poetical discourses, on the other hand, would be those in which we do not find traces of authoritarianism and social coercion, representing a synthesis that respects different voices.

LANGUAGE IN A CRITICAL PERSPECTIVE

From Gramsci's perspective of cultural studies, in the capitalistic society, education has a clearly defined political function: forming intellectuals in many levels whose functions in civil society are to organize the hegemony, the population's "spontaneous consensus". This "consensus" arises from the prestige that bourgeoisie has in society and the state coercion structure that legally insures the discipline of those who "consent". However, this "common sense" must be counterattacked in all the coalitions, including the media, using the critical journalism perspective (Gramsci, 1991).

To Gramsci, as well as to Freire and Gur-Ze'ev, the post-industrial revolution, modern and postmodern politics[1] (1) are marked by class struggles that are objectively expressed through exclusion/oppression and subjectively through ideology, which reflect false reality. This makes the oppressed see the oppression as something natural and the ideology, as something immaterial that permeates and directs all the layers of society, such as media and education.

In this sense, Antonio Gramsci defends, along with Marx, the thesis that the force of material class domination in society is at the same time dominant as intellectual class, in the sense of the ideology of the ruling class. According to Darrel Moen (1998) and Stuart Hall (2003), Gramsci moved forward in Marx's ideology theory, adding hegemony—comprehended as a "false consciousness"—to it. Hegemony expresses the subordinate class' consent to bourgeoisie domination, presenting itself as the other face of power: that of consciousness and language domination by the reproduction of ideology.

This "spontaneous consent" that people have regarding the existence of a coercive system in society is transmitted/reinforced by school, whose function is to form the intellectuals who will maintain, reproduce and perfect the oppressive system under capitalism. The intellectuals produced by schooling are classified as organic or higher level intellectuals: creators of many sciences, philosophy, art, and the like; and the lower level intellectuals: administrators and divulgers of the existing intellectual richness. Gramsci believed that in a transforming perspective, the school would have the role of forming intellectuals that would organize/form a new culture, with the objective of contributing to the creation process of hegemony other than the dominating hegemony, for it is in the "consciousness arena" that the elites make use of their organic intellectuals to maintain the domination. Thus, consciousness must be freed from the bourgeoisie hegemony and must originate a new culture with new values, and consequently, a new social order.

We can find a similar analysis in the Critical Theory's perspective (Adorno, Horkheimer, 1994) where the technique (such as movie and radio) keeps the whole cohesive. As a result, the technique is inserted in the Instrumental Rationality, where the means are above the ends. By becoming business, it reifies people's consciousness through publicity.

> Despite all the illustration and information that is widespread (even with its help) the "Halbbildung" became the predominant structure of the contemporary consciousness, which requires a more wide-ranging theory (Adorno, 1996, p. 388).

On a Subject level, Tognolli (2001, p. 85), asserts that a society "whose relationships occur only through fixed words and access codes instead of mediations and social incidents will generate individuals that will speak and think through clichés—or they will speak and think significants without any meaning." What once was a thought, gives place to non-thought, to automation. To him, language jargon, cliché, is, above all, programming. His hypothesis suggests that computers can absorb key-words and foster the culture of superficiality. Endorsed by Eugene Provenzo's arguments, Tognolli asserts that we already have simplified words, the newspeaks, something similar to the language of the new Oceania, in George Orwell's novel, 1984, "a simplified language to be used by the masses"(p. 177). This process of key-words and clichés can be simply a part of it: we have a simplified language for the human beings' consumption, which can make mass culture even more superficial.

The idea of the individual and the human being's subordination to technique is also highlighted by Lazarte (2000, p. 47), who questions this viewpoint, not as a "Neo-Luddite", "but inverting the order, thinking primarily of the human being and his/her problems, and only then, how technology can contribute to solve them".

By analyzing technology, Marcuse (1970, 1999) defines it as a mode of production, and at the same time, an entirety of the tools, devices and inventions that distinguish the age of machinery as a way to organize, perpetuate, or modify social relations. By doing so, technology can promote freedom, as well as dictatorship, but he highlights that what has been noticed under the capitalistic regime is its dictatorial use.

> For "totalitarian" is not only a terroristic political coordination of society, but also a nonterroristic economic-technical coordination which operates through the manipulation on needs by vested interests (Marcuse, 1970, p. 3).

The language of the media mediates between the master and his/her dependents, and testifies to identification and unification. In the prevailing modes of speech, "the contrast appears between two dimensional, dialectical modes of thought and technological behaviour of social 'habits of thought'" (Marcuse, 1970, p. 85). Marcuse analyses the expression of these habits of thought, the tension between appearance and reality, tend to disappear. The former has no other content than the publicized and standardized word that becomes *cliché* "and, as *cliché,* governs the speech or the writing; the communication thus precludes genuine development of the meaning" (p. 87).

Feenberg (2004, 2005) reflects on the essentially hierarchal nature of technique, which generates a technocratic administration and so originates a dystopic system.

> Heidegger and Marcuse proposed radical critiques of technology that go far beyond the clichés with which we are familiar. Their formulations open up a space for fruitful reflection even if we cannot find satisfactory solutions in their work. That task is left to us. We have an advantage: a far richer experience of technical politics than was available to these precursors. Perhaps out of this experience constructive responses will come to the challenges to modernity they raised so provocatively (Feenberg, 2008, p. 11).

Kellner (2006) describes the impact of technology, the new media of communication today as a complex variety of groups and movements, "both mainstream and oppositional, reactionary and democratic, global and local"(2006, p. 185).[...] "The Internet is thus a contested terrain, used by left, right, and center of both dominant and subcultures to promote their own agendas and interests" (p. 197).

FINAL CONSIDERATIONS

Gur-Ze'ev (2000, 2003, 2005, 2007) asserts that, despite the fact of capitalistic domination in the globalized and self-controlled world, unpredictability and therefore uncontrollability are still possible. This possibility makes individuals revive what is forgotten or deconstructed in the postmodern age: Eros, reflection, transcendence and ethics in a historically placed dialogue. Nevertheless, to Gur-Ze'ev the fulfillment of the critical spirit is not guaranteed, given that the individual, as well as the dialogue, are not more than a Utopia.

> I claim that the aim of education is the normalization of human beings and the leveling of all into mere *things*. [...] The aim of normalizing education is to make the subject forget the *totally Other* than the present order and their unfulfilled human potential (Gur-Ze'ev, 2007, p. 126).

In this sense, Paul virilio alerts (1995):

> We have to acknowledge that the new communication technologies will only further contribute to democracy if, and only if, we oppose from the beginning the caricature of global society being hatched for us by big multinational corporations throwing themselves at a breakneck pace on the information superhighways.

To Adorno (1995), in opposition to the culture industry's mass production and violence, *debarbarizing* is the education's most urgent task. In order to achieve that goal, he suggests activities that involve reading, auditions, and conjunct assistance with students using magazines, radio, songs, and commercial films (we would also add software, sites, hypertexts, and so on) highlighting the falsehood of the speeches present in each of them.

As a result, we see that the main battle between the dominant and subordinate classes is set in the superstructure (social consciousness and State—Bottmore, 1983) and more precisely, in the language arena. From a cultural studies' perspective, Gramsci's asserts that the overcoming of hegemony occurs due to catharsis, comprehended as a "passage from the purely economical (or egoistic-passionate) moment to the ethical-political moment, that is, the superior elaboration of structure into superstructure in men's consciousness" (Gramsci, 1991, p. 53).

And how is this done? Let us recall Marx (1986, p. 12) and his third thesis about Feuerbach, in which he postulates that "The coincidence of circumstance modification with human activity or self-alteration can only be conceived and comprehended rationally as revolutionary praxis."

In a transforming or revolutionary process, intellectuals, given their technical capability, would act as thinking individuals who organize subordinate classes (Gramsci, 1991). Their mission is not professional; however, as participants of the construction of a new culture for the mass coalition, they would direct the ideas and aspirations of the class to which they organically belong, considering that all men are intellectuals; they think, though not all of them have entirely developed this ability, given the bourgeoisie hegemony. This means that the struggle for consciousness emancipation through critical language demands, above all, a non-violent critical language. If this were to take place, a technocratic logic would have been used, that of the bourgeoisie, the oppressor. And thus, it requires emancipation.

On the other hand, Marcuse (1970) argues that underneath the conservative popular base is the substratum of the outcasts and outsides, the exploited and persecuted of other races and other colors, the unemployed and the unemployable.[...] Their opposition hits the system from without and therefore not deflected the system; its is and elementary force which violates the rules of the game and, doing so, reveals it as a rigged game (Marcuse 1970, p. 256–257).

At the beginning of the fascist era, Walter Benjamin (*Apud* Marcuse, 1970, p. 257) wrote: "Nur um der Hoffnungslosen willen ist uns die Hoffnung gegeben. It is only for the sake of those without hope that hope is given to us."

In *Critique of Violence* (1978), Benjamin analyzes:

Is any nonviolent resolution of conflict possible? Without doubt. The relation-ships of private persons are full of examples of this. Nonviolent agreement is possible wherever a civilized outlook allows the use of unalloyed means of agreement. Legal and illegal means of every kind that are all the same violent may be confronted which nonviolent ones as unalloyed means. Courtesy, sympathy, peaceableness, trust, and whatever else might here be mentioned, are their subjective preconditions (Benjamin, 1978, p. 289).

So, in order to reach emancipative, democratic, nonviolent and hopeful discourse in education, it is necessary to act as a friendly guide (Gramsci), in a dialogical-loving (Freire) and reflexive pedagogy (Gur-Ze'ev), which is the foundation of democracy, baring a technological conception that goes beyond the rule of techno-cracy and technoburocratic rationality (Marcuse, Feenberg, Kellner), where the language can be used as an expression of multiple and nonviolent voices (Bakhtin) that does not only mean a consensus, but above all, a poetic speech.

NOTES

[1] Modernism in Philosophy can be viewed as "a movement based on the belief of knowledge advancement, developed from experience and scientific methods". (Peters, 2000, p. 18). Jean François Lyotard (Lyotard, 2000), on the other hand, believes that "The word (postmodern) is used in the American continent by sociologists and critics. It designates the state of culture after the transformations that affected the rules of [ ] science, literature and art games from the XIX century." (p. XV). [...]" The Skepticism regarding metanarrative is believed to be postmodern [...] The narrative speech loses its actors (funteurs), the great heroes, the great dangers, the great perilous and the great objective" (Peters, 2000, XVI)."In the computer age, the question of knowledge is now more than ever a question of government" (Lyotard, 1984, *Apud* Peters, 2001, p. 132). As thinks Peters, such discourse represents the neoliberal attempt to develop a new metanarrative, a unifying and totalizing story. "The goal of education, under these conditions, becomes its optimal contribution to the best perfor-mance of the system. This goal demands the creation of two kinds of skills indispensable to the maintenance of the economic and social system: those necessary to enhance competitiveness in the world market and those necessary for fulfilling the need for its internal cohesion" (Ibid.).

REFERENCES

Adorno, T. W., & Horkheimer, M. (1994). *Dialética do Esclarecimento. Fragmentos Filosóficos*. Tradução de Guido Antonio de Almeida. Rio de Janeiro: Zahar editor.

Adorno, T. W. Teoria da Semicultura. (1996). Tradução de Newton Ramos-de-Oliveira, Bruno Pucci e Cláudia B. Moura. Revista *Educação e Sociedade* (pp. 388–411, ano XVII, n. 56).

Adorno, T. (1995). *Educação e Emancipação*. Tradução de Wolfang Leo Maar. Rio de Janeiro: Paz e Terra.
Bakhtin, M. (1986). *Marxismo e Filosofia da Linguagem*. Tradução de Michel Lahud e Yara Frateschi vieira. São Paulo: Hucitec.
Benjamin, W. (1978). *Reflections. Essays, aphorisms, autobiographical writings*. (E. Jephcott, Trans., P. Demetz, Ed.). New York: Shocken Books.
Bottomore, T. (1983). *A dictionary of Marxist thought*. USA: Basil Blackwell Publisher Ltd.
Faraco, C. A., et al. (Org.). (2001). *Diálogos com Bakhtin*. Curitiba: UFPR.
Feenberg, A., & Barney, D. (Ed.). (2004). *Community in the digital age. Philosophy and practice*. Lanham, MD: Rowman & Littlefield Publishers.
Feenberg, A. (2004). *Teoria Crítica da Tecnologia. Nota autobiográfica*. Texto original "Critical theory of technology". Tradução da equipe de Tradutores do Colóquio Internacional "Teoria Crítica e educação". Unimep, UFSCAR, UNESP. http://www.sfu.ca/%7Eandrewf/critport.pdf. 05.2004.
Feenberg, A. (2005). Heidegger and Marcuse. *The catastrophe and redemption of history*. New York, London: Routledge.
Feenberg, A. (2008). Heidegger, *Marcuse and the critique of technology. Selected talks*. http://www.sfu.ca/~andrewf/ Heideggertalksfu.htm. 12,2008.
Freire, P., & Shor, M. (1986). *Medo e Ousadia*. Tradução Adriana Lopes. São Paulo: Brasiliense.
Freire, P. (1987). *Pedagogia do Oprimido* (17th ed.). Rio de Janeiro: Paz e Terra.
Freire, P. (2000). *Pedagogia da Indignação*. São Paulo: UNESP.
Freire, P. (2001). *Extensão ou Comunicação?* (11th ed.). Rio de Janeiro: Paz e Terra.
Gramsci, A. (1991). *Os Intelectuais e a organização da cultura*. Tradução de Carlos Nelson Coutinho. Rio de Janeiro: Civilização Brasileira.
Gramsci, A. (1991). *Concepção Dialética da História*. Tradução de Carlos Nelson Coutinho. Rio de Janeiro: ed. Civilização Brasileira.
Hall, S. (2003). O Problema da Ideologia. In L. Sovik (Org.). *Da Diáspora. Identidades e Mediações Culturais* (pp. 265–293). Tradução de Adelaine La Guardia de Rezende *et alli*. Belo Horizonte: UFMG; Brasília: UNESCO.
Geogegan. (1987). v. *Utopian Marxism*. London: Methuen.
Gur-Ze'ev, I. (2000). e possivel uma educacao critica no ciberspaco? (N. Ramos-de-Oliveira, Trans. of "Critical education in the cyberspace?"). *Comunicações, 9*(1), 72–98 (Portuguese).
Gur-Ze'ev, I. (2003). *Destroying the other's collective memory* (Counterpoints; Vol. 141). New York: Oxford, Peter Lang Publishing.
Gur-Ze'ev, I. (2004). A teoria crítica e a possiblidade de uma pedagogia não-repressiva. Zuin et al. In S. P. Cortez (Ed.), *Ensaios Frankfurtianos* (pp. 13–41).
Gur-Ze'ev, I. (2005). *Critical theory and critical pedagogy today—toward a new critical language in education* (I. Bachinuch, Ed., Studies in education). Faculty of education, University of Haifa.
Gur-Ze'ev, I. (2006). A Bildung e a Teoria Crítica na era da educação pós-moderna. Tradução: Newton Ramos-de-Oliveira. *Linhas Críticas* (v.12, n.22, pp. 5–22). Brasília.
Gur-Ze'ev, I. (2007). *Beyond the modern-postmodern struggle in education. Toward counter-education and Enduring improvisation*. Rotterdam: Sense Publishers.
Gur-Ze'ev, I., Masschelein, J., & Blake, N. (2002). Reflexo, Reflexão e Contra-Educação. Tradução de Newton Ramos-de-Oliveira. Revista eletrônica *Outras palavras*—v., n. 1, ano 2, outono de
Kahn, R., & Kellner, D. (2004). Virtually democratic: Online communities and Internet activism. In A. Feenberg & D. Barney (Ed.), *Community in the digital age. Philosophy and practice* (pp. 183–200). Lanham, MD: Rowman & Littlefield Publishers.
Kellner, D. (2000). *A Cultura da Mídia. Estudos Culturais: identidade e política entre o moderno e o pós-moderno*. Tradução: Ivone Castilho Benedetti. Bauru: Sagrado Coração.
Lazarte, L. (2000). Ecologia cognitiva na sociedade da informação. *Revista Ciência da Informação, 29*(2), 43–51.
Lima, V. (2001). *A mídia: Teoria e Política*. São Paulo: Perseu Abramo.
Lyotard, J. (2000). *A condição pós-moderna*. Tradução de Ricardo Correa Barbosa. Rio de Janeiro: José Olimpio.

Marcuse, H. (1970). *One dimensional man. Studies in the ideology of advanced industrial society.* Boston: Bacon Press.

Marcuse, H. (1999). *Tecnologia, Guerra Fascismo* (editado por Douglas Kellner). São Paulo: editora unesp.

Marx, K., & Engels, F. (1986) *Ideologia Alemã. Feuerbach.* Tradução de José Carlos Bruni e Marco Aurélio Nogueira (2nd ed.). São Paulo: Hucitec.

Matejka, L. (1973) On the first russian prolegomena to semiotics.In V. N. Volosinov (Ed.), *Marxism and the philosophy of language* (L. Matejka & I. R.Titunik, Trans., pp. 161–174). Cambridge: Harvard.

Moen, D. G. (1998, March). Analysis of social transformative movements in advanced capitalism: A neo-gramscian approach. *Journal of Policy and Culture, 3.*

Moraes, R. de A. (2006a). Aula virtual e democracia: Uma pedagogia crítica no ciberespaço. In Anais do *IV SENAED—Seminário Nacional ABED de Educação a Distância, "Apoio ao Aluno para Sucesso da Aprendizagem"*, Brasília—DF. http://www.abed.org.br/seminario2006/pdf/tc004.pdf.5.2006

Moraes, R. de A., Dias, A. A. C., & Fiorentini, L. M. R. (2006b). As Tecnologias Da Informação E Comunicação Na Educação: As Perspectivas De Freire E Bakhtin. Anais do *VIII Congreso Latinoamericano de Ciencias de la Comunicación*—ALAIC; UNISINOS. http://www.alaic.net/ponencias/UNIrev_Moraes_e_outros.pdf. 7.2006

Peters, M. (2000). *Pós-Estruturalismo e a Filosofia da Diferença.* Tradução de Tomas Tadeu da Silva. Belo Horizonte: Autêntica.

Peters, M. (2001). *Poststructuralism, marxism, and neoliberalism. Between theory and politics.* USA: Rowman & Littlefield Publishers, INCl.

Pucci, B. (1995). *Teoria Crítica e Educação.* Petrópolis: Vozes.

Tognolli, C. J. (2001). *A Sociedade dos Chavões. Presença e lugar—comum na comunicação.* São Paulo: escrituras editora.

Virilio, P. (1999). *A Bomba Informática.* Tradução de Luciano vieira Machado. São Paulo: estação Liberdade.

Virilio, P.. (1995, August). Speed and information. Cyberspace alarm. *Le monde diplomatique* (P. Riemens, Trans.). http://www.ctheory.net/articles.aspx?id=72

AUTHOR INDEX

427

SUBJECT INDEX

Lightning Source UK Ltd.
Milton Keynes UK
12 October 2010

161164UK00001B/4/P

9 789460 912702